Reaping the Whirlw

From reviews of the first edition of *Reaping the Whirlwind*:

'Griffin has reached a better understanding of the Taliban in his book than I have come across anywhere else ... Essential reading to anyone who wishes to understand its nature.'
John Simpson, BBC

'A necessary book ... a meticulous dissection of the limits of power in a violently sectarian society.'
LATimes

'Griffin's writing is elegant, flashing in the sun.'
Post-Gazette, Pittsburgh

'Filled with the dramatic moments, ironies and political intrigues that color the Taliban's rise ... Griffin writes engagingly.'
New York Times Book Review

'Griffin helps us to understand the complexity of current Afghan political culture.'
Choice

'A detailed account of the Taliban ... Griffin has compiled a useful interim study of an extraordinary and little known movement.'
Times Literary Supplement

'Level-headed and plausible in an area which is always going to be filled with the maddest sort of conspiracy theories, and, best of all, seeks to understand and even sympathise with the Taliban's aims – something much more difficult than just complaining about them.'
Philip Hensher, *The Spectator*

'Essential reading for anyone interested in the politics of the region, refreshingly free from any preconceived ideology.'
The Tablet

'It is this complicated story – the rise of the warlords and their subsequent vanquishing by the Taliban – that Michael Griffin describes in his splendid book.'
New Statesman

'Griffin has produced a detailed and heavily researched book which meticulously charts all the different Afghanistan factions, their relationships, their victories and defeats.'
Marxist Review

Reaping the Whirlwind

Afghanistan, Al Qa'ida and the Holy War

Revised Edition

Michael Griffin

Pluto Press

LONDON • STERLING, VIRGINIA

First published by Pluto Press as
Reaping the Whirlwind: The Taliban Movement in Afghanistan, 2001

Revised edition published 2003 by Pluto Press
345 Archway Road, London N6 5AA
and 22883 Quicksilver Drive,
Sterling, VA 20166–2012, USA

www.plutobooks.com

British Library Cataloguing in Publication Data
A catalogue record for this book is available from the British Library

ISBN 0 7453 1916 5 hardback
ISBN 0 7453 1915 7 paperback

Library of Congress Cataloging in Publication Data
Griffin, Michael.
  Reaping the whirlwind : Afghanistan, Al Qa'ida and the holy war /
Michael Griffin.—New ed.
      p. cm.
Includes index.
  ISBN 0-7453-1916-5 (hbk.)—ISBN 0-7453-1915-7 (pbk.)
  1. Afghanistan—History—1989–   2. Taliban. 3. Islamic fundamentalism—
Afghanistan. 4. Islam and state—Afghanistan. 5. Islam and politics—Afghanistan.
I. Title.

  DS371.2.G739 2003
  958.104'6—dc21

                                                                    2003008499

10   9   8   7   6   5   4   3   2   1

Designed and produced for Pluto Press by
Chase Publishing Services, Fortescue, Sidmouth EX10 9QG, England
Typeset from disk by Stanford DTP Services, Towcester
Printed and bound in Canada by
Transcontinental Printing.

For Wendy Edson, with love

Contents

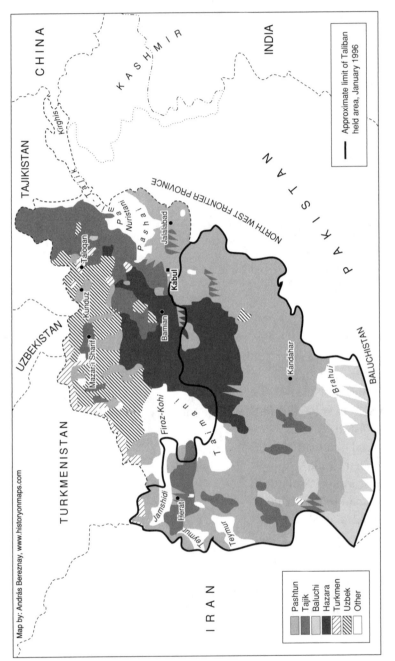

Map by: András Bereznay, www.historyonmaps.com

Afghan ethnic

Pashtun
Tajik
Baluchi
Hazara
Turkmen
Uzbek
Other

Approximate limit of Taliban held area, January 1996

CHINA

KASHMIR

INDIA

TAJIKISTAN

UZBEKISTAN

TURKMENISTAN

IRAN

PAKISTAN

BALUCHISTAN

NORTH WEST FRONTIER PROVINCE

Kirghis

Nuristani

Pashai

Taloqan

Kunduz

Mazar-i Sharif

Jalalabad

Kabul

Bamian

Firoz-Kohi

Jamshidi

Herat

Teymur

Teymur

Taimani

B r a h u i

Kandahar

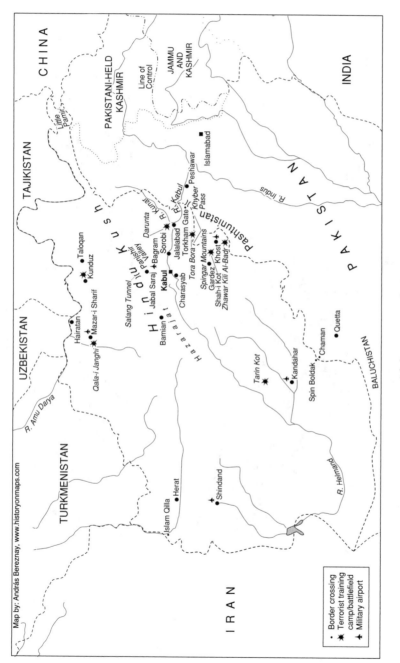

Map by: András Bereznay, www.historyonmaps.com

Afghan general

CHINA

TAJIKISTAN

UZBEKISTAN

TURKMENISTAN

IRAN

PAKISTAN

INDIA

PAKISTANI-HELD KASHMIR

JAMMU AND KASHMIR

Line of Control

BALUCHISTAN

Pashtunistan

Hindu Kush

Hazarajat

Little Pamir

R. Amu Darya

R. Helmand

R. Indus

R. Kabul

R. Kunar

Panjshir Valley

Salang Tunnel

Taloqan

Kunduz

Mazar-i Sharif

Hairatan

Qala-i Janghi

Islam Qilla

Herat

Shindand

Bamian

Charasyab

Jabal Saraj

Kabul

Sorobi

Bagram

Darunta

Jalalabad

Torkham Gate

Khyber Pass

Peshawar

Islamabad

Tora Bora

Spingar Mountains

Gardez

Khost

Shah-i Kot

Zhawar Kili Al-Badr

Tarin Kot

Kandahar

Spin Boldak

Chaman

Quetta

Legend:
- · Border crossing
- ✳ Terrorist training camp/battlefield
- ✦ Military airport

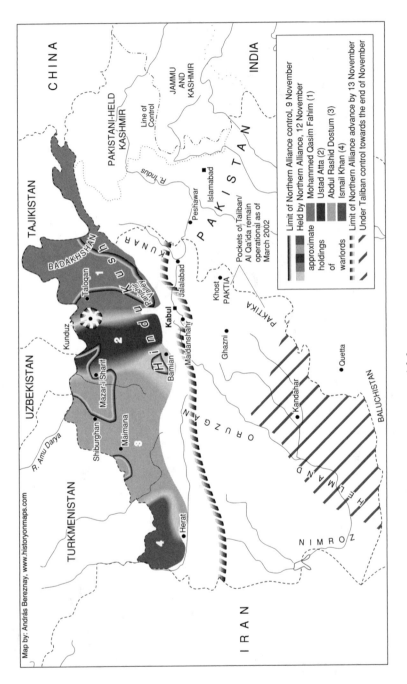

Map by: András Bereznay, www.historyonmaps.com

CHINA

TAJIKISTAN

UZBEKISTAN

TURKMENISTAN

IRAN

PAKISTANI-HELD KASHMIR

Line of Control

JAMMU AND KASHMIR

INDIA

PAKISTAN

R. Indus

Peshawar
Islamabad

BADAKHSHAN

Taloqan
Kunduz

Mazar-i-Sharif

Shiburghan
Maimana

R. Amu Darya

Panjshir
Valley

H i n d u   K u s h

Bamian

Kabul
Maidanshahr

Jalalabad

KUNAR

Khost
PAKTIA

Ghazni

ORUZGAN

PAKTIKA

Kandahar

Quetta

BALUCHISTAN

Herat

N I M R O Z

H E L M A N D

1

2

3

4

Limit of Northern Alliance control, 9 November

Held by Northern Alliance, 12 November

Mohammed Qasim Fahim (1)

Ustad Atta (2)

Abdul Rashid Dostum (3)

Ismail Khan (4)

approximate holdings of warlords

Pockets of Taliban/ Al Qa'ida remain operational as of March 2002

Limit of Northern Alliance advance by 13 November

Under Taliban control towards the end of November

Afghan war

List of Abbreviations

ACBAR	Agency Coordinating Body for Afghan Relief
ACF	Action Contre la Faim
AIG	Afghan Interim Government
b/d	Barrel per day
BJP	Bharatiya Janata Party
BP	British Petroleum
CDA	Council for the Defence of Afghanistan
CENTCOM	US Central Command
CIS	Commonwealth of Independent States
DEA	Drug Enforcement Agency
DSS	Diplomatic Security Service
ECHO	European Community Humanitarian Office
ECU	European Currency Unit
FM	Feminist Majority
GDD	Geopolitical Drugs Despatch
GIA	Groupe Islamique Armée (Algeria)
HUA	Harakat ul-Ansar
HUM	Harakat ul-Mujahedin
IB	Intelligence Bureau
ICRC	International Committee of the Red Cross
IRP	Islamic Revival Party
ISAF	International Security Assistance Force
ISI	Inter Services Intelligence
JI	Jamaat-i Islam
JUI	Jamiat ul-Ulama-i Islam
MSF	Médecins Sans Frontières
NGOs	Non-governmental organisations
NWFP	North West Frontier Province
OMON	Russian acronym for Special-Purpose Militia Detachment
OPEC	Organisation of Petroleum Exporting Countries
PDPA	People's Democratic Party of Afghanistan
PEACE	Poverty Eradication and Community Empowerment
PHR	Physicians for Human Rights
PFLP	Popular Front for the Liberation of Palestine
PKK	Kurdish acronym for Kurdistan Workers Party

PPP	Pakistan People's Party
SCF	Save the Children Fund
SLORC	State Law and Order Restoration Council
SOC	Special Operations Command
TAP	Turkmenistan–Afghanistan–Pakistan gas pipeline
TTA	Transit Trade Agreement
UAE	United Arab Emirates
UF	United Front
UIFLA	United Islamic Front for the Liberation of Afghanistan
UNDCP	United Nations Drug Control Programme
UNICEF	United Nations Children's Emergency Fund
UNHCR	United Nations High Commission for Refugees
UNITA	Portuguese acronym for National Union for the Total Independence of Angola
UNOCHA	UN Office for the Coordination of Humanitarian Assistance to Afghanistan
WFP	World Food Programme
YWCA	Young Women's Christian Association

Preface

'I am in blood
Stepp'd in so far that, should I wade no more,
Returning were as tedious as go o'er.' William Shakespeare.

Scarcely half a dozen writers were interested in the Taliban and Al Qa'ida when the 11 September attacks trumpeted the arrival of a new style of warfare and the collapse of the certainties that raised up New York's skyline and an international conviction in the United States' unshakeable power.

In spite of my own book's apocalyptic title, I had not foreseen the scale of damage Al Qa'ida was capable of inflicting on the US mainland, having catalogued in detail its crude techniques of communication and attack, and the dysfunctional personalities of the few of its members who had then come to light. Indeed, completion of the book was repeatedly held back by the whirlwind's persistent failure to arrive.

Since 'terror', or the threat of terrorist attack, became the element in which we are all compelled to swim, a whirlwind of hyperbole has engulfed the quiet backwaters in which the book was written, flattening facts, obscuring patterns and sweeping what hard information existed about Al Qa'ida into drifts of superlative, but undifferentiated, threat. If the purpose of the first edition was to provide a future generation of Afghans with an *aide memoire* for their history, the intention of the second is to capture the dynamic of great events that passed with such impassioned speed they risk blurring into myth, or collective false memory.

What attracted me most while researching the first edition of *Reaping the Whirlwind* was the sense that some conscious design lay behind the emergence of the Taliban in 1994 and that its authors could best be identified by examining the facilitating role the movement came to play in some of the decade's hottest issues: the politics of Central Asian energy, the heroin trade in Afghanistan, cross-border terrorism in Kashmir and the nuclear race between Pakistan and India.

Pakistan and Saudi Arabia were clearly sympathetic from the outset, supplying the Taliban with weapons, intelligence, cash and, after the capture of Kabul in 1997, diplomatic recognition. Initially, US support was harder to determine – beyond the first Clinton administration's legitimate interest in securing alternative sources of energy even if that involved regimes that discriminated against women or violated human rights. Washington may not have played a decisive role in the Taliban's rise to power, but nor did it display any strong objections when its former allies in the Cold War organised a 'regime change' in Afghanistan that immediately gave Al Qa'ida an unassailable safe haven throughout Clinton's second administration. That may have been a sin of omission on Washington's part, allowable under the principle of plausible deniability, but it prompts one to ask how well informed Pakistan and Saudi Arabia were of Al Qa'ida's ultimate objectives and to look for evidence that they ever tried to frustrate them.

It was only after Al Qa'ida blew up the US embassies in East Africa and Osama bin Laden stepped fully formed into view that a more intriguing picture began to unfold. Although the FBI investigation in Kenya quickly identified the perpetrators of the two attacks and their links with Al Qa'ida, the CIA appeared neurotically averse to taking any more direct action against bin Laden, a stance attributed then and now to the fear that, in so doing, it risked exposing more devastating evidence of its incompetence or complicity. As a result, the titular head of Al Qa'ida enjoyed virtual impunity for the next three years, a state of grace actually enhanced after George W. Bush succeeded to office in January 2001.

The current edition of *Reaping the Whirlwind*, a revised version rather than a floor-to-ceiling rewrite, is an attempt to track the evolution and consequences of the 11 September conspiracy while completing the original task of a cradle-to-grave account of the Taliban – even if few Afghans would agree that the movement is finally dead.

The transcripts of the East African bombers' trials in early 2001 – two years after they confessed to agents of the FBI – provide a useful measure of the data base that existed on Al Qa'ida and its US links at that time, some of which rose to greater prominence later that year. Evidence of a concurrent 'turf war' between the FBI and State Department in the first months of the Bush administration indicate points in time when Khaled Sheikh Mohammed, the alleged architect of the 11 September attacks, might possibly have been apprehended. The business interests that linked the Bush and bin Laden dynasties in Texas – Saudi Arabia's 14th province – furnish a sub-text to the White House's apparent softening in its negotiations with the Taliban for bin Laden's extradition during the cycle of executive slippage that occurs when one administration is replaced by another. 'Manual of a Raid' is an attempt to extract from the official, unofficial and Al Qa'ida versions a coherent narrative of the lives of Mohammed Atta and his fellow conspirators up until the morning of 11 September.

In our era, the dissemination of news of civilian casualties in war can be more damaging than any battlefield weapon: disentangling fact from smoke in the US war in Afghanistan was especially difficult. With Americans reeling from 11 September, besieged by anthrax, and a Pentagon anxious about its masculinity, US conduct of the information campaign in Afghanistan was a model of containment. As well as its agenda-setting daily briefings, the Pentagon was abetted by a national media, sharply aware of its patriotic duty and the needs of an audience for whom the defeat of the Taliban was merely a step towards the greater goal of finding bin Laden and tearing out his liver.

In so dominating the programme, that single quest abbreviated any further coverage of more obvious lines of enquiry, notably the extent of Saudi or Pakistani support for the Taliban and Al Qa'ida, stories that became irrecoverable after the 'axis of evil' speech in which President Bush urged us to look everywhere for the sponsors of terror – except there, as Daniel Pearl learned at the cost of his life. News from the battlefield was similarly tainted by the obsession with bin Laden. But for the scrupulous investigation of key US 'victories' by Philip Smucker of *Christan Science Monitor*, Seymour Hersh at the *New Yorker*, Susan B. Glasser and Bradley Graham of the *Washington Post* and Brendan O'Neill of *Spiked*, it would have been impossible to assemble a narrative of the war without a dangerous reliance on the Pentagon's accounts.

Another story lost for ever is a true account of the size and capability of Al Qa'ida. Distinguishing between those who were Afghan Taliban, a foreign volunteer, an Al Qa'ida mercenary or a martyrdom recruit living thousands of miles away was a central confusion of a war on terrorism ultimately incapable of defining its target clearly but which, in time, would learn to draw some advantage from that fact. From the several hundred known fighters in bin Laden's 055 Brigade, their number proliferated into tens of thousands, with German intelligence estimating that a further 70,000 may have passed through his training camps. The hyperbole and firepower later gathered at Tora Bora and Shah-i Kot transformed bin Laden's organisation from an Islamist Jonestown into a metropolis of militants, all the more effective for their remarkable powers of evasion. To suggest, as one Taliban field commander did in February 2003, that Al Qa'ida's strength was never more than 3,500 offends a fundamental article of the new faith and questions not only the ability of the US military, but also its much-vaunted air power.

The source of Al Qa'ida's funding seems to have intrigued me more than US law enforcement agencies, judging from the silence on the issue in the past 18 months. The prevailing theory is that bin Laden's followers were supported in Afghanistan and elsewhere through donations by religious charities and a number of Gulf businessmen, although the cost of financing a worldwide network of terror must run into hundreds of millions of dollars. The most prominent of his identified financiers is the Saudi banker, Khaled bin Mahfouz, a former shareholder in the failed Bank of Commerce and Credit International (BCCI), a relative of bin Laden's by marriage and a major investor in an oil company with interests in Central Asia and Afghanistan. Detained by the Saudi government in 1999, bin Mahfouz has never been formally indicted by the US authorities although he is being sued in a class action by relatives of the victims of 11 September. Figures with close ties to the BCCI pop up with unusual frequency in any in-depth account of Al Qa'ida, a matter that begs further investigation by a better-resourced author.

Finally, I have tried to provide a description of Afghanistan after the Taliban, and particularly the challenge of rebuilding central authority and political legitimacy after more than two decades of war and warlord rule. It is not an optimistic account. As narrator, I was intrigued by a parallel between the situation, at the beginning of this book, of former president Mohammed Najibullah, and that of current President Hamid Karzai, at its end. The former was the UN's protected guest until he was abandoned to the Taliban in 1997 and lynched. The latter was only saved from assassination during a visit to Kandahar by the timely intervention of his US bodyguards. In the poignant words used to describe Najibullah by another president, Burhanuddin Rabbani, '[he] is like a suspended teardrop, about to fall'.

Michael Griffin
26 March 2003

Timeline

1973

17 July — King Zahir Shah is overthrown by his cousin, Prime Minister Mohammed Daoud, with Soviet backing. Afghanistan is proclaimed a republic.

1978

27 April — Daoud is killed in a Marxist coup by the People's Democratic Party of Afghanistan (PDPA). Attempts by the new president, Noor Mohammed Taraki, to impose land reform and compulsory education for women spark a nationwide *jihad*.

1979

September — President Taraki is murdered by his deputy, Hafizullah Amin, who is executed three months later.

24 December — Red Army units seize Kabul airport as four Soviet motorised divisions roll across the northern border. Babrak Karmal, exiled PDPA leader in Moscow, returns as president.

24 December — Start of the Soviet-Afghan war (ended February 1989). Seven mujahedin parties, based in Peshawar, are selected by Pakistan's President Zia ul-Haq to receive the military supplies pouring in from western countries and the Islamic world.

1985

February–April — Mikhail Gorbachev assumes power in Moscow. Occupation forces rise to 140,000 men but entire regions are no-go areas to Soviet and government troops. The US supplies the mujahedin with Stinger missiles.

1986

4 May — At Moscow's behest, Major-General Mohammed Najibullah replaces Karmal as president. As Soviet casualties mount, Gorbachev describes the Afghan imbroglio as 'a bleeding wound', but continues to press for a military solution.

1988

February — Gorbachev announces a ten-month phased withdrawal of Soviet troops, beginning mid-May. The Geneva Accords, signed on 14 April, allow both superpowers to continue to supply arms to the combatants.

1989

14 February — In Peshawar, the 'Seven-Party Alliance of Afghan Mujahedin' announces the establishment of an 'Afghan Interim

Government' (AIG), with Sibghatullah Mojadeddi as president. Shia resistance groups and many key field commanders are excluded.

March–September   Battle of Jalalabad. Mujahedin forces fail to capture key eastern city after a siege claiming 10,000 lives.

29 August   Foreign Minister Gulbuddin Hekmatyar, head of the radical Hizb-i Islami, breaks with the AIG.

1990

6–7 February   The US and the Soviet Union agree that President Najibullah will remain in power until internationally-supervised elections can be held.

29 May   Najibullah announces the introduction of a multiparty system.

25 July   Refugees begin to return home under the UN's Voluntary Repatriation Scheme.

1991

February–March   US discontinues military aid to the AIG and announces it cannot guarantee humanitarian assistance for 1992.

21 May   UN Secretary-General Perez de Cuellar calls for an end to arms supplies to all sides, a cessation of hostilities and elections for a broadly-based democratic government. The AIG rejects any compromise with the Najibullah government.

1992

April   As mujahedin forces converge on Kabul, Najibullah takes refuge in the UN compound. Mujahedin leaders sign the Peshawar Accord, agreeing to a power-sharing period of transitional rule leading to elections. Hekmatyar is not a signatory.

24 June   Professor Burhanuddin Rabbani is declared transitional president of the 'Islamic State of Afghanistan' for six months. Hekmatyar's forces fire missiles and rockets into Kabul.

July–August   Fighting erupts between mujahedin factions in Kabul. The UN evacuates staff and relocates its offices to Islamabad.

30 December   In defiance of the Peshawar Accord, Rabbani is confirmed as president for a further two years by a 'Council of Wise Men'. Five of the nine key party leaders boycott the council.

1993

19 January   Government launches an offensive against Hekmatyar, who responds with a month-long rocket bombardment of Kabul. Thousands of civilians perish.

7 March   Under the Islamabad Accord, Rabbani's term is reduced to 18 months and Hekmatyar is brought in as prime minister. Fighting resumes two days later over the unresolved status of Defence Minister Ahmad Shah Massoud and General Dostum, the former communist in control of northern Afghanistan.

16 June   Hekmatyar is sworn in as prime minister, Massoud resigns.

1994

1 January	The Battle for Kabul intensifies as General Dostum forms alliance with Hekmatyar. Fighting continues throughout the year. A blockade halts deliveries of relief food and medicine.
14 February	Ambassador Mahmoud Mestiri is named head of a Special UN Mission with a mandate to restart the peace process. He tables proposals for a ceasefire, the creation of a neutral security force and the summoning of a *Loya Jirga*, or representative council, to oversee the formation of a transitional government.
October	Kandahar falls to an obscure militia of religious students, or *taliban*, led by Mullah Mohammed Omar, who calls for 4,000 volunteers from Pakistan.
11 November	The UN appeals for $106.4 million to meet the humanitarian requirements of Afghanistan for the next twelve months. Fighting during the year has killed 7,000, injured around 100,000 and made more than half a million homeless.

1995

February	Taliban force Hekmatyar to abandon his bases at Charasyab and Maidanshahr, ending the first siege of Kabul.
20 March	Following the killing of Abdul Ali Mazari, leader of the Shia Hizb-i Wahdat, Taliban forces are expelled from Kabul by government troops.
5 September	Herat falls to the Taliban. Local warlord Ismail Khan flees to Iran with 8,000 followers.
6 September	Pakistan's embassy in Kabul is set ablaze by rioting Afghans.
October	Second siege begins as the Taliban rocket the capital and tighten the blockade. At the UN General Assembly, Deputy Foreign Minister Abdul Rahim Ghafoorzai accuses Pakistan of orchestrating the Taliban movement.
10 November	UNICEF suspends assistance to education in Taliban-controlled regions.

1996

3 April	One thousand Moslem clergymen elect Mullah Mohammed Omar as Amir ul-Momineen, or Leader of the Faithful.
26 June	Following a peace deal with Rabbani, Hekmatyar reassumes his title as prime minister.
5 September	Taliban launch offensive in eastern Afghanistan, capturing Jalalabad.
26 September	Massoud abandons Kabul.
27 September	Taliban take control of Kabul, hang Najibullah and declare Afghanistan a 'completely Islamic state'.
7 October	Rabbani, Dostum and Karim Khalili, new leader of Hizb-i Wahdat, announce formation of an anti-Taliban alliance, the Council for the Defence of Afghanistan.

1997

13 May	Afghan opposition forms new government under Rabbani in Mazar-i Sharif.
19 May	General Abdul Malik, governor of Faryab, mutinies and allies with the Taliban. Dostum flees to Turkey.
24 May	Taliban forces enter Mazar-i Sharif.
25 May	Pakistan recognises the Taliban government, followed by Saudi Arabia and the United Arab Emirates.
28 May	General Malik, in alliance with Hizb-i Wahdat, turns on Taliban. Hundreds killed and 2,000 captured as fierce fighting drives them from the city.
10 June	Mullah Mohammed Omar makes his first public visit to Kabul to rally morale.
August	Taliban blockade the Hazarajat.
October	UNOCAL announces trans-Afghanistan pipeline consortium.

1998

23 February	Osama bin Laden calls on Moslems to 'kill the Americans and their allies – civilian and military'.
17 April	US ambassador to UN Bill Richardson holds peace talks with the Taliban.
13 July	Two UN staff murdered in Jalalabad.
7 August	US embassies in Kenya and Tanzania are attacked with grievous loss of life.
8 August	Between 4,000–5,000 people, including nine Iranian diplomats, are killed as Mazar-i Sharif falls to the Taliban.
20 August	US cruise missiles attack four terrorist training camps near Khost.
21 August	After the murder of a UN observer in Kabul, the UN and the International Committee of the Red Cross withdraw foreign staff.
21 October	UN defers decision on recognition.
8 November	US posts $5 million reward for information leading to the capture of bin Laden: Taliban respond with offer to try him in Afghanistan, finding him 'innocent' of any crime by the end of the month.
6 December	UNOCAL announces its withdrawal from the pipeline consortium.

1999

12 February	Taliban claim that bin Laden has vanished.
21 April	Taliban recapture Bamian.
May	Pakistan-backed fighters transgress the 'Line of Control' in Kashmir, provoking an international incident with India.
4 July	Bin Laden 'discovered' near Jalalabad.
4 July	Prime Minister Nawaz Sharif of Pakistan signs Washington Agreement.
6 July	US imposes trade sanctions on Afghanistan.

28 July	Taliban launch three-pronged offensive against Massoud, capturing Bagram airbase.
4 August	Ethnic cleansing of Shomali Plain; Massoud launches successful counter-offensive.
24 August	Attempted assassination of Mullah Omar.
20 September	US warns Pakistan's military command against a *coup d'état*.
7 October	ISI chief Lieutenant-General Khawaja Ziauddin flies to Kandahar to denounce the presence of 'terrorist training camps' on Afghan soil.
12–13 October	Nawaz Sharif dismisses army chief General Parvez Musharraf, replacing him with Ziauddin. Troops loyal to Musharraf seize TV centre and arrest Sharif. Musharraf pronounces himself 'Chief Executive'.
15 November	UN imposes sanctions on Afghanistan.
24 December	Twentieth anniversary of the Soviet invasion.

2000

February	Hijacking of Ariana Airlines flight to Stansted, London.
26 March	In a five-hour visit to Islamabad, President Bill Clinton urges a swift return to democracy.
5 September	After 33 days' fighting, Massoud's northern capital, Taloqan, falls to a combined force of Taliban, Al Qa'ida and Pakistani regulars.
12 October	Washington warns it will attack Afghanistan if bin Laden is found responsible for the bomb attack on the USS *Cole* in Yemen, which kills 17 sailors.
19 December	UN tightens sanctions, imposing an arms embargo, closing Taliban offices abroad and bans Taliban officials from international travel.

2001

3 January	The trial, *in absentia*, of Osama bin Laden and scores of others implicated in the East African embassy bombings commences in Manhattan.
January	Bin Laden's son, Mohammed, marries the 14-year-old daughter of his military chief, Mohammed Atef, at a ceremony in Kandahar.
26 February	Mullah Mohammed Omar orders the destruction of the standing Buddhas of Bamian.
17 March	Taliban expels BBC.
5 April	Massoud addresses the European Parliament in Strasbourg.
16 April	Taliban deputy leader, Mullah Rabbani, dies of liver cancer.
25 May	Secretary of State Colin Powell announces $43 million increase in aid to Afghanistan.
5 August	Taliban arrest eight Western aid workers and 16 Afghans for 'spreading Christianity'.

17 August	FBI arrests Zacarias Moussaoui on immigration charges after a Minneapolis flight instructor becomes suspicious when he asks for advanced tuition on flying commercial aircraft despite possessing only rudimentary aviation skills.
31 August	Prince Turki al-Faisal is relieved of his post as the head of Saudi foreign intelligence.
9 September	Two Al Qa'ida operatives, posing as journalists, assassinate Ahmad Shah Massoud with a bomb hidden in a video camera.
11 September	At around 7.55 a.m., hijackers take control of American Airlines flight 11 and United Airlines flight 175, flying them into the North and South Towers of the World Trade Center in Manhattan, causing the buildings to collapse and the deaths of thousands of people. At 8.00 a.m., hijackers seize control of United Airlines flight 93 which, after a successful resistance by passengers, crashes in rural Pennsylvania, killing all on board. At 8.10 a.m., hijackers seize American Airlines flight 77 after it leaves Dulles International Airport, crashing it into the Pentagon in Virginia, causing the deaths of 189 people.
14 September	Secretary of State Colin Powell names bin Laden the leading suspect in the attacks of 11 September.
15 September	President George Bush tells armed forces to prepare for a long war against terrorism.
17 September	A Pakistani delegation visits Kandahar to persuade the Taliban to surrender bin Laden. Bin Laden says he 'did not plan the recent attacks' in a statement to the Al-Jazeera satellite channel. Pakistan 'seals' the Afghanistan border; 200,000 flee Kandahar, fearing US attack.
19 September	The US orders the deployment of over 100 fighter, bomber and support aircraft to forward bases in Gulf as part of 'Operation Infinite Justice'. Amid widespread rioting, Musharraf defends on television his decision to support the US hunt for bin Laden.
20 September	A council of religious scholars recommends to Mullah Omar that he 'persuade Osama bin Laden to leave Afghanistan whenever possible ... and choose another place for himself'.
23 September	Pakistan withdraws diplomats, but maintains its official recognition of the Taliban. US lifts sanctions on India and Pakistan.
25 September	'Operation Infinite Justice', code-name for the US war on Afghanistan, is changed to 'Operation Enduring Freedom' to meet religious objections in the Moslem world.
26 September	Saudi Arabia cuts diplomatic ties with Afghanistan.
1 October	Riyadh denies the US use of Saudi bases to attack any Moslem state. A car bomb kills 38 people in Srinagar, Kashmir.
4 October	For the first time in its 52-year history, NATO invokes Article 5, which calls for a collective response to an armed attack upon any of its members.

5 October	British Prime Minister Tony Blair presents Parliament with a dossier of evidence incriminating bin-Laden in the attacks of 11 September.
6 October	Bin Laden says the US has declared war on Islam and calls on Moslems to defend their religion in a video broadcast by Al-Jazeera.
7 October	Musharraf dismisses or replaces three pro-Taliban officers, including the head of the ISI, General Mahmoud Ahmad. The air war in Afghanistan begins with 50 Cruise missiles launched from British Navy vessels after dark, and simultaneous raids by 40 US aircraft on Taliban air defences and Al Qa'ida training camps. Four Afghan de-miners working for the UN are among the first victims in Kabul.
8 October	Pro-king, tribal leader Hamid Karzai enters Afghanistan to orchestrate Taliban defections in his native province of Uruzgan.
10 October	US claims air supremacy.
19 October	US confirms that it is supplying the Northern Alliance with money and ammunition.
20 October	Jalaluddin Haqqani holds talks in Islamabad on the possible formation of a 'broad-based' government comprising 'moderate Taliban'. More than 100 Rangers and Delta Forces mount the first US ground missions near Kandahar, with the loss of two dead and twelve wounded.
21 October	US aircraft launch bombing raids on Taliban frontlines near Bagram for the first time in a bid to 'resolve' the conflict before winter.
26 October	Former resistance leader Abdul Haq is executed after being captured trying to rally opposition against the Taliban in Nangarhar.
1 November	The US intensifies air attacks on Taliban frontlines amid widespread criticism of its campaign as the war enters its fourth week.
3 November	Bin Laden denounces the UN for its role in the creation of Israel in a video broadcast by Al-Jazeera.
7 November	US military admits to the presence of 50 Delta Forces inside Afghanistan liaising with Northern Alliance commanders.
9 November	Taliban withdraw in disarray from Mazar-i Sharif, scattering to Kunduz or the south.
11 November	Northern Alliance claims the capture of Taloqan, Pul-i Khumri and Bamian, while Herat is poised to fall.
12 November	Alliance forces advance to within four miles of Kabul before halting.
13 November	Alliance forces enter Kabul, as Taliban stream south towards Kandahar. US steps up bombing of Kunduz, the last remaining Taliban stronghold in the north.

17 November	Mohammed Atef, bin Laden's military commander and chief lieutenant, dies in a bombing raid near Kabul.
20 November	Alliance agrees to attend Bonn talks.
26 November	Taliban and Al Qa'ida forces in Kunduz surrender. Jalalabad commander Hazrat Ali claims bin Laden is hiding with over 1,000 Al Qa'ida fighters in his underground fortress at Tora Bora.
27 November	Ferocious fighting over four days kills 170 Al Qa'ida prisoners after they seize weapons at Dostum's citadel at Qala-I-Janghi, outside Mazar-i Sharif. 'Mike' Spann becomes the first American to die in combat in Afghanistan.
1 December	Northern Alliance concedes the transfer of power to a broad-based interim administration. Hamid Karzai is confirmed as interim chairman a day later, after the UN-recognised former president Rabbani agrees to step aside.
6 December	At the urging of his advisers, Mullah Mohammed Omar agrees to transfer power in Kandahar to the pre-Taliban warlords, Naqibullah and Gul Agha Shirzai.
7 December	Taliban surrender in Kandahar, Mullah Omar is permitted to escape.
9 December	US begins carpet-bombing of Tora Bora.
11 December	US judiciary presses criminal charges against Zacarias Moussaoui, the first and only alleged conspirator arrested in connection with the 11 September attacks.
13 December	The Pentagon releases a private video of bin Laden, found a month earlier in Jalalabad, in which he demonstrates fore-knowledge of the 11 September attacks and the operational method of its perpetrators. UK agrees to lead peacekeeping mission in Kabul. Five terrorists kill nine police and government workers in a 45-minute gun battle in the Indian parliament building in New Delhi. The Indian government accuses Pakistan of responsibility.
15 December	Bin Laden is heard communicating by radio in Tora Bora.
17 December	US and British Special Forces search Tora Bora for intelligence materials and signs of bin Laden, without success.
21 December	Some 7,000 suspected Taliban and Al Qa'ida fighters are detained in Afghanistan, pending their release, trial or further question-ing at a US military facility, initially identified as either the Pacific island bases of Guam or Wake.
22 December	Hamid Karzai is inaugurated as chairman of the interim government in Kabul. Sixty-five supporters of Karzai are killed in a US air attack while travelling to the inauguration ceremony.
26 December	Bin Laden appears gaunt but calm in a 35-minute video filmed three months after the 'blessed attacks' on the US, implying he survived the assault at Tora Bora. Two days later, President Bush concedes bin Laden may 'never be caught'.

2002

3 January	President Bush appoints National Security Adviser, Afghan-American Zalmay Khalilzad, as his Special Envoy to Afghanistan.
5 January	Encircled by pro-US Afghan forces in a village in Helmand, Mullah Mohammed Omar escapes by motorcycle, accompanied by bodyguards.
6 January	Search for bin Laden at Tora Bora ends amid speculation that he has made good his escape, though whether to Pakistan, Somalia, Yemen or Chechnya is unknown.
8 January	Karzai orders all armed men to return to barracks after looting claims 49 lives in a week.
11 January	As reports emerge that hundreds of Taliban and Al Qa'ida fighters have escaped in large numbers to Pakistan, the first Al Qa'ida prisoners are flown manacled and blindfolded to the US base of Guantanamo Bay in Cuba for questioning.
21–22 January	Donors in Tokyo pledge $4.5 billion to Afghanistan for a five-year reconstruction, with $1.8 billion due in the first twelve months.
1 February	Sixty civilians die in Gardez after two days of clashes between rival governors.
1 March	UNHCR launches a repatriation programme for Afghan refugees.
4 March	Seven US Rangers are killed when two helicopters participating in Operation Anaconda in mountains south of Gardez are hit by enemy fire. US forces sustain a further fatality and 40–60 casualties in the 18-day operation, the largest deployment of US ground troops in the war.
3 April	A 110-strong force of British Marines arrives in Bagram, vanguard of a total deployment of 1,700 to support US efforts to clear Al Qa'ida fighters from Paktia and Paktika.
8 April	Four die when a bomb explodes close to the convoy of Defence Minister Mohammed Fahim, visiting Jalalabad to supervise the government's ban on opium production. Days earlier, over 160 former supporters of Gulbuddin Hekmatyar are arrested on suspicions of conspiring to overthrow the Karzai administration.
15 April	Al-Jazeera television broadcasts the final bin Laden tape into which a recording has been spliced of Ahmed al-Haznawi, one of the 11 September hijackers, promising to 'kill Americans in their heartland'.
17 April	President George W. Bush calls for a 'Marshall Plan' for Afghanistan and pledges US engagement 'until the mission is done'.
18 April	Zahir Shah returns to Kabul after a 30-year absence, but depends for security on an Italian bodyguard.
2–30 May	A series of British-led missions in southeast Afghanistan, code-named Ptarmigan, Snipe, Condor and Buzzard, uncovers caves,

	documents and weapons, but fails to locate either Taliban or Al Qa'ida remnants.
13 May	The EU Special Envoy to Afghanistan denounces the 'Auschwitz' prison conditions under which 2,000 former Taliban and Pakistani prisoners are held in Mazar-i Sharif.
15 May	US discloses that the war in Afghanistan has cost $17 billion since it commenced on 7 October.
22 May	The number of refugee returnees surpasses 650,000.
30 May	Afghanistan, Pakistan and Turkmenistan sign an agreement to build a gas pipeline linking the Daulatabad gas field with the Pakistan port of Gwadar.
11–19 June	Despite reports of intimidation and bribery during the selection process, 1,600 delegates to the *Loya Jirga* arrive in Kabul to debate the composition of the two-year government that will prepare Afghanistan for democratic elections. Hamid Karzai is approved as head of state by 1,295 of the 1,575 who vote, amid complaints that the US put pressure on Zahir Shah to step aside. Karzai's choice of cabinet members, revealed on 19 June, is criticised because it continues to favour Northern Alliance and incorporates warlords with histories of human rights violations.
19 June	Karzai is sworn in as head of state as Britain announces major reductions in its ISAF and Marine presences and the UN reports that more than 1 million refugees have returned to Afghanistan.
1 July	Nearly 50 civilians are killed and 117 injured when a US plane drops a 2,000 lb bomb on an engagement party in Mullah Omar's home district in Uruzgan. It is the fourth such attack since January.
6 July	Veteran Jalalabad warlord Haji Abdul Qadir, the only Pashtun vice-president in Karzai's government, is assassinated in broad daylight while driving to his Kabul office.
18 July	The number of refugee returnees exceeds 1.2 million, the largest repatriation since the Iraqi Kurds returned home in 1991.
23 July	Hamid Karzai replaces his Afghan bodyguard with 46 US Special Forces troops.
21 August	*Newsweek* reports UN and NGO findings that at least 1,000 captured Taliban asphixiated to death while being held in containers in Mazar in January.
3 September	Hizb-i Islami leader Gulbuddin Hekmatyar declares *jihad* and calls for the withdrawal of foreign troops from Afghanistan.
5 September	Hamid Karzai narrowly escapes assassination in Kandahar within hours of a car bomb explosion which kills 30 civilians in the Kabul central market. Suspicion falls on Taliban, Al Qa'ida and Hekmatyar.

1   The Killing of Najibullah

'But Najib knows full well his days are numbered. He is like a suspended tear drop, about to fall.' Professor Burhanuddin Rabbani, 20 March 1992[1]

The story begins on 28 September 1996 in Afghanistan's capital, Kabul, with a photograph taken the day after its capture by the Taliban.

Two men had been strung up by their necks from an elevated traffic island outside the Argh, the presidential palace, in Ariana Square. The taller one is drenched in blood from his face to the knees of his *shalwar kamees*, the Afghan's traditional baggy trousers, but the location of the wound is not immediately apparent. His throat and upper torso are bound in a cat's cradle of rope; his fingers sculpted into a still life of what look like his last throes. The other man, dressed casually in jeans and trainers, had been executed more dispassionately. The pockets of his coat and his mouth bulge with afghanis, the country's much-debased currency, as a token of his killers' contempt.

Reporters said the crowd cheered on seeing the dead bodies of former communist president, Mohammed Najibullah, and his brother, Shahpur Ahmadzai, the chief of security until his government fell in April 1992. But the only jubilation is in the faces of two Taliban fighters, frozen in one another's arms and laughing before the corpses in the euphoria of a vendetta that has finally been settled. The bystanders – mostly teenage boys or old men – look uncertainly round as if shell-shocked, although the Taliban victory spells an end to the random rocket and artillery attacks that plagued their lives since Najibullah's fall from office. There are no women in the frame.

Afghans had every reason to detest 'Najib', as he was known to friend and foe alike. As director of Khad, the secret police network set up after the Soviet invasion on Christmas Eve 1979, he was said to have ordered the deaths of 80,000 enemies and orchestrated scores of terrorist acts in the tribal trust areas of Pakistan, from where the Afghan freedom fighters, the mujahedin, launched their operations, and in Peshawar, their logistical headquarters. In 1986, when Soviet premier Mikhail Gorbachev decided to withdraw from a war he called 'a bleeding wound', Najib replaced Babrak Karmal as Afghanistan's president, going on to defy Western security predictions by holding the country together for three years after the last Red Army soldier pulled out in February 1989.

But his subsequent efforts to negotiate a transfer of power with the UN in exchange for his own resignation foundered as the US and the Pakistan-backed mujahedin, scenting total victory, pressed for a military solution. Najib had sought to shore up his regime by buying the support of disaffected groups among Afghanistan's substantial Tajik, Uzbek and Hazara minorities, re-equipping them as ethnic militias to fight against their former comrades in the mujahedin. But, when the formidable Uzbek militia, commanded by General Rashid Dostum in the northern capital of Mazar-i Sharif, mutinied in January 1992 and then allied with Ahmad Shah Massoud, the capable commander of the Tajik-dominated Jamiat-i Islami party of mujahedin, Najib's government was doomed.

On the night of 15 April, as the president tried – with the UN's help – to escape through Kabul airport to seek political asylum in India, he was recognised by Jamiat troops. He sought sanctuary instead in the UN compound where he lived in pampered imprisonment for four and a half years, pumping iron to keep his weight down, watching satellite TV and fretting over his kidney stones.[2] Najib also began to make a translation of Peter Hopkirk's classic, *The Great Game*, a study of the imperial intrigues between Britain and Russia which led to Afghanistan's birth as a buffer state in the nineteenth century. 'Afghans keep making the same mistake,' he told the visitor, 'they ought to learn.'[3]

For only the second time in 250 years, Afghanistan would be governed by its Tajik minority, headed by President Burhanuddin Rabbani with Massoud as his military chief. Najib posed this supposedly interim administration with a curious dilemma. Publicly, Rabbani demanded that Najib stand trial for war crimes committed during the Soviet occupation, a process that could be expected to rally support for his beleaguered regime, but he could not physically take the ex-president into custody. Najib's abduction from UN property would infringe international law and alienate the diplomatic community on whose recognition and humanitarian aid the Rabbani regime sorely relied.

In the limbo that ensued, a strange symbiosis evolved between the fallen commissar, with 15 years of Cold War intrigue to his credit, and the inexperienced mujahedin, who had not only taken the reins of power but, in many cases, were riding the same horses as the communists they had deposed. Among the many members of Rabbani's regime who regularly consulted Najib at the fortified UN house in Wazir Akhbar Khan, Kabul's most prestigious district, was Rabbani's Minister of Security,

General Mohammed Qasim Fahim, who had taken over Najib's old job as head of Khad.[4]

As the Taliban entered Kabul's eastern suburbs on 26 September 1996, Fahim invited the former president to accompany Massoud's retreating forces north to Jabal Saraj at the mouth of the Salang Tunnel, the only passage through the palisades of the mighty Hindu Kush.[5] But Najib feared for his life outside the protective custody he enjoyed in the capital and resolved to remain with his brother in what he believed to be the inviolable shelter of the UN compound. Early on Friday 27 September, the Afghan *chowkidars* – the night-watchmen who also guarded him – melted away and he began frantically to call the UN to provide new security. But the senior UN staff had also evacuated Kabul, abandoning him to his gruesome fate.[6]

By some accounts, he went willingly with the squad of Taliban sent to fetch him and, as a fellow-Pashtun, may have even harboured some hope he could negotiate for his life.[7] By others, he and his brother were dragged from the compound and taken to the Argh, where Najib was tortured, shot and hung in public view. A doctor who examined his body said that there was bruising on his upper torso – probably from rifle butts – a bullet injury in the upper abdomen, his fingers had been broken and his brains blown out at close range. Reports that he had been castrated were not confirmed.[8]

'We killed him because he was the murderer of our people,' said the Taliban leader, Mullah Mohammed Omar, from his base in the southern city of Kandahar.[9] But as the photograph and circumstances of Najib's death flashed around the world, there was a feeling of revulsion against Kabul's new rulers and a trickle of sympathy for a man who enjoyed remarkably little of it in his lifetime. A week after his death, the Taliban tried to counteract what had turned into a public relations disaster, by re-categorising his murder as a crime of passion, rather than justifiable homicide. On 1 October – day six of Taliban rule – the new deputy foreign minister, Sher Mohammed Stanakzai, told journalists: 'Under his leadership, our country was destroyed. It was the anger of our people which killed him.' He swore Najib's killers would be brought to justice.[10]

They never were. Kabulis, born weavers of unverifiable theories, recalled that the father and two brothers of Mullah Mohammed Rabbani, a former resistance fighter and head of the Taliban's governing council in Kabul, was pushed out of a helicopter at Najib's order after they were captured in a mujahedin raid on Kandahar.[11] Nor, it was suggested, could the US or Pakistan, the movement's widely-rumoured sponsors, allow the still influential ex-president to survive, lest he unite the more liberal elements in Afghanistan's political diaspora. With the death of Babrak Karmal, Najib's predecessor, from liver cancer in a Moscow hospital three months after the fall of Kabul, it seemed the last links with Afghanistan's communist past had been broken.

In truth, ordinary Afghans had never really bayed for Najib's blood, not even in the rural areas which bore the brunt of a ten-year resistance war in which 1.5 million died and a third of the country's 20 million people were forced into exile. Known as the Butcher of Kabul, for his professional pro-clivities, and the Ox, because of his wrestler's build, Najib was an arch-survivor, who manipulated ideology, ethnicity, religion or the nation-alist card, as and when necessity required. This – and a ruthless pragmatism – were essential requirements for any putative ruler of the whole of Afghanistan, a country whose thin veneer of modernity was constantly tested by more anchored ethnic and social divisons. Moreover, Najib's roots in the Amadzhai clan of the Pashtun, Afghanistan's largest tribe and its rulers for over two centuries, had added a certain legitimacy to his claim to the right to rule, in spite of a history of Soviet collaboration. He was, in short, the devil that was known.

It was grudging, but it was a kind of respect and it deepened as the struggle to fill the void caused by his fall from power devastated the capital and reduced its people to a penury they never experienced throughout ten years of Soviet occupation. Little wonder that Kabulis tended to associate Najib with the rule of law, functioning administration, good salaries, higher education, full bellies on subsidised food, heat, light and enter-tainment. If his continued survival at UN expense seemed the consummate act of this shrewd, political beast, however, he unwittingly came to represent all that had befallen Afghanistan since the end of the Cold War: a hostage from an inconvenient piece of history relegated to a long-drawn-out wait on death row. On the holiest day of the Moslem week, the executioners arrived.

A month before his enforced seclusion, Najibullah had given one of his last interviews to a US reporter.

We have a common task – Afghanistan, the USA and the civilised world – to launch a joint struggle against fundamentalism. If fundamentalism comes to Afghanistan, war will continue for many years. Afghanistan will turn into a centre of world smuggling for narcotic drugs. Afghanistan will be turned into a centre for terrorism.[12]

Najib may have been up to his chameleon tricks again, playing on America's growing awareness that President George Bush's much-trumpeted

'New World Order' – the outcome of a secret war waged in the mountains of Afghanistan – had simply ushered in a different set of geopolitical threats and riddles. Mazar-i Sharif had joined the rebels two months earlier, however, and the president may have already begun to write the resignation speech he delivered on television a week after the interview.

In the light of what was later to transpire, the comments had the ring of real insight.

*   *   *

As Massoud's forces withdrew to his stronghold in the Panjshir valley, creating a twelve-mile (20 kilometres) tailback on the road to Jabal Saraj, the Taliban set about imposing their idiosyncratic vision of Islamic propriety upon Kabul's cowed population. As in Herat, another Tajik city conquered by the movement one year earlier, the first official edicts focused on the rights of females and the Taliban concepts of what constituted public decency.

These had been moulded in the Pashtun regions of the south, where women are traditionally excluded from public life and girls' attendance at schools is regarded as 'un-Islamic' and a sure path to family dishonour. It was a philosophy with fewer converts in Kabul whose culture, after 35 years of Western tourism, US influence and Soviet occupation, had more in common with the secular republics of Central Asia than with Kandahar, the origin of the Taliban movement and the source, for those who lived in the capital, of an almost agoraphobic fear of the ways of the Afghan wilderness.

'All those sisters who are working in government offices are hereby informed to stay at home until further notice,' Radio Kabul – renamed the Voice of Sharia – announced on 27 September. 'Since *satar* [the Islamic dress code for women] is of great importance in Islam,' the radio continued, 'all sisters are seriously asked ... to cover their faces and the whole of their body when going out.' Programming at the station, once a comparatively urbane mix of international news, Asian pop, health advice and topical soap operas, was immediately replaced with bulletins of Taliban victories, religious homilies or fresh directives on how citizens should comport themselves.

Tens of thousands of working women, from social workers and secretaries to office cleaners and engineers, were sent home, paralysing a government in which 25 per cent of the staff were female and seriously compromising the efficiency of whatever form of administration the Taliban proposed to introduce afterwards. The decision affected 7,790 female teachers, the backbone of the educational system in Afghanistan, as well as 8,000 women undergraduates at the recently-rebuilt Kabul University, the country's most important seat of learning. The Taliban ban on education was exclusively directed at girls, but many more boys than girls were affected as 63 of the city's schools promptly closed for want of teachers.[13]

Women who did not put on the all-enveloping *burkha*, which covers the body from head to foot and leaves only a narrow grille of lace to look through, risked being beaten by the kohl-eyed Taliban warriors stalking the streets. The glimpse of an uncovered ankle was enough to arouse their righteous fury, with the result that most women preferred to remain at home, rather than expose themselves – or the male relatives forced to chaperone them – to the frightening mood-swings of what quickly came to be seen as an army of occupation.

In 1959, the writer Frantz Fanon described the hallucinogenic experience of female revolutionaries in Algeria who unveiled specifically to penetrate the French quarters unnoticed. '... She has the impression of being cut into bits, put adrift; the limbs seem to lengthen indefinitely ... for a long time she commits errors of judgement as to the exact distance to be negotiated.'[14] In Kabul, women who had gone unveiled throughout their lives found their scope of vision reduced from 90 degrees – without turning the head – to a 30-degree tunnel of claustrophobic mesh which, added to their muffled hearing, posed the constant threat of being run down by traffic or the fleets of silent bicycles that throng the capital. For those who tripped, whether through unfamiliarity with the tent-like covering or on the icy pavements, there was the further danger of exposing skin or under-garment to any passing Taliban.

For those who could not afford the $30 *burkha*, like Kabul's estimated 30,000 war widows, the enforcement of *satar* was tantamount to a formal sentence of house arrest and slow starvation. Denied any right to work, widows without a *burkha* could neither shop nor collect water without fear, while those with one could only go out and beg. Dr Sidiqa Sidiq, a professor at the Kabul Polytechnic Institute and one of the few women to publicly challenge the Taliban's impositions, warned them: 'If you deprive [women] from holding solid and decent jobs and stop them getting education, they will be compelled to resort to immoral activity to rescue their children from poverty.' Dr Sidiq told Afghan women to expect no help from abroad. She subsequently disappeared but, like many dissidents, may have gone into hiding or secretly travelled abroad.[15]

The only exemptions to the new gender decrees were female doctors and other health workers. They were permitted to continue, but pretexts for harassment were abundant in an occupation with a purely diagnostic approach to differences between the sexes. Women doctors were restricted to treating women patients only, but they faced insuperable difficulties both in communicating with their male hospital colleagues and in getting to work on the newly-segregated bus service. The few who remained active did so to prevent the total elimination of the paediatric and gynaecological services needed by their patients, the logical consequence of a Taliban-regulated, all-male, medical establishment.

Women bore the brunt of the new puritanism, but men were also forced to conform – replacing their Western clothing with the *shalwar kamees*; growing long beards; being forced to go to the mosque five times a day to worship; and abandoning toothpaste in favour of the natural root which the Prophet favoured for dental hygiene.[16] TV, kite-flying, the possession of homing pigeons, dancing, music, singing, chess, marbles and cigarettes were all proscribed in a series of radio edicts, whose growing surrealism was crystallised for many in a ban on vendors using paper as a wrapper, in case it was printed with extracts from the Koran and was later defiled by being thrown away. None of this legislation was new. People in Kandahar and Herat were subjected to the same dour medicine when they fell to the Taliban. But in Kabul, a city with a more clearly-defined liberal class and a closer identification with the social policies of the 17-year communist era, the impact seemed all the more arresting, in spite of the ousted government's record of shattered suburbs, human rights abuses and insincere peace efforts.

The focus of the world's press was inevitably the Taliban's brutal eccentricities, but quantifiable benefits did accrue from the first day of their rule in Kabul. After four years of siege, fighting became a thing of the recent past; food and fuel prices fell as roads re-opened to districts previously in enemy hands; and the few *sharia* judgments carried out in the capital transformed the security climate overnight – even as they inflamed human rights activists abroad. What frightened civilians more were the summary punishments, whether against women for breaking *satar* or alleged sympathisers with the Rabbani regime. As many as 1,000 civilians were detained during Taliban house-to-house searches within the first few days, according to Amnesty International, while the International Committee of the Red Cross put the figure as high as 1,800.[17] Scores of men and young boys were press-ganged at mosques they were forced to attend, leaving their relatives in fear that they would be deployed as human mine-clearers at the front.[18] An atmosphere of terror, created by one faction or another, invaded the city following the successive discovery of 16 headless – and unidentifiable – corpses dumped in ruins.[19]

If this was vigilantism in action, the loss of personal freedom, perhaps, was a small price to pay in a city that had known only destruction and siege since the mujahedin takeover in 1992. Human rights abuses by the Taliban were fewer in number than those perpetrated by General Dostum's Uzbek militia and other armed factions during their tenure of the capital. And while several hundred women were severely beaten by the Taliban, not a single rape was reported during their first nine months in power. Perhaps there was substance to the movement's claim that its rigorous enforcement of restrictions on women was dictated by the need to prevent their mainly rural forces from being tempted in unruly directions.[20]

Diplomats spoke of a trade-off between peace and security on the one hand and human rights on the other. That, at least, was the response of John Holtzman, deputy chief of mission at the US embassy in Pakistan. He told reporters in early October that the Taliban could play a useful role in restoring strong, centralised government to Afghanistan, a position echoed privately by relief veterans who, after two years of fruitless peace negotiations led by the UN, saw in the Taliban, with all their prejudices, a peculiarly Afghan solution to a problem that had defied international peacemakers since 1992. Robin Raphel, the US assistant secretary of state for South Asian Affairs, by contrast, described the Taliban the previous May as 'highly factionalised' and lacking in strong, consistent central leadership, and she had met the leaders on two occasions.[21]

Such contradictory readings of the same phenomenon were not only due to under-research, for the Pentagon had been equally at sea after the Soviet invasion in distinguishing between the main mujahedin parties, split as they were along finely-calibrated ethnic, social and sectarian lines. The newer confusion was more a measure of the Taliban's inherent opaqueness as a political and religious force, even after two years in the relative limelight ignited by its battlefield successes. Even as Kabul succumbed, nothing was known for certain of its military organisation or political agenda, while Mullah Mohammed Omar, the Taliban leader, had never once been photographed or interviewed. This information gap was a fertile ground for speculation about military support to the movement from Pakistan, Saudi Arabia and the United States, the troika that sustained the mujahedin during the Soviet war, only to despair of their disputes once victory was achieved. How else, it was reasoned, could so homespun a movement have made such spectacular advances in a strategic landscape that had been largely quagmired since 1992?

If the West was puzzled by the Taliban, so too was the Moslem world, which initially applauded its paramount objective of establishing a pure Islamic state in Afghanistan. While Taliban spokesmen employed the rhetoric of Islamist revolution, however, their points of reference were light-years removed from militant struggles waged elsewhere in the Moslem world, struggles that married the principles of traditional *sharia* law with concepts of social justice more rooted in the canons of dialectical materialism. The Taliban could not be criticised for want of grassroots support – at least in Pashtun districts. But the society they envisioned, and had begun to build in southern Afghanistan, went so far beyond comparable movements of spiritual revival that it made the ayatollahs look like liberal progressives. Their gender policies, meanwhile, bore an unmistakable odour of state-endorsed misogyny, given sanction by a questionable parsing of religious texts. Regional guardians of Islamic correctness, such as Iran, Egypt's Moslem Brotherhood and Pakistan's Jamaat-i Islami party, were fiercely critical of the movement's social experiments, which they condemned for 'giving Islam a bad name'. But the Jamiat ul-Ulama-i Islam, a strategic partner in Prime Minister Benazir Bhutto's soon-to-founder government and a vocal Taliban supporter, said it would approve the same penalties for blasphemy and theft, when it finally came to power in Pakistan.[22]

Whether intended or not, Najib's execution sent a stark message to all who had served in the communist or Rabbani regimes: the Taliban would take its vengeance where it willed and would not be bound by the niceties of international law. By December 1996, some 150,000 people had fled the city, heading north to Mazar-i Sharif, or across the border into Pakistan, though Massoud showed no intention of investing Kabul during the bitter winter season. Kabul University staff carried out their own straw poll in eight 48-flat housing blocks at Microrayon, a middle-income residential project built by the Soviet Union, which was on the frontline during the faction struggles of 1994. It revealed that 50 per cent of tenants had left during 1992–96, while 50 per cent of those remaining vacated by the end of the first 100 days of Taliban rule.[23]

Without women, or the many technocrats who had acquired their skills during the Soviet occupation but fled as the Taliban approached, an administration that had always functioned on one cylinder only ground swiftly to a halt. Ministerial positions were parcelled out to Taliban fellow-travellers, some eager to learn, but others scarcely out of their 20s, ignorant of the Dari dialect of Persian spoken in the capital and more anxious about sartorial detail than coordinating the management of a city of 1.2 million people.

While Kabulis suffered their stern directives, aid personnel in daily contact conveyed reports of Taliban officials so out of touch with modern protocols that it was like conversing with a group suffering from a specialised form of autism, one that permitted an awareness of an outside world, but did not allow it to enter. This was especially galling to the UN which, since the Taliban capture of Herat, had counted on the Taliban modifying its restrictions on female employment, as it matured from a popular uprising into a sovereign government with linkages to the donor community. This would also have removed the need for any more forthright condemnation of the Taliban's gender policies in a year that had already witnessed a controversial world women's conference in Beijing and the emergence of what was seen as an 'unholy alliance' between the Vatican and Islamic states to prevent the right to abortion being included in the final declaration. But the Taliban refused to bend to international norms, meeting any warning that aid might, as a consequence, be suspended not with alarm, but with passive acceptance and vague assurances that such matters would be dealt with in the course of time, when all Afghanistan were under their spell.

UNICEF announced the suspension of aid to education in Taliban-controlled regions in November 1995, arguing that the ban on female attendance at schools constituted a breach of the Convention of the Rights of the Child. Save the Children (UK) followed suit, saying that the ban on women's employment made it impossible for the agency to communicate with women, the main carers for children. Oxfam went further after the fall of Kabul, suspending its entire programme of development until female nationals working with the agency were free again to resume their duties.

If the furore over women's rights initially took the new leaders by surprise, it did not stay their hands. Nor did it elicit a more robust reaction from the UN. In New York, the Security Council was prevented from issuing a condemnation of the Taliban due to opposition from China and Indonesia – both of which routinely blocked measures that could be considered as interference in domestic matters – and through the puzzling abstention of the US, only one month away from presidential elections. UN agencies stressed the need for a 'non-confrontational' approach, in the expectation that the Taliban's desire for international recognition would induce a softening in its stance before the momentum of protest built to such a point that the organisation would be forced to the brink of the unthinkable: a unilateral break with a *de facto* government whose every pronouncement made a mockery of the Convention on the Elimination of All Forms of Discrimination Against Women. Afghanistan had ratified that document one year after the Soviet invasion.

They needn't have worried. What remained of the international women's movement was more preoccupied with Indian women stepping into bikinis at the Miss World contest, taking place that winter in New Delhi for the first time, than the beatings handed out for dress code violations 600 miles to the northwest.

Even as the *pax Talibana* settled over Kabul, it appeared that this was a government with which nobody could do business.

*   *   *

Backwoods zealots they may have been, but the fall of Kabul shattered whatever doubts may have lingered about the Taliban's military and logistical capabilities. In the first six months after the Taliban emerged in Kandahar in October 1994, it had taken control of one-third of the country, disarming local populations and imposing an interpretation of Islamic law that was both harsh in the extreme but comfortingly familiar to the Pashtun clans living in the east and south of Afghanistan and in the adjacent tribal trust territories of Pakistan.

The largest tribalised society in the world, the Pashtun share an ethos that combines traditional tribal law with an austere form of Sunni Islam. After more than a decade in the refugee squalor of Pakistan, it had hardened into an amalgam of piety and vendetta which found its highest expression in the defence of women's honour and the common call to arms. The movement was born when a former *mujahid*, Mohammed Omar, mobilised a group of fellow *taliban*, or religious students, and killed a local commander for raping two village women.[24] Whether true or not, the story struck just the right note to capture the spirit of the times and to spark off what, in the early months, had the tenor of a genuine 'victims' revolt.

For the best part of four years, the south had been in the grip of a species of Islamic samurai, gallant fighters once but fallen upon hard times since the end of the *jihad* and determined to fall no further. Their fiefdoms had been carved out as Najib's rule teetered towards its conclusion, sometimes by force of arms but, more generally, through opportunistic alliances between resistance commanders and officers in Afghanistan's armed forces. In exchange for their lives or a role in the postwar dispensation, the latter delivered entire garrisons into mujahedin hands, along with their weapons, ammunition, heavy artillery, tanks and jet fighters. These private ceasefires were often made between members of the same clan or family, profiting from both sides of the Cold War divide, but attached to one another by ties more adamant than ideology.

The outcome was a patchwork of rival warlords, each with his ramshackle facsimile of the Soviet war machine. The loyalty of their fighters, whose numbers fluctuated according to season and military need, was assured through a mixture of patronage, loot and cash, supplemented by a supply of wheat for their families. If the warlord were allied with the government – and that depended upon the strategic value of the assets he controlled – a few sacks of newly-printed afghanis might be delivered every few months to pay the troops and to keep up the appearance of a functioning civil service. But most commanders lacked this influence and resorted to racketeering, opium-growing, the trade in Cold War arms or outright banditry to shore up their volatile enclaves. It was the *jihad* that spawned these gangs and it would take another to sweep them away.

As the legend of the Taliban's invincibility spread in late 1994, the impression grew that the long-suffering Pashtun peasantry had overcome their innate differences of clan and valley to impose, through their own efforts, the peace that had eluded Afghanistan since 1979. The movement was hailed as a living embodiment of the tide of popular rejectionism, but the rejection went far beyond the mujahedin and their communist predecessors to embrace the UN's flagging peace initiative, the perfidious US and an exiled monarch who, since 1933, had done everything in his power to modernise Afghanistan – and to undermine what Mohammed Omar perceived as its authentic social and spiritual harmony. As the clock ticked backwards in the towns captured by the Taliban, it seemed that Omar's army, like some nineteenth-century millenarian movement, was taking on history itself.

But as the Taliban scythed northwards through the countryside towards Kabul, scooping up recruits and arms, the suspicion lingered that its fighters were still 'unblooded'; that the militia obtained its victories through a skilful manipulation of religious intoxication, shared ethnicity and the occasional, token skirmish. The Taliban only rarely met resistance from local commanders who, like the garrison officers before them, preferred to submit to fellow Pashtuns on favourable terms, rather than confront a superior force riding on a crest of popular acclaim. It was a textbook case of the Afghan art of knowing precisely when to change sides.

Few analysts believed the Taliban could use the same bluff on the government's brigades, seasoned by four years of siege and an attritional mode of combat which, far from the hit-and-run tactics that dislodged the Red Army, had degenerated into dogged trench warfare. Ahmad Shah Massoud, President Rabbani's charismatic commander, was rated as a supremely capable strategist in the *jihad* when he was elevated to star status in the media as the 'Lion of Panjshir', surviving eleven blistering campaigns by the Soviet-led forces in his native valley. In the defence of Kabul, he displayed a skill for planning fast-moving, multi-phased operations that were exceptional in a conflict which, since the capture of Soviet weapons in 1992, had been characterised more by brute force than tactical subtlety. His reputation was badly tarnished for failing to protect Kabul from the rockets of the Pakistan-backed Hizb-i Islami faction, led by the Pashtun warlord Gulbuddin Hekmatyar, or to oust his siege forces from thir vantage points to the south and southwest of the city. But as a fellow Tajik, he retained the reluctant support of Kabulis who, though desperate for the fighting to end, anticipated little improvement from Hizb-i Islami whose indiscriminate pummelling suggested they recognised no distinction between troops and civilians.

All the evidence suggests that Massoud regarded the Taliban more as a relief column than a threat, when they first approached the capital in February 1995.[25] Their advance on Hekmatyar's positions divided his force, allowing Massoud time to concentrate on his second enemy, the Shia Hizb-i Wahdat faction, that occupied the Karta Se district in southwest Kabul. The Tajik commander met his Taliban counterparts on two different occasions, supplying mechanics to repair a helicopter abandoned by Hizb-i Islami.[26] Massoud swore on the Koran during one meeting that, if the Taliban succeeded in taking Hekmatyar's other base at Charasyab, he would give them 'the golden key of Kabul' and withdraw to prevent more civilian deaths.[27] But while the Taliban worked on Hekmatyar, Massoud launched a two-week offensive, initially against Hizb-i Wahdat though it culminated in the Taliban's expulsion from all the positions they had won. By 19 March, the first siege of Kabul was over.

President Rabbani's political position improved immeasurably after the loss of Herat in September 1995, an event which rang alarm bells from Moscow to New Delhi. After a long period in the wilderness, the government was courted by delegations, clearly worried by Taliban intentions and what was perceived as Pakistan's more aggressive policy in the region. Shipments of fresh arms arrived from Iran, Russia, Bulgaria and Albania, while Ukraine supplied 30 second-hand fighter-bombers and India despatched technicians and a team of trainers.[28] A counter-attack on Herat was considered imminent – Iran underwriting the cost – to push the

Taliban away from Afghanistan's western border. In May 1996, a humbled Hekmatyar finally ended his feud with Massoud and joined the government's alliance, adding several thousand fighters to the Kabul garrison and reinforcing Rabbani's claims to represent Pashtun as well as minority interests. The reconciliation also ended Hizb-i Islami's blockade from Sorobi, 50 miles to the east, at the entrance of the Silk Gorge on the Kabul–Jalalabad road.

Sorobi is the key not only to Kabul but, via a mountain road winding through the Tagab valley, to Bagram military airbase, 40 miles north of the capital and the government's main supply route. Whoever commands Sorobi is free to advance on Kabul from the east and north, while simultaneously blocking the only feasible road of retreat. Hekmatyar had tried on several occasions to punch his forces through the Tagab defile, forcing Massoud to race brigades across the mountains to deflect them. Frustrated militarily, Hizb-i Islami settled in for a siege, interdicting relief convoys and cutting off the nearby hydro station, the city's only power supply. But the Silk Gorge was an equivocal position to hold. It could be blocked with ease, but penetrated only at the risk of great loss of life. Running for 15 miles between coppery rocks that rise sheer to a thousand feet on either side, the road dives at intervals into man-made tunnels through the cliffs, making it the easiest position in the world to defend.

Hekmatyar's 'defection' to the government played a crucial role in the success of the Taliban's final advance on Kabul, for it set Pashtun against Pashtun. A risky gamble in the best of times, this was particularly true when the Hizb-i Islami commanders opposed to Hekmatyar's new alliance with Massoud once shared the Taliban's objective of overthrowing the Tajik by force – as well as their ethnicity in common. Hizb's notoriously rapacious Sorobi commander, Zardad Khan, reportedly accepted a prize of $50,000–$100,000 in exchange for surrendering his position without a fight.[29]

The likelihood increased three days later with the ambush and killing of 70 commanders from the Nangarhar *shura*, the coalition of factions led by Governor Haji Abdul Qadir which controlled the all-important Khyber Pass, the three eastern provinces and showed a preference for peace, commerce and the export of opium over the tedious complexities of governing Afghanistan. The *shura* were in convoy for negotiations with the Taliban when their vehicles where rocketed at Dakka by a renegade commander, Shah Wali.[30] Haji Qadir, his son Jamal and commander Zaman Gham, a key link in the province's narcotics trade, escaped over the border into Pakistan, while the Taliban forces stormed Jalalabad a few hours later, hoisting their white banner over the Governor's House.[31]

They pressed on without pause to Sorobi, where Massoud's forces had taken up positions alongside the Hizb-i Islami garrison. What happened next is not altogether clear. By some accounts, Massoud had decided to quit the capital and had begun blowing up the ammunition which could not be evacuated north. This convinced his forces, most of them at Sorobi for the first time, that the Taliban had somehow moved to their rear, cutting off their escape to Kabul. Whether through panic or treachery, the result was a shambles. The Taliban stormed through the pass on 24 September and the road was clear to the capital. After two more days of fighting in the eastern suburbs, Massoud finally decided to withdraw to Jabal Saraj, undertaking an organised retreat in darkness while still in contact with the enemy.

'Had we not made an alliance with Hekmatyar,' Massoud told journalists that December, 'Kabul would still be in our hands.'[32] His version of events was that Hekmatyar refused to deploy his troops against the enemy at Sorobi, doubting their loyalty. But the truth lay somewhere between: Massoud had been as much out-generalled as betrayed. The Taliban had captured 200 miles of contested territory in less than three weeks, displaying a sophistication of command and communication that military analysts found hard to square with the militia's humble origins.

The Lion of Panjshir was back where he started a quarter of a century before, leading a demoralised force in an unassailable valley far from the seat of power.

2   City of Night

The roots of the hatred between Massoud and Hekmatyar went deeper than the Soviet invasion, yet the two men, in many ways, were as similar as siblings. Both were engineering students in Kabul in the early 1970s, gravitating to the radical circles that gathered around theology professor Burhanuddin Rabbani, founder of Jamiat-i Islami (Society of Islam), Afghanistan's first truly Islamist party.

Both fled to Peshawar, along with their mentor after the 1973 overthrow of King Zahir Shah by his cousin, Mohammed Daoud, a coup supported by the Afghan army, the Afghan communist party and, covertly, by Moscow. As Zahir Shah's prime minister, Daoud had been an active advocate of 'Pashtunistan', the hypothetical ancestral homeland that was hoped would reunite the Pashtun communities divided by Britain's arbitrary drawing of the Durand Line in 1893. This declaration fixed the 950-mile (1,500 kilometres) border between an indomitable Afghanistan and British India, establishing the tribal trust territories in Pakistan – where Pashtun customary law still holds sway – as a turbulent buffer between them.

With Britain's withdrawal from the sub-continent in 1947, the Pashtunistan grievance rose swiftly to the surface. Pakistan, taking its first steps into independence, immediately found its western frontier disputed by the better-equipped and Pashtun-dominated army in Afghanistan. The issue poisoned relations with Pakistan, and also the US, then moving tentatively into the Cold War vacuum created by Britain's abdication of its imperial role. Afghanistan, as a result, drifted closer to Moscow and, by 1970, some 7,000 officers in the armed forces had received training in the USSR.[1]

In Pakistan, Massoud and Hekmatyar were taken up by President Zulfikar Ali Bhutto, father of Benazir Bhutto, as tools to combat Mohammed Daoud's growing irredentism. From 1974 onwards, 5,000 of their comrades underwent military training in a programme coordinated by Brigadier Naseerullah Babar, inspector-general of Pakistan's 2nd Frontier Corps and soon to emerge as President Bhutto's chief adviser on Afghan policy.[2] The training culminated in a series of Pakistani-backed incursions into eastern Afghanistan in mid-1975 that provoked harsh retaliation against the domestic Islamic opposition to Daoud's rule.

The violence of the government's response split the exiled rebels between those, like Rabbani and Massoud, who sought to develop an indigenous movement capable of sustaining a revolt on a national scale, and others, led by Hekmatyar, who wanted to launch an immediate *jihad* with whatever foreign support was available. Hekmatyar broke away from Jamiat-i Islami to form Hizb-i Islami (Party of Islam), a disciplined political organisation with backers in the Pakistani army and the influential Pakistani Jamaat-i Islami party.

Rabbani's Jamiat-i Islami was formed as a broad-based alliance to counter the strength of the Soviet-Afghan communist party – the People's Democratic Party of Afghanistan (PDPA) – which helped Daoud to power but, in April 1978, overthrew him. Jamiat's split into gradualist and radical elements uncannily echoed a schism in the PDPA between the moderate Parcham and hardline Khalq wings that reflected Afghanistan's fierce distinctions of tribe, language and class and was tantamount to a civil war in embryo.

Founded in 1965, the PDPA suffered its first falling-out four years later when Noor Mohammed Taraki and Babrak Karmal disputed the party leadership. Taraki was a Ghilzai Pashtun from the east where the Pashtunistan question was a more vexatious issue. The Khalq, or 'People', faction that he led dominated the officer corps, the police force and was more exclusively Pashtun, with a particular accent on its rural, more 'proletarian' origins. Karmal, by contrast, was a Kabuli, related by marriage to the royal Mohammadzai branch of the Durrani clan which had ruled for the last 200 years. The Parcham, or 'Banner', faction, which he led and to which Najibullah, incidentally, also belonged, was more broad-based, embracing Dari-speaking, non-Pashtun interests, and those of the urban elite.

Both were oriented to Moscow but, while Parcham favoured a gradualist approach – allowing, for example, Prince Daoud to remain at the helm after 1973, as a symbol of dynastic continuity – Khalq aimed for the liquidation of Mohammadzai rule entirely and a revolution along the lines adopted in Central Asia. The rivalry between the two wings intensified after 1978 when, with the approval of Moscow, Taraki had Daoud and his family murdered, declaring himself president of a 'Democratic Republic of Afghanistan'.

As a Ghilzai, Taraki's right to hold high office in Afghanistan was debatable, while his 'Saur Revolution', a programme of reform launched to forcibly redistribute land, secularise education and unveil women, sparked off *jihad* in every one of Afghanistan's provinces a full year before the Soviet Union's invasion. And when it invaded in December 1979, it was to restore the Parcham moderate tendency, in the shape of Babrak Karmal, and prevent a Soviet satellite state from being engulfed by the same Islamist ferment that toppled the Shah of Iran in the same year. Parcham maintained control of power throughout the ten-year occupation, while Khalq military officers – under close Soviet supervision – directed the war effort.

So entrenched were the prejudices of Afghan society – between Pashtun and non-Pashtun, Ghilzai and Durrani, town and country, traditional and modern – it was evident they would not fade with the Red Army or the PDPA, but reassert themselves in a different guise in whatever political framework was cast up by the post-communist balance of power. After Najibullah fell, Khalq elements were attracted to Hekmatyar, Parcham to Massoud and Rabbani while the two existed in an uneasy equilibrium in Rashid Dostum's northern fiefdom, the least reconstructed of all the remnants of the former PDPA state apparatus.[3] When in the course of efforts to end the faction fighting of 1992–94, the UN proposed a role for the Rome-based ex-king Zahir Shah, it was fumbling in the dark towards a pre-communist era when royal government enjoyed cultural and tribal legitimacy. In so doing, it strayed perilously close to Parcham territory – and Khalq taboos – cancelling out whatever benefits might otherwise accrue.

General Zia ul-Haq, commander of the Pakistani army, toppled Zulfikar Ali Bhutto in 1977, executing him two years later. When the Soviet invasion compelled President Jimmy Carter first to consider, and then approve the clandestine supply of weapons and cash to support the mujahedin's ten-year war of resistance, it was Pakistan's Inter Services Intelligence agency (ISI) that coordinated strategy and monitored which Afghan factions qualified for funding and how it was spent.

A crucial conduit for that financial aid was the Bank of Commerce and Credit International (BCCI), the world's fastest-growing bank until an indictment on charges of money laundering for the Colombian cocaine cartels in 1988 exposed it as a criminal enterprise on a global scale. Established by Gulf states and Pakistani bankers to invest revenues from the region's oil boom, one of BCCI's chief shareholders was Sheikh Kamal Adham, head of Saudi Arabian intelligence from 1960 to 1977 and an intimate of key national security, defence and banking figures in the Carter, Reagan and Bush presidencies. After the bank was wound up in 1991, owing depositors $12 billion, a US Senate enquiry revealed that the BCCI transacted the financial side of many other operations that the CIA needed to keep secret from Congressional oversight – illegal arms shipments, the Iran-Contra affair, covert payments to pro-US 'freedom fighters' – though it had long been aware of its involvement in money laundering, fraud and systematic bribery of figures in high office.

Of the seven parties identified and funded by the ISI, the only non-Pashtun group was Jamiat-i Islami which, after the splits in the mid-1970s, took on the ethnic character of Rabbani and Massoud, both Tajiks from Badakhshan and the Panjshir valley respectively. The Dari-speaking Tajiks comprised some 25 per cent of Afghanistan's population, but formed a majority in the administrative and commercial centres of Kabul and Herat. The remaining six hailed from the eastern Ghilzai or 'minority' Pashtun clans, an indication that the ISI was not addressing solely the Soviet threat as it drew up plans for the resistance, but the danger to its own borders of arming an alliance that included the 'royal' Durranis of the south. As in Bhutto's time, this was to be avoided at all costs if the tribal trust territories of North West Frontier Province were to remain in Pakistani hands.

Hekmatyar was a de-tribalised Pashtun from Kunduz, a northern pocket settled under the nineteenth-century ruler, Amir Abdul Rahman. As a result, he could not play the Pashtunistan card with much conviction, but it is unlikely that he wanted to during a period when all the mujahedin aspirants to sponsorship from Zia, a devout Moslem, and other sources in the Gulf were stressing their Islamist credentials over ethnic or nationalist affiliations. But while all the Peshawar-based parties professed Islamist goals, it was an Islam largely stripped of its local associations of custom and tradition, as it moved into global revolutionary mode in the chase for funding. Hekmatyar and Massoud, the first proponents of this radicalised Islam, had as much in common with the Afghan peasant, with his beliefs in spirits and saints, as the PDPA cadres they defied.

Hekmatyar remained the undisputed champion of Pakistan's interests in Afghanistan until 1994. Hizb-i Islami was allocated more than half of the $6 billion in armaments and cash that were estimated to have been siphoned into the anti-Soviet cause.[4] Some of these resources were used to build a revolutionary party structure, complete with posters, portraits, T-shirts and a smooth propaganda machine. All seven parties maintained offices in Peshawar, but Hekmatyar's privileged standing enabled him to exploit what, during the occupation, emerged as the most valuable outward token of legitimacy – the 3 million 'captive' population of mainly Pashtun refugees living in camps in Pakistan.

On arrival, all males were compelled to register as members of one of the seven exiled parties, whatever their political or religious views. Hizb-i Islami established a towering presence in the camps and the aid distribution network, and incoming refugees quickly realised that 'joining'

Hekmatyar's party was a fast-track to relief. In the eyes of one UN refugee worker, this amounted to a 'reign of terror' but, if so, it was not confined to the camps alone.[5] Throughout the 1980s, a number of liberals, including Mina Keshwar Kamal, founder of the Revolutionary Association of the Women of Afghanistan, and Professor Sayed Bahauddin Majrooh, an independent publisher and journalist, were assassinated in circumstances that implicated Hizb-i Islami,[6] as was Mir Wais Jalil, a journalist with the BBC World Service, who was murdered on 29 July 1994.[7]

The bad blood with Massoud dated back to 1976 when, with the backing of the ISI, Hekmatyar had the Tajik commander arrested on charges of spying for the Daoud government, along with his close friend Jan Mahmad, who was tortured and murdered.[8] Massoud left Peshawar three years later to raise the revolt against the Taraki regime in the Panjshir valley, not to return for a decade. The enmity erupted again in 1982, after Massoud agreed a temporary ceasefire with the Soviets to allow time for his fighters to regroup. That winter, Hizb forces turned their weapons on Jamiat groups in the provinces of Takhar, Badakhshan and Baghlan, where 13 of Massoud's commanders were ambushed and killed.[9]

But their quarrel went beyond personalities or tribal differences to encapsulate their wholly contradictory readings of Afghanistan's post-Soviet future. While Zia held the purse-strings of the *jihad*, Pakistan's Afghan policy would always reflect its own priorities. These were to exploit tribal factors to protect its western border and prevent the survival of a strong, unified Afghanistan with its military muscle – boosted by Soviet training and aid – fully intact. Dismemberment, in that sense, was always in the cards. Pakistan could not dispense with its Pashtun proxies: they constituted 40 per cent of the Afghan population and had historically lorded it over the minorities which, on the battlefield, were experiencing in the war against the Red Army their first taste of self-determination.

Fostering 'upstart' elements within the Pashtun pantheon, such as Hekmatyar, ensured that Afghanistan would pose no further threat after the Soviets were beaten. But removing the Durrani from a central role in the Peshawar-based resistance was a recipe for postwar anarchy, when Tajik, Uzbek and Hazara had been primed by combat for a greater share of power after centuries of Pashtun hegemony. While Hekmatyar was consolidating his political position in Peshawar, however, Massoud had been trying a more grassroots approach to Afghan power-broking, travelling from valley to valley to unite the disparate ingredients of the northern *jihad* into a workable coalition.

Starved of military supplies, due to his alienation from the ISI and distance from the Pakistan border, Massoud could still claim with some honesty that he had never been anybody's stooge, merely an Afghan nationalist with Islamist convictions. By 1988, Jamiat had established an alliance of commanders from Herat to Badakhshan, known as Shura-i Nazar Shomal, or Supervisory Council of the North, that cut across ethnic differences. Prominent among its members was Ismail Khan, the army officer from Herat who led the 1979 mutiny that prompted Moscow's decision to invade. Massoud had considered the formation of an 'Islamic Army', integrating units from different factions into a single force, a project he would take up again in 1992 following the collapse of the Najibullah regime in Kabul.[10] By 1991, his strength was reportedly up to 12,000 trained men.[11]

The hands of Pakistan and, to a lesser extent, the US and Saudi Arabia in the formation of the first post-Soviet government was, in effect, to guarantee that it would fold. In February 1988, Moscow announced it would evacuate its troops by the end of March 1989, a decision interpreted as signalling the imminent fall of Najibullah's regime. But despite a decade of Pakistan and US planning, there was no government-in-waiting to fill the vacuum left by the PDPA. It had to be created from scratch, supervised by the ISI, the CIA and Saudi intelligence service from political elements initially selected for funding and fighting on the basis that they served the best interests of Pakistan, not Afghanistan. The Afghan Interim Government (AIG), led by Sibghatollah Mojadeddi, who headed his own faction, was announced in February 1989, but its composition ignored the eight Shia factions which, with Iranian coaxing, had coalesced into Hizb-i Wahdat Islami (Party of Islamic Unity). No other minority group and – most significantly – none of the senior field commanders was considered for office in the new coalition.

The estrangement between commanders and politicians culminated at Jalalabad in 1989 in a showcase operation, designed both to secure an eastern capital for the AIG and demonstrate that the mujahedin were more than a match for the government's demoralised forces. ISI and Pakistani army strategists drew up plans for a full-frontal assault on a city whose garrison and defences were amongst the best-equipped in Afghanistan, being one step away from the hostile border. Some 10,000 mujahedin died in the six-month onslaught, the single most crippling loss of the war and a devastating exposure of the resistance's weakness when confronted with the challenge of a pitched battle, instead of guerrilla warfare. On 29 August, hours before the attack was abandoned, Hekmatyar quit the AIG.

In February 1990, the US and USSR agreed that Najibullah should remain in power until internationally-supervised elections could be held. Though regarded as a breakthrough in the peace talks, the two superpowers reserved the right to continue supplying their protégés for two more years, an arms race that ensured bulging arsenals on both sides should a ballot, miraculously, be held. Washington's stance reflected, in part, the resurgence of the Khalq faction, a consequence both of Moscow's dwindling interest in Afghanistan and the Parcham Najibullah's accommodating attitude to the non-Pashtun elements in the mujahedin.

A month later, defence minister Shahnawaz Tanai attempted to overthrow Naijibullah's regime, in collaboration with Khalq elements in the military, Hekmatyar and the ISI.[12] Serious damage was inflicted on the Argh and other government buildings, but the coup failed and Tanai fled to the army barracks in Rawalpindi, near Islamabad, while his sympathisers merged with the Hizb forces closing in on the capital. Four years later, Tanai's name was widely reported to have recruited the Khalq diaspora to provide the nascent Taliban with the military and air force skills that its fighters had certainly never acquired in religious school.[13]

In April 1992, Massoud, in alliance with Dostum's Uzbek militia, occupied Bagram airbase 40 miles to the north of the capital. Despite requests from Parcham sympathisers to declare himself head of state, Massoud called on the leaders of the seven Peshawar-based parties to agree on the formation of an interim mujahedin government.[14] It took ten days of debate before the Peshawar Accord was finally announced on 26 April, and the complexity of the terms reflected the prevailing mood of mutual suspicion. Sibghatollah Mojadeddi would be interim president for two months, followed by Rabbani for four months, followed by a grand assembly, or *Loya Jirga*, to select an 18-month interim government, followed by the first democratic elections in Afghan history.

The Accord came too late to prevent the clash between Massoud and Hekmatyar which had long been inevitable. On 25 April, the combined forces of Massoud and Dostum entered Kabul to pre-empt a military takeover by Hekmatyar, camped on the outskirts of the city with his Khalq allies. The army swifly disintegrated along the ethnic lines which had underpinned, but been camouflaged by, the faultline running through the PDPA. The 1st Division at Kargah, the 2nd Division at Jabal Saraj, the 99th Rocket Brigade and the 40th Division at Bagram sided with Massoud, while the 5th Division Sarandoi, a paramilitary police force, joined Hekmatyar, along with officers from the Interior Ministry. The Shia Hizb-i Wahdat was also a major beneficiary, scooping up the 95th and 96th Tribal Divisions, garrisoned in south and western Kabul.[15]

In accordance with the Peshawar Accord, Rabbani assumed the presidency in June 1992 and was immediately challenged by Hekmatyar who demanded the withdrawal from Kabul of Dostum's militia and what he called the 'communist elements' which had merged with Rabbani's government and army. In August, the city came under a massive rocket attack from Hizb-i Islami forces, which claimed some 2,000 civilian lives. Hundreds of bodies lined the streets, whole districts were razed to the ground and the homeless sought refuge in the notorious Pul-i Charki prison, a Khad complex which had housed 12,000–15,000 political prisoners.[16]

The first siege of Kabul had begun.

*　*　*

Four roads snake into Kabul from four cardinal points, bisecting the city octagonally and then dividing it into 16 municipal districts. Set in an amphitheatre of mountains, snow-capped in winter, the city tilts, geographically, towards the Khyber Pass to which it is linked by the thin umbilical of the Silk Gorge, shadowing the Kabul river as it flows downstream to fall on the Indus at Attock. To the north lie the foothills of the Hindu Kush and the folds of the Panjshir valley, Massoud's green and narrow country. Abdul Rasul Sayyaf, leader of Ittehad-i Islami, held the western access in 1992, congregating his force at the spa town of Paghman, where King Amanullah used to race elephants. Hekmatyar's men had taken up position in the villages of Charasyab and Maidanshahr, a few miles to the southwest.

Kabul had expanded in that direction in the 1920s, along what the traveller Robert Byron called 'one of the most beautiful avenues in the world', to Darulaman Palace, which housed the Ministry of Defence.[17] Overlooked by the 6,500-foot (2,000 metres) of Television Hill, the neighbouring districts of Karta Se and Qalaye Shada would never entirely be part of Kabul, in spite of the proliferation of new embassies and faculties. Their inhabitants were Shias from the Hazarajat massif, which gave them birth and then promptly expelled them, because there was not enough land to go round. In Kabul, they made a living in service: as *chowkidars* and domestics, barrow wallahs and labourers. The Shia destiny in Afghanistan had always been to slave.

Kabul had passed a pleasant war, largely free from attack. When the Soviets left, Najibullah's Afghanistan wallowed for a while on $3 billion a year in subsidies – on food, fuel, jobs, housing, but mainly on defence to prevent the rip-tide of Islamic extremism, represented by a mujahedin victory, from lapping against the USSR's southern borders. The residential project of Microrayon in east Kabul, built to house 140,000 people, gives some indication of the lengths to which Soviet planners would go in their efforts to create, and then to recruit, an Afghan political class.

Life in those apartments encapsulated some of the worst civic experiences that were available in the post-Cold War world. Weapons once wielded by a superpower that had mortally overreached itself were now directed at a city that consisted chiefly of mud, medieval wells and wood-burning stoves, however ambitious the outward symbols of nationhood built by the former kings and communists in Kabul. In the four years that elapsed after Najibullah's fall, the slaughter in Kabul became so unrelenting that Afghans would ponder, amid the desolation and the international solitude, whether or not it mattered that there was no enemy there apart from the pallid, post-Soviet citizen and the domestics he had never quite managed to shake off.

The purpose, it seemed, was to kill off the city and its attitudes and skills, to wipe the slate clean, quell government itself, the source of all the communist mayhem in the rural areas. What Genghis Khan achieved at Balkh, near Mazar-i Sharif, Hekmatyar tried at this other historic crossroads. It was, probably, never consciously in his mind as his missiles hammered at the fabric of Kabul, but 45,000 Kabulis testified to the thesis with their lives, and several hundred thousand more departed the scene, too broken to remain.

Nearly 300,000 Kabulis had fled to Jalalabad by the end of 1994, while 1,000 more escaped from the capital every day to join them.[18] The refugee population of Sar Shahi, the largest camp, was so highly qualified that it was referred to as the 'University of Kabul in exile'. There were 500 experienced secondary school teachers, along with scores of doctors, laboratory technicians, health workers, senior civil servants, former army officers and engineers, the product of decades of Soviet investment in Afghanistan's human resources.

No city since the end of the Second World War – excepting Sarajevo – suffered the same ferocity of violence as Kabul from 1992 to 1996, but even Sarajevo was a side-show by comparison and its agonies were certainly never ignored. An official of the International Committee of the Red Cross, one of only three foreign organisations to remain after the rocketing of January 1994, said: 'Afghanistan seems to have disappeared off the face of the earth.' This was true both figuratively and literally, as first 50 per cent

– rising to 80 per cent in 1996 – of the built-up areas of Kabul were turned into rubble resembling Dresden after the fire-bombing.

Clusters of worshippers in a mosque, passengers in a minibus, children gathering wood or women in a bread queue exploded, only to step forward in a bromide report in the back pages of the Pakistani press. These vignettes of daily violence took place against a general meltdown of life support systems in a city of 1.2 million which, while never modern at heart, had come to depend upon the utilities of urban life. First, the lights went out, and then the water stopped running. The sewer system, rubbish disposal, revenue collection, salaries, free medicine, the postal service, the comfort of fire and the law one by one faded from memory, while food and fuel had to run blockades in the east, south and the north that were only inter- mittently relaxed to permit the transit of relief goods.

The city's ability to function was further undermined by the flight of the 50,000-strong Sikh and Hindu minorities, who had been at the centre of the money market and the commercial system in Najibullah's Kabul.[19] Despite the absence of bullion or other reserves, the afghani remained broadly stable throughout the mujahedin interregnum, responding more to the food blockades than the fact that the Rabbani government simply had more cash printed up whenever the treasury was empty. One finance minister admitted that Afghanistan's entire budget of $200 million was financed by new notes printed in Russia.[20]

This was just one of the mysteries of surviving Kabul under siege. By winter 1995, the cost of fuel-wood was so high that it cost a dollar a night to light a fire, forcing families to choose between keeping warm or cooking a meal – if they could afford the food. In a household survey one year later, it was learned that it cost around 1 million afghani a month for a family of six to survive but average wages were equivalent to one-tenth that amount.[21] A UNICEF survey of 1,100 war widows found that they lived on nothing more than green tea, *naan* bread and a little yoghurt.

Were the figures flawed? How could they have been, unless Kabulis had a parallel life support system that still defied detection?

*   *   *

There were two flies – excluding Hekmatyar – in the bloody ointment smeared over Kabul before it fell to the Taliban in September 1996. The first was Rashid Dostum, the mutinous general from Mazar-i Sharif whose 1992 alliance with Massoud made Najibullah's downfall inevitable. The nearest the factions ever came to unanimity was on the need to exclude

Dostum from any future power-sharing formula. He had served the communists – until it proved wiser not to – while the 20,000-strong Jawzjani militia, which he personally raised under Najibullah, fought mercilessly against the mujahedin at the sieges of Jalalabad, Khost and Gardez. These Uzbek fighters inspired even greater fear among civilians, who named them *galamjam* – or 'carpet-thieves' – a term that Afghans diversified to embrace anyone with bad intentions. But Dostum controlled the Bagram military airbase and his combined force of 40,000 well-trained regulars, backed by tanks and squadrons of fighter and bomber aircraft, was a threat which Massoud could neither dispense with nor ignore.

The second factor in the post-Soviet equation was the ethnic question. Exacerbated by the alienation of the field commanders from the parties in Peshawar, this underpinned the failure of the mujahedin to devise a viable transitional government, bringing down, in September 1996, Massoud, whose instincts, finely attuned as they were in battle, exhibited a tendency to betray him in politics. His inability – or that of his figurehead president, the pious Rabbani – to deliver a working alliance of Tajik, Uzbek and Hazara to counter Hekmatyar's claim to represent the traditional Pashtun hegemony ensured four years of unremitting conflict.

This outcome was all but implicit under the terms of the Peshawar Accord which glossed over the all-important detail of who should be represented in the Grand Assembly, called to select the 18-month transitional government, when Rabbani's four-month term of office expired. A traditional *Loya Jirga*, composed of the 'great and the good', was certain to call for the return of Zahir Shah, a move that the autonomous ethnic forces cast up by the war were equally certain to oppose. A more democratic approach, based upon proportional representation for the minorities, was beyond Afghan experience and, anyway, raised the thorny question of Dostum and his Uzbeks, still tainted by their communist past. With no real power base to call his own, Hekmatyar played the Islamic card by insisting on an assembly of religious scholars.

Despite his image as a beatific, slightly doddery old man of the cloth, Rabbani behaved with estimable rapacity. He summoned his own 'Council of Wise Men' on 30 December, flying in many of its 1,335 delegates from Peshawar, and was confirmed as president for a further two years – to the outrage of five of the seven mujahedin leaders. Dostum was not invited and Hekmatyar declared Rabbani's constitutional coup an act of war. The fiction of peaceful power-sharing was exhausted even before Sibghatollah Mojadeddi – with a reluctance that verges on the genetic in Afghanistan – even refused to hand power to Rabbani.

Law and order in Kabul had broken down immediately after the mujahedin takeover in April 1992, with rival factions setting up roadblocks every hundred or so yards and indulging in sprees of rape, looting and murder. After Hekmatyar's initial rocketing in April, fighting broke out between Hizb-i Wahdat, strong in southwestern Kabul, and the Saudi-backed, Pashtun forces of Abdul Rasul Sayyaf's Ittehad-i Islami faction over the Shias' exclusion from government. The thriving commercial quarter of Khote Sange went up in smoke.

But the first real onslaught was Hekmatyar's rocket bombardment in early August from Charasyab and Maidanshahr. A single cluster bomb attack on 13 August killed at least 80 people and wounded a further 150. Hekmatyar appeared to be targeting the city's communications, for the TV station, the main printing press, an $8 million airport control tower and Ariana Airlines' domestic fleet were all destroyed, while Radio Kabul and the presidential palace took direct hits.[22] A ceasefire was drawn up through the mediation of Haji Qadir, leader of the Nangarhar *shura*, which guaranteed to deploy a 5,000-strong buffer force of neutral mujahedin to stand between the warring factions.[23]

Rabbani's hijacking of the presidency initially won the support of only Sayyaf, a breakaway Shia group, Harakat-i Islami, and members of the old regime. But after some initial skirmishes, Dostum fell in with the arrangement and, while other faction leaders expressed their disapproval, they remained neutral in the fighting that followed. Hekmatyar stood alone, until the end of January when Abdul Ali Mazari's Hizb-i Wahdat joined in alliance with Hizb-i Islami. Massoud struck first, bombing Hekmatyar's southern bases and the artillery depot at Bagram, east of Kabul. There followed four weeks of fighting, reaching a peak on 8 February in the worst rocketing since August, with missiles randomly falling into civilian areas. When Hizb-i Wahdat attacked from the west, Massoud and Sayyaf joined forces to carry out a combined attack on southwestern Kabul on 11 and 12 February. It was one of Massoud's worst mistakes.

The Hazara had always lived on the defensive. Driven by the Pashtun to the infertile Hazarajat in the nineteenth century, their mujahedin descendants were fighting both for freedom from Soviet rule and greater political representation for a minority that accounted for up to 20 per cent of the population. Pitting the sabre-toting fanatics of Sayyaf's Ittehad-i Islami – another sectarian minority – against a population which would have made better allies than enemies, extended the battle for Karta Se over three wasted years and earned Massoud a place in the Shia chronicle of horrors. On 11 February, government forces and their allies entered the Hazara suburb of Afshar, killing – by local accounts – 'up to 1,000 civilians', beheading old men, women, children and even their dogs, and stuffing their bodies down the wells, '60 at a time'.[24] Local descriptions differ significantly from those of Amnesty International, but are indicative of the event's continuing power to haunt.

Amnesty cited a young nurse who witnessed the incident: 'There were 12 of them. They broke down the door, then they made advances towards my sister and me. My father tried to stop them, but they hit him and then tortured him. They cut off one of his feet and both his hands in the courtyard. One of them threw my father's hands to a dog belonging to one of his commanders.'[25] Such naked massacres were relatively rare, although the rocketing took a different and more consistent toll, killing over 1,000 in February 1993 alone. But the rape or abduction of young women, particularly among minorities, was practised by members of each of the factions, reaching its nadir during the *galamjam* occupation. The Pashtun, it should be noted, counted among Kabul's minorities.

With the exception of Kunduz, Kandahar and Baghlan, the rest of Afghanistan was peaceful throughout 1992, stimulating a massive return of refugees from Pakistan. Nearly 1 million had arrived by the end of the year, attracted by the food for work, seed multiplication and irrigation repair projects established by the UN and other foreign donors.[26] That figure plummeted following the signing of the Islamabad Accord in March 1993, which confirmed Rabbani in office, gave the premiership to Hekmatyar but threw a reckless veil over the status of Massoud, his bitterest rival. Fighting broke out two days later and, while Hekmatyar accepted his post and a desultory peace was restored, he chose to remain at Charasyab, only meeting the president in the presence of armed guards. The fighting came and went during the remainder of 1993, as did the refugee population, dragging their belongings between the capital and the displaced camp or Pakistan and the village.

Dostum, however, had had enough. He had spent most of 1993 in disdain of events in the capital, consolidating his mini-state in the north through a round of diplomatic visits to Pakistan, Uzbekistan, Saudi Arabia, Turkey and Russia. Since 1992, he was excluded from every inter-party discussion about the formation of a new government, despite his military strength and preponderant role in bringing down Najibullah. As dawn broke on 1 January 1994, Kabul awoke to the sound of heavy artillery and the news that Microrayon was ablaze. Allying themselves with troops loyal to Hekmatyar, Dostum's forces attempted to capture the Argh and the Ministry of Defence, attacks which were repulsed. The factions took up positions on opposing sides of the river running through what used to be old Kabul, creating a 20-mile-long front that divided the city into a mosaic of conflicting territories. After two months of intensive rocketing, some 4,000 people lay dead, 21,000 more were injured and 200,000 left the city.[27] In mid-June, the battle-lines began to shift as clashes broke out between Hizb-i Islami and the pro-Rabbani, Shia Harakat-i Islami near Darulaman Palace, inflicting grievous damage on the National Museum and its irreplaceable collection of Bagram and Ghandaran antiquities. Two weeks later, Massoud managed to dislodge the Uzbek militiamen from the fort at Bala Hissar and Maranjan Hill to the southeast, capturing Microrayon and the National Sports Stadium. Hekmatyar responded with a blizzard of revenge rocketings. Some 360 landed on Shahr-i Nau gardens, the Wazir Akhbar Khan diplomatic quarter and residential areas in Khair Khana on 17 July.[28] On 13 August, rockets destroyed the city's central medical stores and three hospitals received direct hits, killing over 30 patients. Many were killed when a building housing 5,000 homeless people was targeted.[29]

With no end to the fighting in sight, the director of the International Committee of the Red Cross, Peter Stocker, announced on 7 October that the ICRC would airlift emergency medical supplies into Kabul, adding that, though the operation would relieve pressure on the hospitals, it could not possibly meet Kabul's other humanitarian needs. No relief food had been delivered since June. 'Living in some areas of Kabul,' Stocker said, 'is now like living in hell.'[30] The prospect of the coming winter, he added, was 'terrifying'.

Meanwhile, in the deep south, a white banner began to unfurl on the 15th anniversary of the Soviet invasion.

3 Warriors of God

It began as a faint susurrus, stirring the palms and leaves, the subtlest alteration in a balance of powers whose nervous bursts of violence had terrorised Kandahar since April 1992. On the fall of Najibullah, a trio of commanders from different factions, dominated by the Jamiat-i Islami warlord Naqibullah and fuelled by profits from the opium trade, seized control of the city of the Cloak of the Prophet, Afghanistan's holiest shrine, dividing it into three well-armed and hostile camps.

If Kabul was Afghanistan's Sarajevo in early 1994, Kandahar could lay reasonable claim to being its South Bronx. This was the view of local merchants trying to revive the border trade with Pakistan, and capitalise on Kandahar's promising position astride the land route from Central Asia. The factions had established roadblocks willy-nilly throughout the southern countryside, levying taxes from passing vehicles and their hapless passengers. Protection was available to those who could afford it, but most of the population could not, having only recently returned from Pakistan to repair their homes and sow their fields.

With no overlord powerful enough to impose a lasting security, Kandaharis were trapped in a crossfire of killing, extortion and rape from members of all three factions, while owing allegiance to none of them. In one incident, two rival commanders in Soviet tanks duelled over possession of a boy lover, killing dozens of people in the local bazaar[1] while, in another, 31 guests at a wedding died when a heroin addict went on the rampage.[2] The grievance aroused by such episodes, fortified by the promise of a return to relationships rooted in Koranic law, fanned the first whispers of resistance to mujahedin rule into a movement that ultimately attained cyclonic dimensions.

Afghanistan was split into four autonomous mini-states and scores of loosely-affiliated enclaves in early 1994. Kabul remained the cockpit of civil war but, in spite of Hekmatyar's bombardments, the disposition of territory across the country varied little. Jamiat controlled the northeast, the thin conduit through Massoud's Panjshir valley and the central provinces of Baghlan, Parwan and Kabul. Hekmatyar held the province of Logar, south of Kabul, the Kabul–Jalalabad road and strategic pockets by the eastern border.

Jamiat-i Islami's most important ally was a former military officer, Ismail Khan, the self-appointed 'emir' of Herat, whose prospering domain, at the crossroads of the Gulf and Central Asian trades, included Badghis, Ghor, Farah and parts of Nimroz provinces. The absence of guns in Herat's crowded streets testified to its stability while the mechanisms of government functioned much as they did in Soviet times, in spite of its isolation from the international aid corridors. General Dostum, in the north, was equally secure, ruling a belt of seven provinces that were all but immune to attack thanks to his control of the Salang Tunnel, the only all-weather route through the Hindu Kush.

The Pashtun regions enjoyed no comparable cohesion. This was partly due to the divisive temperament of Pashtun society, in which a fierce adherence to *pashtunwali*, a tribal code of honour and revenge, placed individual freedom and an eagle-eyed attention to matters of family dignity far above what few prospects existed for dialogue between clans that had historically been unifiable only through *jihad* or the strength of a rare personality. Pakistan's selective seeding of the anti-Soviet resistance encouraged this innate fractiousness by favouring Hekmatyar's radical Islamism over the more conservative – though hybridised – variety practised in the south, where *sharia* law took second place to the *pashtun-wali*, and revolution of any description came in a distant third.

In Jalalabad, military commanders and tribal leaders had sunk their differences in a provincial *shura*, or council, but its durability was due less to any real consensus than the ample profits from the Khyber Pass trade and international relief, both of which would have collapsed with any upsurge of hostilities. Similar alliances existed in Khost, Ghazni and other Pashtun regions in the east but, further south, postwar authority had become thoroughly atomised. Jamiat-i Islami and Hizb-i Islami held some enclaves but, being at each other's throats in the capital, made for poor neighbours in the provinces.

The party that most closely matched the southern profile was Harakat-i Inqilab-i Islami, a traditionalist group led by Mohammed Nabi Mohammedi, which drew its fighters from the network of countryside *madrassa*, or Koranic schools, and their religious students, or *taliban*. After three years' instruction, a *talib* qualified as a village *mullah*, officiating at births, marriages, deaths and providing religious instruction to boys, in exchange for cash contributions or gifts in kind. In rural Afghanistan, religion was the only vocation that required any formal education, though it did not necessarily entail literacy.

Mohammedi was an *alim*, a Koranic scholar, from the Amadzhai – the same clan as Najibullah – and briefly served as vice-president in the Rabbani government, although his forces stayed out of the subsequent fighting in Kabul. This lent him both spiritual and ethnic legitimacy, a vital combination in any candidacy for Afghan leadership. One internal UN document went so far as to suggest that Mohammedi was the personality most acceptable to Rabbani as successor in the unlikely event of his stepping down.[3]

Denied any significant funding during the Soviet war, Harakat was largely dormant by the time the Taliban made their debut. But the political naivety that the latter went on to display and the number of Harakat commanders drawn to their ranks fuelled speculation that the movement did not seek power for itself alone, but was an inspirational police force, designed to clear the way for a more experienced leader to walk into office. None could fathom who that might be, but the notion that behind the *éminence grise* at the head of the movement there was another *éminence grise* waiting to emerge added another dimension to the Taliban's undeniable air of mystery.

The avalanche that fell upon the factions started in the spring of 1994. Two teenage girls from the Kandahari village of Sang Hesar were abducted by mujahedin and repeatedly raped at the local checkpoint. Mohammed Omar, a Harakat commander who had retired to become a *talib* in the neighbouring village of Maiwand, was told of their plight and summoned 30 fellow *taliban* to mount a rescue. After a brief gunfight, the girls were freed and the mujahedin commander hung from a slowly-ascending tank-barrel. Appeals for help rapidly poured in from elsewhere in the district and, thus, the movement of *taliban* was born.[4]

'We were fighting against Moslems who had gone wrong,' Mullah Mohammed Omar reminisced to Rahimullah Yusufzai, one of only two journalists to whom he accorded a face-to-face interview. 'How could we remain quiet when we could see crimes being committed against women and the poor?'[5] The righting of wrongs and punishment for the guilty were the students' first public manifesto, emerging long before the Taliban evolved into a force with sufficient military strength to insist upon the establishment of a pure Islamic state. This 'Robin Hood' quality never vanished from the movement's legend, and even expanded, as it moved east, to embrace the restitution of private property appropriated by the mujahedin.

News of the movement did not filter through to the outside world until mid-1995, after Pakistani journalists confirmed that extraordinary changes were underway in the south. Between the Sang Hesar incident – recounted by a Taliban spokesman – and October 1994, when what evolved into the Taliban emerged from a curious period of gestation, the movement somehow acquired a command structure, skilled manpower, weapons, a strategic plan and funding. Responsibility for the transformation quickly fell on Pakistan, then seeking to build road and rail links through the badlands of Afghanistan in a bid to compete with Iran for the Central Asian export trade.

In the absence of more reliable testimony – and contrary to Taliban claims – what is certain is that the Sang Hesar incident did not immediately spark a popular revolt against the Kandahari mujahedin. Like generations of outlaws before them – and the killing of the Sang Hesar commander qualified them as that – the 30 original *taliban* fled across the border into Baluchistan. On 9 October 1994, Mullah Mohammed Omar, still unknown beyond the confines of his own district, reappeared to announce that a force of 1,500 *taliban* would man traffic checkpoints on the road from the border to Girishk, a town 55 miles (90 kilometres) northwest of Kandahar.[6] Their purpose was the provision of security for a convoy of Pakistani trucks to Turkmenistan which Islamabad intended as the first step towards rebuilding the overland trade route. The *taliban* were funded by local merchants and relied on the hospitality of the surrounding villages, though there was still no indication from where they had come.

The convoy crossed the Afghan border post of Spin Boldak in mid-October, assured of its welcome by a cash advance to the local warlord from Naseerullah Babar, a close confidant of Prime Minister Benazir Bhutto and Pakistan's elderly interior minister. He had traversed the convoy's proposed itinerary through Kandahar and Herat to the Turkmenistan border in September to gain permission for the journey from local commanders. It was too rich an opportunity for any bandit to renounce. Between Spin Boldak and Kandahar, the trucks were waylaid and their cargoes of food, clothes, medicine and soap seized. According to the Pakistani press, the *taliban* stood boldly up to the mujahedin, capturing their weapons and, after three days of fighting, Kandahar fell.

It was a fine frontier tale, soon to become the stuff of legend, but there were enough discrepancies in the account that the hand of the strategist could also be detected. Islamabad denied a press report that Urdu-speaking members of the paramilitary Frontier Constabulary and the ISI were seen fighting alongside the Taliban – by now conferred with the capital letter appropriate to their rising political star.[7] One reliable source recounted that an ex-ISI agent and veteran of the Afghan war, 'Colonel Imam', coordinated the rising from the safety of the Pakistani consulate in Kandahar[8] while another, less objective, claimed that the Taliban attack at Spin Boldak was supported by artillery fire from across the Pakistani border.[9]

The trucks, it transpired, belonged to the National Logistics Cell, the transport arm of the Pakistani army that had ferried supplies to the mujahedin during the *jihad*.[10] We have Babar's word that they contained a goodwill cargo for the people of Central Asia, but they may also have transported Pakistani regular troops, disguised as *taliban*, or the Kalashnikovs, mortars and other firepower needed to capture a city bristling with hard-bitten fighters. The whole story sounded like a whimsy, but traces of any more solid evidence to prove it were swiftly blown away amid the euphoria that swept through the south.

If the caravan were not a Fifth Column, it was certainly an *agent provocateur*. Upon its uncertain fate hung the dignity of Pakistani diplomacy and Mrs Bhutto's bold new strategy in Central Asia. To attack it would be a direct challenge to the powerful eastern neighbour that had stood by Afghanistan throughout the Soviet occupation. If the warlords resisted such a temptation, another ambush would have to be counterfeited. An incident near Kandahar was obligatory in the scenario that Babar had devised.

Naqibullah, Kandahar's most powerful commander, did not oppose the new movement, but the corpses of two other commanders were paraded through the streets suspended from the barrels of tanks.[11] A six-man *shura*, appointed to run the city, announced the dismantling of roadblocks, the confiscation of weapons, a crackdown on crime and drug abuse, and the strict seclusion of women. The Taliban declared that their intention was to purge Afghanistan of all mujahedin and communists – blurred into the same seamless piece of historical fabric – 'who have become killers, thieves and drug traffickers in the name of Islam' – and to end the looting and lawlessness which had characterised the post-Soviet regime.

Such measures were welcomed after years of anarchy and the opening of the roads led to an immediate drop in the food prices. If the banning of videos, football and girls' education was strict by the standards of Kandaharis, whose orthodoxy had been moderated through contact with Pakistan's more heterogeneous culture, the loss was a small price to pay for the restoration of stability, and few complained. These were expendable luxuries and asserting that the Taliban may have erred in their assessment of mujahedin rule was a thankless task, better left to commanders begging for their lives than to citizens, who felt no particular sympathy for either the conqueror or the vanquished.

It is tempting to interpret what happened next – the transformation of the Taliban from a disciplined cadre into a force for national redemption – as a wholly supernatural process, a spontaneous combustion of spiritual zeal and mass hysteria that forged an army that thundered over all the opposition towards a remote utopia. From a distance, the Taliban bore an uncanny resemblance to a horde – the military equivalent of the swarm – and, like a horde, they obeyed no obvious pattern, penetrating into every vent and orifice, hoovering up the vestiges of randomised power and garnering them into a humming storehouse of invincible legitimacy.

There was no obvious hierarchy in this army, no goal beyond the creation of a new spiritual order and the rank-and-file, initially, at least, were acolytes, eyes dilated by faith, antimony and a dream in the far distance. Rumours spread of their purity, their ripeness for martyrdom. Indeed, among all the Afghan combatants, the Taliban alone seemed aware of precisely what they were fighting for as they flung themselves down the road to the capital, waving the white flag of *jihad* and chanting '*Allahu Akhbar*' ('God is great') at a superstitious and demoralised enemy.

But that was the army – or part of it – and a surface description at best: the supposition of popular involvement is moot. The enforcement of law and order, including execution for murder and amputation against highwaymen, won immediate acclamation, as did the public humiliation of local warlords. The establishment of a pure Islamic state, moreover, was an unarguable proposition to a people reared upon the irreducible truths of the Koran. To extrapolate from that convergence of views, however, that the public wholeheartedly endorsed the Taliban's ambitions, throwing their hearts and souls behind the endeavour, underestimates the Afghan's sharp sense of his own individuality and to caricature the range of possible responses in a society unusually dominated by prayer and the rifle.

One of the paradoxes of Afghanistan is that, although composed of 50 ethnic groups often locked in mortal combat, no minority has ever sought to secede and most fully identify with their common nationality. This was signally brought home during the 1994 fact-finding tour by UN peace envoy Mahmoud Mestiri, who received over 300 proposals on ways of settling the post-Najibullah conflict, none of which raised the question of partition.[12] But another paradox is that whatever happens in Kabul only matters in the provinces to the extent that it undermines – or not – the foundations of local power or custom.

This had occurred under both monarchical and communist rule and *jihad* quickly followed, religion being the only language in which such absolutes as justice, solidarity and duty could be expressed simultaneously and with pressing urgency. The preferred Kabul was sickly, riven by internal divisions and forced to pay in cash or patronage for influence at the extremities of its domain. This Kabul already existed under President Rabbani and, as wretched as life had become for its mainly Tajik and Hazara inhabitants, it was not, fundamentally, a Pashtun concern unless it attempted to impose its will locally.

The Durrani clans of the south, it is true, resented the rise of the Tajik, Massoud, and the denial of their traditional role as brokers of government, but this was an unfocused rankling, not a popular call to arms. The Mohammedzai, Afghanistan's historic rulers, had extinguished their claim to legitimacy, first by exchanging their Kandahari roots for the town-houses of Kabul and then, after the overthrow of King Zahir Shah, by taking prominent positions in the communist hierarchy that succeeded the republic and later became the target of Taliban denunciations. Parochial considerations were of far greater concern in the south than the distant gunfire in the capital.

In fact, the spectre of what amounted to strong government had slipped into Kandahar by the back door, offering peace and a pardon in exchange for obedience and the surrender of the weapons that the Pashtun regard as their God-given right to bear. If, therefore, the arrival of the Taliban was a deliverance from mujahedin misrule, it was also an invasion of the Pashtun conception of personal liberty. It was certainly an outright challenge to an economy in which the hiring of fighters provided several thousand families with regular income and food.

There are no contemporary accounts of the weapons-collection programme carried out in the weeks after Kandahar fell, but it must have been a tense period. The Taliban, ostensibly numbering only 1,500 recruits, had no immediate need of arms, having captured a Hizb-i Islami cache at Shin Naray, close to the Pakistani border, on their march to Kandahar in October.[13] This ISI-built store housed an estimated 800 truckloads of arms and ammunition by one account – 15,000 truckloads of ammunition by another – and its fall provided yet another clue to Pakistan's support of the religious students.[14] By February 1995 – four months later – the movement had swollen to 20,000–25,000 men, backed by 200 tanks, artillery, six Mil-17 helicopter transports and a dozen MiG-23 jet fighters.[15] Even if the Taliban strength were exaggerated, it is unlikely that many weapons had been actually taken out of circulation: their owners had merely changed sides, for the guarantee of continuing possession.

The circular, woollen *pakol*, which had been the mujahedin trademark head-gear for 15 years, was tossed aside – along with the old loyalties – in favour of the pure white or black, striped turbans that identified the warriors of God.

*   *   *

There was no mistaking the Taliban as just the latest in a series of Afghan armed factions. Unlike the mujahedin, who fought for food or the government's counterfeit currency, its forces were orderly, mirroring the discipline and obedience drummed into students from an early age by the *madrassa* system. They appeared to know what they were fighting for or, more accurately, what they were fighting against. There was no rape, no individual looting and little indication of the intolerance that would emerge later as they moved out of Pashtun districts of the south and east and into Tajik country.

It was, moreover, an army that advanced, a rare characteristic among the groups which had fought since the Soviet occupation. The Japanese four-wheel-drive pick-ups, which the Taliban had in abundance, transformed a static military landscape by allowing squads of eight to ten commandos, armed with machine guns, grenades and rocket launchers, to move at speed through the least-accessible parts of the countryside. Teams of vehicles, linked by radio or satellite phone engaged in offensive actions, mopping-up operations and hot pursuit simultaneously, leapfrogging one another along a chosen line of advance.[16]

This high-speed command and control, far more than sheer weight of numbers, led to the collapse of Kabul in September 1996, leading some observers to speculate that there were, in fact, not one but two distinctive Taliban armies. The first, composed of just 3,000–5,000 crack infantry, was the force that raced into the capital and pursued Massoud's retreating men into the Panjshir valley, prompting military analysts to doubt that it could have originated unaided in the Pashtun outback.[17] The second, far larger, was made up of ill-trained volunteers from the *madrassa*, turncoat mujahedin and other camp followers. This – the avalanche made palpable – was reserved for use as battle-fodder in the grim set-piece battles on the western front, or to enforce security in the non-Pashtun cities that fell to the movement.

As they proceeded through the south, resistance weakened, as if commanders had fallen into the grip of a virulent disease that sapped their courage and uncocked their weapons. Military boroughs tumbled down, either through the infectious power of Taliban piety or the threat of Pakistani reprisal if they failed to concede. For few southerners doubted

Pakistan's hidden hand behind the movement and the majority of Pashtuns welcomed it. Quantifying the effect on mujahedin morale was a different matter in a country where everyone simply adored a brand-new faction. Here were chances to shuffle the old pecking order, opportunities for new business and jobs for unemployed fighters. The fact that the south was one huge power vacuum undoubtedly helped, although tales of mujahedin atrocities had been much magnified in the Pakistani press to buttress the legitimacy of the Taliban crusade.

In November 1994, Mullah Mohammed Omar called for 4,000 volunteers from Pakistan to help the movement break out from its Kandahar bridgehead.[18] Commanders in the provinces of Uruzgan and Zabul caved in without a shot in November and December, respectively. There was a brief and bloody skirmish in Helmand, the opium-growing capital of the south, but the province was secured in January. Ghazni fell after one-day's fighting and Paktika's formidable Mullah Abdul Salam Rocketi, named for his mastery of Scud and Stinger, surrendered his weapons and territory in February without a shot.

Such capitulations were the product of negotiation as much as intimidation. A Taliban advance on a town or stronghold was preceded by the infiltration by night of a *mullah* or other notable, laden with offers, seeking commanders willing to defect. If the presence of a victorious army did not undermine local morale, the disappearance of dollars and rupees from the local money market, the guarantor of both business confidence and a comfortable exile across the border, usually did the trick. The struggle against the factions was won through an artful blend of currency speculation and outright bribery. This was no novelty in Afghanistan. Selling to the highest bidder was a pragmatic choice for commanders concerned for the loyalty of their supporters and the security of their fiefdoms. And what occurred at the provincial level had its international dimension. Russia sustained Rabbani by printing afghanis to pay his troops and Hekmatyar's money supply was, reportedly, forged in Pakistan for the same purpose. When Hekmatyar cleaved to the government's side in early 1996, Massoud is reported to have given him $2 million in cash to recruit more Hizb-i Islami fighters in Pakistan.[19]

But the Taliban appeared to have deeper pockets. In addition to the hundreds of commanders who succumbed to their offers of cash or rank, it was rich enough to sow wholesale panic by soaking up the foreign exchange in the local money markets. This occurred in Kabul, shortly before it fell, and, even more dramatically, in February 1997 when the northern afghani, valid only in Dostum's territory, plummeted from 15,000 to 100,000 against the dollar in the space of a few days.[20] Common ethnicity was definitely to the Taliban's advantage in specific transactions, particularly when their spreading fame had nourished whatever desire for change already festered in the community of the ruled. The double jeopardy presented by a restive population, willing to rise and fight alongside the Taliban, and right-hand men, who may have already agreed in secret to mutiny, was sufficient to convince most Pashtun commanders to sue for terms.

Uruzgan and Ghazni also contained large communities of Hazara Shias who, though opposed to the government, had grounds for deep suspicion of the religious students. Rumours were rife that the Taliban, so rigorous in reinforcing dress codes and religious attendance, would impose Sunni rituals upon a minority whose preliminary invocation mentions the fourth caliph, Ali, with the same reverence as the Prophet Mohammed. Forced conversion never formed a specific part of the Taliban's religious policy: indeed, in an agenda characterised by a return to first principles, it was conspicuous by its absence. But there was no guarantee that it would not, one day, become the clarion call of another *jihad*.

In an effort to stem these fears as much as to broaden their ethnic base of support, the Taliban took the unusual step of allowing the Shia mujahedin to retain their weapons and operate as an independent but allied force.[21] This rapport looked as if might deepen in February 1995 as the Taliban forces, commanded by Mullah Mohammed Ghaus, the future foreign minister, stormed Hekmatyar's positions at Charasyab and Maidanshahr, outside Kabul. Again, defection played a part in the rout of Hekmatyar's siege engine. Hizb-i Islami forces reportedly refused to fire on the Taliban, but 600 of their Uzbek allies also gave way.[22]

Winter was turning into spring, campaigning season in the central provinces. Mullah Mohammed Omar announced from Kandahar that the Taliban were a neutral, peacekeeping force, appointed by God and popular acclaim to interpose between the factions, disarm them and restore the Islamic law of *sharia* to the country. The assertion had a political precedent in the buffer force of neutral mujahedin, assembled by the Nangarhar *shura* in August 1993 to separate Massoud and Hekmatyar's forces in Kabul. It was broadly in line with UN thinking as well, although Mohammed Omar steadfastly refused to be seen to participate in any peace negotiations that involved mujahedin or communists.

In mid-1994, UN peace envoy Mahmoud Mestiri tabled proposals for an immediate ceasefire, the collection of weapons and the creation of a neutral security force, as a prelude to elections within two years. An international peacekeeping force was categorically ruled out, on grounds of cost and the public's distrust of foreign troops on Afghan soil. The Taliban appeared eminently suited to the role of neutral security force in early 1995: they were disciplined, popular, imbued with moral conviction and had displayed a rare preference for negotiation over combat during the first five months of their campaign. Their defeat of Hizb-i Islami also brought a welcome pause in a conflict that had claimed 20,000 deaths and 100,000 casualties in Kabul, while the movement had established lines of communication with the two remaining combatants in the capital, Massoud and Abdul Ali Mazari, head of the Shia Hizb-i Wahdat.

The prospects for moving the peace process forward seldom looked more promising but, within 40 days of their arrival at the entrance to the capital, the Taliban were in headlong retreat, their alliance with the Shia in ruins and Hizb-i Wahdat finished as a military player in Kabul. The party's strength in the suburbs of Karta Se and Qalaye Shada had relied on the rocket and artillery support provided by its better-armed ally Hekmatyar's bases out to the southwest of the city. After the Taliban captured these positions, Wahdat was vulnerable to the full panoply of Massoud's military power in an attack launched on 6 March.

Mazari offered to surrender Wahdat's crumbling positions and arsenal to the Taliban whom, it was suspected, he also hoped to lure into a direct confrontation with the Kabul commander. But the first promise he could not deliver. Wahdat units turned their weapons on the Taliban's troops and Mazari, a hostage against the value of his own bargain, was taken away by helicopter to Charasyab, where he died in suspicious circumstances. His facial skeleton, a witness said, had been dislocated from the skull, a condition often seen in the victims of high-speed road crashes. There were multiple bullet wounds in the abdomen, inflicted after the first wound but, probably, while he was still alive.[23] The details tended to confirm the popular belief that he had been pushed out of the helicopter, although the Taliban insisted that Mazari, a burly man, had attempted to overpower his guards while airborne. The killing brought the Shia honeymoon with the movement to an abrupt end.

Wahdat cancelled, Massoud turned on the Taliban, who were swiftly expelled from Hekmatyar's positions at Charasyab and Maidanshahr. The defeat exposed their lack of military prowess when pitted against a seasoned force, but may also have helped shed some of the complacency that had set in during their snowballing advance through the Pashtun lands in the previous six months. Exhilarated by conquest and the flood of volunteers flowing in their direction, the Taliban had begun to believe that providence really was with them, at least in the east. Further west, where a second front opened in February 1995, a different story was played out, far from the media's mythologising eyes.

Most of Nimroz province, bordering Iran, surrendered without a fight but the Taliban met stiffer resistance from the forces of Ismail Khan forces, nominally loyal to Rabbani, at Delaram, 210 miles northwest of Kandahar on the Herat road. The Taliban pushed through Farah, thanks to the defection of Khan's local Pashtun allies, forcing the government to airlift troops from Kabul to the former Soviet airbase at Shindand, 60 miles south of Herat, in a bid to hold the line. One analyst called the clash 'the heaviest fighting ... since the battle for Jalalabad in 1989'. The Taliban were finally pushed back to Helmand by late May, thanks partly to the fuel and ammunition provided by Iran which was alarmed by the commotion so close to the frontier.[24]

A ten-day truce in June relieved tensions in the west, but fighting erupted the same month in the north between government forces and Dostum, following the breakdown of peace negotiations and amid accusations that Massoud was planning an offensive along the Salang Highway. On 20 June, the latter captured Bamian from Hizb-i Wahdat, gaining an alternative route across the Hindu Kush to Dostum's provinces of Samangan and Baghlan, a manoeuvre that the Taliban would imitate two years later. For the moment, the Taliban and Dostum gave every indication of working hand in glove, taking it in turns to harry Massoud, in spite of their public statements of mutual detestation.

In August 1995, Ismail Khan launched a second offensive against the Taliban at Delaram, pushing them back to Girishk, where they unexpectedly rallied to inflict a crushing defeat upon the government's allies. Khan's forces fled north in disarray and, after a half-hearted resistance at Shindand, Herat fell to the Taliban on 5 September. Ismail Khan, and what forces he could still muster, fled across the Iranian border to Mashad. The capture of Herat increased the number of provinces under Taliban control to nine out of a total of 32. The movement, its leaders made clear, would no longer be satisfied until all of Afghanistan were united under their command and, for the first time, it became apparent precisely what that regime would look like. What, from a distance, had seemed a sensational flourish of Afghan esoterica was revealed, in the law-abiding alleys of Herat, as a Pashtun aberration that used religious purism as a form of terror and hired bullies to implement it.

Women were prohibited from working, girls' schools shut down and beatings liberally handed out for 'abuses' of the strict dress code. In late

1995, working women who demonstrated against their exclusion were attacked and beaten by Taliban soldiers.[25] Amputations, the blackening of faces as a form of public humiliation and the extra-judicial execution of Ismail Khan's former fighters were reported, while a systematic house-to-house search for weapons forced young men to escape to the mountains. Gone were the days of pious reconciliation. In early 1996, a suspected murderer was inexpertly hung from a crane, taking several hours to die.[26]

The last hope that the Taliban were the peacekeeping force they claimed to be evaporated for Kabulis in October 1995, when their forces reoccupied Hekmatyar's former bases at Charasyab and Maidanshahr and relaunched the siege of the capital after the six-month lull that had followed their defeat the previous May. On 11 November, 170 rockets landed on the city, killing 37 civilians and injuring 52. Massoud launched attacks to push them out of range in November but he failed to dislodge them. In a counter-offensive on 21 November, the Taliban advanced six miles to Pul-i Charki, cutting Kabul's eastern supply route.

That winter was the most cheerless in Kabul's memory. The city had been without electricity since 1993. Amid daily bombardments and sporadic air strikes, the Taliban set up fresh blockades in the south and west. With the Silk Gorge closed by Hizb-i Islami and the Salang Tunnel sealed by Dostum's troops, food and fuel became more scarce, while the afghani lost half its value against the dollar. When temperatures fell below –20 degrees Centigrade, Kabul's orchards and ornamental trees were felled for firewood. On 28 January, the World Food Programme persuaded Hekmatyar to open the road for a convoy of 200 relief trucks and, some days later, the ICRC announced an emergency airlift lasting 25 days.

On 9 March, the Hizb-i Islami leader, Hekmatyar, announced a new alliance with Rabbani and the formation of a Joint Military High Council with Massoud. Hizb-i Wahdat, under its new leader, Karim Khalili, said it, too, would join the new configuration in Kabul, but then began a round of negotiations with the Taliban. Earlier in the month, Rabbani had signed agreements in Tehran, under which Iran pledged training for army officers, the repatriation of all military-age refugees for service in Kabul, the repair of the airport and the provision of funds to win the loyalty of other factions.

Meanwhile, the violence continued. On 15 February, an explosion ripped through an ammunition dump in the Argh, killing 60 outright while hundreds of civilians shopping for the coming Eid were cut by the shattered glass from the nearby Kabul Hotel.[27] Clashes were reported between the Taliban and Ismail Khan's forces in Farah, and a bomb exploded in Herat's Pul-i Ragina quarter, causing even fiercer repression of civilians. In Kabul, rocketing claimed 180 lives and 550 injured in April, peaking on 26 June – the day that Gulbuddin Hekmatyar formally entered the city to take up his position as prime minister – when 220 Katyusha rockets were fired from Taliban positions.[28] Massoud and Hekmatyar responded with joint offensives in Ghor province, in a bid to retake Herat, and against Taliban positions south of Kabul. In late August, Mullah Mohammed Omar ordered the advance that would see the Taliban sweep through the remaining provinces of eastern Afghanistan and end with their possession of the capital.

*   *   *

Kabul was lost not by force of arms, but through a strategic checkmate. As the Taliban embarked on a dazzling campaign through Paktia to Jalalabad, their positions at Charasyab and Maidanshahr fell silent. Jamiat reinforcements were dispatched to Sorobi to strengthen Hekmatyar's forces, whose loyalty had been sorely tested, first by his new alliance with Massoud, but also by the terrifying momentum of the Taliban advance. Waves of martyrs reportedly cleared the minefields laid in the Silk Gorge, a wholly unsporting approach to the Afghan's traditional conduct of war.

The Taliban's bloodless capture of the capital drew a gasp of astonishment from a world that thought it was inured to the tangled politics of Afghanistan. There was little praise for Massoud's retreat, an organised withdrawal under darkness while in contact with an advancing enemy and, no doubt, accompanied by a high quotient of panic. If Massoud were to survive politically, it was vital he move his heavily-laden column of men and machinery to Jabal Saraj, 48 miles north of Kabul, before the Taliban could cut him off along the Tagab valley. The order to pullout was given at 3 p.m. on 26 September, two days after Sorobi was overrun and was still continuing in the early hours of the 27th, as the Taliban mopped up the last resistance at Microrayon estate.[29]

Massoud claimed he withdrew to avoid further loss of civilian life in the house-to-house fighting that would otherwise ensue. It may have been true. But, as so often occurs in Afghanistan, there was also a sense that history was about to repeat itself, this time in a return to the state of military affairs that existed throughout 1994. Some 12,000 Hizb-i Islami soldiers of questionable loyalty were now inside Massoud's capital, along with an unknown number of Pashtun *Ittehad*.[30] If Massoud were to stay and fight it out, he would certainly lose Bagram airbase, his only source of military supply, to the Taliban, who only had to reactivate the rocket positions at Charasyab and Maidanshahr to close the circle. Massoud's capitulation was inevitable, his execution just as probable.

Jabal Saraj is reached by the Soviet-built 'New Road', which leads north through the provincial capital of Charikar, the nearest town to Bagram, en route to the Salang Tunnel. To the east stretches the Panjshir valley and the Khawak Pass, which Alexander the Great crossed in 328 BC while marching south to Kandahar. Seventy miles long and 7,000 feet high, the Panjshir contains dozens of side valleys, sprinkled with stone villages and their fields of wheat, grapes and apples. Massoud conducted campaigns in the valley for a decade and knew it intimately. In 1982, his Tajik forces withstood a 12,000-strong invasion force of mainly Soviet troops, supported by tanks, MiGs and helicopter gunships, at the cost of just 180 mujahedin lives. The Taliban would be hard-pressed to fare better.

Massoud always understood the military importance of securing his rear and contingency plans had been laid for just such a setback, when he entered Kabul in 1992. Rockets, small arms, ammunition, rations, fuel and cash were stored at sites throughout the valley and a supply trail opened to Taloqan in Takhar, where the airport provided an air bridge for supplies from Russia, Iran and Tajikistan, Massoud's major foreign backers. But it was a demoralised force that stumbled into the Panjshir at the end of September. 'I told them: "If you stay with me, consider yourselves to be as good as dead,"' he recalled in February 1997. 'The commanders talked it over with their families. Then they all came back.'[31] His strength was whittled down from 15,000 to 8,000 stalwarts. The remainder defected or fled.[32]

The Taliban's impetus carried them to the mouth of the Salang Tunnel where, in a classic manoeuvre, Massoud turned and struck at their flanks. Basir Salangi, a key Tajik commander, led his men along the mountain ridges by night and ambushed the enemy, dug in on the road, killing 150 men and pushing the main force back to Jabal Saraj.[33] A Taliban attempt to break into the Panjshir was blocked by dynamiting the entry, but enemy pressure continued with rocketing and flanking forays over its icy ridges. On 9 October, Massoud launched a two-pronged attack on Gulbahar, at the mouth of the Panjshir, and, after five days of intensive combat, the Taliban abandoned first Jabal Saraj, and then Charikar, nine miles further south. It was the first Taliban defeat since Ismail Khan's short-lived victory at Delaram in August 1995, and it brought Massoud to within six miles of the capital.

The fighting focused on control of Bagram airbase and Jabal Saraj, which commanded the approach to the Salang and Panjshir valleys, and the old road north through the Ghorband valley and Shia-held Bamian province. Dostum made sure the Salang Tunnel was sealed against any Taliban thrust by blowing up the hillsides on the northern side, but he remained chronically undecided about which side he should back in the struggle. Pakistan was pressing him into a Taliban alliance to finish off Massoud, but it was evident that, with the latter eliminated, the road would be clear for the Taliban to advance on the north. Dostum was everything the Taliban despised.

His 'empire' was an uneasy mixture of former communists and mujahedin, predominantly Uzbek, but with large Tajik, Hazara and Pashtun minorities. Though stable on the surface, what was essentially a loose coalition of provincial, ethnic warlords would rise to a fever pitch of tension with every alteration in Dostum's pattern of external alliances. Abdul Momen, a Tajik commander of the vital Hairatan port on the Amu Darya river, died in mysterious circumstances when Dostum switched sides from Massoud to Hekmatyar in January 1994.[34] Lieutenant-General Rasool Pehlawan, his most important deputy, was gunned down in Maimana in 1996 at a time when Dostum's reopening of the Salang Tunnel was being construed as a sign of his imminent realignment with the Rabbani government.[35] Sayed Mansur Naderi was one of the few original conspirators to have survived since the mutiny which brought down Najibullah and shot Dostum to pre-eminence. The son of the spiritual leader of the Ismaili Hazara – a minority within a minority – Naderi commanded the town of Pul-i Khumri and was responsible for security along the Salang Highway.

Rabbani, Massoud and Hekmatyar all visited Dostum in early October, the Hizb leader going on to Tajikistan and Uzbekistan to drum up support for his flagging cause. Delegations from Dostum and Karim Khalili were in Kabul for talks with the Taliban foreign minister, Mullah Mohammed Ghaus, who publicly invited Dostum to join the new administration 'to prepare the ground for strong central government'. Similar overtures were made on 7 October to Massoud, who 'can have a share in the future government which will be chosen by the people'.[36] But trust was in short supply.

Rabbani's meeting with the northern supremo, the first since 1994, was more productive. A day later, Dostum, Massoud, Khalili and Pir Gailani, head of the Jalalabad-based National Islamic Front, announced the formation of a new alliance, the Council for the Defence of Afghanistan (CDA), but Hekmatyar refused to join. He said he would wage an independent war against the Taliban, but many of his men were known to have defected and Zardad Khan, his Sorobi commander, along with three other Hizb chieftains, had thrown in their lot with Dostum. With few resources and less support, Hekmatyar's role in Afghan history appeared to have ended.

But the CDA was also vulnerable. Massoud spoke optimistically of carrying the war into the Taliban's rear but the three chief protagonists of the alliance had been enemies since 1994, using every possible guile to kill one another, or the comrades closest to them. Alliance in Afghanistan differed from enmity in name only, and each member had reason to suspect the others of seeking a separate peace with the Taliban. Massoud's men, moreover, remained at the centre of the CDA's defensive line: every Tajik death vouchsafed a slightly longer life for the Uzbek and Hazara, shortening the chances for mutiny or defection among Massoud's commanders.

Khalili's fear of betrayal – or of reducing his own opportunities to betray – extended to refusing other alliance members to send their reinforcements into his territory in the Hazarajat. Dostum, facing rampant inflation and the threat of insurrection by his own disgruntled commanders, was still a leading candidate for a coalition with the Taliban, however temporary that might turn out to be. His contribution to CDA joint operations would, in the short term, remain cosmetic – the occasional bombing run over Kabul, declarations of questionable solidarity – while ceaselessly intriguing in a bid to keep his options open.

The defence coalition crystallised on 25 October when the Taliban announced the fall of Qala-i Nau, capital of Dostum's province of Badghis, to a force led by Mullah Yar Mohammed, governor of Herat. The declaration of a *jihad* against Dostum four days later marked the end of a period of shadow-boxing that was dictated as much by the diplomacy of Pakistan, eager to prevent an enlargement of the war, as by Taliban qualms over Dostum's military superiority.

Dostum responded to the loss of Qala-i Nau by airlifting troops loyal to Ismail Khan from their Iranian bases to Maimana in Faryab, where they joined with the forces of Gul Mohammed Pehlawan, the younger brother of the murdered Rasool. In the face of stiff resistance, the force advanced to the Murghab river in central Badghis where, along a ten-mile front, they held the Taliban at bay until winter approached. Some 50,000 people were displaced in more than three months of fighting, many of them Koochi nomads. By January, the UN warned that up to four children were dying daily from hunger and the –10 degrees weather.[37]

North of Kabul, the fighting continued over Bagram and Jabal Saraj. After a desultory month, the Taliban launched an offensive which drove Massoud back to Bagram and forced tens of thousands of Tajiks from their homes in Kalakan, Karabagh and Istalif. Mestiri's succcessor as UN peace envoy, Dr Norbert Holl, described the exodus as 'ethnic cleansing', but the Taliban did permit inhabitants some access to their homes by daylight and worse atrocities were being witnessed in Pashtun areas of provinces under Dostum's total or partial control.[38]

Mestiri had resigned in May on health grounds, but his exasperation was obvious in a final report which said that no peace was possible with the current faction heads. His successor, Dr Norbert Holl, was a former head of the South Asia department in Germany's Foreign Ministry. When he took up his post in July, he benefited from the flurry of alarm that the ultra-orthodox religious movement provoked among the UN's traditional paymasters, the US and the European Union, as well as the regional powers. This did not result in concrete progress, partly through Holl's inability to gain access to the Taliban leader, Mullah Mohammed Omar, but also due to the UN's continued recognition of Rabbani as head of the Afghan government. Holl was not entirely innocent, however: by February 1997, he had won a reputation for arrogance that even the Taliban found difficult to swallow.[39]

The first snow fell in early December, making the roads impassable, but bringing a welcome respite to the frozen combatants. The trophies of victory, so bitterly contested since the fall of Kabul, resumed their usual ordinariness under the white light of winter when Afghan fighters pause for three months of tea-drinking and the resumption of family life. Clashes continued around Karabagh and Bagram, which fell at the end of December. Massoud blamed the loss on a commander who had defected with 2,000 men, but his explanation could not detract from the end-of-term feeling in the air.[40]

Blocked by snow, neither side could advance until the spring thaw. Dostum filled the time with random bombing raids on Herat and Kabul, dropping 25 tonnes on the capital in January when his pilots hit the abandoned US embassy. There was further fighting in Karabagh, but Massoud's men largely went to ground in the Panjshir, leaving undefended the approach to the Ghorband valley, west of Jabal Saraj, and the back door to Dostum's country. Prone to landslide and avalanche, the valley ascends to the heights of the Shibar Pass at 14,000 feet (4,300 metres). The Pashtun farmers of Shinwar and Siagard welcomed the Taliban, pledging 1,000 guns to their crusade, but the pass loomed like the high-water mark of the movement's momentum.[41] They had seen the ruins of Kabul and the decadence at the extremities of a new Pashtun domain, whose heart lay in Kandahar. Why proceed further into the sea of alien steppe, visible from the summit and rolling inconsolably into Central Asia?

The war paused, but the snow went on falling.

4   Mission to Cleanse

Who is – or was – the one-eyed mullah, Mohammed Omar, and what is the nature of his calling? So little is known of his real existence – or so much has been purposefully discounted as a distraction from his value as a symbol – that all that we are left are a few fogged impressions and a handful of conjecture. But this shadowy figure remains crucial to gauging the essence and trajectory of the Taliban movement. He is its presiding genius; the saint on the satellite phone.

Where would his mission end? At the Shibar Pass? The Oxus river? Was he a second Mahdi, conjuring up the elemental 'swarm-life' of Central Asia's Moslems in an ever-expanding *jihad* that must constantly break new ground, or risk implosion? Or simply a modest, local hero who showed his face only to admirers, lest the charm which had overthrown a brutal interregnum and brought about a badly-needed peace would somehow be broken? How much of the plot had God revealed to the Leader of the Faithful?

Eight years after the movement was founded, the Mullah's physical features are unknown outside Kandahar, where he lived simply with his wife and children. He has been described as 40 years of age, 'unusually tall' for an Afghan, alternatively 'heavy-set' or 'distinguished' and, according to one journalist, a speaker of Dari with an Iranian accent – despite being a Pashtun from Maiwand in Kandahar province.[1] His right eye is stitched shut, the result of an encounter with Soviet soldiers when he was a mujahedin commander with Harakat-i Inqilab-i Islami. The left, his few visitors allow, had a 'hawk-like, unrelenting' gaze.[2]

He assiduously cultivated this air of enigma with his refusal to be photographed or interviewed and by delegating all but the most crucial encounters with non-Afghans to underlings. Dr Norbert Holl, the UN envoy charged with coordinating peace efforts in Afghanistan, cooled his heels for six months after the fall of Kabul before being granted a meeting with the *de facto* head of the new government. What scant media access the Mullah permitted tended to reinforce his image as a sphinx-like visitor from another plane of being. In a bizarrely-constructed exchange with David Loyn, the BBC's South Asia correspondent, Mohammed Omar explained, from behind a curtain and via a third party seated inches away, that his reluctance to hold face-to-face interviews was because he did not wish to meet anybody who was not 'helpful' to his cause.[3] While this put the UN and the BBC firmly in their places, it hinted at a fear of contamination, even an element of *noli me tangere*, that was either strikingly authentic or knowingly theatrical.

The atmosphere in his immediate court, by contrast, was relaxed and informal. Commanders came and went, dipping their fingers into the communal pot and contributing at liberty to whatever discussion was going on. The Mullah kept a strongbox by his side, handing out expenses as and when they were required.[4] But this is no more than is expected under the code of *pashtunwali*, in which relations between men are seldom hierarchical. An Afghan leader extends his influence by keeping 'open house' in his *hujra*, the communal room in which men meet, eat and sleep. The provision of credit is an intrinsic part of a relationship which, fundamentally, remains contractual.

There was nothing remarkable, therefore, about the Mullah's accessibility to his followers, but the deference they showed him was unique in an Afghan context. 'Whatever our rank,' explained his liaison officer, Mullah Hashim, 'when we come before him, we consider ourselves as just a simple *mujahid*.'[5] The comment confirms his followers' willingness to discard their rank and prostrate themselves at the feet of their master but, at another level, it shone a light into a non-threatening relationship in which the ultimate *mujahid* categorically refuses to adopt the authority and trappings of the prince.

Afghan kings and the *khan*, who made up the traditional baronial class, maintained power through hospitality and political horse-trading, but descent was a more crucial ingredient in their legitimacy.[6] This is particularly true among the Durrani, who trace their genealogy back to Qais Abdul Rashid, a companion of the Prophet. Even the poorest Durrani regards himself as a *brahmin* in the informal system of clan caste which prevails among the Pashtun, and they are fastidious observers of the four pillars of Islam – prayer, fasting, alms and pilgrimage. But a fifth, invisible pillar exists under *pashtunwali* in the co-dependancy of ancestral virtue and perceived piety.

The generational continuity of rural Afghanistan was interrupted first by the overthrow of King Zahir Shah in 1973 and then by the Soviet war which, in sweeping into exile several million Pashtun, opened the door for the commander to assume the prerogatives of the *khan*. In some cases, a commander would have been chosen to lead the community's resistance to communist rule precisely because he was the son of the local *khan*. After the war, these tended to adopt a more consensual approach to governing. But more often he was an interloper, whose legitimacy during the *jihad* expired when the Red Army withdrew. It was this usurpation that estranged the surrounding community, more than the abuses ultimately committed. In the logic both of the *pashtunwali* and Islam, abuse was the natural consequence of dynastic disruption.

Mohammed Omar was neither of the *khan* class nor a member of the Durrani, which has supplied Afghanistan with its kings since 1747.[7] This lent a certain neutrality to his seemingly accidental role in the orchestration – or re-design – of local power relations after October 1994, for which he anyway showed a studied disregard. He laid claim to a pedigree of a different type – the *talib* – one that married the Pashtun martial tradition with the high ideals of selflessness and piety that are interwoven with tribal concepts of leadership. And religious legitimacy in Afghanistan has the privilege of superseding temporal power during times of emergency, as exemplified by the all-inclusive appeal of *jihad*, which does not jeopardise local authority unless it opposes the tide of 'faith'.

No mujahedin group was without its band of *taliban* during the Soviet war.[8] Young, unmarried and with a tolerance for *shahadat*, or martyrdom, higher than their comrades, they maintained a distinct and separate identity during operations, even eating and sleeping apart. At the war's end, they resumed their spiritual studies, only to watch with mounting disgust the behaviour of the same political order they had helped to install. The *talib* retained the original dignity of the *mujahid*, without the taint which accrued after the Soviets withdrew; he was, therefore, better qualified to embody the spiritual and moral harmonies intrinsic to the Pashtun concept of society, but which had lapsed under mujahedin rule.

Mullah Omar's first public explanation of the Taliban's mission was that it had arisen to restore peace, provide security to the wayfarer and protect the honour of women and the poor. No explicit mention was made of *jihad* and, indeed, it could not have been until the Taliban had acquired the critical mass needed to present themslves as a popular force for change. But *jihad* had become something of a hackneyed concept even to Afghans after the events of 1992, when a government of bloodstained communists which, nevertheless, possessed some of the legitimacy required in the traditional leadership equation, was replaced by home-grown Islamists with talents for little more than libertinism.

The impulse had been hijacked once by the West in a war against the Soviet Union that entailed over a million Afghan deaths. But for all its violence, the Soviet invasion was a footnote in the history of Afghan *jihad*, confirmation merely that the countryside's worst fears of urban politicians had been true. Holy war had been declared one year prior to Moscow's involvement, when the Khalq faction of the Afghan communist party tried to subdue the three Omegas of rural Pashtun society – *zan* (women), *zar* (gold) and *zamin* (land)[9] – by stripping women of the veil and imposing literacy and land reform. The response was *jihad*, the countryside's sole intervention in the civil war which smouldered between Khalq and Parcham and the nearest thing, in Afghan terms, to a referendum.

To invoke the word after 1992 was to risk scepticism or the stink of blasphemy. Jamiat fighters, slain during the siege of Kabul, were eulogised by the Rabbani government as having embraced *shahadat* but, in truth, their body parts had simply been blown away. Even Hekmatyar exploited the word: he declared a *jihad* against the Taliban after his resumption of prime ministerial powers in mid-1996, vindicating the claim with the short-lived crackdown on women's rights and secular amusements which preceded the fall of Kabul.[10] Mohammed Omar used the term more cautiously. He did not resort to calling a *jihad* until October 1996, and it was not against Rabbani's retreating forces, but General Rashid Dostum, whose dyed-in-the-wool post-communism marked him as a less ambiguous theological adversary.[11]

The Mullah's protestations that the Taliban was a wholly indigenous movement, free from Pakistani influence, formed part of the political shorthand which had arisen following the disillusionment of 1992. Any *jihad* with proven foreign support was condemned, in Afghan eyes, to the fate of its predecessor. All parties to the denouement of the Rabbani episode enjoyed the backing of outside powers, but none could own to it for fear of the legitimacy principle which dictated that an Afghan problem could only be solved by Afghans. It was the catch-22 in a country of minorities artificially concocted by foreign powers and, hence, the popular suspicion of a UN peacekeeping force on Afghan soil. In the absence of accord, between Pashtun and Tajik or Durrani and Ghilzai, on the meaning of 'Afghan', however, consensus was only possible through an invidious search engine called 'Islam'.

The scramble for spiritual legitimacy was more complex than its portrayal in the Western media. Far from restoring pre-communist virtue in a frenzy of populist iconoclasm, the Taliban were a cultural revolution in their own right, one that hit at the very traditions which the students purported to uphold. The forces which had fought the *jihad* against the Soviets had been assembled in the name of great scholars or the descendants of Sufi saints: men like Professor Rabbani, a poet and postgraduate of Egypt's prestigious Al-Azhar University; or Pir Sayed Gailani and

Sibghatollah Mojadeddi, the heads, respectively, of the Qadiriyya and Naqshbandi Sufi orders.

These were eminent greybeards at the summit of an ecclesiastical ladder which had extended since the 1970s to embrace the dynamic radicalism of Gulbuddin Hekmatyar and Ahmad Shah Massoud, both of whom learned their politics at the feet of Professor Rabbani. Behind these two key figures in what would later become the Afghan resistance loomed the silhouette of the Ayatollah Khomeini, whose example had inspired a generation of revolutionaries. Hekmatyar had chosen the high road of an Islamic purism, then reaching into every corner of the Moslem world; Massoud, a rearguard nationalism in which the unifying issue of shared faith was tempered by a greater tolerance of Western modernism. The ultimate collision between the two manifestos on ethnic grounds spelled the end of a discourse on Islamic revolution in Afghanistan which had begun to unravel when they fled to Peshawar in 1973.

The culture of the commander was a degeneration of the old *khan* system but the rise of the *mullah*, under the Taliban, proved to be less a return to the elusive values cherished in pre-communist times than the stupefying of a tradition which once traced its origins back to the footsteps of the Prophet. Lineage was more crucial in matters of Afghan religion than in temporal affairs. The *sayed*, the *pir* and the *alim* – Afghanistan's spiritual aristocracy – comprised a legacy that wove together 'High Church' trends in Islamic thought with a popular belief in spirits and anchored them both in the everyday life of the Afghan village. The Taliban buried them all and summoned the *mullah*, who was a cross between a country parson and a Shakespearean clown, to recite the funeral rights.

It is a moot point as to whether the Taliban's rapid ascent reflected disenchantment in the community at large with the customary channels for the transmission of spiritual values. Force of arms, supported by scripture, would always remain the trump among a people who viewed their prosperity as the product of a successful accommodation with impersonal and transient powers. The standing of some *sayed* – direct descendants of the Prophet – and *pir* – the reincarnation of the virtue, if not the person, of Sufi saints – was undoubtedly harmed in the aftermath of *jihad*, as their followers embarked on a spree of freebooting, while the *ulama* – plural of *alim*, or religious scholar – had seen their collective authority as Afghanistan's law-givers consistently undermined by a string of modernising kings and the communist party.[12]

The authority of the *sayed* and *alim* was, moreover, received and largely remote from an illiterate peasantry which, when fate proved intolerable, took its complaints and ailments to the nearest Sufi shrine, where the Pashtun's customary sang-froid was swept away in an orgy of spirit possession. Yet it was far from conclusive that the *mullah* was the institution capable of reviving the Afghan's frustrated religious instincts – or bringing them back to the straight and narrow – or whether *sharia*, the integrated code of justice revealed through Koranic study, fully chimed with the concepts of social equilibrium common among tribal Pashtun.

The *mullah* was not, on the whole, revered for his religious insight. He was a community servant who earned a crust through bone-setting and the selling of religious amulets to protect against the evil eye or the myriad *jinn*, which live in the air and visit illness upon children and women. This was surplus to what he might raise through *zakat*, the tithe on local farm produce which was rendered for his services in the mosque, the *madrassa* and at the graveside. In thin seasons, vilifying the *mullah*, a man who worked with his wit more than his hands, came a close second to cursing the landlord, for most Pashtun are sharecroppers forced to make a punitive reckoning at the end of a hard year's graft. In fat years, they could make a tidy income from trading in opium, the premier crop in Helmand, Zabul and, to a lesser extent, Kandahar.

Nor did ordinary Pashtun thirst for *sharia*, having already in the *pashtunwali* a system of conflict resolution which favoured arbitration and the adjustment of claims over the draconian punishments meted out under Koranic law.[13] The more extreme *sharia* penalties of *hadud* (amputation) and *qisas*, in which an identical harm was inflicted by the victim's family upon the perpetrator of a crime, tended to further inflame tensions in a society with an already striking susceptibility for blood-feuds. Pashtun courts, supervised by *ulama*, preferred the payment of blood-money for the crime of murder and restitution in the case of theft. The suppression of tribal law had preoccupied Kabul since the nineteenth century, when Amir Abdul Rahman sought to undermine local autonomy, and it was resumed by the mujahedin government, which introduced *sharia* law in 1993 without being able to enforce its use outside the towns.

Despite the weight placed by the Taliban on law and order, their judicial procedure was summary and non-consultative. Courts, supervised by illiterate *mullah*, might try a dozen cases in a day in sessions where no provision was made for legal council and where the presumption of innocence was absent.[14] The gravest sentences, moreover, were carried out in public with a clear view to impressing spectators with the terror of the court. In February 1996 in Khost, two Afghans accused of murder were riddled with bullets in front of 20,000 people by the fathers of their victims in accordance with *qisas* (retaliation in kind – an eye for an eye).[15] In Herat, a young man was publicly hung from a crane, having confessed to killing two Taliban. Spectators said that he had been clearly beaten 'close to death' before arriving at the execution spot. In several of the 20 or so reported *hadud* cases, hands or feet were summarily axed by Taliban guards without the benefit of a court appearance.[16]

Determining whether the rise of the *mullah* was tantamount to the 'dumbing down' of a richer spiritual – and legal – tradition is hampered by the opacity of the Taliban movement and the convergence of its religious and military agendas. The young *taliban*, who rallied to the cause, and many of their leaders were the product of the Deoband school of Sunni thought, founded 130 years earlier in Uttar Pradesh, India which, in the absence of any domestic school of theological studies, had exerted an influence on Afghanistan's spiritual leadership equal to that of Egypt's Al-Azhar University, the *alma mater* of both Rabbani and Abdul Rasul Sayyaf, head of the Ittehad-i Islami party.

The Soviet interlude tilted the balance in favour of Deoband, first by blocking state subsidies to finance religious studies farther afield and, secondly, by driving millions of Afghans into the border provinces of Pakistan, where the *madrassa* system, dominated by the north Indian school, provided one of the few sources of education. Speculation about the nature of that education is vulnerable to Western prejudice because of concern at the effects of religious tuition on the very young but, more specifically, because of the suspicion that Islam's highly prescriptive character makes it more susceptible than other faiths to programmes of ideological regimentation.

The Deobandis represent the extreme of such attempts to regulate personal behaviour, having issued nearly a quarter of a million *fatwa* on the minutiae of everyday life since the beginning of the century.[17] There is eyewitness testimony to children, chained to their lecterns, rocking back and forth as they learn by rote a Koran written not in Pashtun, but in Arabic. Boys enter the system as wards, exchanging life in a poor family for bed, board and an austere catechism that will one day lead to life as a *mullah*. It is tempting to identify in this early separation from female relatives the origins of the extreme misogyny which, even more than the objective of a pure Islamic state, lent cohesion to the Taliban as they marched into, and subdued, non-Pashtun lands. Western countries, ironically, contributed to the rise of Deoband influence in Pakistan's tribal trust territories by providing *madrassa* with aid during the *jihad* to foster a new generation of cadets to fight the Soviets.[18]

But *taliban* misogyny went so beyond what is normally intended by that word that it qualified as a kind of 'gynaeophobia', one so broad that the merest sight of stockinged foot or varnished finger was taken as a seductive invitation to personal damnation. Official Taliban policy, in a very immediate sense, stigmatised females as the evil eye made omnipresent – and a cause for real fear – within the communities which the rank-and-file occupied. They had to be covered, closeted and, where necessary, beaten to prevent more sin from spewing into society. The Taliban penalty for women showing their face in public was set by the Office for the Propagation of Virtue and the Prevention of Vice, a religious police established in Kabul to enforce such restrictions, at 29 lashes.[19]

Part of this anxiety was sexual and could be attributed to the highly-charged tribal rules of *pashtunwali*, by which girls embark on the perilous road to puberty at seven, when they are first sequestered from boys and men.[20] From then, until marriage, youths have no licit contact with the opposite sex beyond the members of their immediate family. In Kandahar, the custom of seclusion had given rise to a rich and colourful tradition of homosexual passion, celebrated in poetry, dance and the practice of male prostitution. Heterosexual romance, by contrast, was freighted with the fear of broken honour, the threat of vendetta and, ultimately, death by stoning, if the heart were found out. In Pashtun society, man–woman love was the one that dared not speak its name: boy-courtesans conducted their affairs openly.

Under *pashtunwali*, stoning or burial alive are the customary penalties for adultery, a crime which is seen as threatening the peace of the entire community. Unlike *sharia*, which requires four witnesses to the sexual act, the merest whisper of impropriety among the Pashtun is sufficient to ruin a woman's honour and put her life in jeopardy. The most widely-reported sentence of stoning under the Taliban occurred in Kandahar in August 1996, when a married man and his widowed mother-in-law were found *in flagrante* and taken out and killed before the local mosque.[21] A second confirmed instance took place in Laghman in March 1997 when a married woman was convicted in a *sharia* court of attempting to flee the district with a man who was not her husband.[22]

Homosexual liaisons were criminalised by the Taliban but, compared with adultery, the punishments were token. 'We have a dilemma on this,' explained Mullah Mohammed Hassan, governor of Kandahar. 'One group of scholars believes you should take these people to the highest building in the city and hurl them to their deaths. [The other] recommends you dig a pit near a wall somewhere, put these people in it, then topple the wall so that they are buried alive.'[23] In the event, couples had their faces blackened and were paraded around the streets. One can hear the Mullah chuckling in his beard as he outlined the theological impasse.

The *talib* grew to maturity on the gruel of orthodoxy, estranged from the mitigating influence of women, family and village. This ensured that early recruits to the movement were disciplined and biddable. If their gynaeophobia appeared the product of a repressed homosexuality on the march, *taliban* cohorts also conjured up echoes of a medieval children's crusade, with its associated elements of self-flagellation and an innocent trust in the immanence of paradise. This second impression would be strengthened following the Taliban's military debacle in Mazar-i Sharif in May 1997.

It was logical that trainee *taliban* should regard the graduates of their course – the *mullah* – as the natural officer class in the movement's subsequent military career. Among the dozen or so Taliban leaders to achieve public prominence, only Sher Mohammed Stanakzai, acting foreign minister and the main point of contact with the outside world after the fall of Kabul, eschewed a title that was invoked to stress seniority and became inseparable from the movement's corporatist image. Well-travelled and fluent in English and Urdu, Stanakzai was, perhaps, too worldly, too 'un-Afghan' to qualify for the newly-empowered honorific title of *mullah*. He had, moreover, spent the *jihad* heading the military committee of Sayyaf's Ittehad-i Islami in Quetta and was, arguably, on probation for his former association with Wahhabi rites and Saudi money.[24]

But it is not safe to assume that the Taliban's other leaders, compared with Stanakzai, were more authentic, religious spokesmen. Despite his near-messianic status, Mullah Mohammed Omar 'has not too much religious knowledge', according to Mullah Mohammed Hassan, who added: 'A lot of scholars know more than he does.'[25] The versatility of the Taliban elite, who alternated as military chiefs, governors, ministers, as well as *mullah*, combined with the engrained Afghan practice of adopting *noms de guerre* – Ahmad Shah Massoud is not his given name – argues in favour of the thesis that the movement merely clothed its membership in ecclesiastical titles to disguise their origins.

This process of clericalisation similarly transformed each enemy defection into a Damascene conversion, just as the enforcement of *sharia*-based edicts in non-Pashtun regions added a patina of religion to what was essentially the imposition of martial law. It also veiled a coat-rack of skeletons. 'Mullah' Mohammed Hassan of Kandahar had nothing to do with the religious world before his emergence as the Taliban's number three, while 'Mullah' Borjan, the movement's Rommel, was a former Afghan army officer who had served under King Zahir Shah. A number of other key military appointments – Shah Sawar, the artillery commander north of Kabul, and General Mohammed Gilani, the Taliban air commodore – were Khalq members of the Afghan national army until 1992, making a mockery of Mullah Mohammed Omar's claim that his goal was to rid Afghanistan of 'time-serving communists'.[26] The title 'mullah' had as much connection with spiritual integrity as the term 'comrade' with solidarity.

Mullah Mohammed Omar's closest intimate in the early years was Mullah Borjan, another Harakat veteran and a graduate of the military academy in Kabul. Under his real name, Touran Abdul Rahman, Borjan was allegedly involved in the palace revolution which led to the death of President Hafizullah Amin in 1979, paving the way for the Soviet invasion. Mullah Borjan was commander-in-chief of the Taliban forces as they progressed from Helmand to the first siege of Kabul in 1995, where he was wounded at Charasyab, before returning to the fray in Jalalabad in late 1996.

Why Mohammed Omar decided to remain in Kandahar, directing operations by satellite telephone, is open to speculation, if he really were the brilliant *jihad* commander that the Taliban so widely claimed. Perhaps he was already too valuable a commodity to risk in a style of combat in which commanders stood roughly the same chance of dying as foot-soldiers. Mullah Borjan had perished, along with eight other fighters, after the pick-up they were driving hit a land mine in the Silk Gorge during the final advance on Kabul in 1996. A simple roadside epitaph commemorates him, along with a copse of the green and white flags that denote martyrdom.

Some Afghans murmured treachery, claiming that Borjan, unlike Mohammed Omar, had harboured pro-monarchical sympathies to the last. Mullah Mohammed Rabbani was commonly regarded as Omar's deputy until his mysterious disappearance from the political scene, shortly after the fall of Kabul. A 38-year-old from the Arghastan district of Kandahar, Rabbani fought with Hizb-i Islami (Khalis) (after its founder, Maulawi Yunis Khalis) during the Soviet war, studying at a *madrassa* in Zabul, Kandahar and Quetta before taking command of Taliban forces in Logar in March 1995.[27]

On 27 September 1996, he was appointed head of the six-man *shura* in charge of the capital. He also sat on Mullah Omar's inner cabinet in Kandahar, along with Mullah Mohammed Hassan, governor of Kandahar; Foreign Minister Mullah Mohammed Ghaus; Mullah Sayed Ghayasuddin Agha, a Tajik from Badakhshan and the only non-Pashtun; Mullah Fazil Mohammed from Uruzgan, security commander for Kabul; and Mullah

Abdul Razzaq, another Khalis veteran and Mullah Borjan's deputy commander-in-chief.[28] A third *shura*, composed of the chief of security, the chief of the armed forces and the chief of police, also met regularly in Kabul to determine policies relating to the maintenance of law and order.

In November 1996, Mullah Rabbani vanished from view amidst a rictus of speculation that he might have been brought down by internal disagreements. As a Durrani descended from the royal branch, he, too, may have had mixed feelings about what appear to have been Mohammed Omar's growing imperial ambitions, while his rumoured involvement in the revenge killing of Najibullah created additional grounds for suspicion.[29] Stanakzai, then acting foreign minister, said in January 1997 that Rabbani had merely been suffering from 'mental problems' and had travelled to Saudi Arabia and Kuwait for treatment.[30] He returned to his post that month. Stanakzai was subsequently replaced as acting foreign minister by Mullah Ghaus, one of the Taliban's better-educated leaders.[31]

Mullah Abdul Razzaq remained the lone soldier on Mohammed Omar's ruling council, an indication of the subordination of the Taliban military to its political or religious wing. Following a demonstration by 150 women against the closure of bath-houses in Herat in December 1996, Mullah Razzaq replaced another Taliban stalwart, Mullah Yar Mohammed, as governor of Herat, allegedly because he had been too 'soft'.[32] From there, he opened the western front in Faryab against General Dostum in October 1996, leading the Taliban forces into Mazar-i Sharif in May 1997 where he met his death.

Discernible changes in ideological presentation took place during the first year of the Taliban's emergence, notably after its first defeat at the gates of Kabul. These reflected the growing confidence of a movement which had never been strong on consistent policy statements beyond the objectives of ridding Afghanistan of corrupt leaders, the confiscation of weapons and the introduction of *sharia* law. But they also suggested the development within the Taliban leadership of a far harder line on a range of topics, from the value of the UN peace initiative and the future of ex-king Zahir Shah to Mohammed Omar's perception of himself within the Islamic tradition of warrior-priest and the Prophet's promise that a descendant would some day arise to reanimate the faith.

Despite his four-score years – 20 of them spent in Rome – the king over the water had remained a live political issue a quarter-century after the overthrow of the Afghan monarchy. As a direct descendant of the Mohammadzai rulers, his legitimacy was beyond question while the tragedies which subsequently assailed his kingdom, from the rise of the communist party and the Soviet invasion to the mujahedin struggle for power, could all – with a large dose of nostalgia – be blamed upon the disruption of his reign. His last decade on the throne saw the introduction of a constitutional monarchy, general elections, partial press freedom and a build-up of foreign aid that transformed Afghanistan's infrastructure. President Najibullah offered to hand over power to Zahir Shah during the negotiations for a transitional government which preceded his downfall and, after 1994, the UN peace mission consistently returned to the option as the one on which the majority of mujahedin factions appeared most likely to sink their differences.

Though refusing to be drawn into the UN-sponsored peace talks, the Taliban remained vaguely positive about Zahir Shah's future status during 1995. But, on 4 April 1996, Mullah Mohammed Omar was publicly anointed as Amir ul-Momineen, or Leader of the Faithful, by 1,000 *ulama* in Kandahar, a move that was interpreted as a challenge to all Moslems in the region, but particularly the Shia minority.[33] The following November, he entered the grand mosque in Kandahar, removed its holiest relic and a symbol of monarchical legitimacy, the Cloak of the Prophet, displaying it later to an excited crowd. He issued instructions by radio that mosques should no longer end their prayers with the customary invocation for long life of the old king. The Taliban's previous offers of a warm welcome home to Zahir Shah were modified to include the description of him as a 'criminal', who would be answerable for the crimes of the past 40 years.[34]

'Many people in Pashtun areas were thinking of Zahir Shah in the beginning,' said Massoud in February 1997. 'They thought the US was behind the Taliban and that the US would support Zahir Shah. They saw the Taliban as a temporary phenomenon. But when the Taliban declared its enmity for Zahir Shah, there was a lot of disappointment among educated people.'[35]

While it presented a veneer of unprecedented Pashtun unity, divisions were not far from the surface, as might be expected from a movement in which a sizeable proportion of its manpower had already changed sides, while others had only donned the turban for the sake of convenience. An early analysis of friction within the Taliban identified three distinct groups: the more devout, waiting for guidance from Allah; those seeking an accommodation with Massoud's Jamiat, in exchange for the implementation of *sharia* law; and a Khalq-influenced element which sought to reimpose Pashtun hegemony in the guise of Islamic reaction.[36]

The first defections became apparent in early 1996 when two Taliban commanders, fearing loss of authority in their personal fiefdoms, joined the Ittehad forces in Paghman, west of Kabul.[37] Similar disaffection was reported from Logar, Gardez, Maidanshahr and Paktia in the run-up to the capture of Kabul, usually over Taliban heavy-handedness towards local customs or the refusal by civilians engaged in blood feuds to hand over their weapons.[38] By December 1996, aid workers in Kabul said that the Taliban were no longer sure of who was actually in their ranks and that their harshness to the Kabuli population was a symptom of that uncertainty.[39] This tended to confirm the contention of Robin Raphel, the US assistant secretary of state for South Asian affairs, that, for all its success, the Taliban remained a highly factionalised movement, held together chiefly by the charisma and vision of Mullah Mohammed Omar.[40]

The Mullah's continued residence in Kandahar after the fall of Kabul was similarly scoured for symbolic content. All other Afghan faction leaders had attempted to maintain a presence near, or inside, the capital as the first crucial step towards winning international recognition for the legitimacy of their claim to power. This, more than popular acclaim, had been a vital factor for Afghan rulers since the Third Afghan War which, after 80 years of British rule, won Kabul the right to deal as equals with the West and its neighbours. Mohammed Omar, by contrast, gave every indication that he disdained any worldly endorsement: Kabul was not even worth a flying visit from its new conqueror. He remained in Kandahar, rejecting the advances of a stream of foreign dignitaries until June 1997 when the sapping defeat at Mazar finally prised him from his reclusion.[41]

He appeared, anyway, to have an able deputy in Kabul in the shape of Maulvi Rafiullah Muazin, general president of the Amr Bil Marof Wa Nai An Munkir – Office for the Propagation of Virtue and the Prevention of Vice or, more demotically, the Department of What is Right and What is Wrong. Edicts were issued by Maulvi Raffiullah with great diligence to prevent: sedition and 'female uncovers'; idolatry; the British and American hairstyle; interest charges on loans; the washing of clothes by young ladies in the streams of the city; music and dancing at wedding parties; the playing of the drum; the taking of female body measurements by tailors; and sorcery.[42] His deputy, Maulvi Inayatullah Baligh, a former career bureaucrat with the Rabbani regime, commanded a team of 100 religious inspectors to enforce this flood of *fatwa*, which would mount to include the shaving of male pubic hair, the whitewashing of windows to prevent the accidental sight of women residents and the outlawing of 'squeaky shoes'.

Rafiullah had the ear of Mohammed Omar but there were a multitude of signs that, by virtue of his position at the head of Amr Bil Marof Wa Nai An Munkir, he tended to exceed instructions. Baligh, at least, was an enthusiastic lieutenant, telling one journalist: 'Whenever we catch them doing immoral things, we can do anything we want. We can execute them, we can kill them.'[43] When Radio Sharia announced in December 1996 that 225 Kabul women had been beaten in a single day for violating the department's dress codes, Mohammed Omar was persuaded by Afghans to issue a restraining order which was circulated to the Ministry of Information and police stations around Kabul.

The text of the Taliban leader's 'advice' was illuminating since it demonstrated two facts: that the Taliban were certainly not above the law and that Kandaharis, at least, had begun to take steps to curb the excesses of the rank-and-file. Two innocent women were killed in Kandahar in December 1996 by the guardians of morality but, when two alleged robbers were beaten to death by the Taliban at Qishla Jadid military base, the movement was taken to court and fined around $13,500 ('2,000 lakh afghani').[44] Mohammed Omar's letter also referred to cases of people beaten with electric cables. 'Don't be cruel and don't be dishonest with the Islamic government treasury,' it began, before describing the specific case. 'Such kinds of punishment and beating,' it continued, 'need the permission of the Imam and Emir, otherwise the doer of such actions will be punished under *qisas* (those who make a great sin).' Radio Sharia immediately ceased publicising the punishments.

By late October 1996, a new organogram of power began to take shape in Kabul as fresh, generally capable Taliban 'technocrats' were appointed to replace the ministers of the ousted regime. In spite of Mohammed Omar's avowed intention to purge the government of its communist elements – many of whom were undoubtedly fighting alongside the Taliban forces – it was evident that this project had been deferred, perhaps indefinitely, due to the difficulty it presented to the creation of a functioning administration.

Some Taliban-watchers put the share of former Harakat members in the ministerial line-up as high as 60 per cent, with Pashtuns wholly predominating.[45] Warming to their new roles and the interaction they afforded with representatives of foreign donors or the aid community, many Taliban bureaucrats spoke *sotto voce* of the need to reopen girls' schools, desegregate health care and create income opportunities for widows. Such attempts at compromise, however, failed to result in any significant change in the existing status quo, possibly out of deference to more conservative opinions within the largely rural infantry, then laying down their lives on the northern fronts.

'The three-man *shura*,' rationalised one aid worker, 'is more powerful than the six-man *shura*. But then there is the one-man *shura*, which is Raffiullah. He is more powerful than either of them. As a result, though ministers are saying: "All right. You can let women work, so long as they are properly covered." Raffiullah is saying: "I don't care who said what. It is not allowed."'[46] With few or no Tajiks, Uzbeks and Hazaras represented at any one of the concentric rings of power which emanated from Mullah Mohammed Omar, the prospects of achieving a lasting peace without maintaining an apparatus of repression and conditions of martial law remained slight.

As late as October 1996, the movement appeared at odds at the highest levels about its ultimate purpose and the role of its inspirational leader. On 6 October, Foreign Minister Mullah Mohammed Ghaus stated categorically that the Taliban were only a 'caretaker administration', which would take measures towards the establishment of a broad-based elected government in Afghanistan, once security had been assured throughout the country.[47] This was, in a sense, a return to policies outlined early on in the movement's career when the Mullah announced his intention to disarm the factions and to introduce *sharia* law. It even left a window open for the return of Zahir Shah, in one role or other. But Mullah Ghaus was contradicted just two weeks later in a published interview with Mullah Wakil Ahmad Mutawakil, then Mullah Omar's private secretary. 'For us,' he said, 'consultation is not necessary ... We abide by the Emir's views, even if he alone takes this view ... There will not be a head of state. Instead, there will be an Amir ul-Momineen.'[48]

At that late stage, it was not wholly clear – even to the Taliban – whether it was a movement of liberation or of tyranny.

5   Burning Down the House

'This is the work of the Lawrences of Arabia of the ISI [Inter Services Intelligence],' said Abdul Rahim Khan Mandokhel, an opposition senator for Baluchistan, the province from which the Taliban launched their crusade.[1] It was a colourful comment, satirising the way in which operatives of the Pakistani intelligence service had come to view their part in the Afghan war and more clandestine exploits across the Oxus river to destabilise Soviet Central Asia.[2] But it was not borne out by the evidence and Mandokhel's use of the plural was all the more appropriate. Pakistan's power structure had radically altered since the mysterious air crash in December 1988 that cost the lives of General Zia ul-Haq and the cream of the officer class who planned and implemented Pakistan's Afghan policy during the Soviet occupation. New powers and personalities had emerged to challenge the ISI's authority. If there were 'Lawrences of Arabia' out in the Afghan *dasht*, they were working for different masters and, probably, at cross-purposes.

By 1991, the geopolitical world was spinning so fast that countries unable to escape from the shivering ranks of former Cold War clients and into the club of the New World Order were in danger of falling off altogether. Enemies were greeted as long-lost friends, while seasoned alliances turned to crumbling treaty documents. After a decade transfixed by the Soviet threat, the US swivelled its sensors elsewhere in the world: the Gulf, Somalia, China and the Balkans. Pakistan was among the first to experience the acuteness of US ingratitude. Washington cut aid from $660 million a year during the Soviet war to zero in 1990 and launched an avid courtship of India, Pakistan's historic nemesis, previously aligned with Moscow. Seen from New Delhi, America's former sweetheart looked more and more like a serial home-wrecker. Having turned a blind eye to Pakistan's nuclear programme throughout the Afghan war, Washington woke to the reality of a turbulent Islamist state, dominated by the military and with a nuclear strike potential trained on India. Islamabad's assistance to rebels in Kashmir, meanwhile, had so escalated in 1991 that the US threatened to declare it a 'terrorist' state, along with outcasts such as Libya, Iraq, Iran, North Korea and Cuba. The special relationship was over.

It had been showing strain since 1989, chiefly over the ISI's Afghanistan policy. To protect Pakistani interests, the ISI had used US and Gulf funding to foster a resistance which was dominated by Hekmatyar, the most anti-Western of all seven parties in Peshawar. As the Red Army's phased withdrawal reached its conclusion, the State Department tried to correct the imbalance by channelling aid directly to the commanders in the field, particularly to Massoud. The ISI blocked this tactic by drawing on Saudi funding, estimated at $400 million in 1989, most of which ended up with Hizb-i Islami.[3]

The ISI stayed loyal to its protégé throughout the post-Soviet years, conniving at Hekmatyar's attempted coup with Afghan Defence Minister Shahnawaz Tanai in March 1990; the putsch of April 1992; the siege of 1992–93; his alliance with Dostum which led to the joint assault of January 1994; and the reconciliation with Massoud in March 1996, Hekmatyar's last, desperate gamble to stay in the game. An uninterrupted supply of weapons and fuel crossed the Pakistani border at Spina Shaga, Hizb-i Islami's strongest military base, which fell to the Taliban in August 1996.[4] Stripped of resources as it was after the death of Zia and the end of US funding, would the ISI also create the force that drove its oldest ally in Afghanistan from the field?

Not only the geopolitical world had tilted since the collapse of the Soviet Union. The return to power of Benazir Bhutto in 1993 coincided with a relaxation of the army's grasp on power, the result of the 1989 decision by then chief of staff, General Aslam Beg, to try to bridge the gulf between civilian and military that opened with the execution of Benazir's father ten years earlier. Bhutto rode to office on the appeal of her personality cult and a popular rejection of efforts to create an Islamic state in Pakistan, complete with proposals for the abolition of interest rates, a mandatory death penalty for blasphemy and the compulsory wearing of veils.

Spores from the anti-Soviet war had already drifted across the border to take root in Baluchistan, Malakand, Swat and Bhutto's home province of Sind, where a campaign of urban terrorism by the Mujahir Qaumi Movement, an ally of Bhutto's Pakistan People's Party (PPP) in her short-lived 1989 government, had turned entire districts in Karachi, the commercial capital, into no-go zones. One of her first acts as prime minister was to appoint her late father's Afghan adviser, Naseerullah Babar, interior minister. A Pashtun and former governor of North West Frontier Province (NWFP), Babar was a brusque, retired general who boasted in private that 'having made Hekmatyar, he could break him just as easily'.[5]

It may have been bravado: border politics had been transformed since Babar was last in office.

The 100-year treaty marking the Durand Line lapsed in 1993, but the Pashtunistan issue had all but died out with the demise of a strong and unified Afghanistan. To ensure it remained buried, Bhutto and Babar spent the next three years driving military roads into the more inaccessible valleys and bringing the tribal trust areas into the federal system by creating an NWFP assembly. But if the fear of separatism which had been the motor of Pakistan policy in Afghanistan since 1947 was finally silenced, what was left to replace it?

Another Bhutto appointee was Foreign Minister Sardar Asif Ali, who sought to open a new page in Islamabad's external relations. A decade of war and military rule had ended with Pakistan diplomatically isolated, with the exception of China, its ally against India, and Saudi Arabia, which maintained close ties to contain Iran from the east. Responsibility for that isolation lay largely with the ISI and its activities in Afghanistan, Kashmir and the Indian Punjab. Asif Ali took pains to moderate the Islamic rhetoric that repelled the Americans, and develop relations with landlocked Central Asia. Though only interior minister, Babar was so close a confidant of Bhutto that he was entrusted with the foreign policy task of turning the dream of a Central Asian hinterland into reality. In June 1994, Pakistan announced its intention of building rail and road links with Turkmenistan, a project the World Bank endorsed with a $1.5 million loan. On 14 September, Babar declared that he would travel the length of the Chaman–Torghundi road to negotiate safe passage for a convoy of trucks bearing gifts for the peoples of Turkmenistan and Uzbekistan.

It was a reckless and improbable journey, worthy of the grand old man of Pakistan's Afghan policy-making. The convoy was timed to arrive in Ashgabat in late October, when Bhutto was due to celebrate Turkmenistan's independence day. As poor as the Turkmens undoubtedly were, they did not, perhaps, need to be reminded of it on that particular day and 30 dusty trucks hardly amounted to a Marshall Plan. There was some indication that Babar's diplomatic odyssey across war-torn Afghanistan was frowned upon in senior government circles and only went ahead because of his position as Bhutto's 'favourite uncle'.

The 1993 elections contained another surprise. The mainstream Islamist party, Jamaat-i Islami (JI), which had channelled Gulf funding to Hekmatyar and enjoyed close ties with General Zia and the ISI, saw its share of the national vote collapse from 11 to 7 per cent. Qazi Hussain Ahmad, the JI leader, lost his constituency and was forced to resign. In

August 1996 – under investigation herself – Bhutto would accuse the Qazi of 'minting money' during the *jihad*.[6] The JI appeared, however, to have retained its ties with the military and intelligence services: in May 1996, Qazi Hussain Ahmad spent ten days shuttling between Hekmatyar and Massoud in a last-ditch bid to sew up an alliance to fend off the swiftly-advancing Taliban.[7]

The place of the Islamist party closest to the seat of civilian power passed to Jamiat ul-Ulama-i Islam (JUI) a Deoband-influenced grouping with a power base in Baluchistan and NWFP, where Bhutto had never mustered much support. It was an odd alliance: the Oxford-educated, female prime minister with a fine line in saris, and Maulana Fazl ul-Rahman, the JUI's firebrand leader, who took even extremism to extremes. Out of the need for a patina of Islamic respectability, Bhutto took what, in retrospect, was the momentous decision of appointing Fazl ul-Rahman to the sensitive post of chairman of the standing committee on foreign affairs in the National Assembly. In October 1996, one month after the fall of Kabul, he told a public meeting in Peshawar that the JUI would create an 'Afghanistan-like situation' in Pakistan, if 'anti-Islamic and nationalist' elements in the government did not revise their opinion of the Taliban. 'For the first time in 50 years,' he said, 'Afghanistan was able to have a pro-Pakistan government in Kabul.' All the others, he added, had been pro-Indian.[8]

The rise of such a loose cannon into the decision-making heartland of Pakistan's foreign relations was another outcome of the Afghan war. Saddled with a sophisticated war machine designed to project Western interests into Central Asia, Pakistan was spending around 35 per cent of its budget on defence in 1993 and still could not stand down its forces due to the perceived threat from India. Investment in education had crumbled to 2.3 per cent of the gross national product – almost half the average for developing countries. Like many fringe Islamic parties, the JUI flourished by offering country boys a free Koranic schooling and board in a network of *madrassa*, sprinkled in villages, orphanages and refugee camps across Pakistan's poorest states. Many were financed by the US, Britain and Saudi Arabia, as part of their humanitarian programmes. In a political climate marred by shameless corruption, this was a constituency ripe for the plucking. Once the JUI had attained a position of influence in the National Assembly, it could expand its local power base with *ex gratia* payments from the PPP and through the access the party provided to wealthy patrons in Pakistan or overseas.

Many first-generation Taliban had confirmed ties with the JUI's *madrassa* system and Mullah Mohammed Omar's appeal to the organisation's lawyers for help to prepare a Taliban constitution suggests that he had been one of its students at some time or another.[9] But the JUI's support for the movement was displayed in more practical ways: in September 1996, regular examinations were postponed to allow some 2,000 students to cross the frontier to gain practical experience in *jihad*, and the *madrassa* remained a reservoir of manpower throughout the Taliban reign.[10] In a flip comment on 27 September – which suggested that his relationship with Maulana Fazl ul-Rahman was not all it might have been – Babar said that the Taliban conquest of Kabul was 'only a change of guard, from JI to JUI'.[11] Another change of guard had occurred in Islamabad.

For 45 years, Afghan policy had been determined by the Pashtun and Baluchi commanders-in-chief of the Pakistani army, operating for the most part on the east–west axis that connects Peshawar with Kabul and passes through Ghilzai lands. Under Bhutto, it shifted to the vertical, linking Karachi with Central Asia through Quetta and Kandahar. That policy was controlled by Punjabis and Sinds, passed through Durrani country and it now needed stability, not desolation, in Kabul. The end would be the same: a Pashtun-dominated government attentive to Pakistani interests. But it would arise from a policy of uniting the disparate clans of the Pashtun nation, rather than dividing them and that posed conundrums that had not really been addressed since before the Soviet invasion. How long would an Afghanistan, united through Pakistani devices, remain loyal to Islamabad when both Iran and India were certain to dangle glittering alternatives, if it were to behave contrarily? And how long would it take a movement of soaring national rebirth to rediscover its place on the map, and set a new course for fabled Pashtunistan? 'You cannot buy an Afghan,' according to a British colonial saying, 'but you can rent one at a very high price.'

Despite some secrecy surrounding the *madrassa* syllabus, JUI schools were ill-equipped to provide more than the spiritual ethos and *esprit de corps* of the Taliban movement. The military know-how came from elsewhere. Twenty-six Pakistani Taliban, captured by Massoud in late October 1996, admitted they had received 40 days' training in the use of Kalashnikovs under ISI supervision.[12] Pakistan's Frontier Constabulary, over which Interior Minister Babar had command, was also cited as a source of the Urdu-speaking fighters often sighted in the Taliban ranks.[13]

But these were foot-soldiers, not the tank drivers, mechanics, fighter pilots, supply clerks, rocketeers, radio operators, munitions experts and other specialists that constitute even an unconventional modern army and who were undoubtedly in the Taliban van as it set off northwards from Kandahar. Afghan gossip – the only available information resource – would implicate General Tanai, a Khalq sympathiser who, after the failed ISI-backed coup attempt of 1990, had taken refuge in the ISI barracks at Chaklala, near Rawalpindi.[14] Tanai's influence among former army professionals, sources say, allied with elements of the Pakistani military and what remained of the Harakat Inqilab-i Islami of Mohammed Nabi Mohammedi, provided the skilled steel which underlay the raw populism of the Taliban. The movement's battle captains, according to one Western military analyst, used the 'same tactics as Pakistan's trained strategists, which had nothing to do with the hit-and-run tactics of guerrilla movements'.[15]

But a fifth party – in addition to Babar, the JUI, the Pakistani army and General Tanai – is credited with playing a role in the rise of the movement. This was the Intelligence Bureau (IB), another mysterious tentacle of the military establishment, and one whose funds Babar was accused of siphoning off in 1990 to help defeat a no-confidence motion against Mrs Bhutto.[16] Bhutto could never wholly trust the ISI, which had been instrumental in killing her father and was constantly poised to unseat her, or any other civilian head of state. The existence of a 'dirty tricks' alternative is credible at a time when her administration was seeking to devise an Afghan strategy, independent of the conventional channels and, feasibly, in direct opposition to long-established ISI policy.

'If [Taliban] numbers are about 30,000, as they claim, and each of them would require $100 for daily and military expenses then, Mr President, a very important question should be asked: who is paying more than $88 million a month for their expenses?' Abdul Rahim Ghafoorzai, Rabbani's deputy minister of foreign affairs, was addressing the UN General Assembly in New York on 4 October 1995.[17] These were not numbers plucked from the air: he had been briefed by someone with a grasp of military budgets. 'As far as logistical support,' he continued, 'according to [our] calculations, in order for the Taliban to have their transport vehicles, tanks and other armoured vehicles running, they need more than 15,000 gallons of fuel each day. This is aside from almost the same amount of fuel they require as reserve. Again, who is providing them with such huge logistical support?'

The Rabbani government had much to gain from painting the Taliban as a foreign-backed adventure into Afghan territory. It stripped away some of the legitimacy the movement had earned through the imposition of peace and stability in the lawless south. By contrast, Rabbani always allowed that Hekmatyar had an authentic constituency, even though he transparently enjoyed Pakistani support. Mahmoud Mestiri, the UN special envoy, was in two minds about it. Shortly after the fall of Herat in September 1995, he said: 'The power of the Taliban is mysterious. I think that they are getting money and help maybe from Pakistan.' But he recanted three months later, claiming that, in spite of evidence that the Taliban knew how to fly MiGs and helicopters, there was no hard proof of Pakistani support.[18] By then, he was, arguably, a man broken by the night-marish complexities of Afghan peacemaking.

Testimony to Pakistani aid, prior to the final advance on Kabul, was never more than anecdotal. Fuel, munitions and trained fighters undoubt-edly crossed the border, both from Quetta and through NWFP, and the government was swift to open consulates and banking branches in cities conquered by the movement. But there is little to indicate a systemic programme of assistance, such as accompanied the operations against the Soviet Union. It is certainly dubious that Islamabad possessed the disposable funds to which Ghafoorzai referred in New York, particularly if the ISI were simultaneously backing Hekmatyar, as appeared to be the case throughout 1995 and until mid-1996. The evidence suggests that support for the Taliban was less a central plank of Pakistani foreign policy, which remained the prerogative of the military, and more a rogue project, triggered by Babar and his friends, to win Afghan policy back to the civilian side in the ongoing tension within Pakistan's administration. The funds, at least, came from elsewhere.

Bhutto's second term of office was cut short by Zia's constitutional legacy, the Eighth Amendment, which enabled the president, always beholden to the military nexus, to dismiss a government when it 'erred' or strayed too far from the narrow freedoms permitted it by an overmighty army. The charge of corruption was the Sword of Damocles hanging over every civilian government in Pakistan, and it usually stuck.

'Those who would ignite the fire in our country,' Ghafoorzai told the UN in New York, 'will burn themselves.' It is a metaphor so commonly used by ordinary Afghans when talking about Britain, the Soviet Union and Pakistan that it has achieved the resonance of a proverb.

*   *   *

Hekmatyar had begun to look like history in mid-1994, when Bhutto and Babar decided to concentrate on opening trade links with Central Asia. The Islamabad Accord of 7 March 1993, which had brought him into government as prime minister, collapsed days afterwards. It was the last time that Pakistan, Iran and Saudi Arabia sat down with faction heads to hammer out an Afghan settlement that suited all their interests. Hekmatyar's final bid for power had begun on 1 January 1994, with a searing attack on the capital in alliance with Dostum. That, too, failed to dislodge Massoud. By June, Dostum's troops were evicted from the city and Hizb-i Wahdat forced out its positions in the ruins of Kabul University, while Hekmatyar settled in for an attritional blockade from Sorobi. The bombardment continued, the hardship intensified but the international community began to denounce the killing with a little more vim. Hekmatyar's momentum was well and truly lost.

If Pakistani politicians were growing disenchanted with Hekmatyar's progress, so too were Saudi princes. Islamabad's Afghan policy had been entrusted to the military but Riyadh's remained squarely in the hands of the external intelligence service, the Mukhabarat, headed since 1977 by Prince Turki al-Faisal, nephew of the ailing King Fahd. Hekmatyar's public display of support for Saddam Hussein in the Gulf War did little to enhance relations and Saudi Arabia was also antagonised by his terrorist associations and the 1994 alliance with the Hizb-i Wahdat. Despite the opportunist nature of most Afghan coalitions, this one guaranteed on the surface a Shia component in a post-Rabbani government. That was anathema to the Saudis who, anyway, had hedged their Afghan bets by maintaining support to the Wahhabi faction Ittehad-i Islami, an ally of Massoud. But the more Rabbani leaned towards Tehran, after the fall of Herat, the more Riyadh would support his chief adversary. This came to look increasingly like the purist Taliban, rather than the radical Hekmatyar, in the light of the defeat at Charasyab and his more promiscuous alliances. In late 1995, envoys from Saudi Arabia, Bahrain and Qatar were separately sighted in Kandahar, a favoured location for the princely sport of falconry. The question of money might then have raised its head – but it may have been partridge breaking cover.[19]

Babar's wheeze had had a domino effect, transforming the balance of Afghan power in the south and southwest. But the Taliban, like every renegade Afghan force that Britain, the Soviet Union or Pakistan had concocted, were not, ultimately, the interior minister's creatures. Asking whose creatures they truly were, in fact, may be a futile errand when religious vision, clan rivalry, Saudi dollars and geopolitical ambition are woven together on such an impetuous loom as the nature of Pashtun leadership. The movement's success, moreover, surprised its own leaders as much as their enemies, heightening expectations of what more could be attained in a conflict which, experience suggested, was conducted against bullies and the ghosts of old reputations. Instead of turning left at Kandahar to unlock the Central Asian road, the Taliban headed north, toward the Tower of Victory at Ghazni, which led through Shia country and the apple-growing oases of Wardak.

Such an unbridled rampage had critical consequences in a region so sensitive that the slightest change in the political ionosphere could shut down diplomatic relations altogether. Repulsed at Kabul in March 1995, the Taliban pressed on to Herat. If Pakistan regarded Kabul as its strategic backyard in its endlessly recycled quarrel with India, Tehran felt the same sense of possessiveness toward Herat, a city which was once Persian and still exuded that culture's supple love of poetry, perfume and gardens. The remains of the five filigreed minarets of the *madrassa*, built by Shah Rukh in the sixteenth century and demolished by the British three centuries later, sneered at the simplistic absolutes of its Pashtun conquerors.

'The Taliban,' spluttered the state-controlled newspaper *Jomhour-i Islami*, 'are an American hand-fed group, which is fed, equipped, guided and supported by Saudi petrol dollars through Pakistan's 2nd Division ... Pakistan, since long, is not cutting its coat according to its cloth and has crossed the red line, the criterion of which is Iran's national security limits.'[20] The loss to the Taliban of Shindand, 100 miles (160 kilometres) south of Herat, had grave consequences for it denied Iran the air bridge that it used to arm Hizb-i Wahdat and place a protective arm around the Shia communities of the Hazarajat. This had always formed part of a *quid pro quo* with the emir of Herat, Ismail Khan, which included the provision of fuel, ammunition and other facilities during his unsuccessful bid to repel the Taliban advance in late 1995.[21] To maintain supplies to the region, Tehran now had to rely on Bagram and Massoud, who had battled Wahdat since 1994. New trade-offs had to be contracted with former enemies.

The loss of Herat on 5 September 1995 brought the Taliban within 80 miles of the Iranian border. Tehran went ballistic, but evidence of US and Saudi backing remained circumstantial in late 1995 – and it remained so throughout 1996. Even Pakistani control was beginning to look tenuous after January 1995 when the Taliban broke their cables to advance on Kabul. That decision may have been taken to prevent Massoud reinforcing Ismail Khan's forces, then fighting hard to defend the road through Farah to Shindand, but Jamiat was pinned down by Hizb and Wahdat in Kabul and the Taliban intervention had a totally opposite result. The siege of Kabul was lifted, ushering in an unusual period of calm for its inhabitants and unprecedented respectability for the Rabbani regime.

Ghafoorzai's speech to the UN that October was the culmination of a long-sought, diplomatic honeymoon. It was brought about, in part, by a more widespread appreciation of one of the fundamental principles underlying Afghan governance: the preceding regime is always preferable to the one that comes after it. That yearning for times past had embraced Zahir Shah, Najibullah and, with the Taliban's entry on the scene, it finally came to claim Rabbani. His coalition of moderate Islamists and former communists appeared the lesser evil in mid-1995, especially when seen against the vandalism visited on the capital by Hizb-i Islami.

After the Taliban's defeat at Kabul, it also looked like a contender, badly mauled but still on its feet. Delegations from the US, the EU, the Central Asian republics, Saudi Arabia and Iran all came to pay paid court to a president who, with an enthusiasm that verged on hubris, accepted an invitation to mediate between the government and Islamic rebels in Tajikistan, a war that Massoud and Hekmatyar had fostered from its infancy. It was a role the old prelate had long coveted: in the six-month hiatus in the siege, Rabbani took strides towards seeming statesmanlike. Schools were reopened, plans were laid for rebuilding Kabul University, embassies flew in and a multitude of humanitarian organisations galloped diligently into town.

Echoes of Great Game history had begun to ripple through Kabul with the fall of Herat in September 1995. Blessed with the memory of more humiliating setbacks – notably the mob-killing of Alexander Burnes in 1841 – Britain had pulled out its diplomats in February 1989, leaving a skeleton staff in charge of the embassy mansion in Parwan Mena. The cellars were emptied, the chandeliers extinguished and a dust-cover thrown over the nineteenth-century pianoforte. Under an agreement over the division of imperial assets reached nearly half a century earlier, ownership of the building was finally transferred to Pakistan in early 1995. Whatever else Islamabad was up to, it retained a diplomatic presence in Kabul until September that year.

The day after the fall of Herat, tens of thousands of demonstrators forced their way through the mansion's wrought-iron gates, egged on, Pakistani diplomats reported, by Massoud's security troops. One of the Pakistanis allegedly shot a high school student from an upper window, driving the crowd into an even greater frenzy. The embassy was set on fire, one of its employees was killed – along with five Afghan soldiers, Ghafoorzai claimed – and several others seriously injured, including the military attaché, Brigadier Ashraf Afridi. Pakistan immediately withdrew its delegation and expelled Afghan diplomats from their offices in Islamabad, Peshawar and Quetta.

The trace elements of a more coherent Pakistani conspiracy may have coalesced after this episode. There was no direct diplomatic contact between Islamabad and Kabul for eight months after the embassy's sacking. All calls – and they were few – were re-routed through Tehran and Iran's Afghan troubleshooter, Deputy Foreign Minister Alauddin Broujerdi. It was a unique and perilous estrangement. Babar's primary goal was achieved – the road was clear all the way from Chaman to Torghundi – but the cost had been enormous. The ISI's man, Hekmatyar, was soundly beaten, abandoning his weapons and documents as he scampered away from Charasyab, but the Taliban's limitations were also made plain to all. Setting aside what little was known of the movement's organisational weaknesses, it clearly lacked the military skills to take on Massoud. The ISI may have decided then to change horses and throw in its lot with Babar's unpredictable protégés.

The Taliban success in Herat, however, had rattled windows from Ankara to Beijing. Instead of installing a friendly government in Kabul, Islamabad had driven Rabbani right into the arms of Saudi Arabia's hated rival and their joint competitor in the race for influence in Central Asia. Dostum was facing pressure from Russia, Uzbekistan and Iran to bolster Rabbani or, at the very least, open the Salang route to allow fuel and military supplies to pass. India, a discreet ally of Iran, was helping to strengthen Massoud's air power.[22] China, which tacitly backed Islamabad's sparring exercises against India, announced plans for an air link with Kabul and the reopening of its embassy.[23] Tensions soared as word spread that Iran might lend armour and other resources to Ismail Khan, whose bid to recapture western Afghanistan was considered imminent. At the end of October, Washington dispatched Robin Raphel, assistant secretary of state for South Asia, to the region to find out what the hell was going on. The entire neighbourhood was overheating.

The winter of 1995 was characterised by a burning desire for reconciliation. Bhutto visited Tehran in November to calm things down, while Iran's Broujerdi shuttled between Kabul, Mazar, Bamian and Kandahar in a bid to stitch up a domestic consensus. In January 1996, Iran's foreign minister, Ali Akbar Velayati, flew to Islamabad for talks with Bhutto and his counterpart, Sardar Asif Ali. From Washington, the US said it was pressuring Islamabad to show more commitment to the UN peace effort, a disingenuous claim in view of its own lack of support. Proximity talks between Pakistan and Afghanistan, under Iranian mediation, took place in Tehran in mid-February. This was a region desperate to restore dialogue and the status quo, rather than press for further advantage. By April, one analyst sunnily reported that Pakistani support to the Taliban had 'petered out', in exchange for a commitment by Iran not to back a counter-offensive led by Ismail Khan in the west.[24]

The factions were no less frantic, though their objective was not containment but the creation of new military configurations in time for the next campaigning season. Rabbani contacted Hekmatyar, Dostum and the Nangarhar *shura* and also sent a delegation to Torkham Gate to confer with the ISI.[25] Taliban representatives flew to Islamabad to meet Dostum and Hekmatyar, allegedly at the behest of Pakistan. In mid-February 1996, Afghanistan's consul-general announced that, if all the parties could agree on a mechanism for transferring power to an interim government, Rabbani would step down and Massoud withdraw from the capital. Rabbani had promised as much before, counting on the factions' inevitable inability to agree on terms as an excuse for not resigning. He should have left office the previous March.

But now it was different. Hekmatyar no longer harried the capital and he had adopted a more conciliatory approach to his enemies. With ISI support ruptured or waning, he was in danger of being wholly marginalised, as was Jamaat-i Islami, Hekmatyar's main political backer in Pakistan. Viewed in another light, the ISI had seen over 20 years of investment in Afghanistan's future governance flushed away in the two short years since Bhutto had come to power. The Pashtun professed continued unanimity with Dostum and Hizb-i Wahdat, but he put out feelers for a defence pact with the Taliban, which Mullah Omar rejected. On 9 March, Hekmatyar announced a new alliance with Rabbani and the formation of a Joint Military High Council with Massoud. Electricity was restored in Kabul for the first time in three years. Hizb-i Wahdat, under its new leader Karim Khalili, said it too would join the new configuration. Earlier in the month, Rabbani had signed a military cooperation pact with Tehran, under which Iran pledged training for army officers, the repatriation of all military-age Afghan refugees for service in Kabul, the repair of the airport and the provision of funds to win over other factions.[26]

This was the second juncture at which a more considered meeting of minds may have taken place between the Pakistani government and military, the US and Saudi Arabia. Rabbani, Massoud and Hekmatyar had now become intimately bound up with Washington and Riyadh's profound fear of Iranian expansionism. But the involvement of Jamaat's Qazi Hussain Ahmad in the mediation between the three Afghan leaders added to Islamabad's subsequent diplomacy toward Kabul, still argued against a consistent and unified Pakistani policy to either the government in Kabul or the Taliban. Amid a flurry of meetings by the 'Afghan cell', Islamabad's policy-making unit for Afghanistan, the Pakistani press speculated that a major strategy review was under way, with Bhutto and Babar looking for a face-saving way out of the embassy dispute that could lead to the normalisation of bilateral relations.[27] That was obtained before the month was out: Kabul apologised, agreeing to pay millions of dollars in compensation and to assist in the repair of the building. Two months later, in May 1996, Islamabad welcomed Afghan Transport Minister Abdul Ghaffar, who flew in to discuss the construction of a gas pipeline and road and rail links to Turkmenistan. The energy theme had reached a crescendo in October 1995 with the signing of an accord in Ashgabat between the Turkmen government and a US–Saudi joint venture to build a $2 billion gas pipeline across Afghanistan to Pakistan. It coincided with the revival of US interest, demonstrated by Robin Raphel's visit to Mazar, Kabul, Jalalabad and Islamabad in the same month.

Pointedly, she did not pay calls on the Taliban in Kandahar or Herat, the preferred route for the pipeline but would, when she returned in mid-April. But Senator Hank Brown, who sat on the US Senate Intelligence Committee, had met with them a month earlier and invited the Taliban to send delegates to a conference in the US timed for July. Pointedly, neither Hekmatyar nor Sayyaf were on the guest list.[28] Brown was so disappointed with the drift of the UN peace mission that, on his return to the US, he urged President Clinton in writing to insist on Mestiri's replacement as peace envoy, arguing he had 'squandered' whatever influence he once had with the factions. Mestiri, understandably, was 'very disturbed' by the letter.[29]

Raphel remained pessimistic about the prospects of peace and less impressed by the Taliban's cohesion. 'These weaknesses,' she said, 'combined with Ahmad Shah Massoud's growing strength, appear to be shifting the balance against [the Taliban] somewhat and will prevent them from achieving their stated goal of taking Kabul.' She concluded that they had 'reached the limit of their expansion'. It was an intriguingly downbeat assessment from a country that most Afghans assumed was the movement's secret sponsor.[30]

The Taliban responded to the new alliance in Kabul with their own initiative: a congress of *ulama*, drawn from the 15 provinces under their control, whose decisions would be binding on the movement's *shura*. Whether this was out of fear for a combined Massoud–Hekmatyar force or the suspicion that the moral high ground of a peace settlement was slipping from their grasp, it had a distinctly defensive air. Having consistently rejected Mestiri's peace proposals on the grounds that they favoured Rabbani, or involved mujahedin and communists, a Taliban spokesman relented: 'If we are satisfied that Rabbani would establish Islamic rule in Afghanistan, we have no quarrel with individuals.'

By May, the Taliban appeared to have sewn up an agreement with Hizb-i Wahdat but Khalili thought better of it and announced he would join the coalition with Rabbani and Hekmatyar. The merger was approved by Hekmatyar's former colleagues in the Supreme Coordination Council, but it rankled badly. Five days later, Mestiri threw up his hands in exasperation and resigned, declaring it was impossible to come up with a workable peace formula. Whether his resignation was due to the intransigence of the faction leaders or the absence of US commitment was unclear, but it marked the end of UN initiatives until after Kabul fell on 27 September. When his successor, Dr Norbert Holl, took up his post at the end of July, Dostum had reopened the Salang Tunnel for supplies from Russia and Uzbekistan. But the Taliban were moving so swiftly through the east by then that all Holl could muster were vain appeals for a ceasefire.

This was a sleaker, more assured Taliban that sliced through the countryside like a wind. Weapons were never a problem, but fuel and high-speed transport undoubtedly had been. The revitalised Taliban clearly enjoyed an abundance of both, and the palm-greasing of local mujahedin was more frequently reported. Rumours persisted that Pakistani professionals were directing operations, with 1,000 fighters entering Afghanistan in the month prior to the fall of the capital.[31] All attempts by Rabbani and Hekmatyar to arrange a power-sharing agreement with the Taliban were rebuffed. But the links between the movement and its alleged sponsors remained deeply tenuous, implied more than confirmed, and the shape of Pakistani diplomacy, yet again, belied the thrust of the general accusations.

On 12 August, Pakistan announced it would reopen its embassy in Kabul and allow the purchase of food and fuel to relieve the capital.[32] On the 27th – a month before the government was routed – Jamaat-i Islami said it would open a Kabul office to facilitate the alliance it had been instrumental in moulding.[33] But, on the 24th, Kabul reported the defection to Bagram airbase of a Taliban transport plane with seven Pakistani military officers on board.[34] Were these diplomatic feints, disinformation, or evidence of a profound rift in relations between Pakistan's military, interior and foreign policy institutions?

The Taliban's capture of the capital produced mixed feelings in Islamabad. Mrs Bhutto, only 39 days away from her own dismissal, called it a 'welcome development', qualifying that approval with the hope that the Taliban would moderate their gender policies. Nawaz Sharif, her future successor as prime minister, said her Afghan policy had been a total shambles, which had 'turned friends into enemies'. Jamaat-i Islami called it a US-sponsored plot to divide Afghanistan along ethnic and linguistic lines. Being so closely identified with the movement's origins, Babar had no other choice than to express unadulterated joy at their conquest. 'The rise of the Taliban,' he declared, 'is of great advantage to Pakistan. This is the first time there is a government which has no links with India, or anybody else.'[35]

But Afghan history had shown time and again that a government without external links is a government without a future. And the thousands of volunteers from Pakistan, who flocked to the Taliban standards, were now at liberty to return to NWFP to sow their own individual whirlwinds. Babar may have been putting on a brave face, but Ghafoorzai's prediction looked certain to come to pass.

6 The Zahir Option

The Zahir question floated to the surface of Afghanistan's diminishing options in the year before the Rabbani regime capsized – though not necessarily with more buoyancy than in the past. Mujahedin leaders routinely gave their approval to wistful but untenable peace propositions as a way of gaining time and shifting the blame to their rivals when the project, predictably, guttered.

It was a ritual of Afghan diplomacy, a theatre that pitched wildly between histrionic defiance and abject lullaby and which meshed impeccably with the Möbius strip of a moral dictum once attributed to General Zia: 'Moslems have the right to lie in a good cause.'[1] But it was not without its grace notes: dragging out negotiations allowed UN mediators to return to Islamabad with the dim notion that, with just a little more consultation, a little more time, some path to peace might ultimately emerge from the savage Afghan labyrinth. Everyone's face, in short, was saved.

The UN peace initiative in Afghanistan was only two years younger than the Soviet war itself, harking back to 1981 when Secretary-General Kurt Waldheim appointed Perez de Cuellar to mediate between Moscow and the main sponsors of the mujahedin, the United States and Pakistan. One year after the Soviet withdrawal, on 14 February 1990, the Office of the Secretary-General in Afghanistan and Pakistan was created, with Bevan Sevan at its helm, to supervise the transfer of power from President Najibullah to a transitional coalition of mujahedin parties and the non-communist old guard. When that transfer skidded off the rails in April 1992, leaving Najib a prisoner in the UN's Kabul office and Massoud in command of the capital, the UN hastily withdrew from the affray, as had the United States one year earlier.

Sevan's successor was the former Tunisian foreign minister, Mahmoud Mestiri, a smooth-shaven, stooped figure with snow-white hair and piercing blue eyes. From his appointment by Boutros Boutros-Ghali on St Valentine's Day 1994 to his resignation a little over two years later, he shuttled between the faction leaders and regional capitals at the helm of a peace mission which, by comparison with the $3 billion lavished upon the UN's Transitional Authority in Cambodia, looked distinctly down-at-heel. With the air of a harassed schoolmaster and just a handful of helpers,

Mestiri, in the view of close observers, was little more than a sacrificial offering by an international community which, if it did not actively wish his failure, stood poised to blame it upon the indecipherable rivalries of the leaders with whom he was supposed to negotiate – rather than its own lack of political will.

That some of these leaders continued to receive armaments from the country upon which Mestiri depended for office space and the UN for its relief effort was not lost upon his mujahedin interlocutors who had scant respect for an organisation which had retained an unbroken presence in Kabul throughout the Soviet occupation, only to evacuate it in August 1992 after the first upsurge in intra-mujahedin hostilities. In February 1993, four UN staff were assassinated in Nangarhar on the road to the Khyber Pass, an indication that one faction at least had begun to regard the organisation as fair game.

The UN's failure to denounce Pakistan's covert assistance to Hekmatyar, before Mestiri arrived on the scene, in addition to his own reluctance to incriminate Islamabad in the subsequent rise of the Taliban, branded the peace mission as *parti pris*, at worst, and pusillanimous, at best. From the Afghan point of view, the charade was quite transparent: while the mission publicly deplored the violence wreaked upon Kabul by Hizb-i Islami, it was precisely upon an escalation of the siege – which, in turn, could only occur by turning a blind eye to Pakistan's support – that the UN appeared likely to achieve its own objectives. And that entailed forcing Rabbani into such a desperate position that he would have to step down.

In that sense, Hekmatyar was serving two masters and blood would have more blood, however plaintive the would-be peacemaker. It remains significant that, during his entire 27-month mission, Mestiri was never able to rig up even a symbolic pledge by the regional powers to observe an embargo of arms to the factions. The Jamiat government, reasonably enough in the circumstances, portrayed any political solution which had Pakistani support as contrary to the true interests of sovereign Afghanistan, of which it was, tortuously, still the UN-recognised representative.

'Everyone blames Mestiri,' said the Afghan intellectual Homayoun Assefy after the former's resignation in May 1996, 'but nobody helps him. Everybody criticises him, but everybody also puts obstacles in his way.'[2] Not least the factions who saw in the UN special negotiator a dunce who could be summoned or sent on mendicant circles of mediation secure in the knowledge that there could be no reward for his wanderings without Pakistan's approval – and that would never be forthcoming without US pressure. Bereft of the mandate to send in a peacekeeping force, because of the UN's fear of becoming as hopelessly mired as the Soviet Union before it, he entered this lion's den with neither stick nor carrot, a silvery after-image of the might that the US once deployed to 'liberate' Afghanistan from the Soviets, but would not spare to curb the ravages of its protégés.

Mestiri's mission triggered a surge of expectation among ordinary Afghans that belied the cynicism elsewhere apparent. Over two months in 1994, the envoy talked with hundreds of people from all walks of life – governors, tribal and religious leaders, commanders, students, women's representatives, intellectuals, peasants and refugees – while receiving the Afghan equivalent of ticker-tape receptions in Mazar-i Sharif, Herat and Kandahar. They 'implored' the UN 'not to abandon or fail them and that it be involved at every stage of the political process', Mestiri noted in his report.[3]

His welcome from Rabbani, soon to break his oath to step down in June, and from Hekmatyar, whose bombardment of Kabul continued unabashed, was somewhat less affable, in view of an unguarded remark by the envoy early in his travels that the two men were no more than the 'leaders of armed gangs'. Mestiri wrote:

> The impression that one gets is that many of the soldiers fighting for either side are reluctant to risk their lives in this struggle. Most of the combatants appear to be young men and adolescents, many of whom may be illiterate. Over and over, the Mission was told that the majority of those fighting were doing so for the money, since this was one of the only ways to make a living, especially in Kabul.[4]

In May, Mestiri took his roadshow to the other key players in the Afghan imbroglio – Iran, Saudi Arabia, Russia, Turkey and the US. All pledged whatever assistance the UN considered necessary to bring about a ceasefire – without interrupting whatever support they clandestinely provided to one or other of the factions. The mission concluded with the publication of a set of proposals that, in retrospect, were a triumph of wishful thinking. In tune with its mandate to conveyance, rather than impose, a peace agreement, the UN undertook to help create a transitional authority that would oversee a ceasefire, implement the collection of weapons, create a neutral security force and summon a *Loya Jirga*, or representative council, to prepare for democratic elections within two years.

The *Loya Jirga* was a doubtful mechanism, but the closest Afghan power-broking had ever come to a consultative exercise. Last employed by Najib to rubber-stamp the 1988 constitution, written by the Soviets prior to their withdrawal, it dated back to 1747 when Ahmad Shah was 'elected' king of the Afghans by a selective process of acclamation. The *jirga* was seductive in historical and customary terms but, as an institution, it failed to represent the comparatively urbane Kabul middle class, who did not ride to *bushkashi* matches on thoroughbred stallions or dress in the robes of the *ulama*. Legitimacy was sketchily observed, but not the broader diversity of Afghan opinion that Mestiri specially solicited during his first trip. Dissent, anyway, had always played a walk-off role in Afghan king-making.

This was particularly the case with the modern version, tainted as it was by Afghan communism. But Afghanistan lacked any variant through which less polarised voices could be heard, so it was to a *Loya Jirga* of faction heads, commanders and spiritual leaders that the UN mission leaned when it contemplated the means of achieving a ceasefire. And to Zahir Shah, a hazy paradigm of national unity and fledgling democracy, whose personal bodyguard in the 1950s had dressed in cast-off SS uniforms, until a notorious encounter between one of their number, the then US ambassador and a Kabul swimming pool.[5] Zahir's credentials were impeccable, but his purpose, amid the gunfire, remained cloudy.

He ascended the throne in 1933 on the assassination of his father, Nadir Shah, at a school prize-giving. But two regent uncles ruled in his stead for the next 30 years, to be succeeded – apparently with his approval – by the king's cousin, Mohammed Daoud, who honed the Pashtunistan issue into a razor-sharp threat to regional peace. Zahir Shah was that rarest of Afghan phenomena, a reluctant ruler. Only in 1963 did he finally come into his kingdom, to preside over a decade-long dismantling of the Afghan monarchy's autocratic powers until he was overthrown by Daoud in 1973 while seeking medical treatment in Europe. It is probable that he survived the murderous politics of his country thanks to this timely intervention – unlike its perpetrator who was slaughtered, with his family, during the pro-communist coup of 1978.

Zahir's potential as head of an interim government of reconciliation was recognised by Najib during his negotiations with the UN's Bevan Sevan in 1991–92. Support for his return was particularly strong in the refugee camps of North West Frontier Province and Baluchistan where, two years later, Mestiri was handed a petition for his restoration by tribal leaders claiming to represent over 1 million Afghans.[6] But in Islamabad Zahir Shah was still seen as a threat. Enfeebled by 80 years of history and the conflagration in his kingdom, the old man living on *gnocchi* in Rome nevertheless summoned up the ghost of Pashtunistan, a bleared memory in Afghan eyes, but an abiding menace to Pakistan's elusive sense of wellbeing.

Lacking any tradition of legitimacy at home, Islamabad tended to become overwrought at the slightest hint of it beyond the Khyber Pass –

and the influence it might exert on Pakistan's half-tamed Pashtun population. The military establishment, in particular, was bent on preventing Zahir's return. Benazir Bhutto attempted to arrange the ex-king's restoration in her first government of 1988–90, only to be thwarted by Hamid Gul, head of the ISI, and Aslam Beg, chief of the army.[7] Pakistani interests were better served by a continuation of strife and the meltdown of Afghanistan's military capability, than a government of national reconciliation. Islamabad paid attentive lip service to the need for peace in Kabul, but resorted to shabby tactics whenever asked to facilitate Zahir Shah's return: visa denied.

Against all the odds, the tide was running with Mestiri in late 1994 and early 1995. The Taliban's conquest of Kandahar failed to dent the peace initiative and may have given it a fillip by setting in motion the process of consolidating the south under a single overlord, whose origin and appeal to traditional values appeared to offer a more conciliatory approach and wider support for the ex-king's cause. But this could only become 'bankable' in the peace account if the Taliban were, as Bhutto and their own leaders insisted, a truly indigenous phenomenon rather than a subterfuge that used religion and local grievance to effect a virtual annexation of the south.

In December 1994, Rabbani announced that he would step down, in line with UN planning, but two days later he extended his term to June 1995. Mestiri extracted a compromise whereby Rabbani agreed to surrender power to an interim council on 21 March. Discussions moved on to 'modalities': a council, composed of two representatives from each province, along with 15–20 'eminent' Afghans, was to constitute the 'mechanism council' or interim authority, while a committee of 30 military officers was charged with recruiting and training a 'neutral' security force. Afghan advisers assured Mestiri that, despite the faction fighting, a neutral force was still feasible because of the popular desire for peace.

The Taliban's arrival at the gates of Kabul in February 1995 stopped that process in its tracks. Whether it was their intention – or that of their sponsors – is impossible to confirm, given the movement's shadowy motives and the mujahedin's justified reputation for making ephemeral pledges for short-term gain. The abdication of power by an Afghan warlord was, indeed, unprecedented – with the exception of Zahir Shah – and Rabbani's decision to step down, however faint-hearted, was certainly extracted under duress. But if the Taliban's subsequent military humiliation by Massoud proved that it was still incapable of taking the capital by force, it also killed the Zahir option by relieving the pressure on Rabbani to continue negotiations with the UN and his besiegers. The noose, which had tightened around Kabul since the siege began in 1992, became the rope with which the Rabbani regime would hang itself.

In that light, the Taliban's first bid for possession of the capital could be viewed either as a simple military miscalculation or an outflanking tactic of Machiavellian cunning. It may, conceivably, have been both for the process of negotiation tends ineluctably toward convergence, however unwilling the participants to concede. And for all his political weakness, Mestiri was on a roll in late 1994, cheered on by the thousands of Afghans and scores of local interests not implicated in the battle for Kabul, but alarmed at the speed with which Afghanistan and its people were vanishing from the international map of the world.

In defeating Hekmatyar, the Taliban ushered in the regime's halcyon days which were to last until the fall of Herat in September 1995, a loss that Rabbani later confided was far more of a setback than his expulsion from the capital a year later.[8] Trapped between a hostile Pakistan to the east and a Taliban army in the west that gave every indication of behaving in conformity with Islamabad's larger strategy, the collapse of the Jamiat government became a matter only of time and tighter logistics. An earlier capture of Kabul would have yielded a wholly different outcome, given the scope for an extended war of resistance from the Panjshir valley and the western provinces. If there was method to the Taliban's manoeuvres, it was governed by an intelligence of acute psychological and strategic insight.

The Zahir question was mooted with undimmed seriousness after the Taliban's initial defeat but, as Jamiat strengthened its control of the capital and briefly succumbed to hubris, it was evident that control of the peace initiative had passed from the UN to Pakistan and its military. On 28 May, US Under-Secretary Robin Raphel re-entered the diplomatic fray after a protracted absence from the Afghan scene, urging an arms embargo, without setting very much store by it. In June, Zahir's cousin, General Abdul Wali Khan, flew for the first time from Rome to Islamabad where he told Mrs Bhutto and Foreign Minister Asif Ali that, while the king was willing to join a transitional government, he would not seek to resume the crown.[9] Analysts viewed the apparent reconciliation as theatre, intended either to placate Washington but, more probably, to taint the king's cause through association with its fiercest opponent. By late 1995, Raphel went to Rome herself to talk to the ageing heir apparent.

Mestiri was less sanguine. In a blunt presentation to the UN Development Programme's donor conference in Stockholm in June 1995, he admitted his peace efforts had failed; a new formula was needed and the ethnic war so feared now loomed. 'The Pashtuns, Uzbeks and Hazaras,' he said, 'have been alienated ... There is either a national solution in which all segments of society participate freely, or there is continued conflict, leading to a possible ethnic war and the break-up of the country.'[10] Attempts to revive the negotiations by involving the Taliban came to nothing and, in November, Mestiri publicly condemned the Taliban's refusal to cease rocketing Kabul.[11]

Six months later, Mestiri asked to be relieved of his post because of ill-health. He said peace was impossible, that none of the faction heads – his unwilling collocutors for over two years – were viable future leaders of the country. 'Afghanistan needs somebody much stronger, much more famous, more healthy and younger,' observed one Islamabad-based diplomat of the disappointed envoy. As if a course of aerobics in California was more suitable training for bringing the mullahs and the mujahedin to terms.

* * *

Four months to the day after Mestiri resigned, ex-president Najibullah was dragged out of the UN compound by Taliban, tortured and lynched on the traffic-control island in front of the Argh. Mestiri's successor, Dr Norbert Holl, was a career diplomat from the German Foreign Ministry's South Asia department who took up his post in July. The rapid pace of military events in late 1996 sidelined further UN initiatives, while Mullah Mohammed Omar's refusal even to meet Dr Noll underlined that, if the Taliban were open to a ceasefire, they did not look to the international community to deliver it.

Snatches of the Zahir refrain lingered in the air as the Taliban closed on their prey. On 30 August, during a visit to Islamabad by a member of the US Congress, Dana Rohrabacher, Pakistan conceded it was not averse to the king playing some role in a settlement and, four days later, General Dostum fell in line, on condition that Uzbek rights and interests were protected. Even Hizb-i Wahdat, a Hazara faction with no love, retrospective or otherwise, for the traditions of Pashtun monarchy, declared its support for the Zahir plan in September – though no such plan existed on paper. Rabbani, characteristically, remained aloof from the topic, while appearing to ponder a five-point proposal for joint government, offered by the Taliban. These were the gestures of drowning, not waving.

Pakistan's interior minister, Brigadier Naseerullah Babar, the mastermind behind the Taliban seizure of the capital, had no difficulty gaining access to the mullahs in Kandahar. He denied direct involvement – in spite of the embarrassment of Pakistani professional and irregular soldiers in the Taliban ranks – but it was evident from Islamabad's dispatch of a diplomatic delegation to Kabul the day after the city fell that Pakistan had taken on the role of the movement's public relations adviser. On 1 October, the Taliban drove the last nail into the king's cause with the taunt that he was welcome to return 'as a private citizen, as king, as president, or as criminal'.[12]

More pressing negotiations were in hand. The Taliban's grasp of Kabul was by no means secure: the city had been surrendered without fight to volunteers high on bravado, by a general whose ability to convert rout into victory was legendary. Massoud gave a vivid demonstration of this talent in the first week of October when he turned on the pursuing Taliban at Jabal Saraj, sending them packing to within six miles (10 kilometres) of the capital. Massoud could not be defeated, Babar and his advisers concluded, but he could be cooped in the Panjshir and stripped of his supply line to Taloqan if only General Dostum could be won over.

Hekmatyar's ally in the first siege of Kabul, Dostum had been groomed for years by Islamabad. It extended him all the honours due a visiting head of state and he was considered an integral part of Pakistan's project of opening trade and energy links with landlocked Central Asia. His relations with Massoud, moreover, were riddled with political and personal animosities though, as leaders of ethnic minorities, both received cash and arms from members of the Commonwealth of Independent States to withstand the Taliban's dervish army. But alliance was anathema to Kandahar, which never once seriously contemplated sharing power with any faction. It was unlikely to start with a former communist mercenary.

Yet Babar's advice prevailed. To prevent the war from widening, he embarked on a five-day peace mission, flying between Kandahar and Mazar-i Sharif. Dostum expressed concern about the security of his forces in the west, where the Taliban had launched an offensive from Herat. Babar proposed a twelve-man commission, divided equally between the Taliban and the northern warlord, to rule the country under supervision of the UN and the international Moslem forum, the Organisation of the Islamic Conferences.[13] But building structures for peace in Afghanistan rarely produced more than the micro-structures of war. Talks were expanded to include Massoud and Hizb-i Wahdat, but they collapsed when the Tajik commander insisted that the Taliban must first withdraw from Kabul before agreeing a ceasefire. The dismissal of the Bhutto government on 5 November ended further attempts at mediation.

Babar's attempt to seduce the north ran parallel with a secret ISI operation to impose the Taliban stamp over all Afghanistan. The ISI had established a station, commanded by Brigadier Ashraf Afridi, at the Taliban base of Charasyab in mid-1996 to coordinate the second siege and orchestrate the final assault on the capital.[14] A Pashtun in his early 50s, Afridi was earlier linked to training fighters loyal to Hekmatyar during the Soviet occupation but he had more recent cause to resent Rabbani. As military attaché, he was injured and seriously humiliated during the sacking of the Pakistani embassy in September 1995.

After the capture of Kabul, Afridi moved his headquarters into the city where it supervised the transport of arms and other supplies from depots in Peshawar and Rawalpindi. Pakistani officers and NCOs, disguised as Afghans, allegedly accompanied the weapons to the Taliban frontline positions, where they assumed direct control for training their undisciplined charges. By mid-April 1997, Dostum's deputy, Mohammed Mohaqiq, reported the presence of 5,000 Pakistani troops in the Kabul area.[15] Dostum still refused to play ball with Islamabad, but a new game was about to be devised.

*   *   *

With the rounding-out of the year, the Taliban offensive resumed. An early *Eid al-Fitr* was observed in a frozen but snow-free Kabul with 85 mm artillery and a stream of celebratory tracer fire: clusters of crimson jewels, alternating velocity and formation, like shifting patterns of hot wax dripping up toward a glimmer of high-altitude moon. The city had seen worse, but the carnival atmosphere that traditionally accompanied the end of Ramadan, even under mujahedin rule, had vanished.

Jabal Saraj fell to the movement in January 1997, forcing Massoud across the Hindu Kush to Andarab, east of Doshi. On the 25th, Dostum's troops blew up the bridge and an avalanche-protector north of the Salang Tunnel, rupturing a link between north and south that had lasted 30 years. Three weeks later, an auxiliary tunnel, six miles south of the main structure, was sabotaged. This blocked the road from Jabal Saraj to the Salang, delaying any further northward advance, but it prevented Massoud from opening a second front to the rear of the Taliban, then grappling in sub-zero temperatures with Hizb-i Wahdat over the Shibar Pass at the head of the Ghorband valley.

If Shibar fell, the Taliban would stream into Wahdat's capital in the Buddhist temple complex of Bamian and the Shia heartlands of the Hazarajat, while a second force switched north along the old royal road to Doshi and Pul-i Khumri, the keystone of Dostum's defences. The latter was held by Sayed Jaffer Naderi, son of the spiritual leader of the Shia Ismailis, a tenacious minority in the northern provinces. Naderi was a Birmingham-educated former Hell's Angel with a taste for hashish, heavy metal rock and Pekinese dogs.[16] These interesting traits were unlikely to save his skin were the Taliban to induce a crisis of conscience among his followers.

On paper, Dostum looked impregnable. He boasted an air force of 28 fighters and bombers while his army of 25,000–40,000 men retained the surface discipline of regular uniforms and professional officers, many of whom joined up during the Soviet era.[17] After the loss of Kabul, his confidence was bolstered with the promise of 500 nearly-new tanks from Moscow and the Central Asian republics, of which 50 T-62s and 72s were delivered in the New Year.[18] With their flat, semi-desert terrain, Dostum's seven provinces were tailor-made for the tank warfare for which his forces were specially trained. His supply lines across the Amu Darya were impregnable.

But, in practice, the anti-Taliban alliance, the CDA, never looked more tenuous. 'We are not united,' said one of Naderi's troops in the ghost-town of Khinjan, just north of Salang, 'and so we will break.'[19] Though comprising over 153 mujahedin and militia commanders – a 'Who's Who of the *jihad*' – it was held together less by common interest than common fear – and the seasonal freeze in military activity which, in turn, had reduced opportunities for treachery.[20] As the spring melt set in, the incompatibilities of the CDA's mercurial parts soon appeared.

The same could be said of the ruling Junbish-i Milli-i Islami, Dostum's National Islamic Movement. Its existence lent a patina of political coherence to what was fundamentally a coterie of clan chieftains, whose richly-braided uniforms could not disguise that the roots of their power lay in the tribal militias created by Najibullah and the vicious bloodletting that followed Dostum's mutiny in 1992. By Afghan standards, Mazar was a wealthy, secular town with a sumptuous mosque, a university admired throughout Central Asia and 16 accessible TV channels. But it was held together by aid, whether Western or Russian, a counterfeit currency printed in Uzbekistan and a personality cult of ruthless braggadocio in which Dostum's moustachioed face boomed out from hoarding to hoarding, now a carbon copy of the president he had betrayed, now a backwater Saddam Hussein. It was all paper.

And it was highly flammable. Exchange rates in the Kefayat money market in central Mazar oscillated wildly as the warring season drew near and Dostum's commanders, sniffing defeat in the wind, leached out whatever hard currency was available to feather a future for their wives across the Amu Darya. In January, the northern afghani plummeted to 100,000 against the dollar, compared with 20,000 in Kabul, causing rice prices to triple and cooking oil to appreciate five-fold.[21] In February, the incipient panic was shelved when the currency recovered to 26,000 in a single 24-hour period, a revival that many attributed to a secret transfusion of dollars from Russia or Iran, the countries with most to lose should Dostum's line turn to marshmallow before the Taliban showed their faces.

The jitteriness in Mazar was transmitted as pre-shock to the men dug in at the Taliban's expected point of impact. Ill-fed, cold, demotivated and often abandoned by their officers, there was nothing left but to wait and listen to the rumours or the radio. Control of the airwaves was a far more effective weapon for the Taliban than control of the skies. Radio Sharia's bulletins of captured towns and trophy defections – though often far from the truth – fuelled misgivings at the front that resistance was futile, while appeals for reconciliation under Islam or withering attacks upon the morality of their absent commanders sedated fears that the Taliban intended harm to the soldiers' homes or families.

Marooned in the ice of the Shibar Pass, Khalili's Hizb-i Wahdat proved the only group impervious to Taliban bribery or disinformation during the extraordinary turn of events of early 1997. One can only guess whether this was due to Iran's iron hand or the greater fear of Sunni supremacism, but the line continued to hold against fierce artillery and tank attacks, and despite Taliban claims that Wahdat commanders had been bribed to stand aside. The breakthrough came instead in the west where Governor Abdul Malik Pehlawan, Dostum's foreign minister, later joined by the ousted emir of Herat, Ismail Khan, had spent months fighting off Taliban commanded by Mullah Borjan's former second-in-command, Mullah Abdul Razzaq, who was the new governor of Herat.

On Tuesday 20 May, Taliban radio announced that its troops had captured the Shibar Pass and were within three miles of Bamian. On the same day, General Abdul Malik Pehlawan and his brother, Gul Mohammed Pehlawan, who commanded 511 Division, mutinied, carrying 4,000 troops with them and leaving Dostum's western flank exposed.[22] A third Taliban force claimed to be attacking Kunduz on Dostum's east. The motive for Malik's rebellion was his conviction that it was Dostum who ordered the assassination of his elder brother, Rasool, in Maimana in 1996 and the subsequent murder of another close companion, Mullah Abdul Rahman Haqqani, over tea in Mazar-i Sharif two weeks prior to the mutiny.[23]

But Dostum's security bodies allegedly discovered a plot by Malik to shoot down his helicopter in February and other sources suggested that

Malik merely surrendered to the atavistic temptations of wealth and power.[24] Brigadier Ashraf Afridi had visited Maimana with a delegation of ISI brass in mid-May to persuade Malik to rebel,[25] while General Shahnawaz Tanai, Najibullah's former defence minister and suspected sponsor of the Taliban, had attended a 1996 memorial service for Rasool in Peshawar, testimony to his close personal links with what can only be regarded as the Pehlawan mafia.[26]

Massoud airlifted troops to the airbase in Dostum's fiefdom of Shiburghan, 130 miles west of Mazar along the Silk Route, in a bid to shore up the line but, by 20 May, Malik had added the provinces of Sar-i Pul and Jawzjan to his growing collection. As late as Friday, three days after the mutiny, reporters in Mazar still described a city going about its ordinary chores. That normalcy turned to panic one day later as news arrived that Shiburghan had fallen to Malik's forces without a fight on Saturday morning, followed shortly after by the return of the first of Dostum's frightened rabble.

The general fled, with 135 of his commanders, to the border crossing at Termez where, beneath a giant portrait of himself, he was forced to jettison his vehicles, his cash and most of his pride before guards allowed him to cross Friendship Bridge and into Uzbekistan.[27] In the few hours that remained before Malik reached Mazar at dusk on Saturday, citizens availed themselves of the hiatus to go on a looting spree of aid workers' property that was as frenzied as it was indiscriminate. The next day, a convoy of twelve UN vehicles also departed for Termez.

Sunday 25 May 1997 was a red letter day, marking an apogee of both Taliban and Pakistani ambitions. Malik's euphoric troops announced their arrival the previous night with a fanfare of gunfire in the western suburbs that provoked not the slightest retaliation. The next morning, fleets of Taliban pick-ups roared into town after a headlong night drive from Herat, while additional forces were flown in from Kabul and Kandahar, with a delegation of Taliban leaders that included Foreign Minister Mullah Mohammed Ghaus and Mullah Abdul Razzaq.

By the end of the day, some 2,000–3,000 Taliban fighters were inside the city, commanded by Qazi Gargari.[28] Further south, the Jamiat commander Basir Salangi, who played a crucial role in blocking the Taliban's thrust into Panjshir the previous October, embraced God and ceded the Salang Pass, allowing 2,000 Taliban to drive through the tunnel.[29] In Islamabad, Foreign Minister Gohar Ayub Khan announced Pakistan formal recognition of the Taliban government which, he said, 'genuinely comprises the various ethnic groups in Afghanistan'. A day later, Saudi Arabia followed suit.[30]

Whatever agreement General Malik made with the Taliban or their Pakistani intermediaries was set aside as soon as the Pashtun warriors were installed within the city. He met with Mullah Razzaq that Sunday morning to talk over a power-sharing arrangement in the north, prior to a joint address to a meeting of 3,000 leading citizens in the mosque of Hazrat Ali, Mazar's spiritual focal point. Malik tried to reassure his listeners: 'The Taliban came here not to create problems, but to resolve them.' Speaking in Pashtu, which few listeners could comprehend, Mullah Razzaq banned women from work and education, imposed the *burkha* and introduced summary punishments for murder and theft.[31]

None of this went against the Uzbek grain – excepting the language in which it was expressed – but hundreds in the congregation stalked out of the mosque. More crucially, perhaps, Mazaris had not experienced gunfire in the city since Dostum's mutiny in 1992 and the 'silver lining' argument that won over potential opponents of Taliban rule in Kabul and elsewhere carried less weight in the north. Ethnic undercurrents, the conqueror's swagger, fear of Taliban reprisals and the loss of autonomy all played a part in determining what happened 72 hours later but, when it happened, it was with a speed and ferocity that defied attempts to find evidence of logic or planning. 'This alliance,' said one of the last aid workers in the city 'is one bullet away from disintegrating.'[32]

Accounts differ as to where that bullet came from. A face-off between Malik's men and a 100-strong band of Taliban on the outskirts of Mazar demonstrated there was absolutely no doubt in the latter's mind as to who was responsible for 'security'.[33] Elsewhere, Taliban commandeered General Malik's vehicles and defaced billboard posters of his dead brother, Rasool, as well as Dostum. The two men's images, in the nature of things, were all but indistinguishable.

However, the provocation that carried most resonance, given their unflagging resistance on the Shibar Pass, happened in a poor Shia district where a Taliban squad attempted to disarm members of a local Hizb-i Wahdat faction formerly allied with Dostum. A fire-fight ensued in which eight Taliban lost their lives. When the Shias agreed to the collection of the bodies by pick-up, the Taliban took the opportunity to launch a second attack. Within minutes, the warren of alleys to the north and south of the central mosque turned into a killing field as Shia and Uzbek, militia and citizen, embarked on a hunt for Taliban stragglers, few of whom had any experience of battle, let alone urban warfare.[34]

An estimated 350 Taliban, little more than *madrassa* freshmen, perished during an 18-hour street battle that lasted through the night of Tuesday

27 May and into the next morning when 2,000–3,000 of their comrades surrendered to Malik's forces.[35] Among them was Foreign Minister Mullah Ghaus who 'escaped' to Kunduz province in late July, probably in exchange for a large ransom.[36] Mullah Razzaq was reportedly killed in the fighting though, given the fierce personal animosity between Afghan warlords, it is more probable that he was executed.[37] He was quickly joined by 2,000 of his troops, whose remains were unearthed from eight mass graves in Shiburghan, Dostum's stronghold, when the old fox returned from Turkey to reclaim his inheritance from the Pehlawans.[38]

The rump of the Taliban invasion force fell back to Pul-i Khumri, but Massoud had retaken Gulbahar and Jabal Saraj, cutting off their retreat, and troops loyal to either Malik or Sayed Jaffer Naderi harried them from the north and south. In June, Mullah Mohammed Omar took the unprecedented step of visiting Kabul to rally morale and appeal for fresh volunteers from Pakistan to replace his losses.[39]

But across the Amu Darya, where he fled after the Mazar débâcle, a Pakistani diplomat conceded: 'Recognising the Taliban was a big mistake.'[40]

7   The New Emirates

While the Taliban appeared bent on hurling Afghanistan back to the medieval age from which the Soviet Union had inadvertently rescued it, at another level the movement's successes were curiously well-tailored to the realities of a region, which is forecast to challenge the Middle East as a source of energy in the twenty-first century.

All of the foreign powers that armed the Afghan factions throughout the 1990s were playing for much higher stakes in the international in-fighting that permeated the politics of the Caucasus and Central Asia after the dissolution of the Soviet Union in December 1991. Cut off from natural trading partners to the west or south by over a century of Soviet domination, the new republics found themselves blessed with an astonishing wealth of oil and gas, but no way of getting them to market, save through the network of pipelines pointing into Russia, a colonial power in sharp decline that had historically milked their resources at bottom-rouble prices.

The struggle to command – or restrict – this energy windfall embroiled the US, Russia, Turkey, Iran, Saudi Arabia and Pakistan, winning comparisons with that earlier saga of geopolitical manoeuvring, the Great Game. The first Great Game pitted the intelligence services of Tsarist Russia and the British Raj against one another in a bid for ascendancy over the independent khanates and kingdoms that lay between Asia's two most powerful empires in the nineteenth century. It only subsided when the two powers reached agreement on the frontiers of Afghanistan, an artificial state contrived solely to end the friction between their conflicting spheres of interest.

The second version had been conducted over a broader geography and by corporations as much as states, but it was no less epic and still far from resolution. In ten years, the new game spawned four small but remarkably ugly wars, fired the long-standing Kurdish insurgency in Turkey and dangerously intertwined the flammable worlds of geopolitical rivalry, Islamist revolution and state terrorism on a canvas stretching from Dagestan to China's Xinjiang province. The tensions in the new Great Game, like those of its prototype, were exacerbated by the weakness of many of the states concerned, the enormous prize at stake and the fact that none of the sponsors admitted to being in an open state of war.

The conflicts in Nagorno-Karabakh, Abkhazia, Turkish Kurdistan and Chechnya in the 1990s were all linked by a single, golden theme: each represented a distinct, tactical move, crucial at the time, in determining which power would ultimately become master of the pipelines which, some time in the twenty-first century, will transport the oil and gas from the Caspian Basin to an energy-starved world. Global demand, like global population, will double in the next 25 years and Azerbaijan, Kazakstan and Turkmenistan sit on the largest known reserves of unexploited fuel on the planet.[1] These resources offer the West a unique opportunity to break free of its dependence on the Gulf, which still furnishes 40 per cent of US demand, and a chance to command a reserve that will stabilise the future price of a scarce commodity. The Gulf has suffered three major wars and the producers most crucial to Western interests – most pointedly Saudi Arabia – are alarmingly susceptible to destabilisation, whether through terrorism, outright invasion or the social pressures building up within their oppressive regimes.

From early on, Moscow insisted that Caspian exports be transported through the Russian pipeline system to its Novorossiysk terminal on the Black Sea, ensuring handsome transit fees for its treasury and a continuing stranglehold on the independence of its constituent republics. Instability along prospective alternative routes through the Caucasus to the Black Sea, added to a US trade boycott of Iran, the cheapest path to the open sea, effectively imposed a blockade on resources whose potential has tied up billions of dollars' worth of Western investment. Western companies were desperate to prevent this new energy from falling into the hands of Russia's large but ill-endowed oil and gas monopolies. After the Soviet Union disintegrated in 1991, Washington continued to acknowledge Russian hegemony in the so-called 'near abroad' – the former Soviet republics other than the Baltic States – lest they fall prey to fundamentalist forces from within or outside. But the prospect of Moscow controlling the Caspian's projected 2 million barrels per day (b/d) oil output, in addition to the 7 million b/d flowing west from oilfields in Siberia, raised fears that one crisis-prone energy partner in the Gulf was being exchanged for another, with far greater scope for economic mayhem.

To Saudi Arabia and Iran, divided by military suspicion as much as religious differences, the Caspian represented a further threat to revenues already depleted by low oil prices and an enfeebled OPEC. If they could not stop the emergence of a new generation of oil-rich emirates to the northeast, they could pre-empt the loss of future income by investing in their development and exploitation – at the expense of their rival where possible. Both states assiduously courted the regimes in the Caucasus and Central Asia throughout the 1990s with offers of soft credits, technical partnerships – or assistance in rebuilding their religious inheritance after nearly a century of communism.

The other key player was Turkey, which has linguistic and cultural links with all but one of the Central Asian republics and was thought to offer an alternative role model of how a modern state could accommodate secular values within Islam. As Russia's main competitor for the energy transport business, Ankara tabled its own proposals for pipeline itineraries through Georgia or Armenia and onto national territory. But the long-running Kurdish insurrection, which sapped the government with no appreciable end in sight, continued to put investors off.

The Taliban's conquest of Kabul followed swiftly upon the Rabbani government's surprise announcement in February 1996 that it had signed an agreement allowing for the construction of a $3 billion pipeline across Afghan territory connecting the newly-discovered Yashlar gas field in Turkmenistan with the Indian Ocean.[2] Having lost Herat and Kandahar to the rebels, the government was in no position to guarantee security along the route proposed for the scheme, but the news marked a turning point in what had become an acrimonious and dangerous dispute over the routing of Caspian energy. The mooting of a trans-Afghanistan pipeline opened a brand-new chapter in the latterday Great Game and signalled the arrival of another player on the scene, Pakistan. Bleeding $1.5 billion a year in energy imports, Islamabad stood to profit grandly if the pipeline could be delivered. After years amid the rubble of the post-Cold War world, Afghanistan was propelled from the periphery to the very heart of the energy wars in the region.

A trans-Afghanistan pipeline could preserve the US boycott of Iran, break the Russian monopoly on Central Asian energy and still emerge geographically closer to the faster-growing energy markets in Asia. It also met the requirements of the US and Saudi Arabia, the two countries with easiest access to oil industry finance and the greatest interest in the continued isolation of Iran.

Earlier plans for energy routes had presumed the building of west-flowing pipelines beneath the Caspian to funnel oil and gas from Central Asia into new infrastructure designed to export Azerbaijani production to Europe. But the fastest growing demand in the twenty-first century energy market lies among the large and increasingly wealthy populations of China and India. By redirecting the flow, oil and gas from three virgin producers could travel southeastwards via Afghanistan to Pakistani ports on the Arabian Sea.

By September 1996, the Taliban's solipsistic mullahs controlled the entire pipeline route, the seat of government and the key to the treasure buried in the Caspian hub. Their success in dislodging Massoud may have been greeted with delight in company boardrooms but, with so much at stake if the pipeline were built, it was more intriguing to speculate on the reaction of Russia.

*   *   *

Oddly, Afghanistan is no stranger to the oil and gas industry. Dostum's mini-state in the north had prospered since 1992 from bartering crude oil from Shiburghan province with Uzbekistan for the refined fuels, arms and the other equipment needed to run his war machine. By contrast with most Afghan cities, Mazar-i Sharif experienced a business boom in 1995 with five-storey office blocks shooting up around the shrine of Hazrat Ali, the Shi'ite caliph, and its markets bursting with produce from Central Asia and the Far East.

Soviet geologists had estimated Shiburghan's potential at around 50,000 tonnes a year, more than sufficient to support a small refinery and to turn Afghanistan into a net exporter.[3] Other promising geological areas had been identified at Karakum in the northwest, the Afghan-Tajik basin in the northeast, Tirpul, to the west of Herat and the Helmand and Kundar-Urgun basins in the southwest. But if the Afghan geology qualified it as a minor province in the new oil empire, it was equally evident that the true wealth lay in natural gas. Non-associated gas was discovered in Sar-i Pul in the 1950s and larger fields in Jawzjan and Faryab came on stream during the 1970s. By 1984, Afghanistan was exporting around 2.4 billion cubic metres a year to the Soviet Union, earning an impressive $315 million, or half the country's total export revenue.[4]

Before the Soviet forces retreated in February 1989, the gas fields were capped to prevent sabotage, denying Afghanistan its main source of export earnings. Efforts by Najibullah in the early 1990s to reactivate the industry came to nothing and Afghanistan found itself in a similar predicament to its fellow, landlocked, Central Asian republics: they had potentially vast resources but the transport infrastructure travelled in a direction opposite to where the money lay. Russia preferred to sell its own Siberian on the hard-currency market in Western Europe and sideline Central Asian stocks to poorer neighbours, such as the Ukraine, Belarus and Armenia. And to underscore its stranglehold, Moscow unilaterally imposed 'gas-for-debt' swaps to pay for earlier weapons deals, or offered only half of the world price, which Turkmenistan was forced to accept in its 1995 negotiations with Gazprom, the Russian monopoly which controls nearly a quarter of the world's natural gas supply.[5]

No less than during the Soviet era, the interests of Russia's energy companies in the 1990s reflected the foreign policy of the state, much as the British East India Company was the cat's paw of London's imperial ambitions during the first decades of the Raj. So closely were they intertwined, in fact, their respective managements were interchangeable. Prime Minister Viktor Chernomyrdin created a personal fortune and political empire as head of Gazprom's board of directors until mid-1996, when he was replaced by another prominent politician, Deputy Prime Minister Alexander Kazakov. With little capital to spare, and strategic objectives to pursue as much as profit margins, Gazprom and Lukoil, Russia's largest oil company, were compelled to turn to political intimidation as a means of ensuring their seat at the feast being prepared around the Caspian. Whenever the new republics tried to forge genuine political independence from President Boris Yeltsin's Russian Federation, they were swiftly overtaken by destabilisation or civil conflict, usually camouflaged as ethnic insurrection. These mini oil wars served the dual purpose of reasserting Russia's dominance in the 'troubled' Caucasus and undermining the feasibility of alternative pipeline routes that did not pass through Russian territory.

Azerbaijan's so-called 'deal of the century', signed in 1994, gives some insight into how much is involved in the region. The production-sharing agreement between the state oil company and a consortium of nine Western companies, led by British Petroleum (BP), promised to provide the government in Baku with a dazzling $118 billion over 30 years from just three offshore oilfields – the Azeri, Chirag and Guneshli. The consortium planned to build production of 160,000 b/d to 700,000 b/d by the end of the century.[6] US companies believe there could be four times this amount of oil in the Azerbaijani share of the Caspian Sea. In Kazakhstan, Chevron had invested $1 billion of a projected $20 billion in the offshore Tengiz field, one of the world's largest with reserves estimated at 1 billion tonnes. Richard Matzke, the company's president, called the stake 'Chevron's biggest and most important project since the opening of Saudi Arabia about 50 years ago'.[7] Turkmenistan contains the world's third largest natural gas reserves and a total of 7.4 billion barrels of oil. But none of this energy had reached markets in significant volumes due to the constant wrangling over pipeline routes. By the end of 1995, Chevron was losing tens of millions of dollars every day from its Tengiz investments, which had yielded less than one-tenth of its planned production of 700,000 b/d.[8]

The oil transport issue arose very early on. After Boris Yeltsin took power in Moscow in 1991, the Soviet ex-general, Dzhokhar Dudayev, declared Chechen independence, with the active encouragement of Turkey and Saudi Arabia. Chechnya contains no oil or gas reserves, but it is crucial to oil exportation from the new emirates because the Caucasian pipeline system, which links Baku to Novorossiysk, passes through Grozny, the capital. If Moscow lost control of Grozny, it would automatically be disqualified in Baku. Azerbaijan and Georgia also tried to break away from Moscow's baleful influence in the early 1990s and seek closer economic integration with Turkey, Russia's competitor in the Caucasus. Western oil companies had proposed two alternative routes onto Turkish soil through Georgia and Armenia, bypassing the Grozny intersection altogether. Azerbaijan and Georgia tested the limits of their recent independence in 1991 by refusing to join Moscow's new collective security organisation, the Commonwealth of Independent States (CIS), on the grounds that Russia had fomented the Armenian uprising in Nagorno-Karabakh and supplied Abkhazian secessionists in western Georgia with weapons. The then-presidents Abulfaz Elchibei of Azerbaijan and Zviad Gamsakhurdia of Georgia were soon overthrown by armed rebels, to be replaced by politicians more amenable to Moscow's way of thinking.

Haydar Aliev, a former member of the Brezhnev politburo, was brought to power in Baku while his predecessor, Elchibei, was in London to sign the oil production-sharing agreement with BP. Aliev promptly renounced the budding alliance with Turkey and brought Azerbaijan back within the confines of the CIS. In a further bid to appease Russia – and the parallels with racketeering were becoming inescapable – the third field in the 'deal of the century', Guneshli, was unceremoniously detached from BP's original proposal and handed over for exclusive development by Lukoil, which was granted a 10 per cent share of the whole project.[9] In 1993, President Eduard Shevardnadze of Georgia gave in to pressure from Moscow to extend the life of Russian military bases on the frontier with Turkey, seriously compromising his country's sovereignty.

The message to Western energy companies was uncompromising: Caspian energy would be exploited only with the participation of Russian energy companies and under the protection of the Russian security umbrella. Washington had no particular objection to that, having a grander ambition in the survival of the Russian Federation under Boris

Yeltsin, and the protection of its investments in Western Siberia, by a larger energy supplier by far. When Chechnya's declaration of independence deteriorated into open war in the winter of 1994, the US never officially queried Moscow's right to dispatch an invasion force, settling instead for expressions of concern over the handling of a crisis that would go on to devastate Grozny and claim 80,000 lives.

When the Russian invasion backfired so spectacularly – prompting ordinary Russians to draw parallels with the Soviet débâcle in Afghanistan – Moscow was finally forced to concede over the pipeline question. Chechnya's successful resistance destroyed for ever the myth that Russia could impose its military will within the federation, let alone the wider Caucasus or the 'near abroad'. This had the consequence of downgrading the security arguments in oil circles that had reluctantly favoured the use of Russia's pipeline network. The Chechen war revealed it was as vulnerable to sabotage as any of the alternatives.

In October 1995, the BP-led consortium, which includes Exxon, Amoco, Norway's Statoil, UNOCAL, Ramco, McDermott International, the private Saudi concern Delta-Nimir, Turkey's TPAO and Lukoil, agreed to a compromise. From 1996 onward, the 'early oil' from Baku would be transported through both the Russian and Turkish pipeline systems.[10] The agreement satisfied some of Russia's concerns, while broadly meeting US requirements, which were the earliest possible end to the dispute and the provision of a dual-route system to prevent the emergence of a transport monopoly. But it was little more than a face-saving solution, designed to break the logjam in the Caucasus, rather than lay the foundations of a transportation system to last for 30 years, the average life-span of the production contracts. Oil began to flow, but up to a ceiling of only 700,000 b/d – a fraction of the capacity under development around the Caspian. More important, the sums the consortium earmarked for upgrading the Russian pipeline ($60 million), and for opening a second export route through Georgia to the Black Sea ($250 million), were paltry by the standards of long-term, oil industry planning.[11]

They underlined the oil giants' general air of caution and suggested that, far from being the looked-for breakthrough, the agreement was more a truce, or breathing space, in the pipeline wars waged across the region.

*   *   *

Turkmenistan has the best chance, among the Central Asian republics, of becoming the first 'new sheikhdom' of the twenty-first century. With 11 per cent of the world's gas reserves and large tracts of its desert geography still unexplored, it earned over \$1 billion a year from energy exports in 1997. Little wonder if the ex-communist president, Saparmyrat Niyazov, has felt confident enough to embark on a spending spree, mortgaging future deliveries of energy and the 1.5 million tonne cotton crop to pay for new railways, presidential pavilions, five-star hotels and a \$200 million theme park. The self-styled Turkmenbashi, or 'Leader of the Turkmens', has promised to turn his 4 million subjects into the beneficiaries of 'a second Kuwait'. They cannot wait. Turkmenistan suffered the worst poverty levels of the Soviet Union when it was ruled by Moscow, and has entered an irreversible ecological decline with the drying up of the Aral Sea, lifeblood of the cotton that dominates local farming to the detriment of grain. In the capital, Ashgabat, food shortages are worse than in Soviet times.

As the only country in the region with significant onshore deposits, Turkmen ambitions were best-placed to avoid being derailed by the bidding quarrel over drilling rights in a divided Caspian Sea. But Moscow – in the shape of Gazprom – continued to control the export routes for Turkmen gas and oil which, at current volumes and prices, could command over \$7 billion in revenues each year. Ashgabat steadily raised its prices after independence in 1991, from 6 roubles per 1,000 cubic metres to 870 roubles in 1992, but Turkmen gas remained among the cheapest in the world. Most is still sold to the Ukraine and other CIS members, struggling economies with scant dollars, with the result that Turkmen gas continued to be plundered after independence in the same manner it had before. In a round of negotiations with Gazprom in 1997, Ashgabat won a hike to \$42 per 1,000 cubic metres, but this was still half world levels and there was no guarantee that the user would ever pay.

President Niyazov had worked hard to create new trading relations to replace those which existed at the time of the Soviet Union. Turkmenistan was the only state in Central Asia to have developed close ties with Iran, the others having been frightened off by the US boycott, or Russian anger. In May 1992, the two countries agreed to extend the Iranian railway system from Mashad to the Turkmen city of Tedzen, at a cost of \$500 million. A \$7 billion gas pipeline linking Turkmenistan to Europe through Iran and Turkey was also under consideration, though financing was difficult due to the US boycott. Iran provided Turkmenistan with an alternative supply of cash through swap deals. Under this arrangement, Turkmen gas is trucked or railed to Iran, where it is traded for the equivalent value of Iranian gas on the foreign market.

Alarmed that it was losing out in the Central Asian oil rush, Pakistan launched a vigorous initiative to entice Turkmenistan into its own sphere of influence. In August 1994, President Niyazov visited Islamabad to sign accords on transport and energy and, in October, Prime Minister Bhutto attended the independence celebrations in Ashgabat, rubbing shoulders with President Akbar Rafsanjani of Iran, President Suleyman Demirel of Turkey, Rashid Dostum and Ismail Khan. It was the same month that the Taliban were first sighted in Kandahar, liberating from mujahedin control a convoy of Pakistani trade goods destined for the people of Ashgabat.

The idea of a gas pipeline from Turkmenistan to Pakistan had been simmering for some years, but it seems to have been seriously discussed in the months leading up to Turkmen independence day. Generals Dostum and Khan sniped at one another through the Pakistani media sent to cover Mrs Bhutto's visit but, whatever their political differences, they were in harmony when it came to negotiating the trans-Afghan leg of the proposed route. Energy transport could bring wealth, while the diplomatic and commercial linkages which the work entailed might amount to international recognition for their fragmentary domains.

Pakistan suggested in 1994 the building of a railway across Afghanistan, connecting Tedzen with Karachi. While this project seemed optimistic, in view of the security breakdown, Islamabad officials protested that they had received assurances from the relevant Afghan factions. The independent Argentine company, Bridas, claimed it had similar guarantees, when it unveiled its own proposal for a Turkmenistan–Afghanistan– Pakistan (TAP) gas pipeline in July 1995. Bridas was the first international energy company to take a stake in the infant Turkmen republic, setting up a 70:30 joint venture in 1991 to explore and develop the Yashlar field, 280 miles (450 kilometres) east of the capital in the Karakum desert. In January 1995, after three years' work and what it claimed was $1 billion in investment, it found it had a major discovery on its hands. Yashlar contained $20 billion worth of gas, sufficient to feed growing demand in Pakistan and India and to provide a surplus for sale to the Far East.[12]

In March 1995, President Niyazov and Prime Minister Bhutto signed a memorandum of understanding for the construction of an 810-mile pipeline from Yashlar to Pakistan's largest gas field at Sui, in Baluchistan. Bridas's contract with the Turkmen government stipulated an option to build the transport system to international markets. A feasibility study was carried out by Bridas's technicians under an agreement signed that April, working with representatives from the oil ministries of both countries. Negotiations with Afghan leaders began shortly afterwards. 'Agreements have been reached and signed, that assure us a right of way and the backing of the various groups in the conflict, authorising us to build the gas pipeline through Afghan territory,' Bridas's chairman, Carlos Bulgheroni, declared confidently in March 1996, one month after President Rabbani made his own announcement.[13] The deal awarded Bridas an exclusive right to build, operate and maintain a sub-soil pipeline from the Turkmen border to the Pakistan boundary for the next 30 years.

It was a remarkable concession, even for a war-torn country that had seen no foreign investment in two decades. Bridas's project was an 'open' pipeline, with spur-lines shooting off to supply Kabul, Lahore, Islamabad and Karachi as and when required. President Islam Karimov of Uzbekistan had also been considering a pipeline to ferry Uzbek gas across Afghanistan to Sui. Bridas's 'open' line would accommodate both his resources and the capped, but still recoverable stocks lying under Dostum's territory. And Bridas, in principle, had exclusive rights to the business – as well as 70 per cent of the Yashlar strike.

In practice, everything began to fall apart before the ink on the contract was dry. The Taliban expelled Ismail Khan from Herat in September 1995, introducing another unknown element into the pipeline equation, but worse news was to come from Ashgabat. On 21 October, Turkmenistan signed a contract with two new partners – the Los Angeles-based UNOCAL and Saudi-owned Delta-Nimir – to build a $2 billion pipeline across Afghanistan to the Pakistani coast. That pipeline would be a 'closed' or dedicated line, pumping gas for export only, and from an entirely different source, the Delidibide-Donmes field.[14]

UNOCAL was one of the high-stakes rollers from the western shores of the Caspian, where it controlled 9.5 per cent of the Azeri, Chirag and Guneshli fields in Azerbaijan. With revenues of $8.4 billion in 1995, it is involved at every level of the oil industry from exploration and transport to the development of clean-air fuels to meet California's exacting environmental standards. Over the past 30 years, it had become a major investor in Thailand, Indonesia and Burma, where a $1 billion joint venture in the Yadana offshore gas field was the single largest foreign investment since the suppression of the democracy movement in 1988.

Its Saudi collaborator in the Afghan project was a 'strategic partnership' between Delta Oil, owned by a Jeddah-based group of 50 prominent investors close to the royal family,[15] and Nimir Petroleum, owned by Khalid bin Mahfouz, who also controlled Saudi Arabia's largest bank, the National Commercial Bank, where King Fahd and many of the 4,000 princes in the House of Saud keep their swollen accounts. Considered the 'king's treasurer', five years earlier bin Mahfouz was exposed as one of the principal shareholders in the collapsed Bank of Commerce and Credit International (BCCI), along with Sheikh Zayed bin Sultan, the ruler of Abu Dhabi, and the former Saudi intelligence chief, Sheikh Kamal Adham. In exchange for his patronage, bin Mahfouz received over $176 million from the BCCI and only escaped indictment for fraud in 1991 by agreeing to pay a $225 million settlement with the bank's receivers.[16]

His partner in Afghanistan, and the moving force behind Delta Oil, was another of the kingdom's billionaire 'commoners', Mohammed Hussein al-Amoudi, an Ethiopia-based businessman who also owns Corral Petrol and the Capitol Trust Bank, with offices in London and New York. The two business clans, with a combined value of $5 billion, were equal partners in the Saudi firm Marei bin Mahfouz & Ahmed al-Moudi Group while their three oil companies had joint ventures in Central Asia with Amerada Hess and Texaco, in addition to their stake in the BP-led 'deal of the century' in Azerbaijan.

Were the trans-Afghan pipeline to go ahead, UNOCAL and Delta-Nimir would be the only non-Russian energy companies with interests on both sides of the Caspian basin.

Three months before Kabul fell to the Taliban, Bridas filed a suit in Houston that alleged it had been cheated out of developing its Yashlar investment because of UNOCAL's 'interference'. Company lawyers claimed $15 billion in damages, equivalent to the company's share of the estimated gas reserves. The Argentinians had succumbed to the curse of Central Asian energy prospecting: they had plenty to sell, but the only transporter was their biggest commercial rival. 'They are not going to put Bridas gas into UNOCAL's pipeline,' said a Bridas lawyer. 'Nobody was interested in this field while it was a wildcat. These guys took the risk and are entitled to the rewards.'[17] He claimed Bridas had invited UNOCAL into the TAP project in early 1995, but the US company said it preferred to negotiate directly with the government.[18]

Delta-Nimir had assumed responsibility for negotiating the rights of way for the pipeline across Afghanistan, a task made easier after it recruited Charles Santos, a former political adviser to the UN peace envoy, Mahmoud Mestiri, and a man well known to all the faction heads.[19] UNOCAL, meanwhile, hired Robert B. Oakley, former US ambassador to Zia's Pakistan and a linchpin in coordinating the anti-Soviet *jihad*, to advise on its negotiations with the increasingly successful Taliban.[20] Initially, the movement opposed the project because of 'Pakistan's insistence on controlling the pipeline in its entirety'.[21] But when Islamabad agreed to share the profits, the project obtained the mullahs' blessing. Indeed, all the faction leaders were enamoured of pipelines. Whatever the military ramifications, they were viewed as conduits for peace, patronage, investment and international recognition. Rabbani's announcement that it had overcome its reservations, interestingly, coincided with the first hard signs that Washington's interest in Afghanistan was reviving.

But Kabul had backed the wrong pipeline: the announcement came four months after the Turkmen government signed the UNOCAL contract, effectively disqualifying Bridas as a negotiating partner. At any event, it was unlikely that Kabul would ever be in a position to guarantee security for a project likely to take from two to three years to complete. Its writ ran in just three central provinces, inspiring one Taliban wit to describe President Rabbani as 'the mayor of Kabul'.[22] The Taliban, on the other hand, controlled the preferred route in 1995, and had only been kept out of the capital by the adroit generalship of Massoud, with military assistance from Russia, Iran and India.

The interests of Russia and Iran had been broadly similar in Afghanistan since the appearance of the Taliban. Russia was committed to containment, for fear the movement would ignite the smouldering Islamist movement across Central Asia. To that end, Moscow began supplying the government with weaponry from the start of 1995, as well as the Uzbek, Turkmen and Tajik warlords who ruled the intervening lands. Iran conceived the Sunni Taliban as a US-sponsored gambit designed to gnaw at its eastern borders and diminish Tehran's influence both in the Shia regions of Afghanistan, and Central Asia as a whole. There was also symmetry over oil. A trans-Afghanistan pipeline would jeopardise Russia's control over Central Asian energy, while Iran risked seeing its eastern rival, Pakistan, re-establish the rapport it had enjoyed with Washington during the Cold War, but this time in the defence of US energy interests. With all Afghan parties to the conflict endorsing the pipeline plan, it was essential to both countries that no faction should accumulate sufficient military power to dominate Afghanistan country entirely and so turn it into reality. The oil issue had not entirely displaced internal security as Russia's and Iran's primary concern in Afghanistan, but it had become passionately bound up with their geopolitical futures.

By September 1996, the Taliban appeared close to defeating that objective. UNOCAL vice-president Marty Miller announced after the capture of Kabul: 'We have been in negotiations with the Taliban and they have been very supportive of the project.'[23] UNOCAL called the Taliban's success 'a positive development',[24] while the US announced it would dispatch a diplomat to Kabul for talks with the new government. With the US elections barely one month away, Washington swiftly backtracked.

But as the Taliban advance bogged down outside the Panjshir valley in October and Dostum abandoned his neutrality to side with Massoud, it was clear that the loss of the capital was not the knockout blow it was first thought. The pipeline would have to be shelved, until the shelling ceased. On 4 October, UNOCAL's Robert Todor informed reporters: 'International lenders have told us that the project is not currently financeable.' But he began to court the Taliban by establishing a UNOCAL office in Kandahar and inviting Taliban leaders to visit the company's headquarters in Sugarland, Texas.[25]

In early November, the fighting spread northwest to Badghis and Faryab and rumours flew that Ismail Khan's troops were massing for an invasion from across the Iranian border. It appeared that the next round in the new Great Game was about to begin.

8   Nest of Vipers

The US and Saudi Arabia had a further motive for venturing back into Afghanistan, one that had nothing to do with the welling hydrocarbons beyond its northern frontiers, but which impinged no less upon their shared oil and security interests. In the four years that elapsed between Washington abandoning the mujahedin to their murderous devices and the resumption in 1994 of what would blossom into a furtively active role in the region, a striking reappraisal had taken place in the State Department and among the US intelligence agencies which inform its decisions.

This reassessment addressed the region's growing instability as a result of the spread of Islamist extremism. It mattered less whether the immediate trigger for the change in US policy were the destabilisation of near-nuclear Pakistan, the hot wars in Kashmir and Tajikistan or even the transformation of India from a derelict command economy into potentially the world's largest middle-class constituency. Important as these considerations were, they remained secondary to the recognition in the US capital that, far from washing its hands of its Afghan proxies after the termination of direct diplomacy in 1992, it had, in fact, brought the vengeful bastard of its Cold War affair back into the happy home. For a new and far less predictable threat to domestic security was now at large in the shape of a nimble Islamist conspiracy that transcended national and sectarian differences and was quite able to deliver devastating vengeance not only in Asia, Africa and the Middle East, but on US territory itself.

The vague spokes of what, in time, would sharpen into a global wheel of terror all appeared to converge on Afghanistan, although the controller was ritually identified as Iran's intelligence services. In the absence – when the UN peace plan was discounted – of any more committed strategy for bringing the rule of law to a country that had blanked all memory of government in the years since Najib's fall, the Taliban, on the face of it, could be viewed as supplying a uniquely eccentric alternative – whatever fears the movement raised that it would pour yet more petrol on the fire. Arson had rarely been a US qualm in Afghanistan.

From being the Armageddon of the great powers in the 1980s, Afghanistan had become their rubbish tip: a graveyard for peace overtures and reconstruction plans – and a sanctuary for graduates of Islam's most influential *jihad*. What in the West had been seen exclusively as a duel of the Cold War, with both sides using Afghans as proxies, had served in the East as the forcing ground for an entire generation of Islamist freedom fighters, men who had looked in turn at their blue-eyed Soviet or US paymasters and could not, finally, tell the difference. Inspired by their successes in the clash against the Red Army, they fanned out to raise insurgencies in their own lands.

The Afghan *jihad* united the Moslem world like no other twentieth-century event until Bosnia, another milestone in the wider conflict between Western secularism and radical Islam. For a decade, it was the East's equivalent of the Spanish Civil War, a rite of passage between the absolute values which wrestled over the destiny of the Moslem century. In Western eyes, the call to *jihad* may have appeared a worthy rallying call when mobilised against the Soviet Union but, as it began to leak out and corrode the governments which had sponsored it in Afghanistan – Saudi Arabia, Egypt and Pakistan – it became speedily demonised. That polarisation quickened after the 1991 Gulf War, which had split the Moslem world into rival camps of governments that either appeased Western foreign policy and energy interests, or openly defied them.

It culminated in an event that was experienced as an act of desecration throughout the Islamic world, both radical and moderate – the garrisoning of 'Christian' US troops in Saudi Arabia, keeper of the pilgrimage sites of Mecca and Medina. But the truly defining moment of the *jihad* to come was the 1993 bombing of New York's World Trade Center, the first foreign-backed act of aggression on US soil since the Japanese attacked Pearl Harbor in 1942. The tremors from the first attacks on the Twin Towers urgently altered the way that the US looked at the post-Soviet and the Moslem worlds. Having manipulated Islam's convoluted, but impotent, quarrels for decades, Washington awoke to the realisation that, in the two short years since the collapse of the Soviet empire, it had replaced Moscow as the only non-Moslem power occupying the lands of the *Umma*, or Moslem community, and, therefore, the most politically convenient target of international *jihad*. Even more surprising, perhaps, was the fact that its civilian and military infrastructures across the world were shown to be defenceless in the face of dedicated and well-planned acts of sabotage.

The literature dealing with state-sponsored terrorism at an international level, or Hizballah International as it was known, was as suspect as it was sensational, being based on information leaked by one or other intelligence service in the countries most affected by Islamist subversion. Like US intelligence estimates of the Soviet military capability in the 1980s, it needed to be treated with extreme caution, particularly at a time when

Tehran had largely replaced Moscow as Washington's foremost *bête noire*. Nonetheless, the conviction gained ground in the early 1990s that Islamist organisations across the world had begun to pool resources in order to maximise the impact of their operations against mutual enemies – the US, Israel and pro-Western Arab governments. In the few reports that saw the light, Tehran's Al-Quds (Jerusalem) organisation was identified as the organising genius of what was characterised, in Washington at least, as a fully-fledged international conspiracy to destroy US installations and take American lives.[1] Afghanistan was identified as its training ground.

No other country in the world offered a better selection of asylum or arms than Afghanistan in the early 1990s. With no effective central government, it offered the possibility of sanctuary to any renegade who, upon coming to terms with the local military commander, could lead an unrestricted life by satellite telephone, immune from intruders and cocooned by the Pashtun's traditional code of extending hospitality to fugitives from state 'justice'. As for weaponry, the US had shipped hundreds of thousands of tonnes to the mujahedin in the previous decade, an armoury that came back to haunt as it surged over the borders and into local flashpoints – Kashmir, Baluchistan, Karachi, Tajikistan, Swat and China's Xinjiang province – all of which shared an Islamist dimension, tending to confirm the fear that much of the region was careering towards 'Afghanisation'.

In 1994, Congress voted an official budget of $18 million for operations to destabilise Iran, a programme that was reinforced by an outright trade embargo the following year, as President Clinton identified 'global terrorism', particularly from the Moslem world, as 'the most significant threat to the West at the end of the twentieth century'.[2] Washington's relations with Islamabad also underwent a sea-change between the Soviet withdrawal from Afghanistan in 1989 and 1994 when, after five years of increasingly stony diplomacy, a new South Asia department was created at the State Department, headed by Robin Raphel, the widow of the former US ambassador to Pakistan, Arnold Raphel, who died in the same air crash as General Zia ul-Haq.

US policy since 1991 had nourished a wave of ill feeling in a population only too conscious of the sacrifices it had been forced to make during a war that was originally sold on the basis of Western solidarity with embattled Islam. The abrupt cessation of an annual $600 million in US aid in 1992; the refusal to deliver military aircraft already paid for; efforts to block Pakistan's emergence as a nuclear state; and the threat to blacklist it as an 'exporter of terrorism' were all interpreted as efforts to hobble Islamabad's geopolitical ambitions and, by extension, those of the entire

Moslem world. The equally abrupt end of US assistance to Afghanistan after 1992, on grounds that it was a narcotics-producing state, had further rankled, leaving several million Pashtun refugees chasing the same jobs as their reluctant Pakistani hosts.

Raphel's first impressions left little doubt as to the motives behind the revival of US engagement. 'Afghanistan,' she told a press conference in 1996, 'has become a conduit for drugs, crime and terrorism that can undermine Pakistan, the neighbouring Central Asian states and have an impact beyond Europe and Russia.' Terrorist incidents in the Middle East, she said, had been definitively linked to training camps on Afghan territory.[3] Her warning was almost a word-for-word echo of Najibullah's prediction four years earlier.[4]

Afghanistan's links with what would evolve into an international Islamist movement of terror had two distinct phases. From 1985 onwards, when Saudi Arabia increased its financial aid to the anti-Soviet *jihad*, some 14,000–25,000 Arab volunteers had made their way to the front to join up with the mujahedin, predominantly with the ISI protégé, Gulbuddin Hekmatyar, or Abdul Rasul Sayyaf, the leader of Ittehad-i Islami and a Riyadh favourite for sectarian reasons.[5] Neither Hekmatyar nor Sayyaf had made any secret of their anti-Western stance, in spite of the military aid they received from the US and Europe. Hekmatyar, whose political ardour was modelled on that of revolutionary Iran – from which he also extracted funding[6] – had long been identified with militant Islamist movements, a trait that endeared him to the pan-Islamist President Zia and private sympathisers in the Gulf. In 1991, Hekmatyar and Sayyaf both denounced Washington's declaration of war against Iraq, refusing to send even token forces to support the Gulf alliance in spite of their debts to the US and Saudi Arabia.[7]

The majority of Arab volunteers came from the non-oil world – Sudan, Chad, Mauritania, Somalia and Yemen – but as many as 5,000 Saudis, 2,000 Egyptians and 2,800 Algerians were also reportedly among their ranks.[8] For their new Pashtun comrades, the so-called 'Arab-Afghans' swiftly earned a reputation for enforced marriages, excessive cruelty and a fanatical intolerance of the local Hanafi rituals, though they fought with conspicuous courage in battles in the border areas adjacent to North West Frontier Province.[9] Arab-Afghans remained visibly active in Khost, Kunar and Jalalabad until 1993, and another force was based in Kunduz, close to the frontier with Tajikistan, another scene of insurrection with a global dimension.[10]

With the demobilisation that followed the Soviet withdrawal, Arab-Afghans were sighted farther afield. Two thousand veteran *jihadis* joined the Groupe Islamique Armée (GIA) in Algeria when the military seized power after the Islamist victory in the elections of January 1992, while other contingents surfaced in Kashmir, Somalia, Yemen, Azerbaijan, Bosnia-Herzegovina, Chechnya, Tajikistan and the Philippines, where they were identified fighting alongside the Moro Liberation Front.[11] With little to offer but fighting skills, a large proportion of the Islamic 'international brigade' graduated to mercenary status – 'rent-a-*jihad*', in one journalist's phrase – particularly after March 1993 when, under pressure from Washington, Pakistan issued a deadline for all Arab veterans of the Afghan war to leave the country. Less predictable was that a core in their ranks would go on to instil panic in the imagination of the world's last superpower.

Nangarhar had developed into a sanctuary for absconding terrorists by 1993. Mohammed Shawky al-Isambouli, brother of the Afghan veteran who led the organisation responsible for assassinating President Anwar Sadat in 1981, sought shelter there after being sentenced to death *in absentia* in 1992.[12] Aimal Khansi, who topped the FBI's 'most wanted' list after the murder on 25 January 1993 of two CIA employees at the agency's Fort Langley headquarters, enjoyed Afghan hospitality for four years until he was lured to a Peshawar hotel in 1997 in a $3.2 million operation that featured agents concealed beneath *burkhas*.[13] In July 1993, Hekmatyar, as prime minister, offered political asylum to Sheikh Omar Abdel Rahman, due to stand trial for his role in the World Trade Center bombing.[14] Another famous fugitive was Ibrahim al-Mekkawi, who had escaped to Pakistan after Sadat's murder and was reported to be running a training camp in Nangarhar. When Islamabad finally signed an extradition agreement with Cairo in March 1997, 1,200 Egyptian militants were reported to be loitering with intent in the tribal trust territories, or over the Afghan border.[15]

Most Arab-Afghans entered Pakistan with the help of the Jamaat-i Islami, the Pakistani wing of the Moslem Brotherhood and the main conduit for military and financial assistance to the war effort from the Arab world. But the largest private recruitment organisation was Al Qa'ida ('The Base'), in Peshawar, financed by Prince Turki al-Faisal, a nephew of King Faisal and head of the Saudi external intelligence service since 1977 when he succeeded to the post vacated by his uncle, Kamal Adham. Adham, who founded the kingdom's spying network, went on to achieve notoriety as a major shareholder in and front man for the Bank of Credit and Commerce International (BCCI), the failed Pakistani and Gulf Arab financial institution that was revealed in a 1991 Senate committee enquiry to have laundered profits from narcotics, nurtured the Pakistani nuclear programme as well as disbursed secret CIA funds to Afghan resistance leaders and their backers in the Pakistani military. Buried in the report is the further finding that 'terrorist organisations ... received payment at BCCI-London and other branches directly from Gulf-state patrons, and then transferred those funds wherever they wished without apparent scrutiny'.[16] In spite of the bank's subsequent breakup, suspicion lingered that the nefarious purposes served by the BCCI throughout the 1980s continued through the 1990s, using the same interlinked networks of individuals from intelligence, military and financial circles, only to further goals that had been modified after the collapse of the Soviet Union.

Al Qa'ida was indirectly administered from the outset by Osama bin Laden, scion of an inordinately wealthy Saudi family construction firm, close to the ruling Saud dynasty, which had its roots in Yemen but had diversified around the world as the Bin Laden Group.[17] In 1992, the head of the bin Laden family had established two fellowships in Islamic studies at Harvard University.[18] Born in 1957 and trained as an engineer, bin Laden had flown to Peshawar within days of the Soviet invasion, staying long enough in the nerve centre of *jihad* to build enduring contacts, based on faith and funding, not only with the mujahedin chiefs, but the ISI and the Arab 'Afghans' – as well as to break irrevocably with the rulers of his own country. When Saudi Arabia suspended its support to the Arab-Afghan cause in 1990, bin Laden set up a private base near Jalalabad, activating links with Saudi exiles in Iran and Syria. Two years later, he was in Sudan, where diplomatic isolation of the military junta had led to an almost last-resort alliance with Iran in exchange for oil. He lived in Omdurman under the protection of Prime Minister Hassan al-Turabi, a spiritual leader of the Moslem Brotherhood and Tehran's closest friend in Africa. While there, his wealth was identified as a primary source of finance for Egypt's militant Gamaat al-Islamiya, headed by the physician Ayman al-Zawahiri. In 1994, Riyadh froze bin Laden's assets and cancelled his passport, effectively declaring him a public enemy.[19]

The details of bin Laden's life have since passed out of the personal and into the realm of legend, a process he actively encouraged in interviews that gilded his image as a blend of the then Khartoum-based assassin, Carlos the Jackal, the Great Gatsby and a latterday Old Man of the Mountains. Estimates of his personal wealth varied wildly from £100 million to $7 billion, a figure allegedly supplemented by his involvement in heroin-trafficking operations run jointly with commanders in

Hekmatyar's Hizb-i Islami.[20] On the one hand, he was the equal of princelings, presenting a model of spiritual gallantry for young Turks in the lower reaches of the Saud family tree: on the other, the intellectual consistency of his graduation from a minor engineer in the Afghan *jihad* to the outlawed symbol of a defiant Islam won him unassailable status throughout the Moslem world. By his own account, Riyadh offered to pay 2 billion Saudi riyals (£339 million)[21] if he would call off the *jihad* he declared against his motherland in late 1996, while one reputable news magazine claimed that he gave the Taliban $3 million to buy the defections which opened the road to Kabul in September 1996.[22]

The allegation that Riyadh had tried to buy back bin Laden's loyalty was curious, for it implied that Saudi Arabia had found some common purpose with a man described by the US State Department as 'one of the most significant financial sponsors of Islamic terrorist activities in the world today'.[23] Bin Laden's name had been variously linked to terrorist operations in Egypt, Yemen, Somalia, Saudi Arabia and the US, although his cloak of mystery was of a kind to which rumours naturally clung. With King Fahd gravely ill and his quarrelling brothers casting round for a way to secure the succession of the dynasty, there can be no doubt that, by the mid-1990s, bin Laden had become a rebel with whom to reckon – and, perhaps, do business. The riddle of whether he was definitively recruited to act as the Mukhabarat's Taliban pointman or, conversely, that the Taliban had received finance from Riyadh to hasten the terrorist's capture may never be answered. But, like the Taliban, bin Laden was a past master of the back channel, the art of bribery and, at least, he spoke the same spiritual language.

Bin Laden's career epitomised Afghanistan's transition from an accidental to a mature terrorist 'state'. After his expulsion from Sudan in 1996, he transferred to Nangarhar where, according to Saudi intelligence, he ran the camp which trained three of the four men arrested for the November 1995 bombing of a US military facility in Riyadh.[24] He was also implicated in the June 1996 bombing of a US air force housing estate at Khobar Towers, Dahran, in which 19 Americans died and hundreds more were injured – although not the Bin Laden Group, which was awarded the $150 million contract for its refurbishment. Sheikh Omar Abdul Rahman, perpetrator of the World Trade Center bombing in 1993, was also a colleague: Abdul Rahman's two sons fought in the *jihad* and he had bin Laden's Peshawar address in his pocket when arrested.[25]

Investigations after the Khobar bombing revealed traces of an organisation that, far from the contemporary media description of a rabble of ill-disciplined fanatics, was truly global in both coordination and reach. Preparations for the explosion at the King Abdul-Aziz air base had commenced at least six months earlier and demanded extensive reconnaissance, the smuggling of explosives from the Middle East and the infiltration into Saudia Arabia of militants, many of whose names would already have been known to Mukhabarat and US intelligence. Some were Tehran-based Saudi Shias, like Ahmad Mughasil, but the Iranian intelligence officers held responsible for masterminding the bombing were allegedly impressed by the commitment of the Islamist opposition within the kingdom.[26] This was an undoubted tribute to bin Laden's example and his far-flung influence.

Bin Laden's significance went even further, if contemporary US intelligence sources were to be credited. According to a scrupulous account in the journal *Strategic Policy* (*SP*), the shadowy figure was an integral part of Hizballah International, a pan-Islamist terrorist conglomerate, conceived by the new Iranian chief of external intelligence, Mehdi Chamran, and designed to carry out precision attacks into the heart of US, Saudi and Egyptian power.[27] Several of these operations, including the Khobar bombing and the assassination of a female US diplomat in Egypt, were sufficiently well-advanced to be incorporated in Chamran's new strategy, formally unveiled by Iran's spiritual leader, Ayatollah Ali Khameini at his Friday sermon of 7 June 1996, and described as carrying the *jihad* into 'all continents and countries'.[28]

A two-day 'terrorist' summit was held in Tehran two weeks later which attracted delegates from militant groups from around the world. Senior leaders from nine well-established organisations, including Palestine's Islamic Jihad and the PFLP, the Lebanese Hizballah, Egyptian Jihad, Hamas, the Kurdish PKK and the Islamic Change Movement in the Gulf agreed to unify their financial resources and standardise training in some 30 states in order to establish 'inter-operability'.[29] A committee of three, composed of bin Laden, Imad Mughaniya of the Lebanese Hizballah's special operations command and Ahmad Salah of the Egyptian Jihad, was appointed to consult every month, under Chamran's chairmanship, to vet and coordinate terrorist 'works in progress'.[30]

SP's senior editor Yossef Bodansky, later appointed director of the US House of Representatives' Task Force on Terrorism and Unconventional Warfare, claimed that a second summit of key leaders was held the following July in the 'biggest training camp for Arab-Afghans', close to the Pakistani border town of Konli – a town that does not appear on any detailed map. Among those present were bin Laden; Ayman al-Zawahiri, the leader of Egypt's main terrorist group; Abdul Rasul Sayyaf; commanders from Hizb-i Islami, Hamas, Hizballah and Algeria's GIA; as well as senior officers from the Iranian and Pakistani intelligence services.[31] Bodansky's detailed account of that meeting suggested that he had somehow gained access to its minutes, but, however compromised that may make it appear, it also raised a number of intriguing queries.

Was it possible that a Shia Iran could successfully bridge the sectarian divide and command the loyalty of militant Sunni factions? Certainly, yes: Hamas and Hizballah both enjoyed Iranian support in efforts to derail the Arab-Israeli peace process in the Middle East and, since the rise of the Taliban, Tehran had swung its influence behind Rabbani, a decision which, in Washington, amounted to the kiss of death for the regime. Secondly, could officers from the Iranian and Pakistani intelligence services, as Bodansky claims, have discovered ground so mutual that they were prepared to contemplate what amounted to treachery? Even this proposition is credible, for there were known to be powerful elements within the ISI still committed to President Zia's Islamist mission, despite Mrs Bhutto's policy of disproving US accusations that Pakistan was actively sponsoring international terrorism.

As a token of good faith, she had extradited Ramzi Yusuf, the alleged mastermind of the 1993 World Trade Center attack, to the US in February 1995, a gesture that was followed by the revenge assassination of two US diplomats in Karachi one month later. Bhutto's apparent realignment with the pro-Western bloc of Arab states prompted a flurry of unclaimed terrorist operations in Pakistan. In December 1995, a suicide attack on the Egyptian embassy in Islamabad left 16 dead, and 31 people were killed after a bomb was planted in one of the busiest shopping areas of Peshawar shortly after.

Despite Bhutto's more conciliatory approach, however, Pakistan was identified as early as 1997 as the 'world's leader in hosting international terrorist organisations', with 63 separate camps for Sikh and Kashmiri separatists, and others training militants for cross-border operations inside India.[32] Pabi refugee camp near Jallozai, 25 miles (40 kilometres) east of Peshawar, was the main operational base for Arab-Afghans, but others were situated on Pakistani soil at Warsak, Miramshar and Sa'ada refugee camps.[33] In May 1997, some 3,000 Arab-Afghans were said to be living in the four camps, reportedly supervised by representatives of Hekmatyar, Sayyaf and the Taliban.[34] Such proliferation, indicative both of Pakistan's lack of control over the border territories and the ISI's continuing tendency to make policy at odds with the government objectives, was matched only in Afghanistan where bin Laden's two camps, Badr-1 and Badr-2 near

Khost, hosted between 1,000 and 2,500 trainees from the Gulf states, Pakistan, Chechnya, Uzbekistan, Egypt, the Philippines and China's Moslem Xinjiang province.[35]

Mindful of his own security, bin Laden then lived three hours' drive to the north of Jalalabad, surrounded by 350 personal bodyguards, in an eyrie that was as impressive as it was vertiginous.[36] Situated at an altitude of 8,200 feet (2,500 metres), at the head of a road he had personally built to facilitate the anti-Soviet war in Kunar valley, the camp was defended by anti-aircraft guns, tanks, armoured vehicles, rocket launchers and Stinger missiles and equipped with generators, computers and a 'huge' database.[37] Bin Laden, like his men – all 'doctors, engineers, teachers' – lived in a cave which

> resembles a room, six metres long and four metres wide. In the middle, there is a library full of heritage and interpretation books, such as Ibn-Taymiyah's *Fatwas*, the *Prophet's Biography* by Ibn-Hisham and so on. There are five beds made of very hard wood. They look like those platforms used in vegetable markets. As for the walls, they are decorated with Kalashnikovs.[38]

Tall, slight and dressed in the by-now traditional attire of *shalwar kamees* topped with a camouflage jacket, bin Laden had a modesty unusual for a man on the run from the world's most extensive intelligence dragnet. His relationship with the Taliban, however, was possibly more immediately perturbing. When he told journalist Robert Fisk in late 1997 that he had 'struggled alongside' the Taliban since 1979, he was speaking metaphorically, though his reference to the 'obvious improvement' since they assumed control in Jalalabad indicated his approval of the religious regime that had been imposed.[39] One of the two media visitors he hosted around that time enjoyed a Taliban escort on the journey from Torkham Gate to Jalalabad.[40] But bin Laden's declaration of *jihad* against US soldiers in Saudi Arabia, during a televised interview with the CNN's Peter Arnett in May 1997, appears to have stretched his hosts' patience.[41] Shortly afterwards, he was persuaded to move with his three wives from Jalalabad to Kandahar, where he set up home close to the airport. The Kandahar governor, Mullah Mohammed Hassan, explained: 'He is a human being and we have to rescue him.'[42]

This was a very different official stance from the one publicised shortly after Kabul fell in September 1996. The Taliban were then prompt to dissociate themselves from international terrorism, ruling out the use of Afghan soil either as a training ground or a haven for foreign extremists. 'If foreign terrorists fall into the Taliban's hands,' said acting foreign minister Sher Mohammed Stanakzai, 'we will punish them.'[43] But this was to encrypt a response to the question posed in the Western mind: in the Taliban equivalent, a terrorist was someone, first and foremost, who damages Islam; all Moslems are brothers; a 'foreigner' is usually non-Moslem; and a Pashtun owed a debt of honour to a Moslem fugitive from justice. One of the most glowing tributes paid to bin Laden in Jalalabad was that he used his own money to hire Haji Qadir's plane to carry Nangarhar notables to Mecca on pilgrimage.[44] Certainly, not the act of a 'terrorist'.

But was he the Taliban's honoured guest or a hostage? Some weeks after Kabul fell, bin Laden was seen in the capital, the VIP passenger in an armoured personnel carrier, in the company of 'a retired, high-ranking Pakistani air force officer'.[45] The Saudi renegade had spent half his life with ISI officers and mujahedin but, even so, that apparent camaraderie was hard to square with the Islamabad–Riyadh axis, then believed to be the motor of the Taliban's success and which, therefore, might rather have sought his extradition to the kingdom to face justice. The sighting led to speculation that he had won a reprieve for his Khost training facilities and Jalalabad base, and strengthened suspicions that he helped finance the Taliban's meteoric rise to power. However, it also preceded the 5 November fall of Mrs Bhutto and Brigadier Babar by several weeks. With the new government of Prime Minister Nawaz Sharif safely ensconced at the end of that month, bin Laden mused that he might spend a little more time among the Waeela tribe in northern Yemen, a suggestion that Sana'a frostily rejected.[46]

Still bin Laden lingered. Mullah Omar had now begun to appraise more confidently the terrorist assets he had inherited since the fall of Kabul, assets that were evidently linked to generous streams of revenue and which appeared to span South and Central Asia with the fibres of an alternative network of diplomacy that was invisible to most. On 10 December, the Taliban information minister said that, though the movement supported the struggle of the Islamists in Tajikistan, it had no 'special relationship' with them. Nonetheless, Tajik opposition leader Abdullah Nouri flew to Kandahar to meet Mullah Mohammed Omar, who observed 'that the rights of the mujahedin should also be given to them'.[47] A practical ally of more immediate consequence, however, was Jalaluddin Haqqani, the Pashtun Hizb-i Islami (Khalis) commander from Khost, who led the army which captured the city in March 1991 and who served as minister of justice in the first mujahedin government. Haqqani exercised absolute control over access to the bin Laden training camps at Badr-1 and Badr-2, which then housed 2,000 terrorist trainees.[48]

Haqqani defected to the Taliban in autumn 1996, well before the fall of the capital – though whether under pressure from Pakistan, Saudi Arabia, or at the prompting of bin Laden remains uncertain.[49] After the capture of Kabul, he installed his menage in a villa in Wazir Akhbar Khan, doing aggressive service as a commander in the winter campaign north of Kabul, where he was accused of 'ethnic-cleansing' Tajik villages in the Shomali Plain. Two years later, in a sign of the gallows humour which characterised much of Haqqani's government career, he was appointed the Taliban minister of tribes. Whatever other services he performed, however, none of the foreigners training in camps under his immediate control were deployed to fight alongside the Taliban in the frontlines in 1996. They were considered too valuable to be wasted as cannon fodder.[50]

The fighters training near Khost included several hundred militants from the Harakat ul-Mujahedin (HUM), parent of Harakat ul-Ansar (HUA), a terrorist group with ISI connections which, in 1993, launched a bloody campaign against Indian rule in Kashmir. HUM's secretary-general, Fazi Rahman Khalil, like many other members in the movement, was blooded in the *jihad* while fighting with Haqqani's forces. There, he had also developed close links with Maulana Fazl ul-Rahman, head of the Jamiat ul-Ulama-i Islam (JUI), Mrs Bhutto's policial ally and, via his network of *madrassa*, supplier of thousands of Taliban recruits.[51] The alliance between the JUI and HUM was so close that one Western intelligence analyst described the HUA as 'essentially the armed wing of the JUI'. HUM also had ties to Al Faran, a Kashmiri militant group which kidnapped six Western tourists in 1995, decapitating one, a Norwegian, shortly afterwards; as well as to the radical anti-Shia party, Sipan-i Saheba, responsible for a wave of sectarian killings in Pakistan, and suspected of involvement in the assassination of several Iranian diplomats in Lahore.[52]

As the scope of the Taliban's extended family of extremist affiliates became apparent, it became obvious that Stanakzai's initial commitment to dismantling the training camp network had been revised. In February 1997, Egyptian intelligence announced that bin Laden was still training 1,000 fighters in Khost, accusing the Taliban of 'breaking their pledge'.[53] Later that year, BBC journalist Rahimullah Yusufzai reported from Khost that training camps, previously used by Hizb-i Islami and Massoud's Jamiat-i Islami, also remained open. They had merely been transferred to Haqqani's lieutenant in Khost, Sayed Abdullah, who had reallocated them for the use of the HUA, then training 50 Arabs and 300 Pakistani or Kashmiri fighters for the operations against India.[54]

Still, bin Laden dallied, though his new accommodation close to Kandahar airport suggested he was prepared to bolt at any moment – though his choice of boltholes was narrowing fast. In May 1997, Iranians had elected the moderate Mohammed Khatami as president, and he initiated tentative moves towards normalising relations with Washington after 18 years of rancour. This closed any immediate prospect of an exile orchestrated by his friends in Iranian intelligence.

But it was also mooted he was, by then, the pawn in a different bargain. Whatever deal the Taliban may have originally undertaken with the Mukhabarat, the issue of international aid had since entered the equation. In early 1998, the Taliban refused to hand over bin Laden until Riyadh paid $400 million in cash.[55] With the relaunch of the peace effort in April 1998, US ambassador to the UN Bill Richardson paid a one-day visit to Kabul, where he urged Taliban leaders to keep bin Laden 'under wraps'. He later told reporters that the Saudi had 'threatened' the mission and become a 'very negative force' in attempts to draw up a ceasefire between the Taliban and the Northern Alliance. Yet no attempt had been made to secure bin Laden's extradition. 'He is a guest,' Richardson explained ruefully, 'and Pashtun traditions do not allow any harm to come to friends and guests.'[56]

Particularly if they are worth more than their weight in gold.

9 Oblivion's Feast

With the capture of Kandahar in October 1994, the Taliban took command of the southern outlet of a smuggling empire that, since the withdrawal of Soviet armed forces, had expanded deep into Central Asia and beyond, opening a back door into Pakistan's heavily-protected market of 135 million people. In this prototype of the regional trading bloc which Interior Minister Naseerullah Babar was keen to create, entrepreneurs inside Afghanistan and an 18,000-strong community of expatriates in the port city of Karachi played pivotal roles as middlemen and hauliers.

There had been half-hearted attempts to curb these 'cross-border movements', as the IMF terms them, but well-established combines with political influence swamped Pakistan's fragile economy with impunity. A flood of manufactures from the CIS, including tyres, vehicle spares and machine parts, along with consumer electronics from the East and barrels of Iranian oil, streamed across the two official customs points at Torkham Gate in the Khyber Pass and Chaman in the south.

Border smuggling was not new: in North West Frontier Province, where Pakistani law does not apply, the black market is a way of life, along with trading in arms and narcotics. But smuggling took off as the old political and economic order wilted. A north–south axis grew up to service the hitherto sealed Central Asian region. New routes swarmed across the 950-mile (1,500 kilometres) border with Pakistan, following the dirt roads used by the ISI to convoy supplies to the mujahedin.

The value of Central Asia's trade with Pakistan shot up from $100 million in 1993 to $350 million a year later,[1] but the proceeds from smuggling were worth infinitely more. Dubai is the main entrepôt for trans-Afghan smuggling, with 80 companies dedicated to trading across the narrow Straits of Hormuz to the Iranian port of Bandar Abbas. From there, cargoes take five days by road to reach the Pakistani border at freight prices at least one-quarter of alternative routes by sea or air. When Iran closed the border in June 1997, after the Taliban expelled its diplomats from Kabul, 1,400 containers bound for Afghanistan piled up in Bandar Abbas after ten days.[2]

The breadth and scale of the black market traffic was a tribute to Afghan resourcefulness and the strength of family ties, which easily outlasted the creation, one century earlier, of the Durand Line. Referred to – only half jokingly – as Pashtunistan's 'Berlin Wall', Afghan merchants transformed the border into a vast Panama Canal, allowing commercial passage between divided hemispheres and the free circulation of otherwise banned commodities and substances.

The concentricity of the drugs, arms and smuggling rings around a single imploded state created the conditions for the birth of a unique, post-modern phenomenon: an illicit trading empire that defied customs, frontiers and laws, connecting New York and Dubai with Osaka and the two Koreas but which was controlled by scarcely literate warlords living hundreds of miles from the nearest bank or fax. Its capital market was the roadside money booth where, amid the bundles of bills from a coterie of nations, the only real currency was trust – and the fear of reprisal, if it were broken.

Though Hizb-i Islami's stranglehold on the Kabul road, and Dostum's blocking of the Salang Tunnel, ensured there was little transit traffic from the north or west, Torkham Gate was hub to a booming re-export operation that circumvented Islamabad's duties on imports. The Transit Trade Agreement (TTA), signed in 1965, effectively handed traders a blank cheque once government mechanisms broke down after 1992.

The TTA entitled Afghan and Pakistani merchants to import unlimited quantities of duty-free goods, allegedly for consumption in landlocked Afghanistan. Along with food, fuel and other necessities, hundreds of millions of dollars of vehicles, TVs, videos and CDs, with consignment notes signed for the penniless inhabitants of Kabul, were duly waived through Torkham Gate by complaisant customs officials. Once inside the territory of the Nangarhar *shura*, these products were routinely transferred to camel and mule for the journey back across the Khyber foothills, where they were reloaded onto trucks to the bazaars of Peshawar.

This trade made Haji Abdul Qadir, the governor of Nangarhar, an extremely wealthy businessman. His fleet of ageing Antonovs, flagged Khyber Airlines in an excess of romance, cost $53 million[3] to assemble and flew regularly from Dubai, loaded with Pancheros, TVs, air conditioners and generators. His mud citadel, at the head of the poppy-growing Surkhrud valley, was outclassed in splendour only by the fortress in Landi Kotal, on the Pakistan side of the border, owned by Haji Ayub Afridi, lord of Khyber heroin dealing, who surrendered to US authorities in 1996. Standing on the tarmac leading nine miles up to Haji Qadir's palace, the only new highway in Afghanistan in over 20 years, it was easy to envisage that the two tycoons regarded themselves as the Murdoch and Maxwell of Pashtun commercial chutzpah.

Smuggling had always been more crucial to Kandahar, which suffers regular drought, forcing inhabitants to rely upon grain imports. The cross-border trade provided one of the few hedges against such eventualities, but it was a riskier investment after 1992 as three quarrelling factions ate into profit margins. The 420-mile road from Herat, crossroads of the Central Asian and Iranian trades, passed through the checkpoints of a myriad commanders, each loosely affiliated with one faction or other, but of a single mind when it came to extorting 'taxes' from passing vehicles.

The importance of this road, Highway One, soared in spring 1995 when the Pakistani authorities limited duty-free eligibility to just a few categories of goods, slashing duty and sales tax on a further 30 items in a bid to cut down abuse of the TTA. The decision coincided with the Taliban capture of Kandahar and the beginning of their advance upon Herat. In March 1995, Babar announced that Pakistan would provide $3 million and workers for the repair of Highway One. The decision enraged the Rabbani government, which assumed that Kabul, not Islamabad, was responsible for road repair in the western extremities of its embattled domain. Yet more traffic shifted to the western route.

If, in the eyes of their Pakistani and Afghan sponsors, the Taliban's primary mission had been to clear the Kandahar–Herat road of bandits, the task was largely accomplished by September 1995, when Herat fell after months of fighting. But this did not bring an end to one of Kandahar's most profitable lines of business. The Taliban showed no interest in disrupting the commercial status quo, which would have indicated that they were serving Pakistani, as opposed to smugglers' objectives. They merely streamlined the movement of illicit goods across Afghanistan by replacing the predatory mujahedin with a single, uniform tax to the benefit of their own treasury.

Along with the equipment and vehicles, looted from Herat's ministries but now heading south, there came a surge of trade, as merchants in Iran, the Gulf and Turkmenistan dispatched goods to the raucous truck-stop in Chaman. And though an electronic purdah descended upon entertainment for Afghans, with TVs and videos smashed or symbolically lynched, trucks piled to the gunwales with the products of Sony and Toshiba trundled unmolested between the potholes towards the border.

Despite tensions between Iran and the Taliban, officials on both sides of the border were convivial when it came to bilateral trade until the closure of the Iranian embassy in Kabul. Some 80 new or reconditioned vehicles, imported from the United Arab Emirates, crossed the border at Islam Qilla every day for onward shipment to Pakistan where, after the falsification of registration documents, they traded at half the domestic rate.[4]

Among them were 400 single-cabined Toyota Hilux pick-ups in mint condition, with smoked glass, exotic decals and plates from the Emirates.[5] They took the familiar route from Bandar Abbas, but never crossed the Pakistani frontier. They were a gift to the Taliban from an unknown benefactor, the ultimate beneficiary, perhaps, of a mission that was still obscure. The same Toyotas would one day be loaded with men and quivers of rockets and RPGs, a white pennant flapping from every aerial. If their style suggested that even the Taliban were susceptible to the swagger of fine engineering, like the 'technicals' in Somalia, the loudest message they conveyed was immediate surrender.

Mad Max. Meet the motorised mullahs.

*   *   *

Behind the warmth that greeted the Taliban after their conquest of the Durrani heartlands lay a shudder of anxiety. In a series of communiques isued by the movement about its goals, Mullah Omar had made clear his commitment to the eradication of opium, the most crucial element of all in the economy of southern Afghanistan. Indeed, Taliban zeal over the issue reinforced perceptions that the movement was receiving covert US support as the only practicable means of stemming the rise in output from the 'Golden Crescent'. In 1994, production peaked at 3,270 tonnes of dried opium, pushing Afghanistan past Burma as the world's largest producer, and creating a regional shortage of acetic anhydride, the chemical used to convert morphine base into heroin.[6]

Always a modest grower for domestic use, Afghan opium production rose to 100 tonnes in the 1960s to satisfy demand in Iran, where a million-strong population of addicts suffered a 16-year ban that was only reversed in 1972. The toppling of the Shah and the Soviet invasion of Afghanistan, cascading one after the other in 1979, overturned not only the balance of power in an energy-producing belt stretching from the Straits of Hormuz to the Arabian Sea. Combined with the failure of rain in the Golden Triangle, they created an upheaval in the way that heroin was supplied to, and distributed in, the West.

While the Soviet occupation blocked the Silk Route along which southeast Asian heroin was moved to distribution points in Turkey, the ayatollahs' narcotics ban forced Iranian dealers over the border into Pakistan. For the next decade, their expertise and capital, wedded to a lawless hinterland where poppy flourished unfettered by authority, won Pakistan supreme position in the European heroin market.

The processing and export of heroin created a black economy in Pakistan of around $8 billion[7] by the mid-1980s – half the size of the official one – and its military regime demonstrated many of the symptoms of a fully-blown narco-government. Among officials incriminated in the trade were Lieutenant-General Fazle Haq, governor of North West Frontier Province and a confidant of General Zia; Hamid Hasnain, another of Zia's cronies and vice-president of the state-owned Habib Bank; and Haji Ayub Afridi, the National Assembly member for Khyber agency, coordinator of Islamabad's Afghan policy and its largest drugs baron by the early 1990s.[8] The number of Pakistani addicts spiralled from nil in 1979 to between 1.2 million and 1.7 million at the end of 1988.

Such a rapid rate of growth was impossible without the active connivance of the ISI which, empowered by CIA funding and arms deliveries, had grown from a modest department of the military into a sophisticated intelligence network with a staff of 150,000 and hundreds of millions of dollars a year at its disposal.[9] The links between narcotics in Pakistan and the military were apparent from the start, with 16 senior officers arrested on drugs offences in 1986 alone. Trucks from the army's National Logistics Cell were regularly discovered trafficking as they returned from supply operations in Afghanistan.[10]

The US also colluded in the development of this new heroin source for fear of undermining the CIA's working alliance with General Zia and the mujahedin. From Peshawar, the office of US Drug Enforcement Agency issued a stream of deflated estimates of cross-border opium production, while failing to obtain from the authorities a single investigation into any of the 40 drugs syndicates then known to be operating in Pakistani territory.[11] It was only after 1989, with the general in his grave – the victim of an unexplained air crash – and the US media again free to consider factors other than the by-then retreating Red Army, that the scale of the ISI's involvement began to emerge.

A decidedly small number of mujahedin commanders actively promoted poppy farming during the war but, as US funding tapered off after the Soviet withdrawal and refugees returned to their fields, its production and export became systematic. The process accelerated with the election in 1989 of Benazir Bhutto, whose early crackdown on poppy-growing in North West Frontier Province and the introduction of the death penalty for trafficking helped shift Pakistan's opium production across the Afghan border, where it was less vulnerable to policing actions.

The province of Nangarhar, adjacent to North West Frontier Province, was virtually depopulated during the Soviet occupation but, after 1989, it was swiftly integrated with the heroin workshops and distribution system established by the Afridi syndicate in Khyber. By 1994 – five years after the Red Army withdrew – Nangarhar was generating 1,500 tonnes of opium, nearly half Afghanistan's total harvest. One year later, it had established its own processing facilities.[12]

Some districts in Nangarhar eschewed the crop altogether, usually on the orders of their local commanders. In Kunar, controlled by Wahhabi forces under Jamil ul-Rahman, opium production effectively stopped from 1990 until his murder a year later. But there were more attractive possibilities in the immediate postwar period, such as the trade in military scrap, arms and timber.

Afghanistan was awash with weapons by the Soviet withdrawal. In addition to the jets, helicopters, tanks and rocket launchers supplied to the Afghan army by Moscow, the US and Saudi Arabia funnelled an estimated $6 billion in guns and money to the mujahedin, often through the channels of the BCCI. After 1987, when Washington stepped up its covert aid programme, arms shipments amounted to 65,000 tonnes a year. Shin Naray, a weapons depot built by the ISI on the border south of Kandahar, housed an estimated 15,000 truckloads of ammunition by 1993, along with 400 of the Stinger missiles that were supplied after 1985 and helped destroy Soviet air superiority.[13]

Much of this weaponry ended up in the tribal trust arms bazaars of Dara, Miramshar and Landi Kotal, where rocket launchers and medium-range mortars are openly displayed for sale, like any less lethal commodity. To prevent Stingers falling into undesirable clutches, the CIA announced a 'buy-back' programme in 1989 that offered $175,000 for each undetonated missile still in mujahedin hands. Congress allocated $55 million for the programme in 1993, but the missiles still found their way into the arsenals of the Kurdistan Workers Party in Turkey, the Groupe Islamique Armée in Algeria, UNITA in Angola and the Iranian mafia, who used them to defend drug caravans against helicopter attacks.[14]

Timber, too, was a booming industry. Hundreds of acres of primary pine and cedar in Kunar and Paktia were hauled down the mountain sides to be sawn into cheap window frames or furniture in Pakistan for export to the Gulf. So attractive were profits, in fact, that their loss provoked the only serious resistance offered to the Taliban in any of the regions which fell under their thrall. After driving Haji Qadir out of Nangarhar, the Taliban introduced a tax of $750 per truckload of timber. Qadir, exiled in Peshawar, but aided by two local warlords, Malik Zarin and Haji Kashmir Khan, reacted with a well-armed attack into Kunar in February 1997 that appeared to rattle the Taliban.[15]

Even outside Kunar, Afghans remained ambivalent about a crop that brought profit and opprobrium in roughly equal measures, but also entailed a massive increase in work. With no opium appetite of their own, farmers justified the switch to poppy on the grounds that its baleful effects were exported beyond the pale of Islam and outside the *pashtunwali*. With the exception of Badakhshan, a Tajik province in the far northeast and the only one with a domestic addiction problem, poppy was almost exclusively a Pashtun trading activity, abetted by clan and family links in the tribal trust areas.

But poppy-growing acquired all the characteristics of a modern agro-business after the Soviet withdrawal. To meet farmers' needs for fertiliser to turn a good profit – nearly half a tonne a hectare – traders set up operations to supply inputs, and the credit with which to buy them. Indeed, opium was the only crop in Afghanistan for which cultivators could expect a cash advance against future delivery. Poppy equalled credit, in fact, and every returning family from Pakistan needed to borrow.

In Helmand and Nangarhar, accounting for 80 per cent of total Afghan production, traditional poppy varieties were replaced in the 1990s by genetically-enhanced seeds that raised quality and potency and boosted yield. In both, irrigated farms formerly owned by the state were set aside by commanders for poppy cultivation. The largest were in the northern reaches of Helmand valley, where the US had developed a massive wheat project in the 1960s, which was controlled for much of the war by Mullah Nasim Akhundzada.

The 'King of Heroin', as he was known was a living rebuttal of the UN's belief that poppy-growing would end if people could be convinced that it was 'against Islam'. Mullah Nasim controlled most of the 250 tonnes of opium grown in Helmand in the 1980s, issuing quotas to farmers that he enforced with threats of murder or castration. This policy detracted not one dot from his religious prestige. Many Afghan drug barons were mullahs, owing to their traditional right to exact *zakat*, the 10 per cent tithe levied on all farm produce, including opium, in exchange for their religious duties.

The only protagonist from the *jihad* repeatedly associated with the downstream end of the opium industry was Gulbuddin Hekmatyar, the ISI's chief protégé and recipient of more than half the CIA's assistance to the Afghan resistance. Hekmatyar's commanders established six laboratories in the Koh-i Sultan district of Baluchistan in the mid-1980s to process opium from Helmand before smuggling it through the ports on the Makran coast, or across the nearby Iranian border.[16] This latter vicinity, where the borders of Iran, Pakistan and Afghanistan all converge, is known by enforcement officers as the 'zero line'.

Heavy fighting broke out in 1988–89 when Hekmatyar's loyalists tried to wrest control of the Helmand valley from Mullah Nasim. One year later, now deputy defence minister in the transitional government, Nasim secured an agreement with the US ambassador to Pakistan, Robert B. Oakley, to suppress poppy-growing in exchange for $2 million in 'aid', a deal that may have included provisions for the return of US-supplied Stingers.[17] The ban immediately tripled opium prices in Baluchistan, sparking off another round of fighting over a resource whose value abroad was now being counted in billions. Mullah Nasim was eventually assassinated, but his brother Rasul, a commander in the Harakat-i Inqilab-i Islami party, retained control of the valley. When the US failed to deliver its promise of funds, opium production resumed with unprecedented vigour.

The ISI was far from ignorant of Hekmatyar's heroin business and actively encouraged it after 1990, when a stunned Islamabad was informed that Washington had terminated all economic and military aid to Pakistan. After a decade of glorious unaccountability, the ISI faced a funding drought that threatened all its operations, while a series of elected – and, summarily, ejected – civilian prime ministers were feeling queasy about the ISI's determination to continue as Pakistan's secret government. In an unusually frank interview in September 1994 – which he later denied – former prime minister Nawaz Sharif disclosed that General Aslam Beg, the army chief of staff, and ISI boss Lieutenant-General Asad Durrani had proposed raising money for covert foreign operations through large-scale narcotics deals.[18] The cut in US funding coincided with a precipitous escalation in the ISI's clandestine activities, not only in Afghanistan, where Najibullah defied Western expectations by clinging to power, but in Kashmir and the Indian Punjab, where Pakistan's brazen support for local insurgents led Washington to threaten to brand it a terrorist-exporting state.

ISI promotion of Sikh separatism was clearly identified in a 1993 CIA report on the Pakistani drug trade which reported that the proceeds of heroin sales were used to fund the agency's purchase of arms, adding: 'Heroin is becoming the lifeblood of Pakistan's economy and political system.' The same report named Sohail Zia Butt, a relative of Nawaz Sharif, as a suspected drug smuggler.[19] The connection between narcotics and the insurrection in Kashmir was more tenuous, though the ISI, Pakistan's Jamaat-i Islami party and Hizb-i Islami were all material backers of the chief, pro-Pakistan terrorist group in the territory, Hizb ul-Mujahedin.

As the 1990s wore on, Badakhshan began figuring more prominently in narcotics dispatches. Analysis of samples of raw opium showed a morphine content twice as high as elsewhere in the country, though Badakhshani farmers used neither fertilisers nor irrigation. More alarming still was the fact that the isolated province, controlled by Rabbani and Massoud, was emerging as a stepping stone for an entirely new means of conveying opiates to Europe, via Tajikistan, Uzbekistan and the Central Asian railway system.

Another rascal from the gallery of regional grotesques, Aliosha the Hunchback, commanded the flow of opium over the Pamir peaks into the Tajikistan province of Gorno-Badakhshan, until his alleged murder by Russian border guards in 1996.[20] Since 1992, the region was controlled by the Islamic Revival Party (IRP), which had waged a bloody war against the Russian-backed regime in Dushanbe, financed by the Afghan heroin trade and IRP supporters in Iran and Pakistan. According to the Vienna-based UN Drug Control Programme (UNDCP), the most significant trafficking event in the region since 1995 had been the amount of Heroin No. 1 (pure heroin) and Heroin No. 3 (crude heroin, or 'brown sugar') transferred from the Makran Coast and the 'zero line' into the new Central Asian corridors.[21]

To conclude that the world's only 'Islamic drugs cartel' underwrote terrorist attacks by Islamist groups may be stretching the imagination. Drug Enforcement Agency (DEA) officials deny any such linkage but, given the US's role in creating the Afghan–Central Asian nexus of drugs, arms and organised destabilisation, it is likely that they would. What is certain is that the US had remarkably little influence over a process that its own agencies had set into motion during the anti-Soviet crusade in Afghanistan in the 1980s.

Hekmatyar, the only Afghan leader with an international profile, runs like a golden thread through this tortuous history of entanglement between the Cold War, the *jihad*, the drugs trade, regional terrorism and the intelligence establishment in two countries. Was he the accidental beneficiary of US opportunism or a kingpin of the narcotics industry, whose ambitions spanned not solely Afghanistan, but the Balkanised heartlands of Moslem Central Asia? And was he, after the fall of Kabul, finally vanquished? His former information officer answered with a particularly cryptic Afghan proverb: 'There are always bones around the wolf's lair.'

* * *

It was into this complex web of high finance and low life expectancy that the Taliban ventured in October 1994, after the capture of Kandahar. The following January, they took control of Helmand, source of 150 tonnes of Heroin No. 1, with a total retail value in the European market of $25.5 billion at 1996 prices. Governor Ghaffar Akhundzada, a relative of the dead mullah, quit the provincial capital, Lashkargah, without a fight but when the Taliban moved into the poppy-growing districts of Musa Qa'leh and Kajaki, his home turf, hostilities finally erupted. The religious students, and the former mujahedin who had rallied to their cause, routed Ghaffar's men, suffering fewer than 50 casualties.

In capturing Helmand, the Taliban could no longer hide behind their reputation as an ascetic, but, essentially, naive revivalist movement with relevance only to the domestic scene. Whether by accident or design, they now controlled a commodity on which global fortunes are built. Within two more years, they would have it all: 2,200 tonnes, with a street value of $37 billion. It was the ultimate temptation for the self-styled Leader of the Faithful.

If the Taliban takeover of Helmand and, subsequently, Nangarhar and the capital were in fact dictated by the political dynamics of heroin, it is worth exploring the potential beneficiaries of such a campaign. Afghan rumour had long identified the US and Saudi Arabia as the Taliban's covert financiers and, whatever their ulterior designs in the Central Asian region, it was clear that the mullahs could also play a role in stamping out the opium industry. After years of war and fragmentation, Afghanistan's main poppy-growing areas were controlled by a single dictatorial authority by the end of 1996. In November of that year, Giovanni Quaglia, director of the UNDCP office in Pakistan stated, somewhat blithely: 'In these circumstances, the problem can be dealt with in ten years.'[22]

Yet the consolidation of opium production under a single authority – like the Central Asian transit trade – was of equal advantage to the downstream processors and distributors of heroin as well. After years of dealing with unpredictable mujahedin, the Taliban streamlined the supply side of the industry and helped it to fight off competition from emerging and more savvy poppy-planters in Colombia and Mexico.

Financial support for the Taliban, in the early days, was provided by Afghan and Pakistani traders, concerned at the high rate of extortion on the transit routes. But parallel backing may also have been furnished by heroin cartels seeking to seize control of its suppliers or, at least, vest them in a caretaker authority that undercut the existing financial arrangements.

Such backers would benefit from the third strand in this hypothesis. The effective transfer of the heroin distribution trade from 'zero line' countries into the hands of the Russian 'mafia', with its logistical advantages and lower enforcement risks, threatened the very lifeblood of the Pakistani economy, if CIA accounts of its size are to be believed. The capture of Helmand and Nangarhar provinces by a friendly force helped to anchor these primary suppliers of poppy firmly in Pakistan's economic sphere of influence, and counter-balanced the attractions of the rapidly-expanding drug empire in the north.

In short, were the Taliban a genuine movement of national revival or a fifth column, playing on popular grievances, to effect radical shifts in the structure of the world's leading illicit industry? Or had they really strayed into the business by accident, gifted amateurs in pursuit of a *jihad* against corrupt commanders?

The advent of the Taliban in Kandahar immediately halved the acreage allocated for poppy for the 1995 season, a trend that farmers initially attributed to fear of reprisals. But wheat prices were booming that year and there had been a significant carry-over from the previous opium crop that further depressed prices. Helmand saw an 8 per cent fall in its crop, but again there were external influences at work. Even in remote areas, Afghan poppy-farmers are highly responsive to the global supply and demand.

During that first season in Kandahar, the Taliban produced a booklet outlining what was permitted under religious law, and what not. It was deeply ambivalent. 'The cultivation of, and trading in *chers* [cannabis],' it read, 'is forbidden absolutely.' In Afghanistan, every village once had a *chersi*, referred to with condescending affection, but all were gone by the following season, along with the hundreds of hectares of cannabis that once surrounded Kandahar. Many users were imprisoned.

'The consumption of opiates,' the document continued, 'is forbidden, as is the manufacture of heroin, but the production and trading in opium is not forbidden.' The Taliban justified the distinction on the grounds that elimination of poppy would push the 200,000 families who grew the crop to the very brink of starvation. But the decision also reflected the reality that the smoking of opium, unlike cannabis, was not a Pashtun vice. One Kandahari farmer put it more succinctly: 'The opium goes to our neighbours, who are our enemies, and to the infidels, who sent the guns here.'

An investigator from the *Geopolitical Drug Dispatch* (*GDD*), which monitored global narcotics markets until its closure on 2000, visited the Kandahar customs shed in November 1996. He reported:

> Even before the heavy padlock is removed, a strong smell emanates from the room. Inside, five tonnes of opium have spent two years waiting ... for the occasional journalist to pay them a visit. The five tonnes, in 50 kg sacks, ooze a blackish paste. In a corner of the room, there are a few dozen kilograms of coarsely refined brown heroin. The room next door contains hashish: 10 tonnes, the customs officer says ... That is what the Taliban's seizures amount to. They date from the movement's first few months in power.[23]

After that brief interlude, it was back to business as usual. It was a pragmatic decision, given that the Taliban needed to retain the support not only of the southern Pashtun, but the mujahedin commanders who had been absorbed into the movement, rather than deposed by it. To tamper with the economic status quo in the south, while pressing forward to Herat and Kabul, was to risk triggering revolts in their rear and stiffening the opposition ahead. The Taliban could not afford a crusade against everyone.

In more ways than one. The *zakat* on opium, formerly paid to village mullahs, was redirected to the Taliban treasury, netting the movement an estimated $9 million from the south's regular output of 1,500 tonnes. Apart from that, the *shura* introduced no interdiction and effected no structural changes in the way that opiates were traded in Taliban-controlled areas over its first two years in power.[24]

In Mullah Omar's home district of Maiwand, production actually doubled to 24 tonnes in 1996. Laboratories continued to operate in Nimroz, Kandahar and Helmand in spite of the ban on processing.[25] Taliban-protected drugs convoys regularly set forth from Herat and Iran, then fighting pitched battles with smugglers, sent a delegation to remonstrate with the governor in 1996. Cases of trafficking by air, from Kandahar to Dubai, were also widely reported.

In Herat, governor Mullah Yar Mohammed took opium's legal status a radical stage further. Customs officials from the regime of Ismail Khan were arrested and beaten until they made restitution to traders, whose opium they had once confiscated when, apparently, it was illegal. One prisoner, a former police officer, was 'beaten for about a week' until he submitted.[26]

Days before the fall of Kabul in September, the deputy speaker of the Organisation for Security and Cooperation in Europe, Willy Wimmer, openly accused the Taliban of smuggling heroin into Hamburg. He added that the Taliban 'clearly enjoyed the support of Russian troops in Afghanistan's border regions with Tajikistan' and demanded that the US and Saudi Arabia explain why they so obviously supported the movement. It was a garbled analysis, but an apposite question.

The US had also pondered about the mullahs' drug habits. A DEA report in November 1996 said that 'the Taliban had reached a *de facto* agreement with cultivators, and perhaps even traffickers, to limit their attack on opium cultivation and domestic drug abuse'. The report was based on the first contacts between the Taliban leadership, the DEA and the US State Department's narcotics subsidiary, the NAS. US satellite imaging, usually so forgiving of Afghan production, determined that there were 3,000 tonnes in the fields, rather than the 2,600 tonnes declared by the UNDCP.[27]

On 11 November, shortly after the DEA report was published, the UNDCP received its first formal note that the Taliban had agreed to take the 'necessary measures' to suppress the production, processing and trafficking of narcotics in Afghanistan. The statement, from the foreign minister, Mullah Mohammed Ghaus, proposed a concerted programme of regional and international cooperation, but stressed 'the principle of non-interference in the internal affairs of states'.

The UNDCP had already devised a four-year $16.4 million programme of law enforcement and crop substitution, which offered some chance of restructuring its own crediblity after years of mis-hits in the largest opium-supplying country in the world. There was a sudden air of optimism, but no shortage of problems. During the DEA's visit to Kandahar, sources said, Taliban officials uttered what, in diplomatic circles, was known as the 'R-word' – recognition.[28]

Collaboration over poppy eradication would occur after state-to-state relations between Washington and Kabul were established and the Rabbani regime surrendered its seat at the UN General Assembly in New York. For the US, whose policy is to recognise states and not governments, this presented neither difficulty nor attraction, but the UN recognises governments. Signature would also mean UN endorsement of Taliban gender policies.

But another contention was whether the Taliban, having taken such a *laissez-faire* approach to local power and trading relations, could actually impose their will upon the opium lords of Helmand and Nangarhar. It is interesting, in this context, to ponder the fate of the Akhundzadas. Wealthy, gifted with dynastic continuity and a talent for killing, they nevertheless appear to have melted quietly from the Helmand scene shortly after the Taliban takeover. Neither the DEA nor the UNDCP, which maintain a constant watch on the region, could recollect the mullah who negotiated with the US ambassador, held a portfolio in the first Afghan Interim Government and who dominated the Helmand poppy trade for over a decade.

That Rasul Akhundzada, his legatee, had been a commander of Harakat-i Inqilab, like Mohammed Omar, is more intriguing since it suggests that what had taken place in Helmand that day was less an act of submission than a gathering of old comrades.[29] But how would Rasul react – and the hundreds of others like him – when the choirboys tried to barter away his patrimony?

10   Hostages

'We've fallen into a black hole, 500 years back in history.' Former communist, reported 8 October 1996.[1]

The bodies of Najibullah and his brother hung in Ariana Square for 26 hours until, at Pakistan's insistence, they were cut down and released for burial in Paktia.[2] Elders of the Amadzhai clan, to which Najib belonged, threatened to sue the UN for failing to protect its most famous son, but the matter was forgotten amid the brouhaha which followed the loss of the capital.[3] Four days after his death, Kabul's international airport was reopened for the first time in a year to welcome the UN's new envoy to Afghanistan. Dr Norbert Holl faced an uphill task.

After an initial spurt of enthusiasm, the US, Pakistan and Saudi Arabia backed away from official recognition, realising that the fugitive Massoud still represented an inescapable threat to a movement whose policies towards women were scandalising newspaper readers in Western capitals and the Moslem world at large. The Tajik was far from beaten: the Taliban, universally unpalatable. Official relations could wait until the movement proved beyond any doubt that it was the inalienable master of Afghanistan. Such ambiguity cast longer shadows at the UN where President Rabbani continued to occupy the General Assembly chair for Afghanistan, even going to Rome in November to attend a UN Food and Agriculture Organisation conference, although, at that point, he represented no more than the impoverished bleakness of the Little Pamirs.

All three powers besides retained the luxury of back channels to Mullah Mohammed Omar, channels that allowed them to test the military winds from a distance and fine-tune future political relations far from critical eyes. The UN, by contrast, had to take most of its decisions in public, on the hoof and with its hands tied by humanitarian considerations – as well as the real physical risk to its staff. Yet for the next two years, the organisation which had so conspicuously failed to prevent genocide in Rwanda and Bosnia was tasked with presenting a coherent Western response to what would become an unprecedented redefinition of human rights violation: the institutionalised suppression of women.

It was not a pretty sight that met the envoy's eyes. Taliban strictures on the participation of females in education affected 106,256 girls, 148,223 boys and the 7,793 women who had taught them.[4] An estimated 150,000 women held jobs in Kabul before Massoud's flight; all went to ground, with the estimated 25,000–30,000 widows who relied upon relief aid for survival.[5] Among the former category were Shafiqa Habibi, the country's foremost newscaster, and her 300 female colleagues at Radio Kabul; Sohaila Sidiq, chief surgeon at the 400-bed army hospital; and her sister, Dr Sidiqa Sidiq, director of the Polytechnic Institute and the first eminent Afghan woman to speak out against the Taliban. 'A movement,' she said three months later, 'no matter how strong, is just a movement. It does not last forever.' But since the fall of the city, she had left her house just four times – usually to attend funerals.[6]

Even with the lights on and the rockets sheathed, Kabul was a dark, unpredictable place. Religious observance, once a desirable, but voluntary ideal, became the benchmark of presumed party loyalty. Men were lashed into the mosque, or a soccer stadium transmogrified into a theatre of Taliban justice, where squealing ambulances ensured, at least, that anaesthetised thieves received the benefit of post-operative treatment. Women were less fortunate. One woman had the tip of her thumb cut off for wearing nail varnish and another was whipped with a car radio antenna for letting her *burkha* slip – while a curtain fell like a deep depression on the majority who failed to qualify for such exemplary punishments. A man who chose not to pray was taken to the street, called *kafir*, or 'godless' and executed.[7] In the first week of October, the Taliban bulldozed 1,400 cans of Heineken and 400 bottles of spirits, leaving the UN guesthouse the sole drinking hole in an otherwise dry city: Agence France-Presse reported an 80 per cent drop in weddings.[8] Though the end of the Taliban siege indisputably improved living conditions in Kabul, 125 Afghan refugees a day shambled across the border to Pakistan in early October, rising to 870 per day by the end of the month.[9]

Under President Rabbani, 200 female staff worked at Kabul's Mullalai hospital but, though the Taliban exempted the medical profession from its ban on women's employment, barely 50 appeared regularly for duty, either out of fear of intimidation at work, or for the practical reason that double the number of vehicles were required to provide *sharia*-friendly transport to male and female staff alike. The six-man *shura* banned women from going out without a male, related chaperone, but men were prevented by the same code from travelling in a bus with unrelated female passengers. As for other transport, wheels skidded in the opposite direction whenever a *burkha*-clad figure tried to flag down a cab. The capital was gripped in a religious gridlock.[10]

'It's a confusing situation,' conceded a field officer with the Swiss NGO Terre des Hommes, struggling to tailor a project for street children to the bizarre new norms.

> Afghan statute law says that children cease to be children at the age of 18. *Sharia* law states that girls cease to be children at the age of 14 and boys at the age of 16. The Taliban say that there is no specific age for boys, but girls cease to be children at the age of seven. There should be no mixing of the sexes after that.[11]

He had smuggled in malnourished ten-year-olds, whose wasted frames belied their ages, but at Kabul's largest state-run orphanage, Taskia Maskan, the new regulation could not be ignored. After the female staff were sent home, the 400-odd girls who lived there were locked up for a year without going outside to play. What had been a regular halt for journalists during the siege of Kabul became a powerful – if unvisitable – symbol of the aid community's abandonment of its core constituency.[12]

'Even a woman has trouble in examining a woman in Afghanistan,' a doctor with Médecins du Monde explained in Herat. 'There are still women doctors, but for how long one doesn't know. If the access of females to medical studies is forbidden, there will no longer be any women doctors to assure a service of gynaecology or obstetrics.'[13] The Taliban allowance that women doctors could continue to practise – though women were prevented from studying for a medical career – convinced the UN and NGOs that further windows might occur in time. But Taliban concessions were determined less by humanitarian logic – in this case, the condition of poor or pregnant women – or Islamic propriety, and more by diplomatic wile. Even that trait would prove to have a short attention span. In mid-October, the *shura* banned women from attending the city's 32 *hammam*, or bath-houses, a six-cent, hot-water rite often enjoyed after sex or menstruation. Combining warmth and a space to socialise in the depths of winter, the excursion was proscribed as 'unIslamic'. The UN warned of an imminent surge in scabies and vaginal infections among a population now denied hygiene, as well as easy access to health care.[14]

The Afghan vagina was a murky area for aid worker and Taliban alike for within it were enscribed the viral fingerprints of its proprietor's way of life and, since this was frequently in the cross-border trade, or in killing, there were ample opportunities for outside contact. Medical care for women, as a result, was tantamount to forensic work for, in curing, it also identified the vector and his respectable charade. The spirit of *omerta* that governed Afghan family life ensured that no word of rape, adultery or bisexuality leaked out to the wider community, but it hung above the husband at prayer, poisoned the hearth and, when laid bare in the Petri dish, shocked the few professionals to have done hard-core gynaecological research in the village. Afghan women stood a greater chance of dying in childbirth than anyone outside Sierra Leone; and they gave birth an average nine times in their lives. In between parturitions, they withstood a sustained siege from second- and third-generation sexually-transmitted diseases. Access to the vagina, in the shape of basic health care, would become the cockpit of a new cold war in Afghanistan.

The UN's role as master of ceremonies in the post-Rabbani era was scarcely mitigated by its humanitarian objectives, for foreign aid had been viewed by most Afghans as a political, even missionary, tool since the 1950s when Prime Minister Mohammed Daoud first initiated the custom of playing off the USSR and US in exchange for development loans. The failure to maintain a balance of debt to the two powers cost Afghanistan its Islam, and Daoud his life, tainting in the process all subsequent aid initiatives with the suspicion of a hidden, malignant agenda. When the West created 'solidarity committees' during the *jihad* to offset the social impact of the Soviet invasion, aid also become entwined with the politics and patronage of military commanders. Even the Swedish Committee for Afghanistan, the respected architect of a seed revolution that swept through the countryside in the early 1990s, was once branded a 'sister organisation' to Hizb-i Islami, for were not its wells built near party headquarters and its clinics, dominated by posters of Hekmatyar, known to deny services to members of other parties?[15] The British NGO Afghan Aid, whose work was in Badakhshan, and the French agency Madera, expelled from Pakistan in 1996, were similarly at risk of being viewed as 'foreign aid' to the Francophone Massoud, rather than humanitarian aid to Afghans. To help in Afghanistan was, ultimately, to take sides, for aid had a long tradition of tilting the ethnic or military playing field. Neutrality was inconceivable.

Nowhere was this more true than in the fields of education and female empowerment, both prioritised by the Afghan communist party and the Soviet occupier over the wishes of their subjects, only to be taken up by the UN as the apparently humdrum elements of any late twentieth-century programme of social development. But education was religious dynamite in Afghanistan: it was no coincidence that Nadir Shah, Zahir's father, was murdered at a school prize-giving ceremony. Educational establishments were centres of influence that challenged the authority of the mosque so, while the fruit of school knowledge – a government salary – was undoubtedly desirable, the means of acquiring it entailed a scary fraternisation with the demonic.

Teachers had been one of the soft targets of the *jihad*, with some 2,000 assassinated and 15,000 forced to abandon the profession for fear of their lives. One Nangarhar commander admitted to burning down the local primary school and slaughtering its nine teachers, because 'that was where the communists were trained'.[16] Postwar school curricula were painstakingly deconstructed – by mullah and educational consultant alike – for the heresies impossible to eliminate from a text that was, at bottom, alien to the people it was intended to serve. And their suspicions were sometimes well-founded: in 1994, UNICEF and several Norwegian NGOs banned the use of textbooks developed during the *jihad* for use in refugee camps by USAID in association with the University of Nebraska in Omaha, on the grounds that the teaching of basic arithmetic in terms of dead Soviet soldiers or working Kalashnikovs only glorified war. Despite their limited information, Afghans grasped instinctively the corrosive effect of too much, or the wrong kind of, knowledge on their children. Against such a backdrop, the ascendancy of the Taliban, a movement firmly rooted in the disciplines of the *madrassa*, was a sure sign that the half-century polemic over the place of secular education in Afghan society was closed.

Widows were doubly victimised by the Taliban. Not only were they denied paid employment, along with other Afghan women, they also lost access to food aid which, under the new government, had to be collected by male relatives. The possibility that they had none was inconceivable and Mullah Ghaus, the new acting foreign minister, said he was 'astonished' at the level of international concern for 'such a small percentage of the working population'.[17] The UN estimated the number of widows at around 800,000 after 17 years of war, a statistic which, like most used in Afghanistan, was deeply flawed, but unusually convenient.

Najibullah had institutionalised the widow by establishing women's councils and assistance agencies to liaise between them, the UN and the social services ministry. Prior to that, she would have expected to enter a Levitical marriage with a brother-in-law while her children were cared for by the extended family. Najib's successor, Rabbani, absorbed the same mechanisms into his own administration, swelling the list with mujahedin widows and the dependants of siege victims, which by the middle of 1996 amounted to some 20,000–30,000 people. They were taken up enthusiastically by donors and with little scrutiny of the distinction between an authentic widow and an impoverished but still married woman, which became hopelessly blurred as the siege tightened and food and mothering both grew scarce.

With no direct access to females in the conservative rural areas, projects for widows provided the easiest means for agencies to nail gender credentials – and the equally-important rubric, 'income-generating schemes' – to their fund-raising masts. 'Widows are and remain an emotive issue,' said Jolyon Leslie, the UN's regional coordination officer in Kabul, 'for whom it has been easy to secure support.'[18] In Kabul, widowhood was the next best criterion – after wealth – for exemption from the conventions that prevented women from working or moving around unveiled – long before the rise of the Taliban. And, in a city in which half the 2 million population lived on relief, widows, at least, had a ticket to eat and that was a tradable asset in the *bazaar* and an extended family similarly beset by poverty.

Few agencies bothered to make projects for widows credible outside the context of the siege. The bakery and sewing schemes supported by the World Food Programme, UNICEF and UNOCHA did nothing to instil self-sufficiency or business skills among their illiterate beneficiaries who were granted a 'salary' of relief food, but below-market prices for their bread or quilts, which were distributed elsewhere under the Kabul emergency programme. A similar flavour of *de haut en bas* infected most UN programmes for women, according to an evaluation report that emerged after the Taliban takeover, but referred to projects conducted under the Rabbani government. 'The pressure to reach women has led to a focus on quantities, at the expense of quality of support offered,' said the writer in tones that accented the need to avoid repeating the past. She went on to identify three classic UN responses to the restrictions introduced by the Taliban. One was 'adaptive', and entailed continuing to operate within the dominant political values, and a second was 'defeatist', whereby all decisions were deferred until the political situation had altered. There was little to choose between them. The third, termed 'challenging', treated every violation of gender equity as a violation of human rights, to which the only coherent response was the suspension of social aid.[19]

The arrival of the Taliban heralded a curious transformation in the widow's already anomalous status. Like other working women, she was sent home and denied the right to roam without a *burkha*, but the gaggle of blue-veiled beggars in the streets were a vivid rebuttal of the Taliban's insistent claim that all women were supported by male relatives and, therefore, had no further need of relief. She owed her political profile to aid and women's organisations created under the communist regime, both anathema to the religious movement. But, while Taliban prescriptions on women in general remained non-negotiable, the widow provided the vehicle for the emergence of an embryonic *lingua franca* between the new government and the international community. According to Leslie, writing in February 1998,

> There is a sense here that the current authorities, like others before them, have manipulated the issue of widows for their own ends. For the time being, this seems to work for both sides. The issue of women's rights has been kept safely distinct from the relief needs, both by the international community and the Taliban.[20]

That distinction had a lengthy pedigree. In November 1995, two months after Herat fell to the movement, UNICEF announced the suspension of all assistance to education in Taliban-controlled regions of the country, arguing that the ban on girls' attendance at schools constituted a breach of the Convention of the Rights of the Child. It was the first apparent attempt to set a policy benchmark in the shadow of the Beijing women's conference earlier that year and to strengthen UNICEF's profile as the lead agency in matters related to women and children. SCF (UK) withdrew entirely from Herat the following spring, saying the new ban on employing Afghan female staff made it impossible for the agency to communicate with women, the main carers for children. But these gestures were not entirely of UNICEF's or SCF's making. Pamela Collett of SCF (US), a doyenne of women's literacy programmes in Mazar-i Sharif, leaked details of what she described as the UN's 'appeasement' of Taliban gender policies to the *New York Times* on 10 November after a training visit to Herat, causing a flurry of backtracking.[21] Peter Hansen, then head of the UN's Department of Humanitarian Affairs, admitted that local women aid workers did risk losing their jobs under the new dispensation and talked of the 'terrible dilemma' facing agencies in Taliban-controlled provinces.

Hours later, UNICEF's chief executive, Carol Bellamy, declared a freeze on support to schools projects, but the decision was more an exercise in damage limitation than a coordinated response by the UN to its first challenge over gender equality, a challenge that came not from the Taliban but one of its own NGO partners. For logic dictated that the Taliban's gender policies tainted every stratum of an aid effort mandated on equality of access, from the provision of relief food and drinking water to the basic arena of health care. Drawing the line at education was sophistry disguised as policy. Under pressure from Pakistan to reduce the number of Afghan refugees, UNHCR was questioning the very ethics of repatriating women to a country where basic human rights and access to health or education were denied. Afghans drew their own conclusion: returnees dwindled to 11,000 in the first five months of 1997, compared to 121,000 in the previous year.[22]

Aid agencies, in their different fashions, were forced to grapple with the consequences of what, implicitly, signalled the Taliban's wholesale rejection of any effort to address the structural – read 'religious' – context of women's marginalisation in society, in favour of a bottomless reliance on unconditional relief. The Taliban decreed that you could feed women, but not help them in more meaningful ways. The quintessence of development – which for aid workers anywhere is shorthand for the empowerment of women and girls – was effectively outlawed. But, with the notable exception of Oxfam, international agencies and NGOs in Kabul believed they still had a job to do saving lives, whatever the rights environment. 'We are addressing humanitarian needs,' said a spokesman for ECHO, the EU's relief arm. 'Obviously witnessing and human rights need to be addressed too, but that is not the work of a humanitarian organisation. The people of MSF, Solidarité and AMI are not equipped. Their job is to keep people alive.'[23]

The confrontation over widows, however, receded within days of the Taliban settling into the capital. WFP projects were individually inspected and permitted to continue, so long as men and women did not work together. Female supervisors were appointed – on condition that they had no contact with male staff in the Kabul office. It was an inefficient and expensive compromise, for expatriate females had to be hired to do the tasks usually done by female Afghans, and it drew agencies deeper into a collaborative relationship with the Taliban on worrying terms. The material needs of widows and their children were secured, but the rest of Afghan women were still locked out of work, school and, by September 1997, all but one of the city's hospitals. Reports circulated of suicide attempts by women who dared not leave their home, but no agency raised the alarm.

In 1998, the larger agencies began to audit the 'widow caseload', with a view to redefining the selection criteria. 'It is demographically impossible,' said Leslie, 'for such large numbers of females to have been widowed, even taking into account the scale of loss of life here in recent years. It will be interesting,' he continued, 'to see the response of the authorities to this. In all likelihood, they will choose to view it as another demonstration of the international community's "lack of commitment to Afghan women".[24]

*   *   *

The UN Charter, which allowed the UN to work vicariously with Najibullah, Rabbani, Hekmatyar and Dostum, hardly equipped the organisation for survival in the treeless prairie of the Taliban's daily discourse, a landscape of utter simplicity dappled only by Manichean shadows. Save the Children's Matthew Bullard gave a succinct account of its climate following the agency's withdrawal from its schools programme in Herat in spring 1996, a trend initiated six months earlier by UNICEF:

> To be fair, the new governor is quite open in his rejection of Western humanitarian aid. He ends each meeting by suggesting that the best thing we could do would be to become Moslems and join the struggle. He specifically offered us our money back. 'All the money you have spent in Herat, you can have it back, and go away'.[25]

Michael Scott, manager of the UN agency Habitat's urban regeneration programme, summarised the communication breakdown: 'The degree of cognitive dissonance and communicative distance we can see and feel now with these new potential partners is unlike anything we may have experienced with previous Afghan factions, authorities or regimes.' He added: 'Neither in the new order does there seem to be any notion of accountability; the real authorities are to this day a nameless *shura*, who mediate the will of the Supreme Authority.'[26]

The UN was not about to ask for a refund but it was concerned about how its money would be spent under the Taliban. Between 1988 and 1992, over $1 billion had streamed into Afghanistan, a 'peace dividend' that turned aid into an industry on a par with heroin and, in the view of some critics, essentially accelerated its transformation into the world's largest opium producer by funding the repair of its myriad irrigation systems. The US pulled out in 1992 for that very reason, citing the Foreign Assistance Act which prohibits aid to narcotic-producing countries. Four years later, the EU had become the UN's largest donor, contributing ECU76 million ($96 million) out of a $134.8 million budget. Nearly half the amount, $41 million, was allocated to Kabul's winter emergency, a programme designed to ease the impact of the Hekmatyar and Taliban sieges, and which sustained many of the 38 foreign NGOs working in the city. While the UN waved its arms about in Afghanistan, it was the EU, in principle, that pulled the strings.

After protracted meetings in the UN Guest House, NGOs responded to the Taliban's new gender regime in a position statement that called for a return of the 'status quo of 11 days ago', the end of discrimination between the sexes, the restoration of women's right to work and study, and guarantees for the safety of their staffs.[27] Secretary-General Boutros Boutros-Ghali, three days later, confirmed the UN's commitment to Afghanistan, but only under the terms of its charter, which states that UN activities must be 'for all without distinction, as to race, sex, language or religion'. He acknowledged the importance of local traditions and cultures, but stressed that they could not be used by UN member-states to override international obligations to uphold basic human rights, including those of women to education and employment.

In the first week of October, the UNHCR suspended seven programmes affecting 8,000 people in Kabul, after the Amr Bil Marof Wa Nai An Munkir warned Afghan women by radio not to work with foreign agencies, 'otherwise, if they were chased, threatened and investigated by us, the responsibility will be on them'.[28] Oxfam reacted by closing down all its programmes, including the multi-million dollar Logar water supply project which would have supplied running water to half the capital's houses. The Oxfam position, defended in the face of intense pressure from donors and its own engineers, was that no effective community water project could be realised without guarantees of access to its chief users, women. In November, Save the Children (US), which had closed land-mine awareness programmes when girls were barred from school, reported a 300 per cent increase in casualties, 'due to civilians moving back into front-line areas following the ousting of the Rabbani regime and to Kabulis throwing away weapons and ammunition under a Taliban crackdown on unauthorised arms'.[29]

The one Taliban leader who stood aloof from the narrow intransigence of the *shura* in Kabul was acting Foreign Minister Sher Mohammed Stanakzai, the English-speaking former representative of Ittehad-i Islami in Quetta, who became its interface with the world after the fall of the capital. He alone seemed to grasp that the quarrel over women's rights was more than rhetoric and had set the movement, and the international community on course to inevitable loggerheads, however constitutionally reluctant the UN system was to take offence, impose sanctions or, in a word, 'suspend'.

He sought to mitigate the Taliban's forced redundancy of women by insisting that laid-off staff would continue to receive their wages – though no salaries had been paid to anyone for three months and Massoud had, anyway, made off with the treasury.[30] He reminded journalists that 'according to Islamic rules, education is a must for women' and he promised that girls' schools would surely reopen the following March, at the end of the traditional, three-month winter holiday.[31] In the same month, his superior, Mullah Rafiullah, then head of the Amr Bil Marof Wa Nai An Munkir, was reined in by Mullah Mohammed Omar after authorising the whipping of 225 women for dress code violations in a single day.[32]

The concession was enough to keep the UN relief operation rolling for three more months, for it chimed with the impression, growing in aid circles, that, while 'you could get nothing at the commanding heights of the régime, you could get a lot locally'.[33] The Taliban were not as monolithic, single-minded or secure in power as was first supposed. Their intransigence in more liberal, non-Pashtun cities was dictated in part by the fear of losing face before the troops, but, as the Soviets had also found, the Taliban writ travelled only a short distance beyond the main roads before meeting the unyielding autonomy of the village. Even when restrictions were categorically announced by radio, private arrangements were still viable at a district level, if they were couched in a dialect that did not challenge political or religious allegiances. 'Taliban' authorities in Ghazni and Khost permitted girls' schools to function within a home context; female health workers continued to make house calls in certain districts of Nangarhar; while, for want of any practical alternative, women in Jalalabad freely travelled in buses with men.[34]

Attacks on Western aid workers had begun before the difference between Rafiullah and Stanakzai over the conduct of external affairs: the one gravely pondering the Koran; the other more attuned to a world outside. In a letter on 18 November, the UN's security chief in Afghanistan, Daniel Bellamy, warned New York that a serious casualty was imminent, citing:

> an escalation of insults, threats and harrassment, culminating in the flight of some local staff, explicit threats against international and local staff and the invasion of UN offices and personal residences by armed Taliban fighters including, in one case, the detention of the UN Team Leader in his own home by 16 armed men for five hours.[35]

Bellamy's correspondence was in angry reaction to a UN agency meeting in Islamabad three days earlier under the auspices of the Department of Humanitarian Affairs in which it was suggested that 'consideration should be given to separating urgent issues related to actions by the Taliban towards the UN from broader issues related to the Taliban policies in the areas of human rights and cooperation with the UN'.[36]

In December, an employee of the International Committee of the Red Cross (ICRC), the agency that had been most stoic during the blitz of 1992–96, was stopped after curfew in the Wazir Akhbar Khan diplomatic quarter, soundly beaten and thrown into a police cell where he was discovered, accidentally, by an ICRC prison-visiting team several days later.[37] The incident was blamed on a 'hooligan' element within the rank-and-file, but top Taliban leaders lived in villas nearby and crossing the boundary between supercilious disdain and outright violence was a decision taken at the highest level. Foreigners interpreted the attack as a premeditated attempt to take the aid community down a notch.

Other encounters followed. Four elderly nuns in Kabul were given the strap in January 1997 for some hazy infringement of the dress code and, in February, aid workers referred confidentially to another confrontation, 'far more serious', that was brought to the attention of Stanakzai himself who 'pleaded that it not "go outside"', lest it affect negotiations over recognition.[38] One month later, French aid workers from Action Contre la Faim (ACF) were raided during a farewell lunch for three expatriate females that was attended by male and female Afghan staff. It was not an honest mistake: aid workers played a conscious game of hide-and-seek with the authorities, by maintaining clandestine contact with former female staff or hoarding the videos, CDs and cassettes banned by the Amr Bil Marof Wa Nai An Munkir. The Taliban were keen to demonstrate they were not to be teased. A tribunal sentenced the two ACF staff to one month in prison, and the Afghan men to one-and-a-half months and between 9 and 29 lashes each.[39]

But it was Afghan NGOs – of which there were a remarkable 240 at the end of 1994 – that were expected to bear the brunt of the Taliban's anger. Their ex-civil service staff had been trained in the Eastern bloc, thrived under Najibullah, consorted with women and still found accommodation with the UN and the mujahedin commanders in the areas where their projects were situated. In the Taliban's prayer-glazed view, they were the epitome of apostasy, their own fireside Satan. The first Afghan NGOs were established in the Soviet war as US-backed relief arms to the seven main resistance parties. More were formed after the UN launched 'Operation Salam' in 1988, a cross-border initiative directed at the return of the 3.3 million Pakistan-based Afghan refugees.

But the real mushrooming occurred after 1992, a year that saw both the US withdrawal from development and the outbreak of faction fighting in the capital. 'It seemed that every other Afghan was starting an NGO,' recalled Nancy Dupree, a writer on Afghan affairs employed by ACBAR, one of two bodies created in Peshawar to coordinate their activities.[40] Afghans brought to the fledgling NGOs the skills of a well-educated elite, and a closer rapport than non-Afghans could hope to achieve, while stripping away the formality that interposed between isolated rural communities and well-endowed foreign agencies. Known – both affectionately and derisively – as 'Bongos' (business-oriented NGOs), the most efficient competitively tendered for development 'contracts' put out by the UN or international NGOs. By 1994, their share of funding amounted to $44 million and some 29,000 professional Afghans sheltered within under the 'NGO system'.[41]

'One of the most positive things about this war,' continued Dupree, 'is that Afghans as well as foreigners, the UN as well as donors, have seen for the first time what they have always talked about in rhetoric: grassroots community participation for community development.'[42] By the mid-1990s, rural Afghanistan was in the throes of the same green revolution that had swept through Indian agriculture more than a generation earlier, and the credit was entirely due to local NGOs, which tapped the same filaments of mass propagation that, essentially, underpinned the *jihad*. By late 1995, the 'NGO system' had evolved into what amounted to the virtual privatisation of the services normally provided by government. That worried the UN Development Programme (UNDP), traditionally the co-ordinator of UN operations, whose role was hardly to tinker with the administrative mechanics of a member-state, however imploded. It also bothered the Rabbani government, too involved with the siege to register the raft of Bongos, but wary of the proliferation of new aid fiefs in its strife-torn territory. In the history of Afghanistan, influence had always shown a tendency to ebb away from the centre.

Hopes that the professional staff of Afghan NGOs, familiar with funding and the protocols which governed it, might fill the skills vacuum and develop into a think-tank for an apparently thought-free Taliban, faded even as Kabul fell. In Jalalabad, where NGOs had multiplied on the back of the displaced emergency, vehicles and motorbikes were looted and Taliban appointees inserted into the staff to ensure compliance with the gender edicts.[43] In May 1997, the US-based international relief and development organisation CARE suspended a food programme for 10,000 widows in Kabul, after Jalalabad Taliban stopped a bus carrying five of its male Afghan employees and beat them with sticks.[44] There were fewer Afghan NGOs in Kabul, where ministries and the presence of foreign NGOs ensured more orthodox project implementation. But the ones that were there experienced a sequence of lootings, first as Massoud withdrew, then as his pursuers commandeered vehicles to carry soldiers to the front at Jabal Saraj.

With the gunfire stilled due to the winter recess, agencies met to consider their options at a long-planned donor conference in the Turkmen capital of Ashgabat on 21–22 January that attracted representatives from 250 governments, agencies, development banks and NGOs – as well as scores of dollar prostitutes. The original intent had been to drum up support for the UN's emergency appeal for 1997, but the Taliban victory in Kabul converted the forum into a session devoted to seeking a unified response to the movement's gender policies. This was not easy. The resources of some agencies were dedicated exclusively to emergency relief: to close programmes down, it was argued, would penalise the recipients rather than their new, perhaps unwanted, rulers. Others, including the EU relief arm ECHO, maintained their work was humanitarian in orientation – as opposed to political – while a consultant for UNICEF, the first agency to withdraw support in Taliban areas, opined that UN programmes never had much of a gender perspective in Afghanistan, focusing as they did upon women's biological rather than social roles.[45] Even education failed to produce consensus. Afghan NGOs and the Swedish Committee for Afghanistan said the total denial of assistance because of the closure of girls' schools would be to 'hold hostage' Afghan boys. Where a convergence of views did occur was on the creative working climate in Mazar where, under Dostum, gender was no obstacle. In the following months, UNDP and its sister agencies allocated $35 million to a Poverty Eradication and Community Empowerment (PEACE) programme in Mazar that was more coherent as an acronym than a strategy, since it lent international support to the Taliban's enemy. The conference produced a list of ten resolutions – in which the Taliban were mentioned second to last – and a commitment to spend $50,000 on a resource centre for gender and human rights issues in Afghanistan.[46]

The deadline was nearing for a more vigorous approach. In an internal memo, UNICEF's regional director Ruth Hayward enquired:

> At what point are we taking orders from a foreign government, let alone jeopardising our success at a local level? ... I urge that criteria for a decision as to when

to suspend activities in a field office, based on programme considerations, not only security ones, be made explicit, if not yet done.[47]

As the lead agency in health and education, UNICEF was the UN's weathervane on issues of gender rights but, between the baying of the Western press and the prospect of the Taliban gradually responding to dialogue, it was a hard judgement to call. 'UNICEF discussed non-discrimination as a criterion to guide decision making about the allocation of resources in Afghanistan,' Hayward continued. 'The idea was to apply this systematically, taking into account both security and efficiency concerns. Did we go far enough? I doubt it. Can we now go further? I hope so.'[48]

Stanakzai was replaced over the winter by Mullah Ghaus, a more hard-headed player in daily contact with Mullah Mohammed Omar in Kandahar. In March, UN representatives met the minister of education, who agreed to permit girls up to nine years old to return to schools, then due to reopen by April. Days later, the decision was reversed. The Taliban repeated its pledge to reintroduce schooling for girls when the military situation had 'stabilised', adding for good measure, when 'they have been recognised as a legitimate power base'. UNICEF's Carol Bellamy responded with an irate press release restating her organisation's commitment to non-discrimination.[49]

But the system to which UNICEF belonged was insufficiently robust in its response to Taliban gender policy, and the conduct of 'constructive dialogue' over widows had only coined the language of complicity.

11   Ignoble Grave

'Wherever you go, we will catch you. If you go up, we will pull you down by your feet; if you hide below, we will pull you up by your hair.' Mullah Manon Niazi, August 1998

The encounter at Mazar in May 1997 cost the lives of at least 2,500 Taliban, but as many civilians were killed in an anti-Pashtun pogrom in the city later orchestrated by General Abdul Malik and the Hazara Shia leaders.[1] The ethnic war, predicted by Mahmoud Mestiri, flexed its jaws. In December – one month after the first of eight mass Taliban graves came to light in the desolate Dasht-i Leili near Shiburgan – sources claimed that a further 20,000 Pashtun non-combatants had vanished from Faryab, Jawzjan, Balkh, Badghis and Samangan, the provinces abandoned by the Taliban in their desperate escape from the northern bloodbath.[2] The allegation was never confirmed, but nor was it thoroughly investigated either by the UN or Amnesty International, both of which were subsequently castigated by Kabul for their indifference to atrocities committed by the CDA – now renamed the United Islamic Front for the Liberation of Afghanistan (UIFLA) in honour of the uneasy new alliance between Malik, Khalili and Massoud.[3]

The Mazar reversal placed the movement in the same military deadlock it had occupied one year earlier. Massoud blocked any southward retreat by again blowing up the Salang Tunnel, while his troops in the Shomali Plain, from which 200,000 people had fled, prevented any relief force reaching the besieged Taliban in Pul-i Khumri.[4] The utter collapse of the advance into the north, meanwhile, again emphasised the Taliban's insouciant attitude to the basic rules of military engagement. Instead of a measured advance, consolidated by securing supply lines and strategic towns en route, they had gambled 5,000 lives on what was assumed at the highest levels to be a mere victory procession. The miscalculation triggered the single worst massacre since the rise of the movement in October 1994 and it would lead to even more copious spillage of blood the following year. It also raised again the riddle of how, if the Taliban were indeed receiving military guidance from Pakistani experts, their forces could race to such an unmitigated disaster.

The defeat, however briefly, reassured Central Asia that the Taliban was a stoppable phenomenon. Pakistan, Saudi Arabia and the UAE did not retract their diplomatic recognition, although, in a bid to prevent Malik joining Massoud, Islamabad announced that Mullah Mohammed Omar had agreed the north should retain its 'unique culture' and invited its leaders to peace talks.[5] Malik countered with a proposal to convene a *Loya Jirga*, along lines so similar to those drawn up by Mestiri in 1994 that the name of Zahir Shah was among those called to attend. Against the counsels of his now closest allies, Russia and Iran, Malik sent an emissary to Washington and the UN in New York to drum up support for the plan.[6]

Significant changes had taken place in both the US and the UN administrations since the fall of Kabul. After months of rancorous debate, in which US demands for accelerated budgetary reform at the UN figured prominently, the General Assembly finally agreed upon Ghana's Kofi Annan as the replacement for the outgoing secretary-general, Boutros Boutros-Ghali. He took up his post on 1 January 1997, the same day that former US ambassador to the UN, Madeleine Albright, became the nation's first-ever female secretary of state and the executor of President Clinton's second-term pledge that 'concerns related to women will be incorporated into the mainstream of US foreign policy'. Though no radical feminist, the uniqueness of Albright's appointment and remit ensured that gender issues would assume greater weight in the US's ambivalent relations not only with the Taliban, but also with the UN, which still held the key to international recognition. Rabbani's representative continued to occupy Afghanistan's seat in the General Assembly, though that anomaly was due for review at the annual meeting of the UN's Credentials Committee in September 1997.

Recognition was vital if the UNOCAL pipeline were to raise the $2.5 billion funding needed to get it off the drawing board, but there had also been far-reaching alterations in the energy balance of power in the nine months since the fall of Kabul and they proliferated at a dizzying speed as the Credentials Committee meeting drew near. In a bid to pre-empt UNOCAL, Iran had begun work on a 125-mile (200 kilometre) pipeline to link the Turkmen gas field of Korpedzhe to its Caspian port of Kurt-Kui barely one month after the capital succumbed to the Taliban. Though capable of transporting less than half of UNOCAL's proposed gas volumes, the $190 million line, opened in December 1997, became the first energy export route from Central Asia outside Moscow's direct control and it represented a major setback to the US policy of containing Iran through the trade boycott.[7] With one international pipeline in place across Iran, the argument for others could only become more compelling and US contractors risked being left out in the cold because of an increasingly obsolete foreign policy. The election of the moderate Mohammed Khatami as president in May provided further impetus for a review of Washington's Iran policy. UNOCAL was not about to give up, however. In February, a delegation of Taliban leaders flew to its offices in Sugarland, Texas, for a whirlwind of corporate hospitality and, two months later, the company opened a project office in Kandahar, the seat of Taliban power.[8]

In a further change of watch in Washington, Robin Raphel, the assistant secretary of state for South Asia, was replaced in July by Karl Inderfurth, a forthright and ambitious individual with better access to Albright's ear. Neither despaired of doing business with the Taliban, but it was clear by the end of the year that official limits had been drawn around the foundations of any future relationship. 'The Taliban will not change their spots,' Inderfurth said, 'but we do believe they can modify their behaviour and take into account certain international standards with respect to women's rights to education and employment.'[9] US policy-making in Afghanistan, hitherto geared to the exigencies of the scramble for Caspian energy, had been rouged, however unwillingly, with a women's rights sensibility.

The death of so many fighters in Mazar did little to dent Taliban morale: indeed, there were even grounds for optimism. Mullah Mohammed Omar's appeal for more fighters summoned 10,000 willing martyrs from the apparently inexhaustible reservoir across the Pakistani border.[10] Dostum's surprising escape to Turkey – in view of the fact that he owned a home in Tashkent – had critically weakened the northern coalition, for Malik was neither as ruthless nor as intelligent as his former overlord. Herat's Ismail Khan, a Taliban captive since the May mutiny, had flown to an uncertain fate in Kandahar,[11] while another veteran of the Rabbani government, the Pashtun prime minister, Abdul Rahim Ghafoorzai, died on 21 August in a plane crash at Bamian, the victim not of foul play but of the short mountain runway.[12] By then, however, the Taliban had launched a bid to secure the north before the Credentials Committee assembled.

On 10 June, two weeks after the Mazar débâcle, 2,000 Taliban broke out of Pul-i Khumri and drove northeast on their last fuel to Kunduz, where they were welcomed by Arif Khan, a Pashtun ally of Massoud since 1980.[13] Kunduz, Hekmatyar's home area, contained a large Pashtun population and a functioning runway, but resupplying the depleted expeditionary force by air was an impossible logistical task. Logic dictated an attack on Hairatan port, 20 miles north of Mazar-i Sharif on the Amu Darya river, where Uzbek and Russian supplies of fuel and munitions were piled high, alongside UN relief food. In early September, a part of the Taliban force, joined by local Pashtun commanders formerly allied with Hekmatyar, swept out of Kunduz on a 100-mile dash across the north, capturing first Tashkurgan, Hairatan junction and finally Hairatan port. No sooner had they entered the city than they fired a celebratory volley of rockets across the river, killing several Uzbek nationals.[14]

Replenished, they launched a second assault on the northern capital, supported by warplanes and heavy artillery. On 9 and 10 September, Taliban troops lined up and shot 100 Shia civilians in the villages of Qazelabad and Qul Mohammed and, one day later, they seized control of the airport, without quite managing to penetrate Mazar.[15] In a routine display of the quality of northern leadership, Malik abandoned the city for Samangan shortly after the attack began, returning four weeks later, well after it had petered out.[16] Northern troops took advantage of the disorder to ransack aid agency offices, stealing whatever vehicles, equipment and furniture had been overlooked in the other pillage four months previously. Suddenly, out of a clear blue sky, on 12 September, the burly figure of General Rashid Dostum was reported back in the saddle fighting alongside his troops to recapture the supply base at Hairatan.[17]

Dostum said he returned at the request of Massoud, Khalili and Rabbani, although other sources suggest the invitation was issued by the largely autonomous Hizb-i Wahdat militia in Mazar.[18] In a classic display of Afghan *kow-tow*, the two generals met for the first time since Malik's mutiny at Dostum's personal headquarters in Shiburghan on 28 September.[19] The dialogue crackled but, to prevent any further rents appearing in the shredded fabric of the Northern Alliance, a power-sharing formula was agreed whereby Dostum took Jawzjan, Malik retained his pre-mutiny stronghold of Faryab, while his brother, Gul Mohammed Pehlawan, was given command of the north central province of Sar-i Pul.[20] Dostum immediately left for the eastern front, 26 miles (42 kilometres) from the city, where his return was portrayed as having galvanised the rank-and-file – without any reference whatever to his humiliating desertion four months earlier.[21] Hairatan fell to the alliance on 10 October, removing the springboard of the Taliban's second attempt on Mazar-i Sharif.

The assault on Mazar ran in tandem with a Taliban blockade of the Hizb-i Wahdat heartland of Bamian in the central Hazarajat, where heavy rains in 1997 had ruined the harvest in what had historically been a chronic food-deficit area. The Taliban first denied aid agencies road access in August, arguing that local commanders had 'taken the civilians hostage' and that relief food would simply prolong the war.[22] The World Food Programme complained that its 2,400 tonne stockpile in Hairatan and a further 1,400 tonnes in Mazar had all been looted, either by Taliban or Northern Alliance forces.[23] By November, almost one million people faced food shortages while women, attempting to smuggle in grain beneath their *burkhas*, were turned back by Taliban guards.[24] Fighting erupted the same month in Mazar between the factions in the Northern Alliance. Dostum's Jawzjan militia swept west out of Shiburghan, capturing Adkhoi and Malik's capital at Maimana on 24 November. Malik and Gul Mohammed fled across the border to exile in Iran, leaving their brothers in Mazar dungeons.[25]

Little of these events filtered out in detail for, since September 1996, the Taliban had cracked down on foreign journalism, often literally. In a country with no newspapers, no independent radio and only the BBC or Voice of America to provide hard information, media criticism as a rule was immediate and summary. The BBC's Alan Pearce, the only correspondent to witness the fall of Kabul, was hauled from his Land Rover days later and beaten with rifle butts because of the slants perceived in his coverage.[26] Photographing 'living things' was outlawed early on, although Taliban troops could usually be flattered into making exceptions. But the prohibition on contact between the sexes effectively censored any reporting of the main story in Kabul: how Afghan women were coping under Taliban constraints. Poorly indeed, according to one survey of 160 women which disclosed that 97 per cent showed symptoms of major depression and 71 per cent reported a decline in their physical health.[27] In September, the foreign ministry tightened restrictions further by banning commentary and analysis. 'News which could hurt people's feelings,' read the statement, 'cause dissension or ethnic, religious and linguistic discrimination, should be seriously avoided. The news and reports which agencies send abroad must conform with the rules ... and traditions of the country.'[28] 'Serious avoidance' was standard Taliban shorthand for an imminent beating.

The news blackout, ironically, shielded the UN, whose failure to create a coherent strategy out of its policy of 'constructive engagement' had begun to cause embarrassment. Plans to relocate mother-and-children programmes to the north under the hastily-concocted $30 million PEACE programme were, of course, shelved by the fighting in Mazar, Pul-i Khumri and Maimana, while the lack of progress over both girls' education and the provision of relief to the Hazarajat held out little hope for any meaningful improvement. With no sign of change in Afghanistan, voices were raised abroad. In a confusing double negative on 24 June, Amnesty International called for President Clinton to 'state unequivocally that neither a gas pipeline, or counter-narcotics operation, or simply short-term stability are not more important than confronting human rights violations against women, the majority of Afghans'.[29] Two days later, Kofi Annan announced a categorical ban on UN investment in Afghanistan's crumbling services. 'UN agencies,' he said, 'will not engage in the institution-building efforts of the Afghan authorities as long as their discriminatory practices continue.'[30] Two UN agencies, the World Health Organisation and UNHCR, disregarded the injunction by using their allocation of EU funds to rehabilitate Rabia Balkhi hospital, one of Kabul's 22 health facilities. Following a Taliban decree in late 1997, it had been designated the sole institution permitted to accept women patients, though it still lacked light, water or adequate surgical facilities.

Emma Bonino, head of the EU's relief arm ECHO, flew to Kabul on 28 September in what she admitted later was an attempt to 'use the media to draw international attention to a "forgotten crisis"'.[31] Her entourage of 18 journalists included the CNN's star correspondent, Christiane Amanpour, who gave the order to film women patients as soon as they were inside Rabia Balkhi. A squad of Taliban raced to the scene, threatened Bonino with a Kalashnikov and clubbed a CNN cameraman and European aid worker with their rifles. It took three hours of on-the-spot diplomacy to sort out the 'misunderstanding'.[32] The outcry was curiously short-lived, partly because of Bonino's reputation as a Versace-clad radical.

A more effective contribution to the belated but growing furore over women's rights was taking place in the US, coordinated by the Feminist Majority (FM), an alliance of 30 national women's organisations, including the YWCA, the American Nurses Association and the National Organisation for Women. On 30 July, the FM mounted its first pickets at the Pakistani and Afghani embassies in Washington, following up with a campaign of lobbying at Congress, the State Department, the UN and UNOCAL to prevent diplomatic recognition of the Taliban.[33] When the Credentials Committee were safely out of the way, the FM's 30,000 members focused on a postal campaign to political leaders, winning a public condemnation of the Taliban from First Lady Hillary Clinton.[34] On 5 November, a woman with burns over 80 per cent of her body was turned away from another Kabul hospital on the order of a Taliban and subsequently died untreated.[35] The story was widely editorialised in the US press during November's confrontation with Iraq over UN access to its weapons programme, a period of maximum tension during which Madeleine Albright nevertheless took the time to make a symbolic stopover in Pakistan. During a visit to the Afghan refugee camp of Nasir Bagh on 18 November, she denounced the Taliban's 'despicable treatment of women and children and their lack of respect for human dignity'. She told a press conference: 'I think it is very clear why we are opposed to the Taliban.'[36] One week later, the authorities agreed to admit women to most hospitals in the first concrete display of a *sharia* decree being overturned through outside pressure.

Albright's signal cut less ice in Sugarland. In September, the Taliban's energy mullahs flew to Buenos Aires to negotiate with the Argentinian pipeline rival, Bridas which, since the collapse of its scheme in 1995, had followed UNOCAL's example of trying to link up with a Saudi company to win back the contract. Its new partner, Ningharco, was no ordinary firm: it led directly back to the head of Saudi intelligence, Prince Turki al-Faisal, widely credited with having financed the Taliban phenomenon from the outset.[37] Notwithstanding, the formation was announced one month later of the Centgas pipeline consortium, with UNOCAL as lead partner with 46.5 per cent, in association with Delta Oil (15 per cent), Japan's Itochu Corporation (6.5 per cent), Inpex (6.5 per cent), South Korea's Hyundai (5 per cent), Crescent Group of Pakistan (3.89 per cent) and the Turkmen government (7 per cent).[38] The remaining 10 per cent of the deal was earmarked for Gazprom.

Construction was set to begin in 1998. UNOCAL declared it would not move the project forward until the Taliban were recognised internationally, but the company promptly invested $900,000 in the University of Nebraska in Omaha to train 140 Afghans in pipeline construction techniques, and Marty Miller, UNOCAL's vice-president, told the Taliban authorities they could confidently expect between $50 million and $100 million a year in transit fees if the pipeline became operational.[39] FM stepped up its political campaign, winning a gestural commitment from UNOCAL to include Afghan women in any future training programme.[40] By the following March, when FM joined up with Emma Bonino to launch the 'Flower for the Women of Kabul' campaign to draw greater international attention to the state of women's rights, the oil and gender issues had virtually osmosed: 'The price of a pipeline must not be the enslavement of women,' said FM President Eleanor Smeal.[41]

By then UNOCAL was again encountering legal difficulties. Bridas's $15 billion damages suit for spoiling its Turkmen investments was met with demands from UNOCAL that the case should be heard in Turkmenistan or Afghanistan instead. At a preliminary hearing in May 1998, the company's lawyers handed the court a set of over 2,000 separate civil codes from districts along the pipeline route, still in Dari or Pashtu calligraphy, inviting the judge to disentangle the issue of jurisdiction.[42] A decision, understandably, was deferred. But a more menacing legal threat had arisen from its $1 billion joint venture with Burma's ruling State Law and Order

Restoration Council (SLORC) in 1995 to build the Yadana pipeline, a project on which the UN Commission on Human Rights and independent activists had scrupulously documented incidents of murder, rape, torture and forced labour. In early 1998, residents of the Tenasserim region in Burma brought a class action suit against UNOCAL under the 1789 Alien Tort Claims Act, the first time the legislation had been targeted against a non-governmental party. UNOCAL's motion to dismiss the case was denied by the judge, who ruled that if UNOCAL were proven to have been aware of SLORC's forced labour policies, and had financially benefited from them, it would then create liability.[43]

UNOCAL's proposed partner in Afghanistan, meanwhile, was displaying its usual sensitivity to international opinion. In July, the authorities rounded up 2,000 Tajik and Hazara civilians in Kabul, cramming them into Pul-i Charki political prison in an effort to deter their fellows from joining the anti-Taliban alliance.[44] In the same month, Afghans were banned from changing their faith, and Kabulis were invited to 'introduce' to them any remaining Hindu, Sikh or Jewish residents for a chat.[45] In September, women were banned from wearing 'squeaky' shoes lest they impose an untoward awareness of their wearers' existence upon male citizens.[46] In October, an upsurge in *sharia* punishments was reported as the religious police cracked down on beards and whiskers, which had to be sufficiently long to extend out of the bottom of a fisted hand.[47] Defaulters said they were whipped with steel cables, but not necessarily by the Amr Bil Marof Wa Nai An Munkir, for a stricter police force, loyal to Justice Minister Mullah Mohammed Turabi, had since taken to patrolling the Kabul streets.[48]

On 11 November, two Afghan employees of UNICEF were hauled out of a vehicle in Jalalabad and one was given ten lashes.[49] A day earlier, the UN's special rapporteur on human rights, Choong-Hyun Paik, released a report which described the 'cries of prisoners being tortured' in Taliban-held Kunduz; a mullah who raped and killed five women, only to be released 'for being a good "Talib"'; and a remark by a Taliban leader that 'there were only two places for Afghan women: in her husband's house and in the graveyard'.[50] On 12 November, Angela King, the UN assistant secretary-general and special adviser on gender relations, arrived in Kabul but the authorities refused to receive her. One day later, UN coordinator Alfred Witschi-Cestari urged the Taliban to lift the Bamian blockade, describing it as 'among the cruellest things to have happened here this year'.[51] By the New Year, the execution of sentences in the national sports stadium had become the chief source of amusement to crowds of 20,000–30,000 spectators: after a purge of 'weak men' in the ministries,

Mullah Manon Niazi announced that a backlog of 25 alleged murderers and twelve cases of theft would be dealt with.[52] Mullah Omar had taken to presiding personally over the execution of sentence in Kandahar.[53] Dispensing with the customary Kalashnikov, the father of Jalil, murdered at Spin Boldak, used a knife to slit the throat of the alleged perpetrator, amid the chanting of religious slogans.[54]

Two months earlier, a man who could expect much shorter shrift in a Taliban court was publicly accused of serial fellatio in Washington.

*   *   *

Pakistan had little to show by early 1998, after nearly four years of investment in the Taliban. Saudi Arabia and its Gulf allies may have underwritten the cost of military operations and the purchase of enemy defectors, but it was Islamabad that paid the price in diplomatic isolation. Iran, predictably, was at daggers drawn: after three years' probing of its eastern flank by Sunni extremists, the border was closed and communications between the region's two largest Moslem powers had been reduced to monosyllables. That estrangement, at least, had been implicit from the very first draft of the Taliban plan.

But Pakistan's recognition of the movement had put all the governments of Central Asia – with the exception of Turkmenistan – on high alert, while adding a layer of deeper complexity to the Afghan conflict by pre-empting a decision by the UN's Credentials Committee, still the final arbiter on questions of sovereignty. Further attempts to forge the kind of multi-ethnic government envisaged by UN envoy Mahmoud Mestiri were, henceforth, doomed first to renegotiating the status of a locally recognised, militarily secure but still Pashtun-dominated, Taliban rather than addressing the unwinnable character of the conflict itself. A string of delegations from the EU, the UN, Turkey, Uzbekistan, China, Iran and other leading Moslem states visited Islamabad in early 1998 to plead with Prime Minister Nawaz Sharif to press the Taliban to peace talks prior to the formation of a government of all ethnic groups.[55]

Sharif's command of foreign policy was arguably as shaky as his military's control of the Taliban. He had been elected by a windfall in February 1997 – albeit on a turnout of less than 30 per cent of the electorate – to clean up the corruption of Benazir Bhutto's second administration, a mission he pursued vigorously through the law courts without ever seriously getting to grips with the economic malaise that cast her profligacy in such a cynical light. Sharif's influence over foreign affairs, traditionally the realm of the military, was even less assured, except insofar as the cabinet could convert its *de facto* decisions over India, Kashmir, Afghanistan and, ultimately, the nuclear option, to domestic advantage, a vital consideration in a political landscape in which the shrinking, political centre was under constant pressure from the Islamist tendencies of the street.

For all its reputation as the guarantor of order in an otherwise volatile national chemistry, Pakistan's military tended towards the vainglorious in its conduct of foreign policy, currying flamboyant Islamist expectations and caring little for the cost to a civil administration which it treated no better than pen-pushers. The Taliban project had been indelibly felt at home. Thousands of unemployed young men flocked to the *jihad*, while guns, drugs and a bleak, sectarian ideology were re-imported, fostering violence between Sunnis and Pakistan's large Shia minority, and jeopardising in turn relations with Iran, the US and Saudi Arabia, whose interests demanded far more careful pandering. Sharif might have preferred to hedge support for the Taliban with more diplomatic restraints than Mrs Bhutto or Interior Minister Naseerullah Babar, but he was in no position to impose policy on the generals who had run the 'Afghan Cell' since 1979. One analyst suggested that Sharif, a novice in diplomacy, was kept intentionally in the dark about Afghan policy by Foreign Minister Gohar Ayub, going on to describe a ministry that had 'relegated its broader regional policy aims to a handful of Pashtun and fundamentalist policy makers ... who are the driving force of a pro-Taliban policy at the expense of all other interests'.[56] Even the kingpins of the ISI, however, must have been queasily reminded, after the defeat at Mazar, of their former protégé, Hekmatyar, who managed always to draw blood, without ever quite delivering the *coup de grâce*.

The US, considered a sleeping partner in the scheme to impose a Pashtun-led peace – whether to open up Central Asia's energy, or suppress the opium trade – found grounds for altering its priorities between the Mazar defeat and the next *Eid al-Fitr*. Despite his compelling significance in the background, bin Laden had not yet made the leap into contemporary demonology that would occur so explosively less than a year later. And, despite the raised voices of Hillary Clinton, Madeleine Albright and Emma Bonino, the issue of gender rights had not percolated deep enough to cancel the *realpolitik* of gas pipelines. What was to transform perceptions of the region and Afghanistan was the suspicion that, inadvertently, the US had moved from one geological era of foreign policy management to quite another, a transition which would prune a generation of US, Soviet-era advisers and open up an unmapped terrain in which, even as

Pakistan teetered on the brink of eruption, Iran had mysteriously simmered down. As if in confirmation, 1998 was a year littered with anniversaries and precedents.

The transition was set in motion towards the end of 1997 with the creation of the UN's 6+2 Contact Group, a conference of all Afghanistan's immediate neighbours, with the addition of the US and Russia. It was the first successful attempt to assemble in the same room all the surrounding powers – excluding Saudi Arabia – which had stoked the Afghan fire with weapons, fuel and money. More historically, the Contact Group provided an opportunity for the first face-to-face discussions between Washington and Tehran since the hostage crisis nearly 20 years earlier. They discovered they had more in common than either realised: concerns over Iraq; the fight against drugs; instability in Afghanistan; and the future of Central Asia. This epiphany-strewn relationship was nurtured throughout 1998: first, through their studied collaboration over Iranian reactions to Taliban provocation – and the survival of Massoud; and then through Washington's assiduous screening of Tehran from incrimination in the later activities of its former ally, Osama bin Laden.

The warlords spent the winter of 1997 rebuilding their stores. The Taliban blockade of Bamian remained solid, but Iran flew in supplies unmolested until December when the airport was bombed.[57] In the same month, Massoud captured the Tagab valley, east of Kabul, while his continued occupation of Bagram assured a continuing air-bridge from Tajikistan and Iran. In the north, the front between Mazar and Kunduz remained tense: on 13 February, Dostum was injured by mortar shrapnel and he retired to Tashkent for treatment.[58] One week later, Massoud advanced into Laghman, in a bid either to cut the Jalalabad road or to relieve Taliban pressure on the Hazarajat.[59] However, there was little evidence of coordination between the components of the Northern Alliance. In March, faction fighting broke out between Dostum's forces and Hizb-i Wahdat in Mazar, forcing the ICRC again to evacuate the northern capital.[60]

Efforts to further the peace talks had largely foundered the previous October, after the resignation of the UN special envoy, Dr Norbert Holl. He was replaced by Lakhdar Brahimi, an Algerian with a successful history of resolving hostage situations, but he focused on a regional approach from New York, leaving Holl's deputy, James Ngobi, in charge of the Islamabad office. On 25 March, UN relations with the Taliban took a more confrontational stance when it suspended operations in Kandahar, after an edict barring foreign female Moslem employees from going out, unless accompanied by a male relative. Since most UN female staff were recruited from distant Moslem lands, the ban was interpreted as a direct challenge from the Mullah Omar. The decision to suspend operations followed three physical attacks on personnel: one had a coffee pot thrown at him by a Taliban official; another was slapped across the face; and a third assaulted with a table. Fourteen international staff were evacuated and 120 local employees sent home.[61]

It was the US, rather than the UN that set the pace in a bid to head off a return to total war in the spring. On 17 April, America's ambassador to the UN, Bill Richardson, flew to Kabul to meet the Taliban's number two, Mullah Rabbani, becoming the highest ranking US official to visit Afghanistan since Henry Kissinger.[62] 'He must not have with him the idea of imposing the values of Western civilisation under the terms of the defence of human rights and women's rights,' warned the Taliban's *Shariat* newspaper, indifferent to the unique honour bestowed upon the leadership.[63] But that was precisely the message Richardson had brought from Washington. In exchange for a softening of Taliban social policies in accordance with international norms, the US would use its influence to obtain UN recognition.

That was only the first of his business. Attached to the recognition offer was an urgent codicil concerning bin Laden. Over the winter, Saudi intelligence secured the defection of Mohammed bin Mosalih, one of bin Laden's chief accountants, who provided detailed information of the Saudi's extensive network of overseas financial transactions.[64] On 23 February, bin Laden issued a communique announcing the formation of the World Islamic Front, which called on Moslems to 'kill the Americans and their allies – civilian and military'. The release was co-signed by Refai Ahmad Taha, spiritual leader of Egypt's Gamaat al-Islamiya, Ayman al-Zawahiri, head of Egypt's Jihad, Fazi Rahman Khalil of Pakistan's Harakat ul-Ansar and Abdul Salaam Mohammed, chief of Bangladesh's Jihad.[65] Bin Laden had also been linked to two aborted attempts to assassinate President Clinton in the Philippines and Pakistan. The CIA's Counter-Terrorism Center organised a raid to capture the Saudi in the very month of Richardson's visit, a project that was dropped 'because of the potential for casualties among Americans and innocent Afghanis'.[66]

Richardson flew from Kabul to Shiburghan and Faizabad to meet Dostum and Rabbani, but Massoud was not included in the discussions and Mullah Mohammed Omar did not stir from his Kandahari reclusion. Richardson described his visit as a 'breakthrough' on returning to Islamabad – as if US influence could obtain in a day what had eluded the UN for nine years.[67] The Taliban, he said, had agreed to 'broaden girls' access to education' and allow more foreign female doctors to practise, promises that were neither elaborated in his statement, nor carried through. The peace process that all sides had agreed upon entailed the creation of a steering committee of five Taliban and nine opposition representatives charged with assembling a commission of 40 *ulama* to negotiate terms before 27 April – the 20th anniversary of the Saur Revolution which brought the communists to power.[68]

Despite inevitable hair-splitting over what constituted an *alim* – and a short-lived Taliban offensive the day before – the commission met in Islamabad at the appointed date, evidence perhaps of a wistful desire by all sides to give the American something concrete to take home. The Northern Alliance demanded a permanent ceasefire, the exchange of prisoners and an end to the blockade of the Hazarajat. In Taloqan, Massoud expressed his weariness at 'resolutions' devised in Islamabad, while hawks in the Taliban had clearly received no firm notice from Pakistan that the military option was exhausted.[69] On 30 April, Mullah Wakil Ahmad Matawakil, head of the Taliban delegation, flew back to Kandahar with a progress report, never to return.[70] The Richardson initiative collapsed three days later and, on 5 May, fighting flared in the north as the Taliban in Kunduz launched an offensive into Massoud's province of Takhar.

Interest in the outcome was swiftly eclipsed by India's detonation of five nuclear devices in Rajasthan during 11–13 May, barely two months after the Hindu extremist BJP took power in New Delhi. The abrupt nuclearisation of the sub-continent, with the increased potential for open war with Pakistan, earned an immediate embargo on aid and investment from the US, and a demand that India sign the Comprehensive Test Ban Treaty and agree not to arm or deploy its weapons. New Delhi refused. Fifteen days later, Pakistan responded with six trials of a lesser magnitude in Baluchistan's Chagai Hills. The US reaction was muted by the recognition that Islamabad acted in self-defence, but the punishment was identical and cut much deeper. While Moslems around the world celebrated the birth of an 'Islamic bomb', Pakistan suffered the cancellation of a crucial $500 million loan from the IMF, a 30 per cent collapse of the rupee, and food prices soared by 25 per cent.[71]

At 4.7 on the Richter scale, Pakistan's nuclear debut was 2,000 times less powerful than the earthquake which struck Badakhshan and Takhar on 2 June, killing some 5,000 people across an area of 675 square miles.[72] Journalists detected a causal connection between the two events, due to Afghanistan's position on a 'tectonic plate border' – as good a way as any to sum up its importance for the political stability of the region. The June shock measured 7.1 on the Richter scale and tore fissures a quarter of a mile long in Dashtaq, close to the epicentre at Shari-i Bazurg, where a small blue lake suddenly appeared.[73] More than 70,000 people lost homes and livelihoods, but heavy summer rains and the tug-of-war between agencies and factions meant no significant aid reached them till the third week of June. The fiasco was played out in the full glare of the cameras. Troops in Faizabad, aligned with Massoud's Jamiat-i Islami, halted all aid shipments until they were granted their own cut, while companies across the Amu Darya haggled for special war insurance for the use of their helicopters.[74] NGOs condemned the UN's 'obsession' with helicopters, dispatching columns of relief-laden ponies over the passes and into the devastated valleys.[75] The US agreed to find the helicopters to break the blockage, but neither Massoud, Pakistan nor the charter companies across the border would relent.[76]

The earthquake in the northeast was a potent reminder of the permanent need for a relief capability, however unwieldly, but it did little for the UN's standing in Kabul. Within days of the earthquake, Mawlawi Qalamuddin, head of the Amr Bil Marof Wa Nai An Munkir, ordered the closure of the clandestine schools for girls which had sprung up like mushrooms in Shia neighbourhoods after the Taliban took Kabul in 1996.[77] 'These schools were operating illegally and in secret,' said a shocked spokesman, 'moving to different locations every day.'[78] In fact, the authorities had winked at the 100 or so 'home schools' for nearly two years, but Mullah Mohammed Omar had finally reached his momentous verdict on the wisdom of teaching the 'Three Rs' to girls under seven, even in a secluded setting. After the intimidation in Kandahar the previous March, and a humiliating climbdown by the UN in late May, it seems that the Leader of the Faithful, or his deputies, had finally decided to terminate the UN mission in Afghanistan.

On 13 July, two UN Afghan staff, former professors at Jalalabad University, were abducted as they waited for a lift, and their bodies were found in river beds near the city.[79] Days later – in a not necessarily related move – Mullah Rabbani instructed all 38 NGOs working in the capital to move their quarters from Wazir Akhbar Khan to a group of unheated and unlit faculty buildings at the bombed-out Polytechnic, near the Shia neighbourhood of Karta Se. Relief workers protested that this placed them directly in the line of fire, while $1 million in repairs were still needed to bring the buildings to a habitable condition.[80] Two reasons were given out for the order: it was due to the NGOs' covert support to the home schools in the form of books and salaries – or because their premises in the diplomatic quarter had so many windows through which to peer at Afghan women.[81]

Efforts by the UN and the EU to strike a compromise came to nothing, as did warnings of what would befall Kabul's 400,000 indigents were agencies to live up to their threat and shut down programmes altogether. The Taliban insisted that the order had to be obeyed to 'protect our families'.[82] By 21 July, all but one of the NGOs had withdrawn their staff to Peshawar but their vehicles were attacked by Taliban troops as they passed through Torkham Gate.[83] 'If we see them on the street,' said the head of security, 'we will take action under our laws.'[84] The UN estimated that the withdrawal would affect 75 per cent of relief projects in Kabul: Health Minister Mohammed Abbas, a former communist who also served President Rabbani, announced an allocation of $25,000 to meet the immediate needs of the population in the wake of the NGO withdrawal.[85] In what appeared a retort to all who maintained that the Taliban lacked a sense of humour, the authorities ordered the closure of the ECHO office on 23 July, because Emma Bonino had 'used it for the spread of Christianity'.[86] But the Taliban weren't kidding: the 'joke' came closest to defining the true bone of contention between two such alien cultures.

North of the Hindu Kush, the Taliban were again on the march. On 10 July, Maimana and Shiburghan succumbed in quick succession. Dostum attempted a counter-attack through Faryab, but the offensive collapsed and he fled the country a second time.[87] In Maimana, aid workers reported that 25–40 per cent of the conquering army were Urdu-speakers and, a month later, Massoud claimed that there were 1,700 Pakistanis among the 8,000-strong force.[88] When Sar-i Pul fell on 4 August, the UIFLA summoned 9,000 troops to reinforce Mazar but, in the event, only 2,000 Hizb-i Wahdat fighters arrived.[89] So unflustered were the Mazaris by the danger from the west that, when 5,000 'Taliban' entered the city in the morning of 8 August to the sound of gunfire, they assumed it was just another of the frequent fallings-out between the armed factions and simply went about their business.[90]

The force that captured Mazar included Pashtun fighters from nearby Balkh – the 'mother of cities' – under the Hizb-i Islami regional commander, Juma Khan Hamdard, who had remained part of the Northern Alliance in spite of the defection to the Taliban of the Kunduz Pashtuns one year before. Hizb-i Wahdat, suspecting their loyalty, had attacked their positions some weeks earlier, indulging in widespread rape and driving the Pashtun into the arms of the advancing enemy.[91] But the Taliban had grown wary of gift horses, wanting no repeat of Malik's treachery in 1997.

To prove their mettle and avenge their families, the Pashtuns agreed to circle behind the main line of defence at Qala Zainim in the western suburbs, trapping the entire Hizb-i Wahdat garrison of 1,500–3,000 troops, most of whom were picked off on the roads leading north and east out of the city.[92] A contingent of 700 fled south towards the Alborz mountains, along with stragglers from Dostum's and Massoud's forces and thousands of panicked Mazaris. The road was black with people and vehicles. For two days, the Taliban fired Katyusha multiple rockets at the retreating columns, while jets dropped cluster bombs on their heads.[93] Worse befell those who stayed behind.

The Balkhi Pashtuns acted as a shield as the Taliban entered the city, randomly shooting at anybody they met in the narrow streets surrounding the bazaar and in the boulevards that led to the blue and gold shrine of Hazrat Ali – the so-called 'Noble Grave' – where Abdul Ali Mazari, the Hizb-i Wahdat leader slain by the Taliban in 1995, was also interred.[94] They relished their new work. Hundreds of civilians lost their lives in the first hours after the city's capture but the shooting had largely subsided by midday when, again following leads provided by the Balkhis, the Taliban launched a house-to-house search for anyone of fighting age in the Hazara neighbourhoods of Zara'at, Saidabad and Elm Arab.[95]

Those who spoke Pashtu, or whose features lacked the Hazaras' Asiatic physiognomy, sporadically bluffed their way to survival, but most were betrayed by the ultimate shibboleth of not being able to pronounce the Sunni prayers. Discovered Hazaras were usually shot on the spot, preferably in the face or testicles, while some had their throats cut and yet more were carted off to the city jails.[96] One man escaped by throwing himself over the side of the truck. 'I landed on the right side of the road where there was a mosque,' he reported. 'I ran in ... and began to wash, as if I was preparing to pray.'[97] His friends landed on the left and were shot, as were most Hazaras upon arriving at their destination. Mazari Pashtuns who attempted to shelter their Shia neighbours were warned of a similar fate.[98]

The Balkhis' method of dealing with Hazaras was swiftly endorsed by the new governor of Mazar, Mullah Manon Niazi, a Farsi-speaking Pashtun of a Herati mother and one of a handful of sympathisers from minority groups brought into the leadership after the 1997 massacre to support Taliban claims that it was a multi-ethnic coalition, rather than a wholly Pashtun movement.[99] Niazi distinguished himself as governor of Kabul by fast-tracking the programme of public executions and he arrived at his new northern appointment with great enthusiasm.[100] On 9 August – the second day of the takeover – he began a series of speeches on local radio, in mosques and other public spaces in which he denounced the Hazaras for the 1997 massacre – although it was general knowledge that Malik's Uzbeks had carried out the atrocities in Shiburghan – and threatened reprisals at a rate of three Shia lives for every Taliban slain a year earlier.[101] But Niazi went further.

'Hazaras are not Moslem,' he said at one mosque, 'they are Shia. They are *kofr* [*kafir* – infidel].'[102] And, therefore, no better than animals. Seventy men had their throats cut at the tomb of Abdul Ali Mazari in the *halal* ritual reserved for sheep, while Shias were dragged from their hospital beds, taken outside and shot.[103] Niazi forbade relatives from removing the bodies of the dead from the street for five days or 'until the dogs ate them', and Shia mosques were whitewashed, renamed and converted to Sunni places of worship.[104] Of greater moment, perhaps, was the fact that Niazi's official dehumanisation of Shias was understood by the rank-and-file as permission to rape, an event without precedent in the Taliban's four-year career. In one of several recorded instances, a girl from Ali Chopan was among 20–25 girls held for an unspecified time by Taliban and raped every night. 'One Talib told her that now that you are *halal* [sanctified], [she] should go to his parents in Kandahar and wait for him to come and marry her.'[105] From other houses, Hazara girls were taken south to work as *kaniz*, or maids, a fate their great-grandparents might easily have suffered a century earlier when the enslavement of Hazaras was commonplace in Afghanistan.[106]

On their arrival in Mazar, the Taliban had freed Pashtun criminals to make space in the prisons for Hazaras, Tajiks and Uzbeks. As the jails overflowed with the fresh intake, detainees were shifted to prisons in Shiburghan, Herat and Kandahar in containers 20–40 feet long, each of which could hold between 100–150 men in asphyxiating conditions. The shipping container has achieved in Afghanistan a status imbued with architectural, historical, but sometimes a horrifying significance. Plastered with mud and thatched, the boxes that once held Cold War munitions or smuggled cargo were transformed into secure artisans' premises: ordered ranks of them are found outside every town, like so many fast-food outlets at the edge of an American city. They also make excellent prisons. Abdul Rasul Sayyaf, head of the Pashtun faction Ittehad-i Islami, killed Hazaras in Kabul by locking them in a container and building a fire around it.[107] Thirty-five containers left Mazar in the week after the takeover and, in two cases at least, nearly all the prisoners had died from heat or asphyxiation by the time the metal door was reopened. 'In Shiburgan,' said one witness, 'they brought three containers close to the jail. When they opened the door of one truck, only three persons were alive. About 300 were dead ... The Taliban asked [someone I know] and three Turkmen to go with them to the Dasht-i Leili. The Taliban did not want to touch the bodies, so the porters took the bodies out of the containers.'[108]

News of the massacre did not leak abroad until November 1998 when, evading a nationwide dragnet, the first Hazara refugees crossed the Pakistani border to spill out their sombre tales. Human rights organisations later set the death toll as high as 4,000–6,000, while 4,500 men remained in detention as late as October.[109] The Taliban denied all knowledge, but attempts to investigate the killings in Mazar – even by Pakistani journalists with close links to the leadership – were dismissed out-of-hand. 'In the run-up to their bid for international acceptance,' commented a European diplomat, 'imposing this iron curtain is sending very bad signals to the outside world.'[110]

'Bad signals' had already been received in the Hazarajat. Three weeks after the fall of Mazar, the Hazara stronghold of Bamian capitulated but, when the Taliban column streamed into a city that once boasted 40,000 inhabitants, it found only 50 old men – who were promptly shot.[111] The entire citizenry had fled into the famished highlands, fearing hunger less than a fresh encounter with their now rampant enemies. Some Hizb-i Wahdat commanders bowed without offering resistance, but there was heavy fighting in Yakawlang, the party's main headquarters, before the region finally succumbed. 'The clock has been turned back 100 years to a time when the Hazaras were officially denied the most basic of human rights,' commented one Western analyst.[112]

A further casualty was one of two ancient Buddhas, carved 125 feet high in the cliffs overlooking Bamian, which had made it a pilgrimage centre for over 2,000 years. In the whoop of victory, a Taliban tank commander took aim and fired, hitting the figure squarely in the jaw and groin.

12 A Fistful of Dollars

'It's been an amazing run. Hey, every once in a while, we do something right.'
FBI agent[1]

On 7 August, the day before the Taliban stormed into Mazar-i Sharif, bank worker Jack Omukhai visited his wife Elizabeth at the Ufundi Cooperative Building at the corner of Moi and Haile Selassie Avenues in the heart of Nairobi, Kenya. They spoke of 'little things' and, after sharing a cup of tea, he left. Half an hour later, she was dead, one of 263 people – twelve of them American – who perished in a bomb attack on the nearby US embassy that left a further 5,500 injured.[2] The explosion had been planned to the split second. A lesser device was detonated at the US embassy in Dar es Salaam at the same time, killing ten Tanzanians. It was eight years to the day since US troops first touched down in Saudi Arabia to take up positions for the Gulf War in 1990, a date that rankled throughout the radical Islamic world.[3]

The ambassador had warned of poor security at the city-centre location well before February, when bin Laden's threats against US targets, military and otherwise, were first taken seriously, putting all US facilities in a state of high alert. The Nairobi embassy was especially vulnerable. Since the closure of stations in Khartoum and Mogadishu, both in different ways cauterised by failures in US policy in Moslem Africa, Nairobi had evolved into the CIA's chief listening post for an area reaching from Madagascar to former Zaire and Yemen and encompassing the entire, war-prone Horn of Africa. Jomo Kenyatta Airport, meanwhile, had developed into the crossroads of a trading empire that once sailed the Indian Ocean and Red Sea but had adapted seamlessly to flying. Lack of resources, Africa's low priority in Washington and the sheer scale of the Nairobi watch had led to a critical deterioration in preparedness. So far gone was regional intelligence by January 1996 that the CIA publicly discounted 100 of its leading reports on Sudan – officially a 'terrorism-exporting' country and a proven ally of both bin Laden and Iran – after concluding that their source, not American, was a 'fabricator'.[4]

A posse of CIA and FBI agents descended upon Kenya after the bombings to explore every avenue of enquiry from Nairobi to Mombasa on the coast, where Kenya's Sunni minority lived. Suspicion, at first, fell on Ayman al-Zawahiri's Egyptian Jihad, the nearest, active Islamist grouping to Kenya and one that had demonstrated the least qualms when it came to killing civilians. Secretary of State Madeleine Albright offered a $2 million reward for information leading to the perpetrators, but it was a shot in the dark. A day after the explosion, a US official said: 'We have no suspects. Everything is up for grabs.'[5]

Since the Oklahoma City bombing by white terrorists in 1995, Washington had become wary of ritually pointing the finger of blame at 'Islamists'. Yet, in the reams of editorial copy generated by the Kenyan cataclysm, one thesis is singularly absent. Nowhere is there speculation on the possible involvement in the explosions by Sudan, Libya or, more particularly, Iran, states which had all been accused of sponsoring overseas terrorism in the recent past. Even Saudi Arabia had something to gain from counterfeiting a bin Laden operation, in view of the crumbling trade and political embargoes which had characterised recent US policy towards Tehran, hitherto a confirmed backer of the renegade Saudi. Through an apparently silent, but inexorable, process of consensus-building, the Nairobi bloodbath was turned from a possible conspiracy of countries, to one of individuals. Days after the explosion, Radio France International was contacted by the unknown Islamic Army for the Liberation of Moslem Holy Places, which claimed responsibility for both bombs.[6] The communique, according to the Lebanese newspaper *Al-Safir*, was the product of a learned mind, free of religious hyberbole, determined upon its enemy and evidently capable of superb planning.

One day after the bombing, the first suspect in the conspiracy, Mohammed Saddiq Odeh, was arrested in Karachi, having travelled from Nairobi on a Yemeni passport whose photo did not quite match his face. Under intensive interrogation, he confessed to working for bin Laden's Al Qa'ida and to assembling the Nairobi bomb, though he later recanted, accusing Pakistani intelligence of using torture.[7] In late August when, according to the FBI, he was 'singing like a canary', Odeh told a Manhattan court that the plotters left Kenya the day before the attack and that they had shaved their beards so as 'not to raise suspicion'.[8] So much for planning. He refused to repeat his confession to the FBI, into whose custody he was transferred in mid-August, having been first wrung dry by Pakistani and Kenyan intelligence. Odeh, 34, made an unprepossessing holy warrior. A Palestinian from Jordan, he arrived in Kenya in 1994, settling near Mombasa to work as a fishmonger, buying upcountry stock to sell to the city's hotels. In 1997, he moved to the settlement of Witu near the bandit-infested Somali border – an ideal conduit for smuggled explosives – where he opened a carpentry shop, living piously but in poverty. His Kenyan wife said he had travelled to Nairobi only once in the previous five months, but that was untrue. He must have caught the plane to Karachi from the capital and Kenyan carpenters, as a rule, do not fly. He could not account for the fare. The FBI charged Odeh with riding to the embassy in a bomb-laden vehicle and tossing a grenade at the guard. He faced charges of murder on twelve counts, all against American dead.

As such evidence emerged – and it remained tenuous until mid-September – bin Laden was propelled from a shadowy *éminence grise* into a front-page villain. In the absence of solid leads, however, the press focused upon the Saudi's finely-spun web of financial interests and his catalogue of alleged confederates – including, during the *jihad*, the CIA – rather than the case in hand and none took the time to enquire whether the indiscriminate slaughter at the Ufundi Cooperative Building actually chimed with the self-styled seer's recent *fatwa*. That February, bin Laden had issued his public ruling that 'to kill the Americans and their allies – civilian and military – is an individual duty for every Moslem who can do it in any country in which it is possible to do it'. But he relied for listeners, then as in the past, upon the moral authority of his pronouncements and the tragedy inflicted upon so many Kenyans – many of them devout Moslems – formed no part of such a persona. When asked, he strenuously denied any direct involvement in the embassy bombings, while admitting he had 'instigated' them, an equivocation that could equally have stemmed from bin Laden's vanity as America's public enemy number one – or the need to cover up a bungled operation.[9] To admit incompetence would detract from Islamist rapture at this outwitting of US security. Nevertheless, FBI Director Louis Freeh sided with bin Laden, saying he had come to 'no firm conclusions' as to who was responsible for the bombings, and that was several days after the US took its furious revenge.[10]

As Odeh was being questioned in Karachi, other strategic killings were taking place in Mazar. 'At about 12 noon, a group of Taliban came to the door of the consulate-general,' recalled an Iranian diplomat, Allahdad Shahsavan-Qarahosyeni.

> In the mission at the time were all [nine] staff and the [official news agency] IRNA correspondent, Mahmoud Saremi. After asking us to hand over any weapons, they moved us into another room, where they conducted body searches and took our money. One, possibly a Pakistani, asked to use the telephone to call Pakistan. Since Pakistan had undertaken to ensure our safety, he probably wanted to let them know about the state of things at the mission. But the others stepped in and wouldn't allow him to call.

We did not in any way act contrary to their wishes. They asked for the keys to the mission's cars, they asked for fruit juice. We gave it to them. Then they moved us down to the basement, which contained a single desk. Three of their leaders walked in and immediately raised their weapons. They said they were going to kill us and lined us up against the wall. As they fired the first one or two bullets, I decided to throw myself to the ground and it occurred to me that I had to use the only piece of furniture that was there. I dragged the top half of my body under the desk and lay totally flat. All my friends and brothers were falling to the ground and some were martyred in that first instant.

I tried to make not the slightest movement and to control my breathing. I shut my eyes and recited my final prayers. I was, in a way, waiting to witness my own death, but God bestowed his mercy on me. It seems I was destined to live so I could act as an ambassador who could recount the truth, in view of the fact that they wanted to portray events differently. I could see their legs from beneath the desk and I saw them slowly leave. I waited a few moments. The mission was totally silent.[11]

Shahsavan-Qarahosyeni was the only occupant to escape the Mazar consulate and no record exists of how he survived in the city until 12 September when, under open threat of invasion by Iran, the Taliban finally 'discovered' the bodies of his colleagues on a suburban midden. The rattling of Iranian sabres had become deafening in the preceding weeks as spiritual leader Ayatollah Ali Khameini called the Taliban 'lowly and worthless', former President Akhbar Hashemi Rafsanjani vowed revenge and President Khatami contributed the interesting insult 'orthodox savages'. Revolutionary Guards rushed to the border after the diplomats' disappearance, building to a strength of nine divisions, or around 200,000 troops, supported by armour and air power. The US urged restraint, but a stream of militarist and sectarian rage flooded through Iranian loudspeakers.

Mahmoud Saremi's reports from the Shibar Pass, Shiburghan, Mazar and other battlegrounds had made him into a well-known media figure and Iranians listened, first gripped but finally horrified, as the Taliban approached the Shia pilgrimage site and turned it into an abattoir. Now, having captured Massoud's rear base of Taloqan on 11 August after twelve hours of shelling, they were poised to take Bamian, promising slaughter in another populous Shia centre, while the authority of Karim Khalili, the Hizb-i Wahdat leader, was faltering and his party threatened to splinter into three rival factions.[12] Meanwhile, 50 Iranian truckers, accused of transporting arms to the alliance, were in Taliban custody.

Intervention by Iran was inevitable on a variety of counts: histrionic, in the case of the diplomats, Saremi and the drivers; chauvinist, to repel the

Pakistani-backed onslaught against Iranian influence in Afghanistan; religious, to prevent a sectarian massacre in Bamian; and military, to divert Taliban troops from the north and win Massoud and Hizb-i Wahdat a breathing space in which to regroup. As the war rhetoric flew, however, there was little scrutiny of how a diplomatic delegation, widely known to have coordinated supplies of arms to the Northern Alliance, was allowed to remain at its post even as an enemy, bent on revenge for the murder of Taliban prisoners in May 1997, was hammering at the gates and the frontier lay just 30 miles (50 kilometres) distant. The prospect that the diplomats were purposely sacrificed by elements in the polarised Iranian government to create a foreign policy dilemma for President Khatami, then seeking to mend fences in the world outside, rather than declare a state of war, was far from outlandish.

The hunt for evidence to connect bin Laden to the East African bombings galloped parallel – with scarcely a nose between – to Special Prosecutor Kenneth Starr's pursuit of testimony to illuminate the precise nature of President Bill Clinton's relationship with Monica Lewinsky. The former White House intern's secrets had transfixed America since January, when allegations of her sexual relationship with the president were first revealed. The disclosure hurled the US public into a frenzy of prime-time soul-searching, paralysing the workings of government and converting the US's highest office into a worldwide object of mirth. It was against this background that National Security Adviser Sandy Berger, Defense Secretary William Cohen, Joint Chiefs of Staff Chairman General Henry Shelton and CIA Director George Tenet met in Washington on 12 August to examine the US's options in response to the East African bombings, amid 'intelligence reports' that there was to be a gathering of the leaders of Islamist militant groups at bin Laden's training camp at Al-Badr, near Khost, on 20 August.[13]

US intelligence had been aware of the functions of Badr-1 and Badr-2 for at least two years, and possibly longer, but had taken no action for fear of estranging Pakistan and because, a generation earlier, the CIA had itself helped bin Laden establish the camps as a means of furthering the war against the Soviet Union.[14] As revelations of bin Laden's alleged activities tumbled forth from the press, a Senate enquiry appeared long overdue into the indecision displayed by the intelligence services when confronted with a real and present danger, spookily reconstituted from their own past misdemeanours. What precisely had the combined CIA and FBI leadership done to pre-empt bin Laden's two reported assassination bids against President Clinton? What efforts had been made to eliminate the Saudi, or disrupt his network in the wake of the bombings of the World Trade Center and Khobar Towers? Very little in the past two years, according to intelligence analysts. The sole attempt to kill or capture bin Laden, planned sometime prior to Bill Richardson's visit in April 1998, had been aborted due to the expected number of casualties. But was a fear of casualties a convincing enough justification for America's Praetorian Guard to allow a committed assassin to remain on the loose, or was it fear of exposure, or something more unthinkable? Blame-shirking, it seemed, had become a guiding principle of the CIA and the presidency equally in the days after the Nairobi bombing.

For all their posturing, only the intelligence services could identify targets worthy of American vengeance in its fight against this invisible, Islamist conspiracy. The protocols of terror required a minimum of two US strikes, one for each embassy. Intelligence provided three; one was unanimously fictive, the second, a debatable shot in the foot, while a third, in the form of a postscript, served as a gunboat to the distant, but no less alarming, polemic over nuclearisation in the Indian sub-continent. On 14 August, the four US military and spying chiefs briefed Clinton, who approved their plans and, three days later, US citizens were advised to leave Afghanistan.[15] At 6.30 GMT on 20 August, as Monica Lewinsky lay dreaming of the detail she would reveal to the Grand Jury later that day about oral sex and fondling, 70–100 Tomahawk cruise missiles were launched at targets in Khartoum, Sudan and near Khost. The Afghan-directed missiles contained 166 bomblets each of 3.3 lbs and were designed – like Lewinsky's confession, perhaps – to cause maximum damage over a wide area, rather than to take out a single, pinpointable target.

The missiles purred across the Arabian Sea and Pakistani fields before dropping, on a satellite's instructions, into four terrorist training camps in the valleys around Khost. Two were administered by Harakat ul-Mujahedin (HUM), schooling militants to fight in Kashmir; a third, Al-Farooq, trained 'Arabs'; while the fourth, situated ten miles west of the city and controlled by bin Laden, was Al-Badr, otherwise known as Zhawar Kili Al-Badr.[16] The Saudi had called a Pakistani journalist on his satellite phone three hours before the bombing, allowing US electronic tracking to confirm his presence in the camp.[17] In September, he passed a message to the London-based *Al-Quds al-Arabi* saying six followers had been killed, three of them Yemeni, two Egyptians and a Saudi.[18] He was unharmed, having unexpectedly left the camp at first light, but reports of lumbago or kidney trouble circulated for some weeks after and he next appeared in Kandahar walking with the aid of a cane.[19]

HUM's casualties were higher. HUM Secretary-General Fazi Rahman Khalili, whose party was implicated in the murder of four Western hostages in Kashmir, claimed that 21 of his men were killed and 40 wounded in a camp that he called an 'educational institution'.[20] Post-strike conditions at Al-Farooq, the least known of the camps, were not revealed, though the existence of a camp dedicated to training Middle Eastern Arabs should have caused uneasiness. But one of the Tomahawks launched that morning landed – but did not explode – at Kharan, close to the nuclear-testing facility in the Chagai Hills in Baluchistan. It exposed, accidentally or intentionally, Islamabad's amateurish vulnerability as a new-wave, nuclear contender.[21]

President Clinton broke the news of the missile strike at a press conference in the resort island of Martha's Vineyard, calling bin Laden's network 'as dangerous as any state we face'. Under pressure to deny that US foreign policy had degenerated into a tool of the president's legal team, Defense Secretary William Cohen and George Tenet, director of the CIA, responded with remarks that gave flesh to bin Laden's new profile as a psychological mastermind who dwelled in permanent half-light, planning the next urban cataclysm while seeking to acquire chemical, biological and nuclear weapons for more devastating purposes.

The second major target of the 20 August attack was the Al-Shifa pharmaceutical plant near Khartoum, a factory allegedly constructed with bin Laden's financial assistance in the early 1990s and which, US intelligence insisted, was engaged in the production of VX nerve gas. The assertion was founded upon samples of a substance known as EMPTA, easily convertible into VX, that were collected a few months before the strike from the soil near the plant by CIA-trained agents. Washington maintained that Saddam Hussein had evacuated part of his biochemical arsenal to Khartoum prior to the Gulf War and that bin Laden was using the plant to produce weapons of mass destruction.

In fact, it was not bin Laden who owned Al-Shifa at all, but Saleh Idris, a Sudanese multimillionaire with intimate links to the two Saudi tycoons who names crop up time and again in the history of the *jihad*, the BCCI scandal, the scramble for Central Asian energy and Al Qa'ida: Khalid bin Mahfouz and Mohammed Hussein al-Amoudi. Idris moved to Saudi Arabia in 1976 where he was hired to work as an accountant in bin Mahfouz's National Commercial Bank, the largest bank in the world. Within a few years, he became bin Mahfouz's financial adviser, personally leading the negotiations with the BCCI receivers and US financial authorities that led to the banker escaping prosecution in exchange for some $262 million in compensation and fines. Idris attributed his wealth to commissions and occasional business deals with both bin Mahfouz and al-Amoudi, his Addis Ababa-based partner in the Delta-Nimir oil joint venture.[22]

Though the US suspected Idris of acting as a front for bin Laden's continuing business activities in Sudan, Khartoum categorically reiterated that Al-Shifa was nothing more than what it seemed, a factory in one of the world's poorest countries that produced medicines for children and vaccines for Sudan's multitudinous cattle. It called on the UN to hold an independent enquiry. Idris commissioned his own investigation from US security consultants, Kroll Associates while hiring as his lawyers the high-powered Washington partnership Akin, Gump, Strauss, Hauer & Feld, which also represents bin Mahfouz and al-Amoudi. But as far as Washington was concerned, the matter was closed.[23]

* * *

In what followed the US failure to bomb bin Laden into oblivion in August 1998 there was an echo of the attack three years earlier on the Pakistani embassy after the fall of Herat to the Taliban. In both cases, the mob was summoned to the street and a delegation that had breezily presumed immunity to events on the ground – even as it appeared to work hand in glove with the aggressor – discovered it had become the focus of orchestrated, public rage.

It was the UN's turn, after Khost, to suffer for the ambiguity of its role. Protests erupted across Pakistan within hours of the strike and thousands marched though the derelict streets of Kabul to protest in front of the empty US embassy in Wazir Akhbar Khan. In Jalalabad, the UN compound was set ablaze and, across the border, UN staff were hastily evacuated from Peshawar to the capital.

Lieutenant Calo Carmine, a UN military observer from Italy, and the French diplomat Eric Lavertu, were driving to their offices on the morning after the Khost attack, when a pickup loaded with armed men overtook and fired at their clearly-marked jeep. Carmine was hit in the chest, Lavertu in the hand. 'This was not an error, but a reaction to yesterday's American attack,' said the Italian chargé d'affaires.[24] Carmine later died of his wounds. The authorities arrested two Pakistani suspects, leading in time to the macabre scenario whereby the Italian's grieving mother was invited to Kabul to carry out the execution by Kalashnikov in accordance with Taliban justice. In spite of their outrage at the US attack, the Taliban were clearly mortified by the assassination. Armed escorts were provided for the last 20 international staff on their final journey to the Khyber Pass.

Afghanistan had joined the small club of states that could no longer guarantee the safety of their foreign 'guests' – except one.

Pakistan was also rocked by disorder and not solely in the streets. Amid rumours of further strikes, Prime Minister Sharif was accused by the opposition of having received advance warning of the raid – painting him as a collaborator with US 'anti-Islamism' – while columnists speculated that the country might be so destabilised that its nuclear capability could fall into the hands of HUM's Fazi Rahman Khalil or Maulana Fazl ul-Rahman, head of the pro-Taliban Jamiat ul-Ulama-i Islam. Islamabad could not be seen to be hindering Washington's pursuit of bin Laden, but popular opinion would not allow it to assist in his capture. 'The possibility of backlash is there,' said former ISI head Hamid Gul, 'if people feel that the government helped Americans in the "get-Osama" operation.'[25] Whether or not the government had prior knowledge of the strike, the Tomahawks exposed Pakistan as a co-sponsor of 'terrorism' simply by tolerating training camps so close to its borders.

The only US voice raised in Pakistan's defence was that of James Woolsey, CIA director in the first Clinton administration, who deplored the attacks on HUM and warned of the dangers of a pro-Indian bias stealing into US handling of regional policy: 'We do not have a dog in this fight. Depending on who you believe, these people are terrorists or freedom fighters.' He queried the value of the phrase 'states sponsoring terrorism'. In Sudan and Afghanistan, he said, individuals were richer than states: 'it is a case of terrorists sponsoring the state' and 'the state is a victim'.[26]

The US attacks were sufficient to tip the prime minister towards a significant concession to the extreme conservatives, a direction he might in time have chosen anyway to strengthen his power base, but one which nonetheless confirmed the fear that Pakistan, a former Cold War satrap, was sliding inexorably towards 'talibanisation'. Ten days after Khost, Sharif committed his government to introducing *sharia* law by the end of the year. 'Today in Afghanistan ...,' he elaborated, 'I have heard that one can safely drive a vehicle full of gold at midnight without fear. I want this kind of system in Pakistan.'[27] 'That will doubtless bring peace,' responded the Human Rights Commission of Pakistan, 'the peace of the graveyard.'[28]

If Islamabad was anxious about its loss of Islamist 'face', the Taliban were more concerned by the US challenge to their sense of sovereign and personal integrity, the *pashtunwali*. Mullah Mohammed Omar arguably had no dog in the fight either, preferring to address the immediate problem of recognition by persuading the UN to return to Kabul, to seeing his aid-dependent economy further martyred for a cause in which Afghanistan had no obvious stake. It was less than two weeks since the conquest of Mazar and Iran was still in a high lather about its diplomats. Massoud's forces, meanwhile, were bottled up in the valleys of Parwan, Takhar and Badakhshan provinces, clinging to the arms trade through a single river crossing in the far-off Wakhan Corridor. Immediate pursuit was vital to prevent their resupply and reorganisation. But bin Laden was a guest and none of Washington's charges convinced the mullah that his friend was guilty. Omar was in the typically Afghan trap of hearing ultimata from a superpower and the genetic reaction had been mapped out centuries ago. 'Even if all the countries in the world unite,' he said the morning after the raid, 'we would defend Osama by our blood.'[29]

Halfway through September, Saudi Arabia, withdrew its diplomats from Kandahar and cut off the movement's funding. Riyadh's rupture with the Taliban leader was threatening in the extreme. The Saudi intelligence service, Mukhabarat, had cleared bin Laden of involvement in the Khobar Towers bombing in 1997 – much to the disgust of the US – so the 'down-grading' of its diplomatic links with Afghanistan signalled that Riyadh had either been bullied back into some semblance of obedience after the African bombings, or had determined to press more forcefully for bin Laden's extradition. By November the collapse in hard currency inflows from both Saudi Arabia and the UN relief effort had the movement teetering on bankruptcy amid a wave of defections by fair-weather friends in the north.

In spite of the Khost bombing and the disappointing Richardson mission, the US continued its efforts to negotiate the extradition of bin Laden in a series of letters to the Afghan ambassador to Pakistan, Mulawi Saeed ur-Rehman Haqqani. He refused to accept delivery of one such letter on 1 September but, three days later, dispatched a lowly *chowkidar* to take the envelope.[30] It specified Washington's willingness to speed up the process of recognition in exchange for bin Laden – a remarkable offer in view of other bones of contention with the West. 'This seems to be the only hurdle in winning recognition ...,' Mullah Omar said two months later when the overture was finally exhausted. 'Other issues, like respect for human and women's rights and control of drug-trafficking, are no longer mentioned as vigorously as in the past.'[31]

Mohammed Omar was prepared to ground the Saudi, but not to surrender him. After Khost, bin Laden learned an important lesson about the traceability of his satellite phone and calls to the press fell off thereafter. 'We asked him to refrain from military and political activities,' the Mullah said, using the euphemisms of command. 'Bin Laden has accepted our advice and promised to abide by it.'[32] But on 14 September, the irrepressible terrorist sent word to the London-based *Al-Quds al-Arabi*, denying that he had been placed under house arrest, though the paper's editor, Abd Al-Bari Atwan, later relayed the message that 'they put him up in a house, a safe house and prevented any outside contacts' – which amounted to much the same.[33] Atwan was certain of one thing: 'The man has been attacked by the Americans and usually when he threatens, he delivers. We should take this threat as seriously as we can.'[34]

In spite of the Mullah's confidence, evidence against his friend was fast accumulating. On 22 September, German police arrested Mamdouh Mahmud Salim, bin Laden's alleged weapons procurer and accountant, while buying used cars in Bavaria. Two days later, police in London arrested Khalid al-Fawwaz, of the Saudi dissident group Advice and Reform Committee, along with Adel Abdul Mageed Abdul-Abari and five other Egyptians, all known associates of bin Laden. Abdul-Abari had been sentenced to death *in absentia* for a bomb attack in Cairo and was identified as 'instigator' in the killing of 58 foreign tourists at the Luxor temple complex in November 1997. In Texas, FBI agents picked up Wadih el-Hage, bin Laden's former secretary in Sudan, who was also a friend of the Nairobi suspect, Mohammed Saddiq Odeh, and currently managed a Fort Worth tyre shop. He was charged with eleven counts of lying during a Grand Jury investigation into Al Qa'ida's attempts to procure chemical weapons, and for providing logistical support and training to 'the persons who attacked the US and UN forces in Somalia in 1993 and the early part of 1994'.[35] El-Hage's housemate in Kenya, moreover, was Haroun Fazil, a native of the Comoros Islands suspected of coordinating the Nairobi bombing, and who carried a $2 million bounty on his head.[36]

While Taliban leaders weighed the contradictory demands of friendship and financial advantage, the Iranian crisis rumbled on across the western frontier, rising in tenor as the bodies of the diplomats finally surfaced. Around 16,500 Taliban were airlifted to the border to repel an anticipated incursion, and there were suggestions that Iranian air attacks were only averted in mid-August through back-channel contacts between Washington and Tehran concerning the US's imminent plans for Khost.[37] If true, it pointed to a flattering degree of consultation between capitals at loggerheads since the overthrow of the Shah 20 years earlier and casts an intriguing light on the State Department's reluctance to brand the East African bombings as acts of the state-sponsored terrorism pioneered by Tehran. As late as 12 September, the state-owned daily *Jomhouri Eslami* was continuing to play it straight: 'The end is still not clear in the savage genocide which the evil triangle of America, Saudi Arabia and Pakistan have launched, but all indications are that the Taliban and their blood-thirsty backers have sharpened their swords for further crimes against Afghanistan's oppressed peoples.'[38] On 16 September, UK Foreign Office Minister Derek Fatchett applied soothing balm from Qatar: 'We do understand Iranian anguish and frustration, but the best way to resolve that would be through diplomatic, and not military, action.'[39] Five days later, US Secretary of State Madeleine Albright and Iranian Foreign Minister Kamal Kharazi took tea together in New York in the two states' highest-level meeting in 20 years and one of the most surprising rapprochements of the decade.

Whatever US and Iranian intentions, their missiles and threats had bought time for Massoud, a 'caged animal' hemmed in on three sides, who was using one of his last Mil-17 helicopters to ferry personal possessions to Tajikistan in readiness for exile, according one Taliban commander.[40] A visiting French journalist painted a sombre portrait in October of the Lion of Panjshir and his 'Christ-like thinness', a Napoleon stripped of power gazing down through the chopper's windows at the fleeting northern valleys he had fought over for two decades while clearing his mind for the grinding haggle with Russians at the airport in Dushanbe.[41] This was Massoud the Last *Mujahid*: his enemies and allies alike – Rabbani, Dostum, Khalili, Ismail Khan, Hekmatyar, Abdul Malik, Haqqani, Khalis and the rest – had all died, defected or fled the field.

He alone, and the 200–300 Tajik and Pashtun commanders who piled into a mosque in the Panjshir valley to hear him speak, retained the right to wear the *pakol*, the emblem not solely of the *jihad* against the Soviets, but of an Afghan nationalism overtaken by a modern obscurantism. He mocked the 'Ubuesque' regime in Kabul, but talked to his followers as a comrade not as a demagogue, and remained convinced, even after two decades of combat and intrigue, that they were still fighting a war of resistance against Pakistani colonialism. 'We have lost Mazar-i Sharif,' he explained wearily. 'The commander did what the officers of Basir Salangi did here at the Salang Tunnel, when they went over to the Taliban, or Abdul Malik in the province of Faryab. He betrayed, sold out. He delivered his city for a fistful of dollars.' Massoud regretted not becoming the engineer for which he initially studied – a luxury enjoyed throughout the *jihad* by Osama bin Laden.[42] This was a leader with his back to the rocks after 20 years of fighting, now reverting to the same whispered appeal he had employed in the corridors of his youthful rebelliousness. But he was not yet at the end of his charm, or the unique traits which made him

Massoud, a general able to conjure confidence from the bleakest emptiness in the world. A rare personal photograph, one year earlier, captured the love-light streaming in both directions between his eyes and those of his son, then seven and obviously as spoilt as a *khan*. Exile was as unconscionable as breaking that beam.

The loss on 11 August of Massoud's supply base in Taloqan was grave, but it was not fatal to a man accustomed to eluding the Soviets' far superior arsenal, while the Taliban faced the overwhelming task of imposing their will upon the great swathe of territory that fell under their rule after the capture of Mazar-i Sharif. Manpower was the immediate problem. In spite of their ethnic ties, the northern Pashtun minorities previously sided with either Dostum or Hizb-i Wahdat on their terms, and were largely untrustworthy. Massoud's own objective was to open fresh supply lines for food and weapons to the Panjshir valley before the snow. He retained Shomali Plain 30 miles northeast of Kabul, a position that allowed him to pin down Taliban forces in the capital as well as ensure a trickle of munitions through Bagram air base. Heavier weapons, it was hoped, would soon arrive. In early autumn, an entire train carrying 700 tonnes of Iranian ordnance for Massoud was intercepted in Osh, Kyrgyzstan, providing an insight into the scale of regional gun-running.[43]

What Massoud lacked and badly needed were allies, not only for a counter-attack – if he could put one together – but to convince the UN that a multi-ethnic, broad-based resistance to Taliban rule had survived the Mazar defeat. Dostum was out of the picture and Abdul Malik made a less reliable successor. Karim Khalili, the Hizb-i Wahdat chief, fled after losing Bamian.[44] Other Shia chiefs had defected and were rewarded with appointments in a parallel campaign by the Taliban to convince the UN that their government was also broad-based before the Credential Committee met in mid-October.[45]

Massoud's comeback started on 4 September with a two-pronged, pre-dawn attack from Bagram along the New and Old Roads, and a barrage of rockets to knock out the runways at Kabul airport. Hizb-i Wahdat launched a linked attack into Wardak, backed by artillery and tanks. On the 13 and 14 September, 70 more civilians died in rocket attacks on the capital, though Massoud denied responsibility and the casualties occurred in the very Tajik districts that were his own constituency.[46] Kabul braced for a repeat of the sieges of Hekmatyar and the Taliban. On 8 October, Massoud wrote to the US Senate Committee on Foreign Relations, then holding a hearing on Afghanistan.

Against all odds, we, meaning the free world and Afghans, halted and checkmated Soviet expansionism a decade ago. But the embattled people of my country did not savour the fruits of victory. Instead, they were thrust in a whirlwind of foreign intrigue, deception, great-gamesmanship and internal strife ... We Afghans erred too. Our shortcomings were as a result of political innocence, inexperience, vulnerability, victimisation, bickering and inflated egos. But by no means does this justify what some of our so-called Cold War allies did to undermine this just victory and unleash their diabolical plans to destroy and subjugate Afghanistan.

He wrote of the 'dark accomplishment' which had handed his country over to 'fanatics, extremists, terrorists, mercenaries, drug mafias and professional murderers'. He blamed Pakistan, accusing it of fielding 28,000 paramilitary and military staff to stiffen the Taliban occupation. 'Three major concerns,' he concluded, ' – namely terrorism, drugs and human rights – originate from Taliban areas but are instigated from Pakistan, thus forming the inter-connecting angles of an evil triangle. For many Afghans, regardless of ethnicity or religion, Afghanistan, for the second time in one decade, is once again an occupied country.'[47] 'Evil triangles' recur often in the region's rhetoric, but this one emitted the faint chimes of Najibullah's prophecy.

Four days after the meeting in the mosque, a new alliance, composed of the same 200–300 commanders and headed by Massoud, was announced. Unlike the UIFLA and CDA it replaced, the new arrangement adopted a centralised structure of command. On 19 October, it enjoyed its first success with the recapture of Taloqan.[48] According to Taliban sources, the Massoud fighters who defected in August had been issued three guns each, with orders to surrender one to their new overlords and to bury the remaining two for a future uprising. The Taliban were taken as they slept.[49] Similar localised rebellions were reported from Baghlan, Faryab, Jawzjan, Samangan, Kunduz and Balkh the following month.[50] Massoud's spokesman claimed this reduced the movement's share of the country from 90 to 70 per cent.[51]

Resistance was apparently gathering in the 'settled' zones, conquered by the Taliban in 1996. In October, Justice Minister Mullah Mohammed Turabi launched a three-week purge in Jalalabad that scooped up 400 Khalq officers and 21 generals, once part of the Afghan army, but allied for the past two years with the local Taliban.[52] Among the 2,000 detainees were tribal leaders, men with links to the peace movement and children, who were held hostage to force their parents out of hiding. By 1 November, the jails were so full that detainees were transferred to Kandahar where some died.[53] The reasons behind the crackdown were obscure. Massoud claimed that commanders in Jalalabad, Kunar, Nooristan, Laghman and Nangarhar were still loyal and ready to rise at any moment.[54] But rumours also flew of a rift between Mohammed Omar and Mullah Rabbani, with the latter pressing for accommodation with Massoud, a policy endorsed by the remnants of the Afghan officer class. Even General Tanai, Najibullah's former defence minister and a crucial sponsor of the Taliban in its early months, was arrested and Mullah Rabbani vanished to Dubai for two months.[55] Jalalabad's deputy governor, however, stated clearly, without mentioning any names, that the Taliban had narrowly averted a coup. 'They were backed by a foreign power,' he said, 'and were aiming to explode bombs and fuel lawlessness before taking control.'[56]

In December, Mullah Rabbani was forced by articles in the Pakistani press to deny he had resigned: he had been absent from Kabul, he said, merely for reasons of 'stress'.[57]

13   Satellites and Stars

'If you look at the past, we don't think it strange that America will attack us. Unfortunately it is our fate that everyone attacks us.' Mullah Wakil Ahmad Mutawakil, personal secretary to Mullah Mohammed Omar[1]

The US kept up the pressure on Kandahar to yield up bin Laden, as much out of respect for consistency as for any great wealth of evidence. On 4 November, the Manhattan Federal Court issued a sealed indictment – the usual procedure for a fugitive from justice – chronicling 238 separate charges against the Saudi, from participating in the 1993 World Trade Center bombing and funding Islamist groups in New Jersey to conspiring with Sudan, Iran and Iraq to attack US installations. Informed sources said the indictment contained little hard evidential detail on bin Laden's involvement in the East African bombings, for which he denied any responsibility the following December, while still condoning the actions of the 'real' perpetrators.[2]

In a press conference around the same time, at a tent in the desert near Kandahar, he was his usual equivocal self in response to queries as to whether he had acquired yet more terrifying weapons in the struggle to 'liberate' Saudi Arabia, as the CIA had alleged after the destruction of the Al-Shifa plant. 'We don't consider it a crime if we have tried to have nuclear, chemical or biological weapons,' he opined sniffily, adding 'we have a right to defend ourselves and to liberate our holy land.'[3] This was three months after Mullah Mohammed Omar banned the Saudi from media comment and two months after the Manhattan indictment, much of it based on the confession of the former tyre store manager Wadih el-Hage, friend of a suspect in the Nairobi conflagration, Mohammed Saddiq Odeh.[4] El-Hage was charged by the same court with attempting to solicit bio-chemical weapons for Al Qa'ida, putting bin Laden squarely in the frame. The Saudi admitted to an acquaintance with his accuser, though he claimed they had not met in years.[5]

Four days after the indictment, on 8 November, the CIA's Counter-Terrorism Reward Programme dangled a $5 million bounty apiece for information leading to the arrest of bin Laden and 'another man', each of which was more than double the previous reward ceiling of $2 million. The 'other man', bin Laden's apparent equal in the annals of terror, was

Mohammed Atef, also known as 'Sheikh Tayseer Abdullah', a former Egyptian police officer who had served as the Saudi's head of personal security since 1983. The CIA insisted that Atef was the logistical architect of the East African bombings, a charge the Egyptian vehemently denied, saying that Washington's failure to apprehend the real perpetrators led it to blame everything on him and his master.[6] Bin Laden took a very different view of the cupidity of his nearest companions: 'I did not even change one of my bodyguards as a result. None of the "Arab-Afghans" are so cheap as to be purchased by the Americans.'[7]

If bin Laden sounded relaxed at this point, the strain was definitely telling on the Taliban. Karl Inderfurth, the assistant secretary of state for South Asia, had let it be known that there were no alternatives: give up bin Laden or face further bombardment.[8] The day after Washington posted the rewards, on 9 November, Mullah Mohammed Omar approved the creation of a judicial inquiry to examine Western allegations against bin Laden according to principles of *sharia*, fixing a deadline of 20 November for the submission of evidence to implicate the Saudi in acts of terrorism, subversion or sabotage. There was no response from Washington, which was in no position to negotiate an extradition case with a government it did not recognise, and in no mood either to have its own exhaustive investigations, however flawed, dismissed by a cabinet of illiterate and compliant mullahs. The emir was bound to protect the defendant by ties of friendship, the law of Pashtun hospitality and the Taliban's still vaguely defined sense of solidarity with the crusade to liberate the holy places of Saudi Arabia. But he was also of the view that surrendering the Saudi would lead quickly to reconciliation with the US and, quite possibly, a fast track to diplomatic recognition, the return of the UN and an avalanche of donor investment. If so assured, Omar's next moves were either deeply confused, or suicidally honourable.

On 11 November, Chief Justice Noor Mohammed Saqib, the judge in charge of the case, said: 'America is looking for an excuse to fire more rockets on our dear Afghanistan and that excuse is bin Laden.'[9] If the comment gave an inkling of the state of heightened tension in Kandahar, it also underlined the probable outcome if the court decided to acquit. One day later, the Taliban leader flirted with that prospect by ruling that the 238-point indictment against bin Laden was inadmissible evidence, because it was 'old material which was not convincing enough', effectively pre-empting the court's decision.[10] By the evening of 19 November, not a single scrap of fresh testimony had crossed the chief justice's desk, prompting him to extend the deadline a further ten days. On 30

November, Saqib officially closed the case against the Saudi for lack of evidence, declaring the defendant a 'man without sin' and free to go. Mohammed Omar's attempt to solve his bin Laden problem had been a game of legal and political solitaire.

The advancing winter was accompanied by squalls of further bad news. The Taliban's only corporate friend, UNOCAL, suspended work in Afghanistan immediately after the missile attacks near Khost. But as grievous as this blow to its pipeline dream, it announced, was the slide in world oil prices to below $12 a barrel, which forced it to close down three of its four Central Asian offices. On 4 December, the company formally wound up the Afghan venture amid speculation that the Argentinian rival, Bridas, would pick up its share in the Centgas consortium.[11] Two days later, Saudi Arabia held secret talks with President Rabbani, amid rumours that Riyadh had swung its support behind Massoud, because of the emir's protection of bin Laden.[12] The same day, an assassination squad of four Afghans was intercepted and liquidated less than a mile from the Saudi's house in Kandahar.[13] Saudi interest in eliminating the renegade was confirmed in the new year, when a second murder attempt was reported, this time on the orders of Prince Salman bin Abdel-Aziz, governor of Riyadh, for a fee of $250,000. Prince Salman, one of the most influential full-brothers of King Fahd, had worked as deputy minister of petroleum affairs since July 1995.[14] In January, the Taliban accused Massoud of conniving at bin Laden's death with US officials. Even more intriguing than the prospect that Massoud was negotiating a $5 million contract killing with the CIA was the notion – in Taliban eyes, at least – that, after more than a decade, Washington had come to see some virtue in Afghanistan's most resilient military commander.[15]

On 8 December, the UN Security Council passed a motion of censure on the Taliban for its failure to conclude a ceasefire with the alliance; for killing Iranian diplomats the previous August; the slaughter in Mazar-i Sharif; profiting from the narcotics trade; and harbouring terrorists. The only dissenting voice in the chamber was that of Ahmad Khan, Pakistan's UN ambassador, who called the resolution 'one-sided'. Four days later, Prime Minister Nawaz Sharif arrived in Washington to receive what was described as a personal dressing down from President Clinton, both for supporting the Taliban and for providing hospitality to other terrorist groups. By February, reports in the local press alleged the existence of a photograph taken in Lahore of Sharif, then the governor of Punjab, in affable conversation with bin Laden himself.[16] It never came to light.

In US eyes, the case against bin Laden was rock solid. Some 80 alleged confederates had been picked up as far apart as Malaysia and Montevideo, and Washington claimed that the Al Qa'ida network had penetrated over 25 countries, including the US. Officials claimed to have averted seven further terrorist attacks on US embassies in Albania, Azerbaijan, Côte d'Ivoire, Tajikistan, Uganda and Uruguay since the August bombings, as well as another on the US's Prince Sultan airbase in Saudi Arabia.[17] Efforts to freeze bin Laden's fortune – officially revised downwards to a more manageable $250 million – had come to nothing: the funds were disguised behind 80 front companies, while transfers were conducted by unknown intermediaries briefed by satellite phone or note of hand.[18] But a backlash against the theory of a global bin Laden conspiracy was gathering pace. Former CIA official Milton Bearden, with more than a passing involvement in the anti-Soviet *jihad*, warned that Washington was turning bin Laden into a 'North star' for the entire Moslem world. In spite of his connections with the discredited BCCI, the evidence against Saleh Idris, owner of the Al-Shifa pharmaceutical plant in Khartoum, was soon to evaporate, leaving him free to take out a $30 million legal suit for damages.[19] In Kandahar, a different story was rehearsed about the wealth of its guest. Bin Laden was impoverished, living on remittances from an elder brother and unable to fulfil his personal pledge to Mullah Omar of building in the Taliban capital the second largest mosque in the world. To visiting journalists, the Saudi played the family card: he passed the time playing football, riding horses deep into the desert or with his three wives and many children.[20]

In early February 1999, Mullah Omar sent envoys to Washington and Riyadh, asking the former for advice in dealing with their guest, and the other for guarantees that it would take care of his dependants in the event of his surrender. Deputy Foreign Minister Mulawi Abdul Jalil Akhund, meeting Inderfurth face to face for the first time since the Khost raid, reiterated his master's position: 'We cannot expel the Saudi national as he is a guest of the Afghan nation since the *jihad* days.' Inderfurth responded with his sternest warning yet of the consequences if bin Laden were not expelled, a message turned into hard-and-fast policy some days earlier by Richard Clarke, Clinton's newly-appointed anti-terrorism tsar, who said the US reserved the right to retaliate against any country which knowingly harboured terrorists.[21] Deputy Secretary of State Strobe Talbott had accompanied Inderfurth on the flight to Pakistan. He told the Islamabad Institute of Strategic Studies that Afghanistan had become 'the focus of one of the first, most severe and ominous battles of the post-Cold War world – the battle against the forces of terrorism, extremism and intolerance'. But still the Taliban were not named on the State Department's list of proscribed terrorist organisations, unlike many others then enjoying the hospitality of Afghanistan's many training camps.

On 13 February – less than two weeks after the Inderfurth threat – bin Laden vanished. 'He left his residence in Kandahar some days ago without telling us where was going,' the one-eyed Mullah related. 'Contact with him has been broken. We think he is hiding somewhere, perhaps inside Afghan territory.'[22] The Taliban had 'confiscated' his satellite phone four days earlier, stripping him of any further room for financial or defensive manoeuvre, but other motives for the Saudi's evasion emerged as speculation and rumour fused to produce a riddle at once mythic and disingenuous. There had been a shoot-out between bin Laden's personal bodyguards and the Taliban squad assigned to protect, or restrain, him.[23] The emir snubbed his old comrade at the *Eid al-Fitr* feast: 'Bin Laden was made to wait for about two hours outside and, when they met, [Mullah Mohammed Omar] was very cold. Bin Laden understood that he is not wanted anymore.'[24]

But what other havens were accessible? The Taliban's sole diplomatic coup in the preceding three months was the promise of recognition from the breakaway republic of Chechnya, although Yemeni notables paid court to the fugitive in late November to 'discuss future anti-US operations'.[25] An appropriate asylum was possible in either location, but each required a dangerous transit across exposed terrain, as did other mooted bolt-holes in Iraq and Somalia. In the third week of February, the absconder was reported to have crossed the Iranian border, north of Herat; to be in Hekmatyar's reduced strongholds in Kunduz and Baghlan; in Jalalabad, where he needed hospital access for his reported kidney complaint; or about to join forces with Saddam Hussein, a prospect that sent a delicious – but improbable – shiver down the spine of a suggestible Western press. The two men were the fangs of hugely different snakes. The sightings were denied by spokesmen in the various destinations. Mullah Ismail Haqq, leader of the Moslem Ulama Society of Pakistan, brought some common sense to the rescue in February: 'Bin Laden is neither weak nor stupid [enough] to leave Afghanistan and the Taliban is not that ruthless [as] to ask him to leave.'[26] On 24 February, the Taliban said they had sent an envoy to Jalalabad, where bin Laden was holed up in an old Hizb-i Islami base, appealing for him to return to Kandahar. He had demurred, saying 'he felt freer there'.[27] Taliban claims to ignorance of bin Laden's final whereabouts were incessantly undermined by chattering within the movement.

But was bin Laden even alive? Several witnesses – including the emir's secretary, Mullah Wakil Ahmad Mutawakil – claimed in garrulous moments that the Saudi had left Kandahar by night in a convoy of 20 Land Cruisers, accompanied by his teenage sons Ali and Abdullah, his head of security Mohammed Atef, Ayman al-Zawahiri of Egypt's Jihad, the sons of the blind Sheikh Omar Abdel Rahman, ten Taliban guards and his personal security cordon of Arab-Afghans, armed with Stingers to ward off pursuit by helicopter. Swathed in road dust and a halo of satellites and stars, the party headed north to a derelict Hizb-i Islami base at Khagrel in the Sheikh Hazrat mountains, 30 miles (50 kilometres) from Kandahar. Mutawakil insisted he knew nothing of their ultimate destination.[28] By such Pimpernel tactics – and in such august company – bin Laden dissolved into an Islamist mirror image of the Arthurian legend of the wounded king ready to arise with his comrades and sons when the call to battle once again resounded.

A different scenario was suggested by state radio in Tehran, a well-sourced – if little-believed – voice in the region.[29] Bin Laden had been murdered by the moderate faction of the Taliban and disposed of in the *dasht* to rid the emir of his troublesome guest and, quite as credibly, to claim the $10 million reward and relieve Washington of what had become a humiliating manhunt. The *New York Times* reluctantly agreed with Chief Justice Noor Mohammed Saqib that the evidence against bin Laden was skimpy in the extreme. 'Capturing bin Laden alive,' it reported, 'could deepen complications. American officials say that, so far, first-hand evidence that could be used in court to prove that he commanded the bombings has proven difficult to obtain. According to the public record, none of the informants involved in the case have direct knowledge of bin Laden's involvement.'[30] He was culpable only of using words to incite violence by sympathisers thousands of miles away. Trying him, it inferred, would prove more embarrassing than allowing him to melt away from the scene.

A rigorous radio silence was imposed as his convoy slunk away between the sands.

* * *

After the blaze of UNOCAL's gas ambitions at Khost in August 1998, the US, in principle, had no further interest in the fate of Afghanistan, beyond the burning desire to see bin Laden behind bars and the honour of its intelligence services vindicated. But even as Karl Inderfurth threatened blue murder from the wings, on-the-ground relations with the Taliban over bin Laden displayed a remarkable reticence by the Goliath of the post-Cold

War world. Yes, a reward had been posted and, yes, the assistant secretary of state made it abundantly clear that diplomatic recognition would depend upon Mullah Mohammed Omar handing bin Laden over to the US, or a third country, like Saudi Arabia. Elsewhere, an international intelligence operation was rounding up scores of his associates. But there was a remarkable reluctance to take any more direct action in Afghanistan, whether by challenging the Taliban over the Saudi's current whereabouts, or launching a cross-border raid to take him forcibly into custody. Wherever bin Laden was hiding, the Afghan whispering gallery guaranteed it would not remain secret for long.

Why did Washington fail to press its unquestionable advantages, preferring to genuflect to the unfathomable logic of 'Pashtun hospitality' rather than resort to the more dignified alternative of a snatch operation, followed by a high-profile trial in Manhattan? Certainly, there was the risk that US agents would be killed or captured and later presented to the world through the whetted lens of the media, but an operation was feasible with cut-outs, perhaps Arabs affiliated with Israel's Mossad intelligence agency. Big money was committed: a snatch was not beyond the realm of credibility. Admittedly, the pressure on President Clinton was not as sharp as in August 1998 when the Lewinsky affair made any foreign distraction desirable. The *New York Times* divulged part of the answer: the evidence against the Saudi was insufficient to convict on, apparently, any of the 238 counts in the secret Manhattan indictment. But the newspaper held back on the balance of logic. If it were not bin Laden, who then planned the Nairobi bombing and why was US intelligence so dilatory, first to admit that its initial theory had been wrong and, second, in advancing another hypothesis that might point to the real perpetrators? If there were no second hypothesis, of course, then the extravaganza that had become the hunt for bin Laden could as readily be construed as a cover-up, certainly of gross negligence by the US intelligence service when faced with a global threat to US life and property but, possibly, of a more far-reaching scandal.

On 26 January, Congressman Benjamin Gilman of New York, chairman of the International Relations Committee in the House of Representatives, gave a speech at the Indian Consulate to mark the country's Republic Day. He warned the diplomats of Pakistan's and Afghanistan's active promotion of terrorism abroad – particularly in Kashmir – and accused the State Department of 'failing to distinguish between friends and foes'. Gilman, a Jewish Republican, had served under former UN ambassador Jeanne Kirkpatrick and headed various congressional committees on human rights, narcotics trafficking and government reform. Though a fairly mundane recitation to his Indian listeners, his speech ended with a curious inference. Gilman emphasised the importance of bolstering relations with India and the Central Asian states in order 'to minimise the role of the US Embassy in Islamabad in future policy decisions concerning Afghanistan'.[31]

However limited, it was the first public reference by a member of the legislature to the possible existence of a covert US plan to aid the Taliban's rise to power. No motive was forthcoming and whether the Islamabad embassy acted autonomously or followed Washington's orders was not clearly elaborated. But in Gilman's stated view, the probity of its regional influence was in question. Most specifically, his doubts applied to the conduct of US policy in Afghanistan but, in speaking of that country, it was impossible to exclude the embassy's chemistry with the ISI – its historic mediator in Afghan affairs – and the ISI's own diverse portfolio of intrigues in the region. Gilman implied that a rogue US embassy was writing the regional script, contrary to national interests.

Dana Rohrabacher, a Democrat from Orange County, California, was also trying to discover the Taliban's secret sponsors. A colleague of Gilman on the House International Relations Committee, he had woven in and out of the Afghan peace process since a visit to Islamabad in August 1996. Five days after the Khost bombings, Rohrabacher wrote to the State Department requesting the release of cable traffic with Islamabad and Riyadh and all other documents pertinent to recent US policy on Afghanistan, a privilege due his committee. Three months later, Secretary of State Madeleine Albright promised the documents would soon arrive, but her departmental chiefs refused to comply. The following March, Rohrabacher told Inderfurth: 'For the State Department to be stonewalling us does nothing but confirm to us who believe the worst that there is the possibility of some skullduggery going on.'[32] Inderfurth denied the existence of any secret plan, insisting that the US favoured no faction and sought only a 'broad-based' government in Afghanistan.

On 21 May, the committee's chairman, Gilman, wrote to Albright, insisting that the documents arrive by 21 June. 'On numerous occasions,' said an exasperated Rohrabacher one month after the deadline passed, 'I have charged that the Clinton administration, despite statements to the contrary, has conducted a secret policy with Pakistan and Saudi Arabia to tolerate the creation, rise to power and ongoing tyranny [of] the Taliban.' It was now almost a year since Rohrabacher's original request and not a single page had been handed over. 'The urgent matters of terrorism, opium production and massive human rights violations in Afghanistan underscore the urgency of my request,' continued Congressman Gilman.

'In order to better protect US diplomatic missions and American personnel serving overseas, I ask the support of my colleagues to obtain US policy documents on Afghanistan.'[33] To this appeal from America's foremost foreign policy oversight committee, coming barely a year after the killings in Nairobi, there was a resounding silence from the State Department and in the US press.

For reasons best known in the Islamabad embassy, the US was pulling its punches in Afghanistan and keeping schtumm at home. Bin Laden was out of sight and, because there was no demonstrable urgency in running him to ground, his disappearence was clearly as welcome in Washington as in Kandahar. Gilman and Rohrabacher suspected the existence of an understanding, or a secret treaty, between the Taliban and the US, which had made American taxpayers morally accountable for the suppression of Afghan women's rights, the heroin epidemic at home and, by extension, for the victims of bombings carried out by terrorists under Kandahar's protection. However, like any agreement – if indeed it existed – it was made to be broken when conditions were favourable. At what point it may have been 'broken' is impossible to guess for a number of bifurcations had emerged between US and Taliban interests in the previous two years: Richardson's aborted peace mission, the embassy bombings, the Khost attack, UNOCAL's withdrawal from the pipeline project and the refusal to surrender bin Laden.

What is clear is that the intensive diplomacy between Karl Inderfurth and Kandahar over the winter of 1998–99 did little to restrain either the Taliban or its supporters within the Pakistani government. In early October 1998, Mullah Mohammed Omar offered to shut down Afghanistan's entire opium production in exchange for diplomatic recognition, destroying 34 processing laboratories in Nangarhar as a token of his good intentions. No one took the offer seriously: the owners, all Afridis from the Khyber Pass, received advance warning and escaped across the border.[34] Within less than a year, local production soared to over 4,600 tonnes of dried opium, threatening a heroin price war on the streets of the UK and Europe. Taliban influence, meanwhile, was extending to the refugee camps in Pakistan with the government's apparent approval; in November, girls' schools and four refugee universities were closed down.[35] In December, a campaign of assassinations against dissidents at home expanded to include Pashtun exiles in Peshawar, culminating in attempts against the wife of the respected former mujahedin commander for Kabul, Abdul Haq, and his brother Haji Qadir, ex-governor of Nangarhar and an ally of Ahmad Shah Massoud.[36] Soon it targeted former associates of ex-king Zahir Shah, men with track records in the peace movement like former senator Abdul Ahad Karzai, father of Hamid Karzai, the head of the Popolzai clan of the Durrani Pashtuns.[37] At home, the Taliban demonstrated the same sure touch for public approbation. Six members of the Gurbuz tribe were killed in January near Khost when they refused to halt the egg-breaking competition traditionally held to honour the *Eid*.[38] On 3 March, leather jackets were banned and, twelve days later, car dealers were ordered to re-paint their gaudy signs in white and blue.[39]

The peace trail had grown cold since a limited exchange of prisoners of war the previous November. In February 1999, UN expatriates moved cautiously back to their stations after eight months' absence. With contrived timing, representatives of the Taliban and Massoud's Northern Alliance met in Ashgabat on 11 March for talks supervised by the UN's 6+2 Contact Group, comprising China, Iran, Pakistan, Tajikistan, Turkmenistan and Uzbekistan with the US and Russia. Four days later, 'in a spirit of sincerity, mutual respect and frankness', the rivals announced the formation of a new coalition to a less-than-excited planet, agreeing to meet a month later to hammer out the dilemma of who would head this compromise regime, if not the uncompromising Mullah Mohammed Omar? Within the fortnight, the two sides were locked in combat over Bamian, Massoud had resumed the rocketing of Kabul and Taliban officials pouted their utter refusal to negotiate with 'former communists'.[40] After yet another Central Asian summit failed to elicit the requisite outcome some months later, UN Secretary-General Kofi Annan criticised unnamed members of the 6+2 Group for only 'paying lip service to their own stated intentions', pointing out that peace negotiations in Afghanistan somehow always prefaced a new escalation in the fighting.[41]

This latest battle for Bamian re-emphasised the Taliban's now-total indifference to the hearts and minds of the defeated. Hizb-i Wahdat launched its attack shortly after the Ashgabat agreement was announced, profiting from a civilian uprising to seize the Shia city on 21 April. The Taliban recaptured it three weeks later. Two hundred and fifty Shias supected of fighting with the rebel force were locked inside their homes with their families and set on fire,[42] leading Mullah Mohammed Omar unusually to appeal on the radio for an end to the 'revenge killings'.[43] The pattern was echoed in Herat where a reported 25 Shias were lynched after an allegedly Iran-backed civil insurrection.[44] But the Bamian uprising ended with something of a historical flourish, as news came that the Koochi – Pashtun nomads granted grazing rights in Hazara lands by King Abdul Rahman Khan a century earlier – had returned to demand 'back rent' for the grasses lost in the 20 years since the Soviets collectivised local agriculture in 1978. The Taliban had taken a leaf from the dead king's book, in which the Koochis functioned as a trusted but ruthless buffer between Kabul and the rebellious Shias. In those days, a camel's life had been set at six times that of a Hazara; a Pashtun's at 1,000 camels.[45]

In the following month, a covert incursion into Kashmir by 400 Pakistani-backed mujahedin provoked a two-month border dispute with India, which again brought to the fore the likelihood of a conflict in newly-nuclearised South Asia – while deflecting attention from the much heavier concentration of Pakistani manpower now deployed alongside the Taliban. The force of Kashmiri freedom fighters, Afghan mercenaries and Pakistani irregulars sneaked into the snows overlooking the Srinagar–Kargil road in early May, transgressing the 450-mile Line of Control, which had demarcated the Indian and Pakistani sectors of Kashmir since 1949, precisely half a century earlier. The US had imposed sanctions after the nuclear tests the previous year and Pakistan earned international repudia-tion after Khost and the revelation that it had consistently abetted the training of terrorists for bloodshed abroad. Prime Minister Nawaz Sharif, meanwhile, was steadfastly dismantling the civil liberties introduced since the death of President Zia ul-Haq a decade earlier. It was at this juncture, with international political and economic pressures on Islamabad arguably at their most intense, that Pakistan chose to test the legitimacy of the Line of Control – without the risk of committing regular troops in an operation tantamount to an act of war.

Ex-president Burhanuddin Rabbani, still nominally head of the Northern Alliance, was quick to point out similarities between Pakistan's dual strategies in Kashmir and Afghanistan. In both, a far-from-representative domestic movement was beefed up by foreign volunteers and hired 'terrorists', whipped into military shape by retired regular officers and provided with fighting equipment by Pakistan. Afghanistan's London ambassador, Wali Massoud, the brother of the commander, went further: he said the ISI, the Taliban and terrorists from bin Laden's camps at Al-Badr met in Kabul three months earlier to coordinate both the Kargil expedition and the now customary summer offensive against the Northern Alliance.[46] This could so easily have been propaganda, an attempt by Massoud to bask in the same air of outraged innocence displayed by New Delhi throughout the Kargil crisis, but for the intelligence leached out of the field, not by the national security agencies – they shared information with no one – but by independent reporters.

The US never openly pondered the whereabouts of the hundreds, perhaps thousands of Arab and non-Afghan 'terrorists' who scattered like ants after the bombardment around Khost, but were no less dangerous after the disappearance of their mentor. Washington seemed obsessed by bin Laden, to the neglect of threats more immediate to hand. He came eerily back into focus in a 90-minute profile in June on the UAE's Al-Jazeera, a liberal TV station for the Gulf, which gave the Saudi his first chance to speak to his primary constituency in Arabic, an opportunity he would later return to.[47] News of his former disciples took one month more to emerge. In the third week of July, the subjugation of Bamian was claimed as the work not of Taliban, but Pakistani irregulars backed by 400 Arabs, loyal to bin Laden and newly incorporated as the new 'crack' 055 Brigade.[48] Arabs had been spared any role in earlier Taliban campaigns by virtue of their operational value overseas.[49] Now they were bivouacked under canvas with 3,000–5,000 Pakistani irregulars in Rishkor, a former army barracks outside Kabul turned training camp by Kashmir's Harakat ul-Mujahedin, prior to moving up to the front.[50] Transport planes flew in nightly from Pakistan in readiness for the coming offensive, an attack that analysts – and even the UN's special envoy, Lakhdar Brahimi[51] – warned was commanded by Pakistani officers and used seasoned Arab fighters in the vanguard.[52] Miles above the tented plain, the satellites peered selectively.

On Sunday 4 July, journalist Jason Burke awoke with the knowledge that his life would never rise to the same exalted timbre of professional euphoria it had achieved at the moment he opened his eyes. Emblazoned across that morning's *Observer* was his exclusive, revealing that Osama bin Laden was alive, well – though very paranoid – and squatting in an abandoned processing plant at Farm Hadda, the site of a Soviet-era project to develop an olive oil plantation on land irrigated by the Kabul river.[53] Bin Laden was spotted the previous Tuesday in a convoy on the road to Farm Hadda, three miles south of Jalalabad. There may have been three convoys, for pursuit had made the Saudi edgy. He rode in one vehicle, transferring to a second when instinct dictated, relaying messages through an aide to a third, which carried his satellite phone and hung back for fear of surveillance from the skies.[54] He had purged the Afghans from his circle and relied now for security on his trusty Arabs – though ten Arab families immediately escaped from the compound after Burke went public.[55] He anchored his story with quotes from Islamabad diplomats and the Jalalabad authorities who, in the Taliban fashion, avidly volunteered that bin Laden had offered to buy Farm Hadda outright – while denying he had been anywhere in the vicinity.[56] Burke's day was complete before the morning started: he had discovered what US intelligence was unable – or afraid – to find, though Jalalabad lay barely 70 miles away from its listeners across the Khyber Pass.

Five months had passed since bin Laden's disappearence, months characterised by prevarication on both sides but, within days of Burke's report, the trail of bin Laden was piping hot again. Thousands of hours of journalistic replastering went to shore up the shambles erected after his February evasion. From Cairo came the first of a stream of leaks that bin Laden had sustained in his hour of need by some $50 million in donations from prominent families in the Gulf, notably the unidentified proprietor of Saudi Arabia's largest advertising agency.[57] 'There's government money being laundered in the interest of keeping bin Laden away from Saudi Arabia,' charged Yossef Bodansky, head of a counter-terrorism committee in Washington, who went on to accuse Riyadh and Saudi businesses of paying bin Laden protection money to prevent their assets being targeted by Al Qa'ida: in short, to take his vengeance elsewhere.[58]

But relations between Osama, his family and the kingdom's most powerful business and political circles were far more understanding than Bodansky implied, and it was wilfully negligent of US intelligence not to condemn outright the latitude of collusion with his deadly aims and mission. One of the men detained for transfering funds to bin Laden was Khalid bin Mahfouz, 52, the former BCCI shareholder and owner of Saudi Arabia's National Commercial Bank (NCB), and Nimir Petroleum, a UNOCAL partner in the trans-Afghanistan pipeline project.[59] The transaction was discovered in April 1999 when an official Saudi audit revealed a $2 billion hole in NCB's accounts, and evidence of a $3 million transfer into the accounts of two Islamic charities, Islamic Relief and Blessed Relief, which the US then suspected of being fronts for bin Laden. The transfers, which began five years prior to their discovery, were used to finance Al Qa'ida attacks, including the 1995 assassination bid on President Hosni Mubarak of Egypt, according to intelligence sources.[60] By way of punishment, the Saudi authorities bought bin Mahfouz's majority share in NCB, stripped him of his passport and confined him to a military hospital in the northern town of Taef, where he was being treated for a 'drug problem'.[61] But administrative control of the NCB, depending on which report is believed, passed either to bin Mahfouz's brother, Mohammed, or to Mohammed Hussein al-Amoudi, his close friend and associate, head of the Capitol Trust Bank and Delta Oil, UNOCAL's other Saudi partner in Afghanistan.[62]

Meanwhile, in response to the horrendous publicity generated by its black sheep boy, the family firm in Saudi Arabia decided on 28 July to change the name of its mobile phone company from bin Laden to Ba'id ('Remote'). 'With a new name and logo,' said the accompanying press release, 'we reveal our new identity and we define our mission for the future.'[63]

14 The Bicycle Thieves

'In Pakistan, the Constitution has been violated more often than the honour of a woman who regularly walks the streets.' Ayaz Amir[1]

Prime Minister Nawaz Sharif had some idea of what was in store when he flew to Washington for talks with President Clinton on 4 July, the very morning that bin Laden was rediscovered to the wider world. Not until later would it emerge what had transpired behind the closed doors of Blair House, for nothing leaked out and Sharif denied bin Laden was ever discussed.[2] At home – in the best traditions of Pakistani policy-making – the Kargil incursion had briefly restored Sharif's star at the real risk of a nuclear confrontation, though what possible advantage might accrue from such a gamble remained obscure. It could, after all, have been an ISI ploy to distract domestic attention abroad, much as Clinton was believed to have attempted at Khost and Khartoum, when the Lewinsky enquiry was snapping at his heels. Meanwhile, Indian forces were gradually winkling the mujahedin out of their positions above the Srinagar–Kargil road. Sharif had asked for the meeting with Clinton; it is unlikely he relished its outcome.[3]

Three hours after entering Blair House, Sharif signed the Washington Agreement, committing Islamabad to the immediate withdrawal of its forces from beyond the Line of Control and the signing of the Comprehensive Test Ban Treaty by the end of the year. No such concessions were wrung from India, whose moral right to occupy Kashmir was consolidated, rather than held up to international condemnation, while the latter's first play of the nuclear card a year earlier entirely escaped US censure. With one stroke of the pen, Sharif inflicted lasting damage on the nation's prestige and his own ability to rule. He flew home to a country on the edge of mutiny, with army leaders threatening to withdraw support and the opposition united in their demands for his resignation. But he did not return entirely empty-handed: in exchange for capitulating over Kargil, Sharif had won Pakistan's military a free hand for one last gambit in Afghanistan.

Two days after the Washington Agreement, President Clinton announced sanctions against the Taliban, freezing $400,000 in assets held in US banks by the national airline and a further $24 million in conventional trade.[4] With no more forthright condemnation of the thousands of Pakistani and

Arab fighters mustering at Rishkor, the Taliban protectors of bin Laden and the 055 Brigade received the go-ahead to unleash the campaign which, it was fervently hoped, would finally put paid to Massoud.

There had been sporadic fighting in Samangan, Kunduz, Balkh and the Shomali Plain since the collapse of the Ashgabat agreement in the spring, but this was little more than jockeying for advantage in the onslaught to come. The Northern Alliance still held four provinces – Parwan, Kapisa, Takhar and Badakhshan – and was well-supplied with weapons. From his command post in the Panjshir valley in June, Massoud boasted of 20,000 available troops and a journalist saw rows of recently-acquired tanks and multi-barrelled rocket launchers. 'We know they will come soon,' he said, 'but, with God's will, they will cause us few problems.'[5] Another traveller one month later remarked on the valley's 'well-nourished and carefree children ... living on a diet of peaches, apples, apricots, honey, *naan* bread and yoghurt'.[6] In mid-July, the UN summoned the 6+2 Group members to Tashkent in a last-ditch attempt to avert the approaching battle, extracting 'firm assurances' from the Taliban that it would not attack and a joint agreement from neighbouring countries 'not to provide military support to any Afghan party and to prevent the use of their territories for such purposes'.[7] With utter predictability, the storm broke a week later.

At midnight on 28 July, the Taliban launched three simultaneous attacks against the enemy at Tagab, east of Kabul; eastwards from Kunduz to Takhar; and into the 80-mile-long expanse of wheatfields and orchards that make up the Shomali Plain. As in previous years, the objectives were to drive Massoud out of missile range of Kabul, lock him in the Panjshir valley and knock out his supply lines from Tajikistan. But the coordination of the 1999 campaign surprised analysts, who noted the Taliban's three-to-one numerical superiority and the fact that the shock tactic of a rapid advance in pick-ups – the Taliban's preferred mode of attack – had been replaced by stolid infantry movements, reinforced with tanks and artillery.[8] Tagab and Najrab in Kapisa fell swiftly. On 30 July, a force with 30 tanks captured Barikab Hill overlooking Bagram and the airbase fell after a fierce battle. 'It was loud, very hot fighting,' said a witness, 'particularly before dawn.'[9] After three days, the number of dead was set at 1,000 and the bodies of Massoud's men littered the road to Bagram.[10] The loss of the base, a thorn in the side of the Taliban since the fall of Kabul in 1996, was a massive boost to morale. Charikar, Jabal Saraj and Gulbahar all fell in quick succession, Massoud having withdrawn to the Panjshir valley after dynamiting the entrance to delay pursuit. From the north came other promising news. On 3 August, Taliban forces captured Sher Khan Bandar, the river port that underpinned the opposition's supply line. Massoud was again boxed in his lair, but keeping him there, or eliminating him completely, would demand graver sacrifices. 'Two men with Kalashnikovs could hold the passes,' said a Western observer. 'So it really boils down to whether the Taliban can throw men at Massoud faster than he can kill them.'[11]

The Taliban had an alternative plan to their soldiers dying in droves. On 4 August came reports of a massive exodus from the Shomali Plain with people heading for shelter either to Kabul or the Panjshir valley. The UN estimated that 100,000 were on the move, though the opposition put the figure as high as 250,000.[12] In Bamian the locals fled out of fear of Taliban reprisals, but the Tajik inhabitants of Shomali were simply herded out en masse to prevent Massoud relying on the fat of their land. Six thousand Taliban and their Pakistani allies were given the task of clearing the district of Massoud sympathisers, 'killing wantonly, emptying entire towns, machine-gunning livestock, sawing down fruit trees, blasting apart irrigation canals'. They shot anyone young enough to be a soldier.[13] A spokesman said the Taliban trucked 1,800 families to Sar Shahi refugee camp outside Jalalabad for 'their own protection'; it was a 'temporary measure' to prevent civilians being caught in the crossfire during the anticipated counter-attack; they had only dynamited irrigation canals to prevent them being used as trenches.[14] During 8–12 August, 55,000 refugees streamed down the Old Road to Kabul.[15] On 15 August, the UN accused the Taliban of waging a 'scorched earth war', without surrendering to the more candid description of 'ethnic cleansing'. 'Families speak of whole villages being burned to the ground,' said the UN, 'and crops set on fire to prevent them moving back to this once-fertile valley.'[16] Nor did they spare the mulberries, whose fruit had sustained Afghans through hard winters for centuries. The scale of losses only became evident in October. Among a group of displaced Tajiks in Bazarak, north of Jalalabad, a reporter stumbled across an old woman who had sobbed inconsolably for two months, fingering a red flower embroidered on a pink cloth. No one was quite sure what her story was.[17]

With the sound turned down, something stately could still be discerned in the local art of war. Barbarities aside – and, from the evidence, they were largely indulged in by the Taliban or its Arab allies – war was as measured as a gavotte and it was ruled by a pattern of similarly ritual, and largely symbolic, thrusts and parries – much like the local brand of diplomacy. On 4 August, Massoud launched a counter-attack from the mouths of the Panjshir and Salang valleys, retaking Charikar literally as the Taliban slept.[18] He had announced early in the campaign that any captured non-Afghans would be executed and many 'Taliban' prisoners were slaughtered by the displaced men of Shomali, who had rallied to Massoud in an attempt to win back their homes.[19] An alliance spokesman put the number of Taliban dead at 500, including a 'large number of Pakistanis and Arabs', rising to 1,000 by the end of the two-week offensive.[20] On 6 August, Kabul was back within range and Bagram surrounded, its fall to Massoud inevitable. On 8 August, Mullah Omar asked the heads of Pakistani *madrassa* to declare a ten-day holiday so students could assume responsibility for security in Kabul, freeing more seasoned troops to bolster the collapsing frontlines. More than 2,000 started for the capital over the next two days.[21] Meanwhile, the Tajik population continued to stream out of the contested zones, with 200,000 leaving by 30 August.[22] A further 12,000 found respite in the grounds of the former Soviet embassy in Kabul.[23]

The fighting soon subsided to its usual level of low intensity, mostly to Massoud's small advantage, but August was a month of anxious anticipation elsewhere. Afghans scanned the skies for signs of either a fresh US attack to commemorate the first anniversary of the East African embassy bombings, or a second Tomahawk strike, perhaps at Jalalabad, to eliminate the man who escaped vengeance at Khost. In late July, US battleships moored outside Pakistani waters while, from Qatar, came reports of military transports, laden with US special forces, bound for Quetta in preparation for a raid inside Afghanistan.[24] But the two anniversaries came and passed unpunctuated – to an almost audible sigh of relief.

Four days after the Khost anniversary, at 10 p.m. on 24 August, a broken-down fuel truck, parked close to Mullah Mohammed Omar's home in Kandahar, exploded, damaging buildings up to half a mile away. The mullah survived, but among the 40 fatalities were two of his brothers, a brother-in-law, 14 members of his bodyguard, six police, three civil servants and, interestingly, six Arab nationals. One of his sons was injured.[25] Afghans immediately suspected 'America', but the US denied any connection to the bombs, which had been hidden in fuel drums by the perpetrators who escaped hours before the blast. Pakistan and the so-called moderate faction of the Taliban could equally have been to blame, for Mullah Mohammed Omar had demonstrated clearly in the preceding weeks both his inability to win the war and an absolute refusal to settle for peace. In public, the mullah accused no one, calling the assassination attempt an 'act of terrorism' but, privately, he suspected the hand of Iran, and 70 Shias were rounded up for 'interrogation'.[26]

Coming so soon after the Kargil fiasco, the spoiling of Pakistan's ambitions in Afghanistan by Massoud and his ragtag army of mountain fighters was as humbling, as it was public. Indeed, the scourging of the Shomali Plain seemed more the reaction of an injured conventional power than any domestic faction, for the latter were inured to the thin pickings of an Afghan 'victory' and in thrall to the fiat of destiny and the abiding consolation of patience. For the first time since the rise of the Taliban five years before, the UN finally came clean about the movement's foreign support. 'These thousands of young people are not fighting a foreign invasion force as it was when the Russians were there,' said Special Envoy Lakhdar Brahimi. 'They are taking sides in a local conflict.'[27] But he was silent as to whether these 'young people' ever wore Pakistani uniforms. Switching to its civilian hat, Islamabad quickly offered in mid-August to mediate a fresh round of talks between the Afghans, and a mission was sent to meet Massoud's representatives in Dushanbe. It was led, mischievously, by a middle-ranking official in the Interior Ministry, an office that deals with local law and order, and not foreign relations. The alliance rejected its overtures.[28]

Such incongruous alternations between the military and diplomatic wings of government were not unique to Pakistan: what really astonished was the sheer disconnectedness in Islamabad's approach to the policy of dual engagement. It was very well to send to Afghanistan volunteers, advisers, weapons and fuel on a scale that was royal for a country that had travelled far beyond any orthodox definition of bankruptcy. But to do so without preparing for the long series of possible geopolitical endgames – and, in Kargil, ones with nuclear consequences – raised worrying questions about the competence of an institution which, aloof from the Punch and Judy show of Pakistani politics, routinely aspired to the role of natural arbiter in any serious discussion of the national interest. A military manoeuvre is implemented to secure gains that can be later bartered for some critical alteration in the existing status quo, however minute. But Pakistani military staff seemed oblivious to the finer shadings of the region's nuclear balance, with the result that any gains from their military adventures were nervously frittered away by the civilian government during the international panic that inevitably followed.

Little wonder if the army blamed the government for its loss of dignity, but the army had a tendency to shove its face in the path of incoming fists. Afghanistan was the exception: no one much cared what went on in that broken boneyard, though Pakistan had invested far more resources in the outcome of the Taliban adventure than in its recent foray into Kargil. 'The armed forces of Pakistan,' wrote retired Brigadier Usman Khaled on 29 September, 'have been steadfast in playing their role in safeguarding the security of the country. They have sought to safeguard the nuclear deterrent of Pakistan, resisted pressures to withdraw support from the mujahedin in Kashmir and have been steadfast in their support to the Taliban in Afghanistan.'[29] As the mujahedin were forced down from the heights in Kashmir after the signing of the Washington Agreement on 4 July, Afghanistan had become the only arena where the honour of the Pakistani army, its generals and rank-and-file, and the value of their contribution to the nation's 'wellbeing' could feasibly be redeemed.

Bin Laden remained silent after his rediscovery by the *Observer*, but news of his far-flung enterprises again began to surface after 7 August when Russia launched a full-scale military invasion of the rebel republic of Dagestan, Chechnya's neighbour in the Caucasus. Wahhabi rebels, led by a Jordanian veteran of the anti-Soviet *jihad* named Khattab, were financed by bin Laden, Moscow claimed, and he had also visited one of their training camps in Chechnya.[30] Yossef Bodansky, Washington's resident bin Laden expert, envisaged a 'multinational force of more than 10,000 disciplined and well-armed fighters' trained in Pakistan, Afghanistan and Sudan, whose single goal was to carve out an independent Islamic state in the sensitive Caucasus.[31] For two weeks beginning on 1 September, a bombing campaign claimed over 250 Russian lives in blasts at residential buildings in Moscow and Buinaksk, spurring Foreign Minister Igor Ivanov to order Islamabad to stop the use of its territory for the training and dispatch of terrorists to Russian soil. On 20 September, he said that such activities 'could pose a threat to the existence of the existing regime' in Pakistan.[32] Others voices pointed out – with some reason – that the destabilisation of the Caucasus and the birth of a new sovereign state were also well suited to the interests of US oil companies.

Whether prompted by Washington or to ensure his own survival, Sharif finally took steps to distance his government from the Taliban and bin Laden. In a move supportive of the US sanctions in July, Pakistan announced new restrictions on the Transit Trade Agreement whereby luxuries, as well as basic commodities, were routinely imported duty-free to Afghanistan – only to end up on the Pakistani black market.[33] On 20 September, an unnamed Washington official – who could easily have been Assistant Secretary of State for South Asia Karl Inderfurth – 'intimated' US opposition to any 'interrupted democracy' in Pakistan, a comment that lit a fire of speculation around Sharif's future tenure in office and which was interpreted as notice to the Chief of the Army Staff, General Parvez

Musharraf, not to proceed in a direction that had already come to the attention of US intelligence.[34]

At 56, General Musharraf was liberal Moslem who kept Pekinese, played golf and drank his whisky in a White House-like mansion in the suburbs of Islamabad.[35] Trained at the Royal College of Defence Studies and Fort Bragg, he failed in the 1980s to win a recommendation to become secretary for General Zia ul-Haq through his apparent lack of international polish. He was appointed head of military operations, a post which required a weekly phone call to his Indian counterpart, as well as juggling Pakistan's contribution to the UN's peacekeeping operations elsewhere in the world. 'He is a little decisive, a little bold,' hazarded a former superior, Lieutenant-General Farrakh Khan. 'But I would say he is not impetuous, or jumpy.'[36] In October 1998, Musharraf was promoted chairman of the Joint Chiefs of Staff Committee, the pinnacle of the military establishment, not as a tribute to his military prowess, but because he was considered a more malleable partner by Sharif. Selig Harrison, one of the architects of the 1989 Soviet withdrawal, observed that Musharraf, along with a number of other high-ranking military staff, also had 'ties with many of the Islamic fundamentalist groups that have been supporting the Taliban'.[37] It scarcely showed in the figure of the dapper general, but the allegation festered as the logic behind what happened next grew ever more obtuse.

The timing of the American warning about Musharraf was significant. Sharif had planned to meet with him on 20 September to confirm his new post as chairman of the Joint Chiefs of Staff Committee, an act equivalent to brokering a power-sharing arrangement with the military in a bid to hold on to office.[38] However the head of ISI intelligence, Lieutenant-General Khawaja Ziauddin, was in Washington that same day with Sharif's brother, Shahbaz, head of Punjab province. Ziauddin seized that moment to alert Inderfurth to Musharraf's imminent treason, and to request US support for Sharif's counter-ruse of using the bin Laden card – to which Washington attached so much importance – to justify his long-planned assault on the supreme heights of military power.[39] They were the last obstacle to Sharif's ambitions for absolute dictatorship.

Whatever was agreed, both Sharif and Ziauddin underwent remarkable conversions when the latter returned to Islamabad. Two days after the Washington meeting on 20 September, the US reneged on its trade boycott of Pakistan in the previous year by waiving a few minor sanctions and allocating $330,000 for projects tied to the fight against narcotics. President Clinton agreed to a long-awaited state visit in 2000 – the first by a US president in nearly three decades – though the security implications were frightening.[40] In spite of the democratic deficit in Sharif's bankrupt, but nuclearised Pakistan, Washington was giving the prime minister a cautious vote of confidence as its preferred agent of change in a region where the US had amassed a host of unfinished business. US conditions for this support included the closure of the border with Afghanistan, an end to the infiltration of fighters into Kashmir, the disarming of 200,000 domestic Islamists and, above all, negotiating terms with the Taliban for the surrender of bin Laden.[41] But implementing such a wish list would test Sharif's political support to the limit, while setting him on a collision course with the military.

On 7 October Mohammed Rizvi, a Shia controller of programmes at Pakistan TV, was gunned down on his way to work in Rawalpindi, bringing to 40 the number of civilians killed in sectarian violence over the preceding 10 days.[42] On the same day, Ziauddin flew to Kandahar to confront Mullah Omar with 'concrete evidence' of a training camp in Afghanistan specifically set up to launch Sunni attacks against Pakistani Shias.[43] 'Who on earth can believe,' wondered a Pakistani official out loud, 'that it was only last week [that] Islamabad came to know about Pakistanis being given military training in Afghanistan?'[44] Nawaz Sharif flew to Dubai to brief the Gulf states on his plans to withdraw support for the Taliban and push for the extradition of bin Laden.[45] 'Sharif said he insisted that the Taliban stop all activities in Pakistan, hand over Osama bin Laden, or ask him to leave Afghanistan, and shut down all training camps,' said another anonymous official.[46] On 10 October, four Afghans from Kandahar were arrested in Peshawar in connection with other sectarian killings in Karachi and Dera Ismail Khan, apparently following a CIA tipoff.[47] CIA agents were reported to have joined local army and police units in 'Search and Watch' operations inside Afghanistan. 'We have information of at least three teams having entered our country,' said an official in North West Frontier Province, 'whereas others are awaiting the go-ahead from powers that be.'[48]

On 11 October, Mullah Mohammed Omar publicly decried terrorism in all its forms, adding with a tangible poignancy: 'It is beyond justice that today no distinction is drawn between terrorists and mujahedin in the world.'[49] That world had gone forever, alas.

* * *

Musharraf was on the golf links near Colombo in the early afternoon of 12 October when he received a satellite call from a senior officer who told him that Sharif had finally made his move.[50] Profiting from the general's presence at the 50th anniversary of the Sri Lankan army, the prime minister was conniving with Ziauddin in a manoeuvre that would see the ISI chief imposed as head of the armed forces and Musharraf forcibly retired. It was a desperate gamble on the face of it; the lines of military and civilian command had rarely been more polarised, chiefly as a result of the Kargil 'betrayal'. Three days before, Lieutenant-General Tariq Parvez, commander of the Quetta corps – one of nine making up the Pakistani army – was 'retired' by Musharraf for holding an unauthorised meeting with Sharif.[51] In any other semi-democracy, such a conference would have been routine but, after three years of Sharif's rule, the army's ears were as sharply pricked for signs of a putsch by Pakistan's own civilian government as they were to any military threat from India.

But there was a slit of opportunity that could still bring success to Sharif's enterprise. The general was at least three and a half hours flying time from Karachi and five from Islamabad, all that Sharif and Ziauddin believed they needed to win over the corps commanders, and eliminate Musharraf. As the general raced to Colombo airport to catch Pakistan International Airways' flight 1515 back to Karachi, Sharif ordered Pakistan Television to broadcast an announcement of Musharraf's 'retirement' on the five o'clock news. Simultaneously, instructions were sent to Karachi airport denying Musharraf's civilian flight permission to land, redirecting instead it to a remote strip in Sindh where local police received orders to arrest the general.[52]

All nine commanders rejected Sharif's offers, however, effectively dooming his 'civilian' coup even before Musharraf landed, though whether out of loyalty to the general as an individual, or the army as Pakistan's ruling institution, remains unclear.[53] In later reports, Musharraf was portrayed in the heroic style, using the cockpit radio to summon loyal troops to take over the Karachi control tower, while the airliner and its 198 passengers clutched at the sky with only six minutes of fuel remaining. In fact, he owed his sudden promotion more to Lieutenant-General Mahmoud Ahmad, head of the 10th Corps in the Rawalpindi barracks whose proximity to the capital gives it make-and-break power over whoever governs. Ahmad had ordered his soldiers out of barracks an hour before Sharif's planned news broadcast with orders to secure the prime minister's house and black out the television studios. He was later rewarded with the job of head of the ISI.[54] Musharraf made his first appearance as Pakistan's new dictator in an early-morning broadcast in which he accused Sharif of trying to 'politicise the army, destabilise it' and 'create dissension' within its ranks. Along with accusations of criminal conspiracy, attempted murder and hijacking, these amounted to capital charges when Sharif was arraigned before a special 'anti-terrorist' court in Karachi on 20 November.[55]

It was left to a handful of Westerners the following day to mourn the passing of Pakistani democracy. The *Frontier Post*, whose chief editor had been held in prison since the previous April, spoke of a 'palpable sigh of relief among the citizens' while columnist Ayaz Amir wrote of 'the dolt ... who had not the wit to understand that it is only so much incompetent audacity the Furies can stand'.[56] After an embarrassed silence lasting two days, Musharraf finally issued an emergency proclamation on 15 October in which he declared himself chief executive and suspended the constitution, the elected assemblies and the powers of the federal ministries. He committed his regime to rooting out corruption and tax avoidance among the ruling elite, but there would be no immediate return to the 'sham democracy' that had dogged Pakistan since Bhutto's first term.

'There is despondancy and hopelessness surrounding us,' he told Pakistanis in an extended policy address on 17 October.

> The slide has been gradual but has rapidly accelerated in the last many years. Today we have reached a stage where our economy has crumbled; our credibility is lost; state institutions lie demolished; provincial disharmony has caused cracks in the Federation; and people who were once brothers are now at each others' throats.[57]

Musharraf pledged a policy of nuclear and military restraint, troop reductions on the Indian border and a refusal to tolerate Islamist extremism. 'I urge them to curb elements which are exploiting religion for vested interests and bringing a bad name to our faith,' he said.[58]

By and large, Musharraf's performance earned a good press, but he was clearly playing for time. There was a country first to convince and it was crucial to that priority that no substantive inch be conceded on tricky issues of national or military interest. The initial US reaction, not surprisingly, was muted, largely because the new configuration of power was diametrically opposite to the one which the State Department had calculated and planned to achieve with Sharif in September – but also because a full-scale trade boycott had been in force since the nuclear tests of June 1998. Digging deep into a depleted barrel of sanctions, the Clinton administration suspended a $1.7 million health programme, while pressing ahead with a $2.5 million counter-narcotics initiative. Karl Inderfurth didn't think further sanctions would have much effect: 'We have lost touch with a generation of Pakistani military leaders,' he told a Senate Foreign Relations sub-committee on 14 October.[59]

Opinions varied as to what impact Musharraf's rise to power might have on US interests, particularly in regard to nuclear non-proliferation and the pursuit of bin Laden. On 4 November, former CIA chief Milton Bearden told a congressional committee that Musharraf represented 'the last good chance' for the US to influence Pakistan's direction in the new millennium. 'The once outward-looking officer corps ...,' he said, 'whose foundations were laid at Fort Benning and Fort Bragg ..., [is] being replaced by inward-looking officers who have been trained only in religious fundamentalist *madrassa* schools.'[60] This was over-egging the pudding. Selig Harrison took a wholly contrary view. Far from being a 'safe pair of hands' in which to entrust the world's first Islamic bomb, as Bearden appeared to suggest, Musharraf was a very wolf in sheep's clothing. 'Sharif's recent call on the Taliban not to be a haven for terrorists,' he said, 'was one of the precipitating factors in the crystallisation of the desire of the military to take over.'[61] In other words, by pressing Sharif, in pursuit of bin Laden, to shatter the glass wall which had always separated the military and civilian branches of Pakistani power, Washington had only succeeded in forcing a jagged shard deep into the prime minister's throat. A middle ground existed between these two positions that was equally alarming but quite as credible. Before Sharif's overthrow, it had been the fear of losing international legitimacy based upon what Musharraf had dismissed as 'sham democracy' that stood between Pakistan and the Islamist bomb. Now it was a general of the old school, whose example had merely mapped out a more direct course for his Islamist officers to follow.

News of the coup was greeted stoically by the Taliban, still reeling from the Sharif crackdown in his dying days of power. It was a purely internal matter, sniffed Mullah Mohammed Omar, 'in reaction to certain moves by foreign powers against the Pakistani nation'.[62] He was not far wrong at that. In compliance with the now-departed Sharif's demands, troops were instructed on 13 October to disarm non-Afghan volunteers in Jalalabad, confining them to their training camps.[63] On the other side of the Khyber Pass, Musharraf took the step of banning exports of wheat flour, driving up Afghan bread prices by a fifth. The move was construed as a sign that the general wished to remind the Taliban of who was boss, but no further demands were made and the ban was quietly dropped on 17 November.[64]

The Taliban leadership was far more exercised by UN moves in New York to impose deeper sanctions on Afghanistan, than any change of government in Islamabad. On 15 October, the Security Council met to debate a US-drafted resolution to freeze the Taliban's assets in foreign banks and to ban Ariana Airlines jets from landing anywhere but Mecca until bin Laden was extradited. Torn between its staff's reliance on security in the field and New York's need for the release of the US long-delayed funding contributions, the UN appeared to have taken to the political road by prioritising bin Laden's threats to US territory, over the Taliban's maltreatment of Afghan women and children. In a statement on 25 October, the 15-member Security Council roundly condemned the Taliban's offensive of July 1999, the slaughter in Mazar-i Sharif, its provision of shelter and training to terrorists, its reliance on opium revenues, the use of child soldiers, discrimination against women and children, indiscriminate bombing, the burning of crops, the forced displacement of civilians, the separation of men from their families, the murder of the Iranian diplomats, as well as castigating neighbouring countries for fuelling the war with fresh ammunition and weaponry. However, the statement implied, all of the above could be overlooked if – but only if – bin Laden were handed over to the appropriate legal authorities before 14 November.[65] In the meantime, the Credentials Committee had once again allotted the Afghanistan seat at the UN to representatives of the Rabbani government with no objection on this occasion from the Pakistani delegation.[66] The UN sanctions came into force one month later, to the accompaniment of Taliban-organised riots in Kabul. Commented Erick de Mul, then UN co-ordinator for Afghanistan: 'They are saying: "We are at a low level, so it's very difficult for us to have a situation much worse than we already have, so we will be able to get through this period".'[67]

Three days after the coup, and on the same day that the UN Security Council met to finalise its programme of sanctions, four convicted thieves were led into Kabul football stadium to have their hands cut off for stealing $50, a tape recorder, 15 teapots and 18 fruit bowls. Attendances had plummeted since the fall of the capital over three years earlier, with barely 500 spectators taking their seats for the gory, weekly spectacle. A Taliban guard said that security had been stepped up outside after spectators complained that their bicycles were stolen while they were inside watching the punishments meted out for theft, rape and murder.[68]

It was a keen, if unintended, tribute to the Afghan's ability to survive and to profit in even the bleakest of times.

15 Mr Sam vs the Food and Beverage Industry

For the first time since the Taliban captured the capital three years earlier, music echoed eerily through the alleyways of Kabul on 15 November 1999, shattering one of the movement's cardinal taboos. In response to the UN declaration of sanctions, Mullah Omar had granted Radio Sharia unique permission for the broadcast of a solo male singing voice, accompanied by traditional stringed instruments. 'Oh America, you are an enemy of Islam,' he chanted, 'but you haven't heard the roar of Islam.'[1]

For most Afghans, that 'roar' was experienced as a low, dull keening throughout millennium year as the catalogue of usual misery was supplemented by the worst drought in a generation and a further torquing of the duel over Osama bin Laden. When the song faded, the customary silence grew dense with the signals of impending disaster. So much so that, as 2000 progressed, Kabulis became infatuated with the characters and fate of the blockbuster movie *Titanic*, a craze triggered by underground showings of videos smuggled from Pakistan. Popular resistance takes strange, syncretic forms, as the rise of the Taliban itself had proven. In spite of official attempts to cool *Titanic* fever sweeping Kabul's homes and markets – or perhaps because of them – the Liverpool liner was transformed into a marketing logo for cosmetics, clothes, footwear, hairstyles, wedding cakes, vehicles, and even rice. The bakers in Chicken Street were 'seriously advised' by the Taliban newssheets to desist from icing cakes with replicas of the doomed boat and to model their creations on Afghanistan's cultural heritage, but the course was set – and the prospect for collision growing.[2]

The declaration of US sanctions was answered on 12 November with a volley of seven rocket attacks against the US embassy, the UN building, the US Information Center and various government buildings in Islamabad. Pakistani officials said they suspected 'commandos' associated with bin Laden of involvement.[3] Two days later, a man with an Arabic accent telephoned to claim that the Al-Jihad group, based in Kandahar, had carried out the explosions.[4] On the same day, three people were injured when a bomb exploded outside a mosque in Wazir Akhbar Khan favoured by members of the Kabul *shura*.[5] The UN sanctions, in turn, led to a wave of attacks on UN property in Kandahar, Farah, Mazar-i Sharif, Jalalabad and Herat, while tens of thousands of protesters streamed through the streets of Kabul chanting 'long live Osama' and 'death to America', as Taliban guards fired their rifles in the air to control them.[6] Much of the noise in Kabul was orchestrated cabaret – though of a very different order to the public execution of a murderess in Kandahar football stadium, which took place on the day that Mullah Mohammed Omar apologised to the UN for the damage, and normal business was resumed.[7]

But how normal could the business of aid actually be under the combined conditions of global sanctions, a massive food shortfall across the country but particularly in the drought-hit south, 20 years of war, a crack-down on the cross-border trade and a winter that was soon to hit its stride? The US State Department called its boycott 'smart sanctions', using the same weasel word applied to the bombs dropped on Baghdad during the Gulf War: they were 'crafted' toward forcing the Taliban to recognise its responsibilities with regard to terrorism and narco-trafficking, and not targeted against ordinary Afghans.[8] There would be no 'collateral damage'. But the cancellation of Ariana's landing rights in Dubai immediately disrupted the inflow of $4.5 million a week in hard currency, whether for commodity purchases or remittances to cash-strapped families for whom it was the sole means of support.[9]

Médecins Sans Frontières discovered that it was unable to fly medicine and other relief from Dubai because no Security Council member was willing to chair the committee set up to oversee exemptions to the UN prohibition on international landings.[10] Afghanistan's merchants, expected to import 800,000 tonnes of wheat-flour to relieve the local shortage, found peremptory curbs on supply due to Islamabad's fears for its own food supply, its determination to reduce smuggling and a genuine confusion as to whether trading anything across the border was legal under the UN sanctions. A balance was eventually found – thanks to a most unexpected helper – but it seemed that distinguishing between what was relief, private trade, smuggling and sanctions-busting could erupt into the same poisoned dilemma faced by the UN in 1997, when it was compelled to choose between defending women's rights in general, or feeding widows. That helper was the Islamic Republic of Iran. One year after the killing of its diplomats in Mazar-i Sharif, Tehran reopened the border on 21 November, restoring the road link from Dubai.

Perhaps Tehran brought down the barriers to prod the Taliban into surrendering the killers, but it also sought a more articulate conversation with its unruly neighbour on a variety of border issues, notably the high-intensity war on Afghan drug-trafficking which cost the Iranian exchequer

$800 million in 1999.[11] This was only the first in a series of diplomatic shifts that followed the imposition of sanctions. Even as Russia and the FBI agreed to pool their intelligence on bin Laden, whom Moscow accused of training Islamist rebels in Chechnya, the Islamophobe government of Uzbekistan, a former sponsor of Dostum, reluctantly opened talks with the Taliban. In addition, General Musharraf made his first visit to Tehran in December, returning two days later with a pledge that Iran and Pakistan would henceforth coordinate policy on Afghanistan and 'work towards the formation of a broadly-based government consisting of all Afghan factions'.[12] Afghan specialist and former US ambassador Peter Tomsen commented acidly: 'Whereas Pakistan and Iran before separately tried to manipulate the Afghan scene ... now, Musharraf's visit to Tehran indicates that they are going to cooperate together to manipulate the Afghan scene, which is even worse.'[13] But Tehran continued to provide open house to the anti-Taliban opposition: ousted President Rabbani visited in the same month for a war conference with Rashid Dostum, Abdul Malik and Hizb-i Wahdat leader Karim Khalili.

Any hope that Mullah Omar would adopt a more amenable profile in the face of Washington and the UN's combined censure evaporated as the world armed itself for a party at the end of the millennium, that appeared cursed by a reckoning daily closing in. Y2K specialists had long warned of a catastrophe as the clock struck midnight with airliners, shorn of their flight systems, curving like tracer fire through blossoms of valetudinarian fireworks; men on their knees before the mechanisms that once nurtured them. In truth, neither Mullah Mohammed Omar – nor even bin Laden – retained manual control of the loosely-knit Al Qa'ida network that US intelligence accused the latter of building in his 22-year exile in Afghanistan and Sudan. If a grand conspiracy existed, it existed either at the frontiers of the American mind, or in the archipelago of autonomous colonies of conviction that flourished between the paving stones of US immigration policy. The colonists looked to Kandahar, to bin Laden's probity and the shining star of the Taliban Islamic state for inspiration but, as new Americans, they were also saturated with the portents and imagery that surrounded that ultimate year.

With Christmas approaching, an alert policeman intercepted a lone Algerian, 32-year-old Ahmad Ressam, at a remote crossing on the border between Canada and Washington state. In the boot of his rented car were discovered 54 kg of nitroglycerine, several bags of urea and four Casio watches, 'enough to bomb four city blocks into rubble'.[14] Similar timers and ingredients had been used in the 1993 World Trade Center bombing, an apartment bombing in Moscow and the embassy attacks in Kenya and Tanzania. US intelligence said the components bore the unmistakable signature of the simple but deadly bomb-making techniques taught at bin Laden's training camps in Afghanistan. But what was the target? Ressam was found to be carrying a second passport, which had been used to reserve a getaway flight on British Airways through Chicago and New York to London one day later. Investigators said he had booked a room for a single night at a motel a short distance from the Seattle Space Needle and the Seattle Center, the scenes of a grand end-of-millennium spectacle in the home town of Boeing and Microsoft. Days later, the Royal Canadian Mounted Police broke up an Algerian 'cell' in Montreal, with links to the Groupe Islamique Armée and, before the end of the month, a second Algerian, Abdel Ghani Meskini, was arrested in Brooklyn, and charged with conspiring with Ressam.[15]

Simultaneously, in Amman, Jordan, police announced the arrest of 13 Jordanians of Palestinian descent with elaborate ties to bin Laden, this time through another training facility high in the mountains above Kunar province on the Pakistani border. It emerged at their jury-less trial in April 2001 that they had intended to bomb the capital's Radisson Hotel, as well as two sites of popular Christian tourism, Mount Nebom where Moses first gazed upon the Promised Land of Palestine, and a settlement on the river Jordan where Jesus was baptised. One of the defendants, Khalil Deek, was a naturalised US citizen from Palestine, a US army veteran and a computer studies graduate. Investigators said he had spent two years in Peshawar where he shared a bank account with Abu Zubaida, the director of studies and admissions for bin Laden's camp complex. He called the charges against him 'all this hocus pocus'.[16] And despite the ever-accumulating evidence, the voice of another defendant in the dock, Issam Baqawi, had the particular ring of sincerity: 'So what if [police] seized two machine-guns and two pistols from young men who thought of fighting Jews. Is that terrorism?'[17]

Growing suspicions that the Taliban and Afghanistan were situated in the eye of an impending storm of terrorist violence were reinforced when five Pakistani hijackers, armed with knives and obsolete guns, seized control of Air India's flight 814 from Katmandu to New Delhi on Christmas Eve, forcing its 155 passengers to fly to Lahore, Amritsar and Dubai before finally setting down in baking temperatures in the derelict civil airport at Kandahar in the middle of Ramadan. They demanded the release of three jailed Kashmiri militants, including 'Sheikh Omar Sayeed', also known as Ahmed Umar Sayeed Sheikh, a Pakistani-born, British citizen imprisoned for kidnapping British tourists in 1995 who was alleged to have close links to Al Qa'ida. One passenger, homeward bound after honeymooning in Nepal, was unceremoniously killed and dumped on the tarmac, unbeknown to his wife in the rear of the plane. The hijack was seen by the Taliban authorities as a heaven-sent invitation to demonstrate their uncompromising stance on terrorism. Drained by their fasting, they nevertheless threatened to storm the plane if any other passenger were harmed – but three French hostages on board later swore that they had seen the hijackers take delivery of a stack of more effective weapons immediately after landing in the Taliban capital.[18] Pakistan clearly enjoyed the discomfort of Indian mediators shuttling back and forth to Kandahar until their reluctant surrender to the hijackers' terms. Once the freed militants reached Kandahar, the Taliban – basking by now in the glow of a global Christmas TV audience – gave them and the hijackers ten hours to leave the country and they evaporated, bin-Laden-style, in a blizzard of road dust toward the Pakistani border.

Inspired, perhaps, by the Air India episode – though of less global account – was the hijacking in February of an Ariana Airlines flight from Kabul to Mazar-i Sharif by hijackers claiming to seek the release of Ismail Khan, the former emir of Herat, who had been captured by the Taliban during the mutiny that had led to the fall of Mazar in 1998. While hijackers and hijacked stewed in a long-drawn-out siege at Stansted – and the even longer bureaucratic stand-off that constitutes the asylum process in London – Ismail Khan managed to escape after three years in fetters in a windowless cell in Kandahar, along with the son of former Nangarhar governor Haji Qadir. They later gave 'harrowing accounts of torture' to the UN Special Rapporteur on Human Rights in Afghanistan.[19]

With fears of a worldwide Islamist conspiracy mounting higher by the day, US prosecutors began to divulge some of the evidence they held against Osama bin Laden, chiefly in response to bail demands by lawyers for Wadih el-Hage, the Texas-based chief suspect in the Nairobi embassy bombing who had already spent 15 months in prison awaiting trial. It emerged that el-Hage had been on an FBI watch list for years because of his circumstantial links with several of the World Trade Center bombers; that his Nairobi house was searched by federal agents working with the Kenyan police; and that he was later interviewed by the FBI in Texas, still a full year before the embassy attack. Prosecutors described him as 'one of bin Laden's most trusted and dangerous aides, privy to his secrets and a personal courier of his instructions', who had 'militarised' a pre-existing Kenyan 'cell', using the local NGO, Mercy International Relief Agency, which was another alleged conduit for the bin-Laden finance required to conduct such a sophisticated operation.[20]

But the interception of email, fax and satellite phone messages between bin Laden and his minions revealed Al Qa'ida's surprisingly naive grasp of 'spy-craft', which was on a level not far removed from boys playing espionage games with invisible ink. One letter referred to a 'Mr Sam' or 'Mr O'Sam' and repeatedly warned him to beware of 'an opposition company called the Food and Beverage Industry, based in the US'. El-Hage followed this security alert with another letter, in which he wrote: 'Give my regards to Sam and tell him to take extra precautions because business competition is very fierce.'[21]

It was about to get much fiercer.

*   *   *

General Musharraf showed few signs of actively pursuing his 17 October pledge to combat Islamist terrorism, despite the diplomatic woes arising from his dismissal of the Sharif government and the network of *jihadi* cells spreading through the Middle East, the Caucasus and Central Asia nurtured by the Taliban–bin Laden axis. After the Air India hijack, which Indian analysts claimed bore the hallmarks of an ISI-backed operation, Islamabad made no attempt to capture either the hijackers or the three prisoners freed by India, all now safely ensconced on Pakistani soil, or transiting through to sanctuary in Pakistani-controlled Kashmir. New Delhi called on Washington to declare Pakistan a sponsor of terrorism – as the US had been inclined to do earlier in the decade.[22]

Nor, despite the negotiating muscle acquired by Pakistan as a result of the disruption of Afghanistan's food supply, was there any obvious pressure on the Taliban to reduce the number of training camps on Afghan soil, although much of their graduate output was, by most accounts, fighting alongside Taliban forces at the front lines. In early February, Musharraf flew to Kandahar for his first official face-to-face talks with Mullah Omar, a potentially disciplinary meeting that ended with rosy expressions of mutual esteem and hopes for future collaboration. He told Washington that it would have to negotiate directly with Kandahar over bin Laden. In fact, the only progress he could claim with regard to the fight against terrorism was the mid-February appearance before an Anti-Terrorism Court of former prime minister Nawaz Sharif, on charges of conspiracy to murder and kidnap.[23]

Yet Washington felt it had no alternative but to keep the channels open with the new masters of Islamabad,[24] though the diplomatic aperture was constrictive. His domestic credibility crippled by the Lewinsky investigation, Bill Clinton turned to attempts at mediation in long-running conflicts abroad – Northern Ireland, the Middle East, Kashmir – in a bid to preserve the reputation of his presidency for history. At a crucial moment in the Lewinsky saga, Clinton had profited politically from the imminence of the bin Laden menace but, in the brutally precise calculus of presidential accountability, it was neither the product nor consequence of his watch, but of another's and of the intelligence services granted such licence during the Cold War's most apocalyptic proxy conflict. Given the limited time left to his term, the Islamist conspiracy was irremediable and, however unhelpfully Pakistan behaved in the convoluted business of exporting terrorism, it remained, in Washington's view, a sub-plot, or secondary infection, caused by the much graver complication of two nuclear powers at odds over Kashmir.

The primary purpose of the visit that Clinton paid to South Asia in late March was to persuade India and Pakistan to deepen the proximity that emerged after the Kargil escapade, and Musharraf's later decision to scale down Pakistan's military presence along the Line of Control. At best, there was the possibility of progress toward ratification of the nuclear Comprehensive Test Ban Treaty; at least, the prospect that more cautious military heads in both countries could be persuaded to build the fail-safe mechanisms that limit the danger of accidental war. However, when the visit was first agreed, Clinton's expected host was the pliable and democratically elected Nawaz Sharif, not the usurping general who now had him on trial on capital charges. There was justifiable concern that a presidential visit would be interpreted as conferring legitimacy on Musharraf's regime.

In the event, after a five-day visit to India, the president spent less than six hours in Pakistani territory on what was described as a 'stopover', rather than a full state visit. After 80 minutes of talks – in which Musharraf reportedly conceded nothing – Clinton delivered a brief speech on television in which he called for a return to civilian rule and the end of the rivalry over Kashmir, mentioning Afghanistan once but bin Laden not at all. His motorcade then swept out to the airport. The visit to India had been more fruitful. Some months later – in tacit recognition of India's superior field intelligence network in Pakistan, Afghanistan and Kashmir – Washington and New Delhi established a joint working group on Islamist terrorism, sealing the new partnership with the gift of a CD-ROM copy of *The Encyclopaedia of Jihad*, an eleven-volume textbook on terrorism used as a teaching aid in bin Laden's training camps. *The Encyclopaedia* had been found in the home of Khalil Deek, a suspect in the Jordanian millennium plot. It detailed, in the format of a comprehensive manual, accompanied by diagrams, a multitude of do-it-yourself techniques for assassination, bomb attack, the creation of 'sleeper' cells, surveillance, coded communication and the selection of targets for maximum damage, whether infrastructural, psychological or physical. One volume dealt entirely with bioterrorism and the use of botulism and anthrax to contaminate a target's water, food or medical supplies. On the topic of recruitment, the manual had this to say: 'The *mujahid* should be young, so he can start the mission 10 years before the start of the *jihad*.'[25]

The former US ambassador, Peter Tomsen, who had lobbied hard for Clinton to spearhead a new US-led peace process in Afghanistan, considered his Islamabad trip a missed opportunity. 'We cannot expect an effective foreign policy on Afghanistan before this administration ends,' he concluded. 'Whichever party wins in [the] November [elections], it will take at least a year for the next administration to establish the essential analytical framework and policy approach needed to satisfy US interests in Afghanistan and the region.'[26] As first steps towards a more committed US approach, he recommended the appointment of a special US envoy to Afghanistan and the resumption of a direct US aid effort to non-Taliban areas.

Living conditions in Afghanistan continued their relentless deterioration, accentuated by donor distaste for Taliban policies. The drought dried wells and killed crops across the south and centre, causing a massive culling of the livestock on which so many relied and an accelerated exodus to the cities. In addition to one of the world's largest refugee populations – 3 million distributed between Pakistan and Iran – Afghanistan could also lay claim to one of the largest populations of internally displaced: a quarter of a million people were driven from their homes in the 1999 fighting in the Shomali Plain and still had not returned.[27] By the end of 2000, the World Food Programme (WFP) was providing emergency rations for 3 million people, twice the number it had fed before the drought, while a UN appeal for emergency funding to cope was only 60 per cent subscribed. Contributions to the UN's consolidated funding appeal, meanwhile, were so low that by September mine-clearance work was cut by half.[28] Even the good news was bad. With the drought threatening to cut opium output by a third to 3,275 tonnes, Afghans' supply of foreign exchange was expected to shrink from $230 million to $160 million.[29]

Some aid workers believed that the Taliban were finally preparing to relax some of their fiercer strictures after a formal celebration on 8 March of International Women's Day, an event attended by 700 largely out-of-work university professors, engineers, teachers, doctors, nurses and school principals.[30] But a series of incidents and decisions in July quickly put paid to the illusion. A team of Pakistani footballers, visiting for the first international 'friendly' match in over 20 years, was arrested in Kandahar football stadium for wearing shorts in defiance of the Islamic dress code; their heads were shaved and they were expelled. An edict was issued once again banning women from working for the UN or NGOs, forcing the WFP to shut down a training programme for 600 female relief workers.[31] And on 8 July, 71-year-old Mary MacMakin, an American who had devoted over 20 years to running a physiotherapy and rehabilitation centre in Kabul, was arrested and charged with 'spying and spreading anti-Taliban propaganda'.[32]

Other star-gazers were similarly, simply, though far more dramatically, wrong. In the same month came a shower of forecasts from usually well-informed sources of the scattering and imminent demise of the entire Taliban project. 'We believe the Taliban now have little prospect of completing their goal of gaining control over the 15 per cent held by the opposition,' Assistant Secretary of State Karl Inderfurth told the Senate Foreign Relations Committee on 20 July. 'We believe the Taliban have reached their highwater mark.' Citing as indicators the recent assassination of the governor of Kunduz, continuing sabotage at Kabul airport, the growing refusal of Afghans to be recruited to fight Taliban battles, equipment shortages and splits within the movement, he predicted their expulsion from Kabul 'by the end of the year'.[33] Inderfurth's opinion, informed by the best US intelligence and spies inside the Taliban, Pakistani and Indian administrations, was shared by Peter Tomsen,[34] who testified before the same hearing, and by Wali Massoud, the Afghan ambassador in London and brother of Ahmad Shah Massoud.[35]

What was the source of their confidence? A massive airlift of heavy weaponry and hard currency to Massoud could only instigate the beginning of a reversal on the scale predicted in Washington; and, if such a breakthrough did occur, Kabul could hardly be delivered with certainty within the five-month timetable, such are the imponderables of the Afghan battlefield. Inderfurth's conviction, therefore, was based on a different mark of surety: inside knowledge, perhaps, of a second plot to assassinate Mullah Mohammed Omar with the goal of splintering the Taliban into factions; knowledge of a US-assisted mutiny by the so-called moderate wing, led by Mullah Rabbani, with the aim of opening a second front to the rear of the main Taliban force; or knowledge of a secret agreement with General Musharraf to discontinue his support and withdraw before the deadline all Pakistani military personnel fighting with the Taliban. Whatever he thought he knew then, Inderfurth was now to learn the Afghan punishment for counting chickens.

The Taliban opened their summer campaign on the eastern border of Baghlan, cutting Massoud's lifeline to the Panjshir valley on 1 August when Ishkamish fell after heavy air attack. A week later, they seized Bangi, opening the western road to reinforcements from Kunduz for a two-pronged attack on Massoud's northern headquarters in Taloqan city. According to a report in *Jane's Defence Weekly*, later confirmed by NGO staff in the district, around one-third of the 20,000 Taliban mustered for the Taloqan campaign were of Pakistani origin, while a further 1,000 Arabs were identified as fighting with the 055 Brigade, the cohort trained and paid for by Osama bin Laden.[36] 'Some 40 per cent of the Taliban force is made up of non-Afghans,' said Massoud, a claim also backed by Western officials.[37] After an offensive lasting three weeks, the Taliban captured Taloqan for the third and final time on 5 September, choking off Massoud's main river supply routes at Dasht-i Arshi, Imam Sahib and Sher Khan Bandar, as well as airstrips at Taloqan and Khawajagarh. Some 90,000 inhabitants of the district, mostly Tajiks, sought refuge in the caves, valleys and mountains surrounding their villages to avoid the same Taliban purges carried out after Mazar, Bamian and Shomali Plain had fallen in previous years.[38]

Massoud said his retreat was tactical, that his forces left with their weaponry mostly intact. Over the next two weeks, as if in confirmation, he laid vigorous siege to Taloqan from three sides from positions high on the surrounding peaks, even cutting the Bangi approach road to prevent resupply from Kunduz.[39] Morale remained high among the troops of the Northern Alliance,[40] but the Taliban clung to their prize with an uncharacteristic tenacity, in the light of previous altercations when defeat or, at the very least, a semblance of the status quo, was always snatched from the jaws of what had first seemed like a crushing victory over Massoud. Despite the loss of 1,000 lives and 1,500 other casualties,[41] the Taliban consolidated their control of Taloqan, aided by a wave of defections that included the commander at Farkhar Gorge southeast of the city.[42] Massoud and Rabbani insisted Taloqan would be again theirs before the first snows of November, and Russian ammunition planes buzzed into Faizabad, 70 miles east of the fighting, to bolster the coming fusillade.[43] But, at the last moment, Massoud decided to cut his losses and quit, for fear that the demoralised commanders in his Badakhshan hinterland should choose the same moment that he faced his greatest military challenge to forget their longstanding loyalties and seek God. As the first snows fell, Taloqan was still in Taliban hands: the Lion of Panjshir had suffered his most far-reaching defeat since the loss of Kabul four years earlier.

The loss of Taloqan brought the Taliban within shooting range of Tajikistan, sowing panic in the frontline states of Central Asia, but there was no indication of any more aggressive supply of weaponry from Russia, Iran or India on the scale necessary to rescue their protégé from ignominy. Massoud still held Farkhar, parts of Taloqan province and all of Badakhshan, including Faizabad where the UN-recognised president, Burhanuddin Rabbani now held court in a two-storey house that formerly belonged to the governor. The Taliban took their time, advancing slowly along the demolished roads and blown-up bridges to a final reckoning that would determine who controlled the last 5 per cent of Afghanistan and the 370-mile frontier with Tajikistan, from Darwaz to the tip of the serpentine Wakhan Corridor. After the failure to recapture Taloqan, Massoud had little option left but to wage guerrilla warfare, assisted by a loose organisation of 1,500 'freelance saboteurs' to carry out bombings and assassinations behind Taliban lines.[44] The snow, mercifully, intervened, but how had Inderfurth come to be so misled?

Massoud's popular base began to evaporate shortly before the fall of Taloqan. On 14 September Tajikistan closed its border to thousands of Afghans teeming to get across the frontier at the river Pyandj in boats made of animal skins. By early October, 100,000 more had found their way to Faizabad and Kisham districts,[45] while 23,000 trudged down the mountains to cross the Pakistani border at a rate of 500 families each day.[46] In November, Islamabad closed the frontier entirely, saying it had insufficient resources to offer any more hospitality. All that was now left to the Tajik commander was the friable loyalty of his Central Asian backers and an unholy alliance with the belligerent successor to the Soviet Union. In August, after a withering denunciation of the Taliban at the G-7 Summit in Okinawa, President Vladimir Putin's spokesman, Sergei Yastrzhembsky, announced Moscow's intention to launch 'preventive and aggressive' air strikes inside Afghanistan, a move that so alarmed Uzbekistan, always sensitive to signs of Russia's post-imperial designs, that it begged off from signing a collective security agreement in October. On 6 October, soldiers of Russia's 15,000-strong 201 Motorised Division in Tajikistan, widely regarded in the region as a Russian protectorate, closed border checkpoints after the Taliban seized districts close to the river Pyandj, and a further 135,000 refugees arrived pleading for sanctuary.

One week later and several thousand miles away, one of the US Navy's most advanced warships, the $1 billion Arleigh-Burke-class guided missile destroyer USS *Cole*, pulled into Aden harbour in Yemen for routine refuelling where it was rammed and nearly sunk by an explosives-laden rubber dinghy, one of the smallest vessels to take to water. The blast, which killed 17 sailors and wounded 39 others, ripped through the destroyer's half-inch steel armour, designed to withstand 51,000 pounds per square inch of pressure, and put the vessel out of action for two years. The two perpetrators of the suicide attack – whose remains were later described as 'confetti-sized'[47] – were identified by local investigators as Saudi-born Yemeni veterans of the Afghan war. Uncomfortably for President Ali Abdullah Salih, they had been among several hundred former mujahedin, recruited to fight with the Yemeni army during a bloody war of secession that broke out in the early 1990s after the over-hasty unification of the country after the collapse of the Soviet Union.

More compelling still, were the similarities in origin, conviction and, ultimately, in target, between the dead bombers and another Saudi-born Yemeni with strong ties to Sana'a, and a burning hatred of the US military – Osama bin Laden. They had sufficient funds at their disposal to obtain false identity documents, a four-wheel-drive vehicle, the boat and three safe houses in Aden, in addition to the explosives used to such devastating effect.[48] Bin Laden denied any involvement during a telephone conversation to Kuwait's *Al-Rai al-Aam* newspaper[49] but, as the investigation continued, he left his Kandahar home in a convoy of 15 vehicles on 22 October and was last seen heading north towards a base in the Parapamizad Mountains, Oruzgan,[50] where there were Stingers, anti-aircraft guns and 2,700 Arab Afghans to protect him.[51] With US elections due in November, a strike was expected at any time. On 25 October a CNN news crew was expelled from Kandahar because its presence 'increased fears' of a US missile attack[52] while, a week before, Pakistan officially denied Washington the use of its airspace for any such raid. But the Arab press reported US jets hovering over Kandahar[53] amid rumours that a US-backed mercenary force was already inside Afghanistan.

On 1 November, mosques in Pakistan and Afghanistan held special prayers for God's protection of bin Laden.[54]

16   Head of the Snake

'And in Aden, they charged and destroyed a destroyer that fearsome people fear, one that evokes horror when it docks and when it sails.' Osama bin Laden, February 2001[1]

With outstanding offers of matrimony to two different women, neither one aware of the other's existence, the private life of the FBI's top counter-terrorism expert, John P. O'Neill, was about as precarious as his career. He had been on Osama bin Laden's trail since the World Trade Center bombing in 1993. He sifted through the rubble of the Khobar Towers building in Saudi Arabia, coordinated the 500 agents who scoured East Africa after the attacks on the US embassies in Kenya and Tanzania and personally directed investigations into the millennium conspiracy in Washington state. As agent in charge of the National Security Division in New York, O'Neill, 49, was acquainted with every aspect of national counter-terrorism strategy, and he was worried by what he found.

'John had the same problems with the bureaucracy that I had,' recalled Richard Clarke, the White House's National Coordinator for Counter-Terrorism from 1992 to 2001. 'A lot of people who were working full time on terrorism thought it was no more than a nuisance. They didn't understand that Al Qa'ida was enormously powerful and insidious and that it was not going to stop until it really hurt us. John and some other senior officials knew that. The impatience really grew in us as we dealt with the dolts who didn't understand.'[2] Clarke was speaking with the advantage of hindsight.

Born in Atlantic City, O'Neill joined the FBI after completing a master's degree in forensic science at George Washington University. He maintained, half tongue-in-cheek, that he owed his choice of career to the actor Efrem Zimbalist Jnr, who played an unreconstructed G-Man in the TV series, *The FBI*, throughout the 1960s. On his way up the ladder, O'Neill gained a reputation as a relentless, meticulous, but abrasive, operator who ran investigations like a political boss, squeezing the hands of as many enemies as friends along the way. Meanwhile, his taste for the good things at his New York headquarters was expressed in a fondness for Elaine's restaurant, sharp dressing and hanging out with movie stars and his foreign police contacts in Manhattan's bars and nightclubs. 'I wouldn't want to be the terrorist he was hunting,' said Scotland Yard's counter-intelligence chief, Alan Frye. 'I've seen him move heaven and earth.'[3] Then his career went mysteriously wrong.

The notion that a sneak thief might choose to ply his trade at a gathering of G-Men is hard to credit, but that was not really the point at issue in what occurred at the hotel in Tampa, Florida where O'Neill attended an FBI conference in July 2000, three months prior to the suicide attack on the USS *Cole*. He briefly left the meeting to answer a pager, to return to a room emptied of his FBI colleagues, who had broken for lunch without including him. His briefcase had also disappeared. Inside was a draft of the Annual Field Office Report for New York, a document detailing every counter-espionage and counter-terrorism operation in the state, as well as information about a valuable FBI source.[4] It was found several hours later in a hotel nearby and forensic analysis established that none of the documents had been handled, though a number of personal items were missing. Whether the theft was carried out by a petty thief or a colleague was never fully determined, but the damage was done. O'Neill's reputation fell under a cloud as the Justice Department, embarrassed by a series of other high-profile security leaks, ordered a criminal investigation into a man who, in the words of prosecuting attorney Mary Jo White, 'created the template for successful investigations of international terrorism around the world'.[5]

As the enquiry proceeded, O'Neill became entangled in a public spat with the US ambassador to Yemen, Barbara K. Bodine that further harmed his case. Bodine was more than a match for O'Neill. Fluent in Arabic and Chinese, she had worked for Henry Kissinger and Cyrus Vance before being posted first to Baghdad and then to Kuwait City where, as deputy chief of mission during the Gulf War, she withstood a 137-day siege by Iraqi troops that earned her the Secretary of State's Award for Valour. Between leaving Kuwait and taking up her first ambassadorial post in Sana'a in 1997, Bodine had worked as Acting Coordinator for Counter-Terrorism in Washington, where she formed her own distinctive views of the threat posed by Al Qa'ida to the US.

The Cole enquiry was a far cry from investigations into the millennium conspiracy, conducted in the friendly police terrain of North America. Within hours of the explosion on 12 October 2000, 100 FBI agents descended on the sleepy Red Sea port of Aden only to spend the next six weeks playing poker in the Hotel Movenpick while a 'memorandum of understanding' was hammered out with the government, by which time the trail of the attackers had gone cold. The agreement parcelled out varying levels of access and investigative responsibility between the domestic security apparatus and FBI, but the Yemenis ran rings around their American visitors. Under the agreed terms, agents were denied direct access to witnesses or suspects; to unedited transcripts of interviews or videos of interrogations; and were barred from talking to the bombers' neighbours in spite of a letter from President Clinton requesting a 'genuine joint investigation'. After further negotiations, they were at last allowed to question witnesses in person, but agents had the sneaking suspicion they were fed lines rehearsed with the local police.[6] When the State Department advertised a public reward of $5 million for information leading to others involved in the attack, the ministry changed the telephone numbers printed in the local press twice in a single month.[7] And it came as a revelation when the authorities coolly informed the FBI that the attack on the USS *Cole* was not even the first attempt against US shipping in Yemeni waters. A bomb-boat had been launched against the US destroyer *The Sullivans* in Aden harbour ten months earlier, failing only because it sank under the weight of its deadly cargo.[8]

Sweating it out in Aden's torpid air, O'Neill insisted that the investigation observe the proper rules of evidence if the resulting prosecution case were to withstand hostile examination in a US court. More particularly, he wanted the authority to expand the inquiry beyond the six immediate suspects, most taken into custody as early as December, to determine what links, if any, existed between Al Qa'ida's wider network of sympathisers in Yemen and senior members of a government that had long made military use of veterans of the Afghan war to suppress insurrection. The most pressing danger was that the authorities would fast-track the trial and execution of the suspects in their custody in a show of compliance with Washington while destroying any thread of evidence that tied them to a more extensive Al Qa'ida cell in Yemen. Saudi Arabia had used the same tactic in the Khobar Towers investigation.

Two of the men in custody were the low-ranking officials who supplied the bombers with false identification. But another, Jamal al-Badawi, confessed to have received instruction and funding from a former comrade in the anti-Soviet war, Mohammed Omar al-Harazi, a Yemeni-born Saudi from bin Laden's ancestral province of Hadramaut. The Cole conspiracy was planned immediately after the 1998 embassy bombings in Africa, al-Badawi said, and al-Harazi's cousin, known only as 'Azzam', was one of the drivers in that operation. Al-Harazi never admitted to bin Laden's involvement in the Cole attack, al-Badawi said, but his 'tone and manner' led him to believe this was the case.[9] Later interrogation also revealed a connection between al-Badawi and another young Saudi of Yemeni descent, Tawfiq al-

Atash, known as 'Khallad', who had already been identified as playing an organising role in the embassy bombings. That January, he had been photographed by a surveillance video in Malaysia where he met two other unidentified Saudis, though the significance of this information went unrecognised for nine months more.

The same January, the strong personal animosity between O'Neill and Bodine, the cop and the diplomat, erupted into a departmental turf war that virtually shut down the FBI's Cole investigation for the next six months at the cost of vital, missed intelligence. The chief source of rivalry was O'Neill's demand that his agents be allowed to carry rifles or machine guns in the field due to the palpable threat to US citizens in the region. The FBI presence had grown to include some 300 agents and support staff by this time. Bodine at first rejected the request, arguing that unleashing a well-armed US force in a trigger-happy, tribal society was but a short cut to confrontation – and she may well have had the US experience in Somalia at the back of her mind. 'We wanted to avoid the appearance of an invasion,' a State Department official said in explanation.[10] Bodine finally relented, permitting agents to carry 'long rifles' in their vehicles, but she demanded, and obtained, swingeing cuts in the FBI presence in Yemen, first to 50 agents and finally to 13.

O'Neill flew back to New York. '[He] came home feeling that he was fighting the counter-terrorism battle without support from his own government,' wrote Lawrence Wright in an extended profile.[11] Bin Laden himself seemed to scoff at his efforts in a video made that January at the wedding of his son Mohammed and the daughter of Mohammed Atef, his military chief, that circulated widely round the Gulf as a recruitment video. Obviously bursting with pride, bin Laden was moved to declaim a poem glorifying the attackers of the USS *Cole*, and the 'false power' they had humiliated. When O'Neill sought to be readmitted in February, Bodine vetoed his return, claiming his 'aggressive style' threatened diplomatic relations between Washington and the Gulf's only democratically elected government. 'O'Neill's been thrown out of better places than that,' commented an FBI colleague.[12] The last 13 agents returned to the US on 17 June after reports emerged of a conspiracy to kill them, a threat that the ambassador disputed. The State Department defended Bodine's strategy. 'I think Barbara's position would be, if they need to come back in, of course they would come back in,' an official said. But the FBI maintained it was a lock-out.[13]

If O'Neill was becoming paranoid – and there is strong evidence that he was[14] – his condition could only have been exacerbated by the testimony of former US army sergeant, Ali Mohammed, one of the six men arrested for the East Africa bombings, who pleaded guilty on 20 October to plotting with Al Qa'ida to kill Americans abroad. This was barely a week after the Cole attack. Mohammed was the face of Al Qa'ida in a wholly unrecognisable guise: beardless, well educated, disciplined, a US passport holder – and a graduate of one of America's most elite military training programmes. Fluent in four languages and a graduate of psychology, Mohammed had risen to the rank of captain in the Egyptian army when he was sent in 1981 to study reconnaissance, unconventional warfare and counter-insurgency operations with the Special Forces, or Green Berets, in Fort Bragg, North Carolina. On returning home, he became involved in Egypt's Gamaat al-Islamiya and, in 1984, approached the CIA with an offer to supply information. It declined.[15] Instead, Mohammed's name was added to a State Department 'watch list' aimed at preventing terrorists from entering the US. Notwithstanding, he emigrated to California without difficulty one year later, signing up with the US army for an eight-year tour of duty. Two years later, the suspected terrorist on the government black list was teaching Islamic culture to army trainees at Fort Bragg.[16]

In 1988, Sergeant Mohammed informed his commanding officer that he would use his annual leave to fly to Afghanistan to fight the Soviets. Either then, or in 1991 when he returned to Afghanistan, he became acquainted with bin Laden – who dubbed him 'Abu Mohammed al-Amriki' ('The American') in a sign of their intimacy. Mohammed used the skills he had acquired at Fort Bragg to help the Saudi establish his terrorist camps near Khost, later coordinating his transfer to Khartoum and training his personal security force. All the while, he supplied Al Qa'ida and Islamist groups in the US with a torrent of rudimentary but still classified Special Forces' information on surveillance, interrogation methods, explosives, assassination techniques, encryption, the creation of terrorist cells and military training programmes that can only have crowned his credit with his Islamist friends. For seven years, Mohammed travelled undetected on Al Qa'ida business from his California base to Sudan, Afghanistan, Pakistan, Somalia and Kenya – while secretly working as an FBI source on illegal immigration and the World Trade Center bombing.

'At about this time, late 1994,' he said in his guilty plea, 'I received a call [to Nairobi] from an FBI agent who wanted to speak to me about the upcoming trial of *United States* v. *Abdel Rahman*. I flew back to the US, spoke to the FBI but didn't disclose everything I knew. I reported on my meeting with the FBI to Abu Hafs [bin Laden's chief of security, Mohammed Atef] and was told not to return to Nairobi.' Later testimony from an Al Qa'ida defector suggested Atef didn't much trust al-Amriki, fearing he had been planted by US intelligence. Mohammed obtained a list of all 118 unindicted co-conspirators in the World Trade Center attack – upon which his name was prominent – and promptly sent it to bin Laden in Khartoum. For Larry Johnson, former CIA agent and the head of counter-terrorism at the State Department during the first Bush administration, the truth about Mohammed was transparent. 'He was an active source for the FBI, a double agent,' he said, adding: 'The reason he didn't testify [at the embassy bombing trial] was so they wouldn't have to face uncomfortable statements on the FBI ... They're more interested in covering their ass.'[17]

If he truly were a double agent, Mohammed's intimate knowledge of bin Laden's activities and security arrangements, added to his admitted surveillance of the embassy in advance of the bombing, should have been sufficient to prevent the attack, particularly since another defendant in the Nairobi indictment, Wadih el-Hage, had been an FBI suspect for over a year before the explosion. 'I later went to Khartoum where my surveillance files and photographs were reviewed by Osama bin Laden, Abu Hafs ... and others,' Mohammed told the judge. 'Bin Laden looked at the picture of the American embassy and pointed to where a truck could go [in] as a suicide bomber.'[18] That recollection dated back either to 1993 or 1994, testimony to Al Qa'ida's impressive capacity for advanced planning. Either al-Amriki had been a triple agent – itself an indictment of the competence of the FBI – or the FBI had known of the Nairobi plot, but had been powerless for some reason to abort it.

While Mohammed's lawyers bargained for a reduced sentence, two other Nairobi suspects graphically demonstrated their continuing dangerousness even within the confines of the Metropolitan Correctional Center at 150 Park Row in Lower Manhattan. Khalfan Khamis Mohammed, a Tanzanian from Zanzibar Island, and Mamdouh Mahmud Salim, aka 'Abu Hajer al-Iraqi', a Sudanese of Iraqi origin, were being escorted back to their cell after meeting with attorneys when Salim plunged a sharpened plastic comb so forcefully into the eye of 43-year-old prison officer Louis Pepe that it penetrated three inches deep inside his brain, leaving him blinded and permanently disabled. The two men had planned to seize control of the tenth floor of the facility, according to notes found in their cell.[19] Salim, organiser of the escape bid, was a senior member of Al Qa'ida responsible for acquiring the materials needed to make nuclear weapons, according to his indictment and the testimony of the chief prosecution witness in the Nairobi trial. He had travelled widely, visiting Germany five times between

1995 and 1998 where he did business with Mamoun Darkanzali, a Syrian who had lived in Hamburg since 1985.[20] It was near Munich that he was run to ground days after the bombing. 'You have a pistol,' he reportedly told the arresting officer, Rupert Folger, during his interrogations. 'Why don't you use this pistol on me and then the whole thing will be finished?'[21] Because of his assault on Pepe, Salim was not among the four other defendants when the trial of *United States* v. *Osama bin Laden, Mohammed Atef, Ayman al-Zawahiri* and 19 more conspirators opened on 3 January 2001.

On trial were Wadih el-Hage, a naturalised US citizen born in Lebanon; Mohammed Saddiq Odeh, a Jordanian; Mohammed Rashed Daoud al-'Owali, from Saudi Arabia; and Khalfan Khamis Mohammed, the Zanzibari. Salim's jailhouse attack hardly facilitated the task of the defence attorneys, who had lost earlier challenges over allegations of torture while in the custody of foreign police; denial of their clients' rights to unmonitored consultations with lawyers; and extended periods in solitary on the basis that they were still highly dangerous. Sam Schmidt, attorney for the Texas-based el-Hage, claimed his client – presumed innocent – was rapidly losing his wits after more than two years in the Manhattan jail. As well as difficulties of communication both linguistically and culturally, attorneys encountered different interpretations of law: Odeh told lawyer Sandra Babcock that Islamic law prevented him making any allegations against the Kenyan or Pakistani police for his mistreatment outside a *sharia* court, though there were clear indications he had neither been read his Miranda rights, nor offered access to legal counsel during questioning.[22]

The attorneys, provided under the legal aid programme, underwent a four-month check by federal investigators of their medical and tax histories, their sexual and psychological backgrounds, before being given access to the 200,000 pages of crime-scene photos, wiretap transcripts, surveillance videotapes, telephone records, forensic and autopsy reports and defendants' statements – and this was comparatively unclassified material. To examine more restricted evidence, they were driven to an undisclosed location to read federal documents, but could only take notes on what they contained.[23] Facing them across the table in the Fulton Street courthouse was Mary Jo White, lead prosecutor in cases against Mafia leader John Gotti and the World Trade Center conspirators and who, as the defendants filed into the heavily-policed court, was chief prosecutor in charge of President Clinton's last-day-in-office pardon of billionaire financier Marc Rich.

All four defendants had confessed to FBI agents their involvement either with Al Qa'ida or the plot to blow up the East African embassies. Al-'Owali trained in weapons, explosives, hijacking and intelligence in Afghanistan and admitted travelling in the truck-bomb on the morning of 7 August in Nairobi. Odeh, the fish-dealing carpenter from Witu, admitted training the Somali fighters who had killed 18 US troops in Mogadishu in 1993. Khalfan Khamis Mohammed told the FBI after his arrest in Cape Town that, when he received orders from Al Qa'ida to grind TNT for the Dar-es-Salaam bombing, he 'did his duty'. El-Hage admitted to serving as personal secretary to bin Laden in the early 1990s and establishing businesses in Kenya on his behalf after 1994, though he maintained he was involved only in the Saudi's commercial enterprises.[24] But the devil was in the detail, and this was chiefly furnished by the prosecution's three star witnesses, all Al Qa'ida defectors.

First up was Jamal Ahmed al-Fadl, a close aide to bin Laden, who fell out with his boss in 1996 after stealing $110,000 from the Saudi's holding company in Sudan, Wadi al-Aqiq, which controlled his fruit and vegetable farms, a salt pan and construction, trucking and import–export businesses. Al-Fadl, now in a witness protection programme, gave a lurid account of Al Qa'ida's global affiliations down to the day-to-day minutiae of an operation with hundreds of needy dependants, legitimate and militant, all struggling to survive on low wages in a hostile environment for a benefactor rapidly going bust.

Recruits for 'martyrdom operations' signed a *baiyat*, or loyalty oath, to the 'Sheikh', and were encouraged to disguise their religious leanings by shaving beards, dressing in Western clothes and wearing cologne to avoid remark. Bin Laden's two-story office on Khartoum's McNimr Street issued a stream of passports, visas and airline tickets under falsified names, while importing explosives, chemicals and weapons under the pretext of conventional business transactions. Bin Laden had bank accounts in London, Hong Kong and Malaysia, but al-Fadl recalled him saying: 'Our agenda is bigger than business.' Al-Fadl described how he met with suppliers to procure uranium for a nuclear construction programme established by bin Laden in 1993, though he couldn't confirm whether a deal had been arranged. Then he remembered bin Laden's rage as US troops disembarked on the beaches of Somalia. 'Now they have come to the Horn of Africa and we have to stop the head of the snake,' he quoted him saying. 'The snake is America. We have to cut off the head of the snake.'[25]

Essam al-Ridi, the second prosecution witness, was another US citizen of Egyptian origin who met bin Laden in Peshawar in the 1980s. He had emigrated to the US in 1979 to study flying, training and later teaching at the Boardman Flight School in Fort Worth, Texas, where he befriended

Wadih el-Hage. Al-Ridi fought alongside bin Laden's volunteers in Afghanistan, but he had returned to the US in 1985 because, he told the judge, he was 'totally opposing any rich individual coming to Afghanistan to control the government'. But he was still prepared to do business with the Saudi. In 1993 el-Hage asked him to shop around the US for a second-hand airplane so bin Laden could 'ship US Stinger missiles' from Peshawar to his new base in Khartoum. Al-Ridi bought a long-range T-39 military jet in Arizona for $230,000 and flew it to Khartoum, though he spurned bin Laden's offer to work as his personal pilot.[26] Instead, the job went to Ihab Ali, an Egyptian-born naturalised American from Orlando, Florida, who obtained his licence at the Airman Flight School in Norman, Oklahoma.[27] The significance of these two small centres of aviation expertise would also become apparent later.

The private world of Al Qa'ida members, as portrayed in the 8,000-plus pages of transcripts from the embassy bombings, was a wasteland of waiting, worklessness and exile, with children getting ill and wives falling pregnant, and the only redeeming kindnesses coming from the mosque, bin Laden's patronage or a sporadic business opportunity. The testimony is a swirl of names and their multiple aliases, echoed dyslexically by witnesses for whom the federal protection programme and a green card proved more enticing than the 72 maidens that pleasure the holy martyr, according to the Koran. His Egyptian and Libyan recruits face the prospect of torture or execution if they go home and constant surveillance by the Mukhabarat intelligence service in Sudan. Members of the Kenyan cell, organised by Wadih el-Hage after 1994, live in a sweating fear of detection.

'Wadih's wife told me ... that she had heard strange voices in the television when she was trying to adjust the speaker,' read a letter in el-Hage's computer, allegedly written by Haroun Fazil, the Comoros Islander suspected of orchestrating the bombing. 'She told me she heard: "This is it. This is the line ...".' Fazul continues: 'The fact of these matters and others leave us no choice but to ask are we ready for that big clandestine battle? Did we take the necessary measures to avoid one of us falling in the trap? Knowing we were counting on God's blessing with our limited resources.' It is argued that bin Laden moved to Sudan in 1991 to restore his fortunes after the drain of supporting so many recruits to the anti-Soviet *jihad*, though many of his enterprises there subsequently failed. But it seems more likely that the Sudan interlude was a conscious imitation of the Prophet Mohammed's *hijra*, or migration, a ten-year period of exile that winnowed out the weak among his band of supporters and initiated the period of his greatest international success.[28]

The prosecution's third witness was L'Houssaine Khertchou, a 36-year-old Moroccan pilot who broke his *baiyat* with bin Laden in 1995 when one of Al Qa'ida's chief financial officers, whom he identifies as 'Sheikh Sayeed', refused to advance $500 to pay for his wife's Caesarian operation. He was arrested at Nairobi airport on the day of the bombing while returning to Sudan following a genuine job interview as a pilot. El-Hage had not been charged with direct involvement in the bombings, only denying before a grand jury that he had had any communication with bin Laden or Mohammed Atef since 1994. Khertchou's evidence critically damaged his defence because he'd seen him with Atef, could confirm his friendship with Odeh and knew he used his laptop to forge ID papers for visiting Al Qa'ida operatives. El-Hage was clearly plugged into the Saudi's directory of contacts. He was friends with Ali Mohammed, Haroun Fazul and several of the World Trade Center bombers; he travelled to Afghanistan on 'gem-collecting' trips; and one address of his private company, Anhar Trading, was the home of the import–export agent, Mamoun Darkanzali, in Hamburg.

The prosecution produced records from bin Laden's satellite phone, a $7,500 O'Gara Compact M purchased in 1996 through Khalid al-Fawwaz, allegedly Al Qa'ida's procurement agent in London, also among those indicted for the embassy bombings. O'Gara's records in Long Island revealed that 2,200 minutes of talk-time were sold to the distant subscriber of 873–682–505–331 over the next two years. More than 200 calls were placed to Yemen over that period, 143 to al-Fawwaz, 100 to Sudan and Iran, and around 60 each to numbers in Saudi Arabia, Pakistan and Azerbaijan. Only 16 were made to Kenya, but four of them were to el-Hage's home; two, from Atef in 1997, had been wiretapped and the transcripts were read out. After el-Hage returned to Texas in 1997, the number of calls to Kenya shot up to 40. 'There is nothing to prove Wadi El-Hage agreed to kill Americans,' responded his attorney, Sam Schmidt, to this evidence.[29]

It is worth sampling the statements made to FBI agent Stephen Gaudin by Mohammed Rashed Daoud al-'Owali, who admitted he had prepared the explosives and travelled in the truck to the Nairobi embassy. A well-educated Saudi, who trained in the bin Laden camp at Khalden and later fought with the Taliban, al-'Owali procured a fresh identity and passport in Yemen in 1996 and then returned to Pakistan. There, he met a man he knew only as 'Khallad', 'a Saudi in his 20s', who recruited him for a mission to be carried out by the 'Third Martyrs Barracks of the Army for the Liberation of the Islamic Holy Places'. He saw Khallad again on 31 July

1998, when he flew to Nairobi after changing planes in Muscat and Abu Dhabi. But it was another man, 'Saleh', who briefed him about his 'martyrdom operation'. Al-'Owali asked Saleh if Al Qa'ida had any plans to attack targets in the US, the FBI's Gaudin recalled. 'Saleh explained to him there are targets in the US that we could hit, but things aren't ready yet, we don't have things prepared to do that yet.' Poor al-'Owali was in a spiritual quandary after finishing his operation, without actually dying. 'He was fully prepared to die in carrying out the mission,' Gaudin told the court, 'but to die after your mission had already been completed ... is not martyrdom, it's suicide, and suicide is not acceptable in his religion.'[30]

The wealth of facts and clues that emerged from the Fulton Street hearings was the product of hundreds of thousands of hours work by the units under the direction of John O'Neill, yet most of this information could have been obtained two years earlier, instantly and without lifting a finger. Sudan's Mukhabarat had kept tabs on the activities of bin Laden and his entourage from the moment they first set foot in the country in 1991, photographing them, logging their movements, their functions and bank details, and intercepting their communications. Increasingly isolated in the world, and desperate to rebut charges that it sponsored terrorism, Khartoum made repeated efforts after 1996 to share their swollen terror database with the FBI, CIA and Britain's MI6, only to be stonewalled by the State Department headed by Madeleine Albright, who remained stubbornly unconvinced of Sudan's good faith. 'They were opening up the doors,' said the last US ambassador, Tim Carney, 'and we weren't taking them up on it. The US failed to reciprocate Sudan's willingness to engage us on some serious questions of terrorism. We can speculate that this failure had serious implications – at least for what happened at the US embassies in 1998. The US lost access to a mine of material on bin Laden and his organisation.' It was only in May 2000, after four years of ignored appeals, that US intelligence finally cleared Khartoum of the terror allegations, but Mukhabarat's collection of files remained unread until a year later. 'It was worse than a crime,' Carney said, 'it was a fuckup.'[31]

A different terrorist nexus was exposed in Los Angeles from 12 March onwards when the trial commenced of Ahmad Ressam, the Algerian arrested on the Canadian border in December with a vehicle stuffed full of home-made explosives. It transpired that Ressam had arrived in Montreal in 1994 as an asylum seeker, even as French authorities were seeking to question him in connection with the hijacking in Marseilles of an Air France jet by members of Algeria's Armed Islamic Group (GIA) who planned to crash it into the Eiffel Tower. He had survived in Canada on welfare checks, fraud and robbery until April 1998 when he flew to Peshawar to meet Hassan Zainul Abidin, or 'Abu Zubaida', the bin Laden lieutenant responsible for coordinating the transport of recruits to and from Afghanistan. Ressam admitted to spending eleven months in Khalden and Darunta camps learning to blow up infrastructure, such as 'electric plants, gas plants, airports, railroads, large corporations ... and military installations'. He returned to Canada in February 1999 with a manual on explosives, $12,000 and a request from Abu Zubaida to send as many Canadian passports as he could steal for other members of Al Qa'ida. Ressam's target on millennium night had not been the Seattle Space Needle, it turned out, but Los Angeles International Airport (LAX) where he had once deplaned, and which he therefore knew. When three other Algerians in his 'unit' failed to pass through immigration, he decided to carry out the mission alone.[32]

He told investigators his plan. 'I will go to the city of Los Angeles. I will survey the airport ... Then I will bring a cart that is used for luggage. I will put the cart in a place that is not suspicious and then I will observe the reaction of security, how long it took them to observe it.' The next time he visited LAX, he planned to put three suitcases filled with explosives in the passenger waiting area, and walk away. Ressam needed help getting around Los Angeles. He called fellow Algerian Mokhtar Haouari, who had bought stolen passports from him before, telling him he had business on hand that had *shteah* in it. '*Shteah*,' Ressam told his baffled interrogator, 'basically means "dance". But whenever there is something that involves fear and danger, you say it is something that makes you dance.' Haouari selected Abdel Ghani Meskini, an Algerian living in Brooklyn, to watch Ressam tango in America.

These details only emerged after Ressam's conviction, when he finally agreed to collaborate with the FBI in a bid to reduce his 130-year sentence. His defence lawyers had tried to convince the jury that the Algerian was an unwitting courier of the LAX bomb for another wanted man, Abdelmajid Dahoumane, with whom he had concocted the explosives in a Vancouver hotel room the night before his arrest. 'This is about a young man who fled war-torn Algeria,' his attorney said, 'a very quiet person, a religious person and probably a gullible person.' However, after months of badgering by the prosecution, the renowned French investigative judge Jean-Louis Bruguière, a friend of O'Neill's, was finally permitted to take the witness stand on 3 April.[33]

Bruguière had driven a bullet-proof Mercedes and carried a .357 Magnum since finding a grenade attached to his door after the successful operation to return the terrorist assassin Carlos the Jackal to France from Khartoum in 1997. His recent investigations included bomb attacks on the Paris Metro in 1995 and 1996 and the shooting down of the airplane carrying the Rwandan president that triggered the genocide in 1994. In the French judge's stated opinion, Ressam was among the 'higher echelons' of the GIA and was wanted in connection with the Paris Metro bombings. He formed, moreover, an integral part of a conspiracy that stretched from Afghanistan to Paris and, via a mosque in London's Finsbury Park, to Montreal and the US. And he had the evidence to prove his allegations, having travelled to Canada two months before Ressam's arrest specifically to confront him.

But Judge John Coughenour wasn't listening to Bruguière, and he didn't let the jury listen either. In spite of the French judge's 'breathtakingly extraordinary' credentials as an expert, the judge ruled: 'The force of his reputation would carry the risk that the jury would not focus on hard facts. I must conclude that the probative value of his testimony would be outweighed by its prejudice to the defendant.'[34] In layman's terms, that meant that however precisely Bruguière argued Ressam's involvement in an international web of conspiracy, his colourful reputation as a terrorist hunter was likely to blind the jury to the facts in the case. By the oddest of coincidences, Coughenour's decision to disregard the Frenchman occurred on the same day it was reported in the briefest news announcement that senior officials in the new Bush administration had been instructed to avoid any public mention of Osama bin Laden for fear of jeopardising ongoing efforts to persuade the Taliban to a compromise.[35]

For O'Neill, who had been on the case well before the East African bombings in 1998, the millennium and Cole investigations years had revealed patterns in Al Qa'ida's operations and network that were two years stale even as they came out in court.

- Al-'Owali had explained the division of Al Qa'ida operations into four separate components: intelligence, administration, planning and execution. The final group – the suicide bombers themselves – arrived on the scene at the last moment while the others left the country before any attack took place.
- Al-'Owali, Ressam and the 'double agent' Ali Mohammed had given detailed descriptions of the training regimes at Khalden and Darunta camps; the streaming of recruits into units of the same nationality; and the preponderance of Saudis, Algerians and Egyptians among their ranks.

- Conspirators, broadly speaking, belonged to one of two groups; unskilled 'first-generation' fighters against the Soviet Union, who did menial work or lived through petty larceny; or committed Islamists from the post-Soviet era who were disillusioned with the rewards their education and professional talents could bring.
- The man known as 'Khallad', identified as Tawfik al-Atash, coordinated both the embassy and USS *Cole* bombings, travelling freely between Pakistan and the locations of terrorist attacks. He was last sighted in Malaysia in January 2001.
- The man known as 'Abu Zubaida', based in Peshawar, knew the identity of every single graduate of Al Qa'ida's terror academy, since he dispatched them to their destinations and frequently procured their new identity papers.
- Al Qa'ida's activities were supported by an extensive racket in stolen or forged passports – many of them Canadian – stolen credit cards and bank robberies. Yemen had emerged as an important centre for the acquisition of new identities, but Al Qa'ida preferred recruiting US passport holders because of the ease with which they could travel.
- Defendants' testimony pointed to the existence of active Al Qa'ida support cells in Germany, Britain, Canada and the US. El-Hage and Salim had both done business with Mamoun Darkanzali, the Hamburg-based Syrian entrepreneur, and Ressam contacted 'Abu Doha', a cleric in the Finsbury Park mosque, to obtain false passports. El-Hage and Ali Mohammed also had extensive relations with the perpetrators of the World Trade Center bombing.
- Ali Mohammed – whose guilty plea meant he did not have to stand trial – was either an exceptionally deep-cover, double agent, working for the FBI in the heart of bin Laden's network, or an Al Qa'ida mole who had burrowed far into the FBI.

O'Neill had observed one other pattern: the apparent perversity with which the US government seemed to block fresh avenues of enquiry before they could be prised open. In June, he travelled to Paris to meet Judge Jean-Louis Bruguière and other French anti-terrorist officials who introduced him to Guillaume Dasquié, an investigative journalist, the editor of Intelligence Online and an expert on Al Qa'ida's finances. They dined together there and in New York a month later. O'Neill bitterly denounced the State Department for hampering his investigations into the World Trade Center bombing, the East African explosions and the attack on the USS *Cole*. The motive, he said, was to defend US oil interests in Saudi Arabia which, he declared, nurtured, financed and shielded Al Qa'ida. 'All the answers,' he told Dasquié, 'everything needed to dismantle Osama bin Laden's organisation can be found in Saudi Arabia.' He said he intended to make a very public resignation from the FBI to protest the subordination of law enforcement priorities to diplomatic and economic considerations.[36]

Back in Yemen, Ambassador Bodine had undergone her own near-death experience with terrorism in spring 2000 when a Moscow-bound plane on which she was a passenger was seized by Chechen hijackers and flown to Saudi Arabia where they demanded fuel for a flight to Kandahar. She escaped unharmed, but the episode did nothing to soften her feelings towards O'Neill or the FBI, which remained absent from Yemen between June and late August.[37] But long-withheld evidence was beginning to seep out. The search of the home of Cole suspect, al-Badawi, revealed an undated, handwritten letter from bin Laden, containing general instructions for an attack on US ships. Al-Badawi said it had been hand-delivered by the elusive Tawfiq al-Atash. The other suspected coordinator of the Cole attack, Mohammed Omar al-Harazi, far from fleeing the day before the bombing as the Yemeni authorities claimed, had tarried peaceably there for months while the country crawled with FBI agents.[38]

The FBI investigation in Yemen resumed in early September, when Bodine's spell as ambassador ended, but O'Neill was no longer part of it. As soon as the Justice Department saw fit to drop its prosecution into the briefcase episode, the FBI launched its own enquiry and he also learned that details of the affair had been leaked to the *New York Times*. After 25 years in the Bureau, his career was at an end. Determined to jump before he was pushed, O'Neill applied for a job as a private security consultant at a salary three times his government work, and he got it: head of security at the World Trade Center, with offices in the North Tower.[39]

John P. O'Neill's funeral procession was two miles long.[40]

*   *   *

For most liberal Americans, George W. Bush's hair's-breadth victory in the presidential election of November 2000 provided all the evidence needed that big oil and sharp lawyers had succeeded in subverting the nation's democratic procedures. The man who finally emerged as 43rd president from the acrimonious constitutional dispute that followed was, on the face of it, spectacularly ill-qualified for the task of dealing in a balanced, objective manner with the Taliban, bin Laden, Al Qa'ida and the burning issues of energy policy which, in the view of the FBI's John P. O'Neill, had blinded the State Department to the national security threats that bubbled merrily away in Afghanistan throughout the second Clinton term.

Bush had been swept to high office on a tide of soft funding from the energy and defence industries. Payback began immediately after inauguration as Bush shoe-horned into the White House advisers whose views reflected those of the corporations that had sponsored his campaign, or veterans of Ronald Reagan and George Bush Snr administrations who had gone on to trade the insider knowledge and contacts acquired in government service for high-flying second careers in corporate boardrooms.

Bush's running mate, Vice-President Dick Cheney, belonged in both categories since he had served as secretary of defence in Bush Snr's government, overseeing Operation Desert Storm in the Gulf War, before signing up as president and CEO of the Dallas-based Halliburton Company, the world's largest oil-field services contractor with revenues of over $15 billion in 1999. Cheney used his government contacts to expand the company's foreign operations, winning contracts in Saudi Arabia, Azerbaijan, Iraq – where Halliburton helped to rebuild the infrastructure destroyed by US bombing – and in Burma, where it worked with UNOCAL on the notorious Yadana pipeline. With Cheney at the helm, Halliburton also diversified into military contracting, doubling government orders to $2.3 billion, while raking in $1.5 billion in subsidies from the Exim-Import Bank and Overseas Private Investment Corporation. In 2000, the year he stepped down to run for vice-president, Cheney's annual salary peaked at $36 million, while his stock in Halliburton was valued at $45.5 million.[41]

The potential for a conflict of interest at the highest levels of policy-making was equally striking in the case of Bush's new National Security Adviser, Condoleezza Rice, another Bush Snr ex-staffer, who was later snapped up by Chevron to work on its $1 billion investment in the Tengiz oil field in Kazakstan.[42] Other appointees were recruited from Amerada Hess and the ill-fated Enron Corporation. But Rice was an ingenue compared to the wolverines lurking in the $12.5 billion, Washington-based Carlyle Group, the nation's most highly capitalised private merchant bank and a specialist in corporate buyouts and the provision of services to the Saudi military and energy sectors.

The board at Carlyle is dominated by Reagan and Bush veterans, including former Deputy CIA Chief and Defense Secretary Frank Carlucci, its chairman; former Secretary of State James Baker; and former federal budget director Richard Darman. In early 2001, the elder Bush was the group's largest individual investor and its senior adviser, earning $80,000–$100,000 for every speech he made on its behalf.[43] The Bin Laden

Group was also an investor, with an acknowledged stake of $2 million, though many speculate it was more since Carlucci, as former chairman of Nortel Networks, had helped build up the company's satellite phone network in Saudi Arabia.[44] If this alone were sufficient to raise concerns about the new administration's ability to remain impartial in its dealings with Afghanistan, more worrying still was the presence on Carlyle's international advisory board of Sami Baarama, a close associate of Khalid bin Mahfouz, the disgraced Saudi banker and former BCCI shareholder who had lost control the National Commercial Bank (NCB) when $2 billion was found to have been stolen during an audit in April 1999. He was subsequently accused of siphoning funds to Al Qa'ida. Baarama was director of NCB's International and Investment Services Divisions when the money went missing.[45]

The Bush, bin Laden and bin Mahfouz families went back a very long way, as did their connections with BCCI. After leaving Harvard Business School, the younger Bush had returned to Midland, Texas where he set up a series of limited oil exploration partnerships, called Arbusto '78 and Arbusto '79 after the years in which they were incorporated. One of his financial backers was the businessman James Bath, a fellow pilot in the National Guard, who had represented the Houston interests of Osama bin Laden's older brother, Salem, since the death of their father in 1976. Bath helped to finance Bush's first unsuccessful run for the Texas governorship and he also purchased a 5 per cent stake in Arbusto '79 for $50,000, though it was unclear whether the money belonged to him or to his Saudi patron. After Salem's death in a flying accident in 1988, his Texas holdings devolved onto Khalid bin Mahfouz, whose Texan investments Bath also represented: bin Mahfouz, Bath and the BCCI's most prominent frontman, Gaith Pharaon, subsequently became partners in Houston's Main Bank in an apparent bid to evade the Security and Exchange Commission's (SEC) restrictions on foreign ownership of US banks.[46]

Never successful, Arbusto went through a series of mergers until it was absorbed by Dallas-based Harken Energy Corporation in 1986, which Bush Jnr joined as a director for $500,000 in stock and $120,000 in consulting fees. When Harken also ran into trouble in 1987, another bin Mahfouz associate and Pharaon business partner, Abdullah Taha Baksh, purchased 17.6 per cent of the company even as Bush was trying to secure a cash infusion in Little Rock, Arkansas from banker Jackson Stephens, a major underwriter of Bill Clinton's gubernatorial aspirations and a political kingmaker since Jimmy Carter's candidacy two decades before. Stephens had been intricately involved in BCCI's attempts to secure control of another US bank, Washington's First American, in contravention of federal law. He obtained the $25 million for Bush from the Union Bank of Switzerland, BCCI's partner in its Swiss subsidiary, the Banque de Commerce et de Placements, and Harken began to thrive.

Three years later, amid strong indications that his presidential father had called in a favour, Harken inexplicably won a 35-year drilling contract from the emirate of Bahrain, despite its lack of any international or offshore drilling experience. As the share price moved up, Bush sold his stock for $850,000, triggering an investigation for insider trading based on fore-knowledge of the Gulf War acquired from his father.[47] Under questioning, Bush denied any acquaintance with his business partner, James Bath; denied any knowledge of BCCI's involvement in Harken; and, when forced to concede that the relationship had in fact existed, confessed that he had been aware Bath fronted for Saudi investors all the time. 'The number of BCCI-connected people who had dealings with Harken – all since George W. Bush came on board,' the *Wall Street Journal* wondered in its own enquiry, 'raises the question of whether they mask an effort to cozy up to a presidential son.'[48]

There are two intriguing footnotes to this all-but-deleted episode in the president's business history. Robert Mueller, the Justice Department official responsible for the BCCI investigation in 1991, was severely criticised at the time for failing to expose the full breadth and depth of the bank's corrupting influence on officials in the Reagan and Bush administrations, in part because crucial documents continued to be sequestered by British intelligence in London. In March 2001, President Bush appointed Mueller director of the FBI, in spite – or, perhaps, because of – his discretionary feel for issues of banking secrecy and federal law enforcement. As for Robert Jordan, the Houston-based corporate lawyer who defended Bush in his 1990 insider trading investigation, he obtained his reward eleven years later with the appointment as US Ambassador to Saudi Arabia, though he had no obvious diplomatic qualifications. But Jordan worked for Baker Botts, the private law firm of James Baker, Bush Snr's former secretary of state, who was also senior counsel for, and a board member of, the Carlyle Group. And the Carlyle Group, the largest contributor to Bush's 2000 presidential election campaign, had, and continues to have, a commercial relationship of the utmost sensitivity with the ruling House of Saud.[49]

The most powerful Afghan in the world at this point in time was neither Mullah Mohammed Omar nor Ahmad Shah Massoud, but a Dari-speaking Pashtun from Mazar-i Sharif called Zalmay Khalilzad, 50, the naturalised American selected by vice-president-elect Dick Cheney to restaff the

Pentagon for the incoming administration. During the Reagan years, Khalilzad had worked as a policy planner on Afghanistan at the State Department for Paul Wolfowitz, future deputy to Secretary of State Donald Rumsfeld, before moving to the post of under-secretary at the defence department during the first Bush administration. Like Wolfowitz, he was considered a hawk, arguing for the delivery of Stinger missiles to the mujahedin in the mid-1980s, and less successfully, for the total destruction of Saddam Hussein's regime. He had waited out the Clinton years at the Rand Corporation, and worked for UNOCAL as senior consultant in charge of risk assessment for the trans-Afghanistan pipeline project.

The job brought him into close contact with the Taliban leadership, notably in December 1997 when a delegation of mullahs visited UNOCAL's headquarters in Texas. Khalilzad defended the movement in the op-ed pages of the *Washington Post* that same year: 'We should ... be willing to offer recognition and humanitarian assistance and to promote international economic reconstruction. It is time for the US to re-engage.'[50] Two years later, with UNOCAL's plans in shreds, he had dramatically changed his mind, judging from an essay in the *Washington Quarterly*, datelined winter 2000, but written a year earlier. Citing a menace in Afghanistan that threatened US lives 'at home and abroad', the Middle East peace process and the stability of US regional allies, Khalilzad wrote: 'The only problem with engagement is that it is not likely to work. Despite its superficial pragmatism, a closer look reveals that engagement would do little to subdue the Taliban. Indeed, given the Taliban's intransigence, it could even backfire, encouraging Taliban radicalism.' He proposed six measures to weaken the movement, including increased support for the Northern Alliance and cultivating the many Pashtun tribal leaders believed to be chafing under Taliban rule. 'Continued neglect,' he warned, will only lead to further chaos and violence and pose a growing threat to US interests.'[51] In spite of his influential connections and a subsequent posting to Bush Jnr's National Security Council, however, Khalilzad's advice prevailed neither with the new president nor his own line manager, Condoleezza Rice, until it was far too late.

After four acrimonious years of Clinton and Inderfurth, the Taliban had grounds for anticipating some improvement in their relations with the US under a new administration whose eyes were glued to gas and oil trends. As Americans went to the polls the previous November, Mullah Omar had kept his promise to ban opium cultivation in the 95 per cent of Afghanistan under Taliban control, in spite of UN sanctions and the fact that international recognition had never looked more remote. UN field surveys predicted output collapsing from 3,276 tonnes in 2000, to just 185 tonnes in 2001, most of it confined to Northern Alliance territory in Badakhshan.[52] The Taliban felt they were 'owed' for the achievement – though sceptics argued that the ban was pragmatic, designed to prop up the price of the hundreds of tonnes still stockpiled in their warehouses. 'We want to start a new era of reason and dialogue to resolve the outstanding issues with the US,' said a foreign ministry spokesman. 'We hope President Bush will succeed in eliminating hatred and close the chapter of hostile policy against us.'[53]

But the signals they sent were strangely mixed, leading Peshawar-based Nancy Dupree, a well-informed interpreter of Taliban phenomenology, to conclude that Arab fighters loyal to bin Laden had launched an 'internal coup' the previous December, and that Mullah Omar was nothing more than a powerless hostage.[54] Certainly, the broadcast by Al-Jazeera TV of the wedding of bin Laden's son, Mohammed, and the daughter of his Egyptian aide, Mohammed Atef, in January 2001 could not have been more poorly timed if Mullah Omar were genuinely seeking to convince Washington that his guest was harmless and a new leaf had been turned: New York lawyers had spent the same day arguing over which members of the public were qualified for jury service in the trial of the East African embassy bombers, due to open soon after.

On 26 February, Mullah Omar issued a decree, 'based on the verdict of Islamic scholars and the decision of the Supreme Court of the Islamic Emirate', ordering the destruction of the Buddhas of Bamian and all other pre-Islamic figures, including those in Kabul's National Museum, on the grounds that they were idolatrous. Poised 175 feet and 125 feet, respectively, above a valley inhabited by Shias, the twin sandstone figures were the largest standing Buddhas in the world and dated back nearly 1,500 years to the little-understood Gandaran era when Asian faith and Greek art fused to give birth to a hybridised depiction of spiritual values that belonged neither to the East nor to the West. Surprised by the international condemnation his decision provoked, Mullah Omar shrugged: 'All we are breaking are stones.'[55] Sayed Rahmatullah Hashimi, a Taliban envoy then touring the US, said the decision to destroy the statues was taken when UNESCO and EU delegates offered money to protect the figures, but not to help Afghan people. 'When your children are dying in front of you,' he explained, 'then you don't care about a piece of art.'[56] But ordinary Afghans did care, insofar that they were free to say so. After broadcasting a report in which she claimed she had been unable to find a single Afghan who agreed with the Taliban's decision, the BBC's Kabul correspondent,

Kate Clark, was given 24 hours to leave the country.[57] Video footage, screened on CNN, showed the Buddhas being demolished with explosives inserted into holes drilled into their time-smoothed heads, torsos and limbs.

Despite the mullah's unwavering weirdness, and his defiant flaunting of bin Laden, Bush's State Department still made time to listen to its Taliban visitors, some of whom may have hoped to revive old *jihadi* links with Richard Armitage, Deputy Secretary of State under Colin Powell and a former head of the CIA's South Asia office. His career had briefly collapsed at the end of the 1980s after his involvement in the Iran-Contra scandal. Bush's new Assistant Secretary of State for South Asia, Christine Rocca, was another veteran of America's first Afghan war: she had spent 15 years in the CIA's Operations Directorate, where she liaised with mujahedin commanders over the supply and distribution of Stingers. The Taliban's roving envoy, Sayed Rahmatullah Hashimi, met with Armitage and Rocca in Washington in early March, amid speculation that a new dialogue was opening between the Bush administration and Taliban in which the bin Laden issue was set aside in favour of a less confrontational approach to the two countries' relations. Powell opposed the new direction, but he was reportedly overruled by the CIA and the State Department's Bureau of Intelligence and Research, which held their own talks with Hashimi.[58]

The meetings formed part of a five-day visit organised for Hashimi by Laili Helms, the Taliban's unofficial lobbyist in the US. A Jersey City housewife of Afghan birth, Laili's aunt was married to Richard Helms ('Uncle Dick'), CIA director from 1966 until 1973 when he was dismissed by President Richard Nixon for shredding documents detailing the agency's activities in Chile. After Helms pleaded no contest to charges of lying to a congressional committee in 1977, Nixon appointed him ambassador to Iran, where he helped train the Shah's secret police force, the *Savak*. But Helm's truest benefactor was the multimillionaire Iranian businessman Mohammed Irvani, another BCCI frontman with intelligence connections, who provided the funds for their joint consulting company.[59] Though never recognised as an official Taliban representative, Laili Helms's skills as a fixer and her twice-removed relationship with the CIA earned her credit both in Washington and Kandahar. In interview, she dismissed bin Laden as a 'tractor driver', a 'hangnail' the Taliban had inherited from the *jihad*, but she drew the line at the Buddhas. 'That was a very big deal. That was them thumbing their nose at the international community.'[60]

Massoud took advantage of the international outrage over the destruction of the Buddhas to fly to Europe to drum up political support for the

Northern Alliance, raise its ideological profile and, generally, to show his face – which one journalist thought bore 'a striking resemblance to the American singer, Bob Dylan'.[61] It was an unprecedented step into the limelight for Massoud, who had not travelled beyond his Central Asian rangeland for over a decade, preferring to delegate diplomacy with the West to foreign affairs minister Dr Abdullah Abdullah. The decision to come down from the mountains and cut a dash in Paris, Brussels and Strasbourg, was also an effort to counter the Taliban's perceived progress with Washington by opening a new diplomatic front in Europe. 'My message to President Bush is this,' he told journalists in Paris. 'If he isn't interested in peace in Afghanistan, if he doesn't help the Afghan people to arrive at their objective of peace, the Americans and the rest of the world will have to face the problems.'[62] He discussed foreign aid in Brussels and addressed the European Parliament in Strasbourg on the rights of women and democratic elections, much to the frustration of the Taliban deputy interior minister, Haji Mullah Khasar. 'To invite him personally for this meeting is a tyranny against the Afghan people,' he said, 'because they will give him the orders to fight more.'[63]

Massoud's hunch that Washington was warming to the Taliban was not far wrong. On returning to Afghanistan, he learned of the death from liver cancer in Pakistan of Mullah Omar's supposedly moderate deputy, Mullah Rabbani, one of the original band of fighters who captured Kandahar in 1994.[64] Days later, the authorities announced the purge from government service of 9,000 employees considered 'unreliable elements'.[65] In another gesture of inspired diplomacy in late May, the Taliban unveiled plans to compel the several thousand Hindus living in Afghanistan to wear 'labels' to distinguish them from the Moslem majority. 'This is not a discrimination against our Hindu brothers,' soothed the State Department's new friend, Sayed Rahmatullah Hashimi, 'it's for their own security.'[66] But critics in the US and Hindu-dominated India saw the measure as disturbingly reminiscent of the Nazis. The Taliban's only response to the outcry was to ban foreign female aid workers from driving cars because 'it has a negative impact on the environment'.[67]

Though more manic than murderous, these decrees supplied the background to the 25 May announcement by Secretary of State Colin Powell that the US intended actually to increase its aid to Afghanistan in 2001 by $43 million, of which $10 million was allocated to 'other livelihood and food security programmes', a reference to crop substitution projects in former opium-growing areas. The news came on the same day the UN issued an expert panel report that questioned the seriousness of the Taliban's anti-opium measures. 'If Taliban officials were sincere in stopping the production of opium and heroin,' it read, 'one would expect them to order the destruction of all stocks existing in areas under their control.'[68]

Washington's attempts to re-engage directly with the Taliban continued up until 2 August, according to the official record, when the South Asia department head, Christine Rocca, held her last formal meeting with the Taliban representative in Islamabad, Abdul Salaam Zaeef. Three days after, by way of a retort to whatever impasse was reached in that conversation, the Taliban arrested eight Western aid workers from Shelter Now International, together with 16 Afghan employees, and accused them of 'spreading Christianity', a charge carrying a potential death sentence and a minimum five years in prison. It appeared the charges were only too true: against all prevailing notions of common sense, the fundamentalist Christian agency imported films and Bibles, translated into Dari, with the intention of converting Afghans to Christianity. Among the would-be missionaries were two pretty young American women, one hailing from Waco – scene of a more serious misunderstanding over militant religion – in Bush's home state of Texas.

But back-channel communications had continued throughout the summer in a series of mini-conferences, entitled 'Brainstorming on Afghanistan', chaired by Francesc Vendrell, Special Representative of the UN Secretary-General, and attended by political and military figures from Russia, Iran, Pakistan and the Northern Alliance. The Taliban did not send a delegate, relying on Pakistan to relay the tone of the discussions. 'It was clear that the trend of US government policy was widening,' recalled Tom Simons, a former ambassador to Pakistan and one of three Americans, including Karl Inderfurth, to attend the third conference in a Berlin hotel in mid-July. 'People should worry, Taliban, bin Laden should worry – but the drift of US policy was to get away from single issues, from concentrating on bin Laden as under Clinton, and get broader.' Former Pakistani foreign minister, Niaz Naik, who was also at the meeting, remembered things somewhat differently. 'The Americans indicated to us that, in the case the Taliban does not behave and in case Pakistan doesn't help us to influence the Taliban, then the US would be left with no option but to take an overt action against Afghanistan.'[69]

Why the debate should have been made 'broader' than the single issue of bin Laden – just as his role in the East African embassy bombings was tumbling forth in a Manhattan courtroom – defies explanation unless one subscribes to the theory of French journalists, Jean-Charles Brisard and Guillaume Dasquié, who sat listening in New York that same July as FBI agent O'Neill related how his investigations had been frustrated – an allegation the *Guardian* was able to confirm after speaking with FBI sources later in the year. 'There were always constraints on investigating the Saudis,' said one, particularly members of the bin Laden family, but they became more exacting when the Bush administration took over.[70] For their part, the Frenchmen maintained that the administration had adopted the belief that the Taliban were potentially 'a source of stability in Central Asia that would enable the construction of a pipeline across Central Asia', side-stepping the Russian monopoly on oil transportation, and enriching the companies with which the president was so closely identified.[71] At one stage in negotiations, said Brisard, the 'US representative' had told the Taliban: 'Either you accept our offer of a carpet of gold, or we bury you under a carpet of bombs.'[72]

Something almost as remarkable occurred in Riyadh 45 days later on 31 August. It was an event that signalled some Rubicon was crossed under cover of darkness, that an invisible trackway of long-shared direction had forked, its wayfarers departing in opposite directions. Prince Turki al-Faisal had been in charge of Saudi Arabia's foreign intelligence service for almost a quarter of a century. A series of immensely powerful CIA chiefs from both political parties had worked with him since 1977, but not one could match him for wealth, stealth, freedom from oversight and professional longevity. Prince Turki's memory harboured the secrets of a generation; the BCCI project, the Afghan *jihad*, the politics of oil, the making of Pakistan's nuclear bomb, the assassination of President Sadat, the *intifada*, the scramble for Central Asia, the rise of the Taliban, the role of bin Laden, the purpose of Al Qa'ida – and the making of President George W. Bush. In spite of a royal constraint that meant he could never speak openly of these matters, another thing is certain: Prince Turki had always mediated between Riyadh, Washington, Kabul and his countryman and old comrade, Osama bin Laden, however suffused with fog these relationships ultimately became. Less than a month after Christine Rocca's final meeting with the Taliban and only days before the events of 11 September, the plug was mysteriously pulled on the Saudi spy master on 31 August after a lifetime of service. With no explanation, beyond a mild suggestion of ill-health, Prince Turki al-Faisal asked his uncle King Fahd, nominal ruler of Saudi Arabia, to be relieved of his post.

He gave a series of anodyne interviews with the Middle East Broadcasting Corporation in the months that followed, in which he claimed to have met Mullah Omar on two occasions only. 'In my first meeting ... he was very cordial, but in the second meeting, he turned hysterical in his attacks on the kingdom.' Laili Helms had a more engaging story to relate, dating from 1999, when Mullah Omar reportedly agreed to hand over bin Laden.

Prince Turki had flown to Kandahar with his entourage. 'There's just one little thing,' Helms reported the prince as saying. 'Will you kill bin Laden before you put him on the plane?' Mullah Omar called for a bucket of water, pulled off his turban, splashed water on his bare head and sat heavily down, Helms reported. 'You know why I asked for the cold water?' the Taliban leader enquired. 'What you just said made my blood boil.'[73]

The game was now afoot. On 16 July, the Pakistani High Commission in London granted that rarest of privileges, a one-year, multiple-entry visa, to two Moroccans travelling on Belgian passports. They carried letters of accreditation from London's Islamic Observation Centre, a bin Laden front headed by Yasser al-Siri, an Egyptian wanted on charges of planning suicide attacks in 1995. His letter introduced the two men as reporters for a fictitious television station, Arabic News International. On arrival in Pakistan on 25 July, they quickly disappeared into Taliban-controlled territory.[74] Some days later, a British journalist encountered them in a Northern Alliance guesthouse in the Panjshir valley: 'There was a definite hierarchy between them. The first ... was large and dark, but his most curious feature were two blackened indentations on his forehead, which looked like the result of torture with an electric drill.' He said his name was Karim Touzani.[75]

The Moroccans were anxious to obtain seats on the helicopter to Massoud's headquarters in Khawaja Bahauddin, on the Tajikistan border. After waiting several days in Panjshir, they finally flew to the base where they spent a further week recording video interviews with President Rabbani and Massoud's Pashtun ally, Abdul Rasul Sayyaf, while pestering Massoud's press attaché, Assem Suhail, for an interview with the commander-in-chief. An appointment was accordingly set for 9 September. Something about his Arab visitors aroused Massoud's suspicion, and he shouted for his guards but Touzani was able to detonate a bomb hidden in his video camera before they could respond, killing Suhail and himself, and fatally wounding Massoud. The second Moroccan was shot as he tried to escape by hurling himself out of a window into the Amu Darya river.

The night before his assassination, Massoud had a dream in which he commanded his comrades to tie his sash around his waist. They refused, gracefully, telling him that he 'had no more need for his sash as his work for the Alliance was done'. On waking, he recounted the dream to General Mohammed Qasim Fahim, his deputy, and to Sadiq, his wife and the mother of his son and four daughters. 'Walk with me in the garden,' he told two of his children later that morning, 'for when I am gone, you will have no father to walk with.'[76]

17 Manual of a Raid

'I see water and buildings. Oh my God! Oh my God!' Madeleine Amy Sweeney, flight attendant, American Airlines Flight 11.[1]

Mohammed Atta set down his will in 1996 in Hamburg at the tender age of 28, when it seemed he was condemned to live the interminable half-life of a student after what had proven a demoralising search for work in his native Egypt.[2] He had studied engineering with distinction at Cairo University for five years before embarking, at his father's insistence, on a master's degree in urban planning at Hamburg-Harburg Technical University that would last a further seven. 'I told him I needed to hear the word "doctor" in front of his name,' his father said.

Atta's thesis addressed the newly-fashionable topic of how best to conserve traditional Moslem cityscapes in the face of modern encroachments. He used his bursary as a scholarship student to finance a visit to Istanbul in 1994, where he was photographed – tense, unsmiling and vigilant – decked in tropical shirt and faded jeans like any other young tourist. That winter was spent in Syria, studying the fifteenth-century *souk* in Aleppo, the largest market in the world sprawling over four miles of garrulous streets and scented side-alleys. Back in Hamburg, he was hired as a part-time draughtsman by the architectural consultancy, Plankontor: colleagues remarked on his diligence, reserve, the 'careful elegance of his drawing'. 'He prayed in the office,' recalled Helga Rake, 'we'd never had anyone do that before.'[3]

A devout Moslem since his teenage years, Atta's faith did not conflict with visiting Sharky's Billiard Bar – though he did not drink alcohol – or acquiring the technical skills required of a twentieth-century professional career. Contemporaries thought him a prime candidate for assimilation, despite his lack of a girlfriend, or even German male friends beyond the immediate circle of his faculty supervisors. But the handwritten will, discovered after his death, revealed an unsuspected interior world of ascetic disdain that would have shocked his mother, who had dandled him on her lap until the day he went to university.[4] That Atta was contemplating death four years into his course in Hamburg was distressing; that he had barred women from his burial, including his mother and three sisters, sounded suspiciously like invective. 'Neither pregnant women nor unclean people should say goodbye to me,' he wrote from Germany's most promiscuous port of call. 'Women must not be present at my funeral or go to my grave at any later date.' The 18-clause will gave instructions for the washing of his body and genitals, his funeral garments and the behaviour of mourners after his burial. 'An animal should then be sacrificed,' he declares, with a biblical flourish, 'and the meat be distributed among the needy.'[5]

In late 1996, Atta moved into an apartment at 54 Marienstrasse with a 23-year-old electrical engineering student whom he called 'cousin', though there is no evidence of a blood tie between them. The son of a cleric in the United Arab Emirates (UAE), Marwan al-Shehhi was plump, devout and withdrawn, but their landlord esteemed them as quiet tenants who paid with cash on the nail. Soon they were joined by Ziad Jarrah, a Lebanese student of aeronautical engineering who, at 23, was already a qualified commercial pilot. Atta had taken to praying in the back room of a neighbourhood shop, the only Arabic-language mosque in a neighbourhood otherwise populated by more secular Turks. There he encountered a Yemeni-born cleric, Ramzi Binalshibh, with whom he formed a prayer group at university and who became the fourth tenant at 54 Marienstrasse. An Afghan neighbour, two floors up, remembered them murmuring from the Koran as he passed their door, where four pairs of shoes were always carefully aligned. Atta ran into the Syrian merchant, Mamoun Darkanzali, at around the same time. Darkanzali's business dealings had brought him into contact with two of bin Laden's associates in Sudan, Wadih el-Hage and Mamdouh Mahmud Salim.

Atta took an unexplained leave of absence from Hamburg in November 1997 lasting 15 months, a period he may have spent training with Al Qa'ida in Afghanistan. On his return in early 1999, neighbours thought him changed beyond recognition. He dressed in *shalwar kamees*, wore an unkempt beard and rarely laughed now, but he threw himself with a vengeance into his long-neglected thesis on the mediaeval Arab city, winning the highest possible honours when it was submitted that August. 'He was a very nice young man – polite, very religious and with a highly developed critical faculty,' recalled his supervisor, Professor Dittmar Machule.[6] In November 1999, he disappeared again, telling his father he intended to polish his English skills in the US, but first he had business in Prague.

Forget and force yourself to forget that thing which is called the World; the time for amusement is gone and the time of truth is upon us. We have wasted so much time in our life. Should we not use the hours to offer actions that make us closer to God?

By late 1999, when he disappeared into an atmosphere thick with millennial foreboding, Atta had made contacts that could not be explained as the fruit of his Hamburg years and whom, in all likelihood, he met in the months he went missing. Among them were two comfortably-off, Saudi passport-holders, Khalid al-Midhar and Nawaf al-Hamzi, veterans of the Chechen insurrection and Afghanistan's training camps who had resided in California in 1998.[7] US intelligence was aware of al-Midhar's connection with Al Qa'ida as early as December 1999, when he booked two one-way tickets to Kuala Lumpur through a 'logistical centre' in Yemen with known connections to the terrorist network but, for some unaccountable reason, it decided to let him go.[8] Instead it asked Malaysian intelligence to shadow the two Saudis during their visit, in the hope – one can only surmise – that their trail would lead to the identification of more senior operatives in the Al Qa'ida hierarchy. And it did, with calamitous consequences.

On unspecified dates between late December 1999 and early January 2000, while US security was distracted by the scare in Seattle and the widespread pre-millennium malaise, al-Midhar and al-Hamzi met in a Kuala Lumpur hotel with Tawfiq al-Atash, or 'Khallad', architect of the African embassy bombings and the USS *Cole* attack, to discuss in outline the next 'martyrdom operation', while a Malaysian surveillance team took photographs. The CIA's brief to Malaysian intelligence was to watch and record, but not to intervene. By the time the pictures reached Fort Langley in mid-2000 at the earliest, Khallad was long gone, taking with him the CIA's best chance of disrupting the carnage to come. Widely cited then and since as compelling evidence of bin Laden's involvement in terrorism, the pictures from Kuala Lumpur were never made public, with the result that Khallad's face – and the CIA's blunder – are more a mystery now than before the film was shot.

Al-Midhar and al-Hamzi slipped from view, scorning US vigilance by flying from Bangkok to Los Angeles on business visas on 15 January 2000, and going on to take an apartment in Clairemont, San Diego where, true to their training, they were always prompt with the rent. They applied to Sorbi's Flying Club for instruction in piloting Boeings, but were told they had to learn to fly Cessnas and Pipers first. An instructor said al-Midhar had trouble mastering the controls of the plane and became so terrified at times he started to pray. His more worldly companion asked their landlord to stick an advert for a Mexican wife on the internet for him, but there were no replies.[9]

Atta was in deep cover, and remained so for six months more, though a former lecturer spotted him one morning in early 2000 in a Hamburg shopping mall.[10] A fully-trained architect, with a justifiable interest in acquiring English, he faced no hardship in obtaining travel documents for the US, but his plan entailed transporting the entire 'team' at 54 Marienstrasse to the US, and Binalshibh had little to recommend him to the immigration authorities. In mid-May, the Yemeni mailed the first of four entry applications he made in 2000; all were refused in spite of a last-ditch effort to support his request by booking a pre-paid flying course in Florida.[11] Atta could wait no longer. On 2 June, he boarded the bus for Prague to meet Ahmad al-Ani, an officer with Iraqi intelligence, in an encounter monitored by domestic security.[12] A Czech official suggested the meeting had been held to coordinate a terrorist strike on Radio Free Europe, a US station with headquarters in the capital, but it also served as a tripwire, exciting a flurry of activity culminating in the first of a series of financial transfers to Atta one month later.

The day after the meeting in Prague, Atta flew to Newark, New Jersey to be reunited with Marwan al-Shehhi. For the remainder of June, they were transient, living tracklessly on cash. They reconnoitered the Airman Flight School in Norman, Oklahoma, where bin Laden's personal pilot, Ihab Ali, had earned his licence, but returned to Manhattan to replenish their funds with money wired from the UAE. Oklahoma was rejected as a base of operations in favour of Florida, a warmer, more congenial state where anonymity was the rule, not the exception. They chose Hollywood, cut from the coastal palmetto in the 1920s, near Fort Lauderdale and 25 miles from Miami International Airport. Like any newly-married couple, Atta and al-Shehhi opened a joint account at the SunTrust Bank, receiving a first infusion of $10,000 on 19 July, and a further $100,000 in three staggered payments that ended on 18 September.[13] The final transfer of $69,985 caught the attention of a staff member at SunTrust, who filed a 'suspicious transaction report' with the US Treasury's money laundering agency, the Financial Crimes Enforcement Network, but to no avail.[14]

The first $10,000 transfer was for a 25 per cent deposit on two pilot courses on small planes at Huffman Aviation International Flight School in Venice, courses that cost $38,700 when they finished in November. Atta told instructors he was of royal Saudi lineage, and introduced al-Shehhi as his bodyguard. He was remembered as an eager student, 'though not well-liked, whose reluctance to engage in conversation with others was sometimes resented'.[15] But he knew how to study, and was duly awarded a temporary pilot's licence on 21 December.

At this comparatively advanced stage of the mission, it is far from conclusive that Atta, its commander in the field, was precisely aware of what he was expected to do, let alone how. All he knew was that it involved airplanes and cockpit skills. The Al Qa'ida veterans in the San Diego unit were responsible for communications with Khallad, the presumed coordinator, and kept contact with the novice in Hollywood to a minimum to reduce the chance of interception. He was undeniably professional, committed and had the best of their trust, but the operation – whatever the target – brought them into an unfamiliar security landscape, patrolled by alien giants, with a pervasive technology and disdain for both faith and corruption, the saving graces of many previous operations.

The US mission was the first of a kind. It demanded techniques of dissimulation, camouflage and know-how that so far outstripped the expertise required for operations in Africa and the Middle East that it must have seemed to the conspirators that they stood as much chance of success as an individual singlehandedly launching a moon shot. No executive team waited in the wings to ignite the fuse or drive the truck: their mission relied upon men with the ability to stay in character and maintain a punishing momentum for up to two years, while mastering tasks of the utmost complexity down to their finest details. Atta demonstrated his ignorance of its ultimate objective in August 2000, when he enquired about setting up a crop-dusting company in Florida, a query presumed to indicate an interest in dispersing biological or chemical agents by air over US cities. The same question was asked almost a year later in Oklahoma, this time by a freelance who nearly capsized the project.[16]

When the airplane starts moving and heads towards [takeoff], recite the supplication of travel, because you are travelling to God. May you be blessed in this travel.

Atta's Hamburg roommate, the pilot Ziad Jarrah, breezed into the US in June to attend a Boeing aviation seminar, but Binalshibh still faced insuperable problems obtaining a visa.[17] By October 2000, when he made his last unsuccessful application, the Yemeni's role had been downgraded from aspiring pilot to back-up financial coordinator. He wired a transfer to al-Shehhi in September and, a year later, did the same for Zacarias Moussaoui, the 33-year-old Frenchman of Moroccan descent allegedly brought in to replace him. But Moussaoui was, arguably, as conspicuous as Binalshibh, or so French intelligence believed. He had left France in 1993 to take a master's degree in international business at London's South Bank University, where he attended Brixton mosque and lived for the next seven years. In 1994, French authorities opened a file on a certain 'Zacarias', based in London, whom they suspected was paymaster to Algerian terrorists in

France. The investigative judge Jean-Louis Bruguière travelled to London specifically to interview him and search his apartment, but he was refused permission by the Home Office. Moussaoui had never been arrested, either in France or Britain, so the investigation folded. But London friends had noted his politics harden and he was eventually asked to leave the mosque for preaching holy war.[18] In 1997, he travelled with a childhood friend to Chechnya and, one year later, was identified while training at Khalden terrorist camp alongside the Seattle bomber, Ahmad Ressam.[19]

Somewhere along the way, Moussaoui acquired contacts in Malaysia, Khallad's base of operations for the USS *Cole* attack, and he visited it twice in September and October 2000 using money that was hard for a drop-out student to explain. On 29 September, Moussaoui emailed a course enquiry to the Airman Flight School in Norman from an internet cafe in Kuala Lumpur. On his second trip, he stayed with a local Taliban sympathiser, Yazid Sufaat, who gave him a letter of accreditation that introduced him as the North American marketing executive for Infocus Tech, a computer company in which his wife held shares, on a salary of $2,500 per month.[20] Back in London, Moussaoui received a visit from Binalshibh in the first week of December and swiftly returned via Pakistan to Afghanistan, where he remained for two months. By 7 February 2001, he was on the move again, flying to London for two weeks, before boarding a flight for Chicago, where he admitted on his customs declaration form to carrying $35,000 in cash. He arrived in Norman on 26 February, deposited $32,000 in a new account and started learning to fly.[21]

Stuck out in Oklahoma, Moussaoui was a loner by comparison with the two-man teams established in San Diego and Hollywood, but he was at least wired into the Hamburg cell through his acquaintance with Binalshibh. Hani Hanjour, a Saudi who arrived on student visa in December 2000, was a more complete outsider, with no known connections either to Hamburg or the training camps in Afghanistan. What he did have, inexplicably, was a Federal Aviation Administration (FAA) licence to pilot commercial jets, dating from 1999, though he impressed flight tutors – and, perhaps, his co-conspirators as well – as singularly hapless and accident-prone. Scarcely five feet tall and deeply introverted, Hanjour studied English in Tucson, Arizona in 1990, quitting three months later to return home and manage his family's date farm near the city of Taef. Five years on, he was suddenly gripped by the urge to learn to fly in the US. After six listless months in Florida and California, he signed up for a three-month course at the CRM Airline Training Center in Scottsdale, Arizona, returning a year later for more tuition. Hanjour was considered a rotten student. 'He'd be late, he wouldn't show up, he was unprepared, he didn't do his homework,' recalled CRM's controller. When the school refused to readmit him for classes in 1998, Hanjour joined a flight simulator club at Sawyer Aviation in Phoenix, using the facilities for two summers, and then he 'disappeared like a fog'.

Hanjour came to the attention of the local FBI as early as 1996, when Aukie Collins, a convert to Islam and veteran of the war in Chechnya, was asked by the Phoenix bureau to listen out for information about young Arabs taking flying lessons. 'When I said there's this short, skinny Arab guy who's part of this crowd, drives such-and-such a car,' he said, 'I assumed that they would then, you know, start tracing him and see who his contacts were.'[22] They didn't. When the Saudi returned to the US in December 2000, he was the first of a string of volunteers recruited not by Atta, but the mysterious Khallad, or his associates. He headed back to his old stamping ground in Phoenix to resume training at the Pan Am International Flight Academy. His instructors, disturbed by his continued inability to speak English, the first language of international aviation, alerted the FAA, which sent a representative to observe him practise. He was permitted to continue his training.[23]

Down in Hollywood, Atta had learned more about the nature of his task. On 5 November, more than a month before obtaining his pilot's licence, he purchased two global positioning devices from a Fort Lauderdale shop and flight-deck videos for the Boeing 747–200 and Boeing 757–200 from Sporty's Pilot Store in Batavia, Ohio. The $35 videos provide students with detailed information about customary inflight procedures, as well as extensive simulation techniques. On 11 December, he put in a second order for flight-deck videos for the Boeing 767-300ER and Airbus A320–200, as did Al-Hamzi in San Diego. He spent $1,500 for three hours' training on a Boeing 727 flight simulator at the SimCenter, Opalocka, near Miami, where a tutor said he 'got a good feel for manoevering the airplane around, basically turning the airplane left and right, climbing and descending'.[24]

But he had to leave the country to renew his visa. In January, he and al-Shehhi flew to Madrid where they met Imad Eddin Barakat Yarbas, otherwise known as 'Abu Dahdah', a Palestinian with Spanish citizenship and connections with Al Qa'ida dating back to 1995 when he lived in Peshawar and helped Abu Zubaida, bin Laden's fixer in Pakistan, process volunteers. Nothing is known of what was said in Madrid, but the two men had been in contact since Atta's Hamburg days, and Yarba's Spanish cell was then involved in planning additional attacks on the US embassies in

Rome and Paris. He also had lines of communication with Abu Zubaida that were, arguably, less vulnerable to surveillance than those from the US.[25]

On their return, Atta faced a 57-minute grilling at immigration control in Miami International after he let slip his intention to study flying, which his visitor's visa proscribed. What Florida immigration failed to register was that Atta had overstayed his previous visa by more than a month and that the FAA was also threatening to investigate both men for abandoning a rented plane on a taxiway at the same airport when it broke down shortly after Christmas 2000.[26] They were allowed to proceed, however, and drove north to spend two weeks scouting flying schools in Decatur, Georgia, near Atlanta, briefly joining a health club. On 8 April, travelling alone this time, Atta flew to Prague for a second encounter with his intelligence contact at the Iraqi embassy, Ahmad al-Ani, who was expelled from the Czech Republic two weeks later for other reasons.[27] As happened when the two men last met ten months earlier, their conversation set off a frenzy of activity.

All the enemy's devices, and their gates and all their technology do not do benefit or harm, except with the permission of God.

Between 23 April, when Atta flew back to Florida, and 29 June, a second wave of 13 conspirators passed through US airports, seven in May, six more in June. They were a mixed assortment of mainly Saudi, former US residents, students of aviation or runaways with no clearly defined skills – or identities. Abdulaziz al-Omari, allegedly a Saudi pilot and former flight engineer at John F. Kennedy International Airport in New York, brought his wife and four children, building a convincing cover at Vero Beach, 300 miles north of Miami, though his real identity remains open to question. As does the actual name of the man who called himself Waleed al-Shehri, allegedly the son of a former Saudi diplomat in Washington, who studied at Florida's Embry-Riddle Aeronautical University in 1997 and lived in Dayton Beach. His presumed brother, Wail, was another qualified pilot who had left home in December 2000 to be treated for 'mental illness' in the shrine city of Medina, by his father's account. Two other Saudi pilots with the same family name, Ahmed al-Ghamdi and Hamza al-Ghamdi, lived in the 1990s at an apartment block in Pensacola, Florida housing foreign students of electronics, communications and computers at the nearby military training facility. The licence of yet another pilot, Fayez Ahmed, was registered at an address in Tulsa, Oklahoma, where Ahmed al-Ghamdi allegedly obtained his, but a man with the same name as Ahmed had also attended a course at Lackland Air Force Base in San Antonio, Texas – as did another Saudi arrival, Saeed al-Ghamdi, who may have been related to Ahmed and Hamza al-Ghamdi, but who may not have been Saeed al-Ghamdi at all.

Among these seven names, all with apparent expertise as pilots, six had records as students in programmes specifically created to meet the needs of Washington's military or commercial allies. Their bona fides are impossible to confirm, however. Men with the same names and histories later turned up alive in Saudi Arabia and North Africa, claiming to have lost their passports or had their identities stolen: if they did or had been, the thief was remarkably astute as to the type of profile needed for their substitutes to bypass US immigration controls – and where in the kingdom's military database such 'secure' identities could be acquired. Of the other six arrivals in May and June – Salem al-Hamzi, Ahmed al-Haznawi, Ahmed al-Nami, Mohand al-Shehri, Majed Moqed and Satan al-Suqami – nothing is known for certain, though Mohand al-Shehri could have been related to Waleed and Wail, and Salem al-Hamzi to Nawaf al-Hamzi of the San Diego cell. If true, they injected into their deadly enterprise the flavour of an extended family outing.[28]

The men dispersed to cheap apartments or hotels in Hollywood and the nearby resort of Delray Beach, where they lived unflagrantly, training in local gyms, visiting pizza-houses and making themselves discreetly agreeable to their neighbours. Ahmed and Hamza al-Ghamdi took an apartment together with Ahmed al-Nami in the Delray Racquet Club where, despite keeping a low profile, they impressed one resident as being drug dealers because she saw them at night, 'carrying dark bags'.[29] Abdulaziz al-Omari, Mohand al-Shehri and Saeed al-Ghamdi occasionally trained in the FlightSafety aviation school at Vero Beach but, for the most part, the men were on stand-by: they were trained to fit into the landscape, disguise their identities and bide their time. In the same month the new recruits arrived, Atta and al-Shehhi moved out of Hollywood to a condominium in nearby Coral Springs.

One man busier than the rest of the new recruits was the pilot calling himself Fayez Ahmed, a citizen of the UAE. Shortly before entering the US, Ahmed opened an account at the Standard Chartered Bank in Dubai, UAE on the same day that a known associate of bin Laden, Mustafa Ahmed, opened another at the same branch under the name Mustafa Ahmed al-Hawsawi. Mustafa Ahmed, otherwise known as 'Sheikh Sayeed', was almost certainly the conduit – if not exactly the source – of the $110,000 transferred to Atta's SunTrust account the previous year; the $35,000 Moussaoui brought from Pakistan; and the funds that Ramzi Binalshibh, the other member of the Hamburg cell, wired or transferred on various occasions from Europe to Moussaoui, Atta and al-Shehhi. Somewhere outside the bank, the two men met or conferred and this, and subsequent transactions, strongly suggest Fayez Ahmed had greater responsibility than the twelve other new arrivals, amounting perhaps to the role of financial coordinator. Soon after landing in Florida, Ahmed and eight colleagues opened individual accounts at the SunTrust Bank, using cash brought in as travel expenses. Three weeks later, Ahmed gave power of attorney over his account to the faceless financier in Dubai, who arranged for the shipping of his credit cards to Florida. The day the two Dubai accounts were opened was also the fifth anniversary of the 1996 bombing of the Khobar Towers complex in Saudi Arabia. The National Air Traffic Controllers Association in Hawaii warned: 'The airlines are at risk.'[30]

While the conspirators settled in to their briefest of new lives, the operation was again nearly stopped in its tracks after a single, crucial oversight by an over-confident Atta. He was pulled over by a Florida highway patrol car on 26 April for driving without a valid licence and then ducked the subsequent court hearing, which issued a warrant for his arrest on 28 May. In principle, he could have been picked up, expelled and barred from re-entering the US at any time between then and early July, when he again left for Europe. In practice, legislation that would have allowed immigration, police and the motor vehicle authorities to pool information had been introduced to Congress during Clinton's second administration, but never passed.[31]

> *Know that Paradise has raised its most beautiful decoration for you, and that your most heavenly brides are calling you – 'Come, O follower of God' – while wearing their most beautiful jewellery.*

The penury of public information about the true identities of members of the conspiracy renders analysis of each individual's role in it next to impossible, but log entries from commercial sources, such as aviation schools, banks and restaurants, allow for a certain amount of reasonable deduction. Question: how many of the 20 acknowledged participants were truly licensed pilots, rather than cyphers who had travelled on the falsified or stolen documents of bona fide graduates from US military and commercial flying schools? Among the first wave were Atta and al-Shehhi, who graduated the previous December; their Hamburg roommate, Ziad Jarrah from Lebanon; and Khallad's confidants in the San Diego team,

Khalid al-Midhar and Nawaf al-Hamzi – though there is no record they concluded their courses at Sorbi's Flying Club. Elsewhere were Zacarias Moussaoui and Hani Hanjour, more remote from the operational axis, whose isolation may have been designed to insulate them in the event that the Hollywood and San Diego cells were destroyed and they were needed to replace the main protagonists at short notice. However, in a tribute to Khallad's foresight, a third contingency group existed, composed of Fayez Ahmed, Abdulaziz al-Omari and Waleed and Wail al-Shehri, who all emerge from the miasma of shifting identities as probable pilots, with similar names and skills to the ones enscribed on their visa applications forms.

Toward the end of June, with the second wave safely esconced in Hollywood and Delray Beach, the senior conspirators converged on Las Vegas for a summit of aviators, one of six held between May and August. The venue, convenient to San Diego but 2,179 miles flying distance from Florida, suggests the mission's powerhouse lay in the west, but the city also provided opportunities for a hedonism now permitted to martyrs whose lives could be measured in weeks: the Vegas visits, in short, became working holidays. Al-Shehhi paid $20 to Samantha, a lap dancer at the Olympic Garden Topless Cabaret who, in retrospect, thought he looked 'cheap', though one of her three colleagues – also, interestingly, called Samantha – remembered his group as 'quiet, well-groomed, polite, light drinkers – and the opposite of big spenders'. Atta, al-Shehhi, Ziad Jarrah, Hani Hanjour and Nawaf al-Hamzi stayed at the cheap end of The Strip, in the Econo Lodge, where they worked through an agenda that included gripes about expenses, their training progress, the new arrivals, their strengths, their weaknesses and the next phase of the plan.[32] Several had already joined gyms, though Jarrah went one step further by hiring a personal trainer to teach him to kickbox and fight with a knife. Some evenings, Jarrah rented a car and they drove out to the desert to listen in the silence and pray.

Bin Laden later claimed in a video for private consumption that the 'brothers' knew nothing about the operation, 'not even one letter ... until they are there and just before they boarded the planes'.[33] But an operation on so ambitious a scale required detailed reconnaissance by a skilled pilot, able to time an aircraft's flight path, judge when it had reached cruising altitude and observe what visual landmarks could be used to substitute for the crew's navigational equipment and guide a successful hijack to its target. At the barest minimum, a stop-watch and compass would serve to plot the course, but global positioning devices produce preciser results. While the choice of which flights to seize, each taking off in a narrow time-band and with a full load of fuel, could be left to a planner not directly involved in executing the last phase of the mission, one or more of the pilots were needed to reconnoitre the selected flights, since familiarity with each one's flight plan was crucial to knowing the exact moment to take control.[34] There were admittedly security concerns, particularly with regard to those who stood outside the charmed Hamburg circle, but Atta could vouch for al-Shehhi and Jarrah while al-Hamzi was situated even closer to Khallad, its organisational head. Though no evidence was ever revealed to prove the supposition, it is more than likely that, in the months after the Las Vegas conference, both Atta and al-Hamzi flew first-class more than once from Boston to Los Angeles, Newark to San Francisco and Washington to Los Angeles, under assumed names and on tickets purchased through a bank account not yet identified with their operation. What the record does state is that between 27 June and 3 July, Atta flew to both Boston and Newark airports with the express intention of at least studying the plan of the departure areas, if not actually plot the course changes of individual flights.[35]

Atta and al-Shehhi flew from Miami to Zurich on 8 July, withdrawing $1,000 in Swiss francs from a bank machine. Because they intended to spend only two and a half hours at the airport before catching another flight to Madrid, their true destination, they may have met an accomplice to hand over the cash. While waiting for departure, Atta purchased two Swiss army knives and a set of box-cutters, either as gifts or to test security. Once in Madrid, the men rented a car and disappeared for a week. Given their previous friendship and conversations bugged by Spanish police three weeks later, it seems natural that they spent time with Yarbas, the Spanish cell leader, who was aware of his visitors' reasons for being in the US and, anyway, had his own operation to mount, and so could make use of Atta's expertise. Atta's motives for travelling to Madrid are harder to discern. It was convenient for a meeting with his old friend, Ramzi Binalshibh from Hamburg; the latter had longstanding links with Madrid and, when forced to flee Germany in September, it became his first port of entry. But Spain was also a good location to meet more senior Al Qa'ida members, perhaps Khallad himself, men who were barred from entry into the US or otherwise under surveillance – while enjoying a little relaxation: In the last seven months, Atta had made eight, risky round-trip flights and a unknown number of reconaissance trips by air, as well as attending to a rigorous schedule of flight training and the provision of homes, documentation and money to a dozen subordinates. Atta and al-Shehhi checked into a tourist hotel at Salou, south of Barcelona, on 16 July, where police suspect they may have met two unidentified men on undisclosed business.[36] Three days later, more cautious after Atta's previous experience at immigration, they returned to the US through Atlanta, avoiding Miami altogether.[37]

Oh God, may you make my entry to this car a safe entry and my exit a safe exit. May you make my journey an easy one, and may you grant me support and success in all my endeavours.

Al Qa'ida's field forces in the West seemed immune to detection in early 2001, apart from the arrest by Italian police of a six-man cell in Milan in January suspected of planning to bomb the US embassy in Rome. With the arrest of Djemal Beghal in Dubai on 28 July, however, the survival of the entire European network fell into jeopardy when the Frenchman succumbed to torture and fully confessed. His background was similar to Moussaoui's and the two may well have met. Sons of North African immigrants to France, both had been active sympathisers of Algeria's Groupe Islamique Armée (GIA) in the early 1990s, until French intelligence surveillance forced them across the English Channel where they melted into the Islamist ghettoes in London and Leicester. Beghal travelled to Pakistan in November 2000, taking his pregnant wife and two children. Unusually for a 'Westerner', he underwent training near Kandahar, where he claimed to have learned of a pact between the Taliban and bin Laden that resulted in the closure of all training camps not directly affiliated with Al Qa'ida. The pact, he told police, was more of a leadership merger. 'None of the terrorist operations of Al Qa'ida,' he said, 'could have been decided after May 2001, except with the accord of the Taliban and their chief, Mullah Omar.'[38] After giving *baiyat* to Abu Zubaida, Beghal received the singular honour of three gifts from bin Laden: a string of prayer beads, some incense and a toothpick. Abu Zubaida ordered him to organise a bomb attack on the US embassy in Paris, with the help of Al Qa'ida sympathisers in the Netherlands, Spain and Belgium.

Beghal's confession, which he later retracted, led to twelve immediate arrests and sharpened surveillance of Islamists in all three countries, as well as France, for months after.[39] Spanish intelligence had tapped Yarbas's telephone since 1997 without making any major breakthrough. Finally, on 6 August, he received a cryptic call from a man called 'Shakur', who was identified as an intimate of the Hamburg group, though clearly not one of Atta's men for the calls continued throughout September. 'I have cut off all my old contacts and in one month I may see you,' Shakur said in code, adding: 'I have prepared some threads and other things that you will like.'[40]

Despite racking up 57 hours flying time in Norman, Zacarias Moussaoui had not managed a single minute flying solo, a feat achieved by most students in less than half the time. After three months at Airman, Moussaoui quit without his coveted licence. Both his funds and nerves were wearing thin.[41] On 29 July, and over the next two days, he made a number of calls to Binalshibh in Dusseldorf, who contacted the financier, Mustafa Mohammed Ahmed, aka 'Sheikh Sayeed'. Ahmed wired $15,000 to Binalshibh, who forwarded it to Moussaoui from the railway stations in Hamburg and Dusseldorf. A week after the funds arrived, Moussaoui packed his things and hitched a ride with a friend to Minneapolis where, on 10 August, he paid a $6,300 cash deposit on a $19,000 course in flying Boeing 747s at Pan Am International Flight School in the suburb of Eagan. Pan Am owned the school in Phoenix where Hanjour was training and the SimCenter near Miami, where Atta took computer simulated lessons in flying 727s.[42]

In Coral Springs, Atta and al-Shehhi prepared for the last, frenetic furlong. On 6 August, they rented a car from Pompano Beach, Florida and disappeared for a week to research accommodation in the Washington area, returning on 13 August to take another flight to a meeting in Las Vegas with Hani Hanjour and Nawaf al-Hamzi.[43] Atta flew back from Las Vegas a day later through Houston where, in spite of the warrant for driving without a licence, he rented another car for a five-day trip with al-Shehhi into unknown country. The two men clocked up 3,000 miles in five days, enough for a return trip to Washington, but only half the distance to the west coast and back.[44] Minneapolis was no longer an option. A Pan Am flight instructor became suspicious of Moussaoui three days into the course, when his new student became 'belligerent and evasive' and proved ignorant of basic skills, despite enrolling in an advanced course in flying commercial jets. Reports that he asked only to learn how to steer a jumbo, but not to take off or land it were dismissed by his supervisors as fiction.[45]

Pan Am relayed their instructor's concerns to the Minneapolis division of the FBI, which detained him for overstaying his visa on 17 August. In his possession, they found knives, binoculars, fighting gloves, shin guards, a hand-held aviation radio, flight manuals, flight simulator programmes, pilot software for the 747 and written evidence linking him to the Hamburg and Malaysia cells. On 26 August, French intelligence notified the FBI of Moussaoui's links with Al Qa'ida, but the bureau denied the Minneapolis office's increasingly insistent requests for a warrant to search his computer hard drive and telephone records. There was insufficient evidence, they determined, that Moussaoui was either a member of a terrorist organisation or the agent of a foreign power, as required under the Foreign Intelligence Surveillance Act. Six weeks earlier, agent Kenneth Williams in the FBI office in Phoenix had written to headquarters in a similar vein warning of an 'effort by bin-Laden to send students to the US to attend civil aviation universities and colleges'; he referred to Middle Eastern men enrolled in flying classes at Embry-Riddle University, not to Hanjour who was then training at a Pan Am college in Phoenix. Williams's alert was also ignored but the Minneapolis office, 'in a desperate 11th hour measure to bypass the FBI [headquarters] roadblock', notified the CIA's Counter-Terrorism Center of its anxieties – receiving nothing more than a stern rebuke from their supervisor for their pains.[46] Moussaoui stayed in the custody of the immigration authorities until 11 September, when the pieces began to fall into place. On an unspecified date later that August, the FBI and CIA received information from Israeli intelligence that as many as 200 terrorists had already slipped behind US defences and were planning to attack a 'large-scale target'.[47]

Moussaoui was not a major link in the information chain, and so had fewer secrets to impart, but his determination to not collaborate with the US authorities spoke of a resolution that rarely came into focus in the rest of his career. Atta had rented a Piper Archer on 16 August, spending three days unconcernedly trawling the blue skyways over Palm Beach county, and Jarrah followed a similar pattern further south over Fort Lauderdale. Atta may not have heard of Moussaoui's arrest until days after when, in a possible reaction to the loss of a key operative, the mission kicked into high gear. Jarrah drove to Miami and purchased a global positioning device and a manual of the cockpit instrumentation for a Boeing 757. From 25 August through till 29 August, beginning with al-Midhar in San Diego, 14 of the remaining 19 conspirators booked one-way, first-class tickets on breakfast-time flights out of Boston, Newark and Washington, by internet or with cash, at a cost of around $4,500 each – for a total of $84,500 for the entire group. Atta bought a knife.[48]

On 25 August, bin Laden told a Middle East TV crew – with a 'significant and knowing smile' – that the US was going to 'get a surprise'.[49] Two days later, the CIA finally received word that two Al Qa'ida terrorists – Khalid al-Midhar and Nawaf al-Hamzi – had re-entered the US in July, but intelligence could track them no further than a room at the false address they gave in the Marriott Hotel, New York.[50] Shakur called Yarbas the same day. 'I am taking classes,' he told him. 'it will take a month or so ... In the class, we've come to the part on aviation and we have even cut the throat of the bird.'[51]

Check the suitcase, the clothes, the knife, your tools, your ticket ... your passport, all your papers. Inspect your weapon before you leave.

In mid to late August, the San Diego group, including Hani Hanjour, flew east, converging on the low-cost Motel Valencia, outside Laurel, Maryland, 25 minutes from Washington DC and an hour from Dulles International. They were joined by three of the men from Florida, Salem al-Hamzi, Majed Moqed and Mohammed Atta, but Atta quickly flew home from Baltimore. The remaining five moved into a one-room, self-catering apartment at the Motel Valencia on 2 September, paying $280 a week, though an instructor at Gold's Gym where they worked out said they walked around with 'wads' of cash. When he asked Hanjour the meaning of his first name, he was told it was the Arabic for 'warrior'. Hanjour flew over the area three times in a plane rented in Bowie and, on 7 September, the five checked out of the Valencia, not to be seen again until they stepped into the departure area at Dulles.[52]

Back in Florida, it was time for the intense friendship that had made Atta and al-Shehhi all but inseparable since June 2000 to bend to operational necessity. On or around 3 September, al-Shehhi drove with three of the other conspirators to the resort town of Deerfield Beach, where they took rooms in the Crystal Cay Motel. Al-Shehhi stayed at the nearby Panther Motel with a second group of unidentified men, though it probably included Fayez Ahmed, Ahmed al-Ghamdi, Hamza al-Ghamdi and Mohand al-Shehri, all members of his team. Atta had other business to attend to.[53] On 4 September, he made the first in a series of transfers to 'Mustafa Ahmed' of what remained in the mission's bank accounts before they fell into disuse forever: after Fayez Ahmed, Waleed al-Shehri and Marwan al-Shehhi chipped in the balance of their accounts, a little over $42,000 was preserved for future Al Qa'ida operations.[54] On the same day, a security camera captured a white Mitsubishi circling a restricted parking area at Boston's Logan International at least four times in as many days, a sign that Atta, or his New England support team, had begun to survey the airport's best means of access. As if by clockwork, Ramzi Binalshibh and two other members of the Hamburg cell quietly left Germany on 4 September for Madrid, where they caught a plane to Istanbul, another to Karachi and a third to Quetta and the safety beyond the Afghan border.[55]

On 7 September, the day the Maryland team checked out of the Valencia in Laurel, Atta met al-Shehhi and a third man at Shuckum's Oyster Pub and Seafood Grill in Hollywood. Atta played video games and drank what the barman recalled was cranberry juice for four hours at one end of the bar, while al-Shehhi and the other customer knocked back cocktails and seemed to argue. But it was Atta who let fly when the waitress put the bill for $48 on the bar, taking her gesture as a doubt they were good for the money. 'You think I can't pay my bill?', he shouted, 'I'm an American Airlines pilot.' He was either very drunk or deadly sober, but he ripped a bill from a bundle of $50s and left. Further along the coast, another group of Arabs got tight and nasty at Red-Eyed Jack's in Daytona Beach. 'Wait till tomorrow,' one said, 'America is going to see bloodshed.'[56]

Al-Shehhi checked out of the Panther on 9 September, leaving behind a bag containing aeronautical maps, a protractor and a Boeing 757 flight manual. Atta returned his rented car to the agency, pointing out helpfully that the oil indicator light did not work. On 10 September, the three teams in Florida flew to Newark and Logan airport in Boston where the white Mitsubishi waited, along with another vehicle. Atta drove the Mitsubishi west along the Massachusetts Expressway to Exit 13 where, in another reckless confrontation with authority, he loudly refused to pay the $3.10 toll. The booth operator wrote down his licence number as he sped away.[57] Eight of the Boston group registered at hotels in groups of two, as Atta and Al-Omari got a change of car and then drove 110 miles (175 kilometres) north, checking into the Comfort Inn close to Portland International Jetport, 'Maine's Gateway to the World'. During a round of last-minute chores, the men were caught on security cameras at a petrol station, two bank machines and a Wal-Mart shopping centre. They ate pizza and returned to their room to observe the 15 rituals of self-preparation outlined in a handbook for martyrs, copies of which were found afterwards in Atta's suitcase, Nawaf al-Hamzi's Mitsubishi and in the wreckage of United Airlines 93 at Shanksville, Pennsylvania.

The five-page document, taken down by a woman from dictation according to handwriting experts, gives the suicide bomber guidance on how to spend his last night on earth as it inches through the darkness into the measured but heightened reality of a martyrdom operation. Intended to stiffen the martyr's resolve, the notes prescribe ceremonies for the purification of the body, readings from the Koran and invocations specific to every step of a mission in progress, from the donning of shoes and the prayer to say as the vehicle nears its destination to how to execute bystanders with a glad heart – though the targets of this operation, for security reasons, are disguised by initials: 'M', for *matar*, or airport, and 'T', for *ta'irah*, or airplane. Aspirants are urged to consider themselves the true descendants of the companions of the Prophet, whose war for Islam in the ten years after his expulsion from Mecca, is not unlike their own.[58]

Clench your teeth, as did your predecessors before going into battle. In combat, hit firmly as the heroes do, who do not wish to come back to the worldly life. And say aloud 'God is Great,' for saying it causes terror to enter into the hearts of the disbelievers

Atta was nearly late on the dawn of his martyrdom, passing through Portland security with al-Omari at 5.53 a.m., scarcely 15 minutes before their flight was due to depart for Boston. The bag that he checked in never made their connecting plane, American Airlines 11 (AA11), due to take off at 7.59 a.m. from Logan for Los Angeles with a light load of 92 passengers. As he approached his seat in row 8, Atta scanned the faces in business class to confirm that the other members of his squad were present. Then he sat down and called Marwan al-Shehhi on his cell phone, seated in 6C on United Airlines 175 (UA175), a little ahead on the taxiway and due to leave for Los Angeles at 7.58 a.m.[59] Atta's closest friend confirmed his team was aboard, though a last-minute dispute with a driver over parking the white Mitsubishi had nearly upset their plan.[60] Two minutes after AA11's departure, United Airlines 93 (UA93) took off from Newark for San Francisco and, at 8.10 a.m., AA11 was in the air, flying from Dulles to Los Angeles. Within a span of twelve minutes, four planes, each carrying the four tonnes of jet fuel needed for a cross-country flight, had taken off with 272 passengers from three airports.

AA11 was due to fly west across Massachusetts out of Logan traffic control and into the jurisdiction of Cleveland, both of which received bomb threats by telephone at around 8.15 a.m., just as the Hudson valley became visible through the windows in business class. Atta shouted the signal and his squad marched on the cockpit, cutting the throat of one passenger and stabbing two flight attendants en route. Flight attendant Madeleine Amy Sweeney called Logan to report a hijack but, even as she related what was happening, Atta and his men broke into the locked cockpit. One of the pilots switched on a relay microphone as the hijackers burst in. 'We have more planes,' Logan controllers heard a man say. 'Don't do anything foolish ... you won't be hurt.'[61] At 8.28 a.m., the transponder, which allows a plane's route to be monitored, was switched off. Seated in front of the airplane's controls, Atta banked hard to the left, straightening up the Boeing 767 only when its nose pointed along the gun sight of the Hudson toward Manhattan.

UA175 had taken off a minute before AA11, but its route was south to northern New Jersey, before taking a gentle turn west towards California. Al-Shehhi's team waited until the World Trade Center, visible 50 miles away on a morning as clear as 11 September, came into view of the right-hand side of the plane. Once this was sighted, his squad pulled out box-cutters and slashed at flight staff until they reached the pilots' cabin. At around the same time as Atta was completing his unexpected turn south along the Hudson, traffic controllers noticed something was wrong with UA175, now banking in a full circle east over central New Jersey, instead of west, until it lined up to approach New York harbour from the south. Just as suddenly, its light vanished from the screens as the transponder was cut out.[62]

'Anybody know what that smoke is in Lower Manhattan?' asked an unidentified pilot over the common frequency at 8.50 a.m.[63] Two minutes earlier, flying at 494 mph, a speed at which the plane risked breaking apart in mid-air, Atta had crashed AA11 into the North Tower between floors 94 and 99. Al-Shehhi, always the junior partner in their relationship, exceeded his friend's flying skills at the end of it, tilting the 60-tonne Boeing 767 as it hurtled towards the World Trade Center at 537 mph so that it was angled like a dagger when it plunged into the South Tower between the 78th and 84th floors at 9.03 a.m. The South Tower took only 56 minutes to collapse: the North Tower stood for 102 minutes.[64]

Minutes after AA11 struck the North Tower, traffic control in Indianapolis tried to contact AA77, which had failed to respond. Just after crossing the Ohio–Kentucky border at 8.56 a.m., the transponder was turned off so its exact flight path is unknown.[65] At 9.30 a.m. Khalid al-Midhar, the hijackers' leader, told passengers they should call home because they were all going to die.[66] One of them, political commentator Barbara Olson, whose book on Clinton's departure from the White House, *The Final Days*, was about to be published, called her husband from the locked toilet. 'She said they had knives. They had rounded the passengers up at the back of the plane.'[67] At 9.33 a.m., an unidentified object rapidly approaching the prohibited airspace over the White House and the Capitol alerted Reagan National Airport, which ordered a military cargo plane to intercept and identify it. The crew said it was a Boeing 757, 'moving low and fast'. As AA77 flew over the Pentagon with Phoenix-trained Hani Hanjour at the controls, it began to turn 360 degrees to the right, descending nearly to ground level. A pilot who witnessed the crash said the Boeing was in power-drive as it accelerated into the west side of the Pentagon at a speed well over 500 mph.[68]

Far more is known about the hijackers' *modus operandi* on UA93, flying from Newark to Los Angeles with 37 passengers, many of whom held long telephone conversations with loved ones as the plane flew to its doom. With Moussaoui under arrest, the suicide squad was down to four men, with the Lebanese Ziad Jarrah shouldering the role of both team leader and pilot. According to passenger accounts, three men in red bandanas – presumably to identify one another during the scuffle that followed – broke into the cabin and threatened to detonate a 'red box' strapped to the waist of one of them, that they claimed was a bomb. At 9.35 a.m., controllers in Cleveland heard the sounds of a fight and screams on the radio link to the cockpit, which remained open as an accented voice said: 'This is your captain. There is a bomb on board. We are returning to the airport.'

Before Cleveland, UA93 turned 180 degrees to the left and headed for Pittsburgh, flying low and erratically. Inside the plane, one man was stabbed as crew and passengers were herded to the rear by three of the hijackers, including the one with the red box. Jarrah was now alone at the controls. Five of the passengers resolved to tackle the man with the 'bomb' and then storm the cockpit. 'Are you ready, guys?' said one of them. 'Let's roll.' The plane continued southeast, but eyewitnesses said it was so out of control that it was almost flying upside down. At approximately 10.06 a.m., 31 minutes after the hijack, UA93 crashed into the Pennsylvania woods, 80 miles southeast of Pittsburgh, killing all on board. The pilot's last words were only heard after the flight's black box recorder was recovered from the rubble. There was a 'very noisy sound of a confrontation' and a voice, probably Jarrah's, screaming 'Get out of here! Get out of here!'[69]

18   The First Circle

'America is full of fear from its north to its south, from its west to its east. Thank God for that.' Osama bin Laden, 7 October 2001.[1]

Lieutenant-General Mahmoud Ahmad, head of the ISI and architect of the 1999 coup that brought General Musharraf to power, was in Washington the day the World Trade Center exploded and American Airlines flight 77 slammed into the Pentagon. He had arrived on 4 September for a series of meetings at the Pentagon and National Security Council described as 'routine' at the time, although visits to Washington by ISI chiefs had a tendency to presage major upheavals in policy and, after the collapse of US overtures to Kandahar a month earlier, this one was likely to be no exception.[2] His other task was to lay the groundwork for direct talks between Musharraf and India's Prime Minister, Atal Behari Vajpayee, due to take place at the UN General Assembly before the end of September, and a crucial step towards normalising relations between the two trigger-happy nuclear powers.

Ahmad had paid a courtesy call on his CIA counterpart, director George Tenet, one of the only Clinton appointees to survive into the Bush era – and one of the few in the new administration to remember how Musharraf's coup had effectively scotched Washington's last determined effort to lay hands on bin Laden by squeezing the prime minister he ousted, Nawaz Sharif.[3] By contrast, Ahmad was a loyal ally of the Taliban, for confessional as well as tactical reasons, and had met bin Laden on numerous occasions. As he watched the awful calligraphy of hijacked planes on the morning of 11 September, the ISI chief was probably the only man in Washington who could instinctively decipher the flash of God's name as it ripped through the Manhattan skyline, and the signature of its author, a man who had never boasted of the power he disposed, but who could never again keep it secret.

Responsibility for the attacks on New York and the capital was initially claimed by a fringe Palestinian group, but the finger of suspicion halted more persuasively over the name of Iraq before turning, with a gasp of rage and disbelief, to Osama bin Laden and his nexus of half-educated amateurs. On 13 September, Secretary of State Colin Powell confirmed that the administration viewed the exiled Saudi as the leading suspect. 'We will go after that group, that network and those who have harboured, supported and aided that network, to rip that network up,' he told a briefing, 'and when we are through with that network, we will continue with a global assault against terrorism in general.'[4] In the White House Situation Room the same day, George Tenet outlined a nimble plan for the launch of a secret offensive in Afghanistan that involved strengthening the Northern Alliance through an infusion of money, weapons and Special Forces liaison teams, who could then provide 'eyes on the ground' when a more conventional military response – still a month away in view of the great distances involved – could be organised. He conceded that, without Massoud, the Northern Alliance was likely to be rudderless, demoralised and prone to fracture, but Bush liked the idea more than anything Defense Secretary Donald Rumsfeld had to offer.[5]

Meanwhile, Powell realised Mahmoud Ahmad was still in town, barred from leaving by the three-day ban on civilian flights imposed after the hijackers hit their targets. 'Do what you have to do,' Bush told him. Powell and his deputy-secretary, Richard Armitage, a veteran of America's first Afghan war, drafted a list of demands for 'assistance' from Islamabad that amounted to a terse ultimatum to suspend whatever support was given to the Taliban by the Pakistani government and its citizens or else face global censure – and possibly military attack – as a state that had systematically sponsored the terrorism that had gouged into the heart of America. On 13 September, Armitage as much as told General Musharraf through Ahmad to arrest all Al Qa'ida operatives; intercept all arms shipments; end logistical support to bin Laden; give the US access to Pakistan's naval bases, air bases and borders; provide immediate intelligence and immigration information; 'curb all domestic expressions of support for terrorism against the US, its friends or allies'; cut fuel shipments to the Taliban; and stop Pakistani volunteers from joining the Taliban.[6]

'Should the evidence strongly implicate Osama bin Laden and the Al Qa'ida network in Afghanistan,' ran Powell's final demand, 'AND should Afghanistan and the Taliban continue to harbour him and this network, Pakistan will break diplomatic relations with the Taliban government, end support for the Taliban and assist [the US] in the aforementioned ways to destroy Osama bin Laden and his Al Qa'ida network.'[7] 'The American people,' he told Musharraf later that day, 'would not understand if Pakistan was not in this fight with the United States.' He listened as the general pledged 'unstinted cooperation', offering to send Ahmad to Kandahar to negotiate bin Laden's extradition with the Taliban, but Powell wanted more. Ahmad could go to Kandahar, but he would deliver only the bluntest

of messages: surrender bin Laden without conditions, or expect a declaration of war from the US. Ahmad was whisked out of Washington to
Islamabad the next day.[8]

In private, Musharraf doubted he could honour the promise he had just
given on the phone, in view of the pro-Taliban hierarchy running the ISI,
the strength of Islamist feeling in the street and his flimsy control over the
North West Frontier, where thousands of tribesmen owed their allegiance
and livelihoods more to Kandahar than Islamabad. He had no evidence –
even if he wished to reveal it – to convince Pakistanis of bin Laden's
involvement in the 11 September attacks, which had tended to elate
Moslems around the world as the righteous chastisement of an arrogant
power. '[The] training of pilots is the work of a running government,' said
Mullah Mohammed Omar in a message read out by the Taliban ambassador
to Pakistan. 'Osama has no pilots, and where did he train them? In
Afghanistan, there is no such possibility for training.'[9] It was as difficult to
argue with that logic as it was to counter the myth, widely circulating in
Moslem countries, that 4,000 New York Jews had failed to appear for work
at the World Trade Center that fateful Tuesday after warnings from the
attacks' 'real' perpetrator, Mossad. Any attempt to counter such elemental
beliefs among Pakistani militants entailed the leaking of secrets or
documents that could only incriminate the ISI further as the guarantor of
Al Qa'ida's safe haven in Afghanistan and, therefore, a sponsor of terrorism
in the US and against Americans abroad. How much did the US know of
Abu Zubaida and the intimate links he enjoyed with the ISI, the Interior
Ministry and its immigration authorities that had allowed a tide of Al
Qa'ida recruits to surge into Afghanistan through Pakistan, and flow back
out again, without hindrance, to carry terror to distant parts of the world?
Indeed, how much did the general himself know?

As he considered the possible outcomes of confronting the generals who
had brought him to power specifically to protect their investments in the
Taliban and bin Laden, Musharraf knew he faced his greatest test. As 'Chief
Executive' – his own chosen title – he had allowed the dogs of *jihad* to lie
undisturbed, reassured they were vital to Pakistan's foreign policy priorities
and under the ISI's tight command and control. His restraint had led to
the most devastating terrorist attack in history, and a situation where
Pakistan found itself trapped in the line of fire between a bleeding
Washington and the unpredictable creatures in Kandahar, while India
lurked on the sidelines ready to pounce at the first sign of his wavering.
The options facing Musharraf were to embrace the Taliban's pariah status
and share their transparent destiny, or reject them and withstand a howl

of Islamist protest and potential mutiny that could shake the country to its foundations, toss him into history and pass Pakistan's nuclear trigger into the hands of fundamentalists.

Even as he calculated his choices, Musharraf was not without foresight or guile. He had to decide quickly, it was true, but President Bush was under fiercer pressure to deliver a statesmanlike response to a public travelling rapidly through the initial trauma of 11 September to a cold, hard fury that demanded action against its tormentors that was effective and measured, rather than symbolic like the Tomahawk attack on Khost in 1998. Nine months into his administration, a Bush who had yet to come into presidential focus was required both to comfort his people, and prove he could lead them; prepare them for a war with inevitable casualties, while reining in the hawks, who wanted to expand it to include the alleged sponsors of terror, Iraq and Iran; to build a broad coalition of Western and Moslem states committed to bringing bin Laden to justice, whatever the political cost, while suppressing his own personal tendencies, as leader of the world's largest military power, to command the scores of bombers on the aircraft carrier USS *Carl Vinson* in the Indian Ocean, to exact an immediate, unilateral and merciless reprisal.

Musharraf, the soldier, pondered the positive in his apparently hopeless situation. Whatever Bush decided to do, it could not be done quickly without Pakistan's air space, airports or the ISI, which possessed the most recent intelligence on bin Laden's whereabouts, the members of his network and his bases, as well as copious files on Mullah Mohammed Omar, the Taliban leadership and its battle order and strategy. This gave him leverage and, with leverage, came manoeuvrability. The US public wanted bin Laden 'dead or alive', in Bush's tired, Texan phrase, but it appeared less concerned to discover what had made bin Laden possible in the first place – or who – and Washington, eyes narrowing for a long military campaign, seemed happy for things to be left that way. The CIA and State Department had absorbed a torrent of criticism for failing to predict or prevent 11 September: neither wanted more light shed on their associations with Pakistan and Saudi Arabia, both clearly interwoven with the trajectories of the Taliban, bin Laden and, by implication, Mohammed Atta himself.

The US needed these same Moslem states to underpin Powell's global coalition, facilitate the delivery of its aerial power and limit any further damage to the State Department and the US intelligence community. If speed and the efficiency of Washington's planned military action – not the thoroughness of enquiries into the background of 11 September – were the most important criteria of the US response, Musharraf reflected, then evidence of the ISI's past collusion with bin Laden could be safely buried beneath the sound and fury of an approaching battle in which Pakistan appeared to stand shoulder to shoulder with the victim of its own misguided intrigues. Pakistan would become the toast of Washington and the World Bank again, the smoking gun snuffed out by a willed, collective amnesia that sought to slam the door on a shared bad memory. It might just work. On the evening of 14 September, Musharraf summoned his generals to discuss just how much assistance they could realistically offer Washington. They talked until the early hours.[10]

In a five-page memo, sent to Bush the same day, British Prime Minister Tony Blair argued that the swiftest route to persuading Arab opinion of the need for a multi-faith coalition against Al Qa'ida was by forcing Israel's Prime Minister Ariel Sharon to restart the peace process in the Middle East after a year of renewed *intifada*. He urged Bush to provide coalition partners who were vacillating with a detailed dossier of the government's evidence against bin Laden, a synopsis easily culled from testimony in the trials of the embassy bombings and the millennium plot and the USS *Cole* investigation. He advised the US to improve its relations with Iran and to provide the Northern Alliance with military assistance. Bush made two international calls that day. In the first, to Blair, he described his thinking on the coming war against terrorism. 'We focus on the first circle,' he said, 'then expand to the next circle and the next circle.' His second call was to ask Sharon to reduce the level of Israeli violence in Palestine. 'It was not clear that Sharon understood Bush's message,' observed reporter Bob Woodward.[11]

Three days after the suicide attacks, Congress gave its consent to military action against those found responsible, approving a $40 billion emergency package by 420 to 1, half for immediate disaster relief in New York and Washington, with around $12 billion for the armed forces and $8 billion for the newly-emerging concept of 'homeland defence'. With the death toll from the Twin Towers collapse estimated at over 6,300, and body parts coming out of the wreckage, the US peace lobby had never been more marginalised. On 15 September, after the second evacuation of the Capitol in three days and more bomb threats in Manhattan, Bush authorised the call-up of 35,000 National Guard reservists to man roadblocks and guard government offices, airports, power stations and transport infrastructure against further attacks. 'We're at war,' he told the press at Camp David, where Vice-President Dick Cheney lived in seclusion as the guarantor of continuity in the event of Bush's assassination. 'My message is for everybody who wears the uniform to get ready.'[12]

The nation's airports reopened for business the same day and, as a trickle of passengers trusted themselves to the skies, the shares of airline and insurance companies were poised to fall through the floor when Wall Street finally resumed trading after the longest closure in its history. Among the first to escape the lock-down were members of the bin Laden family, fleeing US homes, businesses and colleges lest they be lynched for sharing the same name as the alleged mastermind of 11 September – or '911', as it was tagged after the US dial code that summons the police, fire and paramedical services. The Texas bin Ladens were escorted to a secret assembly point by FBI agents and flown to Washington, where they left for Saudi Arabia on a private plane. Privately owned jumbos, carrying the Saudi deputy defence minister, the governor of Mecca and their 140-strong entourages, also grounded after the attacks, were similarly cleared for take-off.[13] Al-Kalifa bin Laden, Osama's mother, later told Saudi officials that she had been called on 10 September by her refractory offspring to cancel a holiday they had planned together in Syria. 'In two days,' he told her, 'you're going to hear big news and you're not going to hear from me for a while.'[14]

Soon after the call, bin Laden left Kandahar, sent his wives and children to the country and set off with his bodyguard for Kabul. From there, he ordered a statement to be faxed to Al-Jazeera TV in the Gulf, which read out its contents on 17 September. 'I would like to assure the world,' bin Laden announced grandly, 'that I did not plan the recent attacks, which seem to have been planned by people for personal reasons.' He added: 'I have been living in the Islamic emirate of Afghanistan and following its leader's rules. The current leader does not allow me to exercise such operations.'[15] A day later, 500 of his Arab supporters in Kabul swore their personal allegiance to him, vowing to 'fight to the last man', and he once more performed his vanishing act. 'They left behind the vehicles and left on horses,' said the source. 'He must have gone to some place which is not motorable.'[16] Anticipating US attacks, Omar also quit Kandahar for the countryside, but he had time to phone a statement through to Voice of Sharia radio in Kabul in which he asked Afghans to pray, read the Koran and prepare to meet 'a test'.[17] That same day – Monday 17 September – Islamabad announced that Lieutenant-General Mahmoud Ahmad had flown to Kabul at the head of a delegation of military officers to demand the surrender of bin Laden to the Americans within 72 hours. 'Our dream, I cannot say our expectation, is that somehow or other there will be a miracle,' said Foreign Minister Abdul Sattar. 'Time is very short, patience has run out, there is no room for negotiation, it's time for action.'[18]

After his marathon session with the generals on 14 September, Musharraf had told all ISI officers attached to the Taliban as advisers or trainers to return immediately to Pakistan, a decision that rankled with the ISI chief, whose designs appeared entirely at odds with the Pakistani leader's about-turn on Afghanistan. Ahmad had already approved a trip to Kandahar by retired, mid-level ISI officers in defiance of Musharraf's orders, allegedly to advise the Taliban on strategy in the event that the US launched air strikes. He had vetoed Musharraf's proposal for a face-to-face meeting with Mullah Mohammed Omar on 'security grounds', but the parlay – the first in Musharraf's two-year rule – would have broken the ISI's long monopoly on the dialogue with Kandahar and exposed its leaders to a less edited account of the threat building against them across the world.[19] Mullah Mohammed Omar would have refused to see him anyway, having delegated the wrangle over bin Laden to a 'grand council' of 20 *ulama*, or scholars, in what was construed as a delaying tactic identical to the one employed in November 1998 when Karl Inderfurth sought to extradite the Saudi.

Even this early in, Washington had grave misgivings about the ISI's willingness to obey Musharraf's order or share its best intelligence about bin Laden while Musharraf was having second thoughts about his own ability to help in other directions. He ruled out the presence of US troops on Pakistani soil or the use of Pakistani airbases to attack Afghanistan on 16 September out of a real fear of provoking his Islamist constituency, rapidly shaping up as Kandahar's 'Fifth Column' inside his borders.[20] From beyond the Khyber Pass came reports – no doubt exaggerated – of 20,000–25,000 Taliban warriors, massing to attack against any 'neighbouring Islamic country' providing support to US military operations, and the grind of Soviet-built Scud missiles as they lumbered within firing range.[21] As Ahmad flew to Kabul with an ultimatum to surrender, in Powell's words, 'this curse within their country' or face the 'full wrath' of a US assault, his mission seemed doomed to fail. 'On the issue of Osama bin Laden,' said Taliban Foreign Minister Wakil Ahmad Mutawakil on the eve of the talks, 'there has been no shift in our stand. We maintain our old position. We are responsible for the security of all those living in our country.' The ISI chief may even have permitted himself a smile.

Bin Laden and Mullah Omar were not the only ones on the move. Alerted by the ubiquitous BBC Pashtu and Dari services, hundreds of thousands of people who had never heard of the World Trade Center packed what they could and headed anxiously into the countryside, or for the checkpoints of Afghanistan's five neighbouring states, most of whose borders had been shut tight. 'We heard rumours that fighting would start, that another country would attack,' said a woman crossing into Pakistan at Chaman – still passable to traffic in spite of Musharraf's commitment to seal his frontiers. 'I don't know which country it was, but I think the Taliban must have done something bad again.'[22] Normally bustling Kandahar half-emptied as Arab fighters disappeared with their weapons into the mountains, Taliban escorted their families to Quetta and ordinary civilians trekked to the border, paying the required bribes as they went. Mullah Omar had closed Kandahar's *madrassa* the day after the attacks on America, distributed Kalashnikovs to their students and ordered them into immediate military training.[23] From cities across Afghanistan, refugees brought tales of men of fighting age being press-ganged by the Taliban from mosques, religious schools and homes, threatening to shoot anyone trying to escape. 'Tell my house, tell my father and my mother that they have taken me,' shouted one youth from a truck of unwilling recruits being driven to the front.[24] By the time Ahmad finished his first three-hour session with the *ulama* in Kabul, over 200,000 had escaped Kandahar as the threat of air strikes drew nearer.[25]

The last international aid workers – apart from the eight 'evangelists' still in custody – were evacuated the day after 11 September, leaving Afghan colleagues to administer the centrepiece of the UN programme, a vast and elaborate scheme of famine relief for over 3 million drought-affected people, mainly concentrated in a northern belt stretching from Herat to Balkh on the Uzbekistan border. A Taliban prohibition on satellite phones, lest they be used to disclose military secrets, cut all communications with the UN in Pakistan, while insecurity and the shortage of trucks made it impossible to maintain the 10,000 tonnes of grain needed each week to keep hunger at bay. With winter six weeks away and food sufficient for only 10–14 days, the UN predicted the number of Afghans at risk from starvation rising to between 5 million and 7 million, qualifying as the 'world's worst humanitarian crisis', while a further 1.5 million people were expected to try to cross to Pakistan and Iran in a bid to escape bombardment.[26] 'I think we have a responsibility to go back to the international anti-terrorism alliance,' commented one aid official, 'and say: "Look, this is a risk. There is a climate which has been created by the threat of military action. Damage is not caused by missiles alone".'[27]

Ahmad's mission did not augur well. On 18 September, the *ulama* postponed giving any answer to the US ultimatum for 24 hours and, with a flourish of injured dignity, waved a list their own conditions that included diplomatic recognition, the lifting of sanctions and an end to all support for their opponents. The ISI chief flew immediately south to remonstrate with Mullah Omar, who denied any personal influence over the clerics' erratic timetable or their ultimate verdict. 'You want to please America,' he said, 'and I want only to please God',[28] but as Ahmad boarded his plane to fly back to Islamabad, the one-eyed enigma hissed: 'Osama will be the last person to leave Afghanistan.'[29] The *ulama* did not assemble the following day because Mullah Omar had decided overnight to expand the grand council into a fully-blown *shura* by summoning more than 600 scholars by radio – 20 from each of the country's 32 provinces – to debate the US demands and issue a *fatwa* of *jihad* in the event that the US attacked. Afghanistan's ancients travelled through the night to reach Kabul before the deadline expired.

They convened on Wednesday morning in the bombed-out Argh, the palace at the heart of so much Afghan killing, and listened as the education minister read out a message from Mullah Omar. 'Our Islamic state is the true Islamic system in the world,' he told them, 'and for this reason the enemies of our country look at us as a thorn in their eye and seek different excuses to finish it off. Osama is one of these.'[30] The speech didn't sound like a submission, and the chilling image at its centre more closely reflected the sensations of the average American after the obliteration of the World Trade Center and its thousands of occupants, than any US treatment of the Taliban in the recent past. But Mullah Omar was famous neither for diplomacy nor his willingness to concede. 'We appeal to the American government to exercise complete patience,' he ended, 'and we want America to gather complete evidence and find the real culprits.' The travel-weary clerics chewed over the matters till lunch was announced and each was issued with a questionnaire in which to file their judgements on the weighty topics at hand. Their decision would be published on Thursday 20 September, 24 hours past deadline, but its gist was already too apparent in Islamabad.

General Parvez Musharraf stood before the cameras on the evening of 19 September visibly sweating as he struggled to explain to a volatile public his decision to meet US demands for Pakistan's complete and unreserved help in running bin Laden to earth. The 20-minute speech was a carefully pitched appeal that stressed the survival of the nation over Islamic solidarity at a time when, he said, the country faced its gravest crisis since the disastrous war with India in 1971. If he did not help Washington now, Pakistan's very existence would be threatened because India wanted 'to enter any alliance with the US and get Pakistan declared a terrorist state'.

'If we make any mistake, it could culminate in very bad ends,' he said, 'if we make the right decisions, it could be very fruitful for us.' Musharraf told the '10–15 per cent' of Pakistanis who supported the Taliban not to let their emotions get out of hand: the US was not targeting the Taliban, Afghanistan or Islam, only bin Laden. 'Showing strength without wisdom,' he counseled, 'is a kind of foolishness'. Pakistan's 36,000-strong army and air force were on the highest alert – though whether to repel attacks by India, the 25,000 Taliban massing on its border or US ground troops testing the integrity of Musharraf's commitment was not altogether clear. 'Trust me,' he pleaded, 'I have fought in two wars and, by the grace of God, I have never shown any timidity.' He was sweating now, and about to begin his third.[31]

Two days earlier, on 17 September, Bush signed a Memorandum of Notification authorising the CIA to launch a worldwide covert war against terrorism and Tenet received the go-ahead to land agents inside Afghanistan but, even as the *ulama* mulled over their decision, the Taliban were still not squarely in the presidential sights. 'Our goal is not to destroy the Taliban,' Bush said in private, 'but that may be the effect.'[32] On 19 September, Defense Secretary Donald Rumsfeld ordered 100 planes, mainly F-15 and F-16 fighters and B-1 bombers, to fly to forward bases in the Persian Gulf in a deployment code-named 'Operation Infinite Justice'. The Pentagon refused to reveal their destinations for political as much as security reasons, but the US had access to facilities in Bahrain, Kuwait, Saudi Arabia and Turkey, all containing potential wells of sympathy for bin Laden. B-52 Stratofortresses took off for the shared US–British base on the island of Diego Garcia in the Indian Ocean, while a 14-ship armada, led by the carrier USS *Theodore Roosevelt*, steamed eastwards from Virginia to join the 22 warships in Carrier Groups Three and Five and the 150 strike aircraft on the flagship carriers USS *Carl Vinson* and USS *Enterprise*. Aboard were 2,000 marines capable of mounting special operations: in Fort Bragg, the 82nd Airborne, 101st Airborne, 3rd Infantry and 10th Mountain Divisions were on war footing.[33] By an extraordinary coincidence – and at extortionate expense to taxpayers – nearly a quarter of the entire British military complement of 100,000 men were due to arrive in Oman to take part in Swift Sword 2 war games, beginning 15 September, supported by 28 warships including the aircraft carrier *Illustrious*, the helicopter carrier *Ocean* and two nuclear submarines.[34] The deployment, the largest since the Falklands war 20 years earlier, confirmed Britain's deep anxieties about the region's stability long before 11 September. Within ten days of the terrorist attacks, there was sufficient naval and air power in the Persian

Gulf to launch a major war against any power in the region, without in any way undermining US command of the 'no-fly' zones in Iraq imposed after the Gulf War ten years before.

Meanwhile, in the Washington that instigated this frenzied movement of men and weapons, the ambassador for the UN-recognised government of former President Burhanuddin Rabbani was wondering why no one telephoned. 'Everybody is talking about military action in Afghanistan,' he said, 'and the target is the Taliban and we're also against the Taliban, but they haven't been in contact. It's a real surprise.'[35] But the target, in fact, was not yet the Taliban, for the *ulama* had not delivered their judgment and, while the men and machines arrayed against them were intimidating in the extreme, the military's objectives – and how to achieve them – were causing concern to both Bush and General Tommy Franks at US Central Command (CENTCOM). He would ultimately direct the campaign by video link from Florida, 10 hours behind and 5,000 miles (8,000 kilometres) away from real time in Afghanistan. Bin Laden was no Saddam Hussein with thousands of men, tanks and military installations, ripe for demolition from the sky, a factor that rendered obsolete the institutionalised 'Powell doctrine' of using the US's overwhelming airpower to achieve defined goals that had largely shaped its strategy in the Gulf and the Balkans – as well as its criteria for weapons procurement. 'One of our focuses is to get [bin Laden's] people out of their caves,' Bush had told reporters, 'smoke them out and get them moving.' But no amount of airborne technology could achieve that without having 'boots on the ground' to make sure they were out.[36]

Afghanistan's mountains ruled out using tanks across large swathes of the battlefield, while the value of helicopter gunships was sharply reduced without bases in surrounding countries. Musharraf had agreed to share ISI intelligence – the CIA had employed no agents on the ground in years – but he had balked at using his facilities to mount attacks on Afghanistan because of the challenge it presented to domestic stability. The sheer horror of 11 September had helped Bush to prepare the psychological ground for a return of US troops to the fray for the first time since the 1993 Mogadishu débâcle, but they would be dangerously exposed if support choppers were based far out in the Arabian Sea on US carriers. While front pages pumped testosterone with specifications of the enhanced Daisy Cutter cluster bomb, or the unmanned Predator's remote-triggered Hellcat missiles, editorials fulminated about the impregnable terrain, the approaching winter and how every foreign army that had ever trod there washed up in bloody deserts of Afghan regret. 'I pity their mothers and sisters and brothers,' said former Soviet colonel Yuri Shamanov, 'Vietnam will be a picnic by comparison. Here they will get it in the teeth. They will get it good.'[37]

The support of Saudi Arabia, one of only three states to recognise the Taliban, was critical to Powell's ambition of forging an across-the-board coalition against Al Qa'ida similar to the one that enabled him to defeat Iraq in 1991. If Riyadh signed up to the US agenda, the conservative Islamic world would follow, lending its diplomatic weight to a US-led punitive expedition, while offering whatever military assistance was required. The previous June had seen the opening of CENTCOM's futuristic command centre at Prince Sultan airbase, 70 miles southeast of Riyadh, and the linchpin of the hated US military presence that motivated so many Saudis to follow in bin Laden's footsteps. The state-of-the art consoles of Combined Aerospace Operations at Al-Kharj had been designed to enforce the decade-long ban on Iraqi military flights, but they were capable of co-ordinating the movements of hundreds of planes across thousands of miles of airspace. General Franks was counting on Prince Sultan to facilitate the deployment of aircraft from bases in the US to carriers in the Gulf and from there into the skies above bin Laden's camps, in spite of a long-standing agreement that restricted US aircraft on Saudi soil to defensive operations.[38]

A week after 11 September, the senile King Fahd offered 'full cooperation' in Washington's fight against terror, but this commitment had quickly fractured on the diamond-hard dilemma in the Middle East where to side with the US against Al Qa'ida elided politically into extending moral support to Israeli attacks on Palestinian 'terrorists', whom the Islamic world naturally regarded as 'freedom fighters'. Saudi billionaire, Prince Al-Waleed bin Talal, was among the first to discover the yawning double standard in Bush's rhetoric after 11 September when his $10 million contribution to victims of the World Trade Center disaster was publicly rejected by New York Mayor Rudolph Giuliani, after he openly suggested that a link might exist between the hijackers' suicidal impulses and US policy in the Middle East.[39]

Riyadh was in a much better position than Islamabad to stonewall Powell, in spite of its past support for bin Laden, Al Qa'ida and the Taliban or the fact that 15 of the 19 suspected hijackers were Saudi nationals – and all 15 obtained US visas in the capital. If it chose not to endorse the coalition, the US would be driven into unilateral action, with only grudging support from the liberal West, playing into the hands of bin Laden and radicals in the Middle East and Pakistan, eager to denounce any attack on Al Qa'ida as a war against Islam. As the US's largest energy supplier, there was little that Bush could do, however unique the circumstances or America's needs. The Saudis hedged their bets in customary fashion, offering passive support to the US coalition, while systematically thwarting FBI attempts to expose the Saudi roots of the conspiracy which engulfed the World Trade Center. The authorities refused a request to conduct background checks on the Saudi-based hijackers, and frustrated all efforts to freeze bin Laden's assets or audit contributions from charities and individuals that may have funded Al Qa'ida.[40] As for Prince Sultan airbase, Western diplomats said Riyadh simply asked the Pentagon not to insist on a favour that, as a pillar of Islam, Saudi Arabia could not politically afford. 'We do not accept the presence in our country of a single soldier at war with Moslems or Arabs,' Defence Minister Prince Sultan told a local newspaper in mid-September, though the base named after him currently hosted 320 US F-15, F-16 and Stealth fighters and 4,000 military personnel, all poised for the coming fight in Afghanistan.[41]

Bush was preparing to address a joint session of Congress on 20 September when the *ulama* finally reported their findings. 'To avoid the current tumult and similar suspicions in future,' ran their decision, 'the high council of the honourable *ulama* recommends to the Islamic Emirate of Afghanistan to persuade bin Laden to leave Afghanistan whenever possible ... and to choose another place for himself.'[42] The clerics set no term to his departure, advising that bin Laden should leave 'of his own free will', but the decision was an advance on Omar's more intractable stance – though whether he conveyed it to his guest was up to the mullah's discretion. There was, moreover, nowhere for bin Laden to go. 'He has so many enemies,' said Education Minister Amir Khan Muttaqi, 'it's not possible for him to go out on the road and stop a taxi.'[43] White House spokesman Ari Fleischer was not impressed. 'This is about much more than one man being allowed to leave voluntarily, presumably from one safe harbour to another safe harbour,' he said. 'It does not meet America's requirements.'

Eighty million Americans tuned in that night to hear a speech carefully crafted to summarise the Bush administration's response to 11 September and all that had happened in the nine days since, and to witness his reply to the *ulama*, whose verdict was trailed as the decisive moment both in negotiations for bin Laden, and whether the US went to war. It had been worked and reworked to answer those questions, but also to outline a new and aggressive doctrine of global policing whose form had scarcely begun to emerge from the geopolitical architecture that predated the attacks on the US, but which cracked and groaned in the days that followed like iron breaking, or something giving birth. Bush used the staccato building blocks of rhetoric to fashion a primer of terrorism that was interrupted 29 times by applause from the floor. He mentioned bin Laden once only, and then embarked on a list of demands from the Taliban that slid without logic or clearly defined goals into a description of unending struggle and sacrifice. 'Our war on terror begins with Al Qa'ida, but it does not end there,' he said. 'It will not end until every terrorist group of global reach has been found, stopped and defeated.' The US would direct every resource at its command – every means of diplomacy, every tool of intelligence, every instrument of law enforcement, every financial influence and every necessary weapon of war – to the destruction and defeat of Al Qa'ida. 'Americans should expect not one battle, but a lengthy campaign unlike any we have ever seen,' he said. 'It may include dramatic strikes, visible on TV, and covert operations secret even in success.' Bush's speechwriters and advisers had worried over the next phase of the speech, which dealt with states that sponsored organisations like Al Qa'ida. Powell felt there had to be a definite break with the past, or the US would end up declaring war on everybody, so the magic formula 'continues to' was inserted in the text – allowing Pakistan to slink away unpunished: 'From this day forward,' Bush threatened, 'any nation that continues to habour or support terrorism will be regarded by the US as a hostile regime.' The applause was thunderous.[44]

In spite of the thunder, the overthrow of the Taliban was still not an explicit goal of US policy, chiefly because the ears of the soldier-turned-coalition-builder, Colin Powell, were so closely attuned to a man who strangely resembled him, Parvez Musharraf, a soldier in the process of morphing into a statesman, both now at bay amid the whirring of hawks' wings. Musharraf could conceivably shout down the Islamists in the army and ISI, but this was less likely if the US intended to use Pakistan's support to replace the Taliban in Kabul with a Northern Alliance regime sympathetic to Iran, Russia and, particularly, India. After a week of prevarication and intensive, inter-faction lobbying, the Alliance had finally confessed that its legendary commander, Massoud, had truly perished within hours of the assassination bid on 9 September. His Panjshiri supporters attributed his killing to Al Qa'ida suicide bombers and their friends in the ISI, and its precise purpose, they conjectured, was to deny the US the option of an effective surrogate and ally in Afghanistan after Atta's planes collided with their destinations. It was a pragmatic reading of momentous events that was only discounted because of the Alliance's prejudices against Pakistan, Washington's new friend. On 17 September, amidst the throng of his campaign veterans, Massoud was laid in a grave on a barren, wind-swept hill overlooking the Panjshir valley that swiftly turned into a shrine for pilgrims seeking cures from illnesses ranging from epilepsy to madness. 'Massoud has become far greater in death than he ever was in life,' said one Kabul resident. 'It's a cult, but not all of us subscribe to it.'[45]

As the Lion of Panjshir mutated into an unwilling manifestation of traditional Afghan sainthood, leadership of the Northern Alliance had devolved onto his brother, Wali Shah Massoud, the Afghan ambassador in London, and General Mohammed Qasim Fahim, Massoud's deputy commander and former head of Najibullah's secret police network, Khad. In a bid to re-establish credibility after their commander's death, the Alliance launched offensives in Samangan and Takhar to attract Washington's attention, while Dostum advanced on Balkh from the south, capturing Zari district near Mazar-i Sharif on 23 September.[46] In the meantime, Mullah Mohammed Omar had again decided to override the *ulama's* decision, telling Voice of America radio: 'If we give Osama away today, Moslems who are now pleading to give him up would then revile us for giving him up.' He outlined his choices in an interview censored by the State Department, but which saw the light in a *Washington Post* transcript.

> I am considering two promises. One is the promise of God. The other is that of Bush. The promise of God is that my land is vast. If you start a journey on God's path, you can reside anywhere on this earth and will be protected. The promise of Bush is that there is no place on earth where you can hide that I cannot find you. We will see which one of these two promises is fulfilled.[47]

Bin Laden's whereabouts, of course, were a mystery though Alliance commanders insisted their country was awash with shepherds, nomads and spies who could run him to ground, given a modest inducement. 'If the Americans want to know where he is, they should come to us,' said commander Momar Hasan at Dushti Qala, near the Tajikistan border. 'It is really not so difficult.'[48] Heavily influenced by Musharraf, Powell was suspicious of the Northern Alliance: he had learned to treat warlords with caution after Mogadishu. In spite of Bush's threats against harbouring terrorists, Powell feared that overthrowing the Taliban would suck the US into Afghanistan's whirlpool of strife. With no exit strategy in sight for the soldiers Bush told Congress he would have to commit. The US had still not contacted the Taliban opposition nearly two weeks after 11 September, according to official accounts, and when asked on 22 September whether removing the Taliban was now a US objective, Powell's answer was as ambiguous as it was contradictory. 'That is not uppermost in our minds right now,' he answered. 'It wasn't 15 days ago, and it isn't right now, except to the extent that the Taliban regime continues to support Osama bin Laden.'[49]

But Powell's star was beginning to wane in Washington as the Pentagon geared up for war. On Tenet's orders, the CIA's first six-man team flew from Uzbekistan to the 'northwest corner' of Afghanistan on 26 September in a Russian-bought helicopter, stencilled with the number 91101. Composed of two Dari-speaking CIA officers, two former Special Forces commandos, a communications specialist and a paramedic, Northern Alliance Liaison Team Delta was warmly greeted by commanders loyal to Ismail Khan, who asked for beans, bullets, cold-weather boots and, of course, bucks. Million-dollar packages of $20 bills tumbled from the sky to secure the loyalty of the coalition's newest allies – as America's first casualty in the Afghan war, a $40 million Predator surveillance vehicle, was shot down by Taliban only too aware of the CIA presence. Five more liaison teams were subsequently flown out to make contact with anti-Taliban elements in the west, northwest, Mazar-i Sharif and the south, where they also took delivery of laser target designators to guide US planes to their objectives.[50] The CIA had been quick off the mark, but its failure to insert agents into Al Qa'ida after the embassy bombings four years before, or to prevent 11 September were debts that entirely bankrupted its credibility as an efficient intelligence institution. Warnings of its 'risk-averse' and suburban mind-set had resounded from the pages of *Atlantic Monthly* only weeks prior to the attacks by a former agent who summed up the agency's problems thus: 'Operations that include diarrhoea as a way of life don't happen.'[51] Tenet needed a lot of shit and bravado if the CIA's prestige were to be restored before he retired.

As the military build-up continued, so did opposition to the impending US attack. Police used live ammunition to break up a pro-Taliban demonstration in Karachi, in which three people died and a number of cinemas and a UNICEF office were set on fire. 'We hope that these brothers will be the first martyrs in the battle of Islam in this era against the new Jewish and Christian crusader campaign led by the Chief Crusader Bush under the banner of the Cross,' wrote bin Laden in the first of a series of messages and videos sent exclusively to Al-Jazeera television, quickly emerging as his preferred mode of addressing the global audience that now hung on his every word.[52] Across the frontier, Mullah Omar claimed to have called up 300,000 additional fighters to reinforce the 10,000–15,000 hard-core troops in the Taliban army, though most were plucked unwillingly from village and street. Like bin Laden, Omar strove to internationalise his quarrel with the US in a bid to rally Moslem opinion, though he had hitherto shown total indifference to the nuances of Middle East affairs. 'If Americans want to eliminate terrorism,' he said, 'they should withdraw their forces from the Gulf and put an end to the biased attitude on the issue of Palestine.'[53] On 23 September, President Bush announced the lifting of the sanctions imposed by Clinton on Pakistan, making it again elegible for military aid and a rescheduling of its back-breaking foreign debt of $38 billion. Islamabad withdrew its diplomats from Kabul the same weekend, citing security concerns though the Taliban were allowed to retain their representative in Islamabad, with Washington's approval, in order to preserve some line of contact. The UAE had broken off relations earlier and Saudi Arabia followed on 25 September, citing the Taliban's propensity to 'defame Islam and defame Moslems' reputations in the world'.[54] That day, the Pentagon bowed to moderate Moslem sentiment by changing the code name 'Operation Infinite Justice' to 'Operation Enduring Freedom' because 'infinity' was perceived as a property exclusive to God, not the US.

There would be one last attempt to reason with Mullah Omar – or so it was believed in Washington. On 27 September, Islamabad announced the dispatch of a second delegation to Kandahar, composed of ten Pakistani *ulama* from the Deobandi school that had moulded and motivated the Taliban, led by Lieutenant-General Mahmoud Ahmad. Their task was to 'satisfy the conscience of the Pakistanis that they have done everything possible', explained an official.[55] As they took off, the Urdu-language newspaper, *Ummat*, published a second statement from bin Laden. 'As a Moslem, I will not lie,' bin Laden was quoted as saying. 'I was neither aware of these attacks, nor would I support the killing of innocent men, women and children.'[56] In Kabul, demonstrators ransacked the abandoned US embassy, tearing down the presidential seal, even as delegates from the Northern Alliance and Washington took turns to court former king Zahir Shah in his villa in Rome. Taliban troops were reported abandoning their positions across the country while Herat was on the brink of an uprising and, in Paktia and Paktika, tribal leaders expelled Taliban governors and demanded that Arab fighters be removed from their territory. Fear of US strikes and the Taliban's recruiting sergeants had driven over a million Afghans into headlong flight. In Kandahar, however, the one-eyed mullah was blithely serene, telling a journalist: 'We do not expect [an attack], because they have no reason to attack us.'[57] 'America should give up its stubbornness,' he told the visiting Pakistani *ulama*, 'and only then can Afghanistan negotiate.'[58] Other members of the delegation, however, said that, during the flight to Kandahar, the ISI chief had brusquely impressed on them the need to support Mullah Omar. When they stepped back onto the tarmac in Islamabad, the *ulama* endorsed his decision not to give up bin Laden.[59]

'The Americans are crazy,' said one Taliban defector, Hafiz Sadiqulla Hassani, Omar's former bodyguard and an accountant-turned-torturer. 'It is Osama bin Laden who can hand over Mullah Omar, not the other way round.' Hassani boasted how he had been encouraged to devise punishments as gruesome as possible to deter offenders against Taliban edicts, sometimes crucifying violators or beating them till their spines snapped. 'All the important places are now under Arab control,' he said, 'the airport, the military courts, the tank command.'[60] Teams of US Green Berets, Navy SEALs and British SAS, supported by Black Hawk helicopters, were now reportedly searching for bin Laden around Kandahar, though Pakistan had not yet officially sanctioned American use of its bases and the Pentagon badly needed to build up domestic morale by giving the impression that every avenue was being explored to bring the Saudi to justice – even if it wasn't. The habitual speculation over his destination, however, was this time nipped in the bud after the Taliban envoy, Mullah Abdul Salaam Zaeef, was ordered to put the press out of its misery. 'Wherever he is, he's under the control of the Islamic Emirate of Afghanistan,' he said, circuitously, 'and, because of his safety, you know it's only the security people who are responsible for his safety who know his whereabouts, and no one else.' He said the Taliban wanted to see firm evidence of bin Laden's guilt before even considering a handover. Zaeef added; 'He's in a place that cannot be located by anyone.'[61]

Powell had raised the issue of the evidence against bin Laden on 24 September, not for the benefit of the Taliban, but to convince the restless populations of Pakistan, Saudi Arabia, Egypt and Jordan of the justice of US grievances against him. 'I think in the near future we will be able to put out a paper,' he said, 'a document that will describe quite clearly the evidence we have linking him to this attack.'[62] Two reports were forecast: a statement compiled by the State Department for public consumption; and a secret one, for local intelligence agencies, prepared by the CIA and FBI and including details from trusted sources. A day later, Bush froze the assets of 27 individuals and organisations associated with Al Qa'ida, including the business of Mohammed Atta's Hamburg friend, Mamoun Darkanzali, the Al Rashid Trust of Pakistan, publisher of the Taliban newspaper, and the Kandahar-based Wafa Humanitarian Organisation, financed by wealthy Gulf Arabs. But the president disagreed with Powell's argument for widening access to the evidence against bin Laden. 'It's important as this war progresses that the American people understand ... we will not make the war more difficult to win by publicly disclosing classified information,' he said somewhat confusingly, while shelving Powell's report.[63] Tony Blair, however, agreed with Powell. On 4 October, he gave the House of Commons a 21-page dossier containing what he called 'firm evidence' of bin Laden's involvement in 11 September, while admitting that 'evidence of a very specific nature' had been too sensitive to include. 'A range of people were warned to return to Afghanistan because of action on or around 11 September,' he told the Commons, 'and, most importantly, one of bin Laden's closest lieutenants has said clearly that he helped with the planning of the 11 September attacks and has admitted the involvement of Al Qa'ida.'[64] Musharraf responded a day later, saying the evidence against bin Laden was 'enough for an indictment'.[65]

At 8.30 on the evening of Sunday 7 October, the first of 50 cruise missiles was fired from British cruisers and submarines against Al Qa'ida training camps and Taliban military installations, followed by a wave of 15 B-1, B-52 and B-2 Stealth bombers and 25 F-14 and F-18 strike jets in a night bombing campaign to knock out the Taliban's rudimentary air defences. Before the planes returned from their seven-hour round-trip flights, Musharraf moved against the 'Three Musketeers', the restive generals who had brought him to power precisely two years earlier. In what was later described as a 'coup within a coup', Musharraf sent ISI chief Lieutenant-General Mahmoud Ahmad into early retirement, dismissed the Vice-Chief of Army Staff, Lieutenant-General Muzaffar Usmani and kicked the Chief of General Staff in Rawalpindi, Lieutenant-General Mohammed Aziz Khan, into a largely ceremonial post. All three were pro-Taliban in orientation, and profoundly adverse to Musharraf's alliance with the US. Two days later, in what may have been a classic of Indian disinformation, the *Times of India* reported that the real reason for Ahmad's dismissal was that US intelligence had identified him as source for the $100,000 that was wired to Mohammed Atta in Florida between July and September 2000 and used to pay for flight classes. The go-between for the transfer, according to the anonymous article, was Ahmed Umar Saeed Sheikh, or 'Sheikh Omar Sayeed', the Pakistani-born, British citizen imprisoned in India for kidnapping British tourists in 1995, who was freed after the hijacking of Air India flight 814 to Kandahar on Christmas Eve 1999.[66] The story was neither followed up, nor denied.

Even as the first bombers flew towards Afghanistan, bin Laden popped up in the place that Americans least expected, on CNN, which transmitted a video of him with Ayman al-Zawahiri immediately after Bush announced that airstrikes had been launched. Recorded before 7 October, the tape was delivered by courier to the Kabul office of Al-Jazeera. Seated outside the mouth of a mountain cave, and dressed in camouflage with a Kalashnikov close to hand, bin Laden talked to Al-Jazeera's 35 million Arabic-speaking viewers of swords, horses and infidels in short, flowing phrases and with a quiet intensity that convinced many of his piety. He denounced Washington's support for Israel, the UN sanctions against Iraq and America's 'occupying' forces near the holy places of Saudi Arabia. 'To America, I swear by God the great,' he said, his finger pointing directly into the lens, 'America will never dream of security or see it, before we live it and see it in Palestine, and not before the infidel's armies depart the land of Mohammed.'[67]

19   The Storm of Airplanes

'We just sit in the dark, watching the sky, waiting to die.' Jamal Uddin, vegetable seller[1]

The US warplanes that flew into Afghan airspace on the evening of 7 October dropped precision-guided bombs and conventional explosives on Taliban radar facilities in Kabul, Jalalabad, Mazar-i Sharif and Kandahar, as well as on some of 23 alleged Al Qa'ida training camps located in the provinces of Baghlan, Nangarhar, Kandahar and Uruzgan. The first foreign military pilots to see the Hindu Kush since the Soviet occupation, some had flown $2 billion, bat-winged, Stealth aircraft all the way from Whiteman Air Base, Missouri, 17 hours away, before releasing their bombs and banking southwest towards the island fortress of Diego Garcia. As flashes of explosion lit up Kabul airport, the defence ministry at Darulaman Palace and a Scud base, anti-aircraft shells and hand-held surface-to-air missiles streaked futilely into the night sky while the dormant Northern Alliance positions 25 miles to the north erupted as 25 Grad missiles, 122 mm howitzer shells and volleys of mortars surged toward the Taliban trenches.[2]

Despite the darkness – or because of the huge fires they had lit – some of the pilots made out what seemed to be the seething camps of refugees across the terrain below as they skimmed back out towards the carriers USS *Carl Vinson* and *Enterprise* in the Arabian Sea.[3] The view from the ground was quite different. 'Said Sanan', pseudonym of a Taliban officer and Soviet-trained radar operator who deserted the day after the raids, was on duty when the first US bombers flew into Kandahar. At 8.50 p.m., two dots appeared on his yellow screen, at a distance of 145 miles (230 kilometres), but approaching fast; when they came within 40 miles, his commander cut out the power to stop them locking onto the radar's position. The bombers streamed in overhead, blowing up two MiG-21s on the runway as they passed, but without killing the Taliban air force marshal, Akhtar Mohammed Mansoor, as first was feared. That same night and over the following day, the radar system, along with every other transportable, Taliban military asset, was carried off into the mountains. 'You cannot fight against the Americans' technology,' said Sanan, 'educated military men know that.'[4] But educated US generals would have cause to doubt his conviction before the long-distance war in Afghanistan was over.

Following in the contrails of the bombers were two C-17 transporters from Ramstein in Germany, each as wide as a Boeing 747, flying at altitudes so high that crew members risked the bends.[5] Part of what *Time* called America's 'guns and butter' programme, each was filled with 37,000 packages of Meals Ready to Eat (MREs), containing emergency rations of vegetable, fruit and nut-based foods, assembled according to Islamic dietary rules and similar in weight to a hardback book. President Bush had awarded Afghanistan $320 million in food and medical assistance on 4 October, in addition to the $170 million already committed. 'This is our way of saying that, while we firmly and strongly oppose the Taliban,' he said, 'we are friends of the Afghan people.' The plan was for the two densely-packed, flying libraries of nutrition to airlift and distribute some 2 million packets from Germany to Afghanistan over a period of 55 days.[6] Though designed to flutter gently to earth within three-square-mile areas around zones of displaced people selected by USAID, many missed their targets because of the altitude at which pilots were ordered to fly. Opinions on the value of the Pentagon's 'humanitarian' operation were divided. 'Frankly, it's a joke,' said one UN staffer, who said giving peanut butter to people used to bread and rice would provoke an epidemic of intestinal problems, while pointing out that many had also fallen in minefields, inviting graver disaster.[7] In Khost, Islamic scholars issued a *fatwa* banning the famished from eating peanut butter or any other of the MREs' exotic contents. 'America is ridiculing Afghans by bombing us on the one hand and dropping food on the other.'[8] But with most of the emergency relief programme totally shut down, others were more tolerant. 'We had been feeding five million people before this conflict broke out,' a UN official quipped unconsciously. 'You can almost drop [MREs] anywhere and hit someone who is starving.'[9]

Coalition forces pounded the Taliban's meagre air defences by moonlight until 10 October, when General Richard Myers, Chairman of the Joint Chiefs of Staff, announced that 85 per cent of the targets on the Pentagon's priority list of anti-aircraft batteries, radar and warplanes had been destroyed or damaged and 'air supremacy' was assured. The first daytime bombing attacks were launched against 'garrisons, bivouac areas, maintenance sites [and] troop-type facilities' near Kandahar, Kabul and Herat, as well as 'targets of opportunity', such as tanks or convoys, though one pilot admitted Afghanistan 'is not a real target-rich environment'.[10] Less publicly, US bombers began systematically to pursue bin Laden and Mullah Omar through the labyrinth of camps, hideouts and caves originally built to serve the anti-Soviet war, but which the Taliban and Al Qa'ida had commandeered for their own purposes. The first daylight raids on Kandahar concentrated on an area near the airport where the families of bin Laden and his Arab bodyguard once lived, while jets or missiles were ordered to strike targets in Mullah Omar's home district of Maiwand; an alleged training camp in Helmand; the old mujahedin cave complex near Tora Bora; Darunta training camp on the Kabul river; Farm Hadda camp, near Jalalabad; the 055 Brigade's camp at Rishkor, west of Kabul; bin Laden's base in the Parapamizad Mountains in Oruzgan; and its provincial capital, Tarin Kot. The only known Al Qa'ida camp that was not attacked, curiously, was Zhawar Kili, near Khost. Most had been abandoned after 11 September or earlier.[11]

Two of the Mullah's male relatives were killed in Kandahar during the first night of bombing, according to US intelligence, and his Chevrolet Suburban minivan took a hit on the fourth, prompting questions at the daily Pentagon briefing about the status of non-combatants in the war. 'I'm not going to get into that particular case,' replied a clearly ruffled Rumsfeld, 'but people should be put on notice that it is not trees or rocks that cause terrorism; it's people.'[12] In fact, Mullah Mohammed Omar was identified in person on 7 October via the lens of a Predator surveillance aircraft, equipped with Hellfire missiles, as he escaped the bombing of Kabul in a convoy of Taliban military vehicles. The CIA, which controlled the craft, required authorisation from CENTCOM headquarters in Tampa before it could fire its missiles, according to investigative reporter, Seymour Hersh. Whether for 'legal' reasons, as subsequently cited, or the executive inertia implicit in the mechanics of running a remote-control war in Asia from a set of desks in Florida, the order to fire was not granted. When the CIA then asked for permission to attack the building in which Mullah Omar had taken shelter, permission was given only to fire in front of its entrance – in the hope he would come out to see what had occurred. He didn't. The failure to kill the Taliban leader, Hersh claimed, left Rumsfeld 'kicking a lot of glass and breaking doors'.[13]

CENTCOM's remoteness, and the impersonal might of a war machine that had polished its working parts over Baghdad and Belgrade till they gleamed, were disadvantages from the outset in Afghanistan. Here, it confronted 'men in caves', in one memorable phrase, as hungry and ill-shod as the displaced millions then commanding Western sympathies. Too poorly equipped or disciplined to offer any dignified military response to

US air attacks, they were nevertheless capable of a courage under pressure that might shame the household gods of the new American cavalry, the semi-secret Delta Force, the Green Berets and Rangers, pumped with steroids and steak, but relative children in the thin mountain air. Even after 11 September, and its backdrop of economic carnage and renewed terrorist threats, including an unsolved spate of anthrax attacks, the strength of US power in its search for justice qualified as its single most serious military and political weakness. Military restraint is no more a prerequisite of a swift battlefield triumph, than the guarantee of a fair hearing in the media which, being relatively free, is also at liberty to define the terms of a second query about the conduct of a war before an answer to the first has been formulated. Even the most precisely tooled war machines manufacture dead innocents, the meat and drink of editors in the copy drought that comes with media management in times of conflict. Running a modern war, as a result, is a battle of deadlines, driven as much by daily editorial needs as military requirements. The war in Afghanistan, pitting the cream of US might against a single, messianic killer of Americans, was the most deadline-driven of all. Bin Laden knew that, and soon he had it all explained to the Taliban.

By the fourth day of the war, the Taliban charged airstrikes had claimed more than 100 non-combatants, including a family of ten in Kabul and 15 others in Jalalabad where a bomb hit a mosque and adjacent houses.[14] The first independent account of civilian casualties, however, was a UN accusation that a US Cruise missile had hit the demining agency, Afghan Technical Consultants, during a raid on Kabul's airport and TV transmission tower on 9 October, killing four security guards. 'They found only one leg from four people, nothing else,' said a colleague.[15] The bloodiest raid in the war to date hit Karam, a village 38 miles from Jalalabad and site of a recently abandoned training camp, where the Taliban said more than 200 'women, children and elderly' had died.[16] Rumsfeld called the claim 'ridiculous', saying the attack hit a major arms depot instead, but journalists visiting the village under Taliban escort found its houses eviscerated by fire and the remains of an arm sticking out from the rubble: survivors put the death toll at between 50 and 100.[17]

The evidence for such carnage was difficult to evaluate, since most bodies were buried soon after death according to Moslem custom. But the grainy, green footage of a ruined Kabul under bombardment broadcast nightly by Al-Jazeera, the only media outlet allowed to remain in the capital, transmitted images to the world of an apparently unremitting aerial violence against civilians that was, in fact, more suggestive than accurate, though no less effective in moulding public opinion for being so. Facing a succession of violent demonstrations at home, Musharraf sought to prevent them spinning out of control with assurances that air strikes would be 'short' and 'targeted', while Britain's Defence Minister, Geoff Hoon, said the bombing was 'more likely a matter of days than weeks', though Rumsfeld was privately hunkering down for a long haul.[18] As US aircraft for the first time dropped 1,000 lb cluster bombs on Taliban troop concentrations, UN Human Rights Commissioner Mary Robinson articulated what millions in the West and the Moslem world yearned for when she called for a pause in the bombing to permit aid agencies access to the millions of Afghans in desperate need of food before the winter set in.[19]

By the end of the first week of bombing, US and British air forces had flown a total of 131 strike and bomber missions and launched 68 Cruise missiles against airports, air defences, operational headquarters, military bases, training camps and fuel depots, as well as houses where Al Qa'ida operatives or Mullah Omar himself might be sheltering. Sixty-three targets were eliminated and, despite growing public anger over deaths of civilians, a high degree of precision was maintained by extensive use of satellite-guided bombs, which had in-built global positioning chips.[20] But the Pentagon was running out of fixed targets, the kind best suited to guided weapons, and was at a loss at how to proceed with the next phase of the war. Logic dictated the deployment of US forces to engage the enemy on the ground with a switch in focus from high-altitude bombing to the use of Black Hawk attack helicopters to strike moving Taliban targets, but both strategies risked steep increases in casualties, military and civilian. Since 11 September, it had become an article of faith that the Pentagon must not be exposed to the same systems failure that had revealed the hollowness of the CIA's legend, setting tight political restrictions around any US ground deployment, while the death of every Afghan non-combatant chipped away further at the solidarity of Moslem members of the coalition. With the Soviet defeat clear in their memories, the Taliban instinctively grasped the Pentagon's dilemma, dismissing the air campaign as a sophisticated form of conflict avoidance. 'When Americans enter Afghanistan,' scoffed the Taliban envoy to Pakistan, 'there will start the real war.'[21]

But his confidence was misplaced. After a single week's bombing, the survival of the Taliban hinged less upon America's notorious faintheartedness at sending troops into open battle than Musharraf's continued ability to convince the US not to join swords with the Northern Alliance which, though poorly equipped, undermanned and cursed with a dubious human rights past, remained the obvious key to advancing the ground campaign without risk to US lives. Taliban forces had parried Dostum's thrust against the airport at Mazar for the moment, but a shoot-out over an unpaid lunch of pilau and kebabs in the Tajik village of Bazar-i Taleh resulted in the defection of 40 Taliban commanders with 1,200 men and loss of control of a crucial stretch of the Bagram–Bamian road, the most direct supply route for Taliban garrisons in the north.[22] Alliance forces also captured Chagcharan, in Ghor, which closed the Kabul–Herat route but provided a transport link between Ismail Khan, fighting to regain Herat, and Dostum's forces outside Mazar.[23] Near Jalalabad, at a meeting organised by the Taliban, Pashtun tribal elders refused a request to engage Northern Alliance forces, saying they were tired of fighting, though more likely they were waiting to see on which side the military coin would fall.[24]

Musharraf's own vulnerability in the face of domestic Islamist protest, as much as Powell's perception of the 'indispensable' role Pakistan was to play in the war, tilted the coin as it spun carelessly through the air, embolden-ing the leader of the nation that had created the Taliban to demand – and obtain – a veto on its successor to power in Kabul. It was a compelling per-formance. Musharraf offered the US little of military value beyond the use of three isolated, low-grade airbases – Jacobabad, in Sind, and Pasni and Dalbandin, in Baluchistan – for emergency landing and rescue operations, but not the launch of air or ground operations inside Afghanistan.[25] ISI intelligence of bin Laden and Al Qa'ida had led nowhere while Pakistan's borders remained visibly open to suppliers of weapons and fuel for the Taliban – though not to refugees from the bombing. Musharraf threatened to close Pakistani airspace altogether and cancel his support for the war unless he was given an 'ironclad understanding' that US airplanes based in the Arabian Sea would not bomb the Taliban frontlines, or allow the Northern Alliance in any other way to 'draw mileage' from the air campaign. 'If a power vacuum was filled by the Northern Alliance,' Musharraf declared disingenuously – given ISI support to Gulbuddin Hekmatyar's merciless bombardment of Kabul from 1994 to 1996 – 'we would be thrust back to the anarchy and atrocities we saw in the past.'[26]

It was a classic bluff that fed upon US intelligence's long-term neglect of the cut and thrust of inter-ethnic politics in Afghanistan. Washington's over-hasty agreement with Musharraf, however, had critical consequences for a campaign that needed to achieve its objectives swiftly, if it were not to come to grief on the hardline scepticism in the Western media and the imminent onset of the chilling Afghan winter. Exempting the frontlines from direct air attack blunted the campaign's potential to accelerate the Taliban's disintegration, while boosting its men's morale by providing a relative safe haven in which to shelter during raids on their regular positions in and around Kabul. 'For the Taliban, this is the safest place to be at the moment,' said General Baba Jan, Alliance commander on the Bagram front. 'A month ago, there were almost 5,000 Taliban opposing us. Now there are 7,000 during the day and, at night when the bombing starts, over 10,000.'[27] Musharraf's proviso had the secondary, and not unwelcome effect of shielding the hundreds of ex-servicemen and *madrassa* students from Quetta, Peshawar and Karachi, then fighting alongside the Taliban in forward areas north of Kabul.[28] The apparent subordination of the US campaign timetable to Musharraf's political agenda, meanwhile, fostered dark suspicions among the Alliance's commanders of Washington's ultimate intentions in Afghanistan. In spite of their five-year resistance to what they had every reason to assume was a common foe, Washington's policy choices cut across the underlying logic of Afghan strategic alliance: 'My enemy's enemy is my friend'. The price of thus placing diplomatic considerations in Pakistan above military necessity in Afghanistan was the forfeit of immediate US access to the two-mile runways at Bagram airbase, then occupied by Alliance forces. Far more precious than Jacobabad, Bagram might have functioned as a base for US ground and air rescue operations, the re-supply of the Northern Alliance and the airlifting of humanitarian aid, all independently of Pakistan's veto and after the most cursory military intervention against Taliban artillery in the hills over-looking the base.[29]

The information war was also going awry. A 24-hour satellite link to Kabul transformed Al-Jazeera into the CNN of the Afghanistan war while a succession of increasingly brazen tapes from bin Laden were scrutinised by hundreds of millions of viewers, as well as US intelligence, for clues to his whereabouts or plans. Chairman Sheikh Hamad bin Thamer al-Thani rejected White House criticism that Al-Jazeera gave too much airtime to 'Islamic extremists' in its coverage, mischievously citing press freedom. 'We will continue our work in a professional manner, whether in Afghanistan or elsewhere,' he said, 'offering a margin of freedom in the Arab world.'[30] White House spokesman Ari Fleischer questioned the legality of bin Laden inciting his followers to kill Americans on prime-time network TV and the coded instructions that might be imbedded in his diatribes, but his real concern was for the impact of their apocalyptic content on the morale of a nervous US public. 'The storms will not calm down,' the pro-bin Laden preacher Sulaiman Abu Ghaith threatened in one telecast, 'especially the storm of airplanes, until you see defeat in Afghanistan.'[31]

Fleischer's appeal received a better hearing in the US and in Downing Street, where press officers had coined the nickname 'Spin Ladin' because of the Saudi's bewildering success in the propaganda war.[32] The US tried to censor programme content as early as 21 September when the government-funded Voice of America (VOA) was set to air an interview with Mullah Omar. 'We recognise the independence of the VOA,' said a spokesman for the State Department which tried to shelve the broadcast. 'Its Charter says they should explain government policy and present responsible discussion about it. We don't consider Mullah Omar to be responsible discussion.' VOA went ahead and broadcast anyway.[33] Three weeks later after National Security Adviser Condoleezza Rice asked TV networks to 'limit use' of bin Laden tapes to avoid scaring Americans or inspiring his supporters, CNN and CBS agreed to 'screen' any long passages before airing them.[34] The conflict between the right to free speech and the Pentagon's perception of national security would flare up more fiercely after US ground forces went into action for the first time the following week.

By now, around 130 Western journalists had beaten a path to Jabal Saraj, to the rear of the Northern Alliance frontlines 25 miles north of Kabul, creating a consumer mini-boom for interpreters, drivers, electricity, goat meat, laundry, hot water and, of course, information, all paid for in cash at top dollar prices.[35] One entrepreneur dragged a hand-painted menu board out of storage that hadn't seen service since the last hippy passed through 22 years earlier. The Taliban, by contrast, rarely entertained the press – except for those enthusiasts who fell into their clutches disguised under *burkhas*. This suspicion of journalists was about to change, though efforts to woo the Western media often backfired because of an almost overwhelming desire to please. On the day Secretary of State Colin Powell was due to arrive in Islamabad for crucial talks about the conduct of the war and Pakistan's deteriorating relations with India, *Newsweek* published a poll showing that 83 per cent of Pakistanis sympathised with the Taliban while 48 per cent were convinced Israel was responsible for 11 September.[36] One day earlier, on 14 October, the Taliban invited 30 journalists to visit the blasted village of Karam and to see the twisted steel and crater that had once been Jalalabad airport's radar station. In a display of the gaucheness that sank many of the movement's best intentions, a Taliban official told journalists the airport was also the transit route for couriers bringing funds from overseas donors to bin Laden, cancelling whatever sympathy may have accrued from a show of the damage. One, known as 'The Mauritanian', had arrived with three 'sacks' of Saudi riyals, he said, while six Algerians brought briefcases stuffed with dollars.[37]

The first reports of Donald Rumsfeld's frustration with the direction of the war coincided with a Pentagon briefing that US planes were about to hammer the 'Al Qa'ida-dominated' assault troops of the 055 Brigade – though they were mostly scattered at the frontlines where, under the guarantees to Musharraf, they were immune to US attack.[38] The previous week of high-intensity bombing failed to dislodge bin Laden or kill any Taliban leaders, and Rumsfeld was audibly grumbling in Washington over General Frank's inability to come up with a more 'creative' plan. Franks insisted on yet more bombing to 'soften' resistance before deploying ground forces, though the strategy was arguably doing more damage to the coalition than to Al Qa'ida, and one critic compared it to 'shooting mosquitoes with ballistic missiles'.[39] In a sign of a parallel war developing in the Pentagon, Rumsfeld appointed General Charles Holland to the post of operational commander of special forces in Afghanistan, bypassing Franks and reporting directly to the defence secretary and the president. He also ordered an intensification of the war, the first sign of which was the night-time deployment of two low-flying AC-130 Spectre gunships over camps near Kandahar on 15 October. Modelled on the Hercules transport and armed with howitzer, cannons and machine guns, the Spectre fires 2,500 rounds a minute but its mission, this time, was to instil fear and deliver a message: the high-altitude air war now hovers directly above your heads.[40]

'Get Mullah Omar and Osama won't be able to operate,' General Musharraf told CBS Radio and USA Today on the eve of Powell's arrival in an interview he later vigorously denied. 'It could be over in one day if you take out Mullah Omar and his leadership.'[41] Powell's official agenda was to consult with Musharraf over the US strikes against the backdrop of the heightened tension with India created by a suicide bombing at the Jammu and Kashmir state legislature in Srinagar on 1 October in which 38 people died. But it was clearly an opportunity to discuss in more detail what possible Pashtun contribution could be made to a political settlement after the collapse of the Taliban. Musharraf was adamant about the need for 'broad-based' government in Afghanistan, though this was never a major concern of his until the demise of the Kandahari Pashtun hegemony that the Taliban had imposed became inevitable. Caught off-balance with a faulty political compass, the ISI's former protégé in Afghanistan, Gulbuddin Hekmatyar, burned his bridges by announcing he would donate his entire stock of Stinger missiles to the Taliban, but other pretenders to Afghan power proved less maladroit.[42]

Scurrying across the border came the stocky but impressive figure of Mullah Wakil Ahmad Mutawakil, the Taliban foreign minister who, since the death of Mullah Rabbani in May, was widely tipped as his successor as head of a Taliban 'moderate' clique – the existence of which was more speculative than palpable. Hot on his heels was Jalaluddin Haqqani, the anti-Soviet warlord from Khost who had joined the Taliban in 1996 and, since September 2001, served as Mullah Omar's head of southern command: the visit to 'enemy territory' of the equivalent of a five-star general in time of war was an interesting indicator of the state of Taliban morale. During the previous week, US bombers had studiously avoided attacking five training camps controlled by Haqqani around Khost because of ISI suggestions that he might make a stalking horse for the post-Taliban leadership and a valuable asset in manipulating the Pashtun clans in the east.[43] A three-man delegation from the former king, Zahir Shah, led by Hedayat Amin Arsala, a former World Bank official, was also in the capital the day that Powell touched down. 'No, [the] Taliban are not terrorists,' a Pakistani foreign office spokesman told journalists in a foretaste of the bidding war to come, 'we never regarded them as terrorists.'[44] From Mazar to the Shomali Plain, Alliance commanders gritted their teeth.

Though Mutawakil never met Colin Powell officially, his presence in the capital – amid reports of secret meetings with the ISI – triggered frantic speculation in the press of a split at the highest levels of the Taliban. The day before Powell's talks with Musharraf, Mullah Omar said he was willing to 'discuss' handing bin Laden to a third country for trial if the US ended its attacks and supplied evidence of his involvement in the 11 September attacks, an offer swiftly jettisoned by the White House.[45] Mutawakil made the same offer through Pakistani back-channels, receiving a similar reply though from a lower level official. Powell dined with Musharraf at the heavily-guarded US embassy on 15 October, meeting with Foreign Minister Abdul Sattar the following day before going on to address a joint press conference in the evening at which the general listed the groups who 'can play a role' in a new Afghan government, a list that included 'moderate Taliban leaders'. Obviously very jet-lagged and due in New Delhi the next day to defuse yet another potential nuclear confrontation, Powell's grasp of Afghan political reality and what the US had just signed up to seemed sketchy in the extreme. 'If you got rid of the [Taliban] regime,' he said, 'there will still be those who might find the teachings, feelings and beliefs of that movement are still very important and to the extent that they are willing to participate in the development of a new Afghanistan.'[46]

But the location of Musharraf's 'moderate Taliban' – 'Mullah-Lite', in one inimitable turn of phrase – was a mystery. While *ulama* and tribal chiefs were reportedly trying to persuade Mullah Omar to step down and get rid of bin Laden, any influence they had was more than capped by veteran Taliban such as Justice Minister Mohammed Turabi, Defence Minister Mullah Ubaidullah and Mullah Mohammed Hassan, the governor of Kandahar, all of whom backed the emir to the hilt. An insouciant Mutawakil travelled home later in the week, killing any further rumour of his imminent defection in an interview in which he 'reposed full confidence in the leadership of Mullah Omar'. Haqqani, a long-time confidant of bin Laden and an even more unlikely candidate for the role of moderate quisling, broke his silence just before returning to Afghanistan. 'The Afghans are with the Taliban simply because it is an Islamic government,' he told a journalist. 'The so-called broad-based government will, by its very nature, be secular, which will never be acceptable to the Afghans.' He had words of caution for the US that cut to the quick of the Taliban's unswerving morale after nearly two weeks of intensive bombing. 'I tell you, the Soviets were a brave enemy and their soldiers could withstand tough conditions,' he said. 'The Americans are creatures of comfort. They will not be able to sustain the harsh conditions that await them.'[47] This innate contempt for the US soldier, he said, was what sustained Taliban troops at the front. 'Not a single important leader or military commander of the Taliban,' he continued, 'has been killed in the past 12 days of constant US bombardment. Mullah Omar, Osama bin Laden and all other commanders are safe and sound and carrying out their duties.'

The man who chose to see if there truly were a budding 'Southern Alliance' in the Pashtun heartlands was a figure out of *Beau Geste*, with a dash of an Afghan *Indiana Jones*. Hamid Karzai, 43, a Quetta-based aristocrat distantly related to the former king, was deputy foreign minister in the government of President Rabbani until 1994 when his sympathies switched to the then-embryonic Taliban. 'The Taliban were good, honest people ... They came to me in May 1994, saying: "Hamid, we must do something about the situation in Kandahar. It is unbearable." I had no reservations about helping them. I had a lot of money and weapons left over from the *jihad*. I also helped them with political legitimacy.'[48] But the character of his new friends soon altered. 'It was only in September 1994 that others began to appear at the meetings – silent ones I did not recognise, people who took over the Taliban movement. That was the hidden hand of Pakistani intelligence.'[49] Much of his time was spent latterly in the US where brothers and sister ran the 'Helmand' chain of Afghan restaurants with branches in San Francisco, Chicago and Boston. He had come to the attention of Zalmay Khalilzad, former Under-Secretary of Defense in the Bush Snr administration, then out of office but advising UNOCAL on the trans-Afghanistan pipeline scheme. Karzai joined Khalilzad at UNOCAL, periodically meeting with Christine Rocca, Bush Jnr's new Assistant Secretary for South Asia Affairs. 'To us,' said a State Department official, 'he's still "Hamid", a man we've dealt with for some time.'[50] After the coup attempt against Mullah Omar reported in 1999, Kharzai's father, a former Senator in the pre-communist Afghan parliament, was shot dead in Quetta while walking home from prayers by a lone assassin on a motorbike. Hamid inherited his father's title as *khan* of the Popolzai branch of the 'royal' Durranis – from which every Afghan king had been selected for over 200 years – as well as the reverence of 500,000 clan members across Uruzgan and Kandahar provinces. On 9 October, carrying a satellite phone supplied by 5th US Special Forces Group, Karzai and a handful of followers motored across the border to Kandahar unrecognised, and headed north to his ancestral village of Derawat in a bid to raise the tribes.[51]

For ten hours a day after 18 October, a modified EC-130E with forward air conditioner intakes, known as 'Mickey Mouse ears', patrolled the Afghan skies emitting warnings to Taliban on three frequencies not to resist, while another boomed live 'psyops' messages in dialect about Mullah Omar's sex games with his wives while his followers waited below to meet their certain deaths.[52] 'Attention Taliban!' ran one script. 'You are condemned. Did you know that? The instant that the terrorists you support took over our planes, you sentenced yourselves to death ... Our forces are armed with state of the art military equipment. What are you using? Obsolete and ineffective weaponry. Our helicopters will rain fire down upon your camps before you detect them on your radar. Our bombs are so accurate we can drop them right through your windows. Our infantry is trained for any climate and terrain on earth ... You have only one choice ... Surrender now and we will give you a second chance.'[53]

Just after midnight on the morning of 20 October, 100 Rangers wafted down by parachute through a night-goggled, acid-green sky into a drug- and gun-running air strip at Bibi Tera in Helmand province, 80 miles distant from Kandahar. A second group of Rangers and Delta Force commandos, meanwhile, slid down fast ropes from helicopters into a compound belonging to Mullah Omar at Baba Sahib, five miles from the Taliban capital. The two missions' purpose, officially, was to gather intelligence about the whereabouts of the Taliban and Al Qa'ida leaderships, but no prisoners were taken back for interrogation and four US personnel and five Pakistani ground staff were killed at Dalbandin airbase after accidents involving a Black Hawk and a C-130 transport plane.[54] Green-tinted video footage of the raids circulated the globe for the next two days. Asked what message could be drawn from the first US ground attacks of the war, General Richard Myers, Chairman of the Joint Chiefs of Staff, replied that: 'We are capable of, at the time of our choosing, conducting the kind of operation we want to conduct.'[55] But the raid on Bibi Tera proved to be little better than virtual reality, and the other was a near-disaster, inviting comparisons with the Rangers' nightmare mission in Mogadishu, and it effectively disbarred any further US ground interventions in Afghanistan until after the collapse of the Taliban.

'Next time, we're going to lose a company,' said one disgruntled combatant from Delta Force, a unit so secret its members do not acknowledge its existence, let alone talk to the press about bungled operations.[56] Inside sources said that an army pathfinder unit was inserted into Bibi Tera to ensure that the remote and strategically marginal area was first clear of Taliban forces before the Rangers dropped into the air strip – along with the video crew which filmed them leaving a poster of fire fighters raising the Stars and Stripes above a damaged Pentagon. 'It was a television show,' said the source. Over at Baba Sahib, meanwhile, Delta units emerging from a fruitless search of Mullah Omar's home met fierce resistance from Taliban armed with rocket-propelled grenades, taking twelve casualties, three of them serious, as they fought their way back to the waiting gunships. 'It was a total goat fuck,' said one member who, along with other Delta fighters, pinned the blame on Tampa and CENTCOM's remote and heavy-handed operational methods. After the Chinooks flew back to Dalbandin, leaving one undercarriage on the ground in Kandahar, the Taliban found an 'American foot', still in its boot.[57] Accustomed to relying on stealth in intimate groups of four to six operatives, Delta's raid at Baba Sahib involved some 100 fighters and was announced by a fanfare of 16 Spectre gunships which flailed the compound with thousands of rounds of fire, allowing the Taliban time to regroup and set up an ambush as they struggled to escape. 'This isn't the way you run Delta Force,' journalist Seymour Hersh told CNN, 'you can't have this kind of big-scale operation. And so they're throwing a message over the fence to the leadership, really, through me.'[58]

The US air campaign continued for a second week against a diminishing list of targets, striking a relief warehouse of the International Committee of the Red Cross in Kabul on 16 October, and killing 35 civilians when bombs went astray in the Khair Khana and Kalae Zaman Khan residential areas of Kabul, and on a refugee convoy near Tarin Kot in the south.[59] Powell's agreement with Musharraf not to strike the Taliban frontlines seemed to be holding, despite a Northern Alliance pledge on 14 October not to occupy Kabul, but CIA agents, clad in Afghan clothes and bearded like their hosts, were already in place alongside selected anti-Taliban commanders across the country. They found a bedraggled force with few heavy weapons, low on food and diesel, relying on 'Kalashnikovs and horses'.[60] Rumsfeld confirmed on 19 October that the US was supplying the Northern Alliance with money and ammunition, but Yunus Qanuni, a former Massoud adviser and one of the rising stars of the Alliance's political wing, the United Front, denied it three days later.[61] The visit of an eight-man US military delegation from Uzbekistan to Rashid Dostum introduced further dischord in the Alliance, rather than its opposite. 'If the situation continues like this,' said the Tajik commander Ustad Mohammed Atta, 'it will be seen that the US team is trying to create cracks in the United Front.'[62] Preferential access to US money, weapons and more secure communications threatened to upset the precarious balance of power, weakness and mutual suspicion that allowed members of the Northern Alliance to function together at all. Atta numbered the forces controlled by Dostum – one of the few warlords with a US profile thanks to his lobbyist in Washington – at no more than 600 men.[63] Near Taloqan, meanwhile, another of the new wave of emerging post-Massoud commanders, Mohammed Daoud, recounted how Taliban leaders had tried to convince him to changes sides and join an anti-US alliance should American forces enter Afghanistan in strength.

In Pakistan, the ISI persisted with its plans to marginalise the Northern Alliance by paying for 800 southern Pashtun elders and commanders to travel to Peshawar for a grand assembly on the political future of Afghanistan, chaired by Pir Sayed Ahmed Gailani, a former mujahedin leader and spiritual head of the Sufi Qadiryya sect. Before they could confer, however, Abdul Haq, another Pashtun mujahedin legend and the brother of Haji Qadir, former governor of Nangarhar, slipped across the border with seven companions, two satellite phones and 'a lot of cash' on 21 October in a bid to stir a revolt against the Taliban in the east.[64] He was heading for Azra in Logar province, 20 miles from the border and close to his native village. Like his fellow-Pashtun Hamid Karzai further south, Haq had lost loved ones to a Taliban assassin when his wife and son were murdered in Peshawar in 1999 and, to the Afghan way of seeing things, he was similarly a man who had fallen among Americans. But there the comparisons ended, according to journalist Sayed Masood Majrooh. 'Karzai is a political person. Abdul Haq was a commander. He had the confidence of the intellectuals and the tribal people too.'[65]

Haq was friend and informal adviser to Joseph and James Ritchie, two brothers from Chicago who sold an option trading business in 1993 for $225 million to focus on humanitarian work in Pakistan and Afghanistan, where they lived in the 1950s while their father taught civil engineering in Kabul. During the years of neglect under Clinton, the Ritchies effectively ran a 'freelance Afghan foreign policy', subsidising Zahir Shah, meeting with Massoud, lobbying congress and fanning the resistance to the Taliban with gifts of satellite phones and money to key friendly commanders. To improve political access in Bush Jnr's Washington – where they shared a publicist with Delta Oil – the brothers hired Robert 'Bud' McFarlane, a former National Security Adviser to President Ronald Reagan who was forced to resign in 1985 after lying over the Iran-Contra affair. After leaving office, McFarlane went on to build his own energy development consultancy, Global Energy Investors, also based in Washington.[66] The Ritchies had helped Haq financially since 1998, and James Ritchie was in his compound in Peshawar the day that he departed for Afghanistan.

'War is easy,' Haq once said. 'If you don't like someone, you kill him.'[67] Tall, burly and fluent in English, he had lost a lower leg fighting the Soviets but had no great respect for Washington or for CIA officials either, who dismissed him as 'Hollywood Haq', another of the 'Gucci guerrillas' entertained in the 1980s by President Reagan and Prime Minister Margaret Thatcher as the acceptable face of the gallant Afghan resistance. On 11 October he told a journalist:

> They don't care about the suffering of the Afghans or how many people we will lose. And we don't like that. Because Afghans are now being made to suffer for these Arab fanatics, but we all know who brought these Arabs to Afghanistan in the 1980s, armed them and gave them a base. It was the Americans and the CIA. And the Americans who did this all got medals and good careers, while all these years Afghans suffered from these Arabs and their allies. Now, when America is attacked, instead of punishing the Americans who did this, it punishes the Afghans.[68]

Instead of the wholesale bombing of Afghanistan, Haq advised a tightly focused assault on the central leadership in Kandahar. 'The Taliban are like a crystal ball. They are very hard, but brittle. If they are hit in the right way, they will shatter into a million pieces ... If they are destroyed, every Taliban fighter will pick up his gun and his blanket and disappear back home, and that will be the end of the Taliban.'

The CIA rejected his pleas for guns and air support in the days leading up to the mission, and he refused their offer of a satellite phone, lest it be used to position him or listen in.[69] He took his own, pausing at Parachinar to buy arms from local gunsmiths before he traversed the frontier into northern Paktia. In the first villages where he tried to talk round local commanders, he found tribesmen raging at the devastation wrought by US bombers, but pressed on for Azra, lured by the promise of a crucial defection. No name was mentioned, but Haqqani's exercise in profile in Islamabad put him among the principal candidates, and he did live nearby. Haq, an old comrade, never got further than Azra. He turned back after two days on the road, apprehensive of the bands of Taliban that had shadowed his party since the moment it crossed the border. 'I am cut off on a mountain road,' he told his nephew by phone on 24 October. 'There are Taliban ahead and Taliban behind. Can you do something?'[70] His nephew put a call through to the Ritchies, who called McFarlane, who called his contacts in the CIA who called CENTCOM in Tampa to ask for air support, which was refused due to the perceived risk to civilians. An unmanned Predator was dispatched, but it only arrived after Haq's pony had bolted, throwing its rider who limped on his prosthetic device straight into a trap. When another concerned relative called, a Taliban commander answered Haq's phone. On 24 October, he was hung by a metal noose from a maple tree and raked with bullets after a summary trial at Rishkor on spying charges.[71] The execution order, it was reported, came directly from Mullah Mohammed Omar, but the uncharacteristic efficiency of his capture only strengthened suspicions that the ISI had leaked details of his journey and was pursuing a separate agenda with regard to the Taliban's survival. James Ritchie blamed the CIA – 'The US hung him out to dry' – but the millionaire's own role in the death of his friend, a man once known as the 'Lion of Kabul', was far from blameless.[72]

The dramatic circumstances of Haq's capture and execution overshadowed the deeper significance of his failed operation which, like Karzai's in Uruzgan, had initiated neither a single important defection nor any mass uprising by groups hostile to Mullah Omar's rule. Despite the huge arsenal arrayed against them, astonishingly, not one Pashtun commander was yet convinced the balance of power had shifted emphatically enough to justify the negotiation of new alliances in preparation for the collapse or killing of the Taliban leadership. Haq's death or, conversely, the CIA's unwillingness or inability to ensure his survival on such a risky foray, clearly reinforced their wavering loyalty to the reclusive figure in Kandahar. The same message was reiterated in Peshawar where the elders summoned by the ISI first resolved that bin Laden and Al Qa'ida – 'those foreigners who add more to our miseries' – must go, but then ruled out any participation in a post-Taliban government by the Northern Alliance. 'If that [political] vacuum were filled by a particular group through military operations,' the conference communique stated euphemistically, 'it would turn to a new phase of bloodshed and disorder.'[73] The statement could have been plucked straight from a speech by Musharraf, but the impassivity of the commanders, some of whom had come from as far as Kandahar, undermined the notion the ISI had so far successfully fed to Powell of a 'moderate Taliban' wing prepared to join a broad-based government on equal terms with Tajik, Uzbek and Shia under the aegis of the former king. Neither the Northern Alliance nor, more pointedly, Zahir Shah were invited to send delegates to the meeting.

Delta's failure and Haq's death halfway through the third week of bombing hastened the implementation of a review of US strategy by the National Security Council. Over 3,000 bombs had been dropped to date, leading to the destruction of nine Al Qa'ida camps and serious damage or injury at nine Afghan airfields and 24 military barracks, but the Taliban showed no sign of buckling under the assault, or of imploding.[74] 'I'm a bit surprised at how doggedly they're hanging on to power,' said Pentagon spokesman Rear Admiral John Stufflebeem.[75] US supplies of weapons and fuel had still not been delivered to Northern Alliance fighters but, in the first indication that a policy swerve was in motion, bombers struck Taliban trenches and artillery positions at Bagram airbase and Darra-i Suf for the first time on 21 October.[76] 'Basically, the new thinking is to take those cities that are within easy reach of Northern Alliance forces without waiting any longer to be sure we can control in advance all the risks of postwar factional rivalries,' a Pentagon official said two days later. 'The military track has been held up waiting for progress on the political track. We had to get rid of the idea – or rather the illusion – that we could micro-manage the political future.' The air strikes, consisting of a few selectively dropped 500 lb and 1,000 lb ordnance rather than a full-scale carpet bombing of the frontlines, did little to mollify Alliance commanders like Baba Jan. 'If the US did this for 100 years,' he complained, 'it's not enough.'[77] Even US pilots were heard grumbling at the limits put upon their operational capabilities by diplomatic considerations thousands of feet below.[78] With tanks rationed to 100 litres, enough for a single day's operation but not a fast-moving campaign, and a shell allowance of 40 per tank, against the 160 shells necessary for offensive operations, the Alliance was steadily losing ground near Mazar where two commanders were hung in the main square after they were caught distributing weapons to civilians.[79] If Pakistan were adamant the Alliance must not be assisted to enter Kabul, Russia and India insisted that no Taliban, moderate or otherwise, could ever be elegible for future political office in Kabul. Even as the US appeared to hedge its bets over whether to commit to the Alliance, President Vladimir Putin met its new military leader, General Fahim, in Tajikistan on 21 October to discuss the supply of 40 T-55 tanks, 70 armoured vehicles and twelve military helicopters, at a value of $40 million to $70 million.[80] Over the next two weeks on nightly TV, the Alliance's ragged-trousered brigades mysteriously transmogrified into something akin to a regular fighting force through the acquisition of new uniforms, army boots and crude drilling techniques.

Time was not on the coalition's side. The first snow was beginning to fall in the high mountain passes linking the Panjshir valley with Alliance territory adjacent to the Pyandj river, the overland route for military supplies from Tajikistan. The approach of winter not only threatened to bog down the opposition's minimalist progress, it promised to provide an additional layer of defensive cover for the Taliban army and its allies in Al Qa'ida, both better equipped to wait out the freeze than their raw American adversaries. In a week that saw the death count from 11 September shrink by more than half from its peak of 6,500 to 2,445, the issue of civilian casualties in Afghanistan naturally assumed greater prominence.[81] A Taliban claim that over 1,000 non-combatants had perished during the three weeks of air strikes was impossible to verify or refute, but widespread suspicion of the Pentagon's tight control on the scant information coming out of Afghanistan, along with inevitable incidents of 'collateral damage' to the bombing, antagonised both a Moslem world waiting for Ramadan to start on 17 November and the liberal West. On 21 October, a US Navy fighter accidentally dropped a 1,000 lb bomb on what was either a mosque near a military hospital or a 'senior citizens home' in Herat, depending on differing UN and US reports, with the loss of 20–100 lives. A week later, eight 2,000 lb bombs were dropped on the same Red Cross relief warehouse in Kabul that a US bomber visited two weeks earlier.[82] Riyadh, fearful of protests against the war in Mecca involving hundreds of thousands of Moslem pilgrims, begged for the air raids to end. Its anxieties centred on the religious passion sparked by the rites of Leilat-ul-Qadr, the 'night better than 1,000 months', when the Prophet Mohammed was escorted to heaven by angels. At the end of October, an opinion poll revealed that 54 per cent of people in Britain were convinced there should be a bombing pause to allow the resumption of aid to the millions displaced by war.[83] In spite of 11 September, the bombing campaign was increasingly perceived by the public as the work of 'techno-bullies'.

US targeting of the Taliban trenches near Bagram, Mazar and Taloqan continued through the third week of the war, alongside attacks on urban military sites, without much impressing Northern Alliance commanders. 'We are all astonished how America and its allies, this coalition of all world society against terrorism,' said General Basir Salangi, 'drops three bombs every day on the Taliban, and that's it ... It doesn't seem like America has woken up to what's going on. We are not seeing anything like the kind of air attacks they gave Yugoslavia and Iraq.'[84] Journalists massed in Jabal Saraj half-suspected that the swooping F-18s, their roaring engines and the plumes of black smoke left behind were laid on more for their benefit, and the viewers at home, than for any tactical value they represented in the field. Rumsfeld denied US forces were intentionally restrained in order to allow the diplomacy on the formation of a post-Taliban government to progress. 'We have been ready,' he said, 'and we certainly are ready to have the alliance forces move, both north and south.'[85] Bereft of fuel and shot, Alliance forces refused to advance into a Taliban firestorm, while the early news of Hamid Karzai and his mission to forge a 'Southern Alliance' were far from optimistic. The Taliban announced on 1 November that, after a nine-hour night march to Derawat, they had ambushed his party, killed one of its members and arrested a further 25 supporters. Even now they were tracking Karzai and his Green Beret guard through the mountains of Uruzgan. 'We seized 600 new guns, which were dropped in the area by American helicopters, which also pounded the area during our operation,' said the spokesman.[86] The war on terrorism, it appeared, had reached stalemate but, in truth, it was the coalition, and not the Taliban, that was on the back-foot.

Across the border, an unstable Pakistan moved one step closer to religious war on 29 October when six Islamists, chanting 'Allahu Akhbar' ('God is great') sprayed a Protestant church congregation with machine gun fire in the Punjabi town of Bahawalpur, killing 16, including the wife of a US diplomat and their daughter. Gunsmiths in North West Frontier Province speeded up bullet production to meet the needs of the 9,000 armed Pakistani volunteers who had swarmed to the border and were now waiting for the word to join the *jihad* against the US. Kandahar's spokesman in Islamabad, Abdul Salaam Zaeef, politely declined their offer: 'There are plenty of mujahedin at the frontlines. If they did go, there would be a lot of congestion in these areas and the possibility of mass casualties because of American air strikes would become much higher. It isn't wise.'[87] But several thousand armed Pakistanis had already made it to Kabul, in spite of Pakistan's claims to have sealed the frontier, and one Alliance commander was certain it was the 'fanaticism' of foreign fighters, rather than their more amenable Afghan comrades, which kept the lines intact despite the US bombing. 'They are not as weak as the US thought at first,' said the deputy commander in Baghlan. 'If there were not foreigners among them – especially Pakistanis and Arabs – the Taliban would not be able to defend themselves.'

Distinguishing between those who were Afghan Taliban, one of their foreign volunteers, an Al Qa'ida mercenary or a martyrdom recruit thousands of miles away would become the central confusion of a war on terrorism that was ultimately incapable of defining its target clearly but which, in time, would learn to draw some advantage from these blurred lines of fire. One Afghan witness saw at least 30 truckloads of Pakistani fighters crossing at Torkham Gate in mid-October, and a further six when he reached Jalalabad.[88] Further south, the traffic of fuel and ammunition to Kandahar continued unabated, allegedly on the orders of the ISI, though freight was only allowed to transit by night.[89] To the four confusions in the enemy's identity was added a fifth, Washington's nearest but least stable coalition ally. Through shrewd diplomacy, Musharraf effectively spiked the US guns for the first three weeks of the air war, but he was still fighting for his life against Islamists in the ISI and the population at large. Only one thing alarmed US intelligence more than Musharraf being overthrown by pro-Taliban military officers and that was the prospect of Pakistan's arsenal of 24 nuclear warheads falling into the hands of anti-American Islamists. Sultan Bashiruddin Mahmood, one of Pakistan's top nuclear scientists and an expert in uranium enrichment and plutonium production, had enjoyed a close association since his retirement with bin Laden and Mullah Mohammed Omar, whose militant vision he shared. He had set up an NGO, Ummah Tameer-e-Nau, with a fellow scientist from the Pakistan Atomic Energy Commission, Chaudry Abdul Majid, ostensibly to raise relief funds for the Taliban, though intelligence suspected the NGO was merely a cover for providing Al Qa'ida with nuclear weapons technology.[90] On 23 October, Mahmood and Majid were detained by ISI agents at the request of US intelligence and, under extensive interrogation, they admitted to discussing nuclear, chemical and biological weapons with bin Laden during a three-day visit to Kabul the previous August.[91] Less than a week later, a US special forces unit was reportedly on stand-by for an incursion into Pakistan to 'steal' its entire nuclear arsenal, in collaboration with Israel's renowned deep-penetration team, Unit 262, or Sayeret Matkal, which had arrived in the US to prepare for just such a mission shortly after 11 September.[92]

Further embarrassments for the US lay in store as the war entered its fourth week, still with no intelligence on the whereabouts of bin Laden and Mullah Omar, and no sign that the Taliban were about to cave in. Two dozen journalists on a Taliban press trip to Kandahar were taken to the remains of the village of Chowkar-Kerez, 50 miles north of the city, where 25 civilians were killed after a one-hour attack by a Spectre gunship on 22 October. 'There were no tanks or Taliban cars, they just killed innocent people,' said one of the survivors. 'The plane saw us and they opened fire. We don't understand why they did that.' In Kandahar, they saw three ruined ministries, including the Office for the Propagation of Virtue and the Prevention of Vice, but otherwise remarked on the city's normality, with shops open and people going about their business.[93] On 1 November, the Pentagon announced that it would change the colour of its food relief packages from yellow to blue, because they were too similar in shade to the hundreds of bomblets contained in the cluster bombs dropped by US planes. 'Unfortunately, they get used to running after yellow,' said General Myers.[94] Two days later, bin Laden reappeared in a 20-minute video aired by Al-Jazeera, in which he condemned the US bombing campaign for targeting civilians and denounced the UN as a criminal organisation bent on the destruction of Islam. 'Those who refer matters to international legitimacy,' he ruled, 'have become unbelievers in the legitimacy of the Koran.'[95] To cap a week of bad publicity, Foreign Minister Mullah Wakil Ahmad Mutawakil suggested a duel as a means to end the war. 'The Americans have launched propaganda that Mullah Omar has gone into hiding,' he said. 'I propose that Mr Blair and Mr Bush should take Kalashnikovs and come to a specified place where Mullah Omar will appear with the Kalashnikovs to determine as to who will run.'[96]

Since the visit of the US military delegation to Dostum on 19 October, General Holland had ordered the insertion by helicopter from Uzbekistan of more uniformed Special Forces units to work with Alliance commanders on target identification, communications and resupply. One such attempt was driven off by ground fire and others by fog and early ice, but Rumsfeld admitted that more than a dozen – but less than 100 – ground troops, apart from the early CIA teams, were in the north, while others had 'gone in and come out' of the south.[97] Soon after the information was released, B-52s from Diego Garcia launched the first in a series of carpet-bombing attacks on the enemy's positions north of Kabul, near Taloqan and in Balkh, to the west of Mazar, in the most concentrated day of bombing since the war began. A single stick of bombs at Bagram set off 15 explosions over half a mile of trench, sending smoke plumes 1,000 feet high, and it was followed by waves of bombers following the same pattern.[98] Similar attacks, growing in frequency, continued throughout the fourth week, culminating on 5 November with the deployment of 15,000 lb Daisy Cutter bombs, which produce a mist of ammonium nitrate, aluminum and air that, when combusted, incinerates everything within 600 yards. Considered the next best thing to a nuclear device, the tremors from the impact of the Daisy Cutters were felt six miles away. The new bombing strategy wounded up to 300 Taliban north of Kabul in a single incident, while the Alliance's acting foreign minister, Dr Abdullah Abdullah, said 15 tanks were destroyed in another, but accounts of its effectiveness in Taloqan and Mazar were more sketchy.[99] The little-known Kashmiri separatist group, Harakat-i Jihad-i Islami, claimed 85 of its militants were felled in trenches outside Mazar, but the Pentagon wasn't so sure. Taliban in the north may have responded to the carpet bombing by moving men and machines to populated areas. 'They've gotten smarter every day,' a spokesman said. 'They know what we say we're not going to hit – and they go there.'[100]

After almost a week of heavy bombing, Alliance forces commanded by Dostum and Ustad Atta launched a three-pronged attack on Mazar, as thousands of Taliban forces raced from Kabul by pick-up to hit them in the rear. Taliban sources said they had repulsed the attacks and denied reports that 2,000 mounted Uzbeks, along with a handful of US rough-riders, had seized three peri-urban districts as the Alliance claimed, but they conceded the loss of Zahre, 4 miles from the city centre.[101] By some accounts, the collapse of resistance in Mazar, when it finally came on 9 November after five weeks of bombing, was triggered by the fortuitous shooting of a single influential commander, whose evacuation triggered a panic that shot from trench to trench until every Taliban soldier had taken to his heels.[102] But Alliance Interior Minister Yunus Qanuni attributed the débâcle to a sheer lack of tactical know-how. 'They had a front line, but that was their defence line. They did not have a second defence line. So as soon as that line broke, everything broke.'[103] On a nearby hill, watching the columns of Taliban fleeing east and south, was Dostum himself, who claimed to have lost only four men in the four-hour battle to take Mazar, against 90 on the enemy side.[104] But when Alliance troops entered the city at nightfall, they discovered that 1,200 Pakistani and Arab fighters, abandoned by the Taliban in their desperation to leave, holed up at a military base. After rejecting terms for surrender, many died resisting a siege by Shia forces, as did a group of 170 Pakistani, Kashmiri and Chechen fighters hiding in the Sultan Razia girls' school.[105] The school was first bombed from the air and, when that did not achieve the desired effect, it was pummelled by tank fire for 48 hours until the last man was lifeless.[106] Red Cross workers said they collected 300–400 bodies for burial, the vast majority of them non-Afghans.[107] But after four years of occupation and five weeks of humiliation, the Geneva Convention was the last thing on the minds of the Northern Alliance or its US sponsors.

Within 48 hours of Mazar falling, the provinces of Jawzjan, Faryab, Balkh, Samangan and Sar-i Pul all succumbed to Dostum's forces after a minimum of resistance. The Taliban governor of Bamian, Nabi Islam, simply switched sides and joined a now rapidly-expanding Alliance, although this option was only available to locals – Taliban of convenience – and not the Pashtun Taliban from beyond Kabul. A little further south in Parwan, 5,000 nominal Taliban negotiated their safe transfer to the winning side, opening the road from Bamian to the outskirts of the capital. 'When the enemy surrenders, we deal with them as our friends,' said the local Alliance chief, 'like our brothers. There will be no revenge.'[108] In western Badghis, with as much Iranian as US help, Ismail Khan's Tajiks claimed possession of the provincial capital, Qala-i Nau, deserted by the Taliban, and pressed on to retake Herat. There was greater opposition between Kunduz and Taloqan where, despite heavy B-52 activity, opposition forces encountered stiff resistance from Taliban artillery around Kolkata Hill. Three journalists travelling in an Alliance convoy, two French and one German, were killed in an ambush 30 miles from Taloqan, marking the first foreign press fatalities in the campaign. When Taloqan and Herat finally fell on 11 November, the rout of the Taliban was all but complete except for Kunduz, where a pocket of 15,000 Taliban and Al Qa'ida stragglers from garrisons across the north were totally encircled by the Alliance forces. 'The importance of this big defeat, dramatic defeat is not only that they have lost areas, but they have lost their main fighting force,' said Abdullah Abdullah, the Alliance foreign minister.[109]

On the final night of bombing over Kabul, US jets narrowly missed the BBC studios, but finally silenced Al-Jazeera with a direct hit. The Qatar-based station had screened another video on 7 November in which four of bin Laden's teenage sons posed with weapons and held up the wreckage of what the Taliban had alleged was a US helicopter downed near Ghazni the previous weekend. 'Their heroes are only mythical like Rambo,' a Taliban fighter told one of the boys on the tape, with unexpected perspicuity, 'they won't come on the land of Afghanistan.'[110] Bin Laden had anyway made plans for alternative means of accessing a wider audience. The jubilation in the West that greeted the dizzying collapse of the Taliban was marred only by the publication, on the very day that Mazar fell, of an in-depth interview with the Saudi by Hamid Mir, editor of *Dawn* and bin Laden's 'official biographer'. Despite numerous attempts by the US to kill him by bombing Al Qa'ida strongholds in the east and south, he was, in fact, in or around Kabul on the night of 7 November, when Mir was driven blindfolded to 'a place where it was extremely cold and one could hear the sound of anti-aircraft guns firing away'.[111] Over the course of a two-hour talk, an apparently chipper bin Laden chatted about jurisprudence, the state of his kidneys and his wives, but the nub of the meeting was his assertion: 'I wish to declare that if America used chemical or nuclear weapons against us, then we may retort with chemical and nuclear weapons. We have the weapons as a deterrent.' This was the last thing that the US public needed to hear, panicked as it already was by the delivery of a spate of anthrax-tainted letters through the mail that began soon after the 11 September attacks. But while the White House was quick to dismiss the claim as hollow, quicker still was the surge of popular credence that bin Laden truly did possess the 'tools to turn hatred into holocaust', to quote Bush's address about the capability of the modern terrorist at the UN General Assembly in New York.

With half of Afghanistan in Alliance hands and the remainder almost audibly groaning under the strain of further war, Washington attempted to stall the opposition's advance until a viable representative of the fabled anti-Taliban coalition of Pashtun clans could step forward. 'We will encourage our friends to head south over the Shomali plains, but not into the city of Kabul itself,' said Bush wistfully, but there was little he could do about it.[112] US jets continued to relentlessly bombard Taliban positions in the Shomali Plain while Alliance forces from the north travelled through the night to link up with their comrades north of Kabul. Even while his northern empire crumbled into pieces, Mullah Omar issued orders for the Taliban to withdraw from Kabul, rather than fight, after an occupation that had lasted five years. They ransacked the city before going, looting currency shops, government offices, aid agencies, vehicles and whatever remained in the newly-restored museum. On the evening of 12 November, $6 million was stolen from the vaults of the national bank.[113] 'They took whatever they could,' said one witness, 'then they broke all the locks.'[114] Carefully calibrating their advance so as not to clash with the Taliban retreat, Alliance forces began cautiously moving the following day at 11.30 a.m., capturing two forward enemy defence positions in the early afternoon. By evening, the dust of Taliban tanks, personnel carriers, pick-ups, trucks, taxis, cars and, probably, bicycles, all laden with booty, was visible to astonished spectators on the roof of the

Intercontinental Hotel. The retreat south was visible until sunrise, when Kabulis awoke to loot for themselves. As one half of the population carried away fans, air conditioners, blankets and stoves from agency offices and the Pakistani embassy, others dug up the videos, cassette players and CDs long secreted in their yards.[115]

Most observers present marvelled at the lightning speed of the Taliban's collapse and flight: few remarked the discipline which allowed up to 10,000 Afghan and foreign fighters to evacuate the city with their weapons intact without suffering a single serious massacre, in spite of the US bombers that dogged their every mile. The bulk of opposition forces halted four miles north, citing the same humanitarian reasons for not entering Kabul that Taliban officials gave to explain why they had left it but, at 2.15 in the afternoon on 13 November, the first squad of 50 Alliance troops arrived to reconnoitre as gun shots rang out from Shari Nau where a group of Al Qa'ida stragglers was spotted.[116] The bodies of five Pakistanis were hung in the trees, others died in the gutters, but incidents of revenge killing were few in light of the widely aired brutality common to the northern soldier. This vanguard was quickly followed by a convoy of 1,000 Alliance fighters from Charikar, their jeeps festooned with flags and posters of Massoud, in defiance of White House requests not to occupy the city. Qanuni, the Alliance interior minister, insisted that the intervention was necessary to prevent more looting and eliminate any pockets of Taliban resistance. 'The police forces are going to Kabul,' he said, 'not military troops.'[117] But shortly after, thousands of armed troops mounted on tanks, personnel carriers and buses appeared in the suburb of Khair Khana before rolling on into the city, in apparent defiance of Qanuni. They were greeted loudly, but uneasily, by citizens shouting 'Death to Mullah Omar' and 'Death to the Pakistani president'. But when one laughing young soldier on a truck gestured to the women in the crowd to remove the *burkha* they had been forced to wear for more than half a decade, they stared balefully back from inside their cotton cages. 'For now we will leave the *burkha* on,' said one of them. 'We don't know yet who are these people in the city.'[118]

Two days later, the BBC Pashtu service secured an interview by satellite phone with Mullah Omar, who railed at the US and hinted of the revenge to come. 'The plan is going ahead,' he said, 'and, God willing, it is being implemented. Keep in mind this prediction.'[119]

20   The Road to Kandahar

'This brother ... came close and told me that he saw in a dream a tall building in America. At that point, I was very worried ... the secret would be revealed if everyone starts seeing it in their dream. I told him, if he sees another dream, not to tell anybody.' Osama bin Laden[1]

The heavily armed fighters who entered Kabul on 13 November were loyal neither to the Northern Alliance, which Massoud had painstakingly nurtured following the Taliban takeover of Kabul, nor to Jamiat-i Islami, the mainly Tajik party led by Burhanuddin Rabbani, whom the UN still recognised as Afghanistan's legitimate president, in spite of a political eclipse that became quite irreversible after the assassination of his nominal deputy. Kabul's new rulers were hard-bitten *guerreros* from Massoud's native Panjshir, who had filled the levies for the frontlines to the north of the capital, enduring the worst the Taliban could hurl at them. Their first allegiance was to themselves, their valley, the scarred plains of Shomali – and whatever political manifesto his successors chose to attribute to the lips of the martyred leader whose posters snapped above their guns as they entered the city, scattering afghanis as if they were rose petals. But the euphoria of the crowds owed less to their 'liberators' arrival than the departure of the Taliban, the end of US air strikes and the hiatus that both allowed for the resumption of the rights to sing, shave, flirt and trade freely before the guns opened up yet again. Men and women in Kabul, after all, had been forced to hold their breath for half a decade.

Rabbani, vilified for the cruelty of his time in office and sidelined by the ascendant cult of Massoud, prudently chose to remain in Faizabad, as uncertain of his ground now as Zahir Shah was in Rome. A round of talks in Italy between the Northern Alliance and the former king in late October had centred on the creation of a 120-strong Council for National Unity to rule after the Taliban, an interim government that included members from all five parties in the Alliance's political wing, the United Front (UF), and representatives of Zahir Shah and the Afghan diaspora – but no 'moderate Taliban' and only a sprinkling of the Pashtun leaders who had fought alongside the opposition. 'The UF is following the vision of my late brother,' said Wali Massoud, ambassador for Afghanistan in London. 'What he wanted for Afghanistan was to move from these political parties to everything being decided by the people. To go from here towards the *shura*, to the *Loya Jirga*, the Unity Council and eventually elections. That was his aim. So if it is necessary that I relinquish my post, or President Rabbani, we must do it.'[2]

But, on the face of it, the Unity Council was little more than a conclave of warlords and a dead man's vision no warranty for maintaining peace in the capital, particularly when the alliance over which he presided was splitting into parts after the flight of the Taliban. Dostum's Uzbeks and the Tajiks commanded by Mohammed Atta preserved a working relationship at the ramparts of Kunduz, the Taliban's last northern holdout, but this owed more to US bribes than communal tolerance. In Herat, Ismail Khan's Tajiks and the Shia Hizb-i Wahdat, both posing as liberators, growled at each other from checkpoints throughout the city, while 1,000 Hazaras, equipped with machine guns, mortars and rocket-propelled grenades, advanced on Kabul in a bid to 'protect' its Shia minority.[3] The old faces – and the old vices – were also returning to Jalalabad, which the Taliban vacated without fuss on 14 November. However, after a *jirga* that lasted three days, the Nangarhar elders agreed just such a hegemony of old and new that had eluded Pakistan in the early throes of the war and which the UN later failed to pin down. Haji Abdul Qadir, brother of the late Abdul Haq, was reappointed governor, with Haji Zaman Gamsharik again as military commander, but with the surreal addition of Hazrat Ali, a drug lord once aligned with the Taliban, as police chief in the country's second largest opium-growing province.[4] Hazrat Ali was one Darwinian step ahead of his colleagues in the new *shura* of Nangarhar, a poacher-turned-gamekeeper soon to evolve into an entirely separate, and more cunning, species, the 'American warlord'.

Rumours that Gulbuddin Hekmatyar, exiled boss of Hizb-i Islami, was also back in the race, and vying to take his place in the ISI's post-Taliban affections, were given further credence by the news that four journalists, with Australian television, Reuters, *Corriere della Sera* and *El Mundo*, had been robbed and shot dead at his old stamping ground near Sorobi, 35 miles from Kabul, in the Silk Gorge.[5] On the fall of Kabul, Hekmatyar had contacted former commanders, rendered leaderless again by the collapse of the Taliban, and ordered them to rally Hizb veterans and sieze his pre-Taliban stronghold at Charasyab in a first step towards again laying siege to the city.[6] Even as Kabulis revelled in the return to smooth chins, Western dress, Bollywood films and nights free from aerial attack, the scene was set for a return to the nightmare before last in the days leading up to Ramadan.

The UN that had recognised Rabbani throughout the Taliban era was now powerless to impose conditions on the *de facto* UF government which, in view of the ex-president's absence from Kabul, appeared to have dispensed with his services altogether and was bent on consolidating the Panjshiri occupation of the capital in defiance of US opinion. But it was more averse to having to insert a peacekeeping force opposed by the UF, however loudly Kabulis cried out for the law and order last seen vanishing in the dust of the Taliban's baggage train. Dr Abdallah Abdallah, the former Massoud spokesman now promoted to foreign minister, sent out disturbingly mixed messages. He first welcomed the UN's announcement that it would administer Kabul and send a security force, explaining away the Alliance's capture of the capital as sheer accident, but then denied any reason for one the day after. 'After getting rid of the Taliban and the terrorists,' he said, 'there won't be war and won't be a need for international peacekeeping forces.'[7] When 160 US and British Special Forces flew into Bagram a day later, the advance party for a far larger deployment of several thousand peacekeepers from various nations, Abdallah protested that the government had not been fully consulted and insisted the force be cut back to 15 men. For more than an instant, there was a danger that the guns so recently levelled at the Taliban were now taking a bead on troops in the coalition.

High above the vagaries of Afghan peacemaking – a subject in which President Bush expressed no interest in comparison to the hunt for bin Laden – US planes continued to batter the Taliban's remaining positions in Kunduz and Kandahar. Reports arrived in Kabul of a mutiny by 200 loyalists of the former Jamiat warlord, Mullah Naqibullah, previously submissive to Mullah Omar, who had wrested control of Kandahar's airport. The ISI, meanwhile, warned of up to 3,000 Taliban and Al Qa'ida fighters crossing the border with the aim of mounting attacks on either US ground forces or Pakistani targets: the military advantages of 'strategic depth', a concept long cited by Islamabad as justification for its own adventures in Afghanistan, had not been totally lost on Omar or bin Laden either.[8] From Kandahar, Pashtun commanders issued chilling threats to the Alliance not to advance their forces into the south, a thought that had never entered its collective head in view of the far superior damage the Taliban could inflict on itself, given sufficient time. After intensive discussions with his commanders, Mullah Omar submitted to their 'advice' on 16 November and agreed to turn over control of his capital to Mullah Naqibullah and Haji Bashir, another pre-Taliban leader, in exchange for his freedom. The plan promised an imminent end to the US bombing and the creation of a Pashtun coalition qualified to negotiate in UN peace talks as equals, but it lasted only till bedtime on 19 November when the Leader of the Faithful, still in Kandahar, experienced a change of heart. 'I have had a dream,' he told his commanders on waking, 'in which I am in charge for as long as I live.'[9] The single thought that raced through their minds was quickly stifled by the rigours of *pashtunwali*.

Mullah Omar's uncharacteristic vacillation was due to pedigree as well as prophecy for he was being stalked by something he feared more than Spectres: royal blood. The Popolzai nobleman Hamid Karzai had slipped into Uruzgan in early October intending to foment an anti-Taliban uprising among his fellow *khan* in the Durrani tribe, and while he possessed a mere handful of guns, his most powerful weapon was legitimacy. The true details of his quest, probably the only adventure in the war likely to translate to celluloid, may never be known for Karzai was only too conscious as he travelled of spinning a contemporary legend of leadership to pit against those of Massoud and Mullah Omar. One of its most crucial ingredients, if it were to succeed, was that it must seem a wholly Afghan enterprise, free of foreign influence, and that was harder. Karzai had been guarded by an eleven-man Special Forces team, 'Texas One Two', since first setting foot in Derawat. When the Taliban surprised his party in early November, his brother was at pains to refute Rumsfeld's tactless boast that US jets had bombed the assaulting force or that Karzai was removed from harm's way by an American helicopter.[10] Nothing would ever have been made public about what truly befell the Popolzai prince were it not for a tragic accident that allowed Texas One Two's leader, Captain Jason Amerine, a rare display of openness about his secret, behind-the-lines operation.

Karzai chose Derawat as his destination because it lay only two hours' drive from Tarin Kot, where Mullah Omar came to manhood, and it was a fitting place to mount a challenge to his authority that came to resemble a duel between the two orders of Afghanistan, the customary – and the revolutionary fungus that came to feed upon it. 'According to Hamid Karzai, Tarin Kot was the most important city in the psyche of the Taliban,' Amerine said later. 'It was the heartline of where the Taliban movement began.'[11] Texas One Two spent three weeks drilling local Pashtun fighters in the art of US-style combat before the Taliban ambush compelled them to disperse.[12] 'The message that he continued to spread was one of "treat the prisoners well",' Amerine continued. 'If we treated them well, they'd be willing to surrender and we'd be able to reintegrate them into society and the country could heal its wounds.' This apparent magnanimity swayed the elders in Tarin Kot, then guarded by the lightest of garrisons, to evict the Taliban governor, at which point Karzai moved in his forces, numbering in the low hundreds. But Mullah Omar had already sent a column of 500 men in 80 pick-ups and trucks, chiefly Arabs from Al Qa'ida, with orders to 'slaughter the town, kill the women and children, kill the men, leave them in front of their houses and ... make an example of Tarin Kot.'[13] It was nightfall on the first day of Ramadan when the Taliban convoy arrived on the outskirts, six hours after Karzai's men had made their own appearance.

The men of Texas One Two were bidden to break their fast before going to the defence of the town. Almerine summoned Karzai's fighters and set up a firing line on a ridge looking over the main road into Tarin Kot where they waited until dawn. As the first vehicle came in sight, he called in air support. 'It was kind of strange,' he recalled, 'because they just kept coming into the valley and we just kept bombing them.' At a crucial point, Karzai's forces panicked and ran home, but they were cajoled back to the ridge and the Arabs, 'an extremely motivated force', finally withdrew, leaving the valley strewn with the wreckage of bombed and burning vehicles. US intelligence estimated the Taliban had taken losses of more than 300 men.[14] 'That night, all the religious leaders of ... northern Uruzgan came to speak to Hamid Karzai,' Amerine continued.

> I was sitting there when they came in and he was very concerned that maybe they'd be speaking against the Americans being there, but they told [him] that, if it hadn't been for our presence, they'd all be dead. So, from then on, they pretty much had positive things to say about the Americans working with Hamid Karzai's forces ... From then on, I'd say our relationship was sealed.

A day before the action at Tarin Kot, on 16 November, the US stepped up raids on Kunduz, where it reckoned 3,000 Taliban and Al Qa'ida troops still clung on, against Northern Alliance estimates of 10,000–20,000.[15] The figures were never made fully clear, but one third was repeatedly said to be of foreign origin, chiefly Arabs, Uzbeks, Chechens and Pakistanis, many newly arrived after the call to *jihad* was raised in the tribal agencies. Billeted in the Takharistan mosque and the Spinzar, Kunduz's main hotel, each day they travelled to the frontline at Khanabad, ten miles east of the city. The Taliban, Alliance commanders assured, would surrender gladly, given the correct treatment and guarantees of safe passage, but the foreigners, including the men of bin Laden's 055 Brigade, were expected to fight to the bitter end, fearing summary justice and with nowhere else to go. Their status as future prisoners was equally perplexing since they owed allegiance neither to a sovereign state nor a faction in the civil war, but an international organisation committed to terror; they therefore fell through the cracks between the clauses of the Geneva Convention. The gunning down by Al Qa'ida veterans of over 100 would-be Taliban defectors as they attempted to flee the city in the middle of the week reinforced the Afghan's existing prejudices against 'foreigners'.[16] 'They don't care about life,' one Alliance soldier said in disbelief, 'only death.'[17] In spite of this scorn, a superstitious awe seeped into the fighting spirit of the estimated 6,000 Alliance fighters at the frontline, as they weighed the moral enormity of an enemy who was prepared to die in a cause. Dostum and the Alliance's supreme commander, General Mohammed Fahim, protested their every intention of attacking Kunduz at any moment, but preparations somehow were never made. On some mornings, Alliance soldiers slept through the air strikes aimed at softening up Kunduz before their advance.[18]

The lack of courage was not the only setback delaying the Alliance assault on Kunduz; indeed, it was the symptom of a greater political malaise. The largely Pashtun city lay athwart the faultline that divided the Uzbek and Tajik spheres of interest and, once broached, this could only tear the Alliance to ribbons, seeding a new civil war in the north between members of the anti-Taliban opposition. Washington was eager that the city should fall as fast as possible. It would free up Alliance troops to fight its battles to the east and south, while delivering into US hands the supposed treasury of intelligence locked in the minds of the hundreds of Al Qa'ida fighters trapped there. But Kunduz was potentially the jewel in a new necklace of power stretching from Dostum's stronghold at Shiburghan to the fief of General Mohammed Daoud in Taloqan, the cornerstone of an expanded empire in the north. Neither warlord wanted to cast the first stone, preferring to resolve their differences without bloodshed if possible, but neither wanted responsibility for the bloodbath predicted if the Al Qa'ida commanders chose death over surrender.

Mullah Fazil, the most senior Taliban commander in Kunduz and a deputy defence minister, drove out of the city with 600 men in the second week of November determined to secure an armistice and an orderly withdrawal for his men. The negotiations were not easy. Fazil, and his deputy commander, Mullah Dadullah, were war criminals, instigators of the killing of 4,000–6,000 people in the Taliban conquest of Mazar in 1998, as well as the generals of an encircled foe. Dostum, ever the gentleman, listened attentively over tea and biscuits at Qala-i Janghi, his 'Fort of War' on the road to Shiburghan. Fazil agreed to surrender Kunduz and his heavy weapons in exchange for a safe conduct for his fighters: the fate of the

2,000 foreigners was for Dostum to decide. Rumsfeld was less reflective: 'My preference is that they will either be killed, or taken prisoner.' The Defense Secretary undoubtedly had a war to win, but the truth was that his closest ally, Pakistan, also had up to 1,000 soldiers and agents fighting alongside Al Qa'ida in Kunduz, though this was too galling to raise publicly. On 21 November, the US halted air strikes, ostensibly to allow Mullah Fazil time to keep his side of the bargain, but Alliance commanders reported their astonishment at sighting Pakistani military planes landing by night to rescue their trapped co-nationals. At least five transports and helicopters flew safely in and departed by 24 November, evacuating two brigadiers, all military and intelligence officers seconded to the Taliban war effort, and as many enlisted men as they could fit in. In all likelihood, anyone from Al Qa'ida with enough influence at the ISI – or too dangerous to abandon to US interrogators – also secured a one-way seat to safety.[19]

The bombing of Kunduz and Kandahar ran alongside a campaign to kill as many Taliban and Al Qa'ida leaders as possible. Jalaluddin Haqqani, prospective candidate to head the 'moderate Taliban' faction, was victim to the most gruelling persecution. Three satellite-guided bombs hit his family's compound in Wazir Akhbar Khan on the night the Taliban withdrew from Kabul, killing a sister-in-law who was drawing water; on 13 November, another bomb struck a relative's house in Gardez where he was believed to be sleeping; in a third incident, a Haqqani-sponsored mosque and *madrassa* in Khost were bombed on 16 November, killing ten worshippers at their Ramadan prayers and 15 students of religion; and six of Haqqani's bodyguards, along with twelve members of the family that hosted him, were killed the following night in an attack on Tosha, in Paktia province.[20] Haqqani was cursed with a talent for tragic survival, but the week was not entirely without trophies. Bin Laden's security commander, right-hand man and the alleged architect of the embassy bombings, Mohammed Atef the Egyptian, was killed in a bombing raid on 16 November at an undisclosed location near Kabul.[21] Three days later, Dostum reported that Juma Namangani, head of the Islamist Movement of Uzbekistan and a close bin Laden ally, had been mortally wounded in the fighting around Kunduz.[22] But of bin Laden's whereabouts, not even the ghost of a whisper.

Mullah Fazil's offer to give up failed to materialise by 22 November, sparking a further round of daylight raids by B-52 and Alliance rockets that was met by sustained artillery fire from the still-defiant Taliban. After a second round of negotiations in Mazar, Dostum announced he had reached an 'even broader' agreement with Mullah Fazil, under which all forces in Kunduz, including foreigners, would lay down their weapons at Chahar Darreh, a village seven miles from the city. The Taliban contingent, which included seven former governors and numerous senior commanders, would be free either to join the Alliance or return to their homes after being disarmed, but the 2,000 foreign fighters were to be taken away for special questioning. 'The Arabs, Pakistani and Chechen mercenaries,' said an Alliance spokesman, 'will be put before a court.'[23] Dostum wanted to transport the foreigners to hangars at Mazar airport, but his US advisers vetoed that proposal on the grounds it might be needed for military operations. Why not use the spacious stables at his citadel at Qala-i Janghi, they suggested by way of compromise?[24] No UN representative attended this fateful meeting.[25]

The surrender of Kunduz on the weekend of 24–25 November began surprisingly well, with other pockets of Taliban resistance taking advantage of the opportunity to hand in their weapons, but the total fell far short of the Alliance's claim that there had been 15,000 troops in the city. One thousand gave themselves up on Saturday, followed by 450 near Pul-i Khumri. Dostum allowed the Taloqan commander General Daoud the honour of being the first to enter Kunduz.[26] However, Mullah Fazil may have omitted to tell his Al Qa'ida allies, due to submit to Dostum's forces at an assembly point to the west of the city, that they were to be jailed and interrogated after being disarmed. Weakened by fasting and with night falling quickly, Dostum's men failed to body search all 400 of their prisoners before loading them onto trucks and setting off for Qala-i Janghi in the dwindling light. In a foretaste of what was to come, one detonated a concealed grenade when the searches resumed the following morning, killing himself and Dostum's chief of police. The prisoners were herded into the stables where, during the course of that night, a further eight blew themselves to pieces, rather than face certain torture and execution at Uzbek hands. Realising the risk still posed by their captives, the guards resolved to bind their hands before submitting them to interrogation, confirming the foreigners' worst fears.

Two CIA agents, Johnny 'Mike' Spann and an Uzbek speaker, known only as 'Dave', had been specifically assigned to Qala-i Janghi to seek the information that might help run bin Laden to earth. When Mike and Dave asked the first in a string of eight prisoners what he was doing in Afghanistan, he reportedly replied 'we are here to kill you,' and lunged at Mike, who shot him and several others. In the mêlée that followed, foreign prisoners kicked, beat and bit Mike to death, as Dave shot his way to safety.[27] In other accounts, the prisoner had simply grabbed Mike and blew them both up with a concealed grenade; in either case, Spann was the first American to die in combat during the US war in Afghanistan.[28] The fracas quickly developed into a fully blown firefight after the prisoners broke open one of the fort's many armouries and siezed mortar and grenade launchers. Dave called for air cover from US bases in Uzbekistan, but the missile and Spectre attacks only served to drive the mutineers deeper into the mud and timber fabric of Qala-i Janghi. The fighting continued for four long days, growing in barbarism as Dostum's men, supported by Special Forces and British SAS fighters, first tried conventional firepower to dislodge their enemy, before resorting to dousing their hiding places with flaming oil and freezing water.[29] By 27 November, only three of the 400 men who had entered the fortress were thought still to be alive, one of whom had survived on horsemeat down in the cellars. In the clean-up after the battle, the International Committee of the Red Cross discovered the bodies of 170 foreign Taliban strewn around the fort, many ploughed in two by Dostum's tank tracks, while television audiences watched as Alliance soldiers stripped their clothes and shoes or prised out their fillings. 'We are sorry that they were killed,' said one fighter, unconvincingly, 'because they were Moslems. But you also have to remember that they were terrorists.'[30] A further 80 survivors finally emerged from the flooded cellars on 1 December, including a man known to his companions only as Abdul Hamid, but whose passport identified him as John Walker Lindh, aged 20, a Moslem convert from San Francisco. The 'American Taliban', as he was swiftly dubbed, had suffered bullet and grenade wounds and had not eaten in a week. Dave and the late Mike Spann had interrogated Lindh minutes before the fighting erupted. 'He's got to decide if he wants to live or die, and die here,' Dave told Spann during a lull in the questioning. 'We're just going to leave him, and he's going to fucking sit in prison the rest of his fucking short life. It's his decision, man. We can only help the guys who want to talk to us.'[31]

The massacre at Qala-i Janghi could not have come at a worse time for the UF, graphically confirming a not entirely deserved reputation for viciousness that had fouled news reports of its previous spell in power, while failing to acknowledge the roles played in the earlier bloodshed by Pakistan, Hekmatyar and Dostum. Similarly, Washington's refusal to deploy sufficient forces on the ground to ensure a disciplined handover of the Taliban's foreign allies, ostensibly to protect the lives of American soldiers, conveniently absolved it of any direct involvement in the massacre that resulted, while ridding it of the vexing legal problem of what to do with 400 apparently committed – though not convicted – Al Qa'ida fighters. The Pentagon played fast and loose with the Alliance forces, building up their strength with weapons and dollars, while simultaneously castigating their human rights record through the press, even as it reaped the military benefits of their exactions. The atrocities in the Uzbek fort, it was universally inferred, were the fate in store for Kabul if left in Alliance hands, a thesis that faithfully echoed Musharraf's misgivings while portraying him as a caring and impartial spectator of events, which was very wide of the truth.

The Alliance custody of the capital since 13 November, in fact, fell little short of exemplary, considering its inexperience of maintaining security in an urban environment – and the excessive sense of entitlement that snares any rebel army presented with a sudden enemy retreat and a defenceless prize. This behaviour testified both to the soldiers' discipline and their leaders' unusual regard for world opinion, and not only in Kabul where scores of journalists itched to witness the violations they had so fulsomely predicted. The triumvirate that ruled Kabul with apparent unanimity – Yunus Qanuni, Abdallah Abdallah and General Fahim – appeared to share an awareness of how the world of diplomacy turned that was absolutely unique among recent Afghan politicians. Many analysts spent the days after the slaughter at Qala-i Janghi trying to decide if the uprising had been a plan rather than an accident, an audacious plot to turn the tide of war that Mullah Fazil had hatched as he sipped tea with Dostum in his citadel. More ingenious still, however, was the prospect that Dostum himself had timed the massacre so that it exploded across the world's media on the very day that an eleven-man UF delegation touched down in Germany to attend a UN-sponsored conference to determine the composition of the future government of Afghanistan. Whatever the truth of either theory – or neither – the killings at Qala-i Janghi played straight into US and UN hands.

Yunus Qanuni, the man regarded as the real political power in Kabul, had his first taste of media attention on a tourist barge on the Rhine near the Konigswinter palace outside Bonn. He was a Tajik in his mid-40s, who walked with a cane and more closely resembled the Sinn Fein leader Gerry Adams, than the hirsute mullahs and mujahedin who had spoken for Afghanistan for the previous 22 years of war. Until his meteoric rise in the Taliban twilight, Qanuni was Massoud's political adviser; but as the 'caretaker' government's interior minister, he was responsible for security, the issue that was expected to dog the conference until its closure. A week earlier, representatives from 21 donor nations met in Washington with the World Bank to discuss a rapid start to the task of rebuilding Afghanistan, a programme then estimated to cost up to $30 billion. The purpose of the talks in Bonn, which brought together representatives from Zahir Shah and two pro-peace coalitions, known as the Peshawar and Cyprus Groups, was to find an agreement on the shape, composition and strategy of an interim authority to fill the vacuum left by the Taliban and prepare for a *Loya Jirga* and general elections. 'We need to get a transitional authority in the country as soon as possible,' said Ahmad Fawzi, spokesman for Lakhdar Brahimi, the UN Secretary-General's Special Representative for Afghanistan. 'All the parties agree that this is imperative, that speed is of the essence. We can't spend a lot of time on this. It has to be accomplished as soon as possible.'[32] The framework for the political transition envisaged by the UN was virtually unchanged from proposals submitted to the Northern Alliance and the Taliban in earlier rounds of peace negotiation. All that was required was for the four groups present at the talks to whittle a shortlist of 150 candidates down to the 29 seats available in the cabinet, a comparatively easy task by Afghan standards even in Ramadan, that was achieved in a marathon ten-hour discussion on the final night of talks.

What had changed was the nature of the peacekeeping effort. It would take the UN months to obtain sufficient manpower from members to pose a credible military deterrent and it was reluctant to deploy 'Blue Helmets' without a genuine ceasefire agreement lest they be drawn into the fighting as combatants. A multinational force with a UN mandate was a second possibility, but the organisation's preference was for an all-Afghan force, if it were strong enough to defeat any challenge to its authority and sufficiently neutral to reassure ex-Taliban Pashtuns, whom the UN sought to attract into a new government. Security in Kabul remained stable, but Alliance authority stretched no more than 20 miles to the south, 35 miles in the east and 65 miles in the north and west, while local warlords and elders had elsewhere carved the country into more than 20 fractious fiefdoms.[33] With the capital undeniably in his pocket, Qanuni categorically rejected a UN proposal to deploy international peacekeepers. 'We prefer that security is looked after by the Afghan security forces, composed of different ethnic groups and different parties,' he said on 28 November, reiterating this rejection three times more in the face of repeated questioning. But his assertion was qualified a day later when the UF foreign minister, Dr Abdallah, told CNN: 'Our preference would be for an Afghan force, composed of all ethnic groups. But if we have to go for a multinational force, we would consider it positively ... we are flexible in that regard.' Abdallah's counsel seemed to have prevailed the following day when Qanuni told a second press conference that the UF would no longer 'oppose the deployment of foreign troops in Afghanistan'. He blamed his earlier rejections on an error in translation, and called for a new interpreter.

Hamid Karzai, a candidate for the post of chairman in the interim administration, did not go to Bonn, though he called in a message by satellite phone from Uruzgan in which he described the talks as the 'path to salvation'. After the battle in Tarin Kot, Texas One Two escorted his fighters, numbering around 600 men, to a village to the west of Kandahar called De Maymand, though it may well have been the village of Maiwand from whose obscurity Mullah Omar had broken free to lay the foundations of the Taliban movement in 1994. Finding the road clear, they pressed on to Seyyed Mohammed Kalay, 30 miles east of Omar's capital, as Karzai pummelled the keys on his phone with appeals to local commanders to join the Pashtun rebellion.[34] His legend was burnishing nicely and, besides, he had nothing to fear in Germany where the State Department was assiduously protecting his interests. 'The Bonn conference was only for show,' said one of the Pashtun delegates, Haji Attaullah, two weeks later, 'the decisions had been made before.'[35] Ex-president Rabbani, the UN's hangnail, was warned by both the US and Massoud's new class of tyros to bow out quietly and he never showed his face at the conference, which he described later as the 'humiliation of the nation'.[36] Certainly, the avalanche of reconstruction funds that depended upon the success of the Bonn talks was instrumental in moulding their outcome, which reflected the UN priorities of a broad-based administration, secured by an international peacekeeping force, with a symbolic role reserved for the former king. More shocking, in view of Afghan sensitivity to foreign involvement and the make-or-break nature of the conference, was the blatant manipulation of the final list of members in the interim government, due to rule for six months. Abdul Sattar Sirat, an Uzbek and former justice minister until 1973 when he joined Zahir Shah in exile, was unanimous choice for chairman by the king's delegation and his appointment seemed a certainty after a deal with the UF that guaranteed its continued occupation of the defence, interior and foreign affairs ministries. But he was unexpectedly pipped at the post. 'Members of a group representing the former king, Mohammed Zahir Shah, voted overwhelmingly to choose Abdul Sattar Sirat as head of the new government,' complained Haji Attaullah. 'Mr Karzai, who has close ties to the king, received no votes. But all the delegates understood that the Americans wanted Mr Karzai. So, on 5 December, they finally chose him.' A US diplomat at Bonn went further when he did not deny that Washington had 'overruled' the appointment of Sirat. With Karzai's tenure assured, a doubt nagged as to whether the

UN-approved and British-led International Security Assistance Force (ISAF), based around the hundred or so men still marooned at Bagram, were the core of a genuine peacekeeping force, or the palace guard of a new Pashtun leader with no domestic constituency, imposed on the country against the wishes of the UF and former Taliban equally.

On the day Kunduz fell to the Northern Alliance, Chinook helicopters ferried the first units of an eventual deployment of 1,200 Marines from the Arabian Sea to an airstrip 55 miles southwest of Kandahar in the first significant commitment of US ground forces to the Afghan war. The Pentagon said the purpose of Operation Swift Freedom, as it was named, was to force the Taliban to surrender their capital and to hunt down more vigorously bin Laden and his network, but other sources said the dwindling supply of guided bombs and 'troubles with Afghan tribal leaders' were major determining factors.[37] The operation centred on Dolangi, a rudimentary airstrip in the desert once used for falconry trips by an unidentified wealthy Saudi, which bin Laden had since renovated for his own purposes.[38] As engineers set about upgrading the isolated airfield to accommodate ten C-130 cargo flights a day, F-14s shot up a Taliban attack convoy of 15 tanks and troop transports and Marines in Humvees patrolled the vicinity in circles of ever widening radius. Camp Rhino was to evolve into something more than a forward base for the projection of US strength into the southern mountains where Al Qa'ida forces were then thought to be hiding. It was also designed to function as a high-security detention camp for captured Taliban and Al Qa'ida fighters, whose numbers would soar to 7,000 men by the end of December.[39] In the meantime, the sole and precious prisoner in the custody of the Marines battalion at Dolangi was the American, John Walker Lindh.

With the Taliban in disarray outside its last provincial outposts of Kandahar, Helmand and southern Uruzgan, the Pentagon was free to focus on the hunt for bin Laden. His last public sighting was on 10 November in Jalalabad where he addressed a throng of 1,000 local leaders at the Saudi-funded Institute of Islamic Studies, distributing blessings and gifts of cash to the clan heads, in envelopes of $300 to $10,000, depending on the size of their tribal constituencies. Two days later, visibly nervous in spite of a 60-strong armed guard, he was seen at night before driving east in a Toyota Corolla among a column of several hundred cars and military vehicles.[40] His true destination lay 25 miles southeast of Jalalabad in the Tora Bora massif on the Pakistani border where a complex of caves, bunkers and tunnels had been dug out of the limestone in the Soviet war as a mujahedin refuge and supplies store. Taken over by bin Laden in the 1990s, he paid local workers up to $100 a day to renovate and elaborate the subterranean labyrinth until it was spacious enough to house up to 2,000 fighters and provide them with heat, light, sanitation and food.[41] Tora Bora and other known Al Qa'ida facilities had been bombed repeatedly since the outbreak of war to prevent them being used by the network to regroup, but the raids intensified after 16 November when Hazrat Ali, the reformed drug baron who had taken over policing Jalalabad, told his US liaison that bin Laden had been seen on horseback near Malewa, a village close to Tora Bora.

The siege of Tora Bora raged on for four inconclusive weeks, its ferocity mounting incrementally as the 1,000 Al Qa'ida fighters allegedly trapped inside the mountain shelters withstood the Pentagon's heaviest conventional weapons, including laser-guided 5,000 lb 'bunker buster' bombs developed for penetrating Iraqi command centres deep underground during the Gulf War. Unlike Kandahar, where Mullah Omar vowed never to surrender even as thousands of his subjects continued to flee the bombing, the slopes of Tora Bora were too remote to offer much risk of civilian casualties and constituted fair game for a no-holds-barred assault. The Pentagon was desperately seeking an endgame by now, both to punish bin Laden for the carnage of 11 September but, more urgently, to eliminate the possibility that he may have procured the technology for building nuclear or biological weapons, as was indicated by the hundreds of incriminating documents, computer disks and plans uncovered in former Al Qa'ida safe houses in Kabul and other locations. The quintupling to $25 million of the reward issued in 1998 for information leading to his capture had failed to elicit results, a sign of either the reverence in which bin Laden was genuinely held – or the fear of initiating a Cain-like vendetta that would pursue the informant's relatives from generation to generation throughout eternity. But Pentagon thinking about how best to capture Tora Bora demonstrated a naive faith in the relationship that had evolved between Special Forces units and their Afghan allies; it had worked efficiently enough with Uzbeks and Tajiks in the north, but that did not make it a reliable template for joint operations with Pashtuns, whose feelings about their former Taliban overlords – or their Arab friends – were more ambiguous and more subtle.

With insufficient US troops on the ground for the job, CENTCOM and the CIA turned to Jalalabad's new commanders, Hazrat Ali and Haji Zaman Gamsharik, paying them 'several hundred thousand dollars' each, and over $1 million in $100 bills to recruit a force of 2,500 fighters to assault the Tora Bora complex. Lesser commanders received $30,000 to rent four-wheel-drive vehicles and buy supplies, according to an Afghan who handled the money.[42] Attempts by Gamsharik to negotiate the surrender of what was now calculated to be a force of 2,000 Chechen and Arab fighters at Tora Bora turned to dust on 29 November, but he had already achieved a good grasp of the new rhetoric. 'I have always hated terrorism and will continue to hate it till the day I die,' he told a journalist. 'I also hate the prospect of war.'[43] It remained to be seen, of course, whether the most wanted man of modern times would have so widely advertised his journey to a craggy cul-de-sac if he ever had any real intention of staying there.

Karzai's mission made quicker progress after 1 December when the BBC began a series of increasingly upbeat reports from Bonn which culminated in the announcement that the UF had finally agreed to cede power to the Popolzai, with the blessing of the former king. Publicly, Mullah Omar's defiance was unaffected, but he carefully opened back-channel contacts with the chairman-elect through an unidentified aide, a member of Karzai's clan.[44] To the west, a US-backed force led by Karzai's Quetta-based ally, the former Kandahar governor, Gul Agha Shirzai, was battling Al Qa'ida fighters at the airport and had narrowly escaped an assassination attempt by a suicide bomber. Meanwhile, former comrades in Jamiat-i Islami telephoned Kandahar's pre-Taliban military commander, Mullah Naqibullah, with an invitation to return to the fold in exchange for a return to high office. Naqibullah had lived quietly at home in Arghandab since surrendering the city to the Taliban in October 1994. Under the combined pressure of two months of air attacks and an imminent shuffling of power at the top, Taliban ministers were quietly ebbing away. The first was Mullah Khaksar, the deputy interior minister, who remained in Kabul after it fell to the Alliance and then surprised his former colleagues with the news that he had all along been a spy for Massoud and the CIA.[45] By 3 December, twelve senior officials, including a deputy foreign minister, two former governors, a former education minister and the Taliban envoy to the UN, Mullah Hakim Mujahid, had escaped to North West Frontier Province while, in Chaman, Justice Minister Nuruddin Turabi said he was prepared to capitulate with another 20 ministers, *shura* members and commanders.[46]

Karzai denied any direct contact with Mullah Omar during his clandestine tour of the south, which had now lasted six weeks. If true, it was an uncharacteristic oversight for a future Afghan leader, particularly in the light of their shared backgrounds in Uruzgan, Karzai's inital empathy with the Taliban and their interlaced careers as the playthings of foreign powers, one in the ascendant now as the other slid down into the dark. Their positions could easily have been reversed, even at this late stage, as both were to discover as Karzai's objective drew near. After leaving Seyyed Mohammed Kalay, Texas One Two encountered sustained resistance at a bridge over the Arghandab river, which pinned the party down for two days despite continuous US air strikes. By the morning of 5 December, they finally cleared the bridge and moved to a nearby hill overlooking a *wadi* where Karzai was due to receive the formal surrender of a group of local Taliban. As the Bonn delegates prepared to read out the names of the members in the new interim administration, Texas One Two was hit by a satellite-guided bomb weighing 2,000 lb, which killed three of the team and five of its Afghan allies, wounding 40 more, including its leader, Captain Amerine. Still at the foot of the hill, Karzai sufferered only minor cuts from a falling mirror.[47] The killing of Amerine's comrades by friendly fire, rather than in the heat of the battles they had fought with Taliban forces, was why the Texas team leader received permission to recount his unit's tale of courage.

Whether the US attack influenced Karzai's judgement or not, his first decision as prime minister-elect was to announce a general amnesty. 'Let there be no revenge and no vendetta,' he said regally.[48] Abdul Salaam Zaeef, the Taliban spokesman in Islamabad, sought to clarify the offer further, insofar as it concerned Mullah Omar. 'His life will be saved and he will be allowed to live with dignity. He is a *mujahid*, he has worked for the people of Afghanistan and is not guilty.'[49] When pressed to explain what the Taliban leader should do to qualify for amnesty, Karzai said that he must 'completely distance himself from foreign terrorists'. Karzai's first well-meaning foray into the tangled world of Afghan diplomacy brought a swift tug on the leash from Rumsfeld. 'I have not seen or heard anything that would suggest anyone is negotiating anything that would be contrary to what our interests are,' he said.[50] Even if Karzai's offer were genuine, Mullah Omar surmised, America would never permit it to be honoured.

Before the supreme leader of the Taliban fled Kandahar on 7 December, he inserted a codicil into the last will and testament of the movement he had led for seven years. It said that the city that houses the robe of the Prophet Mohammed would revert to the same state of strife that had plagued it when the followers of Mullah Mohammed Omar emerged from the wilderness to impose peace and restore the law, a jurisdiction that swelled to include 90 per cent of Afghanistan until the events of 11 September. In a parting shot at Karzai, a man of pedigree but with no prophetic power, he elected to surrender his capital to Mullah Naqibullah, one of three warlords who had fought over its spoils until the Taliban delivered Kandahar from violence in 1994. This guaranteed a spontaneous return to the state of armed rivalry Naqibullah had historically entertained against ex-governor Gul Agha Shirzai, still fighting to capture Kandahar airport with US air support. Within 24 hours of Omar's agreement to surrender, the two hostile camps seized the Taliban's tanks and vehicles, four of Gul Agha's men had been killed in street clashes and Mullah Naqibullah was once again under siege in Kandahar's bombed-out military headquarters. 'Hamid Karzai … has made a very, very wrong decision in Kandahar by himself,' complained Gul Agha's spokesman. 'He gave equal rights to Mullah Naqibullah, which everybody opposes. It is not good enough for people to throw away their Taliban turbans and put on Naqibullah turbans. We cannot leave the city in the hands of the same people.'[51] Amid the ensuing chaos, Mullah Omar quietly made his excuses and left.

Further north, the battle for Tora Bora was gathering pace, spurred by the recurrent sightings of bin Laden in the vicinity, usually by commanders in the pay of Hazrat Ali, closest to the Pentagon of the three commanders who brought their fighters to the White Mountains. Ali had developed a shrewd appreciation of the West's obsession with bin Laden, letting slip hints throughout the fighting that whetted the appetite for the chase or a headline, but never led further, usually, he explained, because of the greed and treachery of the soldiers hired by his rivals. Ali's and Haji Zaman Gamsharik's men were at loggerheads throughout the operation, openly pulling guns on each other at the slightest suggestion that there had been some infringement of the other's territory. 'It is a competition among rivals,' conceded one of Gamsharik's commanders. 'This is what Afghanistan is. We kill each other.'[52] When the mainly Arab and Chechen fighters who clung so tenaciously to the heights throughout four weeks of punishing bombardment finally gave up on 17 December, only 19 ragged men stepped shamefacedly into the TV lights, ten Arabs and nine Afghans. The US had spent hundreds of millions of dollars on a military operation that snared a total of 54 of the reported 1,000 Al Qa'ida loyalists inside the Tora Bora fortress, and there was not a senior commander among them, let alone bin Laden.[53]

But another reason for the abiding belief that bin Laden was in the area was the sheer resilience of Al Qa'ida's loyalists, hemmed into the Agam and Wazir valleys, with Afghan troops and US special forces in front and the snow-capped peaks towering behind. While B-52s dropped 'bunker busters' to collapse their tunnels, Afghans used tanks and artillery to pound the enemy positions in the foothills, gradually driving them higher up the slopes to Tora Bora, a redoubt of increasingly lavish amenities according to newspaper graphics that portrayed it as a lair worthy of a James Bond villain. An effort to induce them to surrender at the end of four days of carpet-bombing came to nothing, according to a spokesman for Ali's chief rival at Tora Bora, Haji Zaman Gamsharik. 'They said "we want martyrdom, we will succeed". They won't accept.'[54] It was just such a message that two manhunters seeking to preserve a profitable monopoly could be expected to pass on from their prospective victim to a frustrated, but wealthy, paymaster. 'The Americans poured money in their pockets,' said the Jalalabad mayor, Engineer Ghafar, two months after the attacks petered out, 'but it was not a real war. They were just doing these things for the money.'[55]

And it wasn't even a local business. Ali and Gamsharik were US-backed interlopers from the plains, while the surrounding mountain villagers were indebted to bin Laden for his generosity during the building of Tora Bora: after bombing errors killed 170 civilians in Talkhel, Balut and Agam in early December, they were scarcely minded to shift their allegiances unless they were compensated very well.[56] As the two warlords attacked Tora Bora from the north, local leaders arranged for mule trains and guides to escort Al Qa'ida fighters eastwards through the passes to the safety of Pakistan's North West Frontier Province. Between 28 November and 12 December, around 600 of bin Laden's men escaped, including entire families, at rates of $100 to $1,000 per head, depending on seniority. 'Our main responsibility was getting people across the Kabul river to Laipur,' said Malik Habib Gul, an elder in Upper Pachir village. 'To do this, we had to cross the main road, but there was no one guarding it. To the south, [in the direction of Parachinar], only walkers, mostly young fighters, crossed. The snow was deep and the climb was difficult.' Some of Ali's commanders were undoubtedly engaged in similar transactions. Ilya Khel, one of them, was given $5,000 and a satellite phone to interdict the paths east out of Tora Bora, but the Arabs paid him more to let them pass.[57]

Sightings of bin Laden came almost daily even as his militants slipped away from the base. 'I trust them like my mother or father,' Ali said of sources who claimed to have seen the Saudi galloping by moonlight on 25 November, a lean silhouette seated high in the saddle.[58] A week later, he was spotted riding back from Malewa, accompanied by four bodyguards, while another commander said he had picked up a radio signal from Kandahar that absolutely confirmed his presence in Tora Bora. 'How is the Sheikh?', the voice asked, and was told: 'The Sheikh is fine.'[59] 'None of the three [sightings] by themselves is particularly convincing,' commented a Pentagon official, 'but all three coming together might mean something.'[60]

But the most reliable information on bin Laden's movements would only emerge ten days later when the last defenders of Tora Bora eventually capitulated on 17 December. A group of Al Qa'ida prisoners from Yemen, bin Laden's ancestral home, admitted they had seen their leader only once since entering the complex a month earlier, and that was on the '11th day of Ramadan' – 27 November, or fully six days before the Afghans launched their assault. They had drunk green tea together as bin Laden exorted them to 'hold your positions firm and be ready for martyrdom'. Then he melted away into the pine forests.[61] This version of events confirmed a statement by Abu Jaffar, a senior Al Qa'ida member captured early in the battle after stepping on a land mine, who said that bin Laden had fled to Pakistan in the first days of December, though he had later sent a son back to Tora Bora to command in his stead.[62] The constant sightings and the concentration of forces may well have been a ruse, however, ruthless in its disregard for the lives of Al Qa'ida personnel, but no less effective for that. 'I think Tora Bora will prove to have been a strategic deception by Al Qa'ida,' said retired US army general, Wesley K. Clark.[63]

By now, a new apparition of bin Laden had arisen to puzzle and taunt in the guise of a 60-minute 'home movie' uncovered in Jalalabad in November, whose release was delayed until 13 December to allow for proper authentication. Shot in mid-November, the amateur recording showed an affable bin Laden and a taciturn Mohammed Atef at a dinner to honour a visit to Kandahar by Khaled al-Harbi, a veteran of the Soviet war who had fought for Al Qa'ida in Bosnia and lost both legs in Chechnya.[64] Their obsequious visitor is clearly prostrated by the honour of conversing with 'the Sheikh', lavishing praise and apologising for wasting his time, but bin Laden is equally avid for news from home, particularly al-Harbi's overly glowing accounts of the reactions to 11 September of some of Saudi Arabia's leading religious scholars. Indeed, bin Laden's need for the moral approval of his peers and superiors in the dissident spiritual hierarchy of the kingdom is another telling feature of a video, whose verbal indiscretions, informal style and real-time presentation are so at variance with his previous filmic output one can only conclude that the cassette was intended for the Al Qa'ida leader's personal library, or as a souvenir for al-Harbi, but never for outside consumption. Al-Harbi relates how he left the kingdom shortly after 11 September and was smuggled into Afghanistan by a member of Iran's religious police. After a brief exchange of news and Koranic verses, bin Laden swiftly, and without being asked, interjects to reveal the innermost secrets behind what occurred that September morning.

We sat down to calculate the amount of losses within the enemy and we expected the number to be those inside the plane, and for the World Trade Center towers, the number of people that the plane would actually hit. We calculated that the floors that would be hit would be three or four floors. I was the most optimistic of them all, because of my expertise in this profession and this business. I said that the fuel on the plane would melt the iron structure of the building and collapse the area the plane hit, and all the floors above it. This is all we had hoped for.

Bin Laden describes the 'brothers'' mounting excitement as they listened to the radio on 11 September, alongside their chief and Ayman al-Zawahiri. 'That day the congratulations were coming on the phone non-stop. The mother was receiving phone calls continuously.' After a further exchange of Koranic verses and historic parallels ('I'm sorry to speak in your presence,' murmurs al-Harbi, 'but it is just thoughts, just thoughts'), a second segment begins in which the two Saudis stray into the wondrous terrain of vision and premonition. Bin Laden recollects the dream of his close companion, Mohammed Atef, dead in a US bombing raid by the time this tape was screened. 'He told me a year ago: "I saw in a dream, we were playing a soccer game against the Americans. When our team showed up in the field, they were all pilots!" He said: "So I wondered if that was a soccer game or a pilot game? Our players were pilots."' Bin Laden then turns his attention to Mohammed Atef, 'leader of the group', confirming that the majority of the suicide crews were not even aware of their objective, as many analysts suspected.

> The brothers who conducted the operation, all they knew was that they have a martyrdom operation and we asked each of them to go to America, but they didn't know anything about the operation. Not even a letter. But they were trained and we did not reveal the operation to them until they are there and just before they boarded the planes. Those who were trained to fly didn't know the others.[65]

Washington thought long and hard about releasing the tape, before reaching the verdict that any further trauma caused to the relatives of victims of the 11 September attacks was justified by the renewed vigour bin Laden's 'confession' would bring to the US-led coalition, and its continuing assault on Tora Bora. In a timely echo of the man last seen marvelling at the success of his endeavours in the video, bin Laden's voice was picked up on short-wave radio, issuing orders to his men in the icy caverns of Tora Bora – though the Pentagon later discounted this testimony to his continuing presence as a cassette recording, designed to perpetuate the fiction that concentrating US firepower on the mountains would yield the ultimate prize.[66] Two days later, the Pentagon called off the attack on Tora Bora, launching an exhaustive search of the complex, even as the Stars and Stripes was raised over the US embassy in Wazir Akhbar Khan for the first time since 1989.

Fresh from his tribulations in Kandahar, Hamid Karzai flew to Bagram just after midnight on 13 December, as the first snowflakes fell, to hold talks with General Fahim, ex-president Rabbani and the UN Special Envoy Francesc Vendrell in the Argh. A day earlier, Britain agreed to commit 1,500 men to an international peacekeeping force restricted to patrolling Kabul, headed by Major-General John McColl, with the lead elements due to arrive in the run-up to Karzai's inauguration as chairman of the six-month interim administration on 22 December. Rumsfeld, who personally called on Karzai and US forces at Bagram on 15 December, said he thought the maximum strength of the ISAF should be in the range of 3,000–5,000 men, but the US was unenthusiastic about taking part while military operations continued elsewhere in the country. Further south, a company of US Marines, accompanied by weapons disposal specialists, swept out of Camp Rhino on 14 December to establish a new operational hub at Kandahar airport, where even the toilets were said to have been booby-trapped by the evicted pro-Taliban garrison.[67] The Marines were joined by an eight-man team from the FBI's Violent Criminal Apprehension Unit, on orders to question detainees and thwart future terrorist attacks. Not many miles away, nine Al Qa'ida fighters, convalescing in hospital from injuries received before Kandahar fell, responded to all requests to surrender with threats to detonate grenades if anyone tried to enter their hideout in a second-floor ward.[68]

The growing confusion between the military and peacekeeping roles of the foreign powers engaged in Afghanistan – as well as the trustworthiness of their allies on the ground – came into deadly focus on 21 December when a convoy of 14 vehicles was repeatedly attacked by Spectre gunships and US Navy jets in Karezgay, 24 miles west of Khost. The Pentagon was fully satisfied that the convoy's passengers were members of the Taliban and Al Qa'ida 'leadership', fleeing along a back road when they were spotted by US pilots one hour after dusk. When the aircraft turned back to base following a six-hour assault, the 65 dead bodies left behind were quickly recognised as tribal elders and commanders from Khost, who were to have been the personal guests of Hamid Karzai at his inauguration in Kabul the next morning. Two days after the incident, local sources claimed the air strike was ordered as a result of information supplied by a rival warlord in the province, Bacha Khan, who went on to lead the US-backed Afghan forces fighting to winkle Al Qa'ida remnants out from the mountains in the southeast.[69] There was much that was suspicious about the killings, and they would poison both US and Karzai's relations with the Pashtun of Paktia for months.

The convoy was heading for the provincial capital, Gardez, when it was forced to make a diversion to avoid a roadblock erected by the alleged supporters of Jalaluddin Haqqani, the influential warlord from Khost and Mullah Omar's former head of southern military command. Haqqani, it would transpire, was the only high-ranking Taliban leader to command district loyalty both before and after the movement's five-year reign and, though on the run from US forces, he continued to operate the levers of local political power through his surrogates on the Khost *shura*, including his brother Mohammed Ibrahim, who was among those killed when the convoy was attacked.[70] After the fall of the Taliban in Khost and Gardez, *shura* leaders in both cities backed calls for the return of ex-king Zahir Shah, a rallying figure for the Pashtun in the aftermath of Taliban rule and a vital adornment of the incoming Karzai administration, though *persona non grata* with Northern Alliance leaders.

The acceptance of Karzai's invitation by Pashtun leaders, once loyal to Haqqani, was indicative of a successful back-channel compromise over the future governance of Khost and Gardez and, perhaps, even a personal amnesty for Haqqani himself; despite the Pentagon's express intent to eliminate Haqqani, he remained supreme authority in Paktia, Paktika and Ghazni, and was more useful to the new government as a friend, rather than a martyr. The presence of Haqqani's brother among the convoy's warlords similarly argued against the account that it had been deflected from its path by Haqqani's own supporters. But Bacha Khan, the rising 'American warlord' in Khost, envisioned a new fiefdom in 'Greater Paktia' to match those of Dostum and Ismael Khan in the north. Enjoying close links with the Northern Alliance, each had as much as the other to gain were Haqqani's henchmen in Khost and Gardez, former Taliban stalwarts all, to meet an 'accidental' death as the victims of US fire. To label them as the 'leadership' was, after all, only a little lie, given Haqqani's links with Al Qa'ida, even if Karzai currently regarded them as vital partners in the search for a political and military settlement in the southeast. All it took was a phone call. The question facing the Pentagon was not how much it knew about the delicate diplomacy taking place thousands of feet below its planes, but how much it cared to know.

Karzai faced the prospect of assassination every moment he spent in Kabul, whether from Tajik, Uzbek or Pashtun was immaterial. Nevertheless, a rare reticence by the grizzled warlords and a genuine curiosity to see what Karzai's new order might bring in terms of power, patronage and money lured all but Gulbuddin Hekmatyar to Kabul to witness the inauguration ceremony in an interior ministry dominated by portraits of Massoud, who had been an enemy to so many of them. Even Dostum, who had threatened to boycott the government the day after it was announced in Bonn, thought it wiser to attend, taking his seat alongside Rabbani and an empty chair, filled with flowers, that was reserved for Massoud. He was later rewarded with the post of deputy defence minister in recognition of his 'nuisance value', though he never again visited his office in Kabul.[71] Some 2,000 tribal leaders and international representatives, including coalition commander General Tommy Franks, jostled to get past the metal detectors and into the hall, while 40 Royal Marines patrolled outside, despite the absence of any official agreement with Interior Minister Yunus Qanuni on their status. Ismail Khan from Herat had also voiced objections to the new government but, recognising that the job of warlord was possibly neither dynastic nor long-term in the changed dispensation, he consented to his son's appointment as minister of labour and social affairs. But he still made his entrance an hour late, just as Karzai was about to swear the oath. Karzai interrupted his speech to hail Khan from the podium: 'My brother!'[72] The ceremony ended with Rabbani signing a transfer of authority 'certificate', marking the first peaceful handover of power in Afghanistan since 1973. In view of that history – and amid such company – how long could it be expected to last?

The inauguration of the new government marked the conclusion of one of the White House war objectives, the ouster and replacement of the Taliban as rulers of Afghanistan. But it was making far less progress in its priority goal of killing or capturing the Al Qa'ida and Taliban leaders, most of whom had escaped the military onslaught. Only six of the top 30 Al Qa'ida senior commanders on a US government list were confirmed as dead by mid-December, leaving at large more than 20 of the men who helped carry out the 11 September attacks.[73] For each of the 445 Al Qa'ida and Taliban fighters in US captivity in Kandahar, Bagram or on vessels in the Arabian Sea, hundreds more had slipped across the border into Pakistan and Iran, or melted away into the hills.[74] 'Processing' the additional 7,000 Taliban and Al Qa'ida fighters held by Afghan commanders presented US intelligence with insuperable problems, given the shortage of trained personnel with language skills – and the absolutely desperate need for hard information that might lead to bin Laden or prevent attacks on the US with weapons of mass destruction.[75] US authorities had a special interest in questioning 150 Al Qa'ida fighters, taken into custody by Pakistani troops during the battle for Tora Bora, in the hope they would provide clues to bin Laden's location. On the day Karzai was inaugurated, Musharraf expressed his conviction that bin Laden had died at Tora Bora but, one week later, General Fahim, Afghanistan's new defence minister, said the Saudi was in Peshawar and the deputy intelligence chief in Kabul, General Abdullah Jan Tawhidi, named Haji Zaman Gamsharik, the Jalalabad commander who prosecuted the US assault on Tora Bora, as the man who had arranged his escape. The air was thick with accusations and denial.[76]

As for the Taliban leadership, Mullah Omar was reported by Haji Gulalai, new head of intelligence in Kandahar, to have taken refuge with 500 men at a former Al Qa'ida base near Baghran, in Helmand, a 'mountainous region with many caves', 100 miles northwest of the city. Gulalai expressed remarkably little interest in running him to ground, in spite of the $25 million reward on his head, prompting one US official to wonder if Afghans could possibly conceive of how much such a huge sum might buy.[77] Other leading figures in the movement, according to Mullah Khaksar, the former Northern Alliance mole in the Taliban interior ministry, were living in Peshawar or Quetta, or had gone quietly home. The Minister of Culture, Mullah Muttaqi, and the Minister of Justice, Mullah Turabi, were both in Pakistan; former Interior Minister Abdul Razzaq was at Spin Boldak; and Dostum had simply released Mullah Fazil and Mullah Dadullah, the two Taliban commanders at Kunduz, in exchange for ransom. 'The new government could catch most of these people,' said Mullah Khaksar. 'It would not be so difficult as they don't have huge entourages of armed men. But obviously the political situation is not ripe for that.'[78]

Christmas arrived and the US and ISAF forces celebrated with a few treats to add to their Meals Ready to Eat, but the white-bearded figure who appeared on Al-Jazeera the next day was far from seasonal. Seated in front of a burlap curtain, with the gunsight of a Kalashnikov visible at his side, bin Laden seemed gaunt and aged; apparently injured, his left arm hung lifelessly. It was 'three months after the blessed attacks against world atheism', he said, suggesting the 30-minute tape was recorded in the first ten days of December which, if true, confirmed he had made good his escape from Tora Bora. But he referred to the US bombing of Haqqani's mosque in Khost in which '156 worshippers' perished as 'several days ago', though that strike took place on 16 November and the Pentagon had conceded it was in error. 'All that you hear about mistaken strikes is a lie and a sheer lie,' he continued, before launching into a denunciation of US aggression against Moslems in Chechnya, Palestine, Kashmir and the Philippines that tended to cast him as raging, impotent and broken, rather than the omnipresent scourge that the Western media portrayed. His voice floated up from a pit far beneath the cave of his mouth. Then he hit on a truth that could still hurt his US viewers.

> These blessed attacks ... have shown that this arrogant power, America, is based on a great economy which is fragile. Those who committed the act were not the 19 Arab countries. The armies did not move, and the foreign ministers did not move either. Only 19 high-school students, and I hope that God accepts them as martyrs ... More than a trillion dollars lost, with the help of God. And with simple means, they used the enemy's airplanes, and studied in the enemy's schools. They don't need training camps.

Shortly before the tape ended, bin Laden turned to the US as a military power.

> I'd like to stress the point that the fighting going on round the clock in Afghanistan against mujahedin and Taliban has clearly exposed the shortcomings and ineptitude of the American government and their fragile soldiers. Despite their advanced military technology, they have achieved nothing beyond that which depended upon Afghan collaborators.

The tape stops sharp, a message set in glass from a man marooned in some indeterminate species of agony.

By way of confirming bin Laden's principal message, US airplanes attacked the village of Qalai Niazi, three miles north of Gardez, in the early hours of 29 December, killing between 80 and 100 guests at the wedding feast of 15-year-old Inzar Jan, under the mistaken impression that Taliban and Al Qa'ida leaders were also present. A witness described the wads of bloody hair and flesh ground into the earth, torn party dresses of red, blue and yellow, and 'tunnel-like holes, pierced almost vertically into the dry earth for more than 9 metres (30 feet)', the effect of bombs that drill deep into the ground in search of bunkers to explode.[79] In a seemingly unrelated development five days later in Khost, a 14-year-old boy was accused of killing a Green Beret sergeant, Nathan Chapman, in an ambush construed as an angry riposte to the imposition of the US-backed warlord, Bacha Khan, a man widely loathed for his corruption and cruelty. Chapman was the first US soldier to die in combat in Afghanistan, although 17 had already been killed in accidents.[80] The incident underscored Afghans' mounting resentment of the Pentagon's disruption of local power relations that had successfully accommodated – and survived – the Taliban, and the implacable nature of war, American-style. When three former Taliban ministers, including Mullah Ubaidullah, head of defence, gave themselves up a few days later in Kandahar, the US-backed governor, Gul Agha, simply sent them on their way, more wary of arousing local enmities than the ire of his one-time sponsors.[81] The same held good for Mullah Omar, the man Karzai first thought fit to pardon, however roundly he was condemned in conversations between Afghan commanders and US officers or journalists.

However, the hunt for Mullah Omar could be delayed no longer. On 2 January, 20 US Special Forces drove with Haji Gulalai and his men to Musa Qa'leh, where they picked up Helmand's governor, Haji Shir Mohammed, and his men and continued on to Baghran, where the Taliban leader had been pinpointed three weeks earlier, under the protection of Abdul Ahad. Better known as Rais-i Baghran, or the Chief of Baghran, Ahad was described as a major powerbroker in the rise of the Taliban, though his name had never previously come to the fore. The surrounding villages had all been warned in leaflets to acquiesce and turn over Omar, or face airstrikes. The road led for eight hours along a dry riverbed, flanked by steep mountains. The forces of Gulalai and Shir Mohammed reportedly numbered in thousands, while US helicopters and fighter-bombers loitered overhead in case of resistance.'We will not let him go free,' promised Gulalai, 'he is a national criminal. He can't escape if he is in Afghanistan.'[82]

Shir Mohammed entered Baghran first in a final attempt to negotiate with Abdul Ahad, a warrior with a fine appreciation of the code of *pashtunwali*. 'The protection of Mullah Omar,' he said later, gnomically, 'if a person thought it could, may be a particular benefit for one man.'[83] But he was never asked to pay the price for such loyalty. While the men were talking, or as the troops closed in – so worn down were US officers by Haji Gulalai's lying that he was never formally asked to elaborate his version of events – Mullah Omar and four of his bodyguards allegedly broke through the encirclement on motorbikes and accelerated into the hills where they vanished, in spite of all efforts to locate them. Less than 200 local Taliban eventually surrendered, but they were quickly released in exchange for their weapons; no evidence was ever found to prove Mullah Omar had been in the vicinity and the Rais-i Baghran retained his position as chief.

'There aren't any Taliban and Al Qa'ida in Baghran now,' Haji Gulalai told reporters when he returned from the mission.[84] And as far as the eye could see, what he said seemed to ring true for every other town and village in Afghanistan.

21 The Battle of Shah-i Kot

'The smell too was something that he hadn't imagined, a mixture of cedar from the trees dotting the ridgeline, fuel, gunpowder, metal, sweat, blood and something faintly like strawberries.' *Washington Post*, 17 April 2002

The narrative of the war turned elsewhere after Mullah Omar's elegant exit, a Houdiniesque nod to history that was immediately compared to Steve McQueen's dash for freedom on a motorcycle in *The Great Escape*, with the singular difference that the Taliban leader made good his flight while the actor was snagged on a barbed-wire border fence. CNN's output fell from an average of ten stories a day to less than four throughout January. For the most part, they centred on John Walker Lindh, the 'American Taliban', and a related controversy over the legal rights of 20 Al Qa'ida prisoners, who were flown hooded, tranquilised and shackled to the US naval station of Guantanamo Bay on 11 January for further questioning in Cuba.

The 'super-trial' of Lindh promised to redefine both Al Qa'ida and US justice in fresh and unpredictable ways if it ever came to court: a photograph of him naked, strapped to a stretcher and blindfolded while in military custody was a potentially explosive piece of evidence in a trial that would have dominated the headlines during the first anniversary of the 11 September attacks.[1] To what extent would Lindh be held responsible for Al Qa'ida's global activities and at precisely how many levels of the game could an Al Qa'ida player operate, given its myriad areas of specialisation? And what were the chances of Lindh receiving a trial free of prejudice in America after 11 September?

The Guantanamo prisoners had fewer options and even less inkling of what was in store, whether legally or with regard to the duration of their captivity. By the end of January, 158 Al Qa'ida fighters had been shipped to the US enclave, two-thirds of them Saudis according to Interior Minister Prince Nayef, who had led the kingdom's dubious investigation into the bombing of the Khobar Towers apartments more than five years earlier. Riyadh 'would not be satisfied' with the conclusions of the US investigators, he said, and intended to conduct its own interrogations if Washington allowed the prisoners the benefit of Saudi law, a blessing that, in all likelihood, most regarded as less alluring than the room service in Guantanamo, however surly.[2] By coincidence, bin Laden's Saudi chef –

'Osama's favourite meal is fowl, anything with wings' – had been picked up by a pro-US Hazara warlord after the fall of Tora Bora and was crying out for Guantanamo's stern proprieties after two months of Afghan hospitality. 'I say kill me or cut my legs off, but don't tie me up every night and beat me. I'm ready to go to Cuba, or wherever.'[3]

The switch in media focus was understandable. Four months after 11 September, and three since the US retaliated with the war that unseated the Taliban, everybody from journalist to general, but more particularly the TV audience, needed relief from the blizzard of fear the attacks released, a period of repose in which to regain self-possession, reflect on the helter skelter of war and draw lessons for the future, since 'future' was now a more conceivable tense. Omar's belief-defying escape, though mortifying for the Pentagon, provided the punctuation necessary in a narrative that was too breakneck, too vertiginous, however close to home it struck. Bin Laden was not necessarily dead, but neither was there any recent evidence that he was alive, an absence of certainty that consigned him to a limbo of non-existence convenient, for the time being, to both quarry as well as hunter: he stayed circumspect until mid-April, nursing his wounds according to some, although the Taliban defeat in Afghanistan made an Al Qa'ida counter-strike all but inevitable.

If Mullah Omar's motorbike exhaled the sense of an ending amid the exhaust fumes, Al Qa'ida was by no means finished. The only senior officer the US had captured since the war began was Ibn al-Shaykh al-Libi, the Libyan commander of Khalden training camp and a close associate of Abu Zubaida, the mysterious personality bin Laden trusted to handle logistics for recruits like Mohammed Atta and other Al Qa'ida sleepers around the world, men whose fingers toyed with the counter-strike trigger. Al-Libi was arrested in Pakistan and handed over to the US military authorities on 5 January, joining Lindh on the USS *Bataan* in the Arabian Sea. But Ayman al-Zawahiri, Al Qa'ida's second in command and planning alchemist, was safe according to a wife in Cairo, although some of his children had died in the US bombing. A search of his house in Kandahar in December turned up an apparent laboratory for weapons of mass destruction. 'For our own safety we did not touch the bottles,' said local intelligence chief, Haji Gulalai, 'but from a distance we saw there were hundreds of different kinds of containers – small jars and big jars, sealed with metal lids and containing powders and liquids, white and yellowish in colour.'[4]

Elsewhere, hundreds of Al Qa'ida warriors, perhaps even the thousands conjured by the Pentagon, had simply disappeared into the thin mountain air – with rather more success than the Saudi cook – on redundancy payments of $1,400 and more organised by bin Laden before his empire crumbled.[5] Bin Laden's generosity begged questions at both ends of the contracts he issued to his fighters and servants: as rich as he was reputed to be, how could he possibly afford salaries of over $1,000 per month for every *mujahid* fighting with the Taliban or abroad, and still supply the 'escape kits' of clothing, passports, Pakistani rupees and dollars – known as 'squirters' because the recipients could 'squirt' in and out across the Pakistani border – to which each was entitled after the fall of Tora Bora, the event that effectively ended Al Qa'ida's tenure in Afghanistan? At $12,000 a year per fighter, excluding overheads and fighting expenses, his underlying costs spiralled to the margins of belief as Pentagon estimates of the size of his private army rose to 15,000 and 20,000 men (German intelligence assessed the militants who passed through his camps at 70,000).[6] However rich bin Laden had once been, the payroll was way beyond his means alone.

But the Saudi was out of range and the war visibly winding down, at least in Afghanistan. The news was of the tribulations of Hamid Karzai and the British-led ISAF in a turbulent country where time and money were of the essence if it were not to slide back to the lawlessness that preceded the rise of the Taliban and facilitated bin Laden's transformation of it into a safe haven for Al Qa'ida. On 18 January, the Pentagon decided not to renew a $2 million monthly contract with Space Imaging that had given it a monopoly on high-resolution imagery produced by the commercial satellite, Ikonos, denying the media an independent view of events on the ground for the duration of the war.[7] In a further sign that the US was relaxing its guard, the 2,000 Marines based at Kandahar airport since the Taliban disintegrated a month earlier were rotated out to the Arabian Sea and replaced by regular soldiers from 101st Airborne and 10th Mountain Division, although the combined US presence in Afghanistan remained consistent at over 4,000 troops. The first personal accounts of the war began to emerge as Green Berets, certain their security was no longer in jeopardy, spilled out their adventures behind the Taliban lines. Tiger Zero Three, operating near Kunduz, was credited with eliminating more than 1,300 Taliban and destroying 50 tanks, anti-aircraft guns, artillery pieces and command-and-control bunkers. 'We killed a lot of people here,' said one of its members. 'I hate to sound gleeful, but they deserved it.'[8]

The hunt for bin Laden and Al Qa'ida was not over; it had hastened abroad in pursuit of every scattered scent as its members fled their busted *jihad*. US agents, disguised as pilgrims, boarded ships and planes leaving Pakistan for the annual Haj to Mecca in the hope of intercepting stragglers,

while US warships halted vessels heading to the Gulf to search for the Al
Qa'ida suspects hidden in their cargo. President Bush's declaration of war
on terrorism had identified Al Qa'ida cells in 50–60 countries, but lightly
ruled Yemen and Somalia were best qualified as the 'second Afghanistans'
in which the network could regroup and flourish. US naval aircraft scoured
the Red Sea coast for signs that bin Laden's men were heading to the Horn
of Africa. The discovery of a plot by Jemaah Islamiah to blow up US naval
shipping and personnel in Singapore in mid-December heightened
concerns about Al Qa'ida's penetration in Southeast Asia. Jemaah Islamiah,
a local *jihadi* group whose leaders trained in Afghanistan, had obtained 3.9
tonnes of ammonium nitrate fertiliser, twice the amount used in the
Oklahoma City bombing, and was seeking a further 16.7 tonnes.[9]
Meanwhile, 150 US Special Forces flew to the Philippines to coordinate the
military campaign on Mindanao against the Abu Sayyaf rebel group, which
had longstanding associations with Afghanistan.

US counter-terrorist tactics at this point were of a brash, scattershot
character, but by the time Bush made his State of the Union address on 29
January they had solidified into a vituperative military doctrine that
pinpointed Iran, Iraq and North Korea – countries with barely a glancing
acquaintance with bin Laden, if any – as an 'axis of evil' that was even
more urgent for the US to eliminate than the 'terrorist underworld' that
thrived in 'remote jungles and deserts and hides in the centre of large
cities'. He called for a $48 billion increase in the defence budget to meet
the cost of axing the axis, beginning with Saddam Hussein, bringing the
Pentagon's official budget to $379 billion each year. 'The tools of modern
warfare are effective,' he insisted. 'They are expensive. But in order to win
this war against terror, they are essential.' It was a bravura display of how
to blur the distinctions between the different threats to US national
security posed by, for example, bin Laden and North Korea, while using
the former to demand additional investment in a military colossus that
had proven largely ineffectual in the context of Afghanistan.

There was no disputing the cumulative impact of US air power on the
Taliban, though it had punched well below its weight and was a lumbering
and unpredictable beast at best, whatever the claims made for its precision.
Closer up, the Pentagon's failure to commit ground forces at Tora Bora and
its insistence on controlling the war from Florida were among its gravest
errors; as well as facilitating bin Laden's escape, they ripped away the mask
of US military hauteur to expose the culture of caution and milkiness that
lay at the heart of CENTCOM. The decision not to establish a forward
operating base at Bagram, taken out of deference to Musharraf but abetted

by a political phobia for body bags that proved even deeper seated in Washington than the desire for 'infinite justice', denied the Pentagon military autonomy on the ground, forcing it to rely on money, militias and an unreliable Pakistani military to attain its objectives. Despite mobilising an estimated 61,600 troops to scour the wintry border for fugitives from Tora Bora, Pakistani forces arrested scarcely 300.[10] When the US came to bomb the citadel after 30 November, only a few hundred Marines and regular soldiers had arrived in the country, not enough to secure its eastern perimeter though sufficient to prevent a breakout on a massive scale. CENTCOM conceded later that it would have been necessary to improvise an airfield at short notice to deploy the several thousand troops needed to close off the escape paths from Tora Bora; surely this was not beyond the wit of military planners in a fast-moving war situation?[11]

The fact that not a single officer above the rank of lieutenant-colonel ever set foot on the scene of battle in Afghanistan further atrophied Tampa's armchair vision of a war that relied for intelligence on AWAC, satellite, radio signals and footage from Predator drones, anything rather than the assessment of hardened military officers with a grasp of reality in the new ground zero. In another time, the gap between general and grunt in the war on terror would have been defined in terms of class, as well as military effectiveness, with the principal difference that the lives of American soldiers were never knowingly placed in harm's way. 'We didn't put US forces on the ground despite all the brave talk,' said a counter-terrorism official in the Pentagon, 'and that is what we have had to change since then.'[12] He was referring to the only significant US military excursions in the long-promised ground war: the first was a dress rehearsal, the second earned a merciless panning.

The rusted casings of two of the Tomahawks launched against the bin Laden training camp at Zhawar Kili still protruded from the ground four years after Al Qa'ida's strikes on the US embassies in Kenya and Tanzania in August 1998.[13] A former mujahedin logistical base three miles from the Pakistan border, Zhawar Kili was the next focus of US efforts to disable Al Qa'ida when the Special Forces' search of the Tora Bora caves fizzled out at the end of the first week of January. The Zhawar fortress, built with US funding in the early-1980s, was little short of impregnable: in September 1985, Jalaluddin Haqqani's fighters withstood a two-month siege of Zhawar by massed Soviet and communist Afghan forces, supported by airpower and artillery, with nothing heavier than two captured tanks, a 122 mm howitzer and some multiple rocket launchers.[14] Its facilities consisted of 60 mud-brick buildings and 50 caves or tunnels scattered along a ravine no wider than 500 feet (150 metres). Zhawar Kili was the logical place to foregather for the hundreds of Al Qa'ida fighters prised out of their bases across Afghanistan and seeking to decant into the tribal trust areas of Pakistan, one hour's walk away. It was randomly bombed during the first weeks of the war, but came under withering attacks from B-52, B-1, F-18 and AC-130s after 4 January when US intelligence indicated the possible presence there of the enemy. The Pentagon put a figure of '400,000 pounds' on the burden of bombs the base absorbed before 81 Navy SEALS, Air Force commandos, FBI agents and chemical weapons experts, along with a blocking force of 50 Marines, were landed by helicopter on 6 January with orders to search and destroy the complex. They were astonished by what they found. Reinforced tunnels, some running hundreds of yards into the surrounding rock, contained tanks, artillery, anti-aircraft guns, explosives and every kind of mine and munition. One cache was so large that, when it was blown up, the mountains rumbled with secondary explosions for two full days.[15] Zhawar Kili's significance was undoubtedly flagged by Bacha Khan, the warlord who aspired to replace Haqqani in Khost and Ghazni, but whose value to the US was compromised by his tendency to manipulate his Pentagon connections to rain down ordnance on Haqqani's allies, or by destabilising the Karzai government in more direct ways.

Moving Special Forces into Zhawar Kili was a way both to sideline Bacha and his kind, who had demonstrated their venality at Tora Bora, and to test the stamina of US troops at altitude in full body armour and combat loads under conditions of cold, dehydration and fear. What began as a twelve-hour mission, however, turned into nine days of stress when the helicopters assigned to evacuate the force were first delayed, then postponed and finally put back a week due to the Pentagon's nervousness about extracting troops in daylight. The final number involved varied from 75 to 200, depending on the source, although all concurred it was the largest direct-action mission by Special Forces since the Vietnam War.[16] The US force avoided being drawn into firefights, however, preferring to call down air strikes on the handful of Al Qa'ida fighters that they encountered even when they were only 500 yards away. 'That was testing the limits, the edge of what we could, and could not do,' one soldier said later.[17] By the time the operation concluded on 14 January, a US spokesman claimed the Special Forces had captured a dozen Al Qa'ida fighters and rescued an emaciated dog, but it appeared that the main contingent had eluded them. In one of the caves, posters of New York City decorated the wall; in another, they found the foot of a child, still in its shoe.[18] It was a sharp reminder that Al Qa'ida fighters, their wives and children usually faced the bombs together.

Despite its limited cull, the mission was judged an operational success and it brought the additional bonus of clarifying the line of demarcation between the Pentagon's ability to meet its own objectives in the mountain war and its dependence on men like Bacha Khan to do the job for it. This distinction, however, was far less apparent in the settled areas where, out of prudence, the US paid Bacha's marauders salaries of $200 a month to guard the gates of a new forward base near Khost airport, named 'Chapman' after the Green Beret sergeant slain in early January. Bacha was an embodiment of the conflicting US goals of seeking to pursue Al Qa'ida holdouts with whatever tools were available without inflicting political harm on the administration it had planted in Kabul, a government desperate for credibility among the very people Bacha was busy alienating. The provinces of Ghazni, Paktia and Paktika had profound attachments to bin Laden, the Taliban and Haqqani and were their most likely sanctuaries, but a deep-seated nostalgia for Pashtun royalism marked them out as potential allies of Hamid Karzai, still widely regarded as 'the king's man'. However, whether at the behest of the US or the Northern Alliance – with whom Bacha also had ties of alliance and cash – Karzai had made the monumental error in late December of anointing the warlord governor of all three provinces, a decision that prompted outright rebellion and transformed their dormant royalism into an avid movement of secession.

The local favourite for power – and, no doubt, Haqqani's – was Mohammed Shah Zadran, whose several hundred followers gathered at the gates of Fort Chapman in late January to beat drums and perform tribal war dances with an zest not witnessed since before the Taliban. US officers asked Zadran to calm his men, but Bacha's friendship with the Northern Alliance had brought an ethnic dimension to the question of local leadership, an issue that would fester when the Pentagon, desperate for less ambiguous collaborators in the mountains, called in Panjshiris to reinforce their search operations in March.[19] Three days after the demonstration, more than 60 people died when a shoot-out at Bala Hissar fort in Gardez exploded into a full-scale battle between Bacha and Zadran's forces, with both sides trading artillery and rocket fire while US choppers hovered quizzically over the fray without intervening.[20] Bacha Khan and his fighters were driven out of the city on that occasion, but they remained a thorn in everyone's side until early May. 'Americans are not here to take sides in internal matters in Afghanistan,' Khan told a reporter, 'they have a specific mission to follow, which is to hunt Al Qa'ida.'[21] For people living near the Pakistan frontier or Fort Chapman, that looked exactly like 'taking sides'.

The infighting in eastern Afghanistan was Jacobean in its intensity and would eventually threaten the entire post-Taliban dispensation. Pentagon support for Bacha Khan, whom it openly admitted was an 'untrustworthy, power-hungry brute', fed a resentment that surfaced in rocket attacks on Fort Chapman and a second US base at the Bande Sardeh Dam, 40 miles southwest of Gardez, that were generally blamed on Al Qa'ida but, in all likelihood, reflected local grievances. After a quarter century of war, moreover, the border population was armed to the teeth. In another case of 'mistaken identity' attributed to Bacha Khan's biased intelligence, US Special Forces killed 16 Afghans and captured 27 prisoners in a raid on a compound in Hazar Qadam, near Khost, only to discover that they were members of a faction wedded to Karzai. Their weapons cache consisted of 400 60 mm mortar rounds, 300 rocket-propelled grenades, 300 100 mm rockets, thousands of rocket fuses, 250 automatic grenade launcher rounds and more than half a million rounds of small arms ammunition.[22] And that was the arsenal of a friendly faction.

Surprisingly, in view of its status as the Taliban's heartland, US forces enjoyed a better reception in Kandahar than they could ever dream of in Khost or Gardez. Towards the end of February, Governor Gul Agha Shirzai of Kandahar invited 400 US military personnel forces to celebrate the religious feast of Eid al-Adha in a marquee in the grounds of his mansion where Afghan lutes were played live for the first time since 1994. Three women soldiers arose from a carpet strewn with fruit and soda bottles to dance, M-4s bouncing against their breasts as the music and the clapping soared toward the climax. 'I have never seen women dance,' sighed Fazal Karzai, a cousin of the interim prime minister. 'This is the happiest day of my life. I am almost crying.'[23]

The last resistance to the US occupation of Kandahar expired on 28 January as Special Forces troops in Yankees caps and 'I love NYC' buttons stormed Mir Wais hospital with their Afghan allies, after hurling 20 grenades which killed every one of the six Al Qa'ida wounded fighters still holding out in an upstairs ward since the demise of Taliban rule in December.[24] The Special Forces had spent much of the previous month raiding suspected enemy concentrations in teams of up to 300, supported by helicopters but without the benefit of preparatory bombing. Designed to prepare them for combat independent of their conniving Afghan allies, the manoeuvres instilled greater confidence among US ground forces, but yielded little in the way of intelligence or prizes.[25] The forward base at

Kandahar airport came under rocket or mortar attack five times between January and early March, but the raids were in no sense read as part of a concerted campaign to evict the Americans. Governor Gul Agha was not well loved, but nor were Pashtun elders willing to burn the tentative bridges that linked them through the US garrison and Zahir Shah to the new Kabul of Hamid Karzai and the prospects of future aid.

In late January, a Gul Agha factotum reported that an army of 5,000 Taliban, supported by 450 tanks, armoured carriers and pick-ups, had retreated to the mountains behind Gardez after the fall of Kandahar and was now preparing to launch a counter-attack on the US forces below.[26] It was a remarkable claim, in view of the scale of the Taliban collapse in December, but the US had also received signals that several hundred Al Qa'ida fighters were mustering around Sherkankel, a village in the Arma valley, 20 miles (30 kilometres) east of Gardez and 30 miles from the Pakistani border. The US intelligence proved to have been the more accurate when the smoke finally lifted on what turned into America's largest battle of the war in Afghanistan, but the Pentagon was playing a different numbers game by then.

America's 'purchase' on its Afghan problem had become the gossip of the *bazaar* since the fall of Tora Bora when 35 allied commanders – many of them Taliban defectors – stalked into moneychangers' offices with identical sums of $200,000 to trade. 'Everyone knew that the cooperation of the commanders, most of them former Taliban, had been bought,' said an unnamed US officer.[27] By mid-February, word had spread to the remotest reaches of the south after C-130 transports strewed thousands of white envelopes, each containing two $100 bills and a photograph of President George W. Bush. The envelopes bore no message, but leaflets dropped a week earlier depicted Mullah Omar in the unclean guise of a dog on a leash held by bin Laden and threatened recipients: 'Those providing shelter [to Osama bin Laden and Al Qa'ida] will meet a horrible end.'[28] In preparation for its attack on Sherkankel, US planners hired 600 unemployed Afghans in Paktia, gave them new boots, clothes, food and $200 per month and submitted them to four weeks of US-style training in weapons handling, guard duty and how to surround the enemy. 'They didn't give the money to our commanders,' said one of the astonished recruits, 'but straight to us.'[29] Among other tasks, they were told to offer villagers they met $4,000 for each Al Qa'ida fighter captured alive – a far cry from the $50,000 bonanza Al Qa'ida had offered for every dead US soldier.[30] At the prospect of a US-funded jamboree at Sherkankel to rival Tora Bora, 5,000 Afghan fighters from Paktia, Logar and Ghazni descended on the Arma valley as the hour for the launch of Operation Anaconda arrived on 2 March.[31]

Named after a snake that squeezes prey to death before swallowing it whole, Operation Anaconda was designed to encircle and destroy the Al Qa'ida and Taliban forces in Sherkankel, first by blocking their escape routes over the 10,000–12,000-foot passes through the Shah-i Kot mountains and, secondly, by driving them into the gunsights of US troops waiting at the valley's three exits: the classic hammer-and-anvil strategy. Close-order fighting was left to the newly-trained Afghan militia, commanded by Zia Lodin but led by US Special Forces, which was ordered to attack the village from the northwest and drive the enemy to pre-established US positions in the south on mountains dubbed 'Ginger', 'Heather' and 'Eve'. Though universally described as a 'local warlord', Afghans grumbled that Zia was from a different province and, therefore, unfamiliar with the terrain.[32] The US had committed over 1,000 troops from 101st Airborne and 10th Mountain Division to the operation, supported by 200 Canadian and Australian commandos and around 1,500 Afghans, though intelligence estimated that only 150–200 hostiles were hiding out in the valley. The estimate was inaccurate. As many as 600 Al Qa'ida and Taliban fighters with their itinerant families had been savouring local hospitality since mid-December, stocking up on wheat and sugar at nearby markets and buying a satellite dish to keep up with the war – although watching TV was still a sin.[33]

The villagers got wind of a US attack some weeks earlier and offered to give the fighters – Chechens, Arabs and Pakistanis, for the most part – $10,000 to leave them alone but, when they returned next day with wives and children 'dressed in funeral shrouds', they were solemnly given permission to remain.[34] If the villagers were aware of an imminent battle, how much better prepared was Al Qa'ida? The enemy had positioned defences not only in the low-lying terrain around Sherkankel, Zia's principal destination, but thousands of feet higher up amid a horseshoe of caves and bunkers below the treeline on a ridge known as the Whale's Back. Situated at 10,000–12,000 feet, their tenants commanded unrestricted views over the intended US positions at Ginger and Heather and provided interlocking fields of fire over all the territory between. They had stockpiled mortars, cannon, rocket-propelled grenades, anti-aircraft missiles and AK-47 ammunition, as well as 1,000 bags of wheatflour, water and other necessities. Abdul Rahman Beheshti, a TV repairman kidnapped to install the enemy's new satellite dish, who also spent a week as a prisoner in the cave complex, said 'it seemed they already knew that an offensive was going to be launched against them.'[35] This was hardly surprising, retorted General Abdul Qadir Mohammed, Hamid Karzai's chief of National Security and Defence Affairs. 'The problem is that when the Americans give money to one commander, the other commander will get angry and give information to Al Qa'ida.'[36]

The battle of Shah-i Kot, as it became known, cost eight American lives and more than 80 serious casualties, the largest tally since the fiasco in Mogadishu in 1993. A persistent Pentagon claim that US troops had killed 500–700 enemy by the time the battle ended twelve days later failed to disguise either the courage of their adversary, the quality of its leadership, the precision of their escape – or the fact that no one in the US military was ever quite certain who they had been fighting. There was abundant evidence of a medium-sized Al Qa'ida presence in the valley but, uniquely, its supreme commander was an Afghan, Saifur Rehman Mansoor, a nephew of Latif Mansoor, the Taliban's former minister of agriculture, and a renowned commander who had lost one hand and all but one digit on the other while fighting the Soviets. Jalaluddin Haqqani, the province's most proficient commander, was still recovering from wounds sustained in a bombing raid, according to Taliban sources.[37]

That an Afghan should command an Arab was remarkable in the Al Qa'ida code of leadership. Rumour had it that Mansoor defected from the US side in the heat of battle with 400 Afghan fighters, moved by the piteous state of Al Qa'ida and its mujahedin, and that others in Paktia were inspired to join him. But Beheshti had spotted him in one of the caves at Shah-i Kot on the fourth day of Anaconda, quivering with fear as the US bombs thundered down, and Mansoor himself denied there were any 'foreigners' among his men.[38] Villagers who helped enlarge and fortify the bunkers at Shah-i Kot in the preceding months claimed Al Qa'ida had received a day's notice of the US offensive from sympathisers among the Afghan blocking force. This enabled them to dispatch families and the bulk of their force across the passes, leaving behind a rear guard to hamper pursuit.[39] If that were the case – and no captured fighter was ever brought forward to confirm the presence of bin Laden's fighters in the Arma valley – the battle at Shah-i Kot was waged not against Al Qa'ida or Taliban forces, but Pashtun loyal to the *pashtunwali* and its principles of self-rule, and opposed to the overlordship of Bacha Khan, the Northern Alliance or Hamid Karzai, all tainted by personal ambition or US patronage. Mansoor emerges from most accounts of the battle as a tactician equal in skills to Massoud, the only other Afghan commander to have challenged a superpower in all its might and forced it to its knees. As for his followers, far from the suicidal fanatics the Pentagon and press chose to depict, they were agile and intrepid guerrillas, capable of fast and accurate jabs against the ponderous, but better-armed, Americans before retiring unscathed. Under the swiftly shifting lights of the war in Afghanistan, the unknown fighters at Shah-i Kot were practically partisans.

The Pentagon's plan entailed dispensing with Afghan help at the kill in Shah-i Kot, though Zia Lodin's men were expected to flush Al Qa'ida fighters out of their hides around Sherkankel prior to driving them towards the US blocking positions. In contrast to Tora Bora and Zhawar Kili, there would be no advance bombardment in order to maintain an element of surprise: US forces would go in cold, relying on eight Apache attack helicopters for close air support. Before dawn on Saturday 2 March, a battalion of 10th Mountain was ferried by Chinook from Bagram over the snow-blanketed mountains to Ginger and Heather, above the Al Qa'ida forces presumedly clustered down in the valley, while a convoy of 25 Toyota pick-ups, loaded with Special Forces, 10th Mountain and 101st Airborne, ground through fog and mud up toward Sherkankel, Babakul and Marzak villages. Almost immediately, the three separate forces ran into trouble as mortars, rifle-propelled grenades and machine guns locked onto their positions from unsuspected defences prepared much higher up in the mountains. Seventeen Americans were injured at Ginger in a firefight lasting 18 hours, while a Special Force operative and three Afghans died when their vehicle took a direct mortar hit on the approach to Sherkankel. When it tried to turn back, the convoy found the enemy had secured the road: it took US helicopters three attacks to finally release the group. By the end of the first day of action, four of the eight Apaches assigned to Anaconda had been damaged by grenade attacks and returned to Bagram.[40] When the weather worsened the next morning, grounding helicopter support for the next 24 hours, US troops were ordered to withdraw to Gardez while their officers cast round for ways to salvage Anaconda.[41]

There followed two days of intensive B-52 and F-16 attacks on enemy positions on the ridgeline. When the skies cleared on day three, Special Operations Command in Bagram, which had taken over running the mission from Tampa, decided to take a closer look at the enemy's numbers and deployment by landing a SEALs reconnaissance group on Takhur Ghar, a 10,200-foot ridge overlooking Ginger. The eight-man team, Razor 3, should have taken off from Gardez to arrive before dawn, but mechanical problems delayed departure until first light was beginning to break. When the Chinook touched down near the ridge, the crew sighted a machine-gun post 50 yards off and a rocket-propelled grenade slammed into the cargo bay from elsewhere, crippling the aircraft's hydraulic and electrical systems. As the twelve-tonne helicopter shuddered to pull away from the ridge and the pilot, only partially in control, dived down the mountain in a bid to jump-start its engines, Naval Petty Officer Neil Roberts was hurled off the back ramp and into the snow. Predator footage, broadcast live at Bagram, showed Roberts surviving the fall but he was soon overcome. His commanders watched helplessly as three Al Qa'ida fighters dragged him above the tree line where he was executed.

The Chinook limped north, coming to rest four miles from Ginger where another reconnaissance group, Razor 4, was ordered to collect them. The men in Razor 3, unaware of their comrade's fate, wanted to go back for Roberts, but the two groups together were too heavy to fly back to the ridgeline, so the pilot flew the second Chinook back to Gardez to drop off Razor 4. Some 90 minutes after Roberts fell to the ground, his comrades in Razor 3 came into another blizzard of fire as their fresh transport tried to touch down at Ginger. Finding an enemy bunker on the ridge, the SEALs attacked, losing one man and another two injured before withdrawing down the 70-degree slope beneath the covering fire of an AC-130 gunship. Meanwhile, Razors 1 and 2, composed of Rangers, took off from Bagram with orders to extract the SEALs. US signals, by now, were nearly as confused as US intelligence. Because of a radio malfunction, no one could tell Razors 1 and 2 that Razor 3 had retreated from the ridge and was now located much lower down. As their Chinook hovered above Ginger for the third time that morning, a rifle-propelled grenade hit the right engine, plunging the aircraft into snow more than three feet deep. Within seconds of landing, machine-gun fire killed the forward gunner and two men inside while two more died trying to leave through the back ramp. The survivors looked for cover among the rocks. The enemy was grouped in two positions, hiding in trenches behind leaves, logs and branches. Greg, the co-pilot, staggered out of the cockpit, spurting blood from his wrist into the snow. Two more Rangers took shrapnel in the legs and another was wounded in the shoulder. Nearly all the Rangers had been hit. As they crouched around the stricken Chinook, they saw the enemy moving round to their rear.

Two thousand feet below, the second Razor team landed at 8.30 a.m. on a 'space just large enough to get all the wheels down'. Each member of the ten-man group carried 22 lbs of body armour, an M-4 assault rifle, between seven and twelve magazines, a pistol, night-vision goggles, helmet, first-aid kit, rations and 100 oz of frozen drinking water. Many had put on thermal underwear, which they discarded as the sun grew hot. While Razor 3 was inching down the mountain with their wounded, the Rangers in Razor 1 moved up, hurling their armour into the abyss to prevent it being used by the enemy. Some crawled on all fours under the sporadic mortar fire, throwing their M-4 rifles ahead of them and pulling themselves up through the snow to retrieve them. An ascent that was estimated to take 45 minutes lasted two hours. Upon regrouping with Razor 1, the Rangers deployed two four-man teams for a final assault on the bunkers on the ridgeline under cover of machine-gun fire. After a successful attack lasting no more than 15 minutes, they found a deserted network of shallow trenches, scattered with Chinese and Russian ordnance, and the body of an American sandwiched between two dead enemy. Razor 2's commander was convinced of only two enemy kills during the assault, but a military team visiting some days later counted eight. When the sun sank at 5 p.m. after the battle, 'everyone's throat was bleeding, coughing up some blood. Everyone had bad sore throats and dehydration.' Air Force paramedic Jason Cunningham bled to death at 6.10 p.m., two hours before US helicopters finally evacuated his comrades from the longest and coldest day of their lives.[42]

Six men had died and many others were injured in the mission to bring back Roberts, although the drone had already shown that he was dead. However heroic the effort may have appeared to the Rangers and their regimental historian, it cut no ice with their hoary Afghan allies, pragmatic mountain fighters to a man. '[The Americans] made a big mistake,' observed Gardez security chief Said Mohammed Isshaq. 'They went ahead without making trenches, without reinforcing their positions. And then they were cut off. They retreated very badly.'[43] Comparisons with the disaster in Mogadishu were unavoidable – the Rangers had been in the thick of both engagements – but Special Operations Command (SOC) put on a brave face as the resistance continued in the face of repeated attacks by US bombers, fighters and attack helicopters. 'We've got confirmed kills in the hundreds,' boasted SOC head Major-General Frank 'Buster' Hagenbeck, 'we truly have the momentum at this point.'[44] This was more than the total number of Al Qa'ida fighters believed to be lurking in Shah-i Kot when the offensive started, but US intelligence had been forced to revise its estimates upward to more than 1,000 in the face of the enemy's unshakeable confidence in the ground fighting. On 7 March, the SOC ordered up an extra 300 troops, 17 attack helicopters and several A-10 ground attack aircraft as the fighting overflowed into a battle zone estimated to spread over 70 square miles. Hamid Karzai had dispatched 1,000 Tajiks in a column of tanks, rocker launchers and artillery, commanded by the warlord Gul Haider, to reinforce the SOC's wavering

Afghan warlords, and even Bacha Khan rallied to the cause.[45] 'People here are very sad that they have come,' said a shopkeeper as he watched the Tajiks roll into Gardez. 'It will just encourage people to go to Al Qa'ida. We could have done this ourselves.'[46]

Driving snow and high winds set in as the week drew to a close, curtailing air support for ground operations for a further two days. As the US soldiers shivered in the −15-degree chill – few had brought sleeping bags for what was expected to be only a short operation – it was clear that the hammer-and-anvil strategy was now a fantasy; the positions they were still fighting to occupy would block nobody, since the enemy had mostly evaporated. And after wrangling with them at close quarters, US troops had revised their opinion of the enemy's fighting skills. 'They are highly trained, they're in their mid-30s, they're in excellent shape and they fight hard,' said SOC spokesman Lieutenant-Colonel Joe Smith. 'It is obvious from the documentation we've been getting that they are not just peasants.'[47] Perhaps. But Beheshti, the TV repairman held captive at Shah-i Kot throughout the first week of fighting, said he had seen many more Afghans than foreigners in the caves with Mansoor, and it stretches credibility that Al Qa'ida forces could have used the snow-covered terrain, with all its invisible paths, caves and gullies, quite so inventively. Whether Al Qa'ida, Taliban or simple Pashtun, they were far from willing to 'die a martyr's death', the phrase most frequently used to denigrate the clarity and resilience of the Pentagon's enemies in Afghanistan. 'We could hear them laughing at us,' said army specialist Wayne Stanton of the enemy his group had pinned down from a position 200 yards away. 'We were not used to it. They knew every crevice, every cubbyhole, every cave.'[48] Although 'the death toll ... seems to go up and down like the fluctuations of a troubled currency: 100, 500, 200, 800, 300',[49] as the *New York Times* put it, there were only three blackened corpses when the first allies arrived on the scene of battle on 13 March; Chechens by the look of them, the Afghans said.[50] Shireen Gul, the first Afghan commander to arrive in Shah-i Kot, saw ten bodies as he entered the valley from the north and Commander Abdul Wali Zadran counted another 23 as he came in from the south, while the US owned up to taking 20 Al Qa'ida prisoners. The remaining 650, the Pentagon asserted, must have been buried alive in their caves by US bombers, a notion that Gul Haider dismissed as 'propaganda'. 'Most people escaped,' Zadran insisted, 'you can't call that a success.'[51]

Al Qa'ida published its own account of these events and it is worth preserving here until one of the US commanders writes a memoir of what truly happened at Shah-i Kot. After eight days of confused fighting at high altitudes, 400 weary US soldiers were flown back to Bagram on 10 March and replaced by a battalion from the 3rd Princess Patricia Canadian Light Infantry, cold-weather specialists who were ordered to clear the Whale's Back of enemy and search its caves and positions. Described at the time as a 'tactical reappraisal of their battle plan', the US withdrawal coincided with criticisms that the 101st Airborne and 10th Mountain Division had 'failed to adapt to the guerrilla tactics required for fighting in the mountains'.[52] Two days later, the Al Qa'ida website <www.azzam.com>, since removed from the web, published an article from a leading pro-Taliban newspaper in Pakistan that reported the capture of 18 US soldiers near Gardez and subsequent negotiations between Mansoor and General Franks for their safe release. The US withdrawal, the paper maintained, was the price the Pentagon was forced to pay both for the lives of its troops, then allegedly being held hostage in 'underground bunkers' – and the preservation of its military reputation.[53] This account could so easily be dismissed as propaganda – though propaganda of rare sophistication by Taliban and Al Qa'ida standards – were it not for two anomalies. The Gardez authorities, in the Afghan fashion, had attempted to negotiate the enemy's surrender in Shah-i Kot: Beheshti listened in the cave as his captors talked over and rejected the offer. But he saw someone else in the shadows that still obscure the truth about Shah-i Kot: a tall, English-speaking, blond prisoner with a military haircut, who had been stripped and beaten with sticks.[54] Was he one of the American soldiers that Al Qa'ida said it had captured?

The Pentagon insisted on spinning the battle for Shah-i Kot as an 'unqualified and absolute success'[55] in spite of appearances on the ground and the mounting suspicion that the enemy had again run the gauntlet of US bombing and escaped intact across the border into Miramshah, Waziristan. The Canadians, who replaced half the US force on 10 March, scoured the Whale's Back for a further week, clearing enemy positions and rifling through caves for intelligence, but they met only three Al Qa'ida stragglers during their entire tour of duty. An inadvertent admission that the 10th Mountain Division 'doesn't do mountains' and was therefore ill-equipped to fight at high altitudes posed equally troubling questions about the fitness of US military command to plan and conduct an effective counter-guerrilla offensive, skills that had largely been forgotten since the end of the Vietnam War 30 years earlier.[56] While their Afghan allies disparaged US field tactics, American veterans criticised the decision to send men into high-altitude mountain terrain with nothing heavier than mortars. The day after the Canadians were pulled down from the peaks on 17 March, General Franks asked Britain to send 1,700 Royal Marines to take over responsibility for the mountain campaign in Paktia and Paktika, a decision that reflected badly on his confidence in US combat capabilities. When they arrived in early April, the Marines brought with them six 105 mm howitzers, weapons with greater range and power than anything the enemy possessed but, in the event, they proved redundant.[57] Whether through disparity in firepower, or the better-trained troops from Britain, Canada and Australia, Al Qa'ida had chosen the better part of valour. In a series of operations from 2–30 May, named Ptarmigan, Snipe, Condor and Buzzard after game birds or raptors, the British-led forces uncovered caves, documents and weapons but failed to engage once with any concentration of enemy. Surreally, what the Marines did come up against were sex invitations from Pashtun farmers. 'It was hell,' said Corporal Paul Richard. 'Every village we went into we got a group of men wearing make-up coming up, stroking our hair and cheeks and making kissing noises.'[58] Flirting was perhaps an easier way of repulsing the mainly Scots Marines than fighting them.

Neither bin Laden nor Mullah Omar were believed to be in Shah-i Kot when the US launched Operation Anaconda, but there was evidence that Ayman al-Zawahiri, bin Laden's closest collaborator, may have visited two months prior to the fighting. When Al Qa'ida forces first mustered in the valley in January, they had hired local villagers to hollow out the caves with explosives. Several recalled their leader as a 'portly, bespectacled man', referred to as 'Sheikh' or 'The Doctor', descriptions that matched the Egyptian's profile and rank.[59] Across the border, ancillary groups with links to bin Laden continued to operate with impunity, regardless of General Musharraf's claims that the Saudi was dead and his organisation in disarray. On 21 February, a group calling itself the National Movement for the Restoration of Pakistani Sovereignty released a videotape of the execution of *Wall Street Journal* reporter Daniel Pearl, kidnapped in Karachi on 23 January while investigating links between the ISI and militant Kashmiri groups. Less than a month later, the wife and daughter of a US diplomat died in a grenade attack on the heavily guarded Protestant church in Islamabad's diplomatic enclave, barely 350 yards from the US embassy, on the very day that General Franks was due to arrive. The attack gave Franks an excuse to press the Pakistani leader to authorise 'hot-pursuit' operations by US forces against Al Qa'ida and Taliban in the tribal trust areas, a request approved with great reluctance on 27 March.[60] Within hours, a group of US Special Forces and FBI agents, with ISI operatives and Pakistani police at their side, raided a number of Al Qa'ida safe-houses in the Canal Road district in Faisalabad where, after a brief gun-battle, they captured bin

Laden's chief recruiting and logistical officer, Abu Zubaida, along with 65 other members of the organisation. Though wounded in the legs, groin and stomach during the arrest, Zubaida reportedly told interrogators about further plans to assassinate US officials in Pakistan and of a plot to attack an undisclosed target on the American mainland. The second revelation chimed closely with FBI fears there was still an active Al Qa'ida cell on the loose in America.[61]

Whether there was or not, Al Qa'ida's sixth propaganda video was timed to create maximum consternation. The shade of Ahmed al-Haznawi, one of the four hijackers on United Airlines flight 93 when it crashed into the Pennsylvania countryside on 11 September, jolted back into public consciousness on 16 April when Al-Jazeera transmitted a tape of him, dressed in camouflage and a Palestinian headdress, reading his will against the backdrop of a skyscraper in flames. 'We killed them outside their land,' he announced, 'and we will kill them on their own turf.' Pictures of the will, which carried a date and location next to his signature, indicated that the video had been made in Kandahar in March 2001. It was delivered to Al-Jazeera together with a video of al-Zawahiri and bin Laden, seated on carpets before a large colour photograph of a tranquil, riverside scene. Bin Laden was silent throughout and, though the tape offered no clues as to when or where it was recorded, the Saudi was clearly in better health than last seen the previous December. 'This great victory that was achieved is only thanks to God,' intoned al-Zawahiri, while his master looked deferentially down. 'It is not because of our skill or tricks or excellence. It is all because of God.' The next day a rival Gulf satellite station, Middle East Broadcasting Corporation, aired another video, shot in a setting identical to the first, in which bin Laden jubilantly listed the damage caused on 11 September, from $1 trillion in immediate losses and the laying off of thousands of workers to studies that showed that 70 per cent of Americans had suffered psychological distress since the strikes.[62]

Bin Laden's whereabouts by now were anybody and everybody's guess, but Pentagon officials said they had reason to believe that, dead or alive, he remained in the Tora Bora area.[63] On 4 May, 400 soldiers of 3rd Princess Patricia Canadian Light Infantry and specialists from the US Army Criminal Investigations Division, intelligence and the FBI were flown back to the mountains to conduct sensitive site explorations of the Tora Bora caves for traces of DNA that might help identify the remains of bin Laden. Cave number 4, one of four facilities shut down by US bombs, was of particular interest since 40–70 Al Qa'ida fighters were known to have been buried there, but the Canadians failed to gain access despite blasting away the rubble at the cave mouth.

There were more promising signs in nearby Markhangi where the Canadians were told that Al Qa'ida representatives had come in late December and asked for permission to bury 23 of their comrades in the village graveyard. No one knew who they were for certain, though there was conjecture they may have belonged to bin Laden's personal bodyguard. Up to 1,000 people came to the funerals, the villagers said, and the cemetery, with its banners of white and green beneath the frosted Tora Bora ridgeline, had since become a shrine for Afghans seeking miracle cures. One grave more prominent than the others was thought to be Osama bin Laden's last hiding place, but the cadaver inside proved to be too small to match the Saudi's two-metre frame. The visitors excavated all 23 bodies, taking DNA samples over the next two days, before flying back to Bagram with the news.[64] The caves at Tora Bora were blocked for ever, but bin Laden was not among the dead inside. For if two dozen nameless soldiers could ignite the pilgrim passion among simple Afghans, then the grave of the Saudi must surely cry out its presence to the stars.

If bin Laden indeed were dead, where were the flags of mourning?

22 The Raw and the Cooked

'We are like blind people. We can only see the road we came on and the one we have to travel again.' Bismillah Shinware, Kuchi nomad[1]

While most European countries embraced monetary union in the first minutes of 2002, Afghanistan greeted the New Year with four domestic currencies, all called 'afghani' and most of them counterfeit. Currency had been a secondary field of battle since the Taliban came to power in Kabul; a snapshot of money supply faithfully mirrored the splintered pattern of Afghanistan's political power. When former president Rabbani and his forces fled from Kabul in 1996, they had spirited away the printing plates, ushering in a half-decade in which the Taliban, claiming to control 90 per cent of the country, nonetheless relied on the notes trickling across the front lines from the 10 per cent occupied by the Northern Alliance, which still controlled the means of production. Mullah Omar tried to end this state of affairs by banning from circulation any note issued after 1996, but Rabbani's Russian printers simply manufactured new ones replicating the pre-1996 serial numbers. 'It gave the Taliban a sign,' recalled Sayedalla Hashami, a former Rabbani adviser appointed central bank governor by Interim Prime Minister Hamid Karzai in December 2001. 'You think you're smart? We're also smart.'[2]

Four versions of the afghani were circulating in early 2002, some with identical serial numbers and all with different rates of exchange. The first, the cream of the 'old money', dated from before 1973 and bore the face of Zahir Shah in his brilliantined prime. Greatly in demand, it traded at rates 15 per cent stronger than the second category of 'old money', which dated from before 1996, the year the plates went missing. A third category, known as 'new money', had higher or repeat serial numbers and was printed in Russia for the Northern Alliance at a cost of $100 per 5 billion afghani.[3] Yet a fourth set, sneeringly termed 'northern money', was printed by Dostum to make up the payroll for his army and civil service; it traded at half the official rate, but circulated freely in both Taliban and Alliance territories. Each of these four species of money spoke for one or more of the power blocs that Karzai would ultimately have to contend with, and there were others in the wings, armed with dollars, rupees and Iranian rials. The money-changers in Kabul's Shahzada currency market could tell at a glance which of the four they were being offered, but Karzai was considerably less adept.

Many traders grew rich on speculation after the US attack when the 'old money' strengthened from 72,000 afghani to the dollar to 32,000 by the time of the Bonn Accord, in anticipation of a deluge of emergency aid. Remarkably, the price of *naan* fell from 11,000 to 4,000 afghani in one week alone, spurring a trader to observe: 'Now even a beggar can buy bread.'[4] What he probably couldn't afford was a place to eat it. A tide of aid workers, media agencies, businessmen, bankers and educated exiles swept into Kabul after the war to fill the houses formerly occupied by Taliban and Al Qa'ida apparatchiks, forcing rents in Wazir Akhbar Khan up from $500 to $10,000 a month. 'A $70,000 house is now worth $1 million,' said a Kabul real estate agent, 'and, even for $1 million, most owners wouldn't sell.'[5] Hedayat Amin Arsala, Karzai's finance minister and a former World Bank consultant, said Russia had reassured him that it would only print currency ordered by the Afghan central bank, but rumours abounded that Moscow was already greasing the wheels for a fresh outburst of faction fighting and Iran had supplied Ismail Khan with at least 20 truckloads of money since November to secure the loyalty of his forces in Herat.[6] Meanwhile millions of dollars from the US paychecks of the eastern warlords were flooding into Shahzada *bazaar* while untold billions of afghani were under lock and key in their treasuries. Karzai had more pressing battles to fight, but sooner or later he would have to confront the afghani. What he needed more immediately was protection.

An advance guard of 200 British troops had arrived at Bagram on 23 December, forerunners of a UN-mandated International Security Assistance Force (ISAF), drawn from 21 different nations that would swell to 4,800 soldiers and be led for the first three months by Britain. General Mohammed Fahim, Afghanistan's new defence minister and Massoud's military heir, had disputed the need for any peacekeeping force from the outset, arguing that Alliance troops were entirely adequate to provide security for the capital and that an alien presence risked stirring the deep-seated hatred of foreign occupation that sparked *jihad* against the Red Army so many years before. In the ten weeks since the Taliban were overthrown, robbery, car theft and kidnapping had spiralled in Kabul, and one week in January alone witnessed 49 murders.[7] 'Under the Taliban,' said a money-trader forced to pay ransom for his liberty, 'these bandits had no opportunity to commit these dreadful crimes. Now they are taking their chances.' Britain was indeed apprehensive about deploying its soldiers, noting 'the fragility of local consent',[8] but these fears stemmed less from the reactions of Kabulis – who held quite different views of what was 'alien' – than their newest overlords, the Panjshiri fighters whom the US had co-opted to break the Taliban's spirit. Fortified by US aid, the Russian tank deal the previous October and the windfall capture of Taliban weaponry and ammunition, Fahim commanded the second most powerful army in Afghanistan in early 2002, with 10,000 troops camped around Kabul and an estimated 300 tanks and 500 armoured personnel carriers, parked out of sight in the Panjshir valley.[9]

The only possible challenge to Fahim's mastery was the US air and military presence at Bagram but, with the war against Al Qa'ida and Taliban still unfolding in the east, the Pentagon was dead set against any move that would jeopardise its crucial rear base situated in dangerous proximity to the forces massed in the Panjshir valley. Fahim's decision to enter Kabul in November, against the express wishes of President Bush, was the gesture of a man determined not to let advantage slip away, to insist on his right to be part of the post-Taliban power equation whatever Washington's view. By January, his thoughts were more attuned to meeting the diplomatic and political niceties required before the release of what was then thought to be $15 billion in reconstruction aid, but he would brook no serious rivals in his new fiefdom. ISAF was at liberty to patrol the city and featherbed a government selected in faraway Bonn but, like the patrician Karzai, the force of lightly armed foreigners was no more than a hostage in his palm, useful only until he was ready to swat it away. The security detail assigned to protect Karzai, moreover, had been handpicked from his own men. The men and aircraft at Bagram airbase were just as vulnerable to artillery fire from the hills, and both Fahim and the US knew it.

By comparison with the other warlords, Fahim cut a remarkably drab figure on the Afghan stage; he was burly, charmless and taciturn. This lack of colour may have rubbed off from Khad, the secret police service created by the KGB and headed by Najibullah, which Fahim took over in 1992 and swiftly reclaimed after the Taliban crumbled. Karzai narrowly survived a lesson in Khad's interrogation methods in the mid-1990s when, as deputy foreign minister in the besieged Rabbani government and a secret sympathiser of the Taliban, he was arrested by Fahim's agents, only to escape torture when a rocket struck the building in which he was being questioned.[10] Khad thrived in the Taliban era as it redirected the energies of its network of 30,000 staff and informers toward rooting out acts of moral depravity for the Amr Bil Marof Wa Nai An Munkir, the Office for the Propagation of Virtue and the Prevention of Vice. Renamed the National Security Directorate in 2002, all 23 of Khad's departments were headed by Panjshiris who furnished Fahim with the best intelligence in town and its only functioning bureaucracy.

For all his lack of social graces, Fahim was not without guile. He'd witnessed first-hand what US air power could do to tanks and entrenched troops, but concluded rightly that Washington's commitment to Karzai and his government was less robust than its desire to prosecute a war against Al Qa'ida as free as possible from the casualties that so quickly curdle presidential ratings. He had a shrewd appreciation of what he could get away with as well. US policy toward the interim government had been fatally divided since Bonn between those seeking to bolster commanders like Bacha Khan and Hazrat Ali in the interests of hunting Al Qa'ida more efficiently, and more cautious voices which warned that any further empowerment of provincial warlords threatened the very survival of the man appointed to transform Afghanistan from a narco-state into something resembling a working democracy.

The White House started out sympathetically at first with the appointment on 31 December of Zalmay Khalilzad, the former UNOCAL consultant and National Security Adviser, as President Bush's Special Envoy to Afghanistan, a choice that seemed to signal that Karzai, another former employee of the oil company, had acquired special protected status in the bestiary of the US energy mandarins.[11] His appointment was followed by the lifting of the Clinton-era sanctions and the release from US bank vaults of $221 million in Afghan gold reserves, frozen since 1999, to meet a $100 million demand for backpay by Afghanistan's civil servants.[12] But on the issue of expanding ISAF's generally benign influence from Kabul to the bandit-haunted streets of Kandahar, Mazar-i Sharif, Herat and Jalalabad, Washington was profoundly unreceptive. ISAF's broad success in Kabul earned Karzai a sizeable share of the law-and-order vote that tends to inform all Afghan thinking about the benefits of government, particularly the crucial question as to whether overthrowing the Taliban were wise if their own lives were to be plunged back into an atmosphere of fear and brigandage.

Karzai and the UN repeatedly called for the enlargement of the ISAF mission, both to improve stability in the provincial capitals and extend a bridge of communal understanding from the US-backed administration in Kabul to civilians and their leaders in the Pashtun constituencies excluded from the Bonn talks. By early February, British Foreign Secretary Jack Straw was in full agreement, noting: 'The issue is the practicality of it.'[13] The US was glad to provide ISAF with air support when needed and even to underwrite Turkey's assumption of command when the British pulled out the majority of its forces in June 2002. What it would not tolerate was the creation of a parallel military command, under a UN mandate, that might have powers to define or restrict its own scope of operations in the east and south where Bacha Khan, Hazrat Ali and others were still proving useful to the Pentagon's goals, in spite of their shared histories of murder, treachery and heroin trading. The veto was hard to square with President Bush's stated support for the Karzai government and Afghanistan's previous role as the platform for the attacks of 11 September, but it would remain the cornerstone of Pentagon thinking until late 2002. 'We don't want Afghanistan to export insecurity,' commented a senior Bush administration official, 'or become a net importer of security assistance.'[14] While this view simply refused to acknowledge the scale of Afghanistan's security deficit, it was also a measure of the Pentagon's unwillingness to face down Fahim's stranglehold on the new administration in Kabul and the associated risk of opening a second front in the war against Al Qa'ida.

Superficially, the Taliban defeat returned most regions of Afghanistan to the status quo that prevailed after 1992, with Dostum back in office in Mazar, Ismail Khan in command of Herat and the Hizb-i Wahdat leader, Karim Khalili, restored to the now Buddha-less valleys of the Hazara in Bamian. But US intervention had introduced a number of permutations in the map of raw Afghan power, at their keenest on the Pakistani frontier where Bacha Khan was embarked on a mission to usurp the throne of the absent Haqqani, but prevalent to a lesser degree in Jalalabad, Kandahar, Mazar and Herat. Haji Abdul Qadir, once head of the eastern *shura* in Nangarhar and a former ally of Massoud, had been sidelined by the younger Hazrat Ali who, after proving so helpful at Tora Bora, had subsequently earned Fahim's patronage. The US-backed Governor Gul Agha Shirzai of Kandahar claimed to have 20,000 fighters under arms by late January and, like both Hazrat Ali and Ismail Khan, could count on a ready source of income from duties on the haulage trade that should rightly have gone to Kabul. The whereabouts of Gulbuddin Hekmatyar, Pakistan's lapsed favourite, were unknown for the moment though, in an apparent gesture of support for Kabul's US-backed government, Tehran announced his imminent expulsion days after President Bush identified Iran as a leading member of the 'axis of evil'.[15]

Iran and the other bordering states were also preparing for a resumption of the turf wars that troubled Afghanistan until the Taliban came on the scene. The blatant shipment from Mashad to Herat of weapons, land mines and other munitions culminated in the US firing a cruise missile strike at Khan's headquarters in late January, killing 18 of his men.[16] Iran was also resupplying Dostum with vehicles, weapons and cash and, despite being the first country to reopen its embassy after the fall of the Taliban in November, its old friendship with Fahim and the Northern Alliance, now locked into an opportunistic relationship with the US, seemed to have foundered. 'Foreign relations must be established by the Ministry of Foreign Affairs,' commented an exasperated minister in the interim government. 'The commanders don't have a right to have an independent relationship with other countries.'[17] But Fahim was playing an identical game, securing money and advisers from Russia in readiness for future battles aimed at eliminating rivals in the interim government or the north.[18] Bound by its commitments to the US and distracted by its escalating confrontation with India, General Musharraf and the ISI remained quiescent, assuring Karzai of Pakistan's non-interference, but how long that policy would endure in the face of encroachments by other regional powers – including India – was anybody's guess.

Ironically, the search for 'unity and reconciliation' through the apparatus of the *Loya Jirga*, scheduled for June, provided a key motive for the warlords to re-arm and extend their power bases, although the Bonn Accord, in principle, disqualified from the assembly any considered guilty of human rights violations.[19] As Prime Minister Karzai prepared in late January to fly out to a donor meeting in Tokyo to raise funds for reconstruction, Gul Agha was mobilising men to attack Herat and 20 had died in a clash near Mazar between troops loyal to Defence Minister Fahim and those fighting for his official deputy, Rashid Dostum.[20] Despite his seamless relationship with the CIA and Special Forces teams attached to his command, Dostum was one of the 'losers' of the US war, clawing back just two of the seven provinces he controlled prior to the loss of Mazar in 1998, and confronting a new Tajik challenge on his doorstep in Mazar from Ustad Atta Mohammed, commander of Fahim's northern forces. Many of the northern Pashtun commanders who supported Dostum before the Taliban took power were now openly siding with Atta. By the time the Tokyo meeting concluded, with pledges of $4.5 billion in grants over three years – less than a third of the amount expected by UN Secretary-General Kofi Annan – Bacha Khan launched a virulent attack to secure the governorship of Khost.

At least 75,000 Afghans were working for warlords in early 2002, by government estimates, while a further 100,000 armed men roamed the country in search of more regular employment, or for booty.[21] With ISAF security guarantees extending no further than a radius of 15 miles from the Argh, Hamid Karzai had borrowed the same nickname used by the Taliban to ridicule former president Rabbani; the 'Mayor of Kabul'. Within a month, the State Department was won over by the arguments for enlarging the ISAF mission after a CIA report warned of an imminent return to 'violent chaos' if the competition for power in Afghanistan were not quickly curbed.[22] But Defense Secretary Rumsfeld remained adamant that any ISAF expansion risked diverting men and resources from the campaign on terrorism and the probable entanglement of his forces in the quarrels of provincial warlords.

What the Pentagon envisaged was a new national army of 100,000, including police, border guards and air force, constituted around a Quick Reaction Corps of 6,000 men, based in Kabul but ready to deploy at speed to each of seven main cities. The Tokyo aid conference had allocated no funds for Afghanistan's new security architecture, however, and were money to be found, it would take until 2006 at the least for the new Afghan army to reach effective strength – fully two years after the democratic elections provided for under the Bonn Accord. Conceived as a multi-ethnic force, with soldiers contributed from all of Afghanistan's provinces, the first graduates of the British-led training course complained that 90 per cent of the officers were Tajiks appointed by Fahim who, as defence minister, controlled the programme but, in his other capacity as warlord, had a particular interest in defining its composition and morale.[23] In May, the US Congress tabled a motion for $250 million in aid to Afghanistan, additional to the $296 million pledged in Tokyo, with $50 million allocated to building Afghanistan's army, but Fahim was under no pressure to feed, house or pay its recruits. When US military trainers took over from the British in April, 200 of the first batch of 600 graduates had deserted, while the remainder were paid just $30 a month – scarcely a tenth of what they could earn tracking Al Qa'ida for the US in the mountains of the southeast. Many of the first recruits, apparently, thought they had signed up for English language courses.[24]

Five days after the Tokyo aid conference, Marjan the lion finally succumbed to old age. In more than 40 years as the chief attraction at Kabul zoo, the balding big cat had turned into a symbol of Afghanistan's ability to withstand the worst the world could throw at it. He once killed a Taliban member who climbed into his cage out of bravado and then survived the grenade attack from his grief-stricken brother that left the animal lame and blind in one eye. News of Marjan's death was taken as an omen by Kabulis, though whether the metaphor applied to Karzai, the exiled king or the multi-ethnic vision of that other celebrated 'lion', Ahmad Shah Massoud, none could agree.[25]

*   *   *

As Taliban and Al Qa'ida fighters slipped across the border into the tribal areas, Afghan refugees in Pakistan and Iran were beginning the long march home. At the first signs of war, 200,000 civilians had quit the country, fleeing drought and the collapse of the relief distribution system as much as the Taliban press gangs or the US bombing.[26] The number returning home first outstripped those escaping it in mid-December, and, by the end of the month, 60,000 Afghans had arrived safely in their villages. UNHCR began transporting back to the Shomali Plain the 15,000 Tajiks who had squatted in the old Soviet embassy since the Taliban offensive of 1999, while another 138,000 internally displaced were issued with beams, doors, windows, nails, hammers and hinges to rebuild their homes in central Afghanistan. UNHCR was laying plans for an assisted repatriation programme for the 800,000 refugees it thought might choose to return to Afghanistan by the end of 2002. Each family would receive $20 per relative in travel expenses and a kit of blankets, tarpaulins, tools, seeds and enough wheat to tide it over winter. The estimate was surpassed within 15 weeks of the programme's launch on 1 March and, by the end of May, the agency compared the influx to the repatriation of refugees from Kosovo, the largest and most vivid in recent memory.[27] Some mornings saw 350 ornately adorned lorries, packed with refugees returning from Pakistan, parked outside the sprawling UNHCR transit camp at Pul-i Charki outside Kabul, site of the former Khad prison. Three months later, the operation was described as the 'largest repatriation of people in history', exceeding even the 1.2 million Afghans who had gone home a decade earlier, but the refugee agency had long ago run out of money.[28]

A different pattern of migration was underway in northern Afghanistan. The defeat of the Taliban left the Pashtun minority vulnerable to raids from the newly-dominant Uzbek, Tajik and Hazara commanders, whether out of revenge for the privileges it was thought to have enjoyed under Mullah Omar's rule or as a reprisal for the Taliban's own extensive catalogue of horrors. Swiftly disarmed by their new rulers, Pashtun communities found themselves facing summary execution, beatings, looting, kidnap, extortion and rape, often with the express intent of forcing them off their land. By the end of January, thousands of Pashtun had fled for Chaman on the Pakistani border, a figure that soared to 47,000 by 8 March.[29] Conditions in the north had been a subject of widespread speculation since the prisoner uprising at Qala-i Janghi fort and the killing of the CIA's 'Mike' Spann the previous November, after which the media focus naturally followed the war to Kabul, Kandahar and Khost. The UN offices in Mazar were comprehensively looted after the capture of Mazar and the fragmentation of Taliban power between Dostum, Atta and Mohammed Mohaqiq, northern head of the Shia Hizb-i Wahdat, further disrupted what little relief Uzbekistan allowed to pass over Friendship Bridge to the 400,000 northern families most in need. Attacks on local UN and NGO staff were a common occurrence, with half a dozen attempts at killing, kidnapping or raping them in February alone. On 10 April, Shah Sayed, an employee of the UN Food and Agriculture Organisation, was taken from his home and shot by three unidentified gunmen.[30]

More puzzling still was the fate of the thousands of Taliban detained after the surrender of Kunduz on 25 November who, so far as anybody knew, were still being held in northern prisons. The International Committee of the Red Cross (ICRC) estimated the number of Afghan and Pakistani fighters in captivity at around 5,000, with more than half housed in Shiburghan military jail, 75 miles west of Mazar. ICRC's attempts to gain access to the prisoners were rebuffed throughout December by US military personnel, still screening prisoners for information about Al Qa'ida prior to their possible transfer to Guantanamo Bay.[31] Within a week of the US reassigning out its interrogators on 13 January, two investigators from the Boston-based NGO Physicians for Human Rights (PHR) managed to persuade the warden to let them tour the prison. The three prison blocks comprised 18 cells, built for 10–15 men but each housing 80–110 in sub-zero temperatures and under conditions which another visitor, EU envoy Klaus-Peter Klaiber, later said 'look like Auschwitz'. 'The people have nothing on their bones anymore,' he said, 'they are being treated like cattle.'[32] 'Many, many, many prisoners' had died, the prison commander said, chiefly from dysentery, although malnutrition and pneumonia also took their toll.[33]

But the half-starved Taliban in Shirburghan jail were luckier than their comrades. From the snatches of interview permitted with prisoners, PHR learned that as many as 1,000 of the Taliban who surrendered at Kunduz had suffocated to death on the road to Shiburghan after being locked in unventilated freight containers by soldiers working for Dostum. A convoy of 13 such containers, each filled with 150–200 men, had set out from the agreed surrender point at Qala Zeini on 29 November, the first of three allegedly conveying the Taliban to prison. 'They opened the doors and the dead bodies spilled out like fish,' recalled one of the drivers. 'All their clothes were ripped and wet.'[34] In late January, PHR examined three suspected mass graves near Shiburghan in the Dasht-i Leili desert where they found freshly scavenged human bones, prayer caps, shoes and a bulldozer's scrape marks. A local witness reported seeing six container trucks backed onto the site after the end of Ramadan in late December and armed men who covered their noses with blankets as if to suppress a noxious smell.[35] PHR alerted the State and Defense Departments in March to what it had found, but calls for a full-scale enquiry went unheeded by the US and UN until its own excavation in May uncovered 15 corpses whose condition was consistent with reports of asphyxiation.[36] Dostum later conceded that 100–120 prisoners had died of their wounds during the passage, but Taliban survivors argued that the number of dead must be even higher than PHR's preliminary estimate since 8,000 were reliably reported to have surrendered at Kunduz, though only 3,500 were found at Shiburghan one month later.[37] 'The issue nobody wants to discuss,' summarised Jennifer Leaning, one of PHR's investigative team, 'is the involvement of US forces. US forces were in the area at the time. What did the US know, and when and where, and what did they do about it?'[38]

PHR's investigation at Shiburghan was the only time that the killing of Taliban qualified as a matter of public concern or, *pace* the battle of Shah-i Kot, even accurate measurement, though many of the fighters had been press-ganged from the village to the front and thousands of Pashtun families now hungrily sought news of vanished husbands, brothers and sons. Taliban lives became forfeit in US eyes as soon as hostilities opened. Any remorse stirred by their deaths, whether in the relentless bombardment of their trenches or at the hands of Northern Alliance commanders, stemmed more from US fears of the embarrassment caused to the coalition than any questions of conscience, or even the impact the killings could have on prospects for reconciling the Pashtun to the Karzai administration. Though the Pentagon frequently published estimates of the number of Al Qa'ida fighters killed in action, no attempt was made to inventory the Taliban dead, though the exercise might have marshalled data useful for measuring the effectiveness of US air attacks and the accuracy of its intelligence. That assessment was arrived at instead by calculating the number of civilians killed by US action, a topic that attracted only cursory study when it punctuated the helter-skelter narrative of conflict but to which media and military analysts returned with a vengeance when the air war tailed off in December.

'This has been the most accurate war ever fought in this nation's history,' General Tommy Franks told the US Senate in February. Satellite-guided weapons had accounted for 10,000 of the 18,000 bombs, missiles and other munitions fired at Afghanistan between 7 October and 9 February, a total that rose by nearly a quarter to 22,000 after the crucial battles of Zhawar Kili and Shah-i Kot.[39] But it was also the least visible war in US history: no journalist or photographer was allowed close to the killing fields until the uprising at Qala-i Janghi and the chief source of information about the war's progress remained the Pentagon briefing long after the siege of Tora Bora. Prior to the fall of Kandahar in December, the Pentagon had used air power as its main offensive tool, identifying targets through a mixture of satellite imagery, Predator footage, Soviet-era maps or coordinates radioed in by Special Forces teams. Since the primary military targets were situated in urban areas, there had always been a high risk of civilian casualties despite US claims that the accuracy of its weapons systems was '85–90 per cent reliable'. The first witnesses to incidents of what the Pentagon called 'collateral damage' tended to be Taliban spokesmen or Al-Jazeera reporters, whose charges were smoothly dismissed as unverifiable hyperbole by the US military and media equally. When the information came from a more reputable source, such as the UN in the case of the Red Cross warehouse bombed twice in ten days, the incident was written off as regrettable accident, unavoidable in time of war, but sowing doubts, nevertheless, as to just how carefully targeted the bombing campaign had ever been. It was only after Tora Bora, when air power was reduced to playing a supporting role to US and Afghan forces chasing Al Qa'ida on the ground, that the linkage of civilian deaths with the misinformation provided by the Pentagon's Afghan allies against their rivals finally came to the fore.

Professor Marc Herold of the University of New Hampshire made the first attempt to calculate the number of civilians killed in the two months of the war up to 7 December, basing his figures not on Pentagon reports – which he considered corrupted – but news sources from Britain, France, Pakistan, India, Australia, Singapore, Al-Jazeera and the pro-Taliban Afghan Islamic Press. Herold's analysis showed an average of 62 Afghan civilians a day dying during US air raids, reaching a total of 3,767 by the end of the research period.[40] A survey by the Massachusetts-based Project on Defense Alternatives (PDA) used a similar methodology to Herold, but found 1,000–1,300 civilian deaths up to 1 January – one for every twelve bombs or missiles expended – with a further 3,000 fatalities attributable to the air campaign's impact on the 'refugee and famine crises'.[41] Though its estimate was lower than Herold's, the PDA analysis broadly supported his accusation that the US had run a 'dirty' war through a comparison of the number of Afghans who died in the 4,700 sorties carried out by US aircraft up to 10 December with the much lower figure of 500 civilians killed in 13,000 NATO sorties during the Kosovo war in 1999.

The anomaly could be explained by the greater percentage of cluster bombs dropped over Afghanistan and the fact that the satellite-guided weapons of which Franks had been so proud were actually less accurate than the laser-guided bombs used in Kosovo, with 50 per cent falling 32–42 feet (10–13 metres) outside their programmed coordinates, a crucial error factor in densely populated zones.[42] By UN estimates, up to 14,000 unexploded bomblets, the product of over 1,100 US cluster bombs, still littered the Afghan countryside, posing as great a threat to civilians as landmines.[43] The PDA's count was consistent with Human Rights Watch's estimate of 1,000 civilian deaths, 982 by Reuters and a Global Exchange survey of ten provinces – excluding Uruzgan – that uncovered evidence of 824 deaths by 1 January.[44] US news organisations, by contrast, tended either to talk the total down, bewilder readers with the politics of claim and counter-claim or portray civilian casualties as largely the result of Afghan misinformation – until the attack on a wedding party in July brought the human factor into focus in a way that made the issue of dead civilians unassailable. Associated Press suggested a death roll of 500–600 civilians in February while a *Los Angeles Times* investigation of 1,067–1,201 alleged civilian fatalities discounted 754 because they had been reported by the Taliban and 497 others 'that were not identified as either civilian or military'.[45] A UN survey of Kandahar province alone, by way of comparison, found evidence of 415 civilian deaths as a result of US air strikes.[46]

The war had not been the bargain the Pentagon expected when totting up the Taliban's paltry defence capabilities in 2001. Early forecasts cheerfully compared the cost of an Afghan campaign with the 78 days of bombing in the Kosovo war which came in at under $3 billion at 1999 prices. From 11 September to the Taliban retreat from Mazar on 8 November, Operation Enduring Freedom ran up bills of $1.48 billion, a moderate outlay for the one-off deployment of 50,000 men, 400 planes and their combined equipment needs in numerous fighting ships to the region.[47] With the turn of the year, however, prices began to move up. By April, expenditure on the war had reportedly reached $10.2 billion but, one month later, the Pentagon coolly informed Congress that the entire cost of its Afghan operations in the previous eight months amounted to $17 billion, or over $2 billion per month. Out of that figure, an extraordinary $3.7 billion had been spent on surveillance, reconnaissance and intelligence, much of it consumed in the failed search for bin Laden, while the comparatively small amount of $1.76 billion paid for the bombs and missiles that drove the Taliban out of power and Al Qa'ida underground.[48]

For Hamid Karzai, who first flew to Riyadh to collect a $20 million down payment on Saudi Arabia's change of heart before jetting on to Japan, such sums were the stuff of dreams. The Tokyo donors conference was the culmination of a set of international meetings about the future of Afghanistan that began in Washington the previous November when the UN Development Programme, the World Bank and the Asia Development Bank – the last two long absent from the Afghan scene – were tasked with drawing up a 'preliminary needs assessment' (PNA) to present to donors. If the renewed patronage of the two institutions was a milestone commitment to Afghan statehood, the PNA spelled out its limited menu of options while the Afghanistan Reconstruction Trust Fund, set up to ensure that Karzai's government could meet its recurrent obligations, limited how much it could raise or spend. UN Secretary-General Kofi Annan was still hoping for pledges of $10 billion over five years from the 60 donors in Tokyo, but the PNA outlined needs of just $1.7 billion in the first year of reconstruction, $4.9 billion over three. Donors naturally responded to the PNA's more specific list of requirements, making first-year commitments amounting to $1.8 billion, albeit hesitantly in view of what seemed like a self-fulfilling prophecy engraved in the proposal: 'If assistance is not provided quickly to help the government respond to the needs of the population and manage the inflow of aid resources, there is a risk that the fragile political and security environment will unravel and that donor resources will be wasted and international support lost.'[49]

Japan, the host, chipped in $500 million over two and a half years to start the bidding and other donors followed suit, pledging hundreds of millions over variable time frames, according to their gambling instincts. The biggest single-year commitment came from the US, with $296.75 million for 2002, in addition to the $400 million for humanitarian aid committed by President Bush in the aftermath of the attacks of 11 September. 'The American people,' Colin Powell told Karzai in Tokyo, 'are with you for the long term.'[50]

* * *

The bombing campaign reduced the fleet of Ariana, the national airline, to one Antonov-24 turboprop and a 19-year-old Boeing, its six other planes lying broken on the tarmac at Kabul airport. Ariana's international flights had been grounded by sanctions since 1999, except for the annual airlift of pilgrims to Mecca, but the Boeing functioned, having been hijacked through Russia to London in the same year. With no working beacons, pilots flew only when the visibility was good, accentuating Ariana's reputation as 'Inshallah ['God willing'] Airlines'. A postwar weekly service was established with Herat, mainly for currency traders eager to profit from the stronger afghani in the western city.[51] Kabul airport reopened to international traffic on 16 January, after being cleared of unexploded bombs, and Ariana's first international flight took off for New Delhi, a city unvisited in the five years after the Taliban came to power. With the timely gift of three Airbuses from Air India, part of a $100 million dowry from New Delhi, Ariana went back into business, offering a range of services to Tehran, Islamabad, Dubai, Istanbul and Frankfurt.

The minister in charge of civil aviation and the less enviable task of promoting tourism was Abdul Rehman, a medical doctor who joked with journalists about turning Kabul back into a haunt for hippies, as it was in the 1970s.[52] Once a prominent member of ex-president Rabbani's Jamiat-i Islami, Rehman abandoned the party after the Taliban captured Kabul, going into exile in India where he switched his allegiance to Zahir Shah. He had cut a rare profile at the Bonn talks in November, a Tajik from Nuristan but one of eight members in the pro-Zahir Rome Group to win a portfolio in an administration otherwise dominated by Panjshiri Tajiks. Whether Rehman defected for ideological or financial reasons is unknown, but his working relationship with former Jamiat colleagues proved shortlived.

On 14 February, Rehman drove to Kabul airport where a squad of security troops loyal to Interior Minister Yunus Qanuni had been assigned to protect him as he prepared to fly on official business to New Delhi, his former home. A crowd of around a thousand Haj pilgrims, who had waited for days in the cold for a plane to be made available to fly them to Saudi Arabia, was enraged to see the minister and his entourage sweep aboard the solitary Boeing, surrounding it for two hours before forcing him out. Rehman tried to negotiate with his tormentors, trembling as he scribbled a resignation letter for the mob, but he was dragged away, beaten and dispatched with knives. Only then did bodyguards arrive to take his remains to hospital.[53] The murder was taken as a grisly reminder of the passionate savagery coursing through Afghan veins after two decades of war, rather like a 'Unity' football match four days later when police used barbed-wire whips to stop ticketless fans invading a stadium that only recently was the scene of public executions. After the wake at Rehman's home, Karzai surprised journalists by saying the Hajis were not to blame for the killing; the minister had been the victim of a vendetta by high-ranking officials in a Jamiat faction, who used the infuriated crowd as cover. He identified the three perpetrators as General Abdullah Jan Tawhidi, deputy chief of intelligence, General Kalander Beg, deputy to Defence Minister Fahim, and Saranwal Haleem, a prosecutor in the justice ministry. All had escaped, he alleged, disguised as pilgrims on the Boeing to Mecca from where the Saudi authorities had promised to extradite them. Both Tawhidi and Beg were Panjshiris.[54]

The riddle of Rehman's murder seemed to highlight a glaring rift between the pro-Zahir group in the interim administration and the Tajik Panjshiris who controlled its defence, interior and foreign affairs ministries, but Karzai's outburst and its consequences suggested there were other schisms, scarcely visible till now. Prudently, the chairman had attributed his knowledge of the conspiracy to intelligence supplied by Fahim and Qanuni, but the third member of the Panjshiri troika, Foreign Minister Dr Abdullah, poured cold water on Karzai's charges five days later when he asserted that the Hajis had been responsible after all. The three suspects, he said, were present at the airport in their capacity as pilgrims, not as assassins; they merely conveyed to Rehman the mob's demand for his resignation before departing for Mecca to realise their spiritual aspirations.[55] It was the first example, but not the last, of a Northern Alliance minister publicly repudiating the statements of his head of state. The Alliance, he told *Newsweek*, had never once stooped to political assassination. 'There isn't a single plot in our history,' he said. With Panjshiri detectives in charge of the murder investigation, one was unlikely to surface now.

An ISAF barracks was situated a few hundred yards away from the airport but, under the complex terms of the force's deployment, responsibility for security at the facility lay with interior ministry troops alone. The peacekeeping force had reached its maximum strength of 4,800 soldiers in mid-February, limited to a six-month tour at the insistence of France. A senior State Department official reckoned a more realistic assessment of Afghanistan's transitional security needs entailed stationing 25,000 troops over at least two years, but the Pentagon remained unconvinced and a number of governments already contributing to the 19-nation contingent were also wary. 'We are moving toward a decision,' said a Bush official, but at a pace that clearly did not rate among its priorities the expansion of Karzai's authority in the run-up to the *Loya Jirga*, due to determine Afghanistan's transitional administration in June, just four months away.[56] Four days after Rehman's murder, unknown gunmen shot at British paratroopers at a post on a ruined grain silo in west Kabul, triggering a three-minute burst of return fire which cut down a man taking his pregnant sister-in-law to hospital and wounded four others in the taxi in which they were travelling. But mistaken killings and attacks on ISAF personnel were relatively rare compared with US operations in the south and east, though they emphasised the perils of stretching the peace mission further afield.

With no army to call his own, Karzai had only goodwill and patronage to stave off threats to his authority but, despite a wide circle of flattering friends, the latter was in cruelly short supply. A $20 million start-up fund, pledged to the interim government at Bonn, yielded only $8 million by January despite UN chivvying, and $5 million was already spent paying back salaries for hospital staff, police and *chowkidars*.[57] The new operating budget of $460 million, praised at the time for its realism and the promise not to print money to cover it, was underfunded by $257 million, with just India and Pakistan stumping up $10 million each and the US double that amount.[58] The World Bank later made $100 million available to meet the first quarter's needs. There were some early successes. A quick-release grant of $3 million from Japan paid for 12,000 ex-fighters at $2 a day to clear rubble, plant trees or repair buildings in Kabul and 3 million children were back in class when schools reopened in March. It was the first-ever day of formal education for most of the 1 million girls involved. Of the $1.8 billion pledged by donors in Tokyo, however, barely $160 million had arrived by April, most of it earmarked for humanitarian programmes, rather than the massive rebuilding projects crucial to providing an economic impetus and the jobs needed to remove fighters from circulation.[59] Even the large humanitarian agencies complained of the grindingly slow disbursement of the donors' pledges. By the end of April, the World Food Programme had received just $64 million of the $285 million needed to feed 9 million Afghans affected by drought or war – nearly one-third of the entire population – and the UNHCR was $100 million shy of the $271 million required for the refugee repatriation scheme launched in March. Enthused by the prospect of Karzai's royalist credentials, Afghans were returning at a rate of 50,000 a week, but the giddy commitments at Tokyo were receding just as fast.

Whether through bureaucracy, fatigue or sheer lack of conviction that Karzai's administration was truly the last stanza in Afghanistan's ballad of despair, the donors hedged their bets. Release of the funds at first hinged on the hospitality accorded to the ISAF, but the bar was lifted as time passed to include the reception of the aged monarch, the conduct of the *Loya Jirga* and even the prospects of a coup by the young Panjshiris.

Karzai's grip was withering even as donors looked round for signs their funds would not be wasted. His aides described cabinet meetings in which Northern Alliance demands were met without debate and hinted that Rehman's killing was part of a plot to undermine the Popolzai prince.[60] In the provinces, witnesses drew a picture of chaos in the absence of any strong central authority. 'We don't even know who our governor is,' said a Wardak official.[61] Dostum, Ismail Khan and Gul Agha were running autonomous states, while the tri-province area in the southeast had become a tribal trust territory under US martial law. If Pentagon policy continued unerringly to bolster the warlords at the margins of Karzai's domain, other donors' reluctance to meet their promises seemed to reflect a fear of strengthening the Panjshiris at its core. Washington, at least, paid up promptly. 'The problem many governments have is the issue of security,' said Zalmay Khalilzad, the Afghan-American who represented President Bush in Karzai's court. 'They want security restored before economic development starts. Perhaps it is better to start economic improvement to restore security.'[62]

The UN agency with the toughest task after the war was, unfortunately, the one with the least credibility. Like the Taliban half a decade earlier, the advent of Karzai seemed to offer a heaven-sent chance to eliminate for good Afghanistan's production of opium, a crop that sank from 3,700 tonnes in 2000 to less than 200 tonnes the year after Mullah Omar forbade its cultivation. Prices followed into freefall after 11 September as farmers dumped what remained of their stock, tumbling first from $700 a kilo to $190 and then down to $90.[63] In line with his commitments at Bonn, Karzai banned opium growing on 17 January, defying reports that showed farmers responding with gusto to the Taliban defeat by the wholesale replanting of Nangarhar and Helmand with poppy. The UN Drug Control Programme, renamed the UN Office for Drug Control and Crime Prevention after an internal purge, welcomed the move, but was poorly situated to coordinate or fund it. Pino Arlacchi, the Italian mafia-buster appointed to head the agency's $265 million budget in 1997, had been forced to relinquish his post on 1 January after a UN inspection found evidence of financial malfeasance and a style of management described as 'dispotica e dilettantistica'.[64] Britain, France, Holland and Belgium, the agency's leading donors, all froze funding to the agency while the US, too busy fighting the spectres of terrorism to worry about its other war on drugs, was 'out to lunch on the issue', according to a European diplomat. Since 11 September, 140 agents of the Drug Enforcement Agency had switched to riding shotgun as marshalls on civilian flights or been seconded to the FBI.[65]

Faced with the possibility of a heroin epidemic at home, Prime Minister Tony Blair had cited Afghanistan's opium trade as one of many good reasons for Britain backing the US bombing of the Taliban in October. An initial plan to purchase the entire 2002 crop of Afghan opium at black market prices, at a cost of $50 million to $150 million, was jettisoned out of fear it might prompt other farmers, not yet involved, to cultivate poppy for profit.[66] Britain and other European donors took a leaf instead from the EU's Common Agricultural Policy by offering opium growers 'set-aside' payments to destroy their crops but, with the season so far advanced, this would require gunmen to police the scheme, rather than officials with clipboards. Karzai's adviser, Ashraf Ghani, a former professor at Johns Hopkins University in Baltimore and the future finance minister, said he was prepared to offer the farmers $250 per *jirib*, roughly equivalent to one-fifth of a hectare. 'Will people be unhappy?' he said. 'Absolutely. Some are going to make $17,000 per *jirib* if they take it to market.'[67] The day before it launched a well-publicised campaign to enforce the ban, the government announced the arrest in Kabul of 300 supporters of Gulbuddin Hekmatyar and the Pashtun leader Abdul Rasul Sayyaf, along with eight Pakistanis, on suspicion of plotting to overthrow Hamid Karzai. British military intelligence and ISAF reportedly supplied the leads that triggered the arrests.[68]

Confronting the opium trade was Karzai's first attempt to challenge its warlord backers and prove he was worthy of donor confidence, but it involved a frontal attack on an important constituency of poor and exploited Pashtuns. Omar's ban and a four-year drought had turned farmers into little more than serfs for the opium traders and loansharks who supplied them with their seed, fertiliser and markets. One Jalalabad grower had to pay back double the sum he borrowed five years previously, or its equivalent value in opium paste.[69] Depriving these farmers of their crops by force was not a policy that transformed easily into votes. Nevertheless, squads of surveyors from the Afghan NGO Welfare and Relief Committee, with troops in reserve, set out on 3 April for Jalalabad to meet former Nangarhar governor Haji Abdul Qadir, a man who had fattened on the opium trade after the ouster of Najibullah in 1992, but whose role now was to cull it, albeit selectively.

Like many other warlords, Haji Qadir had an acute understanding of Britain's economic role in early Afghan history and it served him well in his critique of Karzai's eradication campaign. 'The British pay only $5 for the labour of destroying each *jirib*,' he said, 'so it's hard to find enough men to do it. Five dollars doesn't go far between 20 men.'[70] With little or no outside supervision, however, the scheme was wide open to corruption. In a parallel operation in Alliance-controlled Badakhshan, eradication teams gave just a handful of farmers compensation, retaining the balance for themselves, while multiplying by four the area they claimed to have destroyed.[71] However, after a campaign lasting two weeks, Qadir proudly announced the confiscation of 2,000 kg of opium, 250 kg of heroin, 400 kg of acetic anhydride and the destruction of Ghani Khel, the largest opium bazaar in the world, though the thousands of kilos seized vanished from the inventory.[72] Violent protests blocked the road from Jalalabad to Khyber Pass, forcing the government to double its offer to $506 per *jirib*, and eight farmers were killed and 35 wounded when security forces opened fire on a demonstration in Helmand province.[73]

A visit to Nangarhar by a high-ranking official could not have been less propitiously timed. Unsigned leaflets had recently circulated in Jalalabad that sanctioned the killing of any government employee. 'Our country has been invaded,' they read. 'All Afghans are obliged to do *jihad* as we did to the Russians.'[74] On 8 April, Defence Minister Mohammed Fahim flew with his northern commander, Ustad Atta Mohammed, to Jalalabad in order to discuss with Governor Hazrat Ali the opium eradication campaign and the Pentagon's proposal to create a national army as a means of improving security. As their convoy approached Jalalabad's busy central crossroads, there was a massive explosion that narrowly missed Fahim's vehicle, but a crowd of flag-waving children, given the day off school to greet the dignitaries from the capital, was mowed down. Amid howls of pain and the crashing of gears, guards extracted the minister from the mêlée and drove him away, leaving four dead and several dozen injured behind. 'It was not just to kill me,' he said later, 'they wanted to send a message.'[75] But who had sent it was none the clearer.

Following so rapidly after the alleged coup plot in Kabul, suspicion for organising the assassination attempt fell equally between Hekmatyar and Haji Zaman, the Nangarhar police chief allied with the US at Tora Bora, but since engaged in a tussle for power with Hazrat Ali, Fahim's preferred vassal. Hekmatyar, for his part, disappeared from Tehran in late February and was reportedly seeking to forge and lead a new Pashtun alliance from what remained of Hizb-i Islami, the Taliban and Al Qa'ida with the aim of destabilising the interim government in advance of the *Loya Jirga*. In fact, a month later Hizb-i Islami promised to support Karzai's efforts to bring 'a lasting peace', while General Zia Lodin, commanding the US-trained Afghan army at Shah-i Kot, was dismissive of Hekmatyar's ability to present a political or military challenge. 'He is a zero, he does not have the money or the men,' he said.[76] Even the evidence of a conspiracy against Karzai proved less than convincing. Around half the 300 men arrested in connection with the plot were released without charge 24 hours later; a confidential memorandum by UN chief negotiator Michael Semple suggested that the detentions may have been motivated by a desire by elements within the government to intimidate leading Pashtun from participating in the *Loya Jirga*. 'The aim is to exclude our people from any future influence,' complained Wahidullah Sabawoon, a former Hizb-i Islami leader placed under house arrest during the intelligence swoop. 'If they arrest us, they know we can't be active political players and that we will be out of their way.'[77]

Zahir had been due to return to Kabul on 25 March for the popular Norouz celebrations that mark the Zoroastrian new year, a time of spring cleaning and spiritual rebirth. But President Bush telephoned Prime Minister Silvio Berlusconi in Rome four days before his departure to warn of 'credible reports' of a plot to shoot down the former king's plane as soon as it crossed into Afghan airspace.[78] His arrival had been keenly awaited and thousands of tribal leaders were expected to descend on Kabul for the occasion, though some intended him harm and few could recall the peace or bounty of his reign. A villa in Wazir Akhbar Khan, formerly the property of a Taliban minister, had been made ready to accommodate him, its approach roads sealed by barbed wire and concrete, with four armoured personnel carriers armed with machine guns stationed outside. A special unit of 150 police was assigned to protect the 87-year-old memento of nationhood, headed by an interior ministry official who was briefly suspended for failing to prevent the killing of Rehman in February.[79] Zahir expressed no specific apprehension of the Kabul to which he was soon to be transferred, but security arrangements for a life considered critical to the legitimacy of the *Loya Jirga* were clearly inadequate. Following two more cancellations, he touched down at Kabul airport on 18 April after three decades in exile, dressed in a stylish Italian leather jacket and flanked by 40 *carabinieri*. A media blackout ensured that no crowd came to greet him, only ministers, diplomats, journalists and a handful of warlords, no doubt rapt at the wizened figure shuffling along the red welcome carpet, tears springing from watery eyes. Gul Agha, the governor of Kandahar, was first to kiss the ex-king's hand.[80] After resting, Zahir paid his first official visit to the grave of his father, whose murder he had watched 69 years earlier.

Both Karzai and the Pentagon were initially emboldened by the popularity of the king at their side. When Bacha Khan drenched Gardez with a barrage of 500 rockets on 27 April, Major-General 'Buster' Hagenbeck signalled an abrupt change in relations with its attack dog in the southeast. 'It's true that Bacha Khan was an ally of ours before,' he told journalists, 'but the old phrase that there are no permanent alliances probably smacks true in this instance.'[81] Karzai returned to the theme some days later when he called Bacha a killer and appointed as governor Hakim Taniwal, a 60-year-old former professor who had spent the previous five years as a Melbourne teacher, now charged with bringing order to Gardez and securing it for the government. One of his first decisions was to invite himself to tea at the fortress of Kamal Khan, Bacha's brother. 'I think we have broken the ice,' Taniwal reported back, but Bacha's instructions to a messenger suggested otherwise: 'Tell Kamal Khan to [expletive] this new governor. [Expletive] him, pack him and send him back to Karzai.'[82]

Despite US concern at the inconvenience Bacha could cause to coalition operations, the warlord had been overtaken in the Pentagon's estimation by Hekmatyar, then reportedly in the vicinity of the capital. In a break with reporting precedent, news was leaked of a Pentagon attempt to assassinate the Pashtun on 6 May with a Hellcat missile fired from a Predator drone. 'We had information that he was planning attacks on American and coalition forces, on the interim government and on Karzai himself,' said a Pentagon official without supplying supporting evidence.[83] It was the first such claim since a fluffed Hellcat attack on Mullah Omar on the first night of the war, but this time against a former US proxy who had some grounds for claiming to represent an alternative Pashtun ideology to that of the Taliban. Hekmatyar was coloured with the same history of killing that tainted Dostum, but boasting of a bid to murder him so close to the *Loya Jirga* was a certain way of boosting his reputation from a ruthless murderer into a victim of what was widely interpreted as an anti-Pashtun bias in Karzai's regime. Mullah Omar and Hekmatyar would ultimately share the same accolade of being the only Afghan leaders of stature not allocated seats in the marquee of national reconciliation that finally parted its flaps on 10 June.

The omens for the long-anticipated assembly did not look auspicious in May. Though the thrust of military operations had switched across the Pakistani border, squads of US troops continued to harry villages in the southeast, poisoning the atmosphere of the imminent parlay. Nine Afghans perished under a volley of missiles near Khost on 18 May while disputing with another clan over a 'swath of trees', although the Australian forces who called in the US raid said they had been shooting at them for hours.[84] Two weeks previously, tribal leaders in seven Pashtun provinces threatened to boycott the meeting on the grounds that the selection procedures failed to exclude warlords and the *Jirga* commissioners had taken on themselves the right to appoint 500 of the 1,500 expected delegates to represent refugees, returning exiles, women and civil society.[85] From Herat, centre of a flourishing democracy movement, came reports of delegates being threatened or detained by Ismail Khan while the UN announced that eight Afghans associated with the selection process had been killed in Kandahar and Ghor. The killings in Kandahar, where the curfew was lifted on 19 May after 20 years in force, were brutal in the extreme. Four soldiers, transporting *Loya Jirga* papers to Shah Wali Kot district, had been beaten, tied back to back, riddled with bullets and hurled off a mountainside. 'I knew them,' said a former Taliban soldier charged with the murders. 'Everything is from God, so I killed them.'[86] 'They are looking for something that will gain them a lot of publicity,' warned Hagenbeck. 'They are looking for something violent that would be, in their eyes and internationally, so spectacular that it would convince the local populace who are now sitting on the fence supporting us that they need to re-embrace the Taliban.'[87] As if by clockwork, a day later Hekmatyar called on Afghans to mount a *jihad* against American and British occupation in a communique that also denied the Predator attack had caused him any injury.

The tent to which the delegates were invited had been donated by Germany and was once used to host beer festivals. Measuring 230 by 130 feet, it was re-erected in the grounds of Kabul Polytechnic, equipped with air conditioning, CCTV and translation facilities, and furnished with fine Afghan carpets. For eleven days in June, it became a *caravanserai* for most of the disparate political and ethnic fragments thrown up by 23 years of war; a Babel of former Taliban, former royalists, former communists, former mujahedin and both former and aspiring warlords struggling to wrap their tongues around the unfamiliar jargon of reconciliation and unity. The Bonn agreement charged the *Loya Jirga* with electing the head of state of an 18-month administration, responsible for drafting a new constitution and creating conditions for free elections, and with approving its structure and key personnel. If successful, it would be the first time in Afghan history that a political leader had been chosen by secret ballot, but delegates grew suspicious of the proceedings from day one.

The UN considered the voting process in the provinces flawed but generally fair, with warlords wary of, or otherwise failing to stuff delega- tions with their own supporters. 'The delegates do represent the whole of Afghanistan,' said UN special representative Lakhdar Brahimi before the

Jirga opened, 'and its people will recognise themselves in the result.'[88] But the commissioners' appointment of 500 chiefly liberal, secular or female delegates – against the 150 submitted by the south in its entirety – was construed as vote-packing, while the last-minute demand that governors be represented led to the assembly being postponed by a day for 'logistical concerns'. 'It's something to do with the carpets,' said a Kabul University delegate of the delay, but a different kind of interior design was being conducted away from the tent.[89] In contravention of procedural rules, but with UN approval, 32 governors and 64 of their closest advisers, all unelected, were permitted to participate as representatives of the 'existing power structure', bringing the total number of delegates to 1,600.[90] When the *Jirga* finally got started on 10 June, Dostum, Ismail Khan, Hazrat Ali, Gul Agha, even Bacha Khan, men with long memories and sharper knives, were seated up front, glowering as the delegates elected by their people arose nervously to utter. 'We were told that this *Loya Jirga* would not include all the people who had blood on their hands,' said one when he raised the issue to a round of applause. 'But we see these people everywhere. I don't know whether this is a *Loya Jirga* or a commanders' council.' Others complained that 'strangers' and 'intruders' had penetrated the tight security around the tent and called for their ejection. Klaus-Peter Klaiber, the EU envoy who had compared conditions in Dostum's jails to Auschwitz, gave a different gloss on the gunmen's presence. 'It tells me only one thing: the interim administration has decided to integrate former warlords into policy-making in Kabul. If they succeed, that will be an achievement.'[91]

Dostum, ever the zephyr of fashion, had mastered the dialect of unity faster than most, shaving his beard, ditching fatigues and hiring the best tailor in Mazar to run up the newest camouflage; Afghan mock-Armani. It was a trend with leaders throughout the country. He had submitted a proposal in April to devolve power along federal lines, a suggestion seen as an attempt to shore up an authority jeopardised by the inroads made by Ustad Atta Mohammed, but Dostum had longer vision. He was tired and developing a middle-aged spread. Publicly, he adopted the lingo of the *Jirga*, shifting allegiance from the Kalashnikov to the 'rule of law' in numerous speeches, but the two weeks leading to the assembly saw three robberies of relief agencies and the gang-rape of an international aid worker.[92] Dostum was far from in control. Despite the pogrom of northern Pashtun, his new loyalty tended to Zahir and the Pashtuns of the south in the belief that a vote for the king was not only popular with Uzbeks, it offered a viable bulwark against the Panjshiris who controlled Karzai. Their position as a minority within a minority rendered them particularly hostile to minorities of different culture, as a quarrel over proportional representation shortly illustrated. Despite differences between them, the Hazaras agreed with Dostum and even Bacha Khan, a friend now only to himself, warned that a government without Zahir at its head was a recipe for armed conflict.[93]

Selecting the head of state was the *Jirga*'s first order of business, a decision that pitted General Fahim, who rejected out of hand any position for the king but would accept Karzai in a pinch, against the votes of the 300 elected Pashtun delegates and their allies among the minorities. To stay informed of murmurs inside the tent, Fahim persuaded the UN to allow Khad agents in the National Security Directorate to reinforce the security provided by German peacekeepers and the hastily trained National Guard (named '1Bang', without any apparent trace of irony), though most of his energies were directed behind the scenes.[94] Zahir never made a pretence of his hatred for high office, but he was bowed down by the curse he carried as a symbol and the incessant calls to Rome after 11 September which had cast him in the role of redeemer and into his high-security prison-house in Wazir Akhbar Khan. Even those calling for his enthronement knew of the cruelty to which they would sentence him if he accepted, which he could not refuse to do, if they asked. Of his children, none had the stamina demanded of power, though they urged him to become head of state and appoint Karzai his prime minister. Three weeks before the *Jirga* opened, Karzai and Fahim had gone to Zahir with a compromise proposal under which he would accept the role of 'Father of the Nation', with the prestige of a head of state and powers to veto the new constitution, award medals and titles for distinguished service to Afghanistan, should there be any candidates.[95] He wavered, torn between the promptings of power, responsibility and an old man's longing for quiet.

The question that echoed in the tent was whether, at this moment of destiny, Zahir Shah chose voluntarily to renounce high office, or whether it was torn from his hands by Karzai, Fahim, the UN or the US, working together or separately. The evidence pointed to a Washington veto on Zahir's candidacy to prevent damaging the prospects of its own favourite, Karzai – a man so close to him in face and pedigree, barring moustache, he even looked like the king, half a century younger, striding towards an alternative to Afghanistan's history of gun rule. Two weeks prior to the *Jirga*, Karzai signed a new agreement to build a gas pipeline from Turkmenistan to Pakistan, further stoking fears of the Pentagon's real motives in Afghanistan. In an act of *lèse-majesté* that was heavy-handed even by US standards of behaviour in Afghanistan, Zalmay Khalilzad emerged at 4 p.m.

on 10 June to tell journalists that, after all, Zahir Shah had decided not to stand for office, fully three hours before the king formally announced his withdrawal and 18 hours before the furious delegates were told the news.

'I don't think it was inappropriate at all given the role we played,' the envoy said of his conduct when taken to task for undermining the *Jirga's* credibility.

> There was no pressure at all. His Majesty had said previously that he was not a candidate but he was ready to serve the people. The night before, there were reports by people associated with relatives of the former king indicating that he was indeed a candidate. Because I have known the former king, I was asked by the UN and Afghans to ascertain whether indeed the position of His Majesty had changed. He said there was nothing to that story. Since I had facilitated this clarification, I was invited to join [the press conference].[96]

Lakhdar Brahimi confirmed this stilted description of what had been a momentous, off-stage event in Afghan history, but could not silence accusations that the *Jirga's* outcome had been gerrymandered outside the delegates' sight-lines, a conviction that increased when former president Rabbani announced he too had withdrawn from the race. Both candidates, one carrying royal legitimacy in Pashtun eyes, the other a UN-recognised president until the Bonn talks, had pulled out of the first representative ballot on Afghan leadership before a single elected delegate could say a word. 'It is for us to decide what role the king has,' said one of the delegates. 'If we want or don't want the king, it is for us to decide and then the king can say whether he accepts or not.'[97] That night, a crowd of 800 elected representatives stood in vigil outside Zahir's villa, silently begging the old man to reconsider.[98] Apart from a single appearance to declare the conference open the next morning, the king stayed away throughout its eleven-day duration, guarding his thoughts in Wazir Akhbar Khan.

With both the king and Rabbani declaring for Karzai, his nomination with 1,050 votes was greeted by a round of enthusiastic clapping to which, observers say, he reacted as if already elected, an impression reinforced at close of day when the conference chairman, law professor Ismael Qasimyar, told journalists that the Popolzai had been elected president 'by applause'. It had to be explained to him later that no vote had actually been taken.[99] Three other candidate names had also come forward: Dr Masooda Jalal, a female paediatrician formerly with the World Food Programme, Mir Mohammed Mafoz Nadai, a Kabul businessman, and Glas Fareq Majidi, about whom little was ever made public. Majidi was disqualified from going forward for lack of nominations, and Fahim publicly threatened the husband of Jalal, 'calling his wife's bid for the presidency un-Islamic and saying she should step down'.[100] Karzai took 1,295 of the 1,575 votes in the formal ballot, but his victory had been indelibly marred by the elimination of his two major rivals. 'He became a consensus candidate,' concluded Khalilzad. 'It looked liked he was going to win, and [as] happens so often in Afghan *Loya Jirga*, when a victory looks inevitable, then they move towards a consensus.'[101] But whether they had moved or been shoved worried the delegates for days.

Dr Jalal's decision to challenge Karzai, despite her sex, was indicative of the powerful forces of change let loose by the *Jirga* – not all of them welcome to men who had previously fought or supported either the mujahedin or the Taliban. Sima Shamar, women's affairs minister in the interim administration and the *Jirga*'s first deputy chair, was denounced as the 'Salman Rushdie of Afghanistan' by the pro-Panjshiri newspaper *Payam-i Mujahid* for allegedly questioning the benefits of *sharia* justice and she received death threats throughout the conference.[102] After Karzai's election, a heated debate broke out in the assembly over the role Islam should play in the new administration, with speaker after speaker from the old guard of mujahedin leaders rising to voice support for an 'Islamic government'. The only public dissenter, surprisingly, was Gul Agha of Kandahar who argued that so much evil had been done in the name of Islam that to call for Islamic government in Afghanistan was 'untrue to Islam'. He was shouted off the stage and, with tempers so frayed, no one dared second him.

A more contentious issue was the composition and powers of a new National Assembly, or Shura-i Milli, an aspect not directly provided for under the Bonn agreement, but of profound concern to those in the *Jirga* seeking to establish checks and balances over executive authority. The debate stalled for days as delegates argued over whether representation should be proportionate to population, an arrangement regarded as favouring the minorities, or whether each province should be represented equally, an approach that was believed to give more votes to the Pashtun. When the vote was cancelled on the fifth day and the debate resumed on the sixth, around 1,000 of the delegates staged a walk-out to escape the 'boring speeches'.[103] On the seventh day, the chairman proposed a compromise that combined elected representatives from the provinces, with others chosen among *Jirga* delegates and yet more reserved for women, experts and members of civil society. When delegates sprang to the microphones to contest the proposal, Qasimyar adjourned the session to let tempers cool. The national assembly issue remained unresolved by the time the *Jirga* had run its course.

Karzai was expected to address the assembly that morning over the *Jirga's* third and most controversial task, approving the 'key personnel' in his new administration. Many in the tent interpreted the phrase as providing them with carte blanche to debate the new president's nominees for ministerial office, an opportunity to correct the ethnic imbalance of the cabinet installed after Bonn and dilute the Panjshiri hold on the defence, police and foreign affairs portfolios. Karzai thought otherwise, initially seeking *Jirga* approval only for the posts of chief justice of the supreme court and the speaker of the as-yet unagreed national assembly. Khalilzad again drew criticism for the manner with which he overruled Karzai's interpretation of the Bonn agreement in a conversation with journalists outside the meeting. 'Whoever said the approval of the *Loya Jirga* is not needed has spoken mistakenly,' he said. 'On that we are perfectly clear.'[104] Karzai promptly postponed his speech to mull over the consequences, but the delegates were gratified by what appeared their last and final opportunity to exercise their mandate.

* * *

As Karzai pondered his choices that night, four rockets were fired into the capital, while Britain announced a reduction in its contribution to ISAF and the withdrawal of 1,600 Marines. He was greeted next morning by an honour guard as he entered the tent to announce his ministerial choices, telling delegates that instead of the five key posts requiring their approval, he had brought with him the full list of 14 cabinet names. In a last-minute concession, Yunus Qanuni agreed to surrender the interior ministry to Taj Mohammed Wardak, an 80-year-old American citizen, but he retained the allegiance of its Panjshiri officials and was given the education ministry as recompense. Fahim and Abdallah held on to their portfolios, but Karzai nominated the defence minister as one of his three vice-presidents, along with Haji Qadir and Karim Khalili, in a clear attempt to build ethnic symmetry at the highest levers of power. If Tajiks dominated the security and intelligence apparatus, the ministries charged with rebuilding Afghanistan – and with most access to donor funds – passed largely to educated Pashtun, with former World Bank official Ashraf Ghani in the key post of finance minister. Notably missing from Karzai's list, however, were Dostum, who declined the post of vice-president because he didn't consider it safe enough to leave Mazar, and Ismail Khan, whose son instead was awarded a cabinet job.[105] But it was also highly unlikely that Haji Qadir of Jalalabad would be considered a suitable representative by the very different Pashtun of Khost, Gardez, Kandahar and Helmand, the cradles of Taliban power.

Karzai's combination of technocrats and warlords pleased neither delegate nor diplomat but, with no Western commitment to expand ISAF to the regions, he arguably had little option but to offer their rulers a share in government – and the spoils of aid. The choice ran counter to the expressed wishes of the majority at the *Jirga* which, despite their disagreements, had broadly sought a more complete break with the past by the exclusion of former faction heads, rather than an accommodation that tended to enlarge their power. Moreover, Karzai appeared to have tricked the *Jirga* into confirming his list by calling for a show of hands, 'without formal vote, written slate or opportunity to discuss' the nominees, though UN guidelines – and Khalilzad – both required it.[106] Only when the delegates raised their hands, more in resignation than acclaim after nine days of frustrating discussion, did Karzai finally announce the hated names of his vice-presidents – without calling for a separate vote on whether or not the *Jirga* approved his selection. 'By these appointments,' said a European diplomat in Kabul, 'Karzai and the Panjshiris have made more enemies than they had before. Karzai has only demonstrated his weakness and his inability to take hard decisions, which will increase instability outside Kabul and infuriate the Pashtuns.'[107]

A week after Karzai's inauguration on 21 June, Zahir's queen, 84-year-old Homaira Shah, died in Rome of heart problems, as if she were bereaved at the final disappointment of her dynastic hopes. The sidelining of the king was bitterly received by the Pashtun, not least because Zahir, feeble as he was, commanded a deference from commanders to which Hamid Karzai, however fit, could never attain entitlement. Both had been exiled and both restored with US assistance, but Karzai's capture of the presidency was seen by many as a second overthrow of the king, comparable to Daoud's coup 29 years earlier. Others found a closer parallel with Babrak Karmal, the Parcham leader imposed as president after the Soviet invasion in 1979, who, like Karzai, could also lay claim to royal descent.

Comparisons with the Soviet occupation did not end there. One night in May, the inhabitants of Band Taimore awoke to the roar of rotor blades and machine-gun fire as 150 soldiers from the 101st Airborne and their Afghan allies raced into the Uruzgan village, yelling and hurling stun grenades. The 85-year-old headman was executed with a bullet to the head, two men were wounded and 55 others handcuffed, blindfolded and taken by helicopter to Kandahar where, on landing, they were crammed into a container, manacled and stripped naked for interrogation before being confined in to a 'miniature version of Guantanamo Bay'. In Band Taimore, their wives and sisters were gagged to stop them screaming, while troops with blackened faces hoisted their *burkhas* to ensure they were not hiding bin Laden or Mullah Omar. 'If they touch our women again,' said one distraught husband, 'we must ask ourselves why we are alive.' Three-year-old Zarghunah awoke at midnight. Frightened by the helicopters, she ran shrieking into an open village well, 60 feet deep, where she broke her back and drowned. 'We were better off under the Russians,' muttered a villager.[108]

'This was a turning point,' commented a former mujahedin in Kandahar, 'especially because of what they did to the women.'[109] A week later, demonstrators won the release of 50 of the prisoners from Band Taimore, though US intelligence retained the remaining five on suspicion of Taliban connections. Attacks on US bases and its Afghan allies had multiplied in the run-up to the *Jirga*, starting with a bomb outside Gul Agha's palace on 1 June, a rocket attack on the Kandahar base three days later and another bomb on 16 June that destroyed two Pakistani fuel tankers supplying the US forces. But worse was to come. At midnight on 1 July, a Special Forces unit hunting Mullah Omar in Uruzgan, along with Afghan irregulars, called in close air support after reporting a burst of automatic fire near Derawat, Karzai's home district. While an AC-130 sprayed the zone with machine-gun fire, a B-52 dropped seven 2,000 lb satellite-guided bombs after reporting anti-aircraft fire in the same area.[110]

In spite of new orders not to 'touch the women', the American unit was doing precisely that at an outlying settlement before finally advancing into the village of Kakrak, the presumed source of hostile fire, at dawn. They found scenes of unparalleled carnage, according to Carlotta Gall, one of the first reporters on the scene.

> The women and children had been sitting on the flat mud roof of the farmhouse, enjoying the cool night air and singing wedding songs, when the first shell struck at 1am. It blasted a huge hole in the roof and sprayed shrapnel across the rooftop and around the courtyard. A second explosion hit the adjoining compound where the men had been sitting in groups in the courtyard, drinking tea and chatting.[111]

Others were sliced into pieces by the Spectre's guns as they struggled to escape the bombs. 'A woman's torso had landed in one of the small almond trees,' Gall continued. 'Human flesh was still hanging on the tree five days after the attack, and more putrefying remains were tangled in the branches of a pomegranite tree, its bright scarlet flowers still blooming.'

The attack killed 48 people and wounded 117 more over four affected villages, but the worst affected was Kakrak. Though survivors insisted US troops and the pilot had mistaken a wedding volley of automatic fire for an anti-aircraft attack, the Pentagon refused to admit any error had occurred and President Bush took five days to telephone Karzai with a condolence that fell far short of an apology. 'The surprising thing,' said Karzai later, 'is that in all four incidents – this one and three earlier – the civilians being targeted are my own people and my strongest allies and in the forefront in the war against the Taliban.'[112] But they also lived in the province where Mullah Omar was believed to be hiding. Intensive searches revealed no evidence of anti-aircraft emplacements in or around the villages, nor any sign that Mullah Omar had been near the place. 'I have asked,' continued Karzai, 'that from now onwards everything should be closely coordinated between the Americans and the central authority of Afghanistan to make sure that no such mishaps happen again.'

A day after the conversation with the US president, Haji Abdul Qadir was shot in the head in broad daylight while leaving the ministry of public works in his car. Two assassins riddled the vehicle with 36 rounds, killing both driver and bodyguard, before fleeing in a white taxi. The ease with which they escaped and Qadir's Pashtun origins led to suspicion for the killing falling on the Panjshiri faction, though the former governor had made so many enemies in a long life of greed and intrigue, most recently for his conduct of the poppy campaign, it was unclear precisely who wanted most to shoot him dead. Former Taliban, Hekmatyar, Hazrat Ali, Haji Zaman, the Khyber drug lords or the meanest poppy grower, cheated of his season's profit, all waited in line before Fahim, whose interests were better served by the vice-president's continued breathing, if he wished to see the arrival of aid funds. Bush's elegiac comments on the murder struck a rather too forgiving note, in view of Qadir's long tolerance of, if not outright involvement in the heroin trade. 'There's all kinds of scenarios as to who killed him. It could be drug lords, it could be longtime rivals. All we know is a good man is dead and we mourn his loss.'[113]

The investigation of Qadir's murder, like that of Abdul Rehman five months before, turned up no real suspects beyond the ten *chowkidars* guarding the ministry. But it underscored the vulnerability of the jewel in the administration's crown, Hamid Karzai, whose safety had been the responsibility of 70 bodyguards provided by the defence ministry, 'simple soldiers who don't know much about organising security', according to one presidential aide. On 22 July, Rumsfeld announced that a team of 45 US Special Forces had moved into the Argh to take charge of the president's protection, not in reaction to any specific threat, he said, but to ensure that 'the Afghan people do not have an interruption in their leadership, having just completed that process'.[114] Fahim viewed the decision as a slur on his loyalty, indicative of the depth of the breakdown in Karzai's trust, but it made lesser Afghans equally uneasy. 'It doesn't create a good feeling for Afghans to see their president have foreign security guards,' said the former mayor of Kabul.[115] 'Whose president will he be if he is not guarded by Afghan soldiers?' asked another.

But there were people who very much wanted to 'interrupt' the leadership. Scarcely a week after the Special Forces took over Karzai's security, a police search of a Toyota Corolla uncovered 400–600 kg of C-4 explosives hidden in its door panels. The driver, described as a 'foreigner', had planned to crash the vehicle into the 'national leadership' convoy, according to an Afghan intelligence statement.[116] The random but often inaccurate attacks against the US and its allies persisted, beginning with a three-hour firefight at an Afghan army base in Kabul on 7 August in which 15 people died. The following day, a sniper shot and wounded a US soldier on patrol in Paktia and, 24 hours later, Jalalabad was rocked by an explosion at a construction company which left ten dead and 25 injured. In spite of their frequency, ISAF took some comfort from the fact the attacks were rarely targeted at causing maximum damage to either the military or civilians. Three explosions in Kabul at the end of August hit an empty cinema, a storm drain by the communications ministry and a ditch in front of the UN guesthouse. The bombers seemingly intended to keep people on their toes, rather than blow them out of their shoes.

Paratroopers from the crack 82nd Airborne Division replaced 10th Mountain Division in July, building to a maximum strength of 4,000 a month later, or half the total US military presence. Though US operations continued to prioritise the southeast, a new forward base had been built over the summer at Topchy, Kunar province, and garrisoned with 500 Special Forces. Their goal was to neutralise the perceived threat from Hekmatyar: a rocket attack was launched against the camp of one of his most senior commanders, Kashmir Khan, at the end of July. But Special Forces also conducted patrols close to Kunar's frontier with Chitral district in Pakistan's North West Frontier Province, intimidating villagers as they went. Further south, in mid-August, Special Forces launched a joint operation around Shah-i Kot and Zurmat with 600 troops from the 82nd in another bid to winkle out the Al Qa'ida loyalists they failed to kill the previous March and to destroy their arms caches. Fresh from Fort Bragg, North Carolina, the men of the 82nd went about their work with enthusiasm but they had much to learn about Afghan hospitality. 'They knocked down doors, pouring into homes, terrifying everybody, beating people, mistreating people,' said the Zurmat mayor. 'Why do the Americans come and search our women?'[117]

Since the raid on Band Taimore, the disrespect shown by US troops to rural Afghans and their womenfolk had been turned into a rallying cry by those opposed to Karzai more on political or religious grounds. Even the Special Forces admitted that the 82nd had ruined relationships they had built up with nearby villages, 'setting back their counter-insurgency and intelligence operations by at least six months'.[118] In the last week of August, Arabic-language pamphlets began circulating in Pashtun districts, signed by the unknown 'Secret Army of Mujahedin', which claimed responsibility for 21 separate attacks against US forces since 1 June. Interestingly, first among the new movement's three goals was 'to avenge the innocent martyrs of the brutal US bombing of Afghanistan', a clear reference to the wedding party massacre in July – but an open invitation also to any Pashtun whose mother or wife had been dishonoured by US soldiers, or whose son had disappeared in the Dasht-i Leili. '*Jihad* against American forces is compulsory,' the pamphlet read, 'and *jihad* against American puppets is also compulsory.'[119]

The State Department was also concerned that Karzai's US bodyguard was too provocative of local tensions. At the end of August it announced that the Special Forces detail would soon be replaced by agents of the Diplomatic Security Service (DSS), the unit providing protection for heads of state visiting Washington, amid accusations the Pentagon was again distancing itself from 'peacekeeping operations' and that DSS's civilian personnel were incapable of operating in the permanent free-fire zone of Afghanistan.[120] The plan, fortunately, was never implemented. Karzai flew to Kandahar on 4 September to attend the wedding party of his youngest brother, Ahmed Wali, and pay respects at the Ahmed Shah Baba shrine, across from the governor's palace, where many of the mujahedin who fought the Soviet Union were buried. He was glad of the break. Three days earlier, a trio of bombs and mines exploded close to the twin symbols of the old Soviet embassy and the US base at Bagram, killing five Afghans and wounding 22, many of them, alarmingly, engaged in mine clearance operations. The battle with the donors was proving equally frustrating. Of the $1.8 billion promised for 2002, they had delivered around $1 billion in grants to the UN and partner NGOs, but only $150 million to the government's reconstruction programme. Karzai had to demonstrate solid progress in the form of roads, repairs, houses and jobs if he were to recapture the energy briefly extinguished by the *Loya Jirga*, but still hanging, unharvested and unpressed, in the post-Taliban sunrise.

The following morning, a small bomb was detonated near Kabul's information ministry, attracting curious onlookers from a market crowded with women shopping for the weekend. Minutes later, a car bomb exploded in front of a nearby shop selling TVs and satellite dishes, killing at least 30 civilians and injuring a further 170 in the most serious blow against the government since the Taliban's overthrow. Karzai heard news of the attack in Kandahar where he had just finished inspecting Governor Gul Agha's recently renovated mansion. 'It's very sad,' he said, 'it's a horrible thing to happen to our people.'[121] A few minutes later, he was driving from the palace to receive the applause of well-wishers when a figure in military uniform stepped out and fired four shots at his window, narrowly missing the president but winging the governor. The assailant was promptly tackled by a young man standing nearby, who forced him to the ground where they were both cut down by the guns of Karzai's American bodyguard. 'He was the only person who reached forward to shake Karzai's hand,' said the brother of the young man, later identified as Azimullah Khaksar, a seller of plastic bottles in the Kandahar bazaar. 'He wanted to kiss his hand.'[122] Blame for the two near-simultaneous attacks was quickly attached to Al Qa'ida, but the would-be assassin in Kandahar had a rather more suggestive history of grievance. Abdul Rahman had been hired only four days before the attack to guard Gul Agha's new mansion, in spite of a history of service with the Taliban that was no serious bar to employment in the new south. What was perhaps more telling were his origins. Rahman hailed from Kajaki district in Helmand, 100 miles to the northwest of Kandahar, but less than a day's walk from Kakrak, Uruzgan, scene of the wedding party killings and the more abusive of the US searches for Mullah Omar.

After midnight, Karzai flew back to Kabul on a C-130 transport while helicopters patrolled the skies over Kandahar. He had a crucial meeting to discuss radios, lubricants, trucks, fuel, spare parts and military helicopters with Defence Minister Sergei Ivanov of Russia, the first in the post to visit Afghanistan since the end of the Soviet occupation. After the meeting, amid the intense security that followed the attempt to kill him, Karzai flew through the Panjshir valley to the black-marble tomb of Massoud at Bazarak to pay his respects before the anniversary of his death, two days shy of 11 September. 'We will continue to go and fulfil the objectives and desires of the man who lies buried under the ground here,' he said.[123]

Ivanov, who had brought a wreath a day earlier, removed his shoes before entering the tomb and bowed. 'If a fight is over and the defeated enemy comes with an offering, like a sheep or other bounty, he is forgiven,' said a former Massoud bodyguard, now watching over his grave. 'When Ivanov bowed before Massoud's grave today, even if he had killed my father, I would have forgiven him.'[124]

Further south that Saturday, the coffin of Azimullah Khaksar was carried to the martyrs' cemetery at Ahmed Shah Baba on a tank. Five hundred people, including Gul Agha, turned out for the funeral of the bottle-seller, whose father flourished a sheet of paper found on his dead body. Azimullah had written: 'God willing, the time has come for me to meet Hamid Karzai. I will kiss his hand. I want to be a martyr for Afghanistan.'

'That was his goal – to meet Hamid Karzai,' said his brother. 'He met his goal.'

Notes

Chapter 1

1. Nancy Hatch Dupree, *Afghanistan Through the Eyes of Pakistani Cartoonists*, Baba, 1994
2. *Sunday Times*, 29 September 1996; *Guardian*, 12 October 1996
3. *Guardian*, 12 October 1996
4. Ibid.
5. *Sunday Times*, 29 September 1996; *Guardian*, 12 October 1996
6. *Daily Telegraph*, 28 September 1996; *Guardian*, 12 October 1996; interview with Terry Pfizer, UNHCR, January 1997
7. *Sunday Times*, 29 September 1996; *Guardian*, 12 October 1996
8. *Guardian*, 12 October 1996; personal interview, January 1997
9. *Sunday Times*, 29 September 1996
10. *Guardian*, 2 October 1996
11. Personal interview, January 1997
12. *International Herald Tribune*, 11 March 1992
13. UNICEF, *Country Programme Management Plan, Strategic Review*, 1996
14. Frantz Fanon, *A Dying Colonialism*, Pelican Books, 1970
15. *Guardian*, 21 October 1996
16. Taliban decree, translated by Acbar, 6 January 1997
17. Amnesty International, *Afghanistan: Grave Abuses in the Name of Religion*, November 1996; personal interview, January 1997
18. Amnesty International, *Afghanistan: Grave Abuses*
19. Personal interview, January 1997
20. *Guardian*, 24 December 1997
21. *The Nation*, 11 May 1996
22. Ibid., 19 October 1996
23. Personal interview, January 1997
24. *New York Times International*, 31 December 1996
25. *Jane's Intelligence Review*, Vol. 7, No. 7
26. Ibid.
27. Personal interview, January 1997
28. *The World Today*, March 1996
29. *The Muslim*, 9 September 1996
30. Ibid., 12 September 1996; *Frontier Post*, 12 September 1996
31. *The Muslim*, 12 September 1996
32. *Frontier Post*, 2 December 1996

Chapter 2

1. John Fullerton, 'The Soviet Occupation of Afghanistan', *Far Eastern Economic Review*, 1983
2. *Asiaweek*, 12 February 1996
3. Barnett R. Rubin, *The Search for Peace in Afghanistan*, Yale University Press, 1995
4. Ibid.
5. Fullerton, '*The Soviet Occupation*'
6. Amnesty International, *Human Rights Defenders in Afghanistan*, November 1996

7. *BAAG*, 10 October 1994
8. *Jane's Intelligence Review*, April 1996
9. Rubin, *The Search for Peace*
10. Ibid.
11. Ibid.
12. Ibid.
13. *Jane's Intelligence Review*, Vol. 7, No. 7
14. Rubin, *The Search for Peace*
15. *Jane's Intelligence Review*, March 1993
16. *BAAG*, 24 August 1992
17. Robert Byron, *The Road to Oxiana*, Macmillan and Co., 1937
18. *BAAG*, 15 April 1994
19. Ibid., 24 August 1992
20. Economist Intelligence Unit, *Country Profile*, 1993–94
21. Personal interview, UNICEF, 1995
22. *BAAG*, 24 August 1992
23. Rubin, *The Search for Peace*
24. Personal interview, December 1997
25. Amnesty International, *Women in Afghanistan: A Human Rights Disaster*, May 1992
26. UNHCR Repatriation Statistics 1992 (published May 1997); *BAAG*, 30 September 1992
27. *BAAG*, 15 April 1994; *BAAG*, 10 October 1994
28. Ibid., 10 October 1994
29. Ibid.
30. Ibid.

Chapter 3

1. *Time*, 31 March 1997; *New York Times International*, 31 December 1996
2. Barnett R. Rubin, *The Search for Peace in Afghanistan*, Yale University Press, 1995
3. UN document, *Profile of Afghan Leaders and Personalities* (undated)
4. *New York Times International*, 31 December 1996
5. Ibid.
6. *BAAG*, 10 October 1994
7. Economist Intelligence Unit, 4/1994
8. Ibid., 1/1995
9. *Jane's Defence Weekly*, Vol. 7, No. 7
10. Economist Intelligence Unit, 4/1994
11. *Time*, 27 February 1995
12. Rubin, *The Search for Peace*; UN Special Mission to Afghanistan, July 1994
13. Amnesty International, *Responsibility for Human Rights Disaster*, September 1995
14. Ibid.
15. *Time*, 27 February 1995
16. Agence France-Presse, 18 November 1996
17. *Jane's Defence Weekly*, 9 October 1996
18. *BAAG*, 16 February 1995
19. Economist Intelligence Unit, 2/1996
20. UNICEF's Marc Powe in a letter on 3 February 1997; *Daily Telegraph*, 22 February 1997
21. *Jane's Defence Weekly*, Vol. 7, No. 7
22. *Time*, 27 October 1995
23. Personal interview, January 1997
24. Economist Intelligence Unit, 3/1995

25. Agence France-Presse, 24 December 1995; UN *Weekly Update*, 2 January 1996
26. *Sunday Times*, 24 March 1996
27. UN *Weekly Update*, 19 February 1996
28. Economist Intelligence Unit, 3/1996
29. Ibid., 4/1996
30. Ibid.
31. *New York Times Service*, 17 February 1997
32. *Jane's Defence Weekly*, 27 November 1996
33. *Independent*, 10 October 1996
34. *Jane's Intelligence Review*, August 1997
35. *BAAG*, 24 July 1996; *Jane's Intelligence Review*, August 1997
36. *The Nation*, 8 October 1996
37. UNICEF's Marc Powe in a letter dated 3 February 1997
38. Economist Intelligence Unit, 1/1997
39. Ibid.
40. Ibid.
41. Powe letter, 3 February 1997

Chapter 4

1. *Guardian*, 4 January 1997
2. *Time*, 31 March 1997
3. *Observer*, 9 March 1997
4. Ibid.
5. *Guardian*, 4 January 1997
6. *New York Times International*, 31 December 1996
7. *Le Monde Diplomatique*, February 1997; private interview, Kabul, February 1997
8. *The Nation*, 19 November 1996
9. Louis Dupree, 'Tribal warfare in Afghanistan and Pakistan', in Akbar S. Ahmed and David M. Hart (eds), *Islamic Tribal Societies*, Routledge & Kegan Paul, London, 1994
10. *The Muslim*, 10 September 1996
11. *Frontier Post*, 20 October 1996
12. *New York Times International*, 31 December 1996
13. V. Gregorian, *The Emergence of Modern Afghanistan: Politics of Reform and Modernisation 1880–1946*, Stanford, California 1969. Cited in Asgar Christiansen, 'Aiding Afghanistan: The Background and Prospects for Reconstruction in a Fragmented Society', SIDA, Stockholm, 1994
14. Amnesty International, *Afghanistan: Grave Abuses in the Name of Religion*, November 1996
15. *Frontier Post*, 11 February 1996
16. Amnesty International, *Afghanistan: Grave Abuses*, November 1996; Amnesty appeal, *Fear of Further Amputations*, 24 April 1997; *Guardian*, 24 October 1996
17. *Daily Telegraph*, 27 July 1997
18. *BAAG*, 15 November 1996
19. *Guardian*, 21 December 1996
20. Personal interview, Kabul, February 1997
21. *Guardian*, 7 November 1996
22. Amnesty International, *Women in Afghanistan: The Violations Continue*, June 1997
23. *Guardian*, 6 January 1997
24. *The Nation*, 19 November 1996
25. *Guardian*, 4 January 1996
26. *Le Monde Diplomatique*, February 1997
27. *The News*, 4 October 1996

28. *The Nation*, 19 November 1996; *The News*, 4 October 1996
29. Private interview, Kabul, January 1997
30. *Pakistan Times*, 11 January 1997
31. UN *Weekly Update*, 2 January 1997
32. Personal interview, January 1997
33. *BAAG*, 24 April 1996
34. Ibid., 1 October 1996; *Guardian*, 4 January 1997; *Time*, 31 March 1997
35. *Jane's Defence Weekly*, 27 November 1996
36. *Economist Intelligence Quarterly*, March 1995
37. *BAAG*, 24 April 1996
38. *Economist Intelligence Quarterly*, March 1995
39. *Guardian*, 24 December 1996
40. *The Nation*, 11 May 1996
41. Reuters, 10 June 1997
42. Taliban prohibition, No. 6240, 26 September 1996
43. *Guardian*, 12 December 1996
44. Taliban edict, 15 December 1996
45. Interview, Kabul, February 1996
46. Interview, Kabul, February 1996
47. *The Muslim*, 7 October 1996
48. *Al-Majallah*, 23 October 1996

Chapter 5

1. *Los Angeles Times*, 23 November 1995
2. *Washington Post*, 19–20 July 1992
3. Barnett R. Rubin, *The Search for Peace in Afghanistan*, Yale University Press, 1995
4. *The News*, 25 August 1996
5. Economist Intelligence Unit, 1/1995
6. *Frontier Post*, 22 August 1996
7. *The Nation*, 6 May 1996
8. Ibid., 19 October 1996
9. Ibid., 2 October 1996
10. *The News*, 2 September 1996
11. *Frontier Post*, 7 October 1996
12. *Time*, 4 November 1996
13. Economist Intelligence Unit, 4/1994
14. *Jane's Intelligence Review*, Vol. 7, No. 7; *Le Monde Diplomatique*, February 1997
15. *Jane's Intelligence Review*, December 1996
16. Personal interview, January 1997
17. Speech to the UN General Assembly, 4 October 1995
18. *The News*, 20 December 1995
19. Economist Intelligence Unit, 3/1995; *The World Today*, March 1996
20. *The News*, 12 March 1996
21. *BAAG*, 15 October 1995; Economist Intelligence Unit, 3/1995
22. *The World Today*, March 1996
23. *BAAG*, 28 March 1996
24. Economist Intelligence Unit, 2/1996
25. *BAAG*, 30 January 1996
26. *The News*, 12 March 1996
27. Economist Intelligence Unit, 2/1996
28. *The Muslim*, 23 May 1996; *BAAG*, 1 October 1996
29. Agence France-Presse, 25 May 1996

30. *The Nation*, 11 May 1996
31. *The News*, 2 September 1996
32. *Frontier Post*, 12 May 1996
33. *The Muslim*, 5 May 1996
34. *BAAG*, 1 October 1996
35. Agence France-Presse, 11 January 1997

Chapter 6

1. Barnett R. Rubin, *The Search for Peace in Afghanistan*, Yale University Press, 1995
2. Agence France-Presse, 25 May 1996
3. UN Special Mission to Afghanistan, July 1994
4. Ibid.
5. Personal interview, February 1997
6. Rubin, *The Search for Peace*
7. Economist Intelligence Unit, 3/1995
8. *The Muslim*, 6 November 1996
9. Economist Intelligence Unit, 3/1995
10. Ibid.
11. *The News*, 20 December 1995
12. *BAAG*, 1 October 1996; *Guardian*, 4 January 1997
13. *Guardian*, 17 October 1996; *The Muslim*, 23 October 1996; *The Nation*, 25 October 1996
14. <www.rediff.com>
15. Ibid.
16. *Guardian*, 12 February 1997
17. *BAAG*, 15 June 1994; *The Nation*, 11 May 1996
18. Economist Intelligence Unit, 3/1997
19. *Guardian*, 12 February 1997
20. Economist Intelligence Unit, 4/1996
21. UNICEF's Marc Powe in a letter on 3 February 1997; *Daily Telegraph*, 22 September 1997
22. *Jane's Intelligence Review*, Anthony Davies, August 1997
23. *Time*, 9 June 1997
24. *Jane's Intelligence Review*, Anthony Davies, August 1997
25. <www.rediff.com>
26. *Jane's Intelligence Review*, Anthony Davies, August 1997
27. *The Times*, 26 May 1997; *Time*, 9 June 1997
28. *Daily Telegraph*, 26 May 1997
29. *Jane's Intelligence Review*, Anthony Davies, August 1997
30. Ibid.; *Time*, 9 June 1997
31. *Daily Telegraph*, 27 May 1997
32. *Time*, 9 June 1997; *Daily Telegraph*, 27 May 1997
33. *Daily Telegraph*, 27 May 1997
34. *Guardian*, 11 June 1997
35. *New York Times*, 25 August 1997; *Jane's Intelligence Review*, August 1997
36. *Economist Intelligence Unit*, 3/1997
37. *Middle East International*, 13 June 1997
38. Amnesty International, November 1997
39. Reuters, 10 June 1997
40. *Time*, 9 June 1997

Chapter 7

1. *Jane's Intelligence Review*, February 1996
2. Bridas Corporation, *Corporate Profile*, 1996
3. Economist Intelligence Unit, *Country Profile, Afghanistan, 1994–1995*
4. Ibid.
5. World of Information, *Turkmenistan*, 1995
6. World of Information, *Azerbaijan*, 1995
7. *Oil and Gas Journal*, 20 June 1994
8. *Jane's Intelligence Review*, February 1996
9. World of Information, *Azerbaijan*, 1995
10. 'Russia, the West and the Caspian Energy Hub', *Middle East Journal*, Vol. 49, No. 2, 1995
11. *Jane's Intelligence Review*, February 1996
12. *Houston Chronicle*, 27 June 1996
13. Carlos Bulgheroni, keynote address, 13 March 1996, TIOGE '96
14. *Transitions*, October 1998
15. Arab Press Service, *Saudi Arabia Petroleum Industry*, 23–30 October, Sunningdale Publications, 1996; *Newsweek*, 10 December 2001
16. Arab Press Service, *Saudi Arabia Petroleum Industry*; <www.fas.org/irp/congress/1992_rpt/bcci>
17. *Houston Chronicle*, 27 June 1996
18. Ibid.
19. *Transitions*, October 1998
20. *New York Times International*, 31 December 1996
21. Frédéric Grare, 'La nouvelle donné énergetique autour de la Mer Caspienne', CERI (Centre for International Studies and Research), No. 23, June 1997
22. *The News*, 16 March 1996
23. Economist Intelligence Unit, 4/1996
24. Reuters, 1 October 1996
25. *Transitions*, October 1998

Chapter 8

1. Yossef Bodansky, 'Rise of HizbAllah International', *Strategic Policy*, Vol. XXIV, No. 8, 3 August 1996
2. Ibid.
3. *The Muslim*, 23 May 1996
4. *New York Herald Tribune*, 11 March 1992
5. Anthony Hyman, 'Arab Involvement in the Afghan War', *Beirut Review*, spring 1994
6. Barnett R. Rubin, *The Search for Peace in Afghanistan*, Yale University Press, 1995
7. Ibid.
8. James Bruce, 'Arab Veterans of the Afghan War', *Jane's Intelligence Review*, Vol. 7, No. 4; *Beirut Review*, spring 1994
9. *Beirut Review*, spring 1994; private interview, Kunar valley, December 1994
10. *BAAG*, 1 October 1993; Economist Intelligence Unit, 1/1996
11. *Jane's Intelligence Review*, Vol. 7, No. 4.
12. Ibid.
13. *Guardian*, 17 July 1997; Joint CIA/FBI statement, 17 June 1997; <www.odci.gov/cia/public_affairs/press_release>
14. *BAAG*, 1 October 1993
15. Agence France-Presse, 17 February 1997
16. <www.fas.org/irp/congress/1992_rpt/bcci/>; *Beirut Review*, spring 1994
17. *Intelligence Newsletter*, No. 300, 28 October 1996

18. *Boston Globe*, 27 August 1998
19. *Nida'ul-Islam*, October–November 1996; <www.cia.com.au/islam/articles/15/ LADIN>; *Intelligence Newsletter* No. 300, 28 October 1996
20. *The Times*, 10 May 1997; *Intelligence Newsletter*, No. 239, 20 April 1994; <www.indigo-net.com/dossiers>
21. *Intelligence Newsletter*, No. 331, 19 March 1997; *Independent*, 22 March 1997
22. *Newsweek* (International Edition), 13 October 1997
23. State Department press release, February 1996; *Sunday Times*, 27 October 1996
24. Chris Kozlow, 'The Bombing of Khobar Towers: Who Did It and Who Funded It', *Jane's Intelligence Review*, December 1997; *Sunday Times*, 27 October 1996
25. *Jane's Intelligence Review*, December 1997
26. Ibid.
27. *Strategic Policy*, Vol. XXIV, No. 8, 3 August 1996
28. Ibid.
29. Ibid.
30. Ibid.
31. Ibid.
32. Thomas Hunter, 'Bomb School: International Terrorist Training Camps', *Jane's Intelligence Review*, March 1997
33. *Intelligence Newsletter*, No. 312, 29 May 1997; *Jane's Intelligence Review*, March 1997
34. *Intelligence Newsletter*, No. 312, 29 May 1997
35. Ibid.
36. *Independent*, 22 March 1997; *Guardian*, 17 July 1997
37. *Al-Quds al-Arabi*, 27 November 1996
38. Ibid.
39. *Independent*, 22 March 1997
40. *Al-Quds al-Arabi*, 27 November 1996
41. 'Osama Bin Laden: Holy Terror?', *CNN Impact*, 12 May 1997
42. *The Times*, 10 May 1997
43. *Sunday Times*, 27 October 1996
44. Private interview, Jalalabad, February 1997
45. *Sunday Times*, 27 October 1996
46. *Guardian*, 28 November 1996
47. Agence France-Presse, 10 December 1996
48. Roger Howard, 'Wrath of Islam: HUA Analysed', *Jane's Intelligence Review*, October 1997
49. <www.afghan-government.com/news/97_11_02.html>
50. <www.rediff.com>
51. *Jane's Intelligence Review*, October 1997
52. International Institute of Strategic Studies, Vol. 4, Issue 8, October 1998
53. *The Nation*, 17 February 1997
54. *Jane's Intelligence Review*, October 1997
55. *Intelligence Newsletter*, No. 331, 19 March 1997
56. Reuters, 17 April 1998; <www.afghanistan-center.com/news>

Chapter 9

1. *Middle East Intelligence*, 17 February 1995
2. Reuters, 10 June 1997
3. Interview, Jalalabad, February 1997
4. *The Nation*, 25 September 1996
5. Interview, Kabul, February 1997

6. United Nations Drug Control Programme (UNDCP), *Afghanistan Opium Poppy Survey*, 1994
7. Alfred W. McCoy, *The Politics of Heroin: CIA Complicity in the Global Drug Trade*, second edition, Lawrence Hill Books, 1992
8. Sumita Kumar, 'Drug Trafficking in Pakistan', New Delhi Institute for Defence Studies and Analyses, 1995
9. McCoy, *The Politics of Heroin*
10. Ibid.
11. Ibid.
12. UNDCP, *Afghanistan Opium*
13. Amnesty International, 'Afghanistan', November 1995
14. Thomas Hunter, 'Manportable SAMs: The Airline Anathema', *Jane's Intelligence Review*, October 1996
15. *Pakistan Times*, 30 September 1996
16. McCoy, *The Politics of Heroin*
17. McCoy, *The Politics of Heroin*; Anon., 'Afghanistan: The Taliban Face an Opium Dilemma', *Geopolitical Drug Dispatch*, No. 63, January 1997
18. *Washington Post*, 12 September 1994
19. CIA Report, 'Heroin in Pakistan: Sowing the wind', reproduced in *Friday Times*, 3 September 1993
20. Anon., 'Tajikistan: Three borders for the labs', *Geopolitical Drug Dispatch*, No. 63, January 1997
21. UNDCP, *Afghanistan Opium Poppy Survey*, 1996
22. *Geopolitical Drug Dispatch*, No. 63, January 1997
23. Ibid.
24. Ibid.
25. Ibid.
26. Amnesty International, *Afghanistan: Grave Abuses in the Name of Religion*, November 1996
27. *Geopolitical Drug Dispatch*, No. 63, January 1997
28. Interview, Islamabad, February 1997
29. *Geopolitical Drug Dispatch*, No. 63, January 1997

Chapter 10

1. *Independent*, 8 October 1996
2. *The News*, 30 September 1996
3. Ibid., 6 October; 30 November 1996
4. UNICEF, *Country Programme Management Plan, Strategy Review Exercise*, 1996
5. *Guardian*, 27 December 1996
6. Ibid.
7. Amnesty International, *Afghanistan: Grave Abuses in the Name of Religion*, November 1996; *Women in Afghanistan: The Violations Continue*, June 1997
8. Agence France-Presse, 6 October and 13 November 1996
9. *BAAG*, 15 November 1996
10. Personal interview, January 1997
11. Ibid.
12. Ibid.
13. Personal interview, December 1995
14. Agence France-Presse, 20 October 1996
15. Personal interview, January 1997
16. Ibid.
17. Economist Intelligence Unit, 4/1996

18. Email, February 1998
19. Carol A. Le Duc and Homa Sabri, *Room to Manoeuvre: Study on Women's Programming*, UN Development Programme, July–September 1996
20. Email, February 1998
21. *Guardian*, 11 November 1995
22. UNHCR fax, 20 May 1998, *Refugee Statistics*, 1997
23. Personal interview, January 1997
24. Email, February 1998
25. Personal interview, April 1996
26. Memo by Michael Scott, *In Lieu of a Conclusions and Recommendations Section – Some Questions*, 12 November 1996
27. Kabul Information Forum, *Position Statement of International Agencies Working in Kabul*, 5 October 1996
28. *The News*, 6 October 1996; UN Assistance to Afghanistan, *Weekly Update*, No. 187; edict by Amr Bil Marof Wa Nai An Munkir, late November 1996
29. Agence France-Presse, 5 November 1996
30. *The News*, 30 September 1996
31. *Frontier Post*, 2 October 1996; *The News*, 23 December 1996
32. Reuters, 3 December 1996
33. Jim Mohan, UNICEF, personal interview, January 1997
34. Paul Barker, CARE, personal interview, January 1996
35. David Bellamy's memo to Qazi Shaukat Fareed, UN Department of Humanitarian Affairs, 18 November 1996
36. Letter to Benon Sevan from Qazi Shaukat Fareed, UN Department of Humanitarian Affairs, 18 November 1996
37. Agence France-Presse, 10 October 1996; *BAAG*, 15 November 1996
38. Personal interview, February 1997
39. Amnesty International, 21 March 1997
40. Nancy Dupree, interview, December 1995
41. ACBAR *Annual Report* 1993/94; David Lockhart, UNDP, personal interview, December 1995
42. Personal interview, December 1995
43. Personal interview, January 1997
44. *Guardian*, 27 May 1997
45. Personal interviews, February 1997; International Forum of Assistance to Afghanistan, Working Paper 14; Le Duc and Sabri, *Room to Manoeuvre*
46. International Forum of Assistance to Afghanistan, *Summary of Proceedings*
47. Internal UNICEF memo, undated, cited January 1997
48. Ibid.
49. UNICEF press release, 1 April 1997

Chapter 11

1. <www.taleban.com/comment.html> *Massacre of Prisoners in Northern Afghanistan*, note handed to UNDP, 22 December 1997
2. Ibid.
3. Ibid.
4. *New York Times Service*, 25 August 1997
5. *US Veteran Dispatch*, June/July/August 1997
6. Ibid.
7. *OMRI*, 14 October 1996; <www.eia.doe.gov/emeu/cabs/turkmen.html>
8. *Washington Post Service*, 12 January 1998; 'Pipeline to Power', *Transitions*, October 1998

9. *Washington Post Service*, 12 January 1998
10. *Jane's Intelligence Review*, August 1997
11. Amnesty International, *Concerned About the Safety of Opposition General*, 23 May 1997
12. UNDP email, September 1997
13. *Jane's Intelligence Review*, August 1997
14. <www.afghan-government.com/news/97_10_10.html>
15. Association for Peace and Democracy for Afghanistan, 24 September 1997
16. Reuters, 15 October 1997
17. RFE/RL, 12 September 1997
18. UNDP email, September 1997
19. Reuters, 15 October 1997; UNDP email
20. UNDP email, September 1997
21. Ibid.
22. Reuters, 8 November 1997; IPS, 26 November 1997
23. Reuters, 8 November 1997
24. Ibid., 13 November 1997
25. UNDP email, September 1997
26. *Private Eye*, 2 October 1998
27. *Journal of the American Medical Association*, 5 August 1998
28. *IPI Report*, Fourth Quarter 1997
29. Amnesty International USA, 24 June 1997
30. Reuters, 10 November 1997
31. *Index on Censorship*, interview with Emma Bonino, 2/1998
32. *IPI Report*, Fourth Quarter 1997
33. *Washington Post Service*, 12 January 1998
34. Ibid.
35. *New York Times*, 5 November 1997
36. Reuters, 18 November
37. *Transitions*, October 1998
38. Ibid., October 1998
39. *Washington Post Service*, 12 January 1998
40. Reuters, 22 July 1997; *Washington Post Service*, 12 January 1998
41. Press release, *Agencia Efe*, 8 March 1997
42. *Transitions*, October 1998
43. *UNOCAL and Slave Trade in Burma*, <www.sf-frontlines.com/mar98/columns/burma.html>
44. News Service Amnesty International, 133/97, 25 July 1997
45. Reuters, 13 July 1997
46. Economist Intelligence Unit, 2/1997
47. Reuters, 11 October 1997
48. Ibid.
49. Ibid., 11 November 1997
50. UN Department of Public Information, *Reporting Human Rights Violations in Afghanistan*, 10 November 1997
51. Reuters, 13 November 1997
52. Amnesty International, *Flagrant Abuse of the Right to Life and Dignity*, April 1998; <www.afghanistan-center.com/news_98_03.html>
53. Amnesty International, April 1998
54. Ibid.
55. *The Nation*, 16 April 1998; <www.afghan-web.com/aop/yest.html>
56. *The Nation*, 16 April 1998
57. Network, *Vision of Islamic Republic of Iran*, 12 September 1998; Reuters, 17 September 1998

58. Afghan Islamic Press, 13 February 1998
59. Ibid.
60. *ICRC Newsletter*, March 1998
61. *International Herald Tribune*, 26 March 1998
62. Reuters, 16 April 1998
63. Ibid.
64. *Intelligence Newsletter*, No. 331, 19 March 1998; *International Herald Tribune*, 1 September, 1998
65. *Al-Quds al-Arabi*, 'Text of *Fatwah* Urging *Jihad* against Americans', 23 February 1998
66. Agence France-Presse, 6 September 1998
67. Reuters, 17 April 1998
68. *Jane's Defence Weekly*, 13 May 1998; Reuters, 17 April 1998
69. *Jane's Defence Weekly*, 13 May 1998
70. Ibid.
71. *International Institute for Strategic Studies*, Vol. 4/8, October 1998
72. Reuters, 2 June 1998; 5 June 1998
73. Ibid.; *The Scotsman*, 31 July 1998
74. Ibid.
75. Ibid.
76. Ibid.; Reuters, 4 June 1998
77. Reuters, 4 June 1998; 6 July 1998
78. Ibid., 6 July 1998
79. Ibid., 20 July 1998; 23 July 1998
80. Ibid., 19 July 1998; 20 July 1998
81. Ibid., 6 July 1998
82. Ibid.
83. Ibid., 22 July 1998
84. Ibid.
85. Ibid., 23 July 1998
86. Ibid.; Agence Europe, 23 July 1998
87. *Jane's Defence Weekly*, 26 August 1998
88. Ibid.
89. Iran Network 1 TV, 4 August 1998; ITAR-TASS news agency, 5 August 1998; Reuters, 17 August 1998
90. Human Rights Watch, November 1998, Vol. 10, No. X; *Middle East International*, 13 November 1998
91. Human Rights Watch, November 1998, Vol. 10, No. X; *Middle East International*, 13 November 1998
92. Ibid.
93. Human Rights Watch, November 1998, Vol. 10, No. X
94. Ibid.; *Middle East International*, 13 November 1998
95. Human Rights Watch, November 1998, Vol. 10, No. X
96. Ibid.
97. Ibid.
98. *The News*, 3 November 1998
99. Amnesty International, *Flagrant Abuse*
100. Human Rights Watch, November 1998, Vol. 10, No. X
101. Ibid; *Middle East International*, 13 November 1998
102. Human Rights Watch, November 1998, Vol. 10, No. X
103. Ibid.
104. Ibid.
105. Ibid.
106. Ibid.
107. Ibid.

108. Ibid.
109. Agence France-Presse, 15 August 1998
110. *Middle East International*, 13 November 1998
111. Ibid.
112. Ibid.

Chapter 12

1. *Washington Post*, 21 September 1998
2. *New York Times*, 10 August 1998
3. *The Nation*, 21 September 1998
4. *New York Times*, 22 September 1998
5. *Independent*, 21 August 1998
6. Reuters, 8 August 1998
7. *Jang*, 5 September 1998
8. *Observer*, 21 August 1998
9. *Time*, 4 January 1999; *Newsweek*, 4 January 1999
10. *Observer*, 23 August 1998; *Sunday Times*, 23 August 1998
11. *Ettela'at*, 17 September 1998
12. *Frontier Post*, 31 October 1998
13. *Time*, 31 August 1998
14. *Jane's Defence Weekly*, 2 September 1998; RFE/RL, 12 September 1997; *Independent on Sunday*, 1 November 1998
15. *Time*, 31 August 1998
16. Ibid.
17. *Sunday Times*, 23 August 1998
18. Al-Jazeera TV, 12 September 1998, cited by Reuters, 14 September 1998
19. *Time*, 4 January 1999; *Electronic Telegraph*, 21 February 1999
20. *Guardian*, 22 August 1998
21. Ibid., 25 August 1998; *Jane's Defence Weekly*, 2 September 1998
22. *Wall Street Journal*, 28 October 1998
23. <www.elwatan.com/journal/html/2001/09/29/evenement.htm>
24. *Guardian*, 22 August 1998
25. *Jane's Defence Weekly*, 2 September 1998
26. *News International*, 5 September 1998
27. BBC World Service, 17 November 1998; Reuters, 17 November 1998
28. Reuters, 17 November 1998
29. *Guardian*, 21 August 1998
30. *Frontier Post*, 4 September 1998
31. *Hindu Online*, 11 November 1998
32. *Jane's Defence Weekly*, 2 September 1998
33. Al-Jazeera TV, 12 September 1998, cited by Reuters, 14 September 1998; *Sunday Times*, 13 September 1998
34. *Sunday Times*, 13 September 1998
35. *Washington Post*, 23 September 1999
36. Ibid., 21 September 1998
37. Ibid., pA27, 6 September 1998; *Guardian*, 5 October 1998
38. Reuters, 14 September 1998
39. Ibid., 16 September 1998
40. *New York Times Service*, 5 October 1998
41. *Le Monde*, 31 October 1998
42. Ibid.
43. *The Nation*, 16 April 1998; *The News*, 3 November 1998

44. *Frontier Post*, 31 October 1998
45. *The News*, 30 November 1998
46. Agence France-Presse, 1 October 1998
47. *A Message to the People of the USA*, 8 October 1998, via the Senate Commission on Foreign Relations
48. *Le Monde*, 31 October 1998
49. *The News*, 3 November 1998
50. Ibid., 12 May 1998
51. Agence France-Presse, 5 December 1998
52. *Fox Research*, 19 October 1998; *Observer*, 1 November 1998
53. Amnesty International, *Detention and Killing of Political Personalities*, March 1999
54. *Le Monde*, 31 October 1998
55. *Fox Research*, 19 October 1998; *The News*, 10 December 1998
56. *Observer*, 1 November 1998
57. *The News*, 10 December 1998

Chapter 13

1. *Guardian*, 1 March 1999
2. *New York Times Service*, 9 November 1998
3. *Time*, 4 January 1999; *Newsweek*, 4 January 1999
4. *Washington Post Service*, 23 September 1998; *Time*, 4 January 1999
5. *Time*, 4 January 1999
6. *The News*, 26 January 1999
7. *Newsweek*, 4 January 1999
8. *The News*, 4 February 1999
9. Associated Press, 11 November 1998
10. *The Nation*, 12 December 1999
11. *New York Times*, 5 December 1998; *Business Recorder*, 4 February 1999
12. *The News*, 6 December 1998
13. Reuters, 6 December 1998
14. *International Herald Tribune*, 1 September 1998; *Electronic Telegraph*, 21 February 1999
15. News Network International (NNI), 1 April 1999 <www.afghan-web.com/aop/today.html> (5 April 1999)
16. *Frontier Post*, 5 February 1999
17. *USA Today*, 11 December 1998; Associated Press, 24 February 1999; *Guardian*, 25 February 1999
18. *Middle East International*, 26 February 1999; *USA Today*, 11 March 1999
19. *New York Times*, 13 April 1999; *Boston Globe*, 15 May 1999
20. Agence France-Presse, 2 January 1999; Reuters, 3 January 1999; *Time*, 4 January 1999
21. *Middle East International*, 26 February 1999; *Far East Economic Review*, 11 March 1999
22. *Newsweek*, 22 February 1999
23. Reuters, 4 March 1999
24. *Middle East International*, 26 February 1999; Agence France-Presse, 30 November 1998
25. *Frontier Post*, 22 November 1998
26. 'Where's Osama?', *Global Intelligence Update*, 18 February 1998
27. *Al-Hayat*, 24 February 1999
28. *Guardian*, 1 March 1999
29. *Global Intelligence Update*, citing Voice of the Islamic Republic of Iran, 18 February 1999
30. *New York Times*, 13 April 1999

31. NNI, 28 January 1999
32. AAR, 6 March 1999
33. AAR, 20 July 1999
34. *Guardian*, 7 October 1999; *The News*, 15 March 1999
35. *Dawn*, 17 November 1998
36. *Guardian*, 24 February 1999; Amnesty International, *Detention and Killing of Political Personalities*, March 1999
37. *The News*, 15 July 1999
38. NNI, 26 January 1999
39. Associated Press, 3 March 1999
40. *Guardian*, 13 April 1999
41. Reuters, 27 September 1999
42. Agence France-Presse, 25 May 1999
43. Associated Press, 25 May 1999
44. Agence France-Presse, 22 May 1999
45. Ibid., 19 June 1999
46. *Times of India*, 14 July 1999
47. Associated Press, 10 June 1999
48. Agence France-Presse, 26 July 1999
49. <www.rediff.com>
50. *Electronic Telegraph*, 22 July 1999
51. Reuters, 30 July 1999
52. *Electronic Telegraph*, 22 July 1999
53. *Observer*, 4 July 1999
54. Ibid.
55. NNI, 21 July 1999
56. *Observer*, 4 July 1999
57. Associated Press, 6 July 1999
58. ABC News, 9 July 1999
59. Ibid.
60. *USA Today*, 19 October 1999
61. <www.onlinejournal.com/archive/11-03-01_Dowling-printable.pdf>
62. *Newsweek*, 10 December 2001
63. *The News*, 28 July 1999

Chapter 14

1. *Dawn*, 15 October 1999
2. <www.stratfor.com> *Special Report*, 9 July 1999; *The Nation*, 1 August 1999
3. <www.stratfor.com> *Special Report*
4. United Press International, 6 July 1999; Agence France-Presse, 20 September 1999
5. *Observer*, 27 June 1999
6. *Middle East International*, 15 October 1999
7. *The News*, 30 August 1999
8. Agence France-Presse, 3 August 1999
9. Ibid., 1 August 1999
10. *Guardian*, 30 July 1999; Agence France-Presse, 1 August 1999
11. Agence France-Presse, 3 August 1999
12. Ibid.
13. *New York Times*, 19 October 1999
14. Agence France-Presse, 4 August 1999; *Guardian*, 6 August 1999
15. UN *Weekly Update* 330, 14 September 1999

16. *International Herald Tribune*, 16 August 1999
17. *New York Times*, 19 October 1999
18. Agence France-Presse, 5 August 1999
19. Ibid., 26 July 1999
20. *The News*, 6 August 1999
21. BBC News, 9 August 1999; Agence France-Presse, 14 August 1999
22. Agence France-Presse, 30 August 1999
23. *New York Times*, 19 October 1999
24. *Frontier Post*, 6 August 1999; Reuters, 9 August 1999
25. *The News*, 11 September 1999
26. Ibid.
27. Reuters, 1 August 1999
28. *The News*, 24 August 1999
29. *Frontier Post*, 29 September 1999
30. *San José Mercury News*, 10 September 1999
31. Ibid.
32. *Times of India*, 20 September 1999
33. NNI, 27 August 1999
34. <www.stratfor.com/asia/specialreports/special81.htm>
35. *Guardian*, 19 October 1999
36. Ibid., 18 October 1999
37. AAR, 13 October 1999
38. <www.stratfor.com/asia/specialreports/special81.htm>
39. *Friday Times*, 1–7 October 1999
40. Ibid.
41. Ibid.
42. BBC News, 8 October 1999
43. NNI, 8 October 1999
44. *The News*, 8 October 1999
45. Reuters, 13 October 1999
46. Ibid.
47. *Frontier Post*, 10 October 1999
48. Ibid.
49. Agence France-Presse, 11 October 1999
50. *Observer*, 17 October 1999
51. *Frontline*, 19 November 1999
52. *Observer*, 17 October 1999; *Frontline*, 19 November 1999
53. *Frontline*, 19 November 1999
54. Ibid.
55. *Guardian*, 18 October 1999
56. *Frontier Post*, 14 October 1999; *Dawn*, 15 October 1999
57. *Frontline*, 19 November 1999
58. *Guardian*, 18 October 1999
59. Associated Press, 15 October 1999
60. *Dawn*, 4 November 1999
61. AAR, 13 October 1999
62. BBC News, 13 October 1999
63. *Frontier Post*, 13 October 1999
64. <www.stratfor.com> 19 November 1999
65. *M2 Communications*, 25 October 1999; UN Document S/PRST/1999/29
66. NNI, 28 October 1999
67. CNN, 15 November 1999
68. Agence France-Presse, 15 October 1999

Chapter 15

1. <www.realworldrescue.com>
2. Agence France-Presse, 16 November 2000
3. Associated Press, 12 November 1999
4. Agence France-Presse, 14 November 1999
5. Reuters, 12 November 1999
6. UN *Weekly Update*, 17 November 1999; NNI, 15 November 1999
7. Associated Press, 16 November 1999
8. <usinfo.state.gov/topical/pol/terror/00120502.htm>
9. *Friday Times*, 17–23 December 1999
10. *New York Times Service*, 17 December 2000
11. *Los Angeles Times*, 21 March 2000
12. *Asiaweek*, Vol. 25, No. 51, 24 December 1999
13. Interview with Peter Tomsen, Azadi Afghan Radio, 29 January 2000
14. Agence France-Presse, 18 December 1999
15. *Washington Post*, 22 February 2000
16. Agence France-Presse, 5 March 2000; *Sunday Times*, 4 November 2001
17. *Washington Post*, 24 April 2000
18. Agence France-Presse, 2 January 2000; *Time Asia*, 17 January 2000
19. UK General Assembly, *Statement of the Special Rapporteur on the Situation of Human Rights in Afghanistan*, 24 October 2000
20. *New York Times*, 24 January 2000
21. Ibid.
22. BBC News, 3 January 2000
23. *Dawn*, 24 February 2000
24. *New York Times*, 9 March 2000
25. *Times of India*, 10 August 2000; *Sunday Times*, 4 November 2001
26. Senate Foreign Relations Committee, testimony by Peter Tomsen, 20 July 2000
27. UN Office of the Coordinator for Afghanistan, *Afghanistan Outlook*, December 1999
28. UN General Assembly, *Statement of the Special Rapporteur*
29. *Times of India*, 21 October 2000
30. UN General Assembly, *Statement of the Special Rapporteur*
31. Ibid.
32. *Guardian*, 9 July 2000
33. Senate Foreign Relations Committee, testimony by Assistant Secretary of State Karl F. Inderfurth, 20 July 2000
34. Senate Foreign Relations Committee, testimony by Peter Tomsen
35. Personal interview with Wali Massoud, July 2000
36. Azadi Afghan News, 9 October 2000
37. *Daily Telegraph*, 3 October 2000
38. Ibid.
39. *Business Recorder*, 24 October 2000
40. *The Times*, 28 October 2000
41. *Daily Telegraph*, 3 October 2000
42. BBC News, 30 September 2000
43. CNN World News, 23 October 2000; *Business Recorder*, 24 October 2000
44. <www.defencejournal.com/2000/nov/talibaan.htm>
45. NNI, 8 October 2000
46. *The News*, 19 and 21 October 2000
47. *New York Times*, 24 November 2000
48. *New York Times*, 24 and 27 November 2000
49. BBC News, 13 November 2000
50. *Guardian*, 7 November 2000; Reuters, 13 November 2000

51. Reuters, 13 November 2000
52. Agence France-Presse, 25 October 2000
53. *Al-Hayat*, 1 November 2000
54. United Press International, 1 November 2000

Chapter 16

1. Associated Press, 20 June 2001
2. *New Yorker*, 14 January 2002
3. <www.chron.com/content/chronicle/special/01/terror/victims/oneill.html>
4. *New York Times*, 19 August 2001
5. *New Yorker*, 14 January 2002
6. *Time*, 10 July 2001
7. *New York Times*, 21 August 2001
8. <www.cnn.com/2000/US/11/09/uss.cole.02>
9. <www.cnn.com/2000/WORLD/meast/12/13/yemen.cole.ap>;
    <www.cnn.com/2000/US/12/20/terrorism.threat.02>
10. <www.vfw.org/magazine/oct01/12.htm>, citing *Wall Street Journal*
11. *New Yorker*, 14 January 2002
12. *Time*, 10 July 2001
13. *Washington Post*, 7 July 2001
14. *New Yorker*, 14 January 2002
15. *New York Times*, 20 May 1999
16. *San Francisco Chronicle*, 21 October 2001
17. Ibid.; <www.yale.edu/lawweb/avalon/sept-11/emerson_001.htm>
18. CNN, 22 February 2001
19. ABC News, 2 November 2000
20. Ibid.
21. <www.cnn.com/2001/US/10/16/inv.embassy.bombings.connections>
22. *USA* v. *Mohammed Saddiq Odeh*: Notice of Motion to Suppress Statements and Evidence, 7 July 2000, Southern District of New York
23. CNN, 26 January 2001
24. <www.pbs.org/wgbh/pages/frontline/shows/binladen/upclose/letters.htm>;
    Newsday, 27 September 200
25. *Chicago Tribune*, 8 February 2001; <cipherwar.com/news/01/bin_laden_trial.htm>;
    Los Angeles Times, 13 February 2001
26. <cipherwar.com/news/01/bin_laden_trial.htm>; CNN, 14 February 2001; *Newsday*, 27 September 2001
27. CNN, 4 May 2001; 16 October 2001
28. <cgi.pbs.org/wgbh/pages/frontline/shows/binladen/upclose/computer.html>
29. CNN, 26 February 2001; <www.cnn.com/2001/LAW/02/22/embassy.bombing>; CNN, 16 April 2001; 16 October 2001; *Chicago Tribune*, 20 April 2001
30. *Newsday*, 27 September; CNN, 16 October 2001; *Financial Times*, 29 November 2001
31. *Vanity Fair*, January 2002
32. *New York Times*, 4 July 2001; <www.pbs.org/wgbh/pages/frontline/shows/trail/etc/fake.html>
33. *New York Times*, 14 March 2001
34. *Seattle Times*, 3 April 2001
35. *Wall Street Journal*, 3 April 2001
36. Jean-Charles Brisard and Guillaume Dasquié, *Bin Laden: La Verité Interdite*, Editions Denoël, 2001; *New York Times*, 12 November 2001
37. CNN, 14 March 2001
38. *New York Times*, 21 August 2001; 7 December 2001

39. Ibid., 19 August 2001; *New Yorker*, 14 January 2002
40. *The Advocate*, 31 October 2001
41. <www.moles.org/ProjectUnderground/pr_archive/cheney000725b.html>
42. <www.corpwatch.org/news/PND.jsp?articleid=1089>
43. Ibid.
44. *Wall Street Journal*, 27 September 2001
45. <www.onlinejournal.com/archive/11-03-01_Dowling-printable.pdf>
46. *American Spectator*, November 1992; *Intelligence Newsletter*, 2 March 2000; <www.thedubyareport.com/txconnect.html>
47. *American Freedom News*, September 2001
48. <www.inthesetimes.com/issue/25/25feature3.shtml>
49. <www.thedubyareport.com/txconnect.html>
50. *Independent*, 13 January 2002
51. *Washington Quarterly*, Winter 2000
52. *Guardian*, 22 October 2001
53. *The News*, 22 January 2001
54. *Guardian*, 29 September 2001
55. Agence France-Presse, 27 February 2001
56. *New York Times*, 14 March 2001
57. BBC News, 17 March 2001
58. <www.bushwatch.org/attack.htm>; *Irish Times*, 19 November 2001
59. <www.fas.org/irp/congress/1992_rpt/bcci/11intel.htm>
60. *Village Voice*, 6 June 2001
61. Reuters, 3 April 2001
62. Associated Press, 6 April 2001
63. Agence France-Presse, 5 April 2001
64. BBC News, 16 April 2001
65. <www.payamemujahid.com/payam/day.htm>
66. ABC News, 22 May 2001
67. BBC News, 31 May 2001
68. *Times of India*, 27 May 2001; *Womensnews*, 26 May 2001
69. *Guardian*, 22 September 2001
70. *Guardian*, 7 November 2001
71. Brisard and Dasquié, *Bin Laden*
72. Ibid.
73. *Village Voice*, 6 June 2001
74. *Independent*, 24 October 2001
75. *Sunday Telegraph*, 30 September 2001
76. *The Times*, 5 October 2001

Chapter 17

1. *Los Angeles Times*, 22 September 2001
2. *The Times*, 3 October 2001
3. *New York Times*, 15 September 2001; *Observer*, 23 September 2001; *New York Times*, 11 October 2001
4. *New York Times*, 11 October 2001
5. *The Times*, 3 October 2001
6. *Guardian*, 15 September 2001
7. CBS News, 27 September 2001
8. *Newsweek*, 20 September 2001
9. CBS News, 27 September 2001
10. *New York Times*, 14 September 2001

11. Grand Jury Indictment of Zacarias Moussaoui, December 2001
12. Associated Press, 27 October 2001
13. Grand Jury Indictment of Moussaoui
14. *Financial Times*, 29 November 2001; Grand Jury Indictment of Moussaoui
15. *New York Times*, 15 September 2001; *Guardian*, 17 September 2001
16. Grand Jury Indictment of Moussaoui
17. ABC News, 27 September 2001
18. <www.cnn.com/WORLD>, 11 December 2001
19. CBS News, 19 December 2001
20. Grand Jury Indictment of Moussaoui; *Los Angeles Times*, 2 February 2002
21. Grand Jury Indictment of Moussaoui
22. ABC News, 23 May 2002
23. *Guardian*, 17 September 2001; *International Herald Tribune*, 21 September 2001; Washington *Post*, 15 October 2001; Grand Jury Indictment of Moussaoui; *Minneapolis-St Paul Star Tribune*, 21 December 2001
24. *New York Times*, 15 September 2001; Grand Jury Indictment of Moussaoui; Associated Press, 12 December 2001
25. *New York Times*, 20 November 2001; Associated Press, 26 November 2001
26. *International Herald Tribune*, 17 October 2001
27. Associated Press, 27 October 2001; <www.cnn.com>, 9 November 2001
28. *International Herald Tribune*, 21 September 2001; ABC News, 27 September 2001; CBS News, 27 September 2001
29. *Time*, 22 September 2001
30. *Guardian*, 1 October 2001; *New York Times*, 12 December 2001; Grand Jury Indictment of Moussaoui; <www.hcfhawaii.com/news/terror_risk.htm>
31. <www.mondaytimes.com.mv/issue46/atta46.htm>
32. *San Francisco Chronicle*, 4 October 2001
33. Video of Osama bin Laden in conversation with Khalid al-Harbi, released 13 December 2001
34. 'The Hijackings: A Pilot's View', <www.ict.org.il/articles/articledet.cfm?articleid=381>
35. <www.abc.net.au/4corners/atta/maps/timeline.htm>
36. <cnn.com/WORLD>, 13 October 2001
37. *Atlanta Journal-Constitution*, 26 September 2001
38. *USA Today*, 3 October 2001
39. *Nouvel Observateur*, 18 October 2001; *New York Times*, 28 October 2001; *Newsday*, 29 October 2001
40. <www.abcnews.go.com/sections/us/DailyNews/WTC_Investigation011120a.html>
41. *Minneapolis-St Paul Star Tribune*, 21 December 2001
42. Grand Jury Indictment of Moussaoui
43. <www.abc.net.au/4corners/atta/maps/timeline.htm>
44. Ibid.
45. *Minneapolis-St Paul Star Tribune*, 21 December 2001
46. *Le Monde*, 15 September 2001; *Washington Post*, 14 May 2002; *Time*, 21 May 2002; *Fortune*, 22 May 2002
47. *Los Angeles Times*, 20 September 2001
48. <www.abc.net.au/4corners/atta/maps/timeline.htm>; Grand Jury Indictment of Moussaoui
49. ABC News, 14 September 2001
50. *Los Angeles Times*, 18 October 2001
51. <www.abcnews.go.com/sections/us/DailyNews/WTC_Investigation011120a.html>
52. *Los Angeles Times*, 20 September 2001; 27 September 2001
53. Ibid., 27 September 2001
54. Grand Jury Indictment of Moussaoui
55. *Time*, 28 January 2002

56. *USA Today*, 14 September 2001; *Observer*, 16 September 2001; *Los Angeles Times*, 27 September
57. *Newsday*, 30 September 2001
58. *New York Review of Books*, 17 January 2002; CBS News, 1 October 2001
59. *New York Times*, 4 November 2001
60. ABC News, 14 September 2001
61. *Observer*, 16 September 2001
62. <www.ict.org.il/articles/articledet.cfm?articleid=381>
63. *New York Times*, 16 October 2001
64. CBS News, 23 February 2002
65. *New York Times*, 16 October 2001
66. *Observer*, 16 September 2001
67. *Sunday Times*, 16 September 2001
68. *New York Times*, 16 October 2001; <www.ict.org.il/articles/articledet.cfm?articleid=381>
69. *Observer*, 16 September 2001; Newsweek, 22 September 2001; *New York Times*, 16 October 2001; <www.ict.org.il/articles/articledet.cfm?articleid=381>

Chapter 18

1. BBC News, 7 October 2001
2. *The News*, 10 September 2001; *New York Times*, 13 September 2001
3. *The News*, 10 September 2001
4. *Washington Post*, 14 September 2001
5. Ibid., 29 January 2002
6. Ibid.
7. Ibid.
8. Ibid.
9. *Guardian*, 15 September 2001
10. <www.merip.org/pins/pin69.html>
11. *Washington Post*, 30 January 2002
12. *New York Times*, 16 September 2001
13. *Independent*, 26 September 2001; *New York Times*, 30 September 2001
14. *New York Times*, 2 October 2001
15. CNN, 17 September 2001
16. *Dawn*, 19 September 2001
17. *Washington Post*, 17 September 2001
18. *New York Times*, 18 September 2001
19. Institute of War and Peace Reporting, 30 October 2001; *Time*, 29 April 2002
20. *Guardian*, 17 September 2001
21. *Financial Times*, 17 September 2001; *Guardian*, 18 September 2001
22. *Guardian*, 21 September 2001
23. *Washington Post*, 3 October 2001
24. *Guardian*, 4 October 2001
25. *New York Times*, 18 September 2001
26. *Guardian*, 17 September 2001
27. Ibid., 4 October 2001
28. *New York Times*, 19 September 2001
29. *Washington Post*, 19 September 2001
30. *New York Times*, 20 September 2001; *Guardian*, 20 September 2001
31. CNN, 19 September 2001; *New York Times*, 19 September 2001; *Guardian*, 20 September 2001
32. *Washington Post*, 1 February 2002

33. *Washington Post*, 17 September 2001; *New Zealand Herald*, 18 September 2001; BBC News, 19 September 2001; *Daily Telegraph*, 20 September 2001
34. *Guardian*, 22 September 2001; <www.abcnews.go.com/sections/world/DailyNews/oman_profile.htm>
35. *Washington Post*, 20 September 2001
36. Ibid., 21 September 2001
37. *Guardian*, 18 September 2001
38. Ibid., 4 October 2001
39. Reuters, 15 October 2001
40. *New York Times*, 12 October 2001; *New Yorker*, 22 October 2001
41. *Guardian*, 4 October 2001
42. BBC News, 20 September 2001
43. *Daily Telegraph*, 20 September 2001
44. *Washington Post*, 20 September 2001; 2 February 2002
45. *Washington Times*, 2 April 2002
46. *Guardian*, 22 September 2001; BBC News, 23 September 2001
47. *Evening Standard*, 26 September 2001
48. *Daily Telegraph*, 3 October 2001
49. *Washington Post*, 25 September 2001
50. Ibid., 2 February 2002; *Time*, 29 April 2002
51. *Atlantic Monthly*, July–August 2001
52. CNN, 25 September 2001
53. CBC, 24 September 2001
54. CNN, 25 September 2001
55. Ibid., 27 September 2001
56. *Guardian*, 29 September 2001
57. *Daily Telegraph*, 29 September 2001; *Observer*, 30 September 2001; CNN, 30 September 2001
58. *Daily Telegraph*, 29 September 2001
59. Institute of War and Peace Reporting, 30 October 2001; *Time*, 29 April 2002
60. *Sunday Telegraph*, 30 September 2001
61. *New York Times*, 1 October 2001
62. Ibid., 24 September 2001
63. *USA Today*, 25 September 2001
64. *Daily Telegraph*, 5 October 2001; *Guardian*, 5 October 2001; <www.number-10.gov.uk/default.asp?PageID=5322>
65. BBC News, 5 October 2001
66. *Times of India*, 9 October 2001
67. BBC News, 7 October 2001; *Guardian*, 8 October 2001

Chapter 19

1. Associated Press, 10 October 2001
2. *Guardian*, 8 October 2001
3. *Washington Post*, 8 October 2001
4. *Guardian*, 23 October 2001
5. *New York Times*, 8 October 2001
6. Ibid.; ABC News, 8 October 2001
7. Agence France-Presse, 11 October 2001
8. Al-Jazeera, 13 October 2001, cited by *Daily Telegraph*, 14 October 2001
9. *New York Times*, 9 October 2001
10. Ibid., 10 October 2001; *Guardian*, 10 October 2001
11. *The News*, 11 October 2001

12. *Jang*, 13 October 2001
13. BBC News, 15 October 2001; *New Yorker*, 22 October 2001
14. Agence France-Presse, 11 October 2001
15. Associated Press, 10 October 2001; *Guardian*, 10 October 2001; *New York Times*, 12 October 2001
16. Agence France-Presse, 11 October 2001
17. Ibid.; *Guardian*, 15 October 2001; *New York Times*, 9 February 2002
18. *Washington Post*, 9 October 2001; *New York Times*, 9 October 2001
19. BBC News, 12 October 2001; *Guardian*, 12 October 2001
20. *Guardian*, 15 October 2001
21. *Chicago Tribune*, 12 October 2001
22. *Jang*, 10 October 2001; *Guardian*, 16 October 2001
23. Agence France-Presse, 12 October 2001
24. *Guardian*, 11 October 2001
25. Ibid., 12 October 2001
26. *International Herald Tribune*, 10 October 2001
27. *Times of India*, 16 October 2001
28. South Asia Analysis Group, Paper No. 345, 22 October 2001
29. *International Herald Tribune*, 9 October 2001
30. Agence France-Presse, 11 October 2001
31. *New York Times*, 14 October 2001
32. *Sunday Telegraph*, 14 October 2001
33. International Press Institute, 2 October 2001
34. *New York Times*, 12 October 2001
35. *Guardian*, 15 October 2001
36. *Newsweek*, 15 October 2001
37. *Jang*, 16 October 2001
38. *Washington Post*, 14 October 2001
39. Ibid., 18 October 2001
40. *Chicago Tribune*, 16 October 2001
41. *Dawn*, 15 October 2001; Reuters, 15 October 2001
42. *Frontier Post*, 15 October 2001
43. *The Age*, 22 October 2001
44. Reuters, 15 October 2001
45. CNN, 14 October 2001
46. Reuters, 16 October 2001
47. *The News*, 20 October 2001
48. *Atlantic Monthly*, September 2000
49. Ibid.
50. *Asia Times*, 29 January 2002
51. Ibid.; *New York Times*, 3 November 2001
52. *Washington Post*, 19 October 2001; *Daily Mirror*, 20 October 2001
53. CNN, 18 October 2001
54. South Asia Analysis Group, Paper No. 345, 22 October 2001
55. *Guardian*, 22 October 2001
56. *New Yorker*, 12 November 2001
57. *Guardian*, 6 November 2001; *New Yorker*, 12 November 2001
58. *New Yorker*, 12 November 2001
59. *Daily Telegraph*, 29 October 2001
60. *Washington Post*, 11 October 2001
61. Ibid., 19 October; *New York Times*, 22 October 2001
62. *The News*, 20 October 2001
63. Ibid.
64. *Washington Post*, 9 November 2001

65. *New York Times*, 20 January 2002
66. Associated Press, 9 November 2001; *New York Times*, 9 November 2001
67. *Sunday Times*, 28 October 2001
68. <www.ceip.org/files/publications/lievendispatch-haq.asp>
69. *Sunday Times*, 28 October 2001
70. Ibid.
71. *New York Times*, 20 January 2001
72. Ibid., 29 October 2001
73. *Guardian*, 26 October 2001
74. Ibid., 24 October 2001
75. Canadian Broadcasting Corporation, 25 October 2001
76. BBC News, 21 October 2001
77. *New York Times*, 26 October 2001
78. *Washington Post*, 23 October 2001
79. CNN, 21 October 2001
80. *Guardian*, 22 October 2001; 25 October 2001
81. *New York Times*, 26 October 2001
82. *Washington Post*, 24 October 2001; 27 October 2001
83. *Guardian*, 30 October 2001
84. Ibid., 26 October 2001
85. Ibid., 23 October 2001
86. Ibid., 3 November 2001
87. *New York Times*, 30 October 2001
88. Ibid., 5 November 2001
89. *Washington Post*, 1 November 2001
90. *Guardian*, 8 November 2001
91. *Washington Post*, 12 December 2001
92. *New Yorker*, 5 November 2001
93. CNN, 31 October 2001; *Washington Post*, 11 November 2001
94. *Washington Post*, 2 November 2001
95. CNN, 3 November 2001
96. United Press International, 5 November 2001
97. *Washington Post*, 30 October 2001
98. *Daily Telegraph*, 1 November 2001
99. Reuters, 4 November 2001
100. *Washington Post*, 6 November 2001; *International Herald Tribune*, 9 November 2001
101. *International Herald Tribune*, 9 November 2001; *Guardian*, 9 November 2001
102. *Guardian*, 12 November 2001
103. *Observer*, 11 November 2001
104. CNN, 9 November 2001
105. Ibid., 10 November 2001; *Guardian*, 12 November 2001; *Observer*, 18 November 2001
106. *New York Times*, 19 November 2001
107. Ibid.
108. *Guardian*, 13 November 2001
109. CNN, 11 November 2001
110. *Guardian*, 8 November 2001
111. *Dawn*, 9 November 2001
112. CNN, 10 November 2001
113. *Philadelphia Inquirer*, 5 December 2001
114. *Washington Post*, 14 November 2001
115. BBC News, 13 November 2001; Agence France-Presse, 13 November 2001
116. BBC News, 13 November 2001
117. Associated Press, 13 November 2001
118. Ibid.
119. *Observer*, 18 November 2001

Chapter 20

1. *Guardian*, 14 December 2001
2. Personal interview, 6 November 2001
3. BBC News, 15 November 2001
4. *Asia Times*, 13 December 2001
5. Associated Press, 20 November 2001
6. *The News*, 20 Novemeber 2001
7. *Guardian*, 15 November 2001
8. *New York Times*, 19 November 2001
9. *Independent*, 20 November 2001
10. *USA Today*, 6 November 2001; *Washington Post*, 9 November 2001
11. <www.dtic.mil/armylink/news/Dec2001/r2001121401-185.html>
12. *Washington Post*, 11 December 2001
13. <www.dtic.mil/armylink/news/Dec2001/r2001121401-185.html>
14. *Washington Times*, 22 January 2001
15. CNN, 17 November 2001
16. *Guardian*, 21 November 2001
17. *Sunday Times*, 25 November 2001
18. CNN, 17 November 2001
19. *Hindustan Times*, 22 November 2001; *Times of India*, 23 November 2001; *New York Times*, 24 November 2001
20. *The News*, 19 November 2001; *Guardian*, 1 December 2001; *The News*, 12 December 2001; <www.cursor.org/stories/jalaluddin.htm>
21. Associated Press, 17 November 2001
22. <www.cacianalyst.org/view_article.php?articleid=60>
23. Reuters, 22 November 2001; *Washington Post*, 23 November 2001
24. *Guardian*, 1 December 2001
25. CNN, 21 November 2001
26. *Independent*, 26 November 2001
27. *The Times*, 28 November 2001
28. *Guardian*, 1 December 2001
29. Ibid., 15 December 2001
30. Ibid., 1 December 2001
31. *Newsweek*, 7 December 2001
32. Press briefing by Ahmad Fawzi, 26 November 2001
33. *Washington Post*, 29 November 2001
34. *Newsweek*, 11 December 2001
35. *New York Times*, 15 December 2001
36. *World Socialist* website, 22 December 2001 <www.wsws.org/articles/2001/dec2001/afgh-d22.html>
37. *USA Today*, 2 December 2001
38. *South China Morning Post*, 27 November 2001
39. *Washington Post*, 22 December 2001
40. *Christian Science Monitor*, 4 March 2002
41. *Independent*, 26 November 2001
42. *Boston Globe*, 10 February 2002
43. *Daily Telegraph*, 30 November 2001
44. *International Herald Tribune*, 6 December 2001
45. *Washington Post*, 1 December 2001
46. *Daily Telegraph*, 3 December 2001; *The Times*, 4 December 2001
47. *Washington Post*, 11 December 2001
48. *Dawn*, 6 December 2001
49. Reuters, 6 December 2001

50. *Guardian*, 7 December 2001
51. Reuters, 8 December 2001
52. *New York Times*, 20 December 2001
53. *Guardian*, 18 December 2001; *New York Times*, 10 February 2002
54. Reuters, 13 December 2001
55. *Washington Post*, 10 February 2002
56. CNN, 1 December 2001; *Independent*, 3 December 2001
57. *Boston Globe*, 10 February 2002; *Christian Science Monitor*, 4 March 2002
58. *Guardian*, 26 November 2001
59. Ibid., 8 December 2001
60. *Washington Post*, 14 December 2001
61. *Boston Globe*, 10 February 2002; *Christian Science Monitor*, 4 March 2002
62. *Guardian*, 13 December 2001
63. *Washington Post*, 10 February 2002
64. Ibid., 18 December 2001
65. *Guardian*, 14 December 2001
66. Ibid., 15 December 2001
67. *Daily Telegraph*, 15 December 2001; *Washington Post*, 14 December 2001
68. *Hindustan Times*, 18 December 2001
69. *Guardian*, 24 December 2001
70. *International Herald Tribune*, 22 December 2001
71. *The News*, 25 December 2001
72. Agence France-Presse, 22 December 2001
73. *Washington Post*, 12 December 2001
74. *Time*, 13 January 2001
75. *Washington Post*, 22 December 2001
76. *Sunday Times*, 30 December 2001
77. CNN, 18 December 2001
78. *Guardian*, 24 December 2001
79. *Washington Post*, 10 January 2001
80. *Time*, 8 January 2002; 27 January 2002
81. *Guardian*, 10 January 2002
82. *Observer*, 6 January 2002
83. *Time*, 9 January 2002
84. *Observer*, 6 January 2002

Chapter 21

1. <www.bayinsider.com/partners/ktvu/news/2002/04/custody.html>
2. CBC News, 28 January 2001
3. *Christian Science Monitor*, 6 February 2001
4. *Daily Telegraph*, 24 December 2001
5. *Christian Science Monitor*, 6 February 2001; <www.usnews.com/usnews/news/articles/020225/25war.htm>; *Newsweek*, 28 February 2002
6. *Newsweek*, 17 December 2001
7. <www.wired.com/news/business/0,1367,49863,00.html>
8. *USA Today*, 7 January 2001
9. <www.sfdonline.org/Link%20Pages/Link%20Folders/02Pf/aus150102.html>
10. *Jang*, 11 January 2001; *Washington Post*, 17 April 2002
11. *Japan Times*, 29 April 2002
12. *Washington Post*, 17 April 2002
13. *Christian Science Monitor*, 17 January 2002
14. <www.globalsecurity.org/military/library/report/2001/010900-zhawar.htm>

15. *Washington Post*, 16 February 2002
16. *Christan Science Monitor*, 17 January 2002; *US News & World Report*, 25 February 2002; *Time*, 28 February 2002
17. *Time*, 28 February 2002
18. *US News & World Report*, 25 February 2002
19. *Christian Science Monitor*, 29 January 2002
20. Associated Press, 2 February 2002; *Washington Post*, 4 February 2002
21. *Washington Post*, 4 May 2002
22. <www.defenselink.mil/news/Jan2002/t01252002_t0125stf.html>
23. *Los Angeles Times*, 26 February 2002
24. Associated Press, 28 January 2002
25. *Christian Science Monitor*, 28 January 2002
26. *The Times*, 25 January 2002
27. *Washington Times*, 7 February 2002
28. BBC News, 14 February 2002
29. *Guardian*, 5 March 2002
30. Associated Press, 6 March 2002
31. Ibid.
32. Ibid., 14 March 2002
33. *Washington Post*, 10 March 2002
34. *Time*, 10 March 2002
35. *Washington Post*, 10 March 2002
36. *Christian Science Monitor*, 22 March 2002
37. <www.azzam.com>, 2 March 2002
38. *Washington Post*, 10 March 2002
39. *Christian Science Monitor*, 18 March 2002; *Soldier of Fortune*, May 2002; *DefenseWatch*, 24 April 2002
40. *Time*, 10 March 2002; *Guardian*, 10 March 2002; *Soldier of Fortune*, May 2002
41. *Guardian*, 4 March 2002
42. *Washington Post*, 24 May 2002
43. Ibid., 4 March 2002
44. *Guardian*, 6 March 2002
45. *Washington Post*, 4 March 2002
46. Associated Press, 8 March 2002
47. Reuters, 8 March 2002
48. *New York Times*, 9 March 2002
49. <www.spiked-online.com/Articles/00000006D851.htm>
50. *Washington Post*, 14 March 2002
51. Ibid.; *New York Times*, 14 March 2002; Associated Press, 16 March 2002
52. *The Times*, 12 March 2002
53. <www.azzam.com>, 12 March 2002
54. *Washington Post*, 10 March 2002
55. *Independent*, 21 March 2002
56. *The Times*, 17 April 2002
57. Ibid., 19 March 2002
58. <www.news.scotsman.com/topics.cfm?id=561752002&tid=1>
59. *Christian Science Monitor*, 18 March 2002
60. *Washington Times*, 27 March 2002; <www.eurasianet.org/departments/insight/articles/eav040302a.shtml>
61. *Guardian*, 4 April 2002; *Dawn*, 10 April 2002
62. *Washington Post*, 16 April 2002; ABC News, 17 April 2002
63. ABC News, 17 April 2002
64. CNN, 7 May 2002; Reuters, 7 May 2002

Chapter 22

1. *Christian Science Monitor*, 4 April 2002
2. *Philadelphia Inquirer*, 5 December 2001
3. <www.afgha.com/sections.php?op=viewarticle&artid=27>
4. *USA Today*, 28 December 2001
5. *New York Times*, 14 May 2002
6. *Los Angeles Times*, 6 January 2002; *Guardian*, 24 January 2002
7. BBC News, 11 January 2002
8. *International Herald Tribune*, 20 December 2001
9. *Guardian*, 16 July 2002
10. *International Herald Tribune*, 26 July 2002
11. *World Socialist* website, 3 January 2002
12. Reuters, 14 January 2002; BBC News, 15 January 2002
13. *New York Times*, 1 February 2002
14. <www.eurasianet.org/departments/insight/articles/eav040902/shtml>
15. BBC News, 10 February 2002
16. *Guardian*, 24 January 2002
17. *Washington Post*, 7 February 2002
18. <www.iiss.org/stratcomfree.php?scID=228>
19. Associated Press, 4 December 2001
20. *Time*, 23 January 2002
21. <www.eurasianet.org/departments/insight/articles/eav072602/shtml>
22. *New York Times*, 21 February 2002
23. <www.eurasianet.org/departments/insight/articles/eav031402/shtml>;
    www.eurasianet.org/departments/insight/articles/eav072602/shtml>; *Guardian*, 16 July 2002
24. *Guardian*, 16 July 2002
25. BBC News, 26 January 2002
26. UNHCR press release, 14 December 2001
27. Ibid., 30 May 2002
28. *Guardian*, 8 August 2002
29. Human Rights Watch, *Paying for the Taliban's Crimes*, April 2002, Vol. 14, No. 2
30. Human Rights Watch, *Precipice: Insecurity in Northern Afghanistan*, June 2002
31. Physicians for Human Rights, *A Report on Conditions at Shiburghan Prison*, 28 January 2002
32. Agence France-Presse, 13 May 2002
33. Physicians for Human Rights, *A Report on Conditions*
34. *Newsweek*, 26 August 2002
35. Physicians for Human Rights, *Preliminary Assessment of Alleged Mass Gravesites in the Area of Mazar-I-Sharif*, 16–21 January and 7–14 February
36. <www.sml.com/au/articles/2002/08/25/1030053009841.html>
37. CNN, 29 August 2002
38. *Newsweek*, 26 August 2002
39. *New York Times*, 9 February 2002; *Guardian*, 10 April 2002
40. <www.thedubyareport.com/civdeaths.html>; <www.media-alliance.org/mediafile/20-5>
41. <www.comw.org/pda/0201strangevic.html≠1.2>;
    <www.comw.org/pda/0201oef.html>
42. <www.comw.org/pda/0201oef.html>
43. *Guardian*, 23 March 2002
44. <www.globalexchange.org/september11/apogreport.pdf>
45. Associated Press, 11 February 2002; *Los Angeles Times*, 3 June 2002
46. *Los Angeles Times*, 3 June 2002

47. Agence France-Presse, 2 December 2001
48. *Bloomberg*, 13 April 2002; *Washington Post*, 15 May 2002
49. <Inweb18.worldbank.org/sar/sa.nsf/91e66bec154b73d5852567e6007090ae/1d31e 61488c32aef85256bd0005dfc39?OpenDocument>
50. Associated Press, 21 January 2002
51. *The Age*, 22 December 2001
52. *Daily Telegraph*, 18 February 2002
53. *Guardian*, 16 February 2002; *Newsweek*, 19 February 2002
54. *USA Today*, 20 February 2002
55. *Newsweek*, 19 February 2002
56. *New York Times*, 2 February 2002
57. <www.dawn.com/2002/01/24/int11.htm>
58. Reuters, 16 July 2002
59. <www.eurasianet.org/departments/insight/articles/eav042502.shtml>
60. *Washington Post*, 25 February 2002
61. Institute of War and Peace Reporting, 11 April 2002
62. <www.eurasianet.org/departments/qanda/articles/eav031502.shtml>
63. *Daily Telegraph*, 18 November 2001
64. <www.expressonline.it/ESW_articolo/0,2393,19153,00.html>
65. <www.mapinc.org/drugnews/v02/n287/a03.html> citing *Financial Times* (undated); <www.narcoterror.org/twowars.htm>
66. Speech by Ben Bradshaw, London, 10 January 2002
67. Associated Press, 4 April 2002
68. *Independent*, 5 April 2002
69. *The Times*, 25 April 2002
70. Ibid.
71. *Today*, BBC Radio 4, 9 October 2002
72. *The Times*, 25 April 2002
73. *New York Times*, 11 April 2002
74. *Newsweek*, 8 April 2002
75. Ibid.
76. BBC News, 11 March 2002; *Observer*, 14 April 2002
77. *Christian Science Monitor*, 12 April 2002
78. <www.eurasianet.org/departments/insight/articles/eav040202.shtml>
79. *Las Vegas Sun*, 15 April 2002
80. <www.eurasianet.org/departments/insight/articles/eav041902.shtml>
81. Reuters, 30 April 2002
82. *Washington Post*, 4 May 2002
83. *New York Times*, 9 May 2002
84. Associated Press, 18 May 2002
85. *Christian Science Monitor*, 6 May 2002
86. *New York Times*, 30 May 2002.
87. Associated Press, 28 May 2002
88. *Independent*, 10 June 2002
89. Reuters, 10 June 2002
90. International Crisis Group, *The Afghan Transitional Administration: Prospects and Perils*, 30 July 2002
91. Associated Press, 12 June 2002; *Central Asia-Caucasus Analyst*, 19 June 2002
92. Human Rights Watch, *Precipice*
93. <www.eurasianet.org/departments/insight/articles/eav061002a.shtml>
94. International Crisis Group, *The Afghan Transitional Administration*
95. <www.eurasianet.org/departments/insight/articles/eav061002.shtml>
96. Agence France-Presse, 15 June 2002
97. Associated Press, 11 June 2002

98. <www.eurasianet.org/departments/insight/articles/eav061002a.shtml>
99. International Crisis Group, *The Afghan Transitional Administration*
100. Ibid.
101. *New York Times*, 14 June 2002
102. International Crisis Group, *Afghan Transitional Administration*
103. Reuters, 17 June 2002
104. BBC News, 18 June 2002
105. <www.eurasianet.org/departments/insight/articles/eav062402.shtml>
106. International Crisis Group, *Afghan Transitional Administration*
107. <www.eurasianet.org>
108. *Time*, 17 June 2002; *Independent*, 6 August 2002
109. Associated Press, 22 June 2002
110. *New York Times*, 2 July 2002; Reuters, 2 July 2002
111. *New York Times*, 6 July 2002
112. <www.eurasianet.org/departments/insight/articles/eav070802a.shtml>
113. *New York Times*, 8 July 2002
114. Ibid., 23 July 2002
115. *Time*, 21 July 2002
116. Associated Press, 29 July 2002
117. *Time*, 7 October 2002
118. Ibid.
119. Associated Press, 2 September 2002
120. *Washington Post*, 24 August 2002
121. Associated Press, 5 September 2002
122. Ibid., 9 September 2002
123. Ibid., 7 September 2002
124. *Boston Globe*, 9 September 2002

Appendix 1
The Who's Who of the Taliban

By Jan Mohammed, Institute for Afghan Studies

As of 1 March 2000

Taliban Leaders, Ministers and Deputy Ministers

Mullah Mohammed Omar	Emir of Afghanistan; Head of the Taliban Movement
Mullah Mohammed Rabbani	Chairman of the Ruling Council; Head of the Council of Ministers
Mullah Mohammed Hassan	First Deputy Council of Ministers
Mulawi Abdul Kabir	Second Deputy Council of Ministers
Abdul Wakil Mutawakil	Minister of Foreign Affairs
Abdul Rahman Zahed	Deputy Minister of Foreign Affairs
Mullah Abdul Jalil	Deputy Minister of Foreign Affairs
Mullah Ubaidallah Akhund	Minister of Defence
Mullah Abdul Razzaq	Minister of Interior Affairs
Mullah Khaksar	Deputy Minister of Interior Affairs
Mohammed Sharif	Deputy Minister of Interior Affairs
Qari Ahmadullah	Minister of Security (Intelligence)
Mullah Nooruddin Turabi	Minister of Justice
Qari Din Mohammed	Minister of Planning
Mullah Abbas Akhund	Minister of Health
Sher Abbas Stanakzai	Deputy Minister of Health
Mullah Abdul Salam Haqqani	Minister of Education
Mullah Yar Mohammed	Minister of Communication
Alla Dad Tayeb	Deputy Minister of Communication
Alhaj Mohammed Isa Akhund	Minister of Mines and Industries
Mulawi Mohammedullah Mati	Minister of Public Works
Mulawi Rostam Nuristani	Deputy Minister of Public Works
Hafez Mohibullah	Minister of Haj and Religious Affairs
Muwlawi Moslem Haqqani	Deputy Minister of Haj and Religious Affairs
Muwlawi Abdul Raqib	Minister of Repatriation
Mullah Mohamed Jan Akhund	Minister of Water and Electricity
Muwlawi Faiz Mohammed Faizan	Deputy Minister of Commerce
Muwlawi Abdul Hakim Monib	Deputy Minister of Frontier Affairs

Taliban Governors

Mullah Niaz Mohammed	Governor of Kabul province
Mulawi Abdul Kabir	Governor of Nangarhar; Head of Eastern zone (see also above)
Muwlawi Khair Mohammed Khairkhwah	Governor of Balkh province; Head of Northern zone

Na'im Kuchi	Governor of Bamian province
Commander Bashir Baghlani	Governor of Baghlan province
Commander Arif Khan	Governor of Kunduz province
Muwlawi Shafiqullah Mohammedi	Governor of Khost province
Muwlawi Ahmed Jan	Governor of Zabol province
Mullah Dost Mohammed	Governor of Ghazni province

Other High Ranking Officials, Ambassadors and Envoys Abroad

Noor Mohammed Saqib	Chief Justice of Supreme Court
Abdul Rahman Agha	Chief Justice of Military Court
Mawlawi Qalamuddin	Head of Department of Prevention of Vice and the Promotion of Virtue
Sayed Mohammed Haqqani	Ambassador to Pakistan
Abdul Hakim Mujahid	Envoy to the UN
General Rahmatullah Safi	Envoy to Europe
Akhtar Mohammed Mansoor	Head of Aviation
Mullah Hamidullah	Head of Ariana Airlines
Alhaj Mullah Sadruddin	Mayor of Kabul
Mulawi Abdul Hai Motma'in	Taliban spokesman in Kandahar
Amir Khan Muttaqi	Ex-Minister of Culture and Information
Mullah Ghaus	Ex-Foreign Minister
Toorak Agha	Ex-Governor of Paktia province
Mullah Baradar	Insufficient data

Appendix 2
Principal Characters

Burhanuddin Rabbani

A theologian and former professor of religion at the University of Kabul, he founded Jamiat-i Islami in 1973. A Tajik from Badakhshan, he is a moderate Islamist. Jamiat's military wing dominated the north during the Soviet war, and had a strong showing in some areas of the west and south. Under the Peshawar Accord, he took over as president in June 1992 for a four-month period. This term was extended twice: to June 1994, under the terms of the Islamabad Accord; and to December 1994 by his unilateral decision. Frequent offers to step down were never realised due to the absence of an acceptable mechanism for the transfer of power. His regime at varying times received support from Saudi Arabia, Iran, Russia and India.

Ahmad Shah Massoud

Son of a Tajik military officer and a former student at the French Lycée in Kabul, he was Jamiat-i Islami's senior commander during the Soviet war and a minister of defence in the first mujahedin government. He forged an alliance with General Rashid Dostum and other generals from the Najibullah regime to capture Kabul in April 1992. Forced to step down following the Islamabad Accord, he retained control of the largest mujahedin army. Between January 1994 and February 1995, he withstood a joint attack on Kabul by the forces of Dostum, Hekmatyar and Mazari, supported variously by Pakistan and Iran. After the loss of Kabul, he retreated to his base in the Panjshir valley, forming a mutual defence pact with Dostum and the Shia leader, Karim Khalili, to resist the Taliban. Widely acclaimed for his skills as a tactician, he subsequently enjoyed the covert backing of Russia. Massoud was assassinated by alleged agents of Al Qa'ida two days before 11 September 2001 in an attempt to deny the US a unifying leader of Afghans on the ground.

Gulbuddin Hekmatyar

A Pashtun from the northern province of Kunduz, former military cadet and engineering student, he founded the radical Islamist Hizb-i Islami while exiled in Pakistan. During the *jihad*, he received the largest share of the US and Gulf military aid distributed by Pakistan and continued to receive military and tactical support from Pakistan's military intelligence service, the ISI, well after the collapse of the Najibullah regime. Despite a well-organised party structure, his domestic power base was limited to two provinces, Logar and Laghman, and strategic positions around the capital. His attack on Kabul in 1992–93 led to the Islamabad Accord, under which he became prime minister. A second siege, in collaboration with Dostum and Shia forces, lasted 13 months until February 1995 when Hizb-i Islami was driven back by the Taliban. After rejoining the Rabbani government in March 1996, he was reappointed prime minister but remained outside the anti-Taliban pact which was formed after the capture of Kabul. Hekmatyar is widely reported to have links with both the narcotics trade and international Islamist terrorist movements.

Rashid Dostum

A general in the northern Uzbek militia under Najibullah, his mutiny and later alliance with Massoud in April 1992 was decisive in bringing the mujahedin to power but he was excluded from the Jalalabad and Islamabad conferences which attempted to create the post-communist political order. During 1992–97, his Junbish-i Milli-i Islami, or National Islamic Movement, ruled over a semi-independent state of seven northern provinces, largely populated by Uzbeks, Turkmens, Tajiks and Ismaili Shias. Dostum controlled Afghanistan's best-equipped forces, its gas supplies and received aid from Russia, Uzbekistan, Turkmenistan, Turkey and Iran. His switch to Hekmatyar's side in January 1994 led to improved relations with Pakistan and Saudi Arabia. His refusal to mend fences with Rabbani after Hekmatyar's defeat was instrumental in the loss of Kabul to the Taliban and directly contributed to his own overthrow following the mutiny of General Abdul Malik, the Uzbek commander of Faryab province. Dostum flew into exile in Turkey from Uzbekistan in late May 1997 but returned to his Shiburghan power base the following August.

Abdul Ali Mazari

Until his murder by the Taliban in 1995, Mazari headed Hizb-i Wahdat, an alliance of eight Shia resistance groups created in 1990 by Iran to counter the influence of the Sunni-dominated, seven-party mujahedin alliance created by the ISI in Peshawar. Iran continued to be a crucial supplier of military aid, both to Wahdat's popular base in Bamian province and to its urban strongholds in southwest Kabul. An ally of Massoud and Dostum in the 1992 capture of Kabul, it switched to the side of Hekmatyar's Hizb-i Islami following attacks on its positions in the city in the following year, although a Shia splinter group, Harakat-i Islami, remained loyal to the Rabbani government. In March 1995, Wahdat surrendered its Kabul positions to the Taliban, resulting in Mazari's death. He was replaced as leader by Karim Khalili, who switched the Wahdat headquarters to Bamian and joined the anti-Taliban pact following the ouster of Massoud's forces from Kabul. Wahdat resistance both at Shibar Pass and in Mazar-i Sharif delivered the Taliban's two most crushing defeats until their eventual ouster.

Abdul Rasul Sayyaf

A Sunni religious scholar of Pashtun origin, Sayyaf co-founded Jamiat-i Islami, for which he served as deputy leader in the early 1970s. From 1980, he headed Ittehad-i Islami, a marginal faction with a following in Paghman and Kabul provinces, and which won disproportionate political influence as a result of lavish funding from Saudi Arabia and Pakistan's Jamaat-i Islami political party. This was chiefly due to Sayyaf's ability to speak Arabic and his vehement anti-Shiism. Sayyaf was the sole Pashtun leader to join the Rabbani administration, in which he was responsible for drafting a new constitution.

Maulawi Yunis Khalis

Anti-Shia, Pashtun religious leader from Nangarhar Province, he fled to Pakistan in 1974 and created his own faction, Hizb-i Islami (Khalis). Highly effective in the field during the *jihad*, Khalis refused to join or recognise the mujahedin governments and did not participate in the Jalalabad or Islamabad conferences. He retained considerable influence, both as 'honest broker' during the first siege of Kabul when he recruited a peacekeeping force of neutral mujahedin, and through his influence with Haji Qadir, governor of the Nangarhar *shura*.

Maulawi Mohammed Nabi Mohammedi

An Amadzhai Pashtun from Logar and a pre-communist MP, Mohammedi founded Harakat-i Inqilab-i Islami, the largest of the three 'traditionalist' resistance groups, so-called to distinguish them from the four 'Islamist' formations. Harakat combined elements from both the urban intelligentsia and the *madrassa* system and controlled several southern provinces. He endorsed both the Jalalabad and Islamabad accords, served as vice-president under Rabbani who was rumoured to favour him as a successor in the event that he would step down. A number of former Harakat commanders, including Mullah Mohammed Omar, joined the Taliban.

Sibghatollah Mojadeddi

'Traditionalist' religious leader from a prestigious Sufi family, Mojadeddi's Afghanistan National Liberation Front was predominantly Pashtun but lacked significant external funding. He was appointed first interim president after the fall of Najibullah, handing power to Rabbani whom he subsequently condemned, without committing his small group of fighters to Hekmatyar's military effort.

Pir Sayed Ahmad Gailani

Western-educated Pashtun of Arab origin and spiritual head of the Sufi Qadiryya sect, Gailani was regarded as one of the most moderate of the mujahedin leaders during the Soviet war. His military force remained small, due to lack of external patronage and, possibly, his blood connections with the former royal family.

Ismail Khan

Born in Farah and a military captain in Herat, he commanded the 1979 mutiny against the 'Saur Revolution' of President Taraki which led directly to the Soviet invasion. A high-ranking member of Jamiat-i Islami's western command, he diversified his alliances after becoming emir of Herat in April 1992 to accommodate Iranian and Turkmen demands and stabilise the province's large Pashtun minority. After the fall of Herat to the Taliban in September 1995, he fled with 8,000 men to Mashad in Iran, only returning in October 1996 to join forces with Dostum's troops in Badghis province. He was arrested in May 1997 by the mutinous General Abdul Malik of Faryab province and handed over to Taliban forces in Mazar-i Sharif, before being flown to Kandahar. He escaped in early 2000.

Index

Compiled by Sue Carlton

MCG-416-557-6545

MGW-760-793-1770